The Help Book

The Help Book

J. L. Barkas

CHARLES SCRIBNER'S SONS / NEW YORK

TO NANCY AND LARRY CRESHKOFF
HANK AND CHARLOTTE GREENE
WITH THANKS

Copyright © 1979 J. L. Barkas

Library of Congress Cataloging in Publication Data

Barkas, J. L.
　The help book.

　Includes bibliographical references.
　1. Social service—Directories.　2. Consumer
protection—Directories.　3. Environmental protection—
Directories.　4. Legal aid societies—Directories.
5. Family life education—Directories.　I. Title
HV41.B268　　362'.0025'73　　79-11291
ISBN 0-684-15194-4
ISBN 0-684-15195-2 pbk.

This book published simultaneously in the
United States of America and in Canada—
Copyright under the Berne Convention

All rights reserved. No part of this book
may be reproduced in any form without the
permission of Charles Scribner's Sons

Illustration on page 42 reprinted from *The Dog Catalogue*
by R. V. Denenberg. Copyright © 1978 by Eric Sudman
and R. V. Denenberg. Used by permission of Grosset &
Dunlap, Inc.

1　3　5　7　9　11　13　15　17　19　V/C　20　18　16　14　12　10　8　6　4　2

1　3　5　7　9　11　13　15　17　19　V/P　20　18　16　14　12　10　8　6　4　2

Printed in the United States of America

The publisher and the author disclaim any liability to any
person, organization, or agency for any loss or damage
caused by omissions or errors in *The Help Book*, whether
such omissions or errors resulted from accident, neg-
ligence, or any other cause. All names, addresses, descriptions, titles, and prices are subject to change.

Contents

Introduction	ix	Childrearing	109
Guide to Using this Directory	xi	Child/Youth Participation Groups	110
A Note on Literature	xiii	Education	111
		Employment	114
1. Adoption and Foster Care	1	Food and Nutrition	115
		Handicaps	116
2. Aging	11	Health	117
Crimes Against the Elderly	21	Legal Rights	119
		Mental Health and Mental Retardation	120
3. Alcoholism	29		
4. Animal Rights	40	**11. Citizen Action**	124
5. Arts	48	**12. Civil Rights and Discrimination**	133
6. Battered Adults	63	**13. Consumer Affairs**	144
		Getting Help to Resolve Your Consumer Complaints	145
7. Business Information	70	How You Can Report to the FDA	159
Credit	83	National Consumer Information Sources	161
Insurance	84		
Crimes against Business	85		
8. Child Abuse	90	**14. Counseling**	166
		Professional Counseling	167
9. Childbearing	96	Peer Counseling (Self-Help Groups)	170
10. Children	102	**15. Courts**	177
Advocacy and Multipurpose Groups	105	Court Watching and Witness Aid	178
State Agencies for Child Welfare	107	State Courts	179

Civil Court	182	Bleeding	270
Small Claims Court	183	Internal Bleeding	271
Family Court	184	Shock	272
Criminal Court	184	First Aid for Eye Emergencies	272
Federal Courts	186	Traffic Emergencies	273
Out-of-Court Dispute Settlements	187	Poisoning	275
		Natural Disasters	279

16. Crime Prevention — 190

- How to Begin a Crime-Fighting Crusade — 191
- Operation Identification — 192
- Direct Help in Preventing Crime — 193
- Technical Assistance — 199
- Information Clearinghouses — 200
- Personal Defense — 201

17. Crime Victims and Witnesses — 206

- Violent Crime Victims — 207
- Crime Victim Compensation — 215
- Property Crime Victims — 218
- Federal Crime Insurance — 219
- Restitution — 220

18. Drugs, Smoking, and Drug Abuse — 223

- Drugs — 225
- Tobacco and Smoking — 228
- Drug Abuse — 230
- Direct Help for Drug Abuse — 231

19. Education — 239

- Local Educational Resources — 241
- State Agencies for Education — 241
- Accreditation — 248
- National Organizations for Education — 255
- Women and Education — 258

20. Emergencies and Disasters — 262

- A Personal Almanac — 263
- Basic First-Aid Supplies Checklist — 269

21. Employment — 285

- Finding a Job — 287
- Retirement — 297
- Unions — 298
- Women and Work — 300
- Worker's Compensation — 303

22. Environment — 309

- Air Pollution — 316
- Energy — 320
- Nuclear Energy — 324
- Land Conservation — 326
- Solid Waste Management (and Recycling) — 328
- Water Pollution — 329

23. Family Planning — 336

- Birth Control — 339
- Abortion — 342

24. Financial Assistance — 346

- Arts — 353
- Education — 354
- Food — 355
- Health — 356

25. Food and Nutrition — 359

- Desirable Weights — 362
- Overeating — 367
- Hunger and Malnutrition — 370
- Food Cooperatives — 371
- Vegetarianism — 371

26. Gambling — 378
27. Gay Liberation — 382
28. Gun Control — 388
29. Handicaps — 395
30. Health — 410
31. Housing — 434
32. Information Rights and Resources — 442
    Freedom of Information Act — 450
33. Juvenile Delinquency — 457
34. Kidnapping, Missing Persons, and Runaways — 467
    Kidnapping — 467
    Missing Persons — 469
    Runaways — 470
35. Law Enforcement — 474
36. Legal Services — 482
37. Media and Communications — 492
38. Mental Health — 500
39. Mental Retardation and Learning Disabilities — 512
40. Multipurpose Organizations — 521
41. Offenders and Ex-Offenders — 531
42. Parenting — 545
    Day Care — 551
43. Political Action — 558
44. Rape and Sexual Assault — 572
    Myths and Facts about Sexual Assault — 572
    Prevention Techniques — 573
    What to Do if You Have Been Sexually Assaulted — 574
    Direct Help — 575
45. Safety — 585
46. Sex Education and Therapy — 600
47. Suicide Prevention — 609
48. Transportation and Travel — 617
49. Veterans — 632
50. Volunteerism — 643
51. Additional Resources — 650
52. Telephone Directory — 661

Introduction

Whether you are thinking about how to reduce crime in your neighborhood or what means of birth control to use, there is probably a group or agency that offers free or low-cost help. The number of organizations offering professional direct services and information or self-help groups has multiplied as quickly as the number of problems warranting assistance.

Free help has always been available from religious, government, or charitable organizations, but today there are also thousands of special-interest groups offering aid. How do you sift through all the choices?

The Help Book is fifty-two books in one. It is a guide to finding information or direct assistance for practically every situation that might arise. It provides referrals and is a basic source for help within the broad areas of health, the family, counseling, education, women's issues, crime, citizen action, emergencies, and employment. The fundamental organizations listed in this reference book will help you locate more specialized ones. You may learn that no one has yet addressed your particular problem and you will find out how to begin your own group.

Although other directories exist, *The Help Book* is comprehensive yet concise, and since helping services change, new and reevaluated listings are constantly needed. For example, the Salvation Army, a long-established organization, has turned its attention to such timely concerns as drug abuse, battered children and adults, sex discrimination, and teenage pregnancies, and should be considered as a source of help alongside newer services such as the Free University Network and the National Organization for Women. Similarly, familiar information-gathering tools, such as booklets and fact sheets, are now joined by innovative telephone tape libraries, such as Tel-Med, Tel-Law, and Can-Dial.

The listings that follow are the result of thousands of questionnaires and telephone and in-person interviews and have been subjected to scrupulous checks by the author, experts in each category, and information or public relations directors for specific entries. Yet the effectiveness of any of these listings is subject to such unpredictable factors as staff changes and funding cutbacks that can alter or limit services.

Thus, despite persistent efforts to ensure the accuracy of each listing, too many unforeseen changes prohibit endorsement of any of these groups. At the same time, exclusion does not in any way indicate disapproval. Space limitations demanded definite restrictions.

A major contribution of *The Help Book*, in addition to the specific listings, is the education it provides in *how* to go about finding help—information that transcends any one source. For example, since self-help groups and lay counselors are not always sufficient, this directory also offers suggestions on how to find a doctor, therapist, or lawyer.

Obviously without the help of literally thousands of others, this book would have remained just a good idea. Behind every listing is at least one person—more likely between two and five persons—who provided initial information, follow-up details and resource materials, and general interviews. They know of my gratitude and since they assisted me for the same reason I wrote this book, they will, I hope, forgive my inability to single out each and every one for a personal acknowledgment.

Guide to Using This Directory

- Telephone numbers have not been included because they change frequently. Check your local directory or the appropriate directory for the listing desired. If it is necessary to call Directory Assistance, check the front pages of your telephone directory for instructions and charge plans. Some telephone companies charge for each request, beyond an allowance, for a number within the same state. Requests placed to out-of-state Directory Assistance bureaus are free. A national area code map can be found in Chapter 52, *Telephone Directory*, or in your local directory. To obtain or recheck toll-free numbers dial 800-555-1212.
- Categories often overlap; be sure to check several cross references. Some groups are problem oriented, such as Gamblers Anonymous, but others embrace several concerns, such as WEAL (Women's Equity Action League) or the YMCA (Young Men's Christian Association).
- Every organization or agency will differ as to how long they take to reply to your written request; try a second time after you have waited a reasonable length of time, from two to three weeks. (Most state agencies took four weeks to handle written inquiries.) Telephone messages, if not returned after two or three days, should be followed up with a second phone call or a written request that mentions your unreturned telephone inquiries.
- *Remember to send a self-addressed, stamped envelope when writing for information or publications.* Many organizations have small budgets and staffs; volunteers may even coordinate all efforts. By enclosing a self-addressed, stamped envelope with your requests or inquiries, you will help nonprofit organizations keep down their operating costs and expedite your reply.
- Direct your communication to the general department that would handle

your request, such as "Information Officer," "Director," "Public Relations Department," "Volunteer Coordinator," etc., to facilitate its reply.
- The author and publisher do not endorse any of these organizations or publications; this is only a directory. No one was charged any fee nor contributed any donation whatsoever for being listed.
- Whenever possible, fees for membership, subscriptions, or publications have been included. Use this information as a guideline, however, since all prices are subject to change.

A Note on Literature

It is impossible to list all free pamphlets, booklets, or even books in each area. For magazine articles, it is best to look up a specific subject in the *Readers' Guide to Periodical Literature*, available at your local public or university library. All major publications are indexed by subject area, author's name, and by month and year of publication. Other key listings of periodicals are the *Standard Periodical Directory, Social Sciences and Humanities Index,* and *Ulrich's International Periodicals Directory*. For further help in finding additional published information, see Chapter 32, *Information Rights and Resources*.

For newspaper articles on a specific topic, consult the *New York Times Index,* available at your local library, indexed since 1851. Two major directories that list newspapers are *Editor and Publisher International Yearbook* (1920 to date) and *N. W. Ayer and Son's Directory of Newspapers and Periodicals* (1880 to date).

Two other excellent guides to finding information are the *New York Times Guide to Reference Materials* by Mona McCormick, 1971 (Popular Library, 600 Third Avenue, New York, N. Y. 10016 $1.50), and *Finding Facts Fast* by Alden Todd, 1972 (William Morrow & Company, Inc., 106 Madison Avenue, New York, N. Y. 10016 $5.95).

The Help Book

1

ADOPTION AND FOSTER CARE

It used to be that only legally married couples of the same religion and race, who were certified as sterile and were below a certain age limit, could adopt a child. They tended to select the "perfect" baby: a healthy infant of their own race. Older or handicapped children were overlooked and either remained in institutions or were brought up in foster homes.

But adoption practices have changed. Single men and women are now adopting children. Parent or parents and adopted child need not be of the same race or religion. Older and handicapped children are finding permanent homes. Many couples with natural children are adopting a second or third child. This modern view of adoption is best described by Elizabeth Cole, director of the North American Center on Adoption:

> Adoption has swung from being a service that finds babies for people who don't have them or who would like more babies to a service that finds families for children who need them. There are many such youngsters. For the most part, they are school-age and adolescent youngsters who have grown older waiting in foster homes and institutions, large groups of brothers and sisters, minority youngsters, and children whose medical or mental difference require special care. Agencies are actively recruiting families for these children, and they are finding more couples and single applicants coming forward.

There are four types of adoption: independent adoptions of minors (arranged directly with the natural parents); adoption of minors through a licensed agency or agent; adoption of minors by stepparents; and adoption of an adult by another adult at least ten years older than the adopted "child." Requirements vary from state to state as to which court has jurisdiction over adoption proceedings, how long a probation period is necessary before the adoption is final, the age at which the child's consent is also required, and whether an adopted child still has the right to inherit through his or her natural parents who die without leaving a will.

Seventy-five percent of all adoptions are arranged through private or public agencies, which are licensed and regulated by the state. Private agency adoptions are more expensive, but one cannot say which service will arrange a "better" adoption. In both services, however, there is a severe shortage of infants for adoption, particularly healthy white babies. One of the consequences of that shortage has been the notorious "black market" baby farms, which have been known to charge as much as $40,000 for illegally arranging such adoptions. In February 1978, for example, the *New York Times* reported that a lawyer had been indicted on 192 counts including conspiracy, perjury, and unlawfully placing children for adoption. In some of the adoption cases, the lawyer allegedly brought unmarried pregnant women from other states to New York City, where he supported them until they gave birth—and then sold their babies for prices ranging from $5,000 to $11,500.

The most controversial issue in adoption today is the sealing of the birth records. "Sealing" refers to the practice—after a legal adoption—of replacing the original birth certificate with a new revised document. The original one is "sealed" and separately filed. It is then up to the "discretion" of the adoption agency whether to reveal the true identity of any of the parties involved in the adoption. Until very recently, practically all agencies would not release any records. Thus, at maturity, and even if an adoptee knew that he or she had natural siblings, the information was not obtainable. The traditional reasoning for this secrecy was that it was for the child's own good, since it was believed that many adopted children were illegitimate. Now, however, the ethics and even the constitutionality of sealed records are being questioned.

Another controversial issue in addition is whether the adoptive parents should tell the child that he or she is in fact adopted. The current consensus is that at some point the child should be told. More than ever before, agencies, society, and the adoption triangle—adoptees, birth parents, and adoptive parents—are asking, "Is all this secrecy necessary?" and answering, "No."

There are over 150,000 foster parents in the United States. In many ways, it is more difficult than ordinary parenting or adoption since the child may still be returned to his or her natural parents, and the foster care placement may therefore be only temporary. The child also may be transferred to another placement home or facility. Foster care may be short-term or for all of the child's dependent years. Abuses are sometimes publicized in the media, such as in June 1978, when a Baltimore woman, who placed her young sons in foster care for a few months, had them returned to her with signs of physical abuse. When such abuses are exposed, there is temporary public awareness of the need to carefully investigate potential foster parents.

But through such organizations as OFFER (Organization of Foster Families for Equality and Reform) and the National Foster Parent Association, higher standards for foster care are being established and enacted. That foster parenting is a unique and demanding skill is finally being recognized: the Foster Parent Dissemination Center of the Child Welfare League of America, in cooperation with the U.S. Children's Bureau of the Office of Child Development, is helping social workers educate foster parents. They emphasize that even though a child's placement is usually temporary, foster parenting is a challenging and important role.

Some of the questions that have to be answered by potential foster parents are: How does caring for a foster child differ from just having a relative or friend visit in one's home? How will the foster child affect the relationships already established in the foster care family, where there are often other foster care or natural children? How does the foster care parent explain why the child's natural parent or parents are unable to care for him or her? How can the foster care family best utilize the services and skills of the cooperating social service agency?

For direct assistance in adoption, consult your local telephone directory in the state, city, or county government listings under any of the following categories: Child Welfare, Health, Social Services, Welfare, Bureau of Adoption, Human Resources, Child Services. To find out what state department offers adoption services, contact your state information office in your state capital. (State agency addresses are listed in Chapter 32, *Information Rights and Resources*.) Or see the listings in Chapter 10, *Children: State Agencies for Child Welfare;* Chapter 24, *Financial Assistance: State Agencies for Welfare;* Chapter 30, *Health: State Agencies for Health;* Chapter 40, *Multipurpose Organizations: State Agencies for Social Services* for agencies that may provide adoption assistance. State agencies may also be able to provide referrals to private licensed adoption services in your area. You might also wish to look up **Adoption** in your local yellow pages.

Another way to locate a recommended adoption service is to contact the national headquarters of the multipurpose organizations that are described below. They will make referrals to local public and private agencies that offer adoption services and are members or associate members of the national group.

These national and North American organizations provide assistance in adoption:

AASK (Aid to Adoption of Special Kids)
3530 Grand Avenue
Oakland, Calif. 94610

BRANCH OFFICE: AASK in Las Vegas
1700 East Desert Inn Road
Las Vegas, Nev. 89109

A free national adoption exchange referral service between licensed adoption agencies and adoptive parents for children who are considered difficult to place in permanent homes. Families register with AASK from all over the United States (registration forms for children or families available upon request). AASK's emphasis is on children over ten, sibling groups, and mentally, physically, or emotionally handicapped children.

LITERATURE: Free fact sheet.

4 / THE HELP BOOK

ARENA (Adoption Resource Exchange of North America)
c/o North American Center on Adoption
67 Irving Place
New York, N.Y. 10003

A North American clearinghouse for licensed adoption agencies that helps find homes for children with special needs (handicapped, minority or large sibling groups, and older children). ARENA maintains a registry of names and photos of waiting children as well as a list of approved adoptive families and tries to bring them together.

LITERATURE: Free descriptive pamphlet; *Arena News*, a monthly newsletter that contains photos and descriptions of "special-needs" children who are available for adoption and short, informative articles and lists (available for a $5.00 tax-deductible contribution). Suggested as a companion to *Adoption Report*, a newsletter of the North American Center on Adoption.

Child Welfare League of America, Inc.
67 Irving Place
New York, N.Y. 10003

Founded in 1920, the Child Welfare League of America is a private organization devoted to developing standards in the areas that have been specified as child welfare services, including adoption, foster parenting, day care, homemaker services, services to children in their own homes, and unmarried parents. Accredited and associate member agencies that provide all of these services, including adoption and/or foster care placement, are listed by state in the Child Welfare League's directory along with the name of the director, the telephone number, and other functions coordinated by the agency.

The league maintains a library on its premises that is open to the public for research on child welfare.

LITERATURE: Extensive publications list available upon request; *Directory of Member Agencies*, published annually each January, available with *Directory of Associate Agencies* ($8.00); *Child Welfare League of America Standards for Adoption Service*, revised 1973 ($5.00); *Guidelines for Adoption Service*, 1971 ($1.75); *Child Welfare*, journal published ten times a year ($8.00); *Foster Parent Associations: Designs for Development* by Helen D. Stone and Jeanne M. Hunzeker, 1974 ($2.75); *Foster Parenting Young Children: Guidelines From a Foster Parent* by Evelyn H. Felker, 1974 ($3.25); "The Parent in the Shadows" by Phyllis Johnson McAdams, reprinted from *Child Welfare*, January 1972 ($.30).

Committee for Single Adoptive Parents
P.O. Box 4074
Washington, D.C. 20015

Founded in 1973, this national organization offers advice to single men and women who wish to adopt children. It works with public and private agencies in legislation and research concerning single-person adoptions and connects single parents living in the same area.

LITERATURE: *Handbook for Prospective Single Parents* ($3.00); source list with updates, an annotated guide to agency or direct sources of children to be adopted (available with $5.00 membership); free fact sheet on the committee and adoption procedures.

Family Service Association of America (FSAA)
44 East 23rd Street
New York, N.Y. 10010

Founded in 1911, this national organization is a federation of about 300 local agencies in over 200 communities that provide a wide variety of direct services, including adoption and foster care. If you cannot find a member agency in your community, the FSAA headquarters will furnish that information.

LITERATURE: *Directory of Member Agencies*, updated annually ($7.00); *Social Casework* journal ($10.00 per year); extensive publications price list.

ADOPTION AND FOSTER CARE / 5

National Associates of Black Social Workers (NABSW)
2008 Madison Avenue
New York, N.Y. 10027

Some of the local chapters of this 140-member national organization are involved in adoption and child welfare programs, such as the Child Adoption Counseling and Referral Service of the New York chapter, and other adoption programs are starting in New Jersey, Texas, and California. Check with the national headquarters to see if there is a local program in your area or for referrals to agencies that are sensitive to the needs of black adoptees and adoptive parents. The organization also deals with other child and social welfare issues.

LITERATURE: Free adoption and foster care brochures; Adoption Annual Report ($.50); *Child Welfare Journal* ($3.00); other journals dealing with mental health and other social welfare topics and journals summarizing annual conferences (cost between $3.00 and $7.00, depending on the journal).

North American Center on Adoption
67 Irving Place
New York, N.Y. 10003

A nonprofit corporation providing consultation and information to adoption agencies and schools of social work that assist citizen groups; provides education for the general public; has exchange services (with ARENA) to aid in the adoption of special-needs youngsters (children living in foster homes or in institutions, school-age children and older, and handicapped or minority children); follows national legislation; and has an information and action center to find families for waiting children throughout North America.

LITERATURE: *Adoption Report* newsletter (available with a tax-deductible contribution marked "For Adoption Report"), issued quarterly and contains legislative updates, book reviews, editorials, and spot photo notices about available children.

North American Council on Adoptable Children (NACAC)
250 East Blaine
Riverside, Calif. 92507

A coalition of adoptive-parent groups and individuals concerned about children in need of adoptive homes. The NACAC is an information clearinghouse for those interested in adopting a child (American or foreign). Public education programs include sponsorship of nationwide Adoption Week, conferences, and special publications.

LITERATURE: *Adopting Children With Special Needs* ($4.00); *Adoptalk* magazine, issued five times a year ($5.00); free information sheet.

U.S. Department of Health, Education, and Welfare
Administration for Children, Youth and Families (ACYF)
Box 1182
Washington, D.C. 20013

This federal agency handles information and referral requests regarding adoption and foster care.

LITERATURE: "The Role of the Agency: Agency and Parent Responsibilities" and "Foster Parent Education" are free leaflets; article reprints on adoption are also available.

These organizations provide assistance in and/or information on foreign adoptions:

F.A.C.E., Inc. (Families Adopting Children Everywhere)
P.O. Box 102
Bel Air, Md. 21014

F.A.C.E. is not an adoption agency, but a national adoptive-parents organization devoted to support, encouragement, and dissemination of information regarding adoption, both in the

United States and abroad. Membership dues include subscription to the newsletter *F.A.C.E. Facts*, which appears monthly. Monthly meetings are held for those in Washington, D.C., Maryland, and southern Pennsylvania areas.

LITERATURE: A complimentary copy of *F.A.C.E. Facts* is sent to those making inquiries; *Adoption Referral Guide*, a pamphlet outlining overseas adoption requirements, availability of children, costs, etc. ($2.25).

Foreign Adoption Center
2701 Alcott Street
Suite 471
Denver, Colo. 80211

A licensed Colorado placement agency providing screening and escort services for adoptions from Guatemala.

Friends For All Children (FFAC)
445 South 68th
Boulder, Colo. 80303

FFAC places Thai children for adoption and will reply to inquiries with a form letter that describes adoption procedures and availability of children through FFAC. There is a $10.00 per month sponsorship program for needy Thai children. FFAC staffs and runs a day-care center for slum children in Bangkok and is supported by private contributions and fees.

Holt International Children's Services, Inc.
P.O. Box 2880
Eugene, Oreg. 97402

Founded in 1956, this nonprofit organization is associated with the Holt Adoption Program, Inc., and arranges adoptions for Korean orphans. In addition, there is a multiservice program to help children in Korea, India, Thailand, and the Philippines.

LITERATURE: Quarterly newsletter; *Hi Families* (monthly); 16mm sound film and two slide presentations available for development and education.

For national organizations that provide assistance after adoption (to the adoptee, birth parent, or adoptive parent), consult any of the following groups for the nearest local affiliate or for information:

Adoption Forum Library
201 West Cuthbert Boulevard C44
Oaklyn, N.J. 08107

A project of the Adoption Forum of Philadelphia (P.O. Box 5607, East Falls Station, Philadelphia, Pa. 19129) providing information to those interested in adoption; bibliographies and copies of pertinent articles are available; quarterly newsletter includes notices, personal items.

ALMA (Adoptees' Liberty Movement Association)
P.O. Box 154
Washington Bridge Station
New York, N.Y. 10033

Founded in 1971 by Florence Fisher, who found her natural parents after a twenty-one-year search, ALMA has several objectives, including "mutual assistance in search" and opposition to sealing the birth and adoption records of an adult. ALMA maintains the International Reunion Registry, has a search committee, and sponsors workshops. Annual dues are $20.00.

LITERATURE: *ALMA's Handbook for the Search* by Emma M. Vilardi (included in membership fee); introductory form letter; *Searchlight*, a quarterly newsletter; questionnaire for adoptee, natural parent, or others.

Board for Certification of Genealogists
1307 New Hampshire Avenue, N.W.
Washington, D.C. 20036

Provides fact sheets on how to get started in tracing your family history, including a list of the names and addresses, by state, of certified researchers who will help for a fee.

Concerned United Birthparents, Inc. (CUB)
P.O. Box 753
Milford, Mass. 01757

A national support group for birth parents, with auxiliary membership open to concerned citizens, whose goal it is to educate the public about the needs of the adoption triangle (birth and adoptive parents and the adoptee); monthly meetings are held in Boston and other branch locations to exchange birth-parent experiences and feelings; membership $7.50.

LITERATURE: Free information booklets; *Understanding the Birthparent* ($1.50); national *Newsletter*, monthly ($4.00 to nonmembers).

National Archives and Records Service
General Services Administration
Washington, D.C. 20408

Since 1950 the National Archives has sponsored intensive three-week genealogical education programs through the National Institute on Genealogical Research; information on these programs is available from the Office of Educational Programs at the above address. The National Archives has custody of millions of records relating to persons who have had dealings with the federal government.

LITERATURE: *Genealogical Records in the National Archives.*

Orphan Voyage
R.D. #1, Box 153A
Cedaredge, Colo. 81413

A membership organization throughout North America, with sixty chapters in several states, that provides advice and suggestions to any person seeking a reunion with biological relatives. Orphan Voyage is a support network for those who need help or encouragement to undertake their own search. Membership dues are $20.00 for the first year; letters and phone calls personally answered by coordinator and founder, Jean M. Paton-Kittson; public education program.

LITERATURE: Reunion File of the United States and Canada (one-time $5.00 registration fee); free information packet; *The LOG* newsletter, issued five times a year ($5.00 to nonmembers).

Parent Finders
1408 West 45th Avenue
Vancouver, British Columbia V3B 1N7
Canada

Founded in 1974 "to promote a feeling of openness and understanding about the whole concept of adoption," this organization provides assistance to adoptees and has branches throughout Canada and an English branch in London. A list of groups is available from the head office. Assistance is provided in obtaining written background information sheets from the appropriate agencies and instructions are given on how to first approach birth relatives; if the adoptee is hesitant, the organization will act as an intermediary. Membership fee; Reunion Registry and Search Committee.

Yesterday's Children
P.O. Box 1554
Evanston, Ill. 60204

Membership organization ($20.00 a year) whose members are primarily adults who do not know their genetic families and wish to find them; works to amend state laws so that adoptees can have access to all birth information and records pertaining to their history; monthly meetings.

8 / THE HELP BOOK

LITERATURE: Newsletter; National Adoption Registry for those birth parents and adoptees who wish to be known (free to members, one-time $5.00 fee to nonmembers); free fact sheet.

These national organizations provide help to those who are or wish to become foster parents:

Concern for Children in Placement (CIP)
c/o National Council of Juvenile Court Judges
University of Nevada
P.O. Box 8978
Reno, Nev. 89507

A program of monitoring children in foster care. In 1974 pilot projects were launched in twelve diverse courts, including Santa Barbara, Calif.; Wausau, Wis.; Lincoln, Neb.; El Paso, Tex.; Providence, R.I.; Salt Lake City, Utah; Portland, Ore.; Columbia, S.C.; Ravenna, Ohio; Denver, Colo.; Honolulu, Hawaii; and Greenville, Miss. In 1976 CIP began work in twenty-five additional juvenile and family courts.

CIP also promotes adoption of special-needs children. A CIP guidebook with accompanying slide show and videotapes are presented to aid volunteer recruitment and community education.

Foster Grandparents
c/o ACTION
806 Connecticut Avenue, N.W.
Washington, D.C. 20525

A federal program in which senior citizens are employed at minimum wages for twenty hours each week to provide friendship and assistance to institutionalized orphans and mentally retarded children.

Foster Parent Education Dissemination Center
c/o Child Welfare League of America, Inc.
67 Irving Place
New York, N.Y. 10003

A national project to assist agencies providing foster care in developing curriculum for foster-parent education; provides information to the public as well as technical assistance on implementing and adopting curriculum to local agency needs.

LITERATURE: Publications price list; brochures about the curriculum; each U.S. Department of Health, Education, and Welfare regional office and each state office of social services has a foster care education packet that can be examined free.

National Foster Parent Association (NFPA)
P.O. Box 16523
Clayton, Mo. 63105

Founded in 1971, NFPA is the only national information clearinghouse and activist organization of foster parents. It sponsors conferences; makes educational materials available for foster parents, social workers, and agencies; conducts research; assists state and private agencies; helps win access to legal aid and special insurance; issued "Bill of Rights for Foster Children" in 1973. Membership dues range from $5.00 (individual or couple) to $30.00 and includes free loan service of all library materials ($.75 handling fee to nonmembers).

LITERATURE: Posters; "Tape of the Month" program; "Bill of Rights for Foster Children"; "Code of Ethics for Foster Parents"; "Statement of David T. Evans [President] Before the U.S. Senate" (1975); free publications price list, *NFPA Resource Center*.

OFFER (Organization of Foster Families for Equality and Reform)
P.O. Box 110
East Meadow, N.Y. 11554

A group of foster families and other concerned citizens addressing themselves to the national and local issues of foster care. OFFER will provide referrals to local groups with similar orientations and lay counseling, and is working toward the reform of state foster care laws. Membership is $15.00 annually.

LITERATURE: Quarterly journal ($5.00 a year); brochures for foster parents explaining adoption means and clarifying New York State foster care law.

ADDITIONAL LITERATURE

Adopting the Older Child by Claudia L. Jewett (1978). The Harvard Common Press, Harvard University, 79 Garden Street, Cambridge, Mass. 02138 ($11.95). An informative book if you're considering adopting an older child.

Adoption: A Guide to Adopting in the New York Area (1977). Adoption Opportunities Committee, New York Junior League, 130 East 80th Street, New York, N.Y. 10021 ($1.00). In addition to annotated listings for New York agencies, there is a general introduction to adoption that is applicable to most states. Three appendices list national organizations that provide adoption exchanges, support groups, and foreign adoption assistance.

"Adoption Advice" by Joan McNamara, in *Woman's Almanac*, pp. 182–186 (1976); compiled and edited by Kathryn Paulsen and Ryan A. Kuhn. J. B. Lippincott Company, 521 Fifth Avenue, New York, N.Y. 10017 ($6.95). Concise but well-written article highlighting basic information and developments to be considered by prospective adopting parents; covers locating a child, gray and black markets, and protecting yourself in independent adoptions.

The Adoption Triangle: The Effects of the Sealed Record on Adoptees, Birth Parents, and Adoptive Parents by Arthur D. Sorosky, M.D., Annette Baran, and Reuben Pannor (1978). Anchor Press/Doubleday & Company, Inc., Garden City, N.Y. 11530 ($8.95). A reevaluation of our current and past adoption policies by the cofounders and codirectors of the Adoption Research Project in Los Angeles.

The Art of Adoption by Linda Cannon Burgess (1976). Acropolis Books, 2400 17th St., N.W., Washington, D.C. 20009 ($8.95). Burgess, who has worked in adoption agencies for over twenty years, returned to forty-five homes where she placed 146 children since 1954. She describes her impressions of the adopted children, now grown, as well as adoption practices in general.

Baby and Child Care by Benjamin Spock (1945, rev. 1976). Pocket Books, 1230 Avenue of the Americas, New York, N.Y. 10020 ($2.50). Contains a concise and informative section on adoption.

Finding My Father by Rod McKuen (1976). Coward, McCann & Geoghegan, Inc., 200 Madison Avenue, New York, N.Y. 10016 ($7.95).

Is That Your Sister? by Catherine and Sherry Bunin (1977). Pantheon Books, 201 East 50th Street, New York, N.Y. 10022 ($4.95). Subtitled "A True Story About Adoption." Sherry Bunin, an adoptive mother who is also on the staff of the New York Council on Adoptable Children, wrote this book with her daughter, Catherine. The photos of the Bunin family, and the text, make it a charming and real way to teach children—adopted or not—about what adoption really means.

Legal First Aid by Henry Shain (1975). Funk & Wagnalls, 666 Fifth Avenue, New York, N.Y. 10010 ($6.95). See Chapter 7, "Adoptions," pages 85–91. Introductory comments are followed by a brief paragraph on the legal aspects of the four types of adoption: agency, stepparent, adult, and independent, with the emphasis on the last. A useful chart lists adoption laws in each state.

A Time to Search: The Moving and Dramatic Stories of Adoptees in Search of Their Natural Parents by Henry Ehrlich (1977). Paddington Press, Ltd., 95 Madison Avenue, New York,

N.Y. 10016 ($7.95). The different searches of eleven adoptees plus a careful case for the opening of birth records.

Twice Born: Memoirs of an Adopted Daughter by Betty Jean Lifton (1975). McGraw-Hill Book Company, 1221 Avenue of the Americas, New York, N.Y. 10020 ($8.95).

We Take This Child: A Candid Look at Modern Adoption by Claire Berman (1974). Doubleday & Company, Garden City, N.Y. 11530 ($5.95). A comprehensive survey of modern adoption alternatives, including single-parent, older, handicapped, black, intercountry, and independent adoptions. Case studies illustrate each major area; key literature is summarized. A selected bibliography and a state-by-state listing of local adoption organizations are also included.

"Where to Write for Birth and Death Records," "Where to Write for Marriage Records," and "Where to Write for Divorce Records" are government publications that may be useful in tracking down birth information. All are available from the Superintendents of Documents, U.S. Government Printing Office, Washington, D.C. 20402 ($.35 each).

See also the following related chapters in *The Help Book:*

CHILDBEARING
CHILDREN
COUNSELING
COURTS
EDUCATION
FAMILY PLANNING
INFORMATION RIGHTS AND RESOURCES
LEGAL SERVICES
MENTAL RETARDATION AND LEARNING DISABILITIES
PARENTING

2

AGING

We all need to know someone like eighty-six-year-old Bill Hennessey to challenge our preconceived ideas about the elderly. "I've just slowed down," says Bill during one of his numerous daily walks. "That's all. Slowed down, but I'm much keener and more knowing in most areas of life than I was at twenty-six." Bill's voice is strong, his ideas are clear, and his words are spoken with deliberation. "Now I analyze much more than I did and I'm not so quick-tempered—in politics, in working relations, in striving for a certain point and not getting it."

For four years I have shouted out, "Hello, Bill," as I walked down our street or, if I had more time, stopped to chat with him. We would talk about the play he is writing or theater in general. Playwrighting is Bill's fourth career. The first, after he was graduated from Swarthmore College in 1921, was as a reporter for a Philadelphia newspaper. After that, he began his second career as an actor. After serving as a Red Cross field supervisor during World War II, he next became a cabinetmaker like his father. When he was thirty-eight he wrote his first play; now he is finishing his third. Last year Bill took a course in Indian folklore for background to his play, which takes place in the Old West. Bill works on his play for about four hours each day; he's also taking an art course. In addition, he began learning Latin a year ago and he studies that two hours a day. "I've never been bored," Bill explains. "The whole thing is to keep busy and not just sit around. You've got to do things. I don't think of my age. I don't think of what's behind me. I think of what's ahead of me."

But when most of us think of aging in America today, we don't think of the Bill Hennesseys. The contemporary image of the 22.9 million Americans who are 65 or over (or 10.9 percent of the population) is of dependent, depressed, and despondent old people living in nursing homes under constant supervision. Yet those cases should be the exception, rather than the norm. Although the rate at which people age has not changed, better health care and living conditions have increased

12 / THE HELP BOOK

the average life span. In 1975, the average age expectancy for American men and women was 72.5 years—68.7 for males; 76.5 for females. How many elderly who are unhappy have purely physically caused ailments? How much grief is due to prejudice against the elderly?

In interviews with the elderly in different places and professions, I found that two groups fare better than others after 65: those who were always self-employed or self-reliant, and those whose dependence on their families is welcomed and encouraged. Those who can no longer work and do not have hobbies or volunteer jobs, or those without children or nearby family, feel lonely, isolated, and useless. These elderly people get caught in a vicious circle of mental and physical problems that seem to be broken only by death.

A movement against "agism," led by such national groups as the Gray Panthers, is trying to eliminate the prejudices and misconceptions that prematurely render our older population "useless." Even though the best guard against an unnecessarily traumatic old age is to learn—and practice—"anti-agism" ways when young, the fast-paced, competitive American society must still make adjustments for the elderly who demand patience and understanding that too few individuals now seem to have.

There is a wide range of direct services offered to the elderly on the local, city, and state levels. A "model" program would offer free or reduced transportation for the elderly, food programs, cultural pick-up and return services and reduced tickets, recreational facilities, employment counseling, toll-free hot line information, medical services, housing information, a telephone reassurance program, crime prevention education, advocacy courses, friendly visitors, escort services, and legal information. Check your government listings in the phone book under **Aging** or **Elderly** for your nearest public office. Or you might ask for a referral or for the local branch of the office for aging in your state, using the list in this chapter.

Numerous federal programs to assist the elderly (in health care, food, housing, social security) are administered through state agencies. Consult your regional offices of the federal Department of Health, Education, and Welfare, Department of Agriculture, and Department of Labor for information on those programs. (Also see separate listings in this book in Chapter 21, *Employment*, Chapter 25, *Food and Nutrition*, and Chapter 30, *Health*.)

The following are the headquarters for national organizations for senior citizens that provide direct services through their local chapters or affiliated groups:

American National Red Cross
17th and D Streets, N.W.
Washington, D.C. 20006

Seeks to enable every older person to maintain independence in community life and, when needed, to insure dignified protection and assistance. Through a nationwide network of chapters, the American Red Cross determines which services are most needed, and senior volunteers are often a mainstay in carrying them out. Contact your local chapter to see which of these free programs are available: transportation; nutrition maintenance; friendly visits to the homebound; telephone reassurance; and volunteer services in hospitals and nursing homes.

LITERATURE: *Caring* and *Telephone Reassurance Service,* free.

Gray Panthers
National Headquarters
3700 Chestnut Street
Philadelphia, Pa. 19104

Founded in June 1970 by Margaret Kuhn and five friends to fight age discrimination, this national network now has fifty-five local chapters and is growing fast. In 1973 it merged with one of Ralph Nader's public citizen groups, the Retired Professional Action Group, helping the Gray Panthers expand their activities into investigations of the hearing aid industry and nursing home reform. Programs and publications of local chapters vary widely.

The national office acts as an information clearinghouse on Gray Panther activities. General age-related announcements and legislation are discussed in their monthly newsletter, *The Network*.

The first national convention was held in October 1975 with delegates from over thirty-three states; the second national convention was held in October 1977. Their motto is "age and youth in action." Anyone can join the Gray Panthers or subscribe to their newsletter ($3.00 a year; sample on request). The major concerns of the Gray Panthers are an end to age discrimination, the abolition of arbitrary and compulsory retirement and discrimination in employment, the enactment of national health-care programs, reduced-fare or free mass transportation, passage of the Equal Opportunity for Displaced Homemakers Act to help older women gain independence and financial security, a national housing project, tax reform, and education reform to include programs and opportunities for all persons at little or no cost to participants.

LITERATURE: Publications price list; advocacy bibliography ($.50); history ($.25); "New Life for the Elderly" by Maggie Kuhn ($.75).

National Alliance of Senior Citizens, Inc. (NASC)
P. O. Box 40031
Washington, D.C. 20016

A membership organization open to all persons aged fifty and older (dues range from $8.00 to $500.00). NASC promotes self-help and volunteer work by the elderly in community and business affairs. One important concern is the reduction of crime against the elderly.

LITERATURE: *Senior Guardian* newsletter; *The Senior Independent* newspaper; *Senior Services Manual* ($2.50) contains valuable basic information as well as clear, brief descriptions on free and federal programs or resources; free descriptive brochure.

National Association of Mature People (NAMP)
2000 Classen Center
P.O. Box 26792
Oklahoma City, Okla. 73126

NAMP, founded in 1975, has twenty-eight chapters throughout the United States and is a nonprofit, nonpartisan, educational organization formed to assist people over fifty-five in attaining maximum value in their lives. Available services include publications, educational programs, social and recreational activities, group travel, financial guidance, counseling, a pre-retirement planning program, and continuing information on social security and Medicare. Discounts for prescription drugs, insurance, hotels and motels, car rentals, and traffic court appearance bonds are available for all members. Membership dues are $4.00, which includes subscription to *Best Years* magazine and the *NAMP Newsletter*.

LITERATURE: A variety of brochures and pamphlets; "Confidence Games"; *NAMP News; Best Years.*

National Council of Senior Citizens, Inc.
1511 K Street, N.W.
Washington, D.C. 20005

14 / THE HELP BOOK

A national membership organization with affiliated groups throughout the United States; offers health insurance plan; holds yearly conferences; opposes mandatory retirement and age discrimination in employment. Membership dues range from $3.50 to $4.00 for individual, non-club seniors to $25.00 for non-seniors.

LITERATURE: *Senior Citizen News*, a monthly newspaper.

National Retired Teachers Association/ American Association of Retired Persons (NRTA/AARP)
1909 K Street, N.W.
Washington, D.C. 20049

In 1958 Dr. Ethel Percy Andrus, a California educator for more than forty years, founded both organizations; combined membership now exceeds 10 million. Their motto is "To serve and not be served." There are nearly 3,000 chapters throughout the United States; membership dues are $3.00. The local chapters are modeled after the national groups, whose programs include: the Consumer Information Program, the Church Relations Office; Generations Alliance Program; the Health Education Programs; the Institutes of Lifetime Learning in Washington, D.C., and Long Beach, Calif.; the Driver Improvement Program; and the Crime Prevention Program. The Retirement Research and Welfare Association has its headquarters in Long Beach, Calif. There is a national pharmacy mail-order service. Many chapters sponsor group travel for foreign vacations and weekend trips within the United States.

LITERATURE: All the publications that follow are sent free with $3.00 membership—*Pharmacy Products List; National Community Service Programs* booklet; *Your Retirement Housing Guide; Your Retirement Home Repair Guide; Your Retirement Health Guide; Tax Facts 1977 for Older Americans;* "Purchase Privilege Program"; *Your Retirement Widowhood Guide; NRTA News Bulletin* newspaper; *AARP News Bulletin* newspaper; *Modern Maturity* magazine; *NRTA Journal.*

The following federal agencies and national organizations on aging are information clearinghouses for the general public, for the elderly, and for people doing research on aging and on available programs for the aging:

Administration on Aging (AoA)
National Clearinghouse on Aging
Office of Human Development Services
U.S. Department of Health, Education, and Welfare
Washington, D.C. 20201

The federal government's key information clearinghouse, AoA publishes a variety of material for older people and professionals in the field of aging.

LITERATURE: Free fact sheets on AoA programs and topics of general interest to older people, such as retirement, housing, and employment; *Consumer Guide for Older People*, a pocket-sized checklist to help the elderly protect themselves against frauds and swindles; *Directory of State Agencies on Aging; To Find the Way*, a brochure describing the types of services available to older people with explanations on how to find and use them; *Publications of the Administration on Aging*, a leaflet listing additional materials on a variety of elderly-related subjects, such as statistics, home-delivered meals, and basic concepts of aging; *Guidelines for a Telephone Reassurance Service* by Virginia Rogers.

American Geriatrics Society, Inc.
10 Columbus Circle
New York, N.Y. 10019

Promotes and encourages research on aging; provides continuing medical education programs for member physicians.

LITERATURE: Monthly newsletters; *Journal of the American Geriatrics Society*.

Federal Council on the Aging
330 Independence Avenue, S.W. #4260
Washington, D.C. 20201

Advisory body to the President, Secretary of Health, Education, and Welfare, Congress, and the Commissioner on Aging in matters affecting the elderly.

LITERATURE: *Commitment to a Better Life: National Policy Concerns for Older Women* (1975); Annual Reports to the President (1975, 1976, 1977); *The Treatment of Assets and Income From Assets in Income-Conditioned Government Programs* (1977).

Gerontological Society
One DuPont Circle, Suite 520
Washington, D.C. 20036

A national organization for researchers, educators, and professionals in the field of aging that sponsors scientific meetings; membership $35.00, students $17.50.

LITERATURE: *Journal of Gerontology; The Gerontologist*.

National Council on Aging, Inc. (NCOA)
1828 L Street, N.W.
Washington, D.C. 20036

A comprehensive, nonprofit organization serving as an information clearinghouse in the field of aging for seniors, professionals, and interested lay persons. There are several institutes within the umbrella association: National Institute of Senior Centers (NISC) coordinates the Senior Centers throughout the country and publishes *Directory of Senior Centers and Clubs: A National Resource* ($10.00), *A National Directory of Housing for Older People* ($5.50), and *Memo*, a monthly newsletter; National Voluntary Organizations for Independent Living for the Aging (NVOILA) has 158 national voluntary organizations and their branch offices working in 300 communities throughout the country to help the elderly stay independent; the National Media Resource Center on Aging (MRC) provides material on aging to editors, writers, academics, and broadcasters to help change the media image of the elderly and publishes a weekly column, *Going Strong*, and booklets, such as *The Myth and Reality of Aging in America;* and the Center for a Public Policy (NCOA) stays on top of pending legislation affecting the elderly.

The NCOA also has a research department and an extensive library. In addition, NCOA sponsors Senior Community Services Aides, a part-time employment program for the elderly operating in about eighteen rural and urban settings; this program offers the elderly opportunities in a variety of areas, including public housing, federal and state agencies, schools, and hospitals.

LITERATURE: *Perspective on Aging*, bimonthly magazine; *Current Literature on Aging*, quarterly abstract journal; *Journal of Industrial Gerontology; Memo;* NVOILA newsletter; free publications list and leaflets available.

National Institute on Aging
National Institutes of Health
U.S. Department of Health, Education, and Welfare
9000 Rockville Pike
Bethesda, Md. 20014

A research center on all physical, psychological, and sociological aspects of aging, including menopause, memory loss, and susceptibility to disease.

National Interfaith Coalition on Aging, Inc. (NICA)
298 South Hull Street
Athens, Ga. 30605

A national umbrella organization for national religious and other organizations interested in the problems of the aging; membership fees range

16 / THE HELP BOOK

from $50.00 to $500.00; provides public information; holds annual meetings and assemblies.

LITERATURE: Fact sheets and brochures; newsletter.

**National Senior Citizens Law Center
(NSCLC)**
1709 West 8th Street
Los Angeles, Calif. 90017

BRANCH OFFICE: 1200 Fifteenth Street, N.W.
Washington, D.C. 20005

Funded by the Legal Services Corporation and the Administration on Aging, NSCLC is primarily concerned with helping the elderly resolve their legal problems. They are assisting in twenty-nine states to stimulate the expansion of legal services for the elderly. NSCLC also acts as an information clearinghouse on the legal problems of the elderly and monitors legislation related to the elderly; retired attorneys and undergraduate students assist on a volunteer basis.

LITERATURE: Descriptive leaflets; *The Washington Weekly Newsletter; Nursing Home Law Letter*, bimonthly publication; publications price list available from National Clearinghouse for Legal Services Order Department, 500 North Michigan Avenue, Suite 2220, Chicago, Ill. 60611.

Select Committee on Aging
U.S. House of Representatives
Room 712, House Office Building Annex 1
300 New Jersey Avenue, S.E.
Washington, D.C. 20515

This committee has four main purposes: to study the problems of the elderly, including income maintenance, housing, health, welfare, education, recreation, employment, and participation in family and community life; to encourage public and private programs and policies to assist the elderly; to coordinate policies between government and private programs; and to review recommendations made by the President or the White House Conference on Aging.

LITERATURE: Fact sheet.

The following listing includes federal employment programs for the elderly that offer direct placement for eligible seniors through their local offices and national organizations that provide information and local referrals for employment of the elderly:

ACTION
806 Connecticut Avenue, N.W.
Washington, D.C. 20525
Toll-free number

The following programs are sponsored by the U.S. government and are coordinated through ACTION, an independent government agency:

Peace Corps: Since the Peace Corps began in 1961, it has accepted older Americans who are willing to live for two years in a foreign country receiving little money and a salary paid at the completion of their service.

RSVP (Retired Senior Volunteer Program): There are about 600 RSVP programs around the country open to Americans aged sixty and older. They receive out-of-pocket expenses while volunteering in a community program, such as helping the handicapped.

Senior Companion Program: Small stipends are paid to senior volunteers who help other adults in need.

Foster Grandparent Program: Low-income seniors sixty and over work with one child for several hours a day.

SCORE (Service Corps of Retired Executives): Started in 1965, SCORE has volunteers who provide information and advice to small-business owners. Out-of-pocket expense reimbursement is available.

VISTA (Volunteers in Service to America): A domestic counterpart to the Peace Corps with volunteers working in the deprived and needy areas of the United States.

Senior Community Aides
National Retired Teachers Association/
　American Association of Retired
　Persons (NRTA/AARP)
1909 K Street, N.W.
Washington, D.C. 20049

The NRTA/AARP sponsors this employment program in over thirty cities throughout the United States. They find part-time work for seniors in public or private service programs, such as child-care centers. They also train and recruit for these positions.

Senior Opportunities for Service (SOS)
Office of Economic Opportunity
Office of Program Review
Washington, D.C. 20506

Persons over sixty whose incomes are below the Office of Economic Opportunity guidelines are eligible for this employment program, which provides nutrition and consumer education and outreach services for older people.

U.S. Department of Defense Referrals Program
Transitional Manpower Programs
Office of the Assistant Secretary of Defense
Washington, D.C. 20201

Retired military personnel can seek counseling and job placement services.

The following federal agencies and national organizations provide information or assistance on nursing and home care for the elderly. Direct services are available through the local affiliates or chapters of the national organizations:

American College of Nursing Home Administrators (ACNHA)
4650 East-West Highway
Washington, D.C. 20014

A professional association of nursing home administrators offering public information, educational, and job training publications, and referrals to state licensing boards.

LITERATURE: Descriptive brochures; newsletter; list of publications; *Journal of Long-Term Care Administration* ($9.00 a year).

American Health Care Association (AHCA)
1200 15th Street, N.W.
Washington, D.C. 20005

A national trade association for long-term care facilities with chapters in each state. The national headquarters serves as an information clearinghouse for the general public on long-term health care; maintains an information center; conducts educational seminars and workshops; acquaints Congress and the Executive Branch with the problems, needs, and roles of long-term care; and promotes high standards of administration and care in nursing homes. Organized in 1946, the AHCA prefers written inquiries.

LITERATURE: Free publications list; *Books for Nursing Homes; A Positive Step;* audio-visual catalog; *Health Career Opportunities;* and *Thinking About a Nursing Home?*

Health Care Financing Administration
Bureau of Health, Standards and Quality
U.S. Department of Health, Education, and
　Welfare
330 C Street, N.W.
Washington, D.C. 20201

This federal agency has absorbed the former Long-Term Care Department. Through ten regional offices, on-site surveys of long-term care facilities are reviewed for the purpose of entering into contract for Medicaid. State administration of Medicare is also supervised and information and publications on nursing homes are available through the headquarters.

LITERATURE: Free booklets on choosing a nursing home facility; publications price list.

National Citizens Coalition for Nursing Home Reform
National Paralegal Institute
2000 P Street, N.W.
Washington, D.C. 20036

Founded in 1975, this national coalition comprises thirty-seven consumer organizations around the country. It is an advocacy group for regulatory and legislative change and an information clearinghouse on nursing homes.

National Council for Homemaker-Home Health Aide Services, Inc.
67 Irving Place
New York, N.Y. 10003

Founded in 1963, this national organization comprises local private and public agencies that deliver homemaker-home health aide services (someone going into the home at times of illness or stress). It also holds conferences and seminars, serves as an information clearinghouse, and maintains a library open to the public.

LITERATURE: *Directory of Homemaker-Home Health Aide Services* ($3.00); *News* quarterly; descriptive brochure.

Nursing Home Information Service
National Council of Senior Citizens
1511 K Street, N.W.
Washington, D.C. 20005

Originally a 1974 project of the National Consumers League, since 1975 the Nursing Home Information Service has been supported by the National Council of Senior Citizens as part of their National Senior Citizens Education and Research Center. The service is an information and referral service supplying names, locations, prices, and services offered by nursing homes in the Washington, D.C., metropolitan area, along with summaries of federal inspection surveys for those homes certified for Medicare and/or Medicaid. It is used by seekers of long-term care, their families, friends, and advocates. Some information on long-term care services in other parts of the country is also available, as well as guidance on finding geriatric assessment services, and establishing Medicaid eligibility.

Veterans Administration Information Service
810 Vermont Avenue, N.W.
Washington, D.C. 20420

A widespread system of nursing homes is one of the benefits for eligible veterans and dependents. Check with your regional representative of the Veterans Administration for further details.

The following is a listing of the state agencies for aging:

Commission on Aging
740 Madison Avenue
Montgomery, Ala. 36130

Office on Aging
Department of Health and Social
   Services
Alaska Office Building
Pouch H026
Juneau, Alaska 99811

Advisory Council on Aging
1400 West Washington
Phoenix, Ariz. 85007

Office on Aging and Adult Services
Social Services Division
Department of Human Services
7107 West Twelfth Street
Little Rock, Ark. 72201

Department of Aging
918 J Street
Sacramento, Calif. 95814

Division of Services for the Aging
Department of Social Services
State Social Services Building
1575 Sherman Street
Denver, Colo. 80203

Department on Aging
90 Washington Street
Hartford, Conn. 06115

Division of Aging
Department of Health and Social Services
2513 Lancaster Avenue
Wilmington, Del. 19805

Office on Aging
1012 Fourteenth Street, N.W.
Washington, D.C. 20005

Aging and Adult Services Program Office
Department of Health and Rehabilitative
  Services
1321 Winewood Boulevard, Room 328
Tallahassee, Fla. 32301

Office of Aging
Department of Human Resources
618 Ponce de Leon Avenue, N.E.
Atlanta, Ga. 30308

Commission on Aging
Office of the Governor
1149 Bethel Street
Honolulu, Hawaii 96813

Office on Aging
Statehouse
Boise, Idaho 83720

Department on Aging
421 East Capitol
Springfield, Ill. 62702

Commission on the Aging and Aged
201 Graphic Arts Building
215 North Senate Avenue
Indianapolis, Ind. 46202

Commission on the Aging
415 Tenth Street
Des Moines, Iowa 50309

Department on Aging
2700 West Sixth
Biddle Building
Topeka, Kans. 66612

Aging Services
Bureau for Social Services
Department for Human Resources
275 East Main Street
Frankfort, Ky. 40601

Bureau of Aging Services
P.O. Box 44282
Baton Rouge, La. 70804

Bureau of Maine's Elderly
Department of Human Services
State House
Augusta, Maine 04333

Office on Aging
State Office Building
301 West Preston Street
Baltimore, Md. 21201

Department of Elder Affairs
110 Tremont Street
Boston, Mass. 02116

Commission on Services to the Aging
Department of Management and Budget
300 East Michigan
Lansing, Mich. 48909

Governor's Citizens Council on Aging
204 Metro Square Building
7th and Robert Streets
St. Paul, Minn. 55101

Council on Aging
Watkins Building
Jackson, Miss. 39201

Office of Aging
Department of Social Services
Broadway State Office Building
Jefferson City, Mo. 65101

Aging Services Bureau
Community Services Division
Department of Social and Rehabilitation Services
P.O. Box 4210
Helena, Mont. 59601

Commission on Aging
P.O. Box 95044
Lincoln, Neb. 68509

Division for Aging Services
Department of Human Resources
101 Kinkead Building
505 East King Street
Capitol Complex
Carson City, Nev. 89710

Council on Aging
14 Depot Street
P.O. Box 786
Concord, N.H. 03301

Division on Aging
Department of Community Affairs
363 West State Street
P.O. Box 2768
Trenton, N.J. 08625

Bureau on Aging
Social Services Division
P.E.R.A. Building
Santa Fe, N.M. 87503

Office for the Aging
Agency Building No. 2
Empire State Plaza
Albany, N.Y. 12223

Assistant Secretary for the Aging
Department of Human Resources
Albemarle Building
325 North Salisbury Street
Raleigh, N.C. 27611

Aging Services
Community Services Division
Social Service Board
State Capitol
Bismarck, N.D. 58505

Commission on Aging
34 North High Street
Columbus, Ohio 43215

Special Unit on Aging
Department of Institutions, Social, and Rehabilitative Services
P.O. Box 25352
Oklahoma City, Okla. 73125

Program on Aging
Department of Human Resources
772 Commercial Street, S.E.
Salem, Ore. 97310

Office for the Aging
504 State Street Building
3rd and State Streets
Harrisburg, Pa. 17120

Department of Elderly Affairs
150 Washington Street
Providence, R.I. 02903

Commission on Aging
915 Main Street
Columbia, S.C. 29201

Office on Aging
Division of Human Development
Department of Social Services
State Office Building
Illinois Street
Pierre, S.D. 57501

Commission on Aging
306 Gay Street
Nashville, Tenn. 37201

Governor's Committee on Aging
Southwest Towers
Box 12786, Capitol Station
Austin, Tex. 78711

Division of Aging
Department of Social Services
345 South Sixth East Street
Salt Lake City, Utah 84102

Office of Aging
State Office Building
Montpelier, Vt. 05602

Office on Aging
830 East Main Street, Suite 950
Richmond, Va. 23219

State Office on Aging
Bureau of Social Services
Department of Social and Health Services
Olympia, Wash. 98504

Commission on Aging
2100 Washington East
Charleston, W.Va. 25305

Board on Aging
Department of Health and Social Services
1120, 1 West Wilson Street
Madison, Wis. 53702

Division of Public Assistance and Social Services
Department of Health and Social Services
Hathaway Building
2300 Capitol Avenue
Cheyenne, Wyo. 82002

CRIMES AGAINST THE ELDERLY

Older persons are particularly vulnerable to violent personal and property crimes. Many cannot afford to move from the neighborhoods they have lived in for sixty or seventy years, even if they are now run-down high-crime areas. Some property crimes, however, are less likely, if the victims know in advance criminal schemes to watch for. Three well-known con games used by the so-called "bunco artist" have the elderly as their most frequent targets:

1. *The Pigeon Drop.* A "helpless stranger" (the criminal) tells an elderly person he (or she) has "found" an envelope filled with money (or is afraid to carry a large amount of money or has just received and cashed an inheritance check). The criminal shows the money, which usually has a $20 or $50 bill on the outside of the roll or stack. "Could you hold it for me?" he asks the victim.

Another "stranger" (a second criminal) comes by and the first criminal asks the second one what to do. The second one usually says the elderly victim looks honest and should be trusted with the money, but she should get some money from the bank as a sign of "good faith."

The victim withdraws her money (usually about $1,000), gives it to the criminal, takes the first envelope, and the criminal goes off with the victim's money; the victim is left with an envelope filled with play money or paper and only $20 in real money. The victim's bank account turns out to be the "found" money.

2. *The Home Repairman.* Someone, usually in a work uniform carrying a prop (such as a tool kit, paint brushes, or flashlight) offers to check some household equipment or machinery, such as a chimney, washing machine, or heating mechanism. When "serious damage" is reported, the victim is asked to make a cash deposit until the criminal comes back with additional repair tools. The "repairman" never returns.

AT HOME

Equip your door with a deadbolt or drop-bolt lock. The lock should also have a highly pick-resistant cylinder protected by a guard plate.

The peephole should be of the wide-angle type which gives a fuller view of the outside area.

Do not open door until you are sure of the identity of your visitor(s).

Always double lock door when leaving, even to put out trash, pick up mail or walk dog.

Do not leave housekey under mat, in mailbox or in any other area near door.

If on returning you find door open or tampered with, do not enter. Leave immediately and notify police.

If you lose your keys or they are stolen, replace lock cylinders immediately.

For fire escape windows the Fire Department-approved 'ferry' gates are recommended. Any key-operated gate is against the law on fire escape windows.

A licensed locksmith will show you a variety of window locks that are available for all types of windows.

If awakened at night by an intruder, lie still, try not to panic, and at first opportunity call police.

Don't volunteer any information to unknown callers on the telephone.

ON THE STREET

Travel and shop with companions whenever possible during the daytime as well as nighttime. There is greater safety in numbers.

If possible avoid carrying a pocketbook. When carrying a pocketbook, keep keys and cash in garment pockets or hidden elsewhere on your person.

When walking, and especially when shopping, hold your pocketbook at all times and keep your hand on the clasp to foil pickpockets.

In the theatre or when dining, keep your pocketbook on your lap. Do not place it on the floor, or on another seat, or on the back of a chair.

Take only necessary items when going out. Leave charge cards at home unless you intend to use them. Carry only the cash needed, not more. Keep all personal papers in a safe place at home or in a safe deposit box at your bank.

If your pocketbook is snatched, let it go. DON'T FIGHT FOR IT. Anything in it worth fighting for shouldn't be there in the first place.

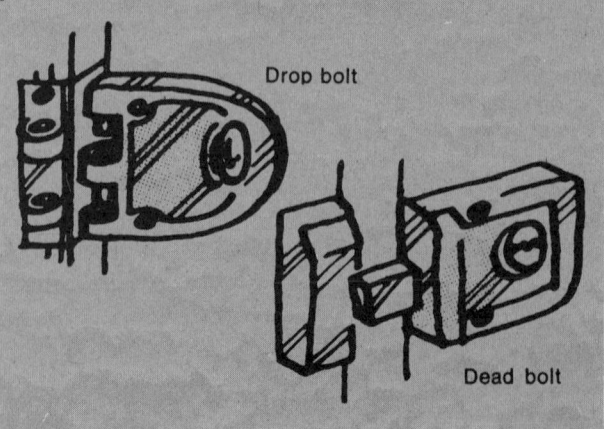

Drop bolt

Dead bolt

Reprinted with permission from "Safety Tips for the Older Person"

WHEN WALKING

The over-65 age group has the highest number of pedestrian fatalities; the 45-64 age group has the second highest. It is therefore particularly important for the older person to observe basic safety rules.

> Never cross against the light.
>
> Cross at the corner, never between parked vehicles or in the middle of the block. Stay within crosswalk.
>
> Watch for cars turning into crosswalk. Before crossing, make certain all cars have stopped.
>
> Never assume the driver will see you or be able to stop in time. Your safety is your responsibility.

CONFIDENCE GAMES

"Con artists" are smooth-talking criminals who aim to separate you from your money through trickery and deceit. They can be men or women working alone or in pairs or groups. They may stop you on the street or call on the phone or ring your doorbell. They may pretend to be repairmen, or building inspectors or assume any other identity. There are many different kinds of confidence games. To avoid becoming a victim:

> Beware of friendly strangers offering goods or services at low rates.
>
> Beware of friendly strangers who tell you they found money and want to share it with you.
>
> Be suspicious of telephone calls from persons claiming to be bank officials who ask you to withdraw money from your account for any reason. Banks communicate in writing on business transactions.
>
> Be alert to any scheme that involves removing your savings or other valuables from safekeeping and turning them over to anyone.
>
> Be suspicious of fortune tellers, "readers," "advisors," etc. If you are asked to turn over money or valuables, notify the police.
>
> Don't hesitate to notify police of any suspicious circumstances.
>
> Remember, YOU DON'T GET SOMETHING FOR NOTHING.

3. *The Bank Examiner.* Either by calling ahead and making an appointment or by coming to the victim's door, a phony bank or savings and loan "investigator" pays a visit. He states that he is checking up on a dishonest employee and asks the victim to "test" the employee by withdrawing money from the bank with the supposed purpose of using it to "trap" the suspected employee. The "investigator" then tells the victim the withdrawn money has to be held as "evidence" but will, of course, be returned after the "thief" is found out. The "investigator" never returns.

These schemes may seem obvious to most people, but the con men and women who use them are skilled and confident in their roles. Education is the best prevention against these fraudulent crimes since the plans follow a predictable pattern.

The unpredictable violent personal crimes or the burglaries committed when the victim is not at home are even more feared and dangerous. Here too education and self-defense are helpful, and many elderly people are learning good crime-prevention skills. For example, the New York City Police Department's Crime Prevention Bureau distributes a leaflet containing the advice on pages 22 and 23 to the elderly on how to be a less-likely victim.

On the national level, information on programs and educational materials on crimes against the elderly are available from:

Center for Studies in Aging
North Texas State University
Denton, Tex. 76203

The center's Improving the Reporting of Crimes Program provides resource and training materials on older victims as well as research into the impact of crime upon adult victims.

LITERATURE: *The Older Citizen's Role in Fighting Crime*, and *Police/Older Victim Relations*, training manuals.

Criminal Justice and the Elderly
1511 K Street, N.W.
Washington, D.C. 20005

A program sponsored by the National Council of Senior Citizens' Legal Research and Services for the Elderly, under grants from the U.S. Department of Justice's Law Enforcement Assistance Administration and the Ford Foundation. This research and resource center has seven demonstration projects associated with it.

LITERATURE: *Criminal Justice & the Elderly*, quarterly newsletter.

National Retired Teachers Association/ American Association of Retired Persons
1909 K Street, N.W.
Washington, D.C. 20049

The National Crime Prevention and Crime Education Program for seniors publishes related booklets. A series of four two-hour crime-prevention sessions, complete with guidebooks and presentation instructions, is also available covering these topics: street crime, burglary, fraud/bunco, and community-police relations.

LITERATURE: *Your Retirement Anti-Crime Guide*, booklet on avoiding all types of crimes; *Guide to Home and Personal Security* (AIM publication); *Preventing Crime Through Education: How to Spot a Con Artist;* brochure on the program.

Local programs for elderly crime victims are not administered through one national agency or organization. Instead, they are provided by different public or private services within each community. Quite often, public programs are sponsored by the police department, the district attorney's office, or the mayor's office. Private programs on crimes against the elderly are operated through local senior citizens clubs or within general crime-victim counseling services. Other possible sources are the Call For Action hotlines throughout the country (see Chapter 13, *Consumer Affairs*), university counseling bureaus, and psychiatric or mental health services.

The following is a sampling of local crime prevention programs for the elderly (adapted and updated from the February 1977 issue of Police Chief *magazine*):

Maricopa County Sheriff's Department
Bureau of Crime Resistance
120 S. First Avenue
Phoenix, Ariz. 85003

Fresno County Probation
Victim Services
P.O. Box 453
Fresno, Calif. 93709

Los Angeles County Department of Senior
 Citizens Affairs
Interagency Task Force on Crime Against the
 Elderly
601 South Kingsley Drive
Los Angeles, Calif. 90005

Sacramento Police Department
Crime Prevention Program
625 H Street
Sacramento, Calif. 95814

Wilmington Crime Resistance Task Force
Wilmington Crime Resistance Program
P.O. Box 1872
Wilmington, Del. 19899

Chief Postal Inspector
Fraud Prevention Program
475 L'Enfant Plaza, S.W.
Washington, D.C. 20260

Special Concerns Staff
Office of Housing Management, HUD
Security Planning for HUD-Assisted Housing
Room N 9108
451 7th Street, S.W.
Washington, D.C. 20410

Jacksonville Sheriff's Office
Sheriff's Jacksonville Community Posse
1041 South McDuff Avenue
Jacksonville, Fla. 32205

Community Services Section
Crime Prevention Unit
Miami Beach Police Department
120 Meridian Avenue
Miami Beach, Fla. 33139

City of St. Petersburg/Junior League of St.
 Petersburg, Inc.
Project Concern
1510 First Avenue North
St. Petersburg, Fla. 33705

Sarasota City Police Department
Crimes Against the Elderly
P.O. Box 3528
Sarasota, Fla. 33578

Lithonia Police Department
Senior Citizen/Invalid Contact Service
6980 Main Street
Lithonia, Ga. 30058

26 / THE HELP BOOK

Evansville Police Department
Symposium on Safety
15 N.W. 7th Street
Evansville, Ind. 47708

South Bend Police
Senior Citizen Lock Project
701 West Sample Street
South Bend, Ind. 46601

Louisville Division of Police
Crime Prevention for Senior Citizens
633 West Jefferson Street
Louisville, Ky. 40202

International Association of Chiefs of Police
Crime, Safety and the Senior Citizen
11 Firstfield Road
Gaithersburg, Md. 20760

Crime Prevention for Seniors
801 Sligo Avenue
Silver Spring, Md. 20910

Detroit Police Department
Cass Corridor Safety for Seniors Project
3165 Second
Detroit, Mich. 48226

Minneapolis Police Department
Crime Cautions for Seniors
Room 130, City Hall
Minneapolis, Minn. 55415

Mid-America Regional Council
Aid to Elderly Victims of Crime
20 West 9th Street
Kansas City, Mo. 64105

Mayor's Office for Senior Citizens
Senior Home Security
560 Delmar Boulevard
St. Louis, Mo. 63101

Omaha Police Division
Crime Prevention Education for Senior Citizens
505 South 15th Street
Omaha, Neb. 68102

Jersey City Police Department
Crime Prevention Unit
282 Central Avenue
Jersey City, N.J. 07307

Bronx Area Senior Citizens Robbery Unit
New York City Police Department
450 Cross Bronx Expressway
Bronx, N.Y. 10457

Jamaica Service Program for Older Adults
Safety Committee of the JSPOA Senior Citizens
    Advisory Council
92-47 165th Street
Jamaica, N.Y. 11433

New York City Department for the Aging
Senior Citizens Anti-Crime Network (SCAN)
150 Nassau Street
New York, N.Y. 10038

New York City Department for the Aging
Senior Citizens Crime Prevention Program
155 West 72nd Street, Room 607
New York, N.Y. 10023

Syracuse Police Department
Senior Citizens Crime Prevention Program
511 South State Street
Syracuse, N.Y. 13202

Cuyahoga County Commissioners
Senior Safety and Security Program
1276 West 3rd Street
Cleveland, Ohio 44113

Mansfield Police Department
Crime Prevention for the Elderly
27 West 2nd Street
Mansfield, Ohio 44902

Eastern Oklahoma Development District
Law Enforcement for the Aged
P.O. Box 1367, 800 West Okmulgee
Muskogee, Okla. 74401

Cottage Grove Police Department
Senior Citizens Crime Prevention Program
28 South 6th Street
Cottage Grove, Ore. 97424

Multnomah County Division of Public Safety
Older Americans' Crime Prevention Research
10525 S.E. Cherry Blossom Drive
Portland, Ore. 97216

CLASP (Citizens Local Alliance for Safer
   Philadelphia)
Senior Safety Program
1405 Locust Street
Philadelphia, Pa. 19102

Dallas Geriatric Research Institute
2525 Centerville Road
Dallas, Tex. 25228

Huntington Police Department
Operation Lifeline
Huntington, W. Va. 25717

Milwaukee County
Neighborhood Security Aid Program
901 North 9th Street
Milwaukee, Wis. 53233

ADDITIONAL LITERATURE

Eating Right for Less (For Older People) by the Editors of *Consumer Reports* (1975). Consumers Union, 256 Washington Street, Mount Vernon, N.Y. 10550 ($2.00). Since the one basic change in eating habits predicated by age is fewer calories (since fewer are expended), this book obviously has value for the overweight as well as the older person. It is a clear, thorough, and specific guide to eating better; even brand names are suggested on the basis of Consumers Union tests.

A Good Age by Alex Comfort, M.D. (1976). Crown Publishers, One Park Avenue, New York, N.Y. 10016 ($9.95). Alex Comfort, whose name is most readily recognizable as the author of *The Joy of Sex*, dedicates this dictionary-format book to his ninety-three-year-old father. Topics covered range from agism, alcohol, arthritis, and bereavement to vitamins, war, wrinkles, youth, and the prudent diet. Michael Leonard's mezzotints and watercolor illustrations are stunning.

Nursing Homes: A Citizens' Guide by Linda Horn and Elma Griesel, introduction by Maggie Kuhn (1977). Beacon Press, 25 Beacon Street, Boston, Mass. 02108 ($8.95). From their experiences working for the Long-Term Care Action Project of the Gray Panthers, the authors tell "how to organize, plan, and achieve nursing home reform in your community." Model programs in over a dozen cities, such as Citizens for Better Care in Detroit, are described in detail along with a few national programs. The book also contains a good resource section.

Options, a free trimonthly newsletter available from the New York City Department for the Aging, 250 Broadway, New York, N.Y. 10007. It contains a wealth of information on free programs available to the elderly in New York as well as book reviews and legislative updates of interest to all working with the elderly.

The Pursuit of Dignity: New Living Alternatives for the Elderly by Bert Kruger Smith (1977). Beacon Press, 25 Beacon Street, Boston, Mass. 02108 ($9.95). Smith, an executive associate of the Hogg Foundation for Mental Health in Austin, Tex., and author of *Aging in America*, suggests that it is far better to find ways to help the elderly cope with the isolation of living alone in their own home than to encourage giving up familiar surroundings (and identity) and moving into a "home." He devotes a chapter to each of the options: day care, home-health service, cooperative housing, and nutritional programs.

The Retirement Threat by Tony Lamb and Dave Duffy (1977). J. P. Tarcher, Inc., 9110 Sunset Boulevard, Los Angeles, Calif. 90069 ($7.95). Lamb, an engineer and inventor who retired in 1971, began a new career counseling senior citizens and coordinating services in Ventura County, Calif. This book grew out of his multifaceted senior survival courses and programs. The book provides such practical information as how much money you will need in your retirement budget, social security and pensions, winning the war against inflation, and preparing for a second career and how to find a job. He also offers his views on how growing older in America could be less harrowing by ending mandatory retirement, establishing a national health care system and guaranteed pension plans, increasing social security benefits, and establishing senior foundations.

Survival Handbook for Children of Aging Parents by Dr. Arthur N. Schwartz (1977). Follett Publishing Company, 1010 West Washington Boulevard, Chicago, Ill. 60607 ($6.95). Dr. Schwartz, director of the Adult Counseling Program at the Andrus Gerontology Center of the University of Southern California, has written a moving and sympathetic book about the predictable crises of aging. It is intended as a guide for the middle-aged person who is overwhelmed by the demands of elderly parents. "Old age can be enormously worthwhile and . . . the younger generation, by helping to make it so, can draw rich dividends" is his message.

Why Survive? Being Old in America by Robert N. Butler (1975). Harper & Row, 10 East 53rd Street, New York, N.Y. 10022 ($5.95).

You and Your Aging Parent: The Modern Family's Guide to Emotional, Physical, and Financial Problems by Barbara Silverstone and Helen Kandel Hyman (1976). Pantheon Books, 201 East 50th Street, New York, N.Y. ($3.95). A good reference book on a wide range of problems, from the loss of physical health to remarriage and sex after sixty-five, with an extensive resource and bibliographic section.

"Every Day Is a Gift When You Are Over 100" by Alexander Leaf, M.D., in *National Geographic* (January 1973).

For other articles on aging, consult the *Readers' Guide to Periodical Literature*, the *New York Times Index*, the *Social Sciences and Humanities Index*, and the *Applied Science and Technology Index*, which are available at your public or university library.

See also the following related chapters in *The Help Book:*

BUSINESS INFORMATION
CIVIL RIGHTS AND DISCRIMINATION
CONSUMER AFFAIRS
COUNSELING
COURTS
CRIME PREVENTION
CRIME VICTIMS AND WITNESSES
EDUCATION
EMERGENCIES AND DISASTERS
EMPLOYMENT
FINANCIAL ASSISTANCE
FOOD AND NUTRITION
HEALTH
HOUSING
KIDNAPPING, MISSING PERSONS, AND RUNAWAYS
LAW ENFORCEMENT
LEGAL SERVICES
MENTAL HEALTH
MULTIPURPOSE ORGANIZATIONS
RAPE AND SEXUAL ASSAULT
VETERANS
VOLUNTEERISM

# 3

ALCOHOLISM

To begin to understand alcoholism's complexities, one has to be closely associated with someone who suffers from the disease. Its depiction in movies, even the memorable *Lost Weekend* or *Days of Wine and Roses*, is mild compared to the unpredictable, frightening, Jekyll-and-Hyde behavior that surfaces in real life. Most alcoholics are ingenious at hiding the severity of their drinking problem; to others, and even to themselves, they are simply "heavy social drinkers." Too often alcoholics, their family, friends, and employers deny that the condition has become uncontrollable and warrants outside help. But since alcoholism is a progressive disease, in which both physical and psychological dependence increase, delaying help may be fatal.

Although today more than ever before, alcoholism is viewed as a disease and not a weakness or character flaw, prejudices against the alcoholic may prevent him or her or the family from getting help. The ramifications for both the alcoholic and the alcoholic's family are severe. "He just acted completely different when he was drunk," an Arizona woman said in describing her father. She grew up and married an alcoholic, whose problem became so bad that "his company put him in a hospital and suggested I come here [a shelter for the wives of alcoholics] because I didn't understand anything about alcoholism."

Few people do know anything about the disease; here are some basic facts about alcoholism, which currently afflicts at least ten million American men, women, and teenagers:

- Susceptibility to alcohol varies with the individual. One person might be unable to stop drinking after consuming only two beers daily for a year, while another might develop the symptoms of alcoholism only after ten years of having consumed huge quantities of hard liquor.
- Since World War II, the number of alcoholic women has doubled.

- 450,000 teenagers are alcoholics; 1.3 million preteens and teenagers drink to excess.
- Alcoholism may be the undetected cause of sexual impotence or mental illness.
- Alcoholism is linked to 50 percent of all road fatalities, 53 percent of deaths in fires, 64 percent of homicides, 21 percent of serious assaults, 30 percent of suicides, 60 percent of abused children, and 22 percent of home accidents.
- Each alcoholic affects seven to ten persons besides himself or herself, and those persons need help in learning how to deal with the alcoholic.

Since diagnosing alcoholism early and accurately may be the only way to realize outside help is necessary, a government publication suggests that you look for the following eight symptoms:

1. A preoccupation with alcohol
2. An increased tolerance of alcohol
3. Gulping drinks
4. Drinking alone
5. Using alcohol as a "medicine" to induce sleep or reduce anxiety
6. Blackouts following a drinking episode, e.g., the inability to recall certain behaviors or statements
7. Protecting the alcoholic supply
8. A yes answer to the question, "Is your drinking ever different from what you would like it to be?" namely uncontrolled drinking.

In the entries that follow, much space is devoted to descriptions of Alcoholics Anonymous, an organization that helps the drinker, and Al-Anon, an organization for the family, friends, and business associates of the alcoholic. These groups provide confidentiality and counseling by peers. Alcoholics Anonymous has been a model for hundreds of groups treating different problems, such as Overeaters Anonymous and Parents Anonymous. However, embracing AA or Al-Anon for help with alcoholism—as hundreds of thousands of recovered alcoholics have successfully done since AA's inception in the 1930s—should not rule out the use of one-to-one counseling or therapy as a means to understanding the more fundamental reasons for the initial reliance on alcohol.

For direct help for alcoholism, see the state agency listings in this chapter or check your telephone directory under state government services for an **Alcoholism** listing. Or you may write for a computer printout listing for your state for public and private in-patient and out-clinic alcoholism facilities, available from the National Clearinghouse for Alcohol Information (see listing that follows).

The following international and national organizations have numerous publications available from their headquarters. For direct help, check your local phone book for the nearest affiliate or chapter in your community. Or write to the headquarters of that agency or organization, listed below, requesting a local referral.

Al-Anon Family Group Headquarters, Inc.
P.O. Box 182
Madison Square Station
New York, N.Y. 10010

Started by the wife of the founder of Alcoholics Anonymous after her husband achieved sobriety, there are now local Al-Anon groups throughout the United States and the world to assist the friends and family of the alcoholic. People can join Al-Anon whether or not the alcoholic is actively drinking and/or admitting his/her problem or seeking help. With slight variations, Al-Anon utilizes the "Twelve Steps" of AA and also has spiritual overtones. Al-Anon members are encouraged to attend open meetings of AA to learn as much as possible about the disease of alcoholism. Often Al-Anon members will form groups among themselves to act as a secondary support system to help them live through (or find the strength to get out of) often unbearable home situations where one member is an active alcoholic. Emphasis is on the life of the nonalcoholic rather than the self-blame or guilt-ridden ponderings associated with alcoholics. Neither AA or Al-Anon, however, are substitutes for one-to-one counseling with a professional to arrive at the roots of the drinking problem, or the reasons for "allowing" the destructive behavior of the alcoholic to continue until it negatively effects—and often destroys—the rest of the family.

LITERATURE: *This is Al-Anon; Purpose of the Al-Anon Family Groups and Suggestions For Those Who Need Help; A Guide for the Family of the Alcoholic; Family Al-Anon—Family Treatment Tool in Alcoholism; Al-Anon Fact File;* fact sheets; publications list.

Alateen
P.O. Box 182
Madison Square Station
New York, N.Y. 10010

Started in 1957 by a California boy whose father was an alcoholic, Alateen is made up of several hundred groups of young people throughout the United States learning to cope with a family member's drinking problem and developing a greater understanding of drinking itself.

LITERATURE: *Youth and the Alcoholic Parent* and *Facts About Alateen for Those in the Helping Professions, Parents and Friends.*

Alcohol Education Project
National Congress of Parents and Teachers (PTA)
700 North Rush Street
Chicago, Ill. 60611

Since 1974, the National PTA has provided funding to its members to develop eight model programs for the primary prevention of alcohol abuse among youths and adults. The national headquarters serves as an information clearinghouse and provides educational materials and referrals as well as assistance for establishing a local PTA.

LITERATURE: *Alcohol: A Family Affair* pamphlet; *How to Talk to Your Teenager About Drinking and Driving* (in cooperation with the U.S. Department of Transportation); *Growing Hurts,* a series of 8 posters on alcohol abuse for the junior and senior high school levels; *How to Talk to Children About Drinking: A Parenting Guide,* a series of four workshops for parents; *Alcohol Alley,* a multimedia curriculum unit for grades 4 through 6;

Project Promise, a series of eight workshops for parents of troubled children who are active substance abusers; *People to People*, a training program for community teams who wish to develop alcohol abuse prevention programs in their schools.

Alcoholics Anonymous, Inc. (AA)
General Service Office
P.O. Box 459
Grand Central Station
New York, N.Y. 10017

BRITISH HEADQUARTERS: P.O. Box 514
11 Redcliffe Gardens
London SW10 9BG,
England

Since AA was founded in 1935 by two men, it has grown into the largest and most effective private, free, self-help organization for the alcoholic. There are over 800,000 members with more than 25,000 local AA groups in more than 92 countries. Total abstinence is believed to be the only long-term cure; the "Twelve Steps," based on religious and psychological principles, characterize the program. Alcoholics are assigned a "big brother" (or "big sister") to aid them in their withdrawal experience; meetings are held virtually every day and night of the week in most major cities. There are closed meetings for members only, and open meetings for those interested in alcoholism or the friends and relatives of alcoholics who want to learn more about the disease. AA is supported solely by contributions and the sale of publications. "Telephone therapy" between AA members is encouraged so that no alcoholic has to go it alone unless he or she wants to. Anonymity is not just a goal; it is a consistent principle; a silence pact is generally stated at the close of each meeting.

LITERATURE: *A Brief Guide to Alcoholics Anonymous*; *Alcoholics Anonymous in Your Community*; *Inside A.A.*; *A.A. Fact File*; free publications list available listing the hundreds of pamphlets, leaflets, and books written about AA (generally by former AA members).

Association of Drinkwatchers, International, Inc. (DW)
P.O. Box 179
Haverstraw, N.Y. 10927

A nonprofit, educational, self-help group established in 1974 with either abstinence or controlled drinking as the therapeutic goal. In *Alternatives for the Problem Drinker*, by Ariel Winters, President of Drinkwatchers, DW is further described: "Drinkwatchers' aim is to put alcohol in proper focus on the periphery of your life rather than in central focus whether that be abstention or moderate drinking. Drinkwatchers is not for extreme cases who need hospital detoxification centers, courts, jails, or medical treatment."

LITERATURE: Monthly newsletter ($12.00 a year); *How To Be a Drinkwatcher*.

National Council on Alcoholism, Inc. (NCA)
733 Third Avenue
New York, N.Y. 10017

A national voluntary health organization founded by Marty Mann, with headquarters in New York and Washington, D.C., NCA also has local affiliate councils on alcoholism and state voluntary alcoholism associations. NCA is an information clearinghouse whose goals are to encourage programs for the early detection of alcoholism and the prevention and treatment of alcoholism. It also works for the removal of the stigma of alcoholism and public awareness about alcoholism. Extensive publications list is free and provides a one-place source of major pamphlets, articles, books, and booklets, with requests filled quickly after receipt of order and payment.

LITERATURE: "The National Council on Alcoholism," a free pamphlet about the agency.

The Salvation Army
National Headquarters
120 West 14th Street
New York, N.Y. 10011

Two programs are offered for male alcoholics—Men's Social Service Centers for the business or family-oriented alcoholic, and Harbor Light Center for the "down-and-out" (skid-row) alcoholic. Contact your local Salvation Army for services in your community. Free counseling is also available for the wives and other family members of the alcoholic.

LITERATURE: *Help for the Alcoholic*, a free leaflet.

Veterans Administration (VA)
Alcohol and Drug Dependent Service
810 Vermont Avenue, N.W.
Washington, D.C. 20420

Free treatment for alcoholism is available at VA hospitals to any honorably discharged veteran.

Women for Sobriety, Inc.
P.O. Box 618
Quakertown, Pa. 18951

Founded by Dr. Jean Kirkpatrick, author of *Turnabout: Help for a New Life*, and executive director, this national organization of self-help groups provides help for alcoholic women to realize their full potential. It maintains a speakers bureau and sponsors community education programs.

Included in the Thirteen Statements of Acceptance "upon which" the members of Women for Sobriety reshape their lives are:

- I have a drinking problem that once had me.
- Negative emotions destroy only myself.
- Happiness is a habit I will develop.
- Problems bother me only to the degree I permit them to.
- I am what I think.

LITERATURE: *Sobering Thoughts*, a monthly newsletter ($10.00 a year).

The following organizations and federal offices do not provide direct help for the alcoholic, but are information clearinghouses or research centers on alcoholism:

Alcohol and Alcohol Abuse Program
National Association of Counties Research Foundation
1735 New York Avenue, N.W.
Washington, D.C. 20006

A research project with publications geared to county officials and those wishing to begin or assess a program.

LITERATURE: *A Practical Manual for County Officials on the Treatment of Alcoholism;* "Alcoholism and Alcohol Abuse Program," a fact sheet issued monthly.

Alcohol and Drug Problems Association of North America (ADPA)
1101 Fifteenth Street, N.W. #204
Washington, D.C. 20005

Founded in 1949 by a group of state alcoholism program directors, this nonprofit corporation now has members throughout North America who are involved in programs and agencies and individuals who are concerned about alcohol and drug problems. Dues range from $10 (student) and $20 (individual) to $300 (program members) a year. They provide a directory of treatment facilities, special reports, employment bank clearinghouse, annual meetings, listings of alcohol/drug problem summer school sessions, malpractice insurance, and a permanent secretariat to the North American Congress on Alcohol and Drug Problems.

LITERATURE: Fact sheet; publications price list.

Center of Alcohol Studies
Smithers Hall
Rutgers, The State University of New Jersey
New Brunswick, N.J. 08903

34 / THE HELP BOOK

One of the leading research centers on alcohol, its uses and misuses, the center publishes CAAL (Classified Abstract Archive of the Alcohol Literature), maintains a library, and has a publications list.

LITERATURE: Free descriptive leaflets on the center and the summer school courses.

Department of Health, Education, and Welfare
Public Health Service
Alcohol, Drug Abuse, and Mental Health Administration
National Institute on Alcohol Abuse and Alcoholism (NIAAA)
5600 Fishers Lane
Rockville, Md. 20857

Geared more to the program director and researcher than the National Clearinghouse for Alcohol Information, this arm of the Public Health Service publishes a wide variety of technical bibliographies and articles on alcohol—including "Alcohol and Crime" and *Alcohol Health and Research World*, a quarterly ($6.40 a year)—and has research laboratories. All individual referral or research requests are answered with the addresses of local treatment and counseling agencies or by manual or automated searches of their files.

LITERATURE: See the listings for the National Clearinghouse for Alcohol Information since all publications listed from NIAAA may be ordered from that address.

Do It Now Foundation
P.O. Box 5115
Phoenix, Ariz. 85010

This national nonprofit organization will mail up to three free pamphlets on any alcohol and drug topic that contain "realistic, truthful, non-hysterical drug information" to students or parents but not organizations.

National Clearinghouse for Alcohol Information (NCALI)
P.O. Box 2345
Rockville, Md. 20852

A comprehensive, fast, reliable computer-run information clearinghouse on all educational, research, and program aspects of alcohol and alcohol abuse. Free publications and wide and updated listings are available by writing to the above address. They will send you an application form so you can be placed on their mailing list.

LITERATURE: Just a few of the hundreds of free publications include *The Clearinghouse: An Information Network*, a leaflet; *In Focus: Alcohol and Alcoholism Media*, a 73-page guide to audio-visuals with annotated bibliography and ordering information; *Someone Close Drinks Too Much* (NIAAA), a booklet with the do's and don't's of helping an alcoholic; *Facts About Alcohol and Alcoholism* (NIAAA), a clear, well-done booklet with basic nontechnical information and where to go for help; *The Drinking Question: Honest Answers to Questions Teenagers Ask About Drinking; Teaching About Drinking* (NIAAA); *How to Help: What You Can Do to Help Your Community Help Alcoholic People* (NIAAA), a short booklet; *Alcoholism: Some Questions and Answers; Alcohol Abuse and Women: A Guide to Getting Help* (NIAAA), a 25-page booklet with short case histories on why women develop drinking problems, a short bibliography, and basic information on alcohol; *Alcohol and Your Unborn Baby* (NIAAA), a short booklet for expectant mothers with nontechnical information on the effects of alcohol on the fetus.

The following is a list of the state agencies for alcoholism programs:

Alcoholism and Drug Abuse Division
Department of Mental Health
502 Washington Avenue
Montgomery, Ala. 36130

Office of Alcoholism and Drug Abuse
Department of Health and Social Services
Anderson-Wilson Building
210 Ferry Way
Juneau, Alaska 99801

Alcohol Abuse Program
Bureau of Community Services
Division of Behavioral Health
2500 East Van Buren Street
Phoenix, Ariz. 85008

Alcohol Abuse Program
Office on Alcohol Abuse and Alcoholism
1515 Building, Room 202
1515 West 7th Street
Little Rock, Ark. 72202

Office of Alcoholism
825 15th Street
Sacramento, Calif. 95814

Alcohol and Drug Abuse Division
Department of Health
4210 East Eleventh Avenue
Denver, Colo. 80220

Alcohol and Drug Dependence Division
Department of Mental Health
90 Washington Street
Hartford, Conn. 06115

Alcoholism Services
Mental Health Division
Department of Health and Social Services
State Hospital, RERW Building
New Castle, Del. 19720

Bureau of Alcoholic Treatment and Prevention
Mental Health Administration
Department of Human Resources
1875 Connecticut Avenue, N.W.
Washington, D.C. 20009

Alcoholism Treatment and Research Center
100 West College Drive
Avon Park, Fla. 33825

Alcohol and Drug Services Section
Division of Mental Health and Mental Retardation
618 Ponce de Leon Avenue, N.E.
Atlanta, Ga. 30308

Alcohol and Drug Abuse Branch
Mental Health Division
Department of Health
1250 Punchbowl Street
Honolulu, Hawaii 96813

Bureau of Substance Abuse
Division of Community Rehabilitation
Department of Health and Welfare
State Office Building
700 West State Street
Boise, Idaho 83720

Division of Alcoholism
Department of Mental Health and
   Developmental Disabilities
160 North LaSalle Street
Chicago, Ill. 60601

Advisory Committee on Addiction Services
Department of Mental Health
5 Indiana Square
Indianapolis, Ind. 46204

Division on Alcoholism
Department of Health
508 Tenth Street
Des Moines, Iowa 50319

Alcohol and Drug Abuse Section
Department of Social and Rehabilitation
   Services
State Office Building
Topeka, Kans. 66612

36 / THE HELP BOOK

Division for Preventive Services
Bureau for Health Services
Department for Human Resources
275 East Main Street
Frankfort, Ky. 40601

Bureau of Substance Abuse
Division of Hospitals
Health and Human Resources Administration
200 Lafayette Street
Baton Rouge, La. 70801

Office of Alcoholism and Drug Abuse
  Prevention
Bureau of Rehabilitation
Department of Human Services
32 Winthrop Street
Augusta, Me. 04330

Alcoholism Control Administration
Department of Health and Mental Hygiene
201 West Preston Street
Baltimore, Md. 21201

Division of Alcoholism
Department of Public Health
755 Boylston Street
Boston, Mass. 02116

Advisory Committee on Substance Abuse
  Services
Department of Public Health
3500 North Logan Street
Lansing, Mich. 48914

Alcohol and Drug Problems
658 Cedar Street
St. Paul, Minn. 55155

Division of Alcohol and Drug Abuse
Department of Mental Health
619 Robert E. Lee Building
Jackson, Miss. 39201

Division of Alcoholism and Drug Abuse
Department of Mental Health
32 North Eighth
Columbia, Mo. 65201

Addictive Diseases Bureau
Adaptive Services Division
Department of Institutions
1539 Eleventh Avenue
Helena, Mont. 59601

Division of Alcoholism
Department of Public Institutions
P.O. Box 94728
Lincoln, Neb. 68509

Program on Alcohol and Drug Abuse
Division of Public Health
Department of Health and Welfare
8 Loudon Road
Concord, N.H. 03301

Department of Health
John Fitch Plaza
Trenton, N.J. 08625

Alcoholism Section
Substance Abuse Bureau
Behavioral Health Services Division
Health and Environment Department
809 St. Michael's Avenue
Santa Fe, N.M. 87501

Division of Alcoholism
Department of Mental Hygiene
44 Holland Avenue
Albany, N.Y. 12229

Alcoholism and Drugs
Division of Mental Health and Mental
  Retardation Services
Department of Human Resources
Albemarle Building
325 North Salisbury Street
Raleigh, N.C. 27611

Division of Alcoholism and Drug Abuse
Department of Health
909 Basin Avenue
Bismarck, N.D. 58505

Alcohol Division
Department of Mental Health
408-A North Walnut Street
P.O. Box 53277
Oklahoma City, Okla. 73107

Programs for Alcohol and Drug Problems
Mental Health Division
Department of Human Resources
2575 Bittern Street, N.W.
Salem, Ore. 97310

Governor's Council on Drug and Alcohol Abuse
Riverside Office Building 1
2101 North Front Street
Harrisburg, Pa 17120

Services of Mental Health, Retardation, and
  Hospitals
600 New London Avenue
Cranston, R.I. 02920

Commission on Alcohol and Drug Abuse
3700 Forest Drive
P.O. Box 4616
Columbia, S.C. 29204

Division of Alcoholism
Department of Health
Joe Foss Building
Pierre, S.D. 57501

Alcohol and Drug Abuse Section
Department of Mental Health and Mental
  Retardation
501 Union Street
Nashville, Tenn. 37219

Texas Commission on Alcoholism
809 Sam Houston State Office Building
Austin, Tex. 78701

Division of Alcoholism and Drugs
Department of Social Services
554 South Third East Street
Salt Lake City, Utah 84102

Alcohol and Drug Information Clearinghouse
State Office Building
Montpelier, Vt. 05602

Substance Abuse Division
Department of Mental Health and Mental
  Retardation
P.O. Box 1797
Richmond, Va. 23219

Office of Alcoholism
Bureau of Social Services
Department of Social and Health Services
Office Building 2
Olympia, Wash. 98504

Division of Alcoholism and Drug Abuse
Department of Mental Health
265 State Office Building 3
1800 Washington Street, East
Charleston, W.Va. 25305

Bureau of Alcohol and Other Drug Abuse
Division of Mental Hygiene
Department of Health and Social Services
One West Wilson Street
Madison, Wis. 53702

Alcohol Abuse Programs
Mental Health and Mental Retardation Services
Division of Health and Medical Services
Department of Health and Social Services
Hathaway Building
2300 Capitol Avenue
Cheyenne, Wyo. 82002

ADDITIONAL LITERATURE

Alcohol and Nutrition by Gary and Steve Null (1976). Pyramid Publications, 757 Third Avenue, New York, N.Y. 10017 ($1.75). A nonpreachy and informative guide to the effect of alcohol on the body, overturning many myths and confirming many suspicions (for example, alcohol and sex *do not* mix, unborn infants *are* damaged by excessive drinking).

Alternatives for the Problem Drinker: A.A. Is Not the Only Way by Ariel Winters (1978). Drake Publishers, Inc., 801 Second Avenue, New York, N.Y. 10017 ($8.95). Winters, president of the Association of Drinkwatchers, Inc., reviews the literature on alcoholism and its treatment. She also suggests controlled drinking and other innovative programs as alternative cures to total abstinence.

Helping Your Alcoholic Before He or She Hits Bottom: A Tested Technique for Leading Alco-

holics Into Treatment by Roque Fajardo (1976). Crown Publishers, Inc., One Park Avenue, New York, N.Y. 10016 ($7.95). The radical part of Fajardo's treatment is that the spouse of the alcoholic is asked to be the reason for provoking the drinker into treatment. (Most authors and agencies say the alcoholic cannot be helped unless he or she admits to alcoholism and to the need for help.) Fajardo is founder and president of the Samaritan Center for Alcoholics in Nashville, Tenn. He points out that the "co-alcoholic" must have courage and love for the afflicted spouse if the threats and provocation are to actively push the alcoholic into treatment. It is a "new" approach worth considering and reading about.

The Booze Battle by Ruth Maxwell (1976). Ballantine Books, 201 East 53rd Street, New York, N.Y. 10022 ($1.75).

Living With an Alcoholic With the Help of Al-Anon (1976). Al-Anon Family Group Headquarters, Inc., P.O. Box 182, Madison Square Station, New York, N.Y. 10010 ($4.50).

New Hope for Problem Drinkers: An Alternative to Abstinence by Phillip T. Drotning (1977). Contemporary Books, Inc., 180 North Michigan Avenue, Chicago, Ill. 60601 ($8.95). In the introduction the author, a former newspaperman, writes: "The book *is* intended for those who are beginning to feel concern about their drinking and want to do something about it *before* their lives become unmanageable, *before* they get caught up in the vicious spiral that leads inexorably to alcoholism, *before* abstinence becomes their only answer."

Turnabout: Help for a New Life by Jean Kirkpatrick (1978). Doubleday & Company, Garden City, N.Y. 11550 ($6.95). A moving account of one woman's fight against alcoholism.

Hazelden Foundation Literature Department, P.O. Box 176, Center City, Minn. 55102. Established in 1956, this company publishes and distributes books, pamphlets, cassettes, cards, audio-visuals, and other materials on alcoholism and other drug dependencies. It serves as a one-point ordering service for numerous organizations, including AA, Al-Anon, the National Council on Alcoholism, and commercial publishers. A catalog and free publications price list is available. Toll-free ordering outside Minnesota.

Kemper Insurance Companies, Long Grove, Ill. 60049. Publishes the following five booklets on various aspects of alcoholism and offers one free copy of each; inquire about ordering larger quantities:

Detour: Alcoholism Ahead . . . For 1 Out of 15 Who Drink (1976). Prepared for supervisors and others who need a basic understanding of alcoholism; includes twenty-six revealing questions developed by the National Council on Alcoholism.

Guide For the Family of the Alcoholic by Joseph L. Kellermann (1977). Well-written and concise description by the director of the Charlotte Council on Alcoholism of those common, family-related consequences of alcoholism. States in nonpunitive terms how the alcoholic "forces" his or her family to become involved in a circular path of denial, overcompensation, anger, and depression.

Management Guide on Alcoholism and Other Behavioral Problems (1976). Although not intended as a model for other companies, this compact booklet explains the policy and procedure services in use since 1974 for alcoholics. Employees of Kemper Insurance who develop alcoholism receive the same benefits and medical procedures as employees with other illnesses who accept appropriate treatment. Two essential components of their program are worth citing: It is confidential and employer intervention is warranted only when job performance is noticeably suffering.

The Way to Go by Kenneth A. Rouse (1976). Intended for the responsible driver who wants to have some basic facts about drinking and driving, including facts about the effect of alcohol on the blood, chemical tests for intoxication, and the thirteen ways drinking drivers deviate from regular drivers.

What to do About the Employee With a Drinking Problem by Kenneth A. Rouse (1975). This is a booklet concerned with convincing employers that nonpunitive alcohol treatment programs are good business sense. It is a companion booklet to *Management Guide on Alcoholism and Other Behavioral Problems*.

See also the following related chapters in *The Help Book:*

**BATTERED ADULTS
CHILD ABUSE
CHILDREN
COUNSELING
DRUGS, SMOKING, AND DRUG ABUSE
EMERGENCIES AND DISASTERS
HEALTH
JUVENILE DELINQUENCY
MENTAL HEALTH
OFFENDERS AND EX-OFFENDERS
RAPE AND SEXUAL ASSAULT
SAFETY
SUICIDE PREVENTION
TRANSPORTATION AND TRAVEL**

4

ANIMAL RIGHTS

Most activities generated by citizens' concern for animal protection focus on a few distinct areas:

- Finding nonanimal ways to experiment for scientific, health, and nutritional reasons (antivivisection)
- Preventing excessively cruel and painful means of capturing and confining animals (humane and antizoo activities)
- Prohibiting the trapping, killing, or imprisonment of animals in danger of extermination (endangered species, conservation)
- Finding other means of nourishment and dress outside the animal kingdom (vegetarianism, veganism, synthetic furs and shoes, nonanimal cosmetics)
- Bettering the care of household pets and curbing their numerical explosion as well as safeguards against their potential threats to the human population (animal shelters, pet adoption centers, spaying, and other birth control methods).

The treatment and rights of animals have concerned humankind throughout history and have been the subject of debate by such philosophers as Aristotle, Voltaire, and Schweitzer. In sixth-century B.C. Greece, Pythagoras, upon seeing his neighbor beating a dog, is said to have cried out that he should stop, "It is the soul of my late friend: I can tell from his voice!" Ancient India ascribed religious and sacred qualities to the cow, a custom that still prevails and is at the base of that country's widespread vegetarianism among the Hindu population. With the nineteenth-century increase in vivisection—the use of dogs, cats, rats, mice, and other creatures for dissection and other scientific purposes—the rights of animals began to involve even more issues than whether a person had the right to hunt, beat, or eat an animal. How many animals are used in vivisection? No one has an exact number. But a Rutgers University study revealed that between 1971 and 1978, 80 million mammals, reptiles, and birds (including 45 million rats and mice, 700,000 rabbits, 500,000 dogs, and 200,000 cats) were used in experiments. Is animal experimentation humane? Legal? In 1978 a Honolulu man who felt that two dolphins being used in a university experiment to teach them communication should be free was convicted of theft and sentenced to six months in prison for releasing them. (Hawaiian law stipulates that dolphins become the personal property of those who capture them.)

Many notables have joined in the cause of preventing the killing of wildlife and certain species in danger of extermination, such as dolphins, coyotes, doves, seals, and whales. But in contrast to the concern for a diminishing wildlife population is the very real household pet explosion. It is estimated that there are 40 million privately owned dogs in the United States; in New York City alone there are about 1.1 million dogs, and as many as 2 million cats. Because of neglect and abandonment, the 450 animal shelters in the United States have become slaughterhouses where an estimated 13.5 million dogs and cats are killed annually. The cost of capturing and killing the unwanted pets as well as leash-law enforcement and animal shelter services is about $500 million yearly. The problem with stray animals is not just the ethical issue of killing those that are captured, but the potential health hazards from dog bites and dog waste. Unfortunately, abandoning an unwanted dog or other pet is still one of the most common ways of getting rid of a pet.

Surgical birth control is one way of decreasing the household pet population, but many owners fail to "fix" their pets because of ethical commitments, indifference, or an inability to pay the fees of private veterinarians. As an alternative, lower-cost facilities, such as the Los Angeles Spaying Clinic, have been successfully established where the cost of neutering or spaying is one-third to one-half the price charged by private veterinarians. Controlling the pet population without resorting to extermination will ultimately be the responsibility of the pet owners. Those goals can be accomplished through public education, leash and dog feces removal law enforcement, and animal birth control.

Your state department of conservation and wildlife, listed in the telephone directory under the state-government listings, will provide you with state laws governing animal welfare, registration, and maintenance. R. V. Denenberg's *Dog Catalog* (see Additional Literature) suggests that you look under the name of your town or county government in the telephone directory to find a municipal pound that accepts stray dogs. To locate a voluntary shelter, check for an organization that uses one of the following names in its title: Society for the Prevention of Cruelty to Animals, Humane Society or Association, Animal Welfare League or Society, Animal Rescue League, Animal Protective Association or League, Animal Shelter, Animal Refuge, League for Animals or Animal League, Animal Havens League,

Dumb Friends League, Animal Friends, Bide-a-Wee Home Association, and Animal Aid Association.

One such local multiservice animal welfare organization, whose services you might look for at your own community-based society is:

American Society for the Prevention of Cruelty to Animals (ASPCA)
441 East 92nd Street
New York, N.Y. 10028

Founded in 1866, the ASPCA provides low-cost hospital service and clinic service for animals whose owners cannot afford to pay private veterinarian costs. Shelters for lost, strayed, or unwanted animals are maintained, and an education program for children and adults in the care of animals is available. The ASPCA campaigns for animal welfare legislation and enforces all animal-protection laws. It has an Animalport at Kennedy International Airport to take care of airborne animals at all stages of their flying experience. (You may wish to check out the policies of this or any other local animal shelter to determine whether unwanted animals are given away for scientific experimentation or are destroyed because of overcrowding.)

LITERATURE: *Animal Protection*, published twice a year.

The following international and national multipurpose organizations and federal offices are concerned with all aspects of the humane treatment of animals:

American Horse Protection Association, Inc.
1312 Eighteenth Street, N.W.
Washington, D.C. 20036

A national organization with state representatives established in 1966 and devoted to the welfare of wild and domestic horses. The Junior American Horse Protection Association was started in 1971 to educate six-to-sixteen-year olds in kindness to horses. It led the battle for passage of the Horse Protection Act of 1970 and is supported by contributions.

LITERATURE: Newsletter; wild horse and information pamphlets.

American Humane Association (AHA)
5351 South Roslyn Street
Englewood, Colo. 80111

Founded in 1877, some two million persons make up this federation of over 1,000 humane organizations that are dedicated to eliminating cruelty toward animals and children. AHA has an office in Hollywood that advises the motion picture industry on animal rights in film production, and it has extensive publications.

LITERATURE: *American Humane Magazine* (see Additional Literature); *Kindness Calendar* (published yearly—imprinting available).

Citizens for Animals
421 South State Street
Clarks Summit, Pa. 18411

A lobby organization that polls candidates for office on issues concerning animals and endorses candidates on the basis of their responses or past records; for example, Governor Hugh Carey of New York State told Citizens for Animals in a pre-election statement that he would lead the fight for the repeal of the Metcalf-Hatch Act in New York (which compels tax-supported public pounds to turn over impounded animals to laboratories for experimentation).

LITERATURE: "The Metcalf-Hatch Act: Why It Must Be Repealed" ($.05).

Committee for Humane Legislation, Inc.
11 West 60th Street
New York, N.Y. 10023

The political arm of the Friends of Animals that maintains a Washington, D.C., staff to draft strong animal protection bills and lobby for their passage in the U.S. Congress.

Defenders of Wildlife
1244 19th Street, N.W.
Washington, D.C. 20036

Founded in 1925, this membership organization is comprised of people who are dedicated to wildlife conservation and conducts public education and research programs to protect all wildlife from inhumane treatment.

LITERATURE: *Defenders of Wildlife* magazine (see Additional Literature).

Friends of Animals, Inc.
11 West 60th Street
New York, N.Y. 10023

A national, nonprofit membership organization of about 60,000 persons in all states that was formed in 1957 to try to reduce and eliminate the suffering of animals. Membership dues range from $5.00 (senior citizens and junior members) to $10.00 (annual) and up (for patrons and donors). Programs include activities to curb baby seal slaughter, hunting for sport, fur trapping, poisoning, bounties, and to promote saving porpoises and pet animal spaying.

LITERATURE: "Who Are Friends of Animals?" (leaflet); "A Time to Choose: Beauty Or . . . ," a color brochure about *Skins*, a film available free to local television stations or a $5.00 rental fee for group showings; fact sheet.

Fund for Animals, Inc.
140 West 57th Street
New York, N.Y. 10019

With writer-personality Cleveland Amory as president, this animal welfare group has attracted more attention than most others. The national headquarters are aided by regional offices in Washington, D.C., Los Angeles, San Francisco, Boston, Chicago, Ann Arbor, and New Orleans. Mainly an educational organization to inform the public about what animal problems exist and, through public pressure and awareness, to alleviate those problems. Projects vary and have included saving the whales to banning the use of the painful steel leghold trap. The Fund maintains responsibility for 159 animal species; in 1976 they succeeded in having those species placed on the federal endangered species list. They have also successfully terminated hunting the mourning dove in Ohio and obtained protection status for the black bear in Pennsylvania. Other projects include having the wolf designated the national mammal and the promotion of birth control methods for animals. Membership dues range from $5.00 (student) to $10.00 (adult) to V.I.P. (Very Important Patron) $1,000.00.

LITERATURE: *So You Want to Do Something About Over-Population of Animals*, by Marge Melgaard (leaflet); *So You Want to Do Something About Trapping!* (leaflet); wolf petitions; publications list; newsletter.

Greenpeace Foundation
2108 West 4th Avenue
Vancouver, B.C. V6K 1N6 Canada

240 Fort Mason
San Francisco, Calif. 94123

An international multipurpose environmental action organization, founded in 1971, that is concentrating on stopping the depletion and inhumane killing of seals in Canada as well as the economics and activities of the worldwide whaling industry. Speakers and films on and about these issues are available; a newsletter is planned.

LITERATURE: Fact sheets; brochures.

Humane Society of the United States (HSUS)
2100 L Street, N.W.
Washington, D.C. 20037

With more than 65,000 members, this national organization, founded in 1954, is concerned with a wide range of animal welfare issues including: the reduction of overbreeding of pets; the elimination of cruelty in hunting and trapping; the elimination of the plight of animals used in biomedical research and testing; an end to cruelty to animals used for entertainment purposes as well as inhumane conditions in zoos; stopping cruelty in transporting animals; the marketing and killing of food animals; promoting the humane ethic in schools, and monitoring animal-related laws. This information clearinghouse on animal cruelty includes a research library and training in-service programs for animal control officers and teachers and disaster relief for animals. Membership dues are $10.00 a year.

LITERATURE: Publications list has extensive materials including posters, educational filmstrips and booklets.

International Fund for Animal Welfare
P.O. Box 193
Yarmouth Port, Mass. 02675

An international animal welfare group devoted to ending the commercial seal hunt in the Gulf of Saint Lawrence and to helping the animal conservation cause in general. Volunteers assist by gathering petitions, participating in fundraising, etc.

LITERATURE: Bimonthly newsletter; films, such as *Seal Song* and *Loneliest Place*, are available on loan.

Millennium Guild
40 Central Park South
New York, N.Y. 10019

Started in 1912 by a prestigious group of ethical vegetarians, the guild's work is now carried on by dedicated radio personalities Pegeen and Ed Fitzgerald. It is an information and advocacy organization concerned about slaughterhouses, vivisection, killing for sport, the use of furs and feathers from slain birds, and advocates a vegetarian diet.

LITERATURE: "Diet and the Arts" by Henry Bailey Stevens; selections from Richard Wagner's essays against vivisection and for vegetarianism; free leaflets, brochures, and fact sheets.

National Park Service
U.S. Department of the Interior
Washington, D.C. 20240

Provides "Adopt-a-burro" and "Adopt-a-horse" service as an alternative to shooting the animals in order to thin out herds. The government will allow you to adopt a burro or horse at no charge for the animal, but the buyer must pay for picking up and transporting the animal to an adequate field or lot.

Society for Animal Rights, Inc. (SAR)
421 South State Street
Clarks Summit, Pa. 18411

A membership organization with about 12,500 members and contributors (voting, $50.00; nonvoting, $15.00) that provides extensive publications and information on all aspects of animal welfare, vegetarianism, fur trapping, vivisection, planned parenthood for pets, cat declawing, rodeos, and so forth.

LITERATURE: Extensive leaflets and booklets available ($.05 each and up); write for listing; films available on loan for $2.00 fee (see Additional Literature).

U.S. Department of Agriculture
Animal and Plant Health Inspection Service
13th Street and Jefferson Drive, S.W.
Washington, D.C. 20250

The service's purposes are the welfare of pets and animals used in research and for exhibition; to regulate the export and import of animals and plant products; to control or eradicate pests and diseases of animals and plants in the United States; and to prevent the entry of foreign agricultural pests and diseases. Inquiries receive a covering letter with a description of the agency, a publication list, and a fact sheet. General consumers may inquire by telephone about what plants and animals they may bring into this country.

LITERATURE: Leaflets include: *Pocket Guide to Federal Requirements on Identifying Cattle for Interstate Shipment* and *Bring a Pet Bird Into the U.S.A.?* Booklets include: *Exotic Newcastle Disease: A New Form of a Familiar Poultry Disease; Animal and Plant Health Inspection Service;* and *Travelers' Tips on Bringing Food, Plant, and Animal Products into the United States.*

The following national organizations oppose the use of animals in experimentation:

American Fund for Alternatives to Animal Research (AFAAR)
175 West 12th Street
New York, N.Y. 10011

AFAAR was instituted to stimulate and encourage vital research without the use of live animals for experimentation purposes. It seeks to pressure government agencies into giving larger proportions of funds for non-animal research.

LITERATURE: "The Role of the American Fund for Alternatives to Animal Research," brochure; "Animal Experiments and Tissues Culture Comparative Costs" by M. Mirkovik, leaflet.

Beauty Without Cruelty
175 West 12th Street
New York, N.Y. 10011

Started in England, this group manufactures cosmetics made without animal products or testing on animals, and stores throughout the United States stock their products.

LITERATURE: Will send a "Compassionate Shopper" guide for everything from belts to shoes, if a stamped self-addressed envelope is enclosed.

National Anti-Vivisection Society
100 East Ohio Street
Chicago, Ill. 60611

A national organization acting as an information clearinghouse and advocacy group against the use of animals in experimentation.

LITERATURE: Free article reprints sent if a stamped self-addressed envelope is enclosed.

Society for the Prevention of Animal Experimentation, Inc.
106 Day Street
South Plainfield, N.J. 07080

President and founder Perry Bruno established this membership organization ($5.00 yearly; donations accepted) as an information clearinghouse that is mainly against the use of animals in experimentation.

LITERATURE: Articles—"You, the Taxpayer and Animal Experimentation" and "Congress—The 'Godfathers' of Vivisection"; fact sheets.

ADDITIONAL LITERATURE

American Humane Magazine is published monthly. American Humane Association, 5351 South Roslyn Street, Englewood, Colo. 80111 ($3.75 a year; $.50 per single copy). This magazine combines *Animal Shelter Shoptalk* and *The National Humane Review.* Articles cover abuse of children, animals, and prisoners; columns include "You and Your Pets," "Stresses Prevention," and "Cruelty Cases."

Animal Liberation: A New Ethics for Our Treatment of Animals by Peter Singer (1977). Avon Books, 959 Eighth Avenue, New York, N.Y. 10019 ($2.50). A treatise on animal rights that is considered a leading contemporary reference in this area.

Animals, Men & Morals: An Enquiry into the Mal-Treatment of Non-Humans, edited by Stanley & Roslind Godlovitch (1972). Taplinger Publishing Co., Inc., 200 Park Avenue South, New York, N.Y. 10003 ($7.95). A collection of essays, mainly by British authorities, on cruelty to animals.

Basic Guide to Canine Nutrition, 4th edition (1977). Gaines Professional Services, 250 North Street, White Plains, New York 10625 ($2.00). Basic information on the nutritional needs of dogs, as well as feeding and management practices; a chapter on the nutrition of cats is included.

Defenders, published monthly. Defenders of Wildlife, 1244 Nineteenth Street, N.W., Washington, D.C. 20036 ($10.00 a year to non-members; sent free with $15.00 a year membership dues). Articles on a variety of animal-welfare and endangered-species issues; columns on pending and passed legislation; book reviews for children and adults.

The Dog Catalog, written and edited by R. V. Denenberg (1978). Grosset & Dunlap, Inc., 51 Madison Avenue, New York, N.Y. 10010 ($14.95 hardcover; $7.95 paperback). In addition to descriptions and illustrations of every recognized breed of dog, plus buying information, there are valuable consumer sections, such as how much money the dog food companies make and what's really in their products.

Eloquent Animals by Flora Davis (1978). Coward, McCann & Geoghegan, 200 Madison Avenue, New York, N.Y. 10016 ($9.95). Readable and informative book on how animals communicate; extensive bibliography.

Ethical Arguments for Analysis, 2nd edition, edited by Robert Baum (1976). Holt, Rinehart, and Winston, 383 Madison Avenue, New York, N.Y. 10017 ($6.95). Includes reprints of newspaper articles and discusses key arguments in a variety of controversial areas, including animals and vegetarianism.

Gluttons and Libertines: Human Problems of Being Natural by Marston Bates (1971). Vintage, 201 East 50th Street, New York, N.Y. 10022 ($2.45). Light tone but thoroughly researched account of some key ethical problems, such as meat-eating and animal treatment.

In Pity and In Anger: A Study of the Use of Animals in Science and *The Dark Face of Science*, both by John Vyvyan (both 1972). Transatlantic Arts, Inc., N. Village Green, Levittown, New York 11756 ($7.50 and $8.75). Two well-written and fascinating histories of the antivivisectionist movement featuring biographies of its early leaders such as Anna Kingsford.

Men, Beasts & Gods: A History of Cruelty and Kindness to Animals by Gerald Carson (1972). Charles Scribner's Sons, 597 Fifth Avenue, New York, N.Y. 10017 ($3.95). Popular book that is well written and filled with anecdotes about the issues and personalities in the modern animal rights movement.

On Abstinence From Animal Food by Porphyry, translated by Thomas Taylor and edited by Esme Wynne-Tyson (1965). Branden Press, Inc., 221 Columbus Avenue, Boston, Mass. 02116 ($7.50). Arguments by Neo-Platonist Porphyry about why one should or should not kill animals that are just as valid today as they were in ancient times.

On the Fifth Day: Animal Rights & Human Ethics, edited by Richard Knowles Morris and Michael W. Fox (1977). Acropolis Books Ltd., Colortone Building, 2400 17th Street, N.W., Washington, D.C. 20009 ($12.50). A collection of essays developed under the auspices of the Humane Society of the United States that deals with man's relation to animals. The contributors—ecologists, philosophers, biologists, lawyers, theologians, and animal behaviorists—delve into issues such as whether man is innately aggressive or if we have a right to demand an end to animal cruelty.

The Recovery of Culture by Henry Bailey Stevens (1963). Weelington Books, distributed by Charles T. Brawford Co., 28 Union Street, Newton Centre, Mass. 02159 ($4.95). Stevens probes man's evolution from a nut and seed gatherer to a meat-eater.

Savage Luxury: The Slaughter of the Baby Seals by Brian Davies (1971). Taplinger Publishing Co., Inc., 200 Park Avenue South, New York, N.Y. 10003 ($7.95). The companion text to Davies's movie, "Seal Song" (see description that follows).

"The Animals Are Crying," a film available on loan from the Society for Animal Rights, 421 South State Street, Clarks Summit, Pa. 18411 ($2.00 loan fee) or for purchase from the Learning Corporation of America, 1350 Avenue of the Americas, New York, N.Y. 10019 (full 28-minute version, $370.00; short 16-minute version, $230.00). A poignant film that demonstrates how people buy animals for pets without being fully aware of the responsibility and costs involved, and that many soon abandon these animals on the road or give them up to shelters that try to find homes but may exterminate those they cannot place. Includes a visit to an animal shelter and talks with pet caretakers.

Argus Archives, 228 East 49th Street, New York, N.Y. 10017, publishes an annotated catalog of films and filmstrips dealing with animal rights, *Films for Humane Education* ($2.50). Each film has the rating and comments it received when screened before an audience. Some related books also available for sale; write for publications list.

"Seal Song," a color film available from the Society for Animal Rights (see address above) for a $2.00 loan fee. This is a powerful and superbly made film by Brian Davies of the International Fund for Animal Welfare that shows the harp seals of Canada. The film climaxes with brief but brutal scenes of the actual clubbing of the seals.

See also the following related chapters in *The Help Book:*

CITIZEN ACTION
CONSUMER AFFAIRS
FOOD AND NUTRITION
LEGAL SERVICES
MULTIPURPOSE ORGANIZATIONS
POLITICAL ACTION

5

ARTS

When unemployed and poverty groups are highlighted in the media, few include the often underpaid and out-of-work performers, visual artists, and writers. (It seems that the plight of the highly skilled but destitute person in the arts is considered far less serious than the plight of unemployed disadvantaged youths, women, or unskilled males.) Yet for all but the lucky few—and even then it may only be for sporadic periods—complete reliance on writing, fine arts, or performing as a steady income is rare. One comprehensive 1978 study, by the U.S. Department of Labor, of the five major performing artists unions found that there is a much higher percentage of unemployment among performing artists than the 19 percent out-of-work rate in the labor force as a whole. The Screen Actors Guild (SAG), American Guild of Musical Artists (AGMA), and American Federation of Television and Radio Artists (AFTRA) reported one-half of their members unemployed; Actors' Equity reported two-thirds unemployment; and the American Federation of Musicians (AFM) reported one-third unemployment. Is it better for writers? It may be better for salaried, staff writers for magazines or newspapers. But it is estimated that only 1,500 free-lance writers in this country are able to support themselves on just the income derived from their own publications.

But it is even becoming more difficult to juggle a "regular" full- or part-time job with one's artistic training and related work. As profit-minded conglomerates gobble up the publishing industry, even the weekend or academic writer is expected to bring in revenue. Teaching jobs, long a second source of income to writers, artists, and actors alike, are getting harder to find or keep. Even the smallest cinematic venture now means hundreds of thousands, and probably millions, of dollars. To produce an off-Broadway show today costs as much as it might have cost to stage a lavish Broadway production ten years ago. As magazines and newspapers seek to prune their budgets, reliance on "staff" rather than "freelance" artists and writers narrows the available markets even further. True, dozens of new markets, especially for magazine writers, are appearing, but their rates—generally from $300 to $750—are far below what a seasoned professional should, and needs to, earn for a major assignment.

Although the rules of the competitive artistic professions do not change simply because there are unions (getting the assignment or the part may still depend upon talent, luck, and who you know) in those arts where rigid wage requirements are observed, the economic gains have been outstanding. For example, the graduated scales and minimum weekly wages developed and enforced by such unions as the Newspaper Guild, Screen Actors Guild, and the Writers Guild have introduced the "living wage" for certain artistic pursuits. However, nonfiction and fiction writers, as well as painters, sculptors, and other artisans, still lack such uniform or unified wage standards. In light of that, it is even more important for artists to band together and, if they cannot officially and unanimously organize, to at least know what the "going rates" are and where they can turn to for public and private financial help as well as free legal assistance.

Public support for the arts in the United States is greater than at any time since the government-funded WPA and related depression-years projects. But it is still a miniscule amount compared to what it should be. In some cities, such as New York, lower-cost housing for artists (such as Westbeth) or for performers (such as Manhattan Plaza) have helped those lucky enough to qualify. (Unfortunately, unrealistic income restrictions and subletting regulations have discouraged many artists from applying.)

Private sources for financial aid are still available, however, from writing organizations that provide emergency loans, artist colonies with low-cost or free residencies, foundations offering grants and research funds, and wealthy individuals.

Although "taking care of one's own" has a long history in the theater—with the Actors Fund and the Home for Actors—those in other arts are beginning to help each other as well. Several very rich and successful painters have gotten together to form an emergency fund plan for other needy artists. Writer resource groups, such as the one founded by two members of the American Society of Journalists and Authors, are small self-help groups that meet monthly to share knowledge, advice, and market tips. In a spirit of dedication to the theater and fellow performers, two years ago actor Ralph Waite founded the Los Angeles Actors Theatre with his own money. No one gets paid and no admission is charged (contributions are suggested), but still this new vital theater has become an innovative force in California. There seems to be an attitude of camaraderie evolving in all the arts that is as determined and pervasive as the big-business profit-concerned trends with which it must coexist.

The following federal agencies and national organizations cover all the arts—performing arts, fine arts, photography, writing, architecture, and so forth:

American Council for the Arts (ACA)
570 Seventh Avenue
New York, N.Y. 10018

A national membership organization that serves as an information clearinghouse for more than 800 state and community arts organizations. Membership dues range from $20.00 (student) to $30.00 (individual) to $500.00 (depending upon size and budget of the membership councils). ACA offers a variety of publication, information, and technical assistance services.

LITERATURE: *A Word from Washington*, a monthly newsletter; ACA reports; ACA Arts Yellow Pages ($7.50); publications list available.

Center for Arts Information
152 West 42nd Street
New York, N.Y. 10036

The Center for Arts Information is an information clearinghouse for and about the arts in New York State. The center maintains a 3,500-volume library and research facility of materials concerning arts administration, programming, and funding sources. Use of the library is by appointment only. Staff is available to answer questions by phone from 1:00 to 4:00 p.m. weekdays. Inquiries will also be answered by mail.

The center publishes organizational listings of importance to arts organizations and artists throughout the United States, not just New York State. Each listing is typescript and well written, with objectives, publications, and offerings succinctly highlighted. There is also a periodic bulletin of practical information and advice for arts administrators and artists. An arts service-organization directory for New York State is being prepared. Listings are free for New York State artists and arts administrators who send self-addressed, stamped envelopes as indicated below. There is an extra charge for profit-making and out-of-state organizations.

LITERATURE: *Organizations Offering Services to Writers in New York State* (business-size envelope, $.15 postage; extra charge for profit-making and out-of-state organizations, $1.00); *Organizations Which Offer Services to Visual Artists in New York State* (business-size envelope, $.15 postage; extra charge, $.50); *Organizations of Interest to Photographers in New York State* (business-size envelope, $.30 postage; extra charge, $1.50); *Community Arts Councils in New York State* (business-size envelope, $.15 postage; extra charge, $1.00); *Publications on Architectural Preservation and History in New York State* (business-size envelope, $.15 postage; extra charge, $.50); *Charities Registration in New York State* (business-size envelope, $.15 postage, plus $.50 handling charge; extra charge, $1.00).

Copyright Office
Library of Congress
Washington, D.C. 20559

With passage of the new copyright bill, which took effect on January 1, 1978, there is now one system of statutory protection for all copyrightable works, whether published or unpublished. Booklets and information are available on what and how to register, exempt nondramatic literary and musical work performance, and so forth.

LITERATURE: "Highlights of the New Copyright Law," circular R99; list of publications; you may have your name added to the Copyright Office mailing list by sending a written request.

National Academy of Television Arts and Sciences
See the listing in Chapter 37, *Media and Communications*.

National Arts Club
15 Gramercy Park South
New York, N.Y. 10003

A membership organization founded in 1898 embracing all the arts. Residence facilities, although few vacancies occur, are attached to the club and available to members. Membership dues are $210.00 a year for resident members, $90.00 for nonresidents. The club holds monthly get-togethers, recitals, contests, and shows of members' works.

LITERATURE: Fact sheets; "Design: Some Garret, Club Life" by Jane Geniesse, *New York Times Magazine* (November 25, 1975).

National Council for Arts and Education (NCAE)
743 Fifth Avenue
New York, N.Y. 10022

NCAE is a nonprofit advocacy group that supports innovative funding proposals to ensure financial stability for arts, education, and cultural activity in the United States. It was founded in 1976 and is open to all interested persons.

LITERATURE: Free information on arts and education legislation.

National Endowment for the Humanities (NEH)
806 Fifteenth Street, N.W.
Washington, D.C. 20506

The NEH has three programs of interest to writers who are involved in scholarly and critical work; Fellowships for Independent Study and Research, Fellowships for Stipends and Professions, and Youth Grants for persons under thirty.

LITERATURE: *A Guide to Programs* is issued each July and may be obtained free by writing to the Program Information Office. Eligibility requirements, application deadlines, and addresses of state arts agencies are given.

Pen and Brush Club
16 East Tenth Street
New York, N.Y. 10003

A national organization of professional women sculptors, writers, painters, and craftspersons.

The following are national organizations for writers of fiction and nonfiction, playwrights, poets, and journalists:

Academy of American Poets
1078 Madison Avenue
New York, N.Y. 10028

A national organization founded in 1934 "to encourage, stimulate and foster the production of American poetry by providing fellowships for poets of proven merit, by granting scholarships, awards and prizes for poetic achievement." There are more than ninety affiliates throughout the United States, and they work with the academy to stimulate the appreciation of poetry.

LITERATURE: Free fact sheets on various fellowships and awards; *Poetry Pilot*, a monthly newsletter-type magazine sent to contributors of over $5.00, containing poems, information on poetry editors, and so forth; free brochures entitled *What Does the Academy Do?*, *People and Prizes*, and *University and College Poetry Prizes: Description and Procedures*.

American Society of Journalists and Authors, Inc. (ASJA)
1501 Broadway, Suite 1907
New York, N.Y. 10036

A national organization whose over four hundred members include notable writers and journalists such as Temple Fielding, Vance Packard, Alvin Toffler, and Betty Friedan. New applicants must meet high membership standards, including publication of at least three full-length articles in respected magazines or books published by recognized major publishers, or a combination of both. Benefits to members include a medical plan, a confidential monthly newsletter with tips on markets and editors, and summaries of talks by guest speakers at the preceding month's members meeting and dinner, a Dial-a-Writer Service, a lecture bureau, use of the New York office for interviewing, and monthly professional workshops with working journalists and representatives of the related media and arts.

Each year a nonfiction writers workshop is held with ASJA members sharing their experience and knowledge, as well as invited non-members—renowned agents, authors, publicists, and editors. Membership dues are $60.00 a year for New York area residents, $45.00 outside New York; there is also a one-time $25.00 initiation fee.

LITERATURE: Fact sheets for prospective members; membership list; membership directory (free to members; $25.00 to all others); leaflet.

American Writers Theatre Foundation
P.O. Box 191
Lenox Hill Station
New York, N.Y. 10021

The purpose of this national organization is to assist new playwrights as well as authors who are interested in adapting their writing for stage production. Selected original plays or adapted works of prose and poetry are given staged readings, workshop presentations, or full productions, all with professional casts. A reading committee selects the scripts; the performance is recorded on tape. The tape is sent free to out-of-town members unable to come to New York; nonmembers are charged a $10.00 fee. The $15.00 membership fee also provides reduced rates for foundation publications and performances.

LITERATURE: *Preview*, a quarterly journal (free with membership, $3.00 to nonmembers); American Writers Theatre Foundation Fact Sheet, free on request; *Adaptations '76*, an annual catalog of adaptations ($1.50 for members; $2.50 for nonmembers).

Authors Guild, Inc.
234 West 44th Street
New York, N.Y. 10036

A membership organization of more than 5,000 writers meeting qualifications standards. Work done by the guild is in the area of book contracts, copyright, subsidiary rights, censorship, and taxes. It publishes an informative bimonthly newsletter, conducts membership surveys on book advances and other financial concerns, and holds an annual meeting in New York City.

LITERATURE: Fact sheets; membership application on request.

Coordinating Council of Literary Magazines
80 Eighth Avenue
New York, N.Y. 10011

A national nonprofit organization that has a program to aid nonprofit literary magazines and publishes a list of magazines.

The Drama Desk
41 West 72nd Street
New York, N.Y. 10023

A membership organization ($20.00 a year) of New York drama critics, editors, and reporters. It holds monthly luncheons with guest speakers;

each time a different theme and aspect of theater is discussed. The Drama Desk Awards are presented annually to theater artists. The organization is dedicated to advancing the theater and keeping drama in the media's eye.

LITERATURE: Fact sheet.

Dramatists Guild, Inc.
234 West 44th Street
New York, N.Y. 10036

A professional organization with initiation and yearly dues that sets professional policies and offers information about markets to its members; meetings and workshops are held in the New York area.

Investigative Reporters & Editors, Inc. (IRE)
220 Walter Williams Hall
University of Missouri
Columbia, Mo. 65211

A membership organization for working reporters, editors, and other persons interested in investigative journalism. IRE sponsors a yearly three-day workshop and meeting, bringing members together and having guest speakers on various legal, creative, and technical aspects of investigative reporting; applications sent on request ($15.00 a year dues). It also occasionally sponsors special projects, such as the nationally noted Arizona project to investigate the murder of journalist Don Bolles. Maintains the Paul Williams Memorial Resource Center at its Missouri headquarters; nonmembers may use it for a $10.00 service charge, plus costs.

LITERATURE: Fact sheets; *The IRE Journal* newsletter.

National Writers Club
1450 South Havana
Aurora, Colo. 80012

Founded in 1937, the club provides literary companionship for freelance writers and prepares publications, writer research reports, and manuscript criticisms; membership dues are $22.00 yearly ($7.50 initiation).

The Newspaper Guild (TNG)
1125 15th Street, N.W.
Washington, D.C. 20005

Founded in 1933, there are eighty-five locals in this 33,000-member organization, which is affiliated with the AFL-CIO. TNG has a library at its headquarters, a research and information department, and collective bargaining and organizing sections.

LITERATURE: *Directory*, issued semiannually; *Constitution*, published yearly.

P.E.N. American Center
47 Fifth Avenue
New York, N.Y. 10013

This is the U.S. branch of International P.E.N., an association of writers—poets, playwrights, essayists, editors, novelists—with centers in Europe, Africa, Australia, and the Americas. Minimum requirement for membership is two books of literary merit published in the United States; a committee reviews applications. P.E.N. American Center holds monthly get-togethers and sponsors a writers-in-prison program and various fellowships for writing excellence.

LITERATURE: *Grants and Awards Available to American Writers* ($2.25), revised annually.

Poetry Society of America
15 Gramercy Park
New York, N.Y. 10003

Established in 1910, this private membership organization ($18.00 annual dues) sponsors public poetry meetings, several poetry contests, and workshops, maintains a poetry library, and every ten years publishes anthologies of member poets' work (titles on request).

LITERATURE: *PSA Bulletin* ($1.00).

Poets & Writers, Inc.
201 East 54th Street
New York, N.Y. 10019

An information clearinghouse for American poets and fiction writers and for teachers, readers, and sponsors of literary activities. Poets & Writers publishes directories about literary matters and answers questions (e.g., copyright, writer colonies, reading series, etc.).

LITERATURE: *Coda: Poets and Writers Newsletter* (see description under Additional Literature); brochure; bulletin published eight times a year and mailed to 750 sponsors of literary activities and to any listed writer or *Coda* subscriber who asks to be on the mailing list; free checklists—"How to Organize a Reading or Workshop" and "How to Publicize Your Reading or Workshop"; other lists; fact sheets on applying for listing in the directories; *A Directory of American Poets* ($3.00 paper, $10.00 clothbound); *A Directory of American Fiction Writers* ($5.00 paper, $10.00 clothbound).

Society of Professional Journalists
Sigma Chi Delta
35 East Wacker Drive
Chicago, Ill. 60601

Founded in 1909, this is a worldwide membership organization ($20.00 a year) with local chapters. National conventions are held each year.

LITERATURE: Annual directory; *The Quill* ($12.00 a year); *How to Apply for a Job in the Media*.

Teachers and Writers Collaborative
186 West 4th Street
New York, N.Y. 10014

Founded in 1967, the Collaborative places artists in schools to work with teachers and students interested in discovering new ways to use language and the arts; it is also a clearinghouse for those seeking jobs or information about teaching the arts.

LITERATURE: *Bright Ideas For Creative Teachers;* "Poetry in the Schools" by Alan Ziegler, in *The American Poetry Review*, vol. 4, no. 2 (1975); *Teachers & Writers* magazine, published three times a year ($5.00 a year).

The Writer's Guild
See entry in Chapter 37, *Media and Communications*.

Writers in the Public Interest (WPI)
17 Myrtle Drive
Great Neck, N.Y. 11021

Founded and directed by author Ronald Gross, WPI has no membership dues and is dedicated to encouraging writers to contribute "to the common good through both paid work at professional rates, and through *pro bono* services where needed." Advisors include such esteemed writers as Kurt Vonnegut, Jr., John Holt, Nat Hentoff, and Gloria Steinem. Workshop roundtables are held in New York City and are summarized in the next month's newsletter. WPI now has a membership of several hundred writers throughout the United States, ranging from novices to well-known professionals.

LITERATURE: WPI descriptive leaflet; newsletters (self-addressed stamped envelope must be enclosed with request).

The following groups provide services to fine artists; they are national in scope:

American Federation of Arts (AFA)
41 East 65th Street
New York, N.Y. 10021

Membership organization ($25.00 active to $500.00 sponsor) has the benefits of *Arts Magazine* and discounts on other related publications. AFA is a nonprofit cultural service organization, founded in 1909, that organizes lower-cost traveling exhibitions to participating institutions; provides film programs for universities; and has an International Exhibitions Committee. All grants and gifts to AFA are tax deductible.

LITERATURE: Free information brochure.

Artist Equity Association (AEA)
2813 Albemarle Street, N.W.
Washington, D.C. 20008

A national organization with individual chapters throughout the United States; a lobbyist; an information clearinghouse on the arts, and action kits. Membership dues are $20.00 yearly and insurance is available.

LITERATURE: Newsletter.

Artists for Economic Action (AFEA)
10930 Le Conte Avenue
Los Angeles, Calif. 90024

A national membership organization concerned with bettering economic conditions for artists through fair and equitable tax laws. AFEA provides technical information to artists on business management, tax and legal matters, and artist-gallery relations, and seeks more media coverage of art activities. Dues are $12.00 for professional artists, $6.00 for associate members.

LITERATURE: Quarterly newsletter ($5.00).

Indian Arts and Crafts Board
U.S. Department of the Interior
Washington, D.C. 20240

A federal agency established in 1935 to promote the development of Native American fine arts and handcrafts—the creative work of Indian, Eskimo, and Aleut people; the headquarters acts as an information clearinghouse and referral service.

LITERATURE: *Bibliography 1; Source Directory 1; Source Directory 2;* fact sheet for consumers concerned about judging and buying genuine handmade Native American arts and crafts.

National Gallery of Art
Department of Extension Programs
Washington, D.C. 20565

Sponsors a program that allows clubs, schools, or individuals to borrow slide shows of great art (complete with text and cassette or record) or 16 mm color/sound films. There are thirty-eight slide programs and twenty-six films to choose from. Write for their catalog.

United Scenic Artists (USA)
1540 Broadway
New York, N.Y. 10036

Founded in 1918, this labor union of professional scenic designers, artists, and costume designers has about 1,000 members who are employed by the media.

The following are national organizations concerned with the performing arts:

Actor's Equity Association
1500 Broadway
New York, N.Y. 10036

A union founded in 1913 for legitimate theater performers; offices in Chicago, Hollywood, San Francisco, and Toronto.

Affiliate Artists Inc.
155 West 68th Street
New York, N.Y. 10023

Founded in 1966, the Appointment Residency Program of Affiliate Artists has allowed more than 200 performing artists (dancers, singers, instrumentalists) to be heard in communities throughout the United States. It is privately funded by major corporations, foundations, individuals, and the National Endowment for the Arts. They hope that the "residencies" will be changed to "residences" so performing artists can earn a living in their chosen professions in a wide range of possible communities. In 1977 there were eighty-five artists operating in 110 different communities. For each eight-week residency, the performing artist is reimbursed $7,000. New programs include PACT-WEEK, a shorter one-week residency.

LITERATURE: Free annual report.

American Federation of Musicians of the United States and Canada
1500 Broadway
New York, N.Y. 10036

Founded in 1896, this national labor union has over 650 locals and over 300,000 members and is affiliated with the AFL-CIO.

LITERATURE: *International Musician*, monthly.

American Federation of Television and Radio Artists (AFTRA)
1350 Avenue of the Americas
New York, N.Y. 10019

This national labor union has over 30,000 members and 33 locals and is affiliated with the AFL-CIO; AFTRA holds an annual convention.

American Theatre Association (ATA)
1029 Vermont Avenue, N.W.
Washington, D.C. 20005

A national organization with a wide range of information about education and community theater programs; offers a Playwrights Program.

Composers and Lyricists Guild of America (CLGA)
6565 Sunset Boulevard, Suite 420
Hollywood, Calif. 90028

Founded in 1954 this national labor union has over 400 members, maintains a New York office, and holds an annual conference.

Directors Guild of America (DGA)
7950 Sunset Boulevard
Hollywood, Calif. 90046

Founded in 1959, this national labor union has over 4,000 members, gives awards, and holds a conference every two years.

LITERATURE: *Action*, bimonthly; *Directory of Members*, updated annually.

League of Resident Theatres (LORT)
233 Broadway, Suite 3505
New York, N.Y. 10007

A national organization of nonprofit professional theaters serving as a communications liaison between member theaters; it also acts on its members' behalf in union negotiations. Founded in July 1966 in Chicago by a group of professional resident theaters, LORT is supported solely by the contributions of its members.

LITERATURE: Free fact sheets; list of theaters with the names of past performances, and current phone numbers, addresses, and the names of managing and artistic directors.

Screen Actor's Guild (SAG)
7750 Sunset Boulevard
Hollywood, Calif. 90046

551 Fifth Avenue
New York, N.Y. 10017

Founded in 1933, this national labor union has 36,000 members, twelve branches, and a general membership national office.

LITERATURE: *Screen Actor*, quarterly magazine ($4.00 a year).

Screen Extras Guild (SEG)
3629 Cahuenga Boulevard, West
Hollywood, Calif. 90068

Founded in 1945, this national labor union has over 3,000 members and sponsors an annual meeting in Los Angeles.

Direct assistance is given to working artists as well as to organizations through the various state arts and humanities councils, although who gets what, and how much, will vary enormously. Many of the state councils on the arts have programs in the following areas: architecture and environmental arts; arts service organizations; dance; film; literature; museum aid; music; special programs; theater; TV/media; and visual arts services. Make sure you know the cutoff date for filing your application for the next year's grants since most councils rigidly follow those deadlines.

What might an arts council provide in the way of aid? Of course there is the outright financial grant, but there may also be other programs, such as artist-in-residence (at schools, other communities), commissioning of works for public buildings and places, ticket subsidies, statehouse exhibitions, awards to improve the administration of an organization, student scholarships, funds for film rentals, speakers' fees, equipment rental or purchase, community-based dance, theater, and music organizations and companies, and so forth. Contact your state arts council office to find out if their office administers all programs, or if you must direct your inquiry to another agency that is already funded by the arts council.

Along with the state arts council are programs known as Volunteer Lawyers for the Arts, usually sponsored by your local or statewide bar association. Volunteer lawyers for the arts provide information on such vital issues as copyright, taxes, gallery relations, and insurance. Some programs, such as the New York City-based Volunteer Lawyers for the Arts (36 West 44th Street, New York, N.Y. 10036) have published booklets, such as *Fear of Filing: A Beginners' Handbook on Record Keeping and Federal Taxes for Dancers, Other Performers, Writers and Visual Artists (Keyed to the 1975 Federal Tax Forms)* by Bill Holcomb and Ted Striggles (with periodic updates) and *The Individual Artist: Recordkeeping, Methods of Accounting, Income and Itemized Deductions for Federal Income Tax Purposes* by Herrik K. Lidstone and Leonard R. Olsen (1976). They also publish a newsletter, *Art & The Law*.

Contact the state agencies below for information on services, on obtaining financial assistance, and about programs of study and/or presentation for the public:

State Council on the Arts and Humanities
449 South McDonough Street
Montgomery, Ala. 36130

State Council on the Arts
Office of the Governor
619 Warehouse, #220
Anchorage, Alaska 99501

58 / THE HELP BOOK

Commission on the Arts and Humanities
6330 North 7th Street
Phoenix, Ariz. 85014

Office of Arts and Humanities
Continental Building
Little Rock, Ark. 72201

Arts Council
115 I Street
Sacramento, Calif. 95814

Colorado Council on the Arts and Humanities
Department of Higher Education
1550 Lincoln Street, Room 205
Denver, Colo. 80203

State Commission on the Arts
340 Capitol Avenue
Hartford, Conn. 06115

State Arts Council
803 Wilmington Tower
1105 Market Street
Wilmington, Del. 19801

D.C. Commission on the Arts and Humanities
1012 Fourteenth Street, N.W.
Washington, D.C. 20005

Fine Arts Council
Division of Cultural Affairs
Department of State
The Capitol
Tallahassee, Fla. 32304

Georgia Council for the Arts
Office of Planning and Budget
Trinity-Washington Building
270 Washington Street, S.W.
Atlanta, Ga. 30303

Foundation on Culture and the Arts
Department of Budget and Finance
State Capitol
Honolulu, Hawaii 96813

Commission on Arts and Humanities
Office of the Secretary of State
322 Statehouse, Annex 3
506 North Fifth Street
Boise, Idaho 83720

Arts Council
111 North Wabash Avenue
Chicago, Ill. 60602

Arts Commission
614 Union Title Building
155 East Market Street
Indianapolis, Ind. 46204

Arts Council
508 Tenth Street
Des Moines, Iowa 50319

Arts Commission
509-A Kansas Avenue
Topeka, Kans. 66603

Arts Commission
100 West Main Street
Frankfort, Ky. 40601

Department of Culture, Recreation, Tourism
Baton Rouge, La. 70160

State Commission on the Arts and Humanities
State House
Augusta, Maine 04333

Maryland Arts Council
Department of Economic and Community
    Development
2525 Riva Road
Baltimore, Md. 21401

Council on the Arts and Humanities
John W. McCormack State Office Building
1 Ashburton Place
Boston, Mass. 02108

Council for the Arts
Department of Management and Budget
State of Michigan Plaza Building
Detroit, Mich. 48226

State Arts Board
314 Clifton Avenue, South
Minneapolis, Minn. 55403

Arts Commission
301 North Lamar Street
Jackson, Miss. 39205

Missouri Arts Council
Community and Economic Development
  Agencies
Department of Consumer Affairs, Regulation,
  and Licensing
611 Olive Street
St. Louis, Mo. 63101

Arts Council
235 East Pine Street
Missoula, Mont. 59801

Arts Council
8448 West Center Road
Omaha, Neb. 68124

Council on the Arts
560 Mill Street
Reno, Nev. 89502

Commission on the Arts
40 North Main Street
Concord, N.H. 03301

State Council on the Arts
109 West State Street
Trenton, N.J. 08625

New Mexico Arts Division
113 Lincoln Avenue
Santa Fe, N.M. 87503

Council on the Arts
80 Centre Street
New York, N.Y. 10013

Arts Council
Department of Cultural Resources
407 North Person Street
Raleigh, N.C. 27611

Council on the Arts and Humanities
Department of English
North Dakota State University
Fargo, N.D. 58101

Ohio Arts Council
50 West Broad Street
Columbus, Ohio 43215

Oklahoma Arts and Humanities Council
640 Jim Thorpe Office Building
2101 North Lincoln Boulevard
Oklahoma City, Okla. 73105

Oregon Arts Commission
835 Summer Street, N.E.
Salem, Ore. 97301

Council on the Arts
2001 North Front Street
Harrisburg, Pa. 17102

State Council on the Arts
334 Westminster Mall
Providence, R.I. 02903

Arts Commission
Boylston House
829 Richland Street
Columbia, S.C. 29201

Fine Arts Council
Department of Education and Cultural Affairs
108 West Eleventh Street
Sioux Falls, S.D. 57102

Tennessee Arts Commission
222 Capitol Hill Building
301 Seventh Avenue, North
Nashville, Tenn. 37219

Texas Commission on the Arts and Humanities
202 West Thirteenth Street
P.O. Box 13406, Capitol Station
Austin, Tex. 78711

Division of Fine Arts
Department of Development Services
609 East South Temple Street
Salt Lake City, Utah 84102

Vermont Council on the Arts
136 State Street
Montpelier, Vt. 05602

Commission of the Arts and Humanities
1215 State Office Building
Richmond, Va. 23219

60 / THE HELP BOOK

Arts Commission
1151 Black Lake Boulevard
Olympia, Wash. 98504

Arts and Humanities Division
Department of Culture and History
B531 State Office Building, 6
1900 Washington Street, East
Charleston, W.Va. 25305

Arts Board
123 West Washington Avenue
Madison, Wis. 53702

Council on the Arts
200 West 25th Street
Cheyenne, Wyo. 82002

ADDITIONAL LITERATURE

WRITING

Alphabetized Directory of American Journalists, developed by Jack Barkley, editor of *Kokomo Tribune* (1977) (updated annually). P.O. Box 231, Kokomo, Ind. 46901 ($7.95 postpaid). Lists some 20,000 journalists, editors, management, and other news-related personnel by name and provides information on what they are doing and how to contact them.

The Business of Publishing: A PW Anthology, with an introduction by Arnold W. Ehrlich (1976). R. R. Bowker Company, 1180 Avenue of the Americas, New York, N.Y. 10036 ($12.95).

Coda: Poets & Writers Newsletter (bimonthly). Poets & Writers, Inc., 201 West 54th Street, New York, N.Y. 10019 ($6.00 a year, $4.50 to writers listed in their directories, $1.50 single copy). Each issue is filled with feature articles, such as "Agents and Authors: *Both* Sides Are Right," news on grants and awards, and advertisements for presses and publications.

How to Get Happily Published: A Complete and Candid Guide by Judith Appelbaum and Nancy Evans (1978). Harper & Row, Publishers, 10 East 53rd Street, New York, N.Y. 10022 ($9.95). A practical book by two seasoned editors that includes such topics as evaluating writing courses, obtaining critical advice, manuscript submission, negotiating a good contract, promotion gimmicks, and suggestions on how to persevere.

Huenefeld Report. The Huenefeld Company, Inc., 119 The Great Road, Bedford, Mass. 01730 ($48.00 a year for 26 issues). The ins and outs of publishing—marketing, direct mail campaigns, editorial development, graphics, production, manuscripts, and remainders.

International Authors and Writers Who's Who, 8th ed., edited by Adrian Easter. Gale Research Company, Book Tower, Detroit, Mich. 48226 ($52.50).

International Directory of Little Magazines and Small Presses, 13th ed., edited by Len Fulton and Ellen Ferber (1977–78). Dustbooks, P.O. Box 1056, Paradise, Calif. 95969 ($8.95).

LMP With Names and Numbers: The Directory of American Book Publishing (updated annually). R. R. Bowker Company, 1180 Avenue of the Americas, New York, N.Y. 10036 ($24.50). An indispensable one-volume guide to book publishing and all related literary matters—agents, conferences, conventions, direct mail promotion, manufacturing, plus information on radio, television, films, and magazine and newspaper publishing. There is a helpful "yellow pages" directory in the back.

TUB: A Magazine of Discovery, P.O. Box 3484, Grand Central Station, New York, N.Y. 10017 ($1.00 for sample copies). Unpublished books are reviewed in *TUB*, which is sent to about 3,000 editors, publishers, producers, and agents. If the capsule description results in a request for the manuscript and a definite contract with a publisher, *TUB* receives a 10 percent finder's fee.

Washington International Arts Letter. P.O. Box 9005, Washington, D.C. 20003 ($16.00 yearly for ten issues). A letter service and digest concerning support programs, patrons, developments in the arts, government, books, publications, humanities, and education.

The Writer, monthly magazine. 8 Arlington Street, Boston, Mass. 02116 ($12.00 yearly). Articles by seasoned professionals on how to write with a monthly listing of markets; also contains book publishing and sales services on all aspects of writing.

Writer's Digest, monthly magazine. 9933 Alliance Road, Cincinnati, Ohio 45242 ($10.00 introductory subscription rate). Interviews and articles on all aspects of writing plus up-to-date market listings and new publications, editor changes, and sources of financial aid. The magazine also publishes numerous books on writing.

Writers Directory 1976–78. St. Martin's Press Reference Department, 175 Fifth Avenue, New York, N.Y. 10010 ($35.00). Details on more than 12,000 writers with a section on publishers' addresses.

A Writer's Guide to Book Publishing by Richard Balkin (1977). Hawthorn Books, Inc., 260 Madison Avenue, New York, N.Y. 10016 ($9.95). An excellent inside look at the publishing process—from manuscript through submission to publication—by literary agent Balkin.

The Writer's Legal Guide by Tad Crawford (1977). Hawthorn Books, Inc., 260 Madison Avenue, New York, N.Y. 10016 ($10.95). Crawford, a lawyer, discusses copyrights, the rights of the writer, contracts, and income taxation.

Writer's Market, edited by Jane Koester and Rose Adkins (updated annually). Writer's Digest, Cincinnati, Ohio 45242 ($13.95). A listing of over 5,000 paying markets for novels, stories, fillers, plays, articles, gags, verse, and photos. There are also sections on play producers, syndicates, foreign book publishers, picture sources, government information sources, author's agents, and audiovisual markets.

FINE ARTS

American Artist, monthly magazine. 1 Color Court, Marion, Ohio 43302 ($15.00 a year).

American Artist Business Letter for Practicing Artists, monthly. 2160 Patterson Street, Cincinnati, Ohio 45214 ($3.00 for single issue, $15.00 yearly subscription). Information on artist-dealer relationships, portrait commissions, taxes; book reviews; market reports.

Arts and Crafts Market, edited by Lynne Lapin and Betsy Wones (updated annually). Writer's Digest, 9933 Alliance Road, Cincinnati, Ohio 45242 ($9.95). Thousands of markets for illustrations, cartoons, crafts, designs, photography, and fine art works. Also includes chapters on arts organizations, art competitions, galleries, including names, addresses, and a brief annotation.

Basic Guide to Photography by Lou Jacobs, Jr. and the editors of *Photographic Magazine* (1973). Petersen Publishing Co., 8490 Sunset Boulevard, Los Angeles, Calif. 90069 ($2.95).

Contemporary Crafts Market Place, compiled by the American Crafts Council (1977–78). R. R. Bowker, 1180 Avenue of the Americas, New York, N.Y. 10036 ($15.95). Comprehensive directory that lists fairs and shows throughout the country. Also lists craft suppliers, courses, books, organizations, and guilds.

Crafts Business Encyclopedia by Michael Scott (1977). Harcourt Brace Jovanovich, orders to *The Crafts Report*, Book Department, 700 Orange Street, Wilmington, Del. 19801 ($10.00). A how-to book for someone who wants to make money marketing home crafts.

Fine Arts Market Place, compiled by Paul Cummings (1977). R. R. Bowker, 1180 Avenue of the Americas, New York, N.Y. 10019 ($19.95). A directory of publishers of art books, art dealers, exhibitions, and museum stores; resource section.

How to Make Money in the Art Market by Richard Blodgett (1975). David McKay Co., Inc., 750 Third Avenue, New York, N.Y. 10017 ($8.95).

Legal Guide for the Visual Artist by Tad Crawford (1977). Hawthorn Books, Inc., 260 Madison Avenue, New York, N.Y. 10016 ($9.95). Comprehensive legal reference—income tax, gallery agreements, artist's rights—by lawyer/writer Crawford.

Syndicate Survival Kit (1977). Cartoonist Guild, 156 West 72nd Street, New York, N.Y. 10023 ($5.00). A report on six syndicate contracts that also includes recommendations and guidelines to help an artist to negotiate with a syndicate.

The Photographer's Handbook by John Hedgecoe (1977). Knopf, 201 East 50th Street, New York, N.Y. 10022 ($16.95).

Photography Market Place, edited by Fred E. Mcdarrah (1977). R. R. Bowker, 1180 Avenue of the Americas, New York, N.Y. 10019 ($15.50). Buyers and sellers guide in the photography field.

PERFORMING ARTS

Audition: Everything An Actor Needs to Know to Get the Part by Michael Shurtleff, foreword by Bob Fosse (1978). Walker & Company, 720 Fifth Avenue, New York, N.Y. 10019 ($9.95). A well-written book intended to help actors and actresses conquer that most difficult experience—the audition—but also helpful to anyone in a nontheatrical interview/audition situation.

Back Stage. 165 West 46th Street, New York, N.Y. 10036. Weekly trade newspaper in the performing arts with feature articles and, most important, announcements for auditions, summer stock, business concerns of actors, playwrights, and others in the theater.

New York Theatre Review. 55 West 42nd Street, New York, N.Y. 10036 ($12.00 a year). A monthly national theater magazine with reports from twelve cities; includes interviews with critics and performing artists, essays, and photos.

Performing Arts Journal. P.O. Box 858, Peter Stuyvesant Station, New York, N.Y. 10009 ($6.00 a year for three issues). Contains interviews with playwrights and directors, essays, short plays, book reviews, and regional theater reports.

Players Magazine. University Theatre, Northern Illinois University, De Kalb, Ill. 60115 ($5.00). Bimonthly that contains articles and provides an ongoing source of information on playwriting markets, contests, and performances.

Show Business, weekly newspaper. 136 West 44th Street, New York, N.Y. 10036. Information on casting of New York, regional, and road companies, plus theater reviews, feature articles, and columns.

Simon's Directory of Theatrical Materials, Services and Information (1975). Package Publicity Service, 1564 Broadway, New York, N.Y. 10036 ($8.95). Information almanac for the United States and Canada listing performing arts books, theaters, unions, play contests, awards, and national organizations and associations.

Theater. Box 2046, Yale Station, New Haven, Conn. 06520 ($8.00 a year for three issues). Formerly *Yale/Theatre*, this magazine contains essays, plays, and interviews with theater writers and performers.

Variety. 154 West 46th Street, New York, N.Y. 10036. Weekly trade newspaper in the performing arts with an emphasis on films.

We're Pleased That You Are Interested in Making the Arts Accessible to Everyone (1976). ARTS, Grand Central Station, New York, N.Y. 10017 (free).

For articles in the areas of the arts, consult the *Art Index, Readers' Guide to Periodical Literature,* and *Social Sciences and Humanities Index,* available at your local or university library.

See also the following related chapters in *The Help Book:*

COUNSELING
EDUCATION
EMPLOYMENT
FINANCIAL ASSISTANCE
HOUSING
INFORMATION RIGHTS AND RESOURCES
MEDIA AND COMMUNICATIONS

6

BATTERED ADULTS

That no adult should be physically or psychologically abused—whether it be husband beating wife, wife beating husband, child beating parent, stranger beating stranger—seems obvious enough. Yet it has become very controversial to direct helping efforts to violence in the family in areas other than that of the battered-wife syndrome. Sociologist Suzanne K. Steinmetz's article on the battered husband published in the 1977–78 issue of the journal *Victimology* (see Additional Literature), generated two immediate overreactions. The first came from members of the women's movement who were also involved in the battered-wife problem. They felt attention to the battered husband would diffuse the "social costs and consequences of violence by the stronger against the weaker." The second surfaced as inaccurate and sensationalized distortions of Steinmetz's inconclusive study; magazines and newspapers wrote articles with headlines like "Study Backs Up Suspicions Husband Is More Battered Spouse."

But while the feminists and academics fight over who is the most beaten, shelters and counseling centers for battered women are beginning to counsel the abusing husband and, if space and time permits, give help to the battered man as well. At issue are not just the number of victims of family violence, or the social, political, and historical causes, but immediate help to prevent the all-too-common escalation of violent assaults into attempted murder or homicide cases. Hopefully the unnecessary and dangerous violence that goes on in an estimated 7.5 million American households will remain the key problem to be solved without any of the victims—husbands, wives, intervening police officers, etc.—becoming political scapegoats.

"Wife-beater Hit With 3-Year Term," read the January 1977 *New York Post* article. "You can't arrest me—that's my legal wife," the accused man was quoted as saying. But he was arrested, tried, and convicted of attempting to murder his wife by stabbing her with a screwdriver, stomping her with his boots, and attacking her with a chair and a bicycle chain as their seven children watched. The case of that thirty-year-old wife represents a legal milestone in this field. Few, if any, husbands had previously received more than ten days in the city or county jail for similar beatings. Some states are even changing their laws so that husbands no longer have the "right" to regard their wives as personal property that can be abused at will.

That victim did not have to withstand her ordeal alone. Many local groups, such as the South Brooklyn Legal Services group, the Center for the Elimination of Violence in the Family, and branches of such national organizations as the YWCA provided legal, emotional, and financial advice and assistance. In the United States, Canada, and England, the previously ashamed and fearful battered woman now need no longer suffer beatings or seek legal redress alone.

Nevertheless, the chronically battered adult—male or female—is the victim of one of the most complicated of crimes because he or she usually knows the criminal (the wife or the husband) and because he or she may even stay with his or her spouse long after the first, second, or third assault. Why? The abused wife may be torn between financial dependency on her husband and her wish to end the beatings. Also, since many cases of wife beating are associated with alcoholism or drug abuse, the husband may be loving when "straight" and resort to beatings only when the Mr. Hyde side of his personality emerges. The beaten husband may stay because he is ashamed, fearful, or he has responded to the wife's violence with verbal or physical abuse of his own. In that way, a cycle of violence becomes the family's way of relating, albeit a destructive and potentially fatal one.

But whether there is more adult abuse today, or whether it is just more frequently reported, beaten wives and husbands are *not* taking it anymore. Wives are founding or finding shelters where they (and their children) can be safe until they decide what their next step will be: family court action, criminal charges, separation, returning home, or divorce. More battered men and parents are speaking out about the physical abuse they endure. And perhaps the result of the increased awareness of the problem is that more batterers are seeking professional help.

So far there is no national social service agency solely concerned with battered adults. The Center for Women's Policy Studies in Washington, D.C., does research in this area, and disseminates information, but is a comparatively small operation. The coordination of emergency shelters is left to a few independent clearinghouse operations—such as Betsy Warrior's efforts through the Women's Educational Center in Massachusetts or the *National Communication Network* and the Feminist Alliance Against Rape newsletter *Aegis* reports on battered women activities; the national Young Women's Christian Association (YWCA) notes this concern in its national newsletter, *Interchange*.

But direct services are still a local phenomenon, even with national organizations such as the American National Red Cross, the Salvation Army, the YWCA, and the National Organization of Women (NOW) providing services on a local community-to-community basis. (Contact your nearest branch of these national organizations to see what help they provide.) Battered women and batterers should remember that good counseling or emergency food, shelter, and clothing are needs that can be met through allied services such as women's groups, YMCA's/YWCA's, crisis intervention counselors attached to local mental health services, and hospitals. More and more cities and smaller communities have emergency shelters and treatment facilities designed especially for battered women and their children, but they are equipped to serve only those who live in their immediate areas. They are often very small facilities, with room for a maximum, often, of twenty-five persons (including children). Some facilities are free; others charge rates that are very low, sometimes only a dollar a night, or have a sliding-scale fee based on ability to pay.

For information about battered adults, contact these national organizations:

Center for Women Policy Studies (CWPS)
2000 P Street, N.W., Suite 508
Washington, D.C. 20036

A national information clearinghouse on sexually and physically abused women and children established in 1972 and involved in various research projects and publications. Requests for information are handled by either making referrals to organizations, individuals, or publications; by sending materials developed by other programs but that CWPS is authorized to distribute; or by fact sheets developed by CWPS.

LITERATURE: *Response*, free newsletter geared to the professional project director or worker in the field of spouse abuse (subscription should be requested only if interest is that specialized).

Domestic Violence and Spouse Assault Project, Inc.
1917 Washtenaw Avenue
Ann Arbor, Mich. 48104

Provides information through its publications, such as *Wife Beating: How to Develop a Wife Assault Task Force and Project* by Kathleen M. Fojtik ($1.50); *Wife Beating: Counselor Training Manual #1* by Mindy Resnik ($2.00); and *Wife Beating: Counselor Training Manual #2* by Barbara Cooper ($2.00).

Family Violence Research Program
Sociology Department
University of New Hampshire
Durham, N.H. 03824

Established in 1970, the program provides at a nominal charge related articles on spouse assault. Send for the price list that describes the available reprints by sociologists Murray A. Straus, Richard J. Gelles, and Suzanne K. Steinmetz.

Women in Crisis
444 Park Avenue South
New York, N.Y. 10016

Sponsored a national conference in May 1979 to establish a communication network to link related services to women.

Women's Rights Program Unit
U.S. Commission on Civil Rights
1121 Vermont Avenue, N.W.
Washington, D.C. 20425

The unit is concerned with the problem of the battered woman; it sponsored a conference on this issue in January 1978.

The following is a sampling of local direct services for battered women:

Rainbow Retreat, Inc.
4332 North 12th Street
Phoenix, Ariz. 85014
(Mainly for alcohol-related abuse.)

Mothers In Stress Service (M.I.S.S.)
1147 Ohio Street
Fairfield, Calif. 94533

Solano Center for Battered Women
P.O. Box 2051
Fairfield, Calif. 94533

Women Shelter
P.O. Box 4222
Long Beach, Calif. 90804

Women's Transitional Living Center, Inc.
P.O. Box 6103
Orange, Calif. 92667

Haven House, Inc.
P.O. Box 2007
Pasadena, Calif. 91105
(Mainly for alcohol-related abuse.)

La Casa De Las Madres
P.O. Box 15147
San Francisco, Calif. 94115

York Street Center
1632 York Street
Denver, Colo. 80260

Women in Crisis Center Shelter
1426 Pierce Street
Lakewood, Colo. 80214

Prudence Crandall Center for Women
Box 895
New Britain, Conn. 06050

House of Ruth Annex
1215 New Jersey Street, N.W.
Washington, D.C. 20001

Hubbard House
1231 Hubbard Street
Jacksonville, Fla. 32206

Dade County Task Force on Battered Women
100 Southeast Fourth Street
Miami, Fla. 33131

Shelter for Abused Spouses and Children
1888 Owawa Street
Honolulu, Hawaii 96819

The Salvation Army
The Emergency Lodge
432 W. Wisconsin Street
Chicago, Ill. 60614

Rosie's Place
23 Dartmouth Street
Boston, Mass. 02116

Transition House
c/o Woman's Center
46 Pleasant Street
Cambridge, Mass. 02139

Elizabeth Stone House
128 Minden Street
Jamaica Plain, Mass. 02130

Respond
P.O. Box 555
Somerville, Mass. 02143

Abby's House
23 Crown Street
Worcester, Mass. 01608

Domestic Violence and Spouse Assault Project, Inc.
1917 Washtenaw Avenue
Ann Arbor, Mich. 48104

Rape/Spouse Assault Crisis Center
29 Strong Avenue
Muskegon, Mich. 49441

Women's Advocates
584 Grand Avenue
St. Paul, Minn. 55102

Center for the Elimination of Violence in the Family, Inc.
P.O. Box 279
Bay Ridge Station
Brooklyn, N.Y. 11220

Victims Information Bureau of Suffolk (VIBS)
501 Route 111
Hauppauge, N.Y. 11787

Hofstra Center for Physically or Psychologically
 Abused Women
Hofstra University
Hempstead, N.Y. 11550

Abused Women's Aid in Crisis
G.P.O. Box 1699
New York, N.Y. 10001

Partners Anonymous
158-18 Riverside Drive
New York, N.Y. 10032

Vera House, Inc.
P.O. Box 62
Syracuse, N.Y. 13207

Akron Task Force on Battered Women, Inc.
146 South High Street
Akron, Ohio 44308

Project Woman
22 East Grand Avenue
Springfield, Ohio 45506

Bradley-Angle House
P.O. Box 40132
Portland, Ore. 97240

National Organization for Women (NOW)
Task Force on Household Violence/Battered
 Women
P.O. Box 843
Portland, Ore. 97207

Women in Crisis, Inc.
Harrisburg, Pa. 17101
(Full address withheld upon request)

Women Against Abuse Emergency Shelter
P.O. Box 12233
Philadelphia, Pa. 19144

Women's Center South
6907 Frankstown Avenue
Pittsburgh, Pa. 15208

YWCA Crisis Center
300 8th Street
Chattanooga, Tenn. 37403

Women's Shelter & Support Service Program
Y.W.C.A.
220 East Union
Olympia, Wash. 98501

Catherine Booth House
The Salvation Army
925 East Pike Street
Seattle, Wash. 98122

Young Women's Christian Association
Battered Women's Program
West 829 Broadway Avenue
Spokane, Wash. 99201

Y.W.C.A. Women's Emergency House
1012 West 12th Street
Vancouver, Wash. 98660

Task Force on Battered Women
3719 West Fond Du Lac Avenue
Milwaukee, Wis. 53216

Calgary Women's Emergency Shelter
 Association
938 15 Avenue, S.W.
Calgary, Alberta, Canada

Ishtar Transition House
Langley, British Columbia, Canada
(Address withheld upon request)

Auberge Transition/Transition House
1355 Dorchester Street West
Montreal, Quebec H3G 1T3
Canada

Interval House
211-5th Avenue North
Saskatoon, Saskatchewan
Canada

Women in Transition Incorporated
143 Spadina Road
Toronto, Ontario M5R 2T1
Canada

Transition House
c/o Vancouver Status of Women
2029 West Fourth Avenue
Vancouver, British Columbia V6J 1N3
Canada

Chiswick Women's Aid
369 Chiswick High Road
London W4, England

National Women's Aid Federation
51, Chalcot Road
London NW 1, England

ADDITIONAL LITERATURE

Battered Wives by Del Martin (1976). New Glide Publications, 330 Ellis Street, San Francisco, Calif. 94102 ($6.95 plus $.50 postage and handling). Basic information on battered wives, including chapters on the batterer and the victim, plus descriptions of several exemplary refuges in the United States.

Battered Women: A Psychological Study of Domestic Violence edited by Maria Roy (1977). Van Nostrand Reinhold Company, 450 West 33rd Street, New York, N.Y. 10001 ($11.95). Anthology of writings by leading researchers and counselors.

Battered Women Info Digest (March 1977). Business and Professional Women's Foundation, 2012 Massachusetts Avenue, N.W., Washington, D.C. 20036 ($.25 for postage and handling). Prepared by the Foundation's Library and Information Center, this *Info Digest* provides concise descriptions of the issues involved in abuse of women, alternatives, resources, and annotated bibliographic references.

Conjugal Crime: Understanding and Changing the Wifebeating Pattern by Terry Davidson (1978). Hawthorn Books, Inc., 260 Madison Avenue, New York, N.Y. 10016 ($9.95).

Interchange, monthly newsletter. National Board of the YWCA, 600 Lexington Avenue, New York, N.Y. 10022 (free). Prints pertinent articles, for example, "The Battered Women" (May/June 1977 issue).

Aegis: Magazine on Organizing to Stop Violence Against Women. Box 21133. Washington, D.C. 20009 ($8.75 for individuals; $20.00 for institutions). A bimonthly newsletter with input from anti–domestic violence groups across the country that is trying to avoid duplication of efforts and to let the various shelters know what the others are doing. It also provides updates on legislative or legal status changes of domestic violence statutes.

Programs Providing Services to Battered Women, compiled by Susan Bancroft (1978). Center for Women Policy Studies, 2000 P Street, N.W., Washington, D.C. 20036 (limited number available free). State-by-state listings of emergency shelters for battered women collected by the center during early 1978 and in typescript format; gives addresses, phone numbers, a brief description of services, and who provides funding.

Scream Quietly or the Neighbours Will Hear by Erin Pizzey, edited by Alison Forbes (1974). Penguin Books, Inc. 7110 Ambassador Road, Baltimore, Md. 21207 ($1.95). Pizzey, founder of the Chiswick Women's Aid Emergency Shelter in England for battered women and their children, tells of her experiences running the shelter; also includes some basic facts about the problem of wife abuse and numerous case studies.

"Spouse Assault," *Victimology: An International Journal*, Emilio Viano, editor-in-chief, numbers 3–4, volume 2, 1977–78, Visage Press, Inc., 3409 Wisconsin Avenue, N.W., Washington, D.C. 20016 ($10.00). A collection of articles, research and project notes, book reviews, and comments on spouse assault including Suzanne K. Steinmetz's controversial article on "The Battered Husband Syndrome." Contributors to the issue are sociologists, criminologists, and those working in public or private spouse assault centers and shelters.

The Violent Home: A Study of Physical Aggressions Between Husbands and Wives by Richard J. Gelles (1974). Sage Publications, P.O. Box 776, Beverly Hills, Calif. 90213 ($11.00 hardcover, $6.00 paper). A sociologist's view of the problem, Gelles discusses the victim and the offender and why the sacrosanct status of the family has heretofore obscured the problem; includes interviews.

Violence in the Family, edited by Suzanne Steinmetz and Murray Straus (1974). Harper & Row Publishers, 10 East 53rd Street, New York, N.Y. 10022 ($7.50). Six scholarly articles on the origins and patterns of spouse assault.

Wife Beating: The Silent Crisis by Roger Langley and Richard C. Levy (1977). E. P. Dutton,

201 Park Avenue South, New York, N.Y. 10003 ($9.95). Reviews the findings of Steinmetz, Straus, Bard, Gelles, and other sociologists who have studied violence in the family and includes case histories, including battered men, and a bibliography.

Working on Wife Abuse, 4th ed. compiled by Betsy Warrior (1977). 46 Pleasant Street, Cambridge, Mass. 02139 ($3.00 plus $.50 postage and handling). Periodically updated, this mimeographed directory lists researchers in the field of battered women as well as refuges, counseling centers, and research projects in progress.

See also the following related chapters in *The Help Book:*

ALCOHOLISM
CHILD ABUSE
CHILDBEARING
CHILDREN
COUNSELING
CRIME PREVENTION
CRIME VICTIMS AND WITNESSES
DRUGS, SMOKING AND DRUG ABUSE
EMERGENCIES AND DISASTERS
EMPLOYMENT
FINANCIAL ASSISTANCE
HOUSING
KIDNAPPING, MISSING PERSONS, AND RUNAWAYS
LAW ENFORCEMENT
LEGAL SERVICES
MENTAL HEALTH
PARENTING
RAPE AND SEXUAL ASSAULT
SUICIDE PREVENTION

7

BUSINESS INFORMATION

Everyone needs business and economic information since credit, insurance, taxes, and retirement plans affect us all. In addition, there has been a renewed interest in small businesses in the 1970s. This growth has been largely through the efforts of three groups that wish to "strike out" on their own—those who have retired (or been retired) from another job, women who want to be self-employed rather than in more conventional office situations, and minority group members who prefer to avoid traditional job discrimination problems.

Even though establishing your own small business may sound like a good idea, rising costs and lower returns necessitate the new or ongoing entrepreneur to be more of a business expert than ever before. Knowing when to go into business, how to get loans, how to advertise, how to get free or inexpensive publicity, and how to get free business counseling may prove to be the difference between good intentions and financial success. The local offices of the U.S. Small Business Administration and the U.S. Department of Commerce offer hundreds of free or low-cost pamphlets, booklets, and brochures for every aspect of business. Volunteer groups, such as SCORE and ACE, offer free counseling by retired executives. Many cities also have their own free executive volunteer corps for information and direct counseling services to new and established businesses.

The Small Business Administration issues a comprehensive "Checklist for Going Into Business" (Small Marketers Aid No. 71) that suggests you ask yourself some vital questions if you are thinking about starting your own business. Since beginning a new business is risky, at best, you will substantially improve your chances of success if you understand what problems you may come up against and work out possible solutions before you even start your enterprise. Listed below are some questions from the SBA's checklist to help you think through what you need to know and do. Answer *yes* or *no* to each question.

BEFORE YOU START

HOW ABOUT *YOU*?

Are you the kind of person who can get a business started and make it go? ____

Think about *why* you want to own your own business. Do you want to badly enough to keep you working long hours without knowing how much money you'll end up with? ____

Have you worked in a business like the one you want to start? ____

Have you worked for someone else as a foreman or manager? ____

Have you had any business training in school? ____

Have you saved any money? ____

HOW ABOUT THE MONEY?

Do you know how much money you will need to get your business started? ____

Have you counted up how much money of your own you can put into the business? ____

Do you know how much credit you can get from your suppliers—the people you will buy from? ____

Do you know where you can borrow the rest of the money you need to start your business? ____

Have you figured out what net income per year you expect to get from the business? Count your salary and your profit on the money you put into the business. ____

Can you live on less than this so that you can use some of it to help your business grow? ____

Have you talked to a banker about your plans? ____

HOW ABOUT A PARTNER?

If you need a partner with money or know-how that you don't have, do you know someone who will fit—someone you can get along with? ____

Do you know the good and bad points about going it alone, having a partner, and incorporating your business? ____

Have you talked to a lawyer about it? ____

HOW ABOUT YOUR CUSTOMERS?

Do most businesses in your community seem to be doing well? ____

Have you tried to find out whether stores like the one you want to open are doing well in your community and in the rest of the country? ____

Do you know what kind of people will want to buy what you plan to sell? ____

Do people like that live in the area where you want to open your store? ____

Do they need a store like yours? ____

If not, have you thought about opening a different kind of store or going to another neighborhood? ____

GETTING STARTED

YOUR BUILDING

Have you found a good building for your store? ____

Will you have enough room when your business gets bigger? ____

Can you fix the building the way you want it without spending too much money? ____

Can people get to it easily from parking spaces, bus stops, or their homes? ____

Have you had a lawyer check the lease and zoning? ____

EQUIPMENT AND SUPPLIES

Do you know just what equipment and supplies you need and how much they will cost? ____

Can you save some money by buying secondhand equipment? ____

YOUR MERCHANDISE

Have you decided what things you will sell? ____

Do you know how much or how many of each you will buy to open your store with? ____

Have you found suppliers who will sell you what you need at a good price? ____

Have you compared the prices and credit terms of different suppliers? ____

YOUR RECORDS

Have you planned a system of records that will keep track of your income and expenses, what you owe other people, and what other people owe you? ____

Have you worked out a way to keep track of your inventory so that you will always have enough on hand for your customers but not more than you can sell? ____

Have you figured out how to keep your payroll records and take care of tax reports and payments? ____

Do you know what financial statements you should prepare? ____

Do you know how to use these financial statements? ____

Do you know an accountant who will help you with your records and financial statements? ____

YOUR STORE AND THE LAW

Do you know what licenses and permits you need? ____

Do you know what business laws you have to obey? ____

Do you know a lawyer you can go to for advice and for help with legal papers? ____

PROTECTING YOUR STORE

Have you made plans for protecting your store against thefts of all kinds—shoplifting, robbery, burglary, employee stealing? ____

Have you talked with an insurance agent about what kinds of insurance you need? ____

BUYING A BUSINESS SOMEONE ELSE HAS STARTED

Have you made a list of what you like and don't like about buying a business someone else has started? ____

Are you sure you know the real reason why the owner wants to sell his or her business? ____

Have you compared the cost of buying the business with the cost of starting a new business? ____

Is the stock up to date and in good condition? ____

Is the building in good condition? ____

Will the owner of the building transfer the lease to you? ____

Have you talked with other businessmen in the area to see what they think of the business? ____

Have you talked with the company's suppliers? ____

Have you talked with a lawyer about it? ____

MAKING IT GO

ADVERTISING

Have you decided how you will advertise? (Newspapers—posters—handbills—radio—by mail?)

Do you know where to get help with your ads? ____

Have you watched what other stores do to get people to buy? ____

THE PRICES YOU CHARGE

Do you know how to figure what you should charge for each item you sell? ____

Do you know what other stores like yours charge? ____

BUYING

Do you have a plan for finding out what your customers want? ____

Will your plan for keeping track of your inventory tell you when it is time to order more and how much to order? ____

Do you plan to buy most of your stock from a few suppliers rather than a little from many, so that those you buy from will want to help you succeed? ____

SELLING

Have you decided whether you will have salesclerks or self-service? ____

Do you know how to get customers to buy? ____

Have you thought about why you like to buy from some salesmen while others turn you off? ____

YOUR EMPLOYEES

If you need to hire someone to help you, do you know where to look? ____

Do you know what kind of person you need? ____

Do you know how much to pay? ____

Do you have a plan for training your employees? ____

CREDIT FOR YOUR CUSTOMERS

Have you decided whether to let your customers buy on credit? ____

Do you know the good and bad points about joining a credit-card plan? ____

Can you tell a deadbeat from a good credit customer? ____

A FEW EXTRA QUESTIONS

Have you figured out whether you could make more money working for someone else? ____

Does your family go along with your plan to start a business of your own? ____

Do you know where to find out about new ideas and new products? ____

Do you have a work plan for yourself and your employees? ____

Have you gone to the nearest Small Business Administration office for help with your plans? ____

Just by answering these questions carefully, you have probably discovered some areas you still need to know more about or do something about—especially questions that you answered *no*. Try to solve those queries on your own, but if you need help, seek out those experts who can share their knowledge. The organizations described in this chapter should help you start—or improve—your business operation.

Contact your county, city, or state department of commerce for information, pertinent seminars, and workshops, as well as counseling and advice on how to start a business. For direct help in business areas, contact your local, county, city, or state government offices listed under these categories in the telephone book: Better Business Bureau, Chamber of Commerce, N.O.W. chapter, Department of Commerce, Small Business Services, Bureau of Economic Affairs, or miscellaneous sources, such as the Economic Development Administration. Many of these agencies make available a group of successful retired businesspersons to provide free counseling and advice. Direct free help is also available through the regional, field, or state office of the U.S. Department of Commerce or the U.S. Small Business Administration (see the listings in this chapter under federal agencies).

The following federal agencies or groups working with federal agencies offer information or assistance in business matters:

BUSINESS INFORMATION / 75

Bureau of Consumer Protection
Federal Trade Commission
Washington, D.C. 20580

A federal office offering help and information regarding advertising complaints.

Consumer Affairs Division
Office of the Comptroller of the Currency
Administrator of National Banks
Washington, D.C. 20219

The Consumer Affairs Division was established in 1974 to gather and provide information in the area of consumer banking problems and to provide a place where consumers could go with complaints against any of the over 4,500 national banks; contact one of the fourteen national bank regional offices before going to the headquarters.

LITERATURE: Free fact sheet.

Consumer Hotline
Commodity Futures Trading Commission
2033 K Street, N.W.
Washington, D.C. 20581

A federal office offering help and information on commodity trading.

Consumer Liaison Office
Securities and Exchange Commission
Washington, D.C. 20549

Handles questions and complaints concerning stocks and bonds.

Economic Research Service
U.S. Department of Agriculture
500 Twelfth Street, S.W.
Washington, D.C. 20250

The service will provide the latest forecasts on production, prices, and supplies of farm and food commodities.

LITERATURE: List of publications; detailed list by subject area of interest; *National Food Situation*, a quarterly; *Agricultural Outlook*, a monthly available by subscription.

Internal Revenue Service (IRS)
U.S. Department of the Treasury
111 Constitution Avenue, N.W.
Washington, D.C. 20226

For taxpayer assistance, call your local IRS office or find your nearest one by looking for that listing on your yearly tax form. Educational courses on taxes and business are offered; problems unrelated to the yearly personal income tax should be directed to the regional or national headquarters.

National Center for Productivity and Quality of Working Life
Washington, D.C. 20036

An independent federal agency founded in 1975 doing research in productivity growth and ways to foster cooperative efforts among groups to achieve its recommendations. The center publishes pamphlets and reports in this area, including alternative work patterns, directories of productivity centers around the world, and public and private sector programs and policies.

LITERATURE: Publications list.

Office of Bank Customer Affairs
Federal Deposit Insurance Corporation
Washington, D.C. 20429

A federal agency offering information on state-chartered banks.

Office of Housing and Urban Affairs
Federal Home Loan Bank Board
Washington, D.C. 20552

A federal agency offering information on banking procedures on federally-insured savings and loans.

Office of Saver and Consumer Affairs
Federal Research System
Washington, D.C. 20551

A federal agency offering information on banking procedures in federal reserve banks.

U.S. Department of Agriculture
Assistant Secretary of Food and Consumer Affairs
Washington, D.C. 20250

A federal department concerned with a number of business and economics issues. It publishes consumer-oriented materials in its annual *Agriculture Handbook*. Short articles, such as "Keeping Records" are distributed free by the Consumer Product Information Center, Public Documents Distribution Center, Pueblo, Colo. 81009. Since a new listing is issued semiannually, make sure what you wish to order is still in print by checking with your local federal information center or writing for a free catalog.

U.S. Department of Commerce
14th Street between Constitution Avenue and E Street, N.W.
Washington, D.C. 20230

Established by Congress in 1903, this multipurpose federal agency has numerous bureaus and services to help business and consumers around the country. The focus of these services is, however, informational; the U.S. Department of Small Business Administration provides more direct services. Some of the original goals of the Department of Commerce were "to foster, promote, and develop the foreign and domestic commerce [and] . . . manufacturing and shipping . . . industries . . . of the United States." Within the department, there are nine subdivisions of interest to business—Bureau of Economic Analysis, Census Bureau, Patent and Trademark Office, National Bureau of Standards, Office of Minority Business Enterprise, National Technical Information Service, Office of Ombudsman for Business, Domestic and International Business Administration, and the Bureau of Domestic Commerce. The Department of Commerce has ten regional offices throughout the United States; the nine subdivisions also have their own regional offices throughout the country.

LITERATURE: *Serving the Nation*, a 36-page booklet about the Department of Commerce; *Toward Economic Progress: The Annual Report of the Secretary of Commerce: The American Economic System . . . and Your Part in It*, a free booklet of basic information available from "Economics," Pueblo, Colo. 81009; *Fourteen Ways the U.S. Department of Commerce Can Help Make Your Business More Profitable*, a free booklet.

Bureau of Economic Analysis: Analyzes economic statistics.

Census Bureau: Takes the national population census every ten years and has a wide range of information available from the last decennial census taken in April 1970.

Patent and Trademark Office: Processes new patents and trademarks.

National Bureau of Standards: Provides information on physical measurements; booklets are available to aid in the shift to the metric system.

Office of Minority Business Enterprise: Established to coordinate a national effort to create new minority businesses and expand those that already exist; field offices in sixteen cities and six other regional offices.

National Technical Information Service: Clearinghouse for the sale of Government-funded research and development reports including Department of Commerce publications.

Office of Ombudsman for Business: Part of the Bureau of Domestic Commerce, this office is designated to cut through traditional red tape by providing a direct line of communication between business, individuals, and the government. It is geared to federal government-based problems; local and state situations are referred to the appropriate agency. Although the Ombudsman has no legal power, it will ask a company that has had a complaint lodged against it for its side in the matter, which sometimes provokes a voluntary solution.

Domestic and International Business Administration: Established in 1972 to handle most general business inquiries. There are forty-three administration district offices within twenty-one satellite offices located in principal cities throughout the United States and Puerto Rico.

Bureau of Domestic Commerce: Part of the Domestic and International Business Administration, the bureau collects, analyzes, and maintains files on U.S. industries as well as related information on labor, taxation, pricing, production, and marketing.

LITERATURE: *Publications for American Business*, free pamphlet with listings by subject available from the Domestic and International Business Administration; *Selected Publications to Aid Business and Industry*, available from the Office of Field Operations; descriptive pamphlets of available services from the Office of Ombudsman for Business; *Situation Reports* on various business concerns such as tips on productivity, labor-management success story in the construction industry, available from the Office of Ombudsman for Business; *A Basic Guide to Exporting* ($.70) and *Expand Overseas Sales With Commerce Department Help* (free), both available from the Bureau of International Commerce, Washington, D.C. 20230.

U.S. Small Business Administration (SBA)
1441 L Street, N.W.
Washington, D.C. 20416

For individual business problems or questions about starting your own business, your regional office of the SBA is where to go for help. SBA is an independent federal agency created by Congress in 1953. Through an extensive range of informational and direct services, the U.S. SBA offers business assistance.

Branch offices in over ninety cities throughout the United States provide such direct help as management counseling, workshops, seminars, financial assistance, and so forth.

SBA has three national volunteer programs for business counseling:

ACE (Active Corps of Executives): These volunteers are active executives in all major industries, educational institutions, and trade associations; they are also drawn from the professions. It is a program that was started to expand on **SCORE**'s services (see below) and to assure that management counseling would be continually updated.

SCORE (Service Corps of Retired Executives): Begun in 1964, it has answered more than 300,000 requests for assistance, providing free confidential management counseling for small businesses having problems as well as to those persons thinking about starting a business or service organization. There are more than 290 local chapters of SCORE throughout the United States.

SBI (Small Business Institute): A management assistance program that operates through the cooperation of faculty and senior and graduate students of leading business schools around the country to give personal counseling to small business owners.

LITERATURE: *SCORE Counselor's Guidebook*; SCORE fact sheet; SCORE descriptive flyer; *Management Assistance*; *SBA—What It Does*; *SBA Business Loans*; *Women and the U.S. Small Business Administration*; *The Facts About Women as Users of SBA Services*; *Business Plan for Small Manufacturers*; *Finding a New Product for Your Company*; "Six Methods for Success in a Small Store." Write for extensive list of free and low-cost publications.

The following are national organizations offering general business and economics information:

Advertising Council Inc.
825 Third Avenue
New York, N.Y. 10022

A nonprofit organization whose membership consists of U.S. business, advertising, and communications companies that contribute their skills and resources in campaigns on national problems. Very effective recent campaigns have included free advertising for booklets offered on the U.S. economic system and exporting; others deal with aging, careers, child abuse, and so forth.

LITERATURE: Free newsletters: *Economic Communicator* and *Public Service Advertising Bulletin.*

American Institute of Cooperation (AIC)
1129 20th Street, N.W.
Washington, D.C. 20036

Founded in 1925, AIC provides information on cooperative business to business leaders and lay persons. It has a national education organization for farmer cooperatives; produces and distributes educational materials; holds conferences; and its National Institute on Cooperative Education usually attracts some 2,500 persons, including students, women, and state council and association leaders.

LITERATURE: *How We Organize to Do Business in America* (free); free descriptive leaflets and brochures.

Business and Professional Women's Foundation
2012 Massachusetts Avenue, N.W.
Washington, D.C. 20036

An information clearinghouse and reference center on working women providing career and educational scholarships and loans and training seminars. The foundation holds five to six seminars (about $125.00) around the country to help strengthen supervisors' skills in the areas of communication, delegating, and coordinating.

LITERATURE: CAP newsletter; publications price list.

Chamber of Commerce of the United States
1615 H Street, N.W.
Washington, D.C. 20062

National federation of over 3,000 chambers of commerce and trade associations, and information clearinghouse on business and economic issues. Contact your local branch for specific aids that they offer.

LITERATURE: Publications price list.

The Conference Board
845 Third Avenue
New York, N.Y. 10022

Research arm of the business community conducting extensive background explorations of business, unions, professional associations, economics, employment, and alternate work programs; promotes media awareness of business problems and trends through press releases and coverage of studies and reports.

LITERATURE: *Across the Board* monthly magazine ($30.00 nonassociates; $15.00 associates and educators); publications price list; free pamphlet on The Conference Board.

Council of Better Business Bureaus (CBBB)
National Headquarters
1150 17th Street, N.W.
Washington, D.C. 20036

A group of independent agencies throughout the country with voluntary self-regulation by supporting businesses and professional firms. When illegal practices are uncovered and the business refuses to cooperate with the CBBB, the matter is referred to the appropriate law enforcement agency. Many branches have voluntary arbitration between the business and the complaining consumer. There are offices in practically every city in the United States, but they vary widely as to effectiveness, size, and scope of operation.

Council of Better Business Bureaus
National Advertising Division
845 Third Avenue
New York, N.Y. 10022

This office investigates complaints against unsubstantiated national advertising.

Council on Economic Priorities (CEP)
84 Fifth Avenue
New York, N.Y. 10011

A $15.00 membership provides for ten CEP free newsletters ($1.00 each for nonmembers) or send for publications list of pertinent literature on business with a stress on affirmative action, environment, and energy. CEP is a nonprofit organization established to collect and distribute objective information on the practices of U.S. corporations in such social areas as consumer practices, political influence, military production, foreign activities, equal employment, and environmental quality.

LITERATURE: *Buyer, Beware!* ($3.00); *Short-changed: Minorities and Women in Banking* ($5.95).

National Alliance of Business (NAB)
1730 K Street, N.W. Suite 558
Washington, D.C. 20006

A volunteer organization of business executives on loan from their companies, working in cooperation with the U.S. Department of Labor and industry to assist in improving employment for the men and women of various minority groups.

National Association of Bank Women (NABW)
111 East Wacker Drive
Chicago, Ill. 60601

With over 17,000 members in fifty states, Canada, and other foreign countries, NABW represents women employed in banks and banking institutions; its objectives include more productive careers for women in banking, public education for banking as a career, the NABW Education Foundation, which has affiliations with undergraduate institutions, a certificate program in management, workshops, and seminars, such as the "Life Planning Seminar," for women bank executives.

LITERATURE: Free fact sheets, including "Careers for Women in Banking"; NABW Membership Directory; *NABW Journal*.

Public Interest Economics Foundation (PIE-F)
1714 Massachusetts Avenue, N.W.
Washington, D.C. 20036

National public interest group acting as an information clearinghouse, research center, and providing a liaison for professional economists and public interest groups and government officials. Its western office (PIE-West, 1095 Market Street #604, San Francisco, Calif. 94103) offers economic analysis and expertise to citizen groups and groups under contract to a government agency.

LITERATURE: Free descriptive leaflets; *PIE Newsletter* ($5.00 a year); send for publications price list.

Tax Reform Research Group
P.O. Box 14198
Washington, D.C. 20044

A nonprofit nongovernmental group that is part of the Public Citizen Group of Nader-inspired organizations. The Tax Reform Research Group, concerned with the reform of federal, state, and local income taxes and property taxes, is an information clearinghouse; performs advocacy and Congressional lobbying; and seeks reform of the IRS.

80 / THE HELP BOOK

LITERATURE: *People & Taxes*, monthly ($7.50 a year, free samples available); *Tax Politics: How They Make You Pay and What You Can Do About It* ($6.95, or $4.95 if you subscribe to *People & Taxes*).

Although the services provided by state agencies for business or commerce will vary, the basic commitment of these government services to the public is in promoting more businesses, spreading up-to-date business and economic information, the encouragement of more minority businesses, and the development or improvement of state training and manpower programs. Quite often free seminars and conferences are held throughout the state on such topics as "How to Start Your Own Business," management techniques, insurance and accounting procedures, inventory control, bookkeeping, and so forth.

Write or phone your local state business office to find out what free leaflets, pamphlets, and brochures are available. Since a great deal of business information must relate to those laws specific to one's state, it is often more productive to seek information from the local and state level on up to the federal level. Also, the state department of economic development may be an umbrella agency for activities to promote revenue in the state, such as tourism and travel. Free maps and brochures may be available.

The following is a listing of the state agencies for economic development:

Industrial Relations Department
Industrial Relations Building
649 Monroe Street
Montgomery, Ala. 36130

Department of Commerce and Economic Development
State Office Building
Pouch D
Juneau, Alaska 99811

Economic Planning and Development
1700 West Washington Street
Phoenix, Ariz. 85007

Department of Industrial Development
205 State Capitol Building
5th and Woodlane
Little Rock, Ark. 72201

Department of Economic and Business Development
1120 N Street
Sacramento, Calif. 95814

Division of Commerce and Development
Department of Local Affairs
500 State Centennial Building
1313 Sherman Street
Denver, Colo. 80203

Commission on Environmental Protection and Economic Development
Department of Commerce
210 Washington Street
Hartford, Conn. 06106

Division of Economic Development
Department of Community Affairs and Economic Development
Delaware State Building
Dover, Del. 19801

Office of Business and Economic Development
District Building
1350 E Street, N.W.
Washington, D.C. 20005

Division of Economic Development
Department of Commerce
G-62 Collins Building
Tallahassee, Fla. 32304

Department of Industry and Trade
1400 North Omni International
Atlanta, Ga. 30303

Department of Planning and Economic
  Development
Kamamalu Building
250 South King Street
Honolulu, Hawaii 96813

Division of Tourism and Industrial
  Development
Office of the Governor
108 Capitol Building
Boise, Idaho 83720

Department of Business and Economic
  Development
222 South College Street
Springfield, Ill. 62706

Economic Development Group
Department of Commerce
336 State House
Indianapolis, Ind. 46204

Iowa Development Commission
250 Jewett Building
914 Grand Avenue
Des Moines, Iowa 50309

Department of Economic Development
503 Kansas Avenue
Topeka, Kans. 66603

Industrial Development Division
Department of Commerce
Capital Plaza Tower
Frankfort, Ky. 40601

Department of Commerce and Industry
P.O. Box 44185
Baton Rouge, La. 70804

Development Office
Executive Department
State House
Augusta, Maine 04333

Department of Economic and Community
  Development
2525 Riva Road
Annapolis, Md. 21401

Division of Economic Development
Department of Commerce and Development
100 Cambridge Street
Boston, Mass. 02202

Office of Economic Expansion
Department of Commerce
Law Building
Lansing, Mich. 48913

Department of Economic Development
Hanover Building
480 Cedar Street
St. Paul, Minn. 55101

Research and Development Center
3825 Ridgewood Road
Jackson, Miss. 39205

Division of Commerce and Industrial
  Development
Department of Consumer Affairs, Regulation
  and Licensing
Jefferson State Office Building
Jefferson City, Mo. 65101

Economic Development Division
Department of Community Affairs
1424 Ninth Avenue
Helena, Mont. 59601

Department of Economic Development
State Office Building
P.O. Box 94666
Lincoln, Neb. 68509

Department of Economic Development
Capitol Complex
Carson City, Nev. 89710

Division of Economic Development
Department of Resources and Economic
   Development
State House Annex, 3rd Floor
Concord, N.H. 03301

Division of Economic Development
Department of Labor and Industry
P.O. Box 1390
Trenton, N.J. 08625

Economic Development Division
Department of Development
Bataan Memorial Building
Santa Fe, N.M. 87503

State Economic Development Board
Alfred E. Smith Office Building
Albany, N.Y. 12225

State Economic Opportunity Office
Department of Natural Resources and
   Economic Development
P.O. Box 27687
Raleigh, N.C. 27611

Department of Business and Industrial
   Development
523 East Bismarck Avenue
Bismarck, N.D. 58501

Economic Development Division
Department of Economic and Community
   Development
State Office Tower
30 East Broad Street
Columbus, Ohio 43215

Department of Industrial Development
Office of the Governor
Will Rogers Memorial Office Building
2401 North Lincoln Boulevard
Oklahoma City, Okla. 73105

Department of Economic Development
Loyalty Building, 9th Floor
317 S.W. Alder Street
Portland, Ore. 97204

Bureau of Economic Development
Department of Commerce
425 South Office Building
Harrisburg, Pa. 17120

Department of Economic Development
1 Weybosset Hill
Providence, R.I. 02903

State Development Board
1301 Gervais Street
P.O. Box 927
Columbia, S.C. 29202

Industrial Development and Expansion Agency
Department of Economic and Tourism
   Development
Joe Foss Building
Pierre, S.D. 57501

Department of Economic and Community
   Development
1007 Andrew Jackson State Office Building
500 Deaderick Street
Nashville, Tenn. 37219

Industrial Commission
719 Sam Houston State Office Building
P.O. Box 12728, Capitol Station
Austin, Tex. 78711

Department of Development Services
104 State Capitol
Salt Lake City, Utah 84114

Economic Development Department
Agency of Development and Community Affairs
Pavilion Office Building
109 State Street
Montpelier, Vt. 05602

Division of Industrial Development
Office of the Governor
1010 State Office Building
Richmond, Va. 23219

Department of Commerce and Economic
   Development
101 General Administration Building
Olympia, Wash. 98504

Governor's Office of Economic and Community Development
B517 State Office Building 6
1900 Washington Street E.
Charleston, W.Va. 25305

Department of Business Development
650, 123 West Washington Avenue
Madison, Wis. 53703

Department of Economic Planning and Development
Barrett Building
Cheyenne, Wyo. 82002

CREDIT

Credit information is available from the following organizations and federal agencies:

Bureau of Consumer Protection
Federal Trade Commission
Washington, D.C. 20850

This federal office is concerned with credit and gives information to the consumer as well as accepts complaints about violation of the federal credit laws.

Credit Union National Association, Inc. (CUNA)
P.O. Box 431
Madison, Wis. 53701

A trade association for U.S. credit unions.

LITERATURE: *A Brief History of the Credit Union Movement; Credit Unions: What They Are, How They Operate, How to Join, and How to Start One.*

Farmers Home Administration (FmHA)
U.S. Department of Agriculture
Room 225-W
Washington, D.C. 20250

Apply for credit from this office if you live in rural America and all other sources for low-cost, reasonable credit have been depleted.

National Credit Union Administration
2025 M Street, N.W.
Washington, D.C. 20456

A federal office covering federal credit unions.

LITERATURE: *Organizing a Federal Credit Union With Standard Amendments and Guidelines* (September 1972); *Federal Credit Unions*, a leaflet; *Your Insured Funds;* publications list.

National Foundation for Consumer Credit, Inc.
1819 H Street, N.W.
Washington, D.C. 20006

Umbrella organization for 200 state chartered, community-sponsored Consumer Credit Counseling Services throughout the United States. The foundation provides educational materials through pamphlets, textbooks, studies, and speeches.

LITERATURE: Write for publications price list or the following booklets ($.25 each)— "Consumer Credit"; "The Forms of Credit We Use"; "Establishing Good Credit"; "Measuring and Using Our Credit Capacity"; "The Emergency Problem, What to Do About It."

Office of Saver and Consumer Affairs
Federal Reserve Board
20th Street and Constitution Avenue, N.W.
Washington, D.C. 20551

If you want to complain about a lender's possible violation of the federal Equal Credit Opportunity Act and are unsure which agency you should contact, write to this office, which will make referrals to the appropriate agency.

LITERATURE: Free leaflets—"Equal Credit Opportunity Act"; "Consumer Credit Protection Act"; "Truth in Lending"; "Consumer Leasing"; "Fair Credit Reporting."

INSURANCE

Federal agencies that offer insurance programs include:

Federal Crime Insurance
P.O. Box 41033
Washington, D.C. 20014

Provides robbery and burglary insurance for businesses and homes. Premiums range from $20.00 to $80.00 for $1,000.00 to $10,000.00 coverage. Participating states are:

Alabama	Massachusetts
Arkansas	Minnesota
Colorado	Missouri
Connecticut	New Jersey
Delaware	New York
District of Columbia	North Carolina
Florida	Ohio
Georgia	Pennsylvania
Illinois	Rhode Island
Iowa	Tennessee
Kansas	Virginia
Maryland	

Office of Manpower
U.S. Department of Health, Education and Welfare
330 Independence Avenue, S.W.
Washington, D.C. 20201

Administers the unemployment insurance system through over 2,000 local employment offices throughout the country; oversees the state-federal system providing job counseling and placement.

National Flood Insurance Program
Federal Insurance Administration
U.S. Department of Housing and Urban Development
451 Seventh Street, S.W.
Washington, D.C. 20410

Provides reasonable flood insurance to individuals and businesses.

Urban Riot Insurance
Federal Insurance Administration
U.S. Department of Housing and Urban Development
451 Seventh Street, S.W.
Washington, D.C. 20410

Provides urban riot insurance to individuals and businesses.

For information about insurance, contact the following national organizations:

American Council of Life Insurance
277 Park Avenue
New York, New York 10017

Free pamphlets available; consumer program for education and financial planning.

Educational Division
Insurance Information Institute
110 William Street
New York, N.Y. 10038

This organization, supported by insurance companies, provides information to the general public and students on auto and home insurance and insurance careers.

LITERATURE: Free booklets include *Insurance For the Home, Auto Insurance,* and *Careers in Property and Liability Insurance*.

Women's Equity Action League
733 Fifteenth Street, N.W.
Suite 200
Washington, D.C. 20005

LITERATURE: *Sex Discrimination in Insurance: A Guide for Women* ($3.00).

Complaints and information requests regarding insurance matters are also handled by most state insurance agencies. Some publish cost comparison tables on companies that do business within their jurisdiction. Free consumer booklets are offered by most state departments. Individual complaints about any type of insurance—life, home, health, and auto—will be followed up and often fast results are possible. State insurance agencies are also able to provide information on licensing as well as research and statistics. Contact your state agency for insurance, listed in your local telephone directory, for further information.

CRIMES AGAINST BUSINESS

The most frequent crimes against a business are shoplifting, vandalism, bad checks, counterfeiting, inventory shortages (employee theft), arson, robbery, burglary, and credit card abuse. A *Convenience Store Merchandiser* survey found that employee theft was responsible for 75 to 85 percent of all inventory shrinkage. These crimes cost U.S. business an estimated $31.2 billion in 1976.

Robbery and burglary losses are crimes that every store—no matter how high-crime or high-risk the area it is in—can be insured against. If you don't already have such insurance, study carefully the entries for the Federal Crime Insurance Program administered by the U.S. Department of Housing and Urban Development. Curbs on shoplifting are also becoming more common. The security directory of a large Detroit department store that apprehended over 5,000 shoplifters in 1976 gave this description of the typical shoplifter: "Most often, the person who steals from us is—in terms of age, sex, race, and economic position—the very same as the person who shops from us."

To report an "economic" nonviolent crime against a business (a so-called "white-collar crime") start at the local precinct level. They will refer you to the appropriate law enforcement agency for additional help, such as the Consumer Complaints Bureau or Fraud Bureau in the District Attorney's Office. (Depending upon the type of crime involved, you might also be referred to the Attorney General's Office or the District Court of the U.S. Court House.) If you telephone in your complaint, you should try to make an appointment to speak to someone about your charges to guarantee that your accusations are taken seriously and pursued.

The following national organizations and federal agencies offer information on crimes against business:

Chamber of Commerce of the United States
1615 H Street, N.W.
Washington, D.C. 20062

Maintains a Crime Prevention and Control office within its national headquarters which publishes pertinent information in this area.

LITERATURE: *White Collar Crime*, 1974 ($2.50); *Marshaling Citizen Power Against Crime*, 1970 ($2.00); *Deskbook on Organized Crime*, rev. 1972 ($2.00).

American Bar Association
Section of Criminal Justice
Committee on Economic Offenses
1800 M Street, N.W., 2nd floor
Washington, D.C. 20036

Conducts research into economic offenses; membership in this section available to law students, lawyers, and non-lawyers as an International, Judicial, Administrative Law, and Educational Associate ($20.00 a year).

LITERATURE: *Report of Criminal Justice Section Economic Offenses Committee*, 1977 ($4.50).

U.S. Department of Commerce
Domestic and International Business
  Administration
Bureau of Domestic Commerce
Fourteenth and Constitution Avenue, N.W.,
  Room 1104
Washington, D.C. 20230

Will answer telephone inquiries about cost of crimes against business and make referrals to published sources. Issues news releases on surveys on crime against business conducted by this bureau.

LITERATURE: *Federal Government Sources on Crimes Against Business*, Nov. 1974 ($.30); *Crimes Against Business: A Management Perspective*, Dec. 1976 ($2.65); *The Cost of Crimes Against Business*, Jan. 1976 ($1.60); *Crime in Retailing*, Aug. 1975 ($1.10). (The above booklets are available for sale from the Superintendent of Documents, U.S. Government Printing Office, Washington, D.C. 20402).

U.S. Securities and Exchange Commission
Officer of Consumer Affairs
Washington, D.C. 20549

For direct help, contact your nearest office of the Securities and Exchange Commission, listed in your telephone directory under "U.S. Government," or call the headquarters for referrals for filing complaints. The Securities and Exchange Commission, established by Congress in 1934, provides information and, through its laws, protection against misrepresentation and fraud in the issuance and sale of securities.

LITERATURE: Free pamphlets—*Investigate Before You Invest* and *Ponzi and Pyramid Schemes*.

ADDITIONAL LITERATURE

Advertising Age: The International Newspaper of Marketing. 740 Rush Street, Chicago, Ill. 60611 ($25.00 a year for 52 issues).

Bicentennial Statistics: A Reprint of Bicentennial Statistics Chapter From the Pocket Data Book USA 1976, U.S. Department of Commerce, Bureau of the Census. Write to Superintendent of Documents, U.S. Government Printing Office, Washington, D.C. 20402 ($.90). A digest of statistics on population, immigration, consumer prices, with charts on selected historical trends including health, education, income, and prices. A useful reference tool for the student, businessperson, or consumer.

The Big Foundations by Maxwell S. Stewart, based on the Twentieth Century Fund Study by Waldemar A. Nielsen (1973). Public Affairs Pamphlet No. 500, 381 Park Avenue South, New York, N.Y. 10016 ($.50). A succinct discussion of thirty-three foundations.

Business As a Game by Albert Z. Carr (1968). Mentor Books, New American Library, 1301 Avenue of the Americas, New York, N.Y. 10019 ($1.50). A guide for the executive on the way up with advice on all matters, such as how to gain raises and promotions.

Business Week. McGraw Hill Building, 1221 Avenue of the Americas, New York, N.Y. 10020 ($26.00 yearly; $1.25 per issue). A weekly magazine containing news, book reviews, reports on business, economics, unions, labor, management, advertising, and resources; usually contains one or two in-depth articles on some business development in each issue.

Complete Guide to Your Own Business by Charles E. Tate, Jr., Leon Megginson, Charles R. Scott, Jr., and Lyle R. Trueblood (1977). Dow Jones-Irwin, 1818 Ridge Road, Homewood, Ill. 60430 ($30.00).

Economic Education: A Guide to Information Sources by Catherine A. Hughes (1977). Gale Research Company, Book Tower, Detroit, Michigan 48226 ($18.00). Directory of available resources for teaching economics in grades one through twelve that includes booklets, pamphlets, tests, games, audio-visual materials, and books.

Finance Facts. Consumer Credit Education Foundation, 601 Solar Building, 1000 Sixteenth Street, N.W., Washington, D.C. 20036. Free monthly containing information on urban family budgets, personal income increases and decreases, consumer price index, and so on.

The Game of Business by John McDonald (1977). Anchor Books, Garden City, N.Y. 11530 ($4.50). Veteran business writer McDonald explores corporate and cooperative games and highlights certain key businesspersons, such as Howard Hughes and Walt Disney.

How Capitalism Works by Pierre Jalée, translated from the French by Mary Klopper (1977). Monthly Review Press, 62 West 14th Street, New York, N.Y. 10011 ($3.95). A simplified analysis for workers, students, and teachers on the capitalist economic system from a Marxist vantage point. The author deals with profit, monopoly, labor power, credit, and inflation.

How to Be Successfully Self-Employed Working for Yourself by G. Hewitt, photos by Tom Gettings (1977). Rodale Press, Emmaus, Pa. 18049 ($9.95). A practical guide to self-employment, including the less conventional freelance jobs—farmsteading, crafts, services, innkeeper, handyman, electrician, photography, real estate, inventor. Inspired by Studs Terkel's *Working*, the book contains valuable and extensive interviews with freelancers. It is more a gift book than a how-to book for those considering the uncertain world of the self-employed.

How to Sell Anything to Anybody by Joe Girard with Stanley H. Brown (1978). Simon & Schuster, Inc., 1230 Avenue of the Americas, New York, N.Y. 10020 ($8.95). Girard, who the 1977 *Guiness Book of World Records* listed as the "number one retail car and truck salesman in the world" shares his selling methods as well as his personal story.

The Money Game by "Adam Smith" (1976). Vintage Books, 201 East 50th Street, New York, N.Y. 10022 ($1.95). Wall Street guide stressing "anxiety, identity, and money" as factors and goals in the money business pursuit.

Murphy's Law and Other Reasons Why Things Go Wrong! by Arthur Block (1977). Price/Stern/Sloan Publishers, Inc., 410 North La Cienega Boulevard, Los Angeles, Calif. 90048 ($2.50). A humorous support, with quotations, of the law that "If anything can go wrong, it will."

People & Taxes. P.O. Box 14198, Washington, D.C. 20044 ($7.50 individual yearly subscription; $12.00 business yearly subscription). Monthly report for the general public on the latest tax news.

Politics and Markets by Charles E. Lindblom (1977). Basic Books, Inc., 10 East 53rd Street, New York, N.Y. 10022 ($15.00). Lindblom, Sterling Professor of Economics and Political Science at Yale, explores American business. He examines democracy, corporate power, private ownership economy, and their restraints.

Should You Incorporate? (1977). Council of New York Law Associates, 36 West 44th Street, New York, N.Y. 10036 (free). A bilingual pamphlet that asks and answers the basic questions about whether someone should incorporate or not as well as how to go about it.

Sylvia Porter's Money Book: How to Earn It, Spend It, Save It, Invest It, Borrow It—and Use It to Better Your Life by Sylvia Porter (1975). Doubleday & Company, Inc., Garden City, N.Y. 11530. The bible for everything you need to know about money—the economics of children, funeral expenses, your rights as a consumer, where to get help. Columnist Porter talks in understandable terms and offers a practical, comprehensive tool for those who need assistance in this area. The book has a valuable resource section and is cross-referenced for easy use.

Tax Politics: How They Make You Pay and What You Can Do About It by Robert M. Brandon, Jonathan Rowe, and Thomas H. Stanton, with a preface by Ralph Nader (1976). Pantheon Books, 201 East 50th Street, New York, N.Y. 10022 ($6.95). Written by lawyers and tax experts in easy-to-understand language.

U.S. Industrial Outlook (published annually). Available at the U.S. Department of Commerce field offices or write to Superintendent of Documents, U.S. Government Printing Office, Washington, D.C. 20402 ($6.75). Forecasts for 200 industries based on the government's business data base.

U.S. News & World Report. 2300 N Street, N.W., Washington, D.C. 20037 ($18.00 a year; $1.00 per issue). A weekly magazine that covers news and business with appeal for the general audience. It contains one or two feature articles each week, plus school and college updates and a letters section with information and opinions.

Woman's Guide to Starting a Business by Claudia Jessup and Genie Chipps (1976). Holt, Rinehart and Winston, 383 Madison Avenue, New York, N.Y. 10017 ($4.95). A good, basic beginning guide written in a lively style with an annotated resource section.

Women Today. Today Publications & News Service, National Press Building, Washington, D.C. 20045 ($25.00 prepaid). A biweekly newsletter with updates and calendar information on various business and career matters relating to women and business; also includes some material on other concerns of women, such as battered wives and sex discrimination.

CREDIT

Borrowing Basics for Women, with an introduction by Bess Myerson (1977). Citibank Public Affairs Department, P.O. Box 939, Church Street Station, New York, N.Y. 10008. A free pamphlet.

Fair Credit Billing Act. Consumer Information Center, Department 649E, Pueblo, Colo. 81009. A free pamphlet.

Women: To Your Credit (1976). Commercial Credit Corporation, 300 St. Paul Place, Baltimore, Md. 21202. A free pamphlet.

INSURANCE

The following is a list of free booklets available from Kemper Insurance Companies, Long Grove, Ill. 60049:

Businessowner's Guide to Insurance
Guide: A Common Sense Introduction to Insurance
How to Buy Car Insurance
How to Buy Home Insurance
We're Glad You Asked: A Consumer Question and Answer Guide to Insurance

Your Insurance Handbook by Richard Guardino and Richard Trubo (1975). Doubleday & Company, Inc., Garden City, N.Y. 11530 ($3.95). A guide to health, life, auto, and property insurance with tables showing the average annual premium and twenty-year cost index for major companies. It also includes addresses of major companies' home offices and a household inventory checklist.

For articles in the areas of business, economics, insurance, credit, taxes, and money, consult the *Business Periodicals Index,* available at your local or university library.

See also the following related chapters in *The Help Book:*

ARTS
CONSUMER AFFAIRS
COURTS
CRIME PREVENTION
EDUCATION
EMPLOYMENT
FINANCIAL ASSISTANCE
INFORMATION RIGHTS AND RESOURCES
VETERANS

8

CHILD ABUSE

In 1977 more than one million American children were physically abused or mistreated. Five thousand victims died from their injuries. Child abuse has always existed, but through the research and writings of a small group of medical pioneers—Drs. Vincent DeFrancis, Ray E. Helfer, C. Henry Kempe, Leontine Young, and Vincent Fontana—the public has become aware of the problem and its consequences to the victims.

Child abuse is a cyclical situation—many abused children grow up to be abusing parents. In addition, an untold number of children with permanent physical and mental handicaps may in fact have been victims of custodial mistreatment. One of the most frequent "weapons" is a hairbrush; but infants and children have also been beaten with bare fists, pool cues, broom handles, T.V. aerials, ropes, straps, and fan belts.

Help for child abuse now centers on self-help groups and telephone counseling for abusive or potentially abusive parents, such as Parents Anonymous (PA), on "hotlines" for reporting suspected abuse, and on local, state, and federal programs to take abused children away from abusing parents with temporary or permanent institutional or foster care placement. But more and more effort is being placed into the diagnosis, and treatment, of child abuse as well as care for the abused child before the psychological scars become permanent. Parents Anonymous recognizes six forms of child abuse: physical abuse; physical neglect; sexual abuse; verbal abuse; emotional abuse; and emotional neglect. Except for sexually abused children, too few physically abused child victims receive concerted attention from counseling services. Sensitizing emergency-room medical personnel to abuse as a possible cause for child injuries will help to get aid to the victim, and the abuser, before it is too late.

To report incidents of child abuse or neglect, or to find public help on the local or state level, contact the Child Welfare Department in your area (listed in the

Government section of your telephone book). Child abuse may also be part of the Bureau of Social Services, Welfare Department, Child Services, Juvenile Probation Department, Health Services, and so forth, in your state or city. Many states and communities now have child abuse hotlines. Check your telephone book to see if such a service is available.

You might also look for a privately funded organization to help in the area of child abuse with the words "Specialized Services for Children" or "Society for the Prevention of Cruelty to Children" in its title. It might offer services similar to those provided by The New York Society for the Prevention of Cruelty to Children, founded in 1875.

The New York Society for the Prevention of Cruelty to Children (NYSPCC)
110 East 71st Street
New York, N.Y. 10021

The NYSPCC was the first child protective agency created to enforce laws to protect children, which is still the goal of the agency. It maintains branches in the other New York City boroughs. Referrals are made to other appropriate social services (such as mental health, alcoholic treatment, drug abuse). NYSPCC is also concerned with the welfare of children under sixteen who are professional entertainers. The society determines what action should be taken if abuse or neglect is suspected. Immediate intervention may be needed and the assistance of Family Court is used where the society will initiate proceedings.

You may also contact the regional office of the U.S. Children's Bureau National Center on Child Abuse and Neglect (see entry below for address) for help in finding local referrals and assistance.

> **Being a parent is one of the toughest jobs in the world.**
> Everyday pressures can become unbearable.
> Many parents need someone to turn to... someone who will listen and try to help.
> If you need help...or know of someone who does...call us. All contacts are confidential. To get help, or give help, call

Developed by the National Center on Child Abuse and Neglect.

The following is a list of national organizations that have local groups or local member agencies providing direct help for parents with child abuse problems and for abused children:

Big Brothers/Big Sisters of America
220 Suburban Station Building
Philadelphia, Pa. 19103

Two national organizations founded in 1903, now merged into one, Big Brothers/Big Sisters of America have a combined network of about

400 agencies serving more than 100,000 children throughout the United States. They are particularly helpful to single parents who are having problems with their child or children. Check your local directory for the nearest branch or contact the national office. Big Brothers and Big Sisters offer volunteer opportunities to work with children and young people needing friendship and emotional support.

Child Welfare League of America, Inc.
67 Irving Place
New York, N.Y. 10003

The Child Welfare League has hundreds of member agencies whose concern is child abuse (see complete listing in Chapter 10, *Children*, and Chapter 40, *Multipurpose Organizations*).

Family Service Association of America
44 East 23rd Street
New York, N.Y. 10010

The association has hundreds of member agencies whose concern is child abuse (see complete listings in Chapter 10, *Children*, and Chapter 40, *Multipurpose Organizations*).

National Center on Child Abuse and Neglect (NCCAN)
Office of Child Development
Department of Health, Education, and Welfare
P.O. Box 1182
Washington, D.C. 20013

NCCAN funds ten regional offices that provide training and technical assistance to states within their region and is charged with dispensing federal funds for the identification, prevention, and treatment of child abuse. There are over thirty demonstration projects that are currently funded through NCCAN, which will provide the name of each regional center, a child abuse specialist, or specific services within your community.

Parents Anonymous, Inc. (PA)
2810 Artesia Boulevard
Redondo Beach, Calif. 90278

PA consists of parents (persons) with child abuse problems and is concerned with the identification, treatment, and prevention of child abuse. There are over 650 local groups, which conduct group-therapy rap sessions and have support groups, based on a "do-it-now" approach. Toll-free twenty-four-hour telephone hotlines are available.

LITERATURE: Free booklets include "I Am a Parents Anonymous Parent," "Child Abuse," "Losing Your Kool With Your Kids?," and "Child Abuse is Scary," a booklet for professionals; *Frontiers*, a quarterly newsletter available with a contribution.

Salvation Army
Headquarters
120 West 14th Street
New York, N.Y. 10011

Check your local directory for the nearest Salvation Army since child abuse is treated as a specific problem by many local units, although the national headquarters does not isolate it from other family distress situations. Write to the territorial office if you cannot find a local branch; their Social Service Department caseworkers are also equipped to handle child abuse or neglect problems. (See also Salvation Army listing in Chapter 40, *Multipurpose Organizations*.)

The following national organizations act as information clearinghouses on child abuse and child neglect:

American Humane Association
Children's Division
5351 South Roslyn Street
Englewood, Colo. 80111

A national association of child protection agencies that conducts research and evaluation programs and also offers consultations to direct services for abused children. Membership dues are $25.00 a year, $15.00 for subscribing members.

LITERATURE: *Guidelines for Schools;* membership classification leaflet; *Children's Division,* a pamphlet; *Publications on Child Protection,* a leaflet; *American Humane,* a monthly magazine ($5.50 a year; $.50 per copy); *Plain Talk About Child Abuse* ($.35); *Child Abuse Legislation in the 1970s,* rev. ed. ($2.50); *Accent on Prevention* ($.05); *Emotional Neglect of Children* ($.10); *Marshalling Community Services on Behalf of the Abused Child* ($.35); *Protecting the Battered Child* ($.35); *Protecting the Child Victim of Sex Crimes Committed by Adults* ($4.95).

California State University
Child Abuse and Neglect Resource
  Demonstration Program
Los Angeles Foundation
5151 State University Drive
Los Angeles, Calif. 90032

The program provides treatment for victims of child abuse and neglect and maintains a resource library.

LITERATURE: Bimonthly newsletter.

Concerns of Children
Mabom Odyssey
Building 13, Wards Island
New York, N.Y. 10035

A child abuse and neglect research and information clearinghouse with a rights advocacy center that has distributed the petition "For the Declaration of Interdependence for America's Children," and makes referrals to local groups concerned with helping the abused child.

LITERATURE: Write for publications list; free fact sheets; slide presentation on the problem of child abuse available for sale.

National Center for the Prevention and Treatment of Child Abuse and Neglect
Department of Pediatrics
University of Colorado Medical Center
1205 Oneida Street
Denver, Colo. 80220

Founded by child abuse identification and treatment pioneer C. Henry Kempe, M.D., this center is concerned with the development of innovative programs to deal with the abused child and the abusing parent(s). It has training programs, an extensive reference library, and audio-visual aids for teaching purposes, and provides technical assistance and consultation services.

LITERATURE: Catalog available upon request.

National Center for Voluntary Action (NCVA)
Technical Services Division
1214 Sixteenth Street, N.W.
Washington, D.C. 20036

A national volunteer agency that offers a packet, "Volunteers in Child Abuse Prevention Programs" ($1.50), listing programs across the country that use volunteers. (See also NCVA listing in Chapter 50, *Volunteerism.*)

National Center on Child Abuse and Neglect
U.S. Children's Bureau
Department of Health, Education, and Welfare
P.O. Box 1182
Washington, D.C. 20013

An information clearinghouse on child abuse and neglect.

LITERATURE: Write for list of publications and film strips developed by the National Center on Child Abuse and Neglect, but available through other federal information services; *Working With Abusive Parents From a Psychiatric Point of View* by Brandt F. Steele, M.D. ($.45 from the Superintendent of Documents); fact sheets.

National Committee for Prevention of Child Abuse
111 East Wacker Drive, Suite 510
Chicago, Ill. 60601

A national membership organization ($10.00 a year) organized to develop a public awareness of the child abuse problem in America by disseminating information to professionals, workers, laypersons, teachers, and students. Provides training and makes referrals to direct services through their directory (see Additional Literature).

LITERATURE: *Prevent Child Abuse* (free); *A Look at Child Abuse* ($3.00); *Child Abuse and Neglect: Model Legislation for the States* ($3.00); *What Every Parent Should Know* by Dr. Thomas Gordon ($2.00); *Caring*, a bimonthly newsletter (for members only); *The Educator and Child Abuse* by Brian G. Fraser; send for more complete publications list.

National Safety Council
444 North Michigan Avenue
Chicago, Ill. 60611

The council has no services for child abuse but does publish and mail a free one-page flyer listing organizations and articles relating to abused children.

Protective Services Resource Institute
Rutgers Medical School
College of Medicine and Dentistry of New Jersey
P.O. Box 101
Piscataway, N.J. 08854

Established in 1975, this information clearinghouse is concerned with educating students, families, professionals, children, and the public about child abuse and neglect. It publishes a monthly newsletter and maintains a library of resource material on this problem. The institute also provides technical assistance to professional service coalitions, has a speakers bureau, and sponsored a national conference on the topic of child abuse in April 1978.

LITERATURE: Catalog ($2.50); free brochures and leaflets including *P.S.R.I. Report* and *Sexual Abuse Proceedings*.

The following is a sampling of local child abuse and neglect helplines and services, arranged by state:

Family Services
Cook Inlet Native Association
P.O. Box 515
Anchorage, Alaska 99510

SCAN Volunteer Service, Inc. (Suspected Child Abuse & Neglect)
Room 135 Hendrix Hall
Arkansas State Hospital
4313 W. Markham
Little Rock, Ark. 72201

CALM (Child Abuse Listening Mediation, Inc.)
P.O. Box 718
Santa Barbara, Calif. 93102

Parental Stress Service, Inc.
154 Santa Clara Avenue
Oakland, Calif. 94610

Parents Anonymous of New York
250 West 57th Street
New York, N.Y. 10019

Children's Advocates, Inc.
21 James Street
Boston, Mass. 02118

ADDITIONAL LITERATURE

By Sanction of the Victim by Patte Wheat (1976). Kable News Co., Inc., 777 Third Avenue, New York, N.Y. 10017 ($1.75). Pulitzer Prize nominee novel on child abuse told from the point of view of an abused twelve-year-old child. The author is also editor of the Parents Anonymous newsletter *Frontiers*.

Child Protection Report (biweekly). 1301 20th Street, N.W., Washington, D.C. 20036 ($50.00 a year for individuals; $75.00 a year for agencies). An "independent newsletter covering children/youth health and welfare services" that reports on research and demonstration projects and new publications.

Helping the Battered Child and His Family by C. Henry Kempe, M.D., and Ray E. Helfer, M.D. (1972). J. B. Lippincott Company, E. Washington Square, Philadelphia, Pa. 19105 ($4.95). The authors describe how professionals can coordinate their efforts to protect children from abuse; they also suggest how a treatment program can be developed in any community.

The Little Victims: How America Treats Its Children by Howard James (1975). David McKay Co., Inc., 750 Third Avenue, New York, N.Y. 10017 ($10.95). Well-written and sensitive summary of the child abuse problem, including interviews with abused children. Sexual abuse is also discussed, and the major researchers and pioneers are noted.

National Directory of Child Abuse Services and Information by the National Committee for Prevention of Child Abuse (1974). 111 East Wacker Drive, Room 510, Chicago, Ill. 60601 ($4.00 prepaid). A 100-page directory listing programs by state with the location, telephone number, contact, sponsoring agency, and a description.

National Directory of Children and Youth Services, compiled by the *Child Protection Report* staff (1978). 1301 20th Street, N.W., Washington, D.C. 20036 ($25.00 prepaid). A directory of government and private service programs now operating in cities and counties throughout the United States; it includes child abuse and neglect among other programs for children and youth, such as juvenile court programs.

Prevent Child Abuse by the National Committee for Prevention of Child Abuse (1976). Available from Prevent Child Abuse, P.O. Box 2866, Chicago, Ill. 60690 (free). A 4-page information and resource guide to child abuse presented in tabloid style; includes a bibliography that lists some publications of the National Committee.

Somewhere a Child is Crying: Maltreatment— Causes and Prevention by Vincent J. Fontana (1973). Macmillan Publishing Co., Inc., 866 Third Avenue, New York, N.Y. 10022 ($6.95). Through case histories, Dr. Fontana shows that generalizations about the abusing parent cannot be made or the motives behind their physical assaults simply pinpointed to anger, poverty, or inappropriate disciplinary treatment.

To Combat Child Abuse and Neglect by Theodore Irwin (1974). Public Affairs Pamphlet No. 508, 381 Park Avenue South, New York, N.Y. 10016 ($.50). Irwin summarizes what child abuse is, suggests causes, and describes the newer approaches to treatment, such as the Comprehensive Emergency Protective Services to Neglected Children in Metropolitan Nashville-Davidson County, Tennessee. He also discusses how concerned citizens can help to solve a national problem.

Wednesday's Children: A Study of Child Neglect and Abuse by Leontine Young (1964). McGraw-Hill Book Company, 1221 Avenue of the Americas, New York, N.Y. 10020 ($2.45). Young, a social worker, discovered an extraordinary number of child abuse cases in the records of a public welfare department and was led to describe how abusing parents compared and differed from non-abusing ones. One of the earliest general books in this area, later researchers have confirmed many of her findings.

See also the following related chapters in *The Help Book:*

ALCOHOLISM
BATTERED ADULTS
CHILDBEARING
CHILDREN
COUNSELING
CRIME PREVENTION
CRIME VICTIMS AND WITNESSES
EDUCATION
EMERGENCIES AND DISASTERS
KIDNAPPING, MISSING PERSONS, AND RUNAWAYS
LAW ENFORCEMENT
LEGAL SERVICES
MENTAL HEALTH
MULTIPURPOSE ORGANIZATIONS
PARENTING
RAPE AND SEXUAL ASSAULT
SEX EDUCATION AND THERAPY
VOLUNTEERISM

9

CHILDBEARING

For a while it seemed those women who had postponed childbearing in order to establish a career first might never begin their families. But by April 1977, a new "baby boom" was reported; the birth rate was up 6 percent from the previous year, and the "over thirty" mother was credited with most of the new births.

Is it better to wait to have children? According to Dr. Roy H. Petrie, assistant professor in the Department of Obstetrics and Gynecology of the College of Physicians & Surgeons of Columbia University, "The problems of pregnancy late in the reproductive life of the female are far fewer than the lay or even elementary medical press would have us believe." Psychologist Albert Ellis has also found that those women who have first had a career and then had children report to him only the virtues of that chronology. "They are often grateful that they have had the child," says Ellis, "and are willing to put up with the interruption of their career, extra work, not getting along that well with their husbands, and other hassles of having children. Those among them who have a basic emotional stability take the whole thing very well and get a good deal more satisfaction and joy from their children" than do younger mothers.

At the opposite end of the spectrum, however, is the increase in babies born to unwed mothers between the ages of fifteen and nineteen—a 75 percent increase from 1966 to 1975. And the list of other controversial developments in childbearing is long: the way in which the child is born—natural versus drug-induced labor; artificial insemination; laboratory fertilization of eggs outside the womb; attention to the nutrition of babies *before* birth; employment during pregnancy; "The Pregnant Patient's Bill of Rights" (developed by The International Childbirth Education Association); drugs during pregnancy; breastfeeding; abortion; genetic counseling; the use of amniocentesis to detect Down's syndrome (mongoloidism) before birth. More than ever, the need for counseling and information for the mother and father—

whatever their age—is keener at this, the most important—and potentially trying—time in their lives.

To find an obstetrician or gynecologist, consult your local medical association for referrals. (See Chapter 30, *Health*, for a more extensive description of how to find a doctor.)

The following federal agencies provide information on maternal health and childbearing. For direct services, they suggest contacting your local or state government health agency for either specific doctors or free childbearing classes. (See the state agency listings in Chapter 30, Health.)

Administration for Children, Youth and Families
Children's Bureau
U.S. Department of Health, Education, and Welfare
P.O. Box 1182
Washington, D.C. 20013

Publishes a variety of materials on maternal care, pregnancy, and childbearing.

LITERATURE: *Prenatal Care* is available from the Superintendent of Documents, U.S. Government Printing Office, Washington, D.C. 20402. ($.75); write for publications price list.

Bureau of Community Health Services
U.S. Department of Health, Education, and Welfare
5600 Fishers Lane
Rockville, Md. 20857

The bureau publishes the following directories (single copies available for free):

Directory of the Bureau of Community Health Services (1974)—a 91-page listing of U.S. Projects operating under grants for community health centers, maternal and child health, health maintenance organizations, and family planning, as well as the cooperating state health departments and related agencies.

Annotated Bibliography on Maternal Nutrition (1970)—199 pages.

Food for the Teen-ager During Pregnancy (1976)—24 pages.

Maternal Nutrition and the Course of Pregnancy: Summary Report (1970)—23 pages.

LITERATURE: For additional listings, write for the *Publications of the Bureau of Community Health Services* booklet.

National Institute of Child Health and Human Development
National Institute of Health
9000 Rockville Pike
Bethesda, Md. 20014

Researches and reports on maternal health and childbearing.

Office of Human Development
U.S. Department of Health, Education, and Welfare
330 Independence Avenue, S.W.
Washington, D.C. 20201

Publishes free or inexpensive pamphlets, leaflets, and fact sheets on various aspects of maternal health and childbearing.

The following international or national organizations all have local chapters that provide direct services for expectant parents; the headquarters offer information and publications as well as referrals:

American Society for Psychoprophylaxis in Obstetrics (ASPO)
1411 K Street, N.W.
Washington, D.C. 20005

A nonprofit educational organization, established in 1960, of physicians, childbirth experts, and parents to help men and women prepare for childbirth with the Lamaze method. ASPO makes referrals to the closest local teacher, physician, and ASPO chapter; there are thirty-one chapters and fourteen affiliates.

LITERATURE: *Professional Bulletin*, quarterly ($.25 for recent issue); *Conceptions*, quarterly newsletter, ($.20 for recent issue); *It's Only Natural* ($.10); "Natural Childbirth: Pain or Peak Experience?" by Deborah Tanzer, *Psychology Today* reprint ($.20); for additional titles, write for publications price list.

Association for Childbirth, International (ACI)
P.O. Box 1219
Cerritos, Calif. 90701

ACI provides information, referral services, parent education classes, and a certified childbirth-educator training program ($5.00 membership).

LITERATURE: *Birth Notes*, newsletter; *Giving Birth at Home* by Tonya Brooks and Linda Bennett, a parent information handbook containing reprints of articles, typescript instructions and data sheets, photos ($8.00); descriptive brochure; publications price list.

Birthright, Inc. (U.S.A.)
62 Hunter Street
Woodbury, N.J. 08096

761 Coxwell Avenue (International)
Toronto M4C 3C5 Canada

Provides an alternative to abortion in unplanned pregnancies through referrals to counseling and legal/medical information sources; emergency housing and furnishing of maternity and childbirth material needs; and referrals to branches throughout the United States. International headquarters are in Toronto, Canada.

LITERATURE: *The Story of Birthright: The Alternative to Abortion* by Louise Summerhill ($1.95 postpaid); write for publications price list; some free pamphlets available.

Home Oriented Maternity Experience
511 New York Avenue
Takoma Park, Washington, D.C. 20012

A supportive, educational, nonprofit organization dealing with home births. There are about thirty-five H.O.M.E. groups in nineteen states making telephone and written referrals.

LITERATURE: "Welcome to H.O.M.E.," free pamphlet; *H.O.M.E.: A Comprehensive Guide to Homebirths* ($3.00 + postage); newsletter (with membership).

International Childbirth Education Association, Inc.
P.O. Box 20852
Milwaukee, Wis. 53220

An educational clearinghouse for complete family-centered maternity care. There are about 300 local member groups, which make referrals to local childbirth classes, hold conferences, and provide information.

LITERATURE: *News*, newsletter; publications list.

National Genetics Foundation, Inc. (NGF)
9 West 57th Street
New York, N.Y. 10019

A direct service providing treatment and genetic counseling to those afflicted with inherited disorders by referrals to the Nationwide Network of Genetic Counseling and Treatment Centers for definitive diagnosis. NGF is also an information clearinghouse on genetic disorders and counseling and provides education programs.

LITERATURE: *How Genetic Disease Can Affect You and Your Family; Can Genetic Counseling Help You?; Over 35 and Pregnant?; Genetic Counseling and Treatment Network* (free publications).

The Salvation Army
National Headquarters
120 West 14th Street
New York, N.Y. 10011

Contact your local branch for confidential advice and help given to unwed mothers. They also provide both prenatal and postpartum medical care, a temporary or long-term place to live, and pregnancy testing and family planning.

LITERATURE: "Yes, There Is Life After Birth," pamphlet.

This national organization offers self-help to those with infertility problems:

Resolve, Inc.
P.O. Box 474
Belmont, Mass. 02178

Headquarters for this self-help support group for infertile people with local chapters throughout the United States. Resolve, Inc. offers counseling and support groups as well as referrals to physicians and other resource services.

LITERATURE: *Infertility: A Guide for the Childless Couple* by Barbara Eck Manning, founder and director of Resolve, Inc. ($3.45).

The following are national information and/or research organizations:

American College of Nurse-Midwives
1012 14th Street, N.W., Suite 801
Washington, D.C. 20005

A national organization founded in 1955 that provides general information on nurse-midwives for pregnant women, their families, and potential consumers of nurse-midwife services. The college has educational programs with guest speakers and an annual convention.

LITERATURE: *What is a Nurse-Midwife?* ($.25); *Journal of Nurse-Midwifery* ($10.00 a year).

American Association For Maternal and Child Health, Inc.
P.O. Box 965
Los Altos, Calif. 94022

A national educational organization founded in 1914 by physicians at Chicago Lying-in Hospital that now has four chapters with over 3,500 members, including professionals, researchers, students, and interested persons. Membership dues are $20.00 for physicians, dentists, and pharmacists; $10.00 for all others. The association sponsors *American Baby* magazine.

LITERATURE: Send for list of available reprints for sale.

Maternity Center Association
48 East 92nd Street
New York, N.Y. 10028

A national, nonprofit health agency concerned with the betterment of maternity care. It is an information clearinghouse with classes and conferences available.

LITERATURE: *Workshops on Expectant Parent Education*, leaflet; *Planning Parents Classes*, leaflet; descriptive booklet; publications price list.

The National Foundation/March of Dimes
P.O. Box 2000
White Plains, N.Y. 10602

Provides birth defects information and supports research.

LITERATURE: *International Directory of Genetic Services* (free); *Facts: 1977* and *Be Good to Your Baby: Before It Is Born* (free booklets); "Family Medical Record" (free leaflet).

National Tay-Sachs & Allied Diseases Association, Inc.
122 East 42nd Street
New York, N.Y. 10017

Tay-Sachs disease is an inherited genetic disorder causing destruction of the nervous system that strikes at about six months of age with death occurring by or during the child's fourth year; a simple blood test can identify carriers. The association conducts research and provides education and prevention programs.

LITERATURE: Fact sheets; newspaper article reprints; *Tay-Sachs: The Killer is Cornered*, leaflet.

ADDITIONAL LITERATURE

Birth by Catherine Milinaire (1974). Harmony Books, c/o Crown Publishers, One Park Avenue, New York, N.Y. 10016 ($5.95). Photographs and descriptions of births in different geographical areas.

Birth Book by Raven Lang (1972). Genesis Press, P.O. Box 11457, Palo Alto, Calif. 94306 ($6.00). Stories and photos from the Birth Center on home birth in a personal scrapbook format.

Birth Without Violence by Frederick Leboyer (1975). Alfred A. Knopf, 201 East 50th Street, New York, N.Y. 10022 ($8.95). A French obstetrician's advocacy of a more peaceful birth; with illustrations.

Choices in Childbirth by Silvia Feldman (1978). Grosset & Dunlap, 51 Madison Avenue, New York, N.Y. 10010 ($14.95). Feldman, a psychotherapist and a mother, discusses the pros and cons of physician/hospital births versus midwife home deliveries. She also probes how to find local help, the psychological aspects of pregnancy and childbirth, and breastfeeding versus bottlefeeding.

Is My Baby All Right? by Virginia Apgar, M.D., and Joan Beck (1974). Pocket Books, 1230 Avenue of the Americas, New York, N.Y. 10020 ($2.25). In addition to being a guide to birth defects, the authors discuss basic reproduction, the stages of pregnancy, and what can go wrong and why. The book concludes with chapters on genetic counseling and sources of help.

Pregnancy, rev. ed., by Gordon Bourne, M.D. (1972, 1976). Pan Books, Ltd., Cavaye Place, London SW10 9PG, England (£1.50) or William Collins Sons & Co. Ltd., 100 Lesmill Road, Don Mills, Ontario M3B 2T5 Canada ($4.50). This complete guide to pregnancy, labor, and motherhood by a British obstetrician and gynecologist is considered one of the best books on the subject for the layperson; illustrated with diagrams; glossary.

Pregnancy After 35 by Carole Spearin McCauley, foreword by Dr. Howard Berk (1976). E. P. Dutton, 201 Park Avenue South, New York, N.Y. 10003 ($7.95). Covers all the topics someone considering childbearing over age thirty-five would be concerned with—risks, genetics, combining career and family, diet and drugs, psychology of pregnancy, postpartum, fathering, single parenting, labor, and delivery.

The Pregnant Patient's Bill of Rights and Responsibilities, International Childbirth Education Association, P.O. Box 1900, New York, N.Y. 10001 (single copies free). Four-page leaflet.

The Psychology of Childbirth by Aidan Macfarlane (1977), part of the "Developing Child" series edited by Jerome Bruner, Michael Cole, and Barbara Lloyd. Harvard University Press,

70 Garden Street, Cambridge, Mass. 02138 ($2.95). Explores the psychology of such prenatal concerns as "life before birth," morning sickness, when and where to deliver, and so forth. Includes footnotes, bibliography, photos.

Thank You, Dr. Lamaze by Marjorie Karmel (1959). Dolphin Books, Doubleday & Company, Garden City, N.Y. ($1.95). The theory and practice of psychoprophylaxis is described in this early work.

Two Births by Janet Brown, Eugene Lesser, and Stephanie Mines, photos by Ed Buryn (1972). The Bookworks, 1409 Fifth Street, Berkeley, Calif. 94710 ($3.95). Outstanding photos depicting two births—honest, memorable, and a joyful gift.

What Every Pregnant Woman Should Know: The Truth About Diet and Drugs in Pregnancy by Gail and Tom Brewer (1977). Random House, Inc., 201 East 50th Street, New York, N.Y. 10022 ($8.95).

You're Not Too Old to Have a Baby by Jane Price (1977). Farrar, Straus and Giroux, 19 Union Square West, New York, N.Y. 10003 ($7.95). The author, who did not have her first child until she was thirty-one, interviewed over two dozen couples who had their first child in their thirties or forties. Includes chapters on who waits to have children and why and whether age makes a difference in childbearing.

The American College of Obstetricians and Gynecologists (ACOG), One East Wacker Street, Chicago, Ill. 60601, has available a publications price list, noting appropriate materials on childbearing, and also publishes the monthly journal *Obstetrics and Gynecology* and the biennial *Directory of Fellows* (the ACOG has 17,000 members).

See also the following related chapters in *The Help Book:*

ADOPTION AND FOSTER CARE
BATTERED ADULTS
CHILD ABUSE
CHILDREN
COUNSELING
FAMILY PLANNING
FINANCIAL ASSISTANCE
HANDICAPS
HEALTH
MENTAL HEALTH
MENTAL RETARDATION AND LEARNING DISABILITIES
MULTIPURPOSE ORGANIZATIONS
PARENTING
SEX EDUCATION AND THERAPY

10

CHILDREN

A profile of children in America today would include the following facts:*

- About 60 million Americans are below eighteen years of age (about one-third the population); 20 million are younger than six years.
- About 17 million children live in families with income levels that are too low to adequately provide for their nutrition and developmental needs.
- The death rate of nonwhite children is about twice that of white children.
- On an average Saturday morning, between 8:00 A.M. and 2:00 P.M., 50 percent of America's children are watching television.
- Forty-five percent of those born in 1977 will live in a single-parent family sometime before the age of eighteen.

Is childhood "changing" in America? Certainly there are now problems associated with childhood that were previously ascribed to adulthood (or late adolescence at the earliest)—drug abuse, alcoholism, sexual promiscuity, and the commission of violent crimes. But while social scientists debate *why* that is so, parents, teachers, and community leaders need to know how to get immediate help for children. Perhaps even more importantly, they need to learn how to stimulate children so that they will independently seek out the help that they need. Yet in reviewing the list of national organizations that deal with child-related problems, it becomes apparent that few groups rely solely on child members. Except for the traditional organizations, such as the Girl Scouts of the U.S.A., and a few newer ones, such as the Childrens Rights Organization and Youth Liberation, children have little direct input into those associations dedicated to coping with their diverse problems.

Perhaps it is that overreliance on adults that inhibits a solution; if a child

*Based on *America's Children 1976* by the National Council of Organizations for Children and Youth, Washington, D.C. (see Additional Literature).

does not deal with, or learn to overcome, genetic or learned problems he or she will probably need even more help as an adult. There are self-help groups for abusing or potentially abusing parents, but what about rap sessions for the abused child? A mother or father may seek information and counseling from an association for the handicapped, but what about the child who has the disability? Is he or she not the one who must ultimately understand, and accept, it?

Instead of stressing radical family or social change, a shift to greater self-determination by children might produce more dramatic and immediate results. For example, the success of the Youth-Tutoring-Youth program of the National Commission of Resources for Youth, Inc. should become a model in other key areas as well. Will we see the growth of a national elementary school student organization as powerful and influential as the National Congress of Parents and Teachers (PTA)? Or do adults secretly fear that more child responsibility will result in the kind of lawless society that emerged in Goldman's *Lord of the Flies?*

Yet from a very early age, children are keenly aware of the realities of the world. They also have strongly developed moral codes. For example, the following story composed by Julia, a five-year-old urban child, emphasizes her own perceptions of the world, her deep commitment to changing that world, and her incorporation of her parent's positive values. It concludes with Julia's need to find a reason for the plight of the disadvantaged in those children's behavior.

The World With the Big Mess
by
Julia Lee Robinson (age 5)

The world is in a big mess. People don't have any food. I want to share my stuff with the world. It's really bad not to have anything.

I have everything I need. I need clothes, food, pajamas, dresses and my mommy and daddy. I would share my food (spaghetti and meat balls, noodles, french fries and potatoes) and my clothes (pajamas, dresses, shirts, slacks.) I'm going to try to find all the people who don't have this stuff. I think they live in New York, America, and all the world.

When I was three, I began thinking about the children who had nothing and I told my mother and father. And that's how I learned, because my mother and father taught me that the people didn't have food and that I should give them some. I'd do a lot of things for them, if they wanted me to. Like clean the house for them and be their helper. If they would like me to visit someone for them, I would do it.

The world is in a big mess because God didn't make them have all they need because they must of been bad when they were up there in heaven where God lives. Maybe they said something bad to God or something bad to themselves and God.

104 / THE HELP BOOK

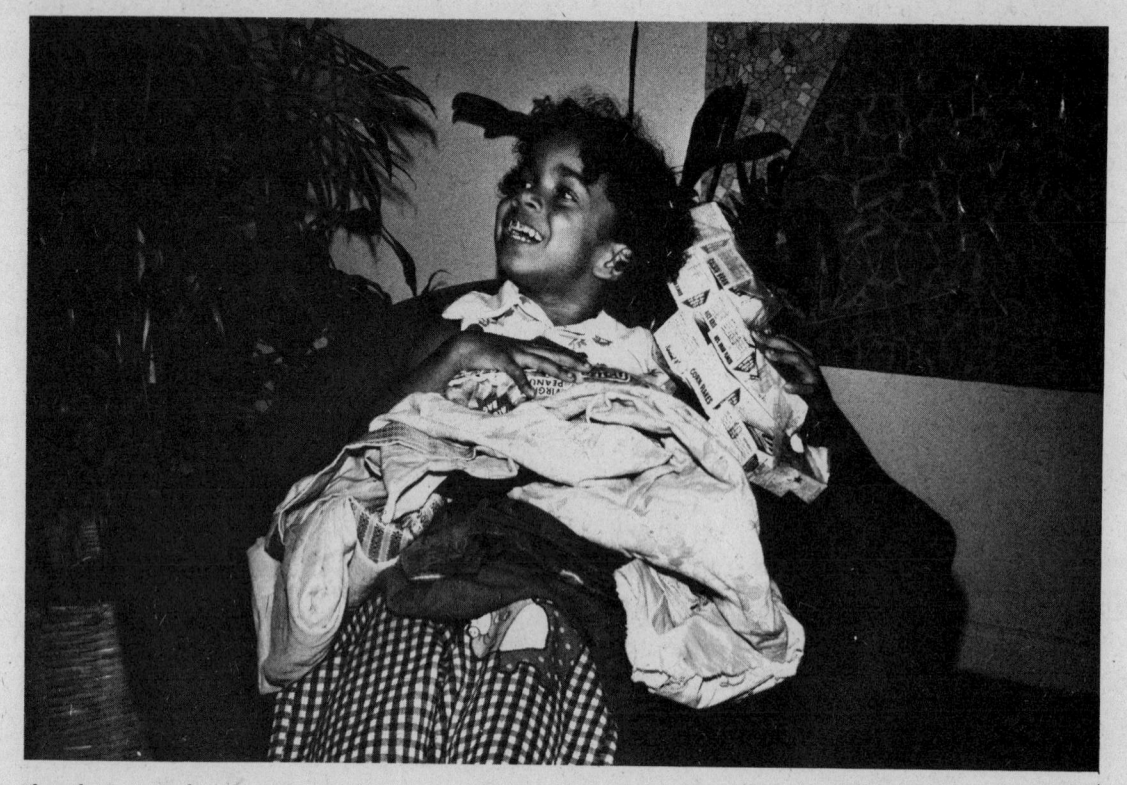

Photo by J. L. Barkas

NOTE: For this chapter, an arbitrary definition of *children* is from infancy through high school.

This chapter on children contains the following subheadings:
- Advocacy and Multipurpose Groups
- State Agencies for Child Welfare
- Childrearing
- Child/Youth Participation Groups
- Education
- Employment
- Food and Nutrition
- Handicaps
- Health
- Legal Rights
- Mental Health and Mental Retardation

The subjects *Childbearing* and *Juvenile Delinquency* are covered in their own chapters, "Day Care" and "Media" are covered in the *Parenting* chapter, and "Runaways" are discussed in the chapter on *Kidnapping, Missing Persons, and Runaways*.

For direct public assistance in child-related areas, contact the local or state departments or agencies in the appropriate category for which you need help, such as mental health, social welfare, children and youth services, education, health, labor or social services. If you are uncertain which office to contact initially, scan your telephone directory under the government listings for your city, county, or state, or call the Office of Citizen Services or Office of Public Information for assistance.

Three national organizations that provide free services for children on a local basis are the Salvation Army, the American National Red Cross, and the United Way. Call your local chapter to see what programs or information is available. You may also consult the annual directory of the United Way, available at most libraries, which lists state community councils or councils for community services, as well as local United Way affiliates. The regional or national headquarters of the Salvation Army or the national headquarters of the American National Red Cross will refer you to your local branch if the telephone book or operator are unable to provide assistance. (See complete listings for these three organizations in Chapter 40, *Multipurpose Organizations*.)

ADVOCACY AND MULTIPURPOSE GROUPS

The following federal agencies and national organizations offer information on a broad range of child/youth concerns and problems (some of the national organizations are also child/youth advocacy groups):

Administration for Children, Youth and Families
U.S. Children's Bureau
Department of Health, Education, and Welfare
Box 1182
Washington, D.C. 20013

ACYF works with states and public and private agencies to improve children, youth, and family services. It is also a point of coordination in the government for children and youth programs. Leaflets and booklets, costing less than one dollar, cover infants, children through age twelve, and adolescents. Most are addressed to parents, such as *Infant Care*. Some are light, such as *Fun in the Making*.

LITERATURE: *Publications of the Office of Child Development; An Adolescent in Your Home* ($.50); *Infant Care* ($1.00); *One-Parent Families* ($.30); *The Pocket Guide to Babysitting* ($.70); *Beautiful Junk* ($.40).

American Academy of Pediatrics
P.O. Box 1034
Evanston, Ill. 60204

This Pan-American association of physicians certified in the care of infants, children, and adolescents publishes a wide range of low-cost leaflets, pamphlets, and booklets on child welfare, including adoption, child health, day care, school health, drugs, environmental hazards, child development, foods and nutrition, handicapped children, learning disabilities, and public health education.

LITERATURE: Free publications price list pamphlet and descriptive brochure on the academy.

Child Welfare League of America, Inc. (CWLA)
67 Irving Place
New York, N.Y. 10003

Founded in 1920, CWLA is a nonsectarian federation of 400 affiliated private and public agencies throughout the United States and Canada. CWLA is a privately supported organization completely devoted to the improvement of care and services for deprived, dependent, and neglected children, youth, and their families. Member and affiliated agencies provide services in one or more of the following areas: adoption, child abuse, day care, foster family care, juvenile delinquency, mental retardation, family therapy, homemaker service, post-adoption services, child welfare legislation, and residential treatment. Regional conferences open to anyone interested in the welfare of children are held at various locations and times throughout the United States. CWLA also has many publications and conducts research on child welfare issues.

LITERATURE: Free publications price list; *Directory of Member and Affiliate Agencies*, updated and published each January ($8.00); *CWLA Newsletter* ($4.00 a year for 5 issues); *Child Welfare* journal ($8.00).

Coalition for Children and Youth (CCY)
The Bowen Building
815 Fifteenth Street, N.W.
Washington, D.C. 20005

An amalgam of 130 national organizations and 1,200 state and local members acting as an information clearinghouse and umbrella coalition for diverse groups and individuals concerned with the welfare of children. Membership dues range from $15.00 (associate) to $200.00 (full voting member). Clusters (work groups that meet regularly to explore issues and options and distribute summary reports to members) include Day Care Alliance, Health, Foster Care/Adoption, Juvenile Justice/Youth Development, and Family/Parenting. CCY also provides legal information. Speakers are available on legislative issues as well as for community education.

LITERATURE: Publications price list and free descriptive brochures; *America's Children/1976*, a factbook ($4.00); *Focus on Children and Youth*, monthly newsletter (free to members); *Directory for Child Advocates* ($3.50).

National Alliance Concerned with School-Age Parents (NACSAP)
7315 Wisconsin Avenue, Suite 211-W
Washington, D.C. 20014

Founded in 1969, this is a national, private, nonprofit, multidisciplinary membership organization that specializes in technical assistance to those working with school-age parents, young families, and sexually-active youth. NACSAP works with parents, community groups, and agencies to develop programs and strategies that can help prevent high-risk adolescent pregnancies. Tax deductible membership dues are $2.00 (young parents), $20.00 (individual), $30.00 (family) and up.

LITERATURE: *National Directory of Services for School-Age Parents* (1976), information on over 1,000 agencies providing a variety of services from maternity homes to birth control ($3.95).

National Center for Child Advocacy
Children's Bureau
Office of Child Development
P.O. Box 1182
Washington, D.C. 20013

Established in 1971, this federal bureau acts as an information clearinghouse on all child/youth problems, including child abuse, childrearing, day care, and so forth; state and national organizations are provided with technical assistance and consultations.

LITERATURE: *Quarterly*, by subscription.

STATE AGENCIES FOR CHILD WELFARE

The following state agencies will either provide the child welfare services you need or direct you to sources of help; they will also provide information on federally funded child welfare programs that they administer locally, such as adoption, day care, food stamps, and services to the blind or prevention of blindness:

Bureau of Family and Children's Services
Department of Pensions and Security
Administrative Building
64 North Union Street
Montgomery, Ala. 36130

Office of Child Advocacy
Office of the Governor
Community Building
Pouch AL
Juneau, Alaska 99811

Child Protective Services Section
Public Welfare Division
Department of Economic Security
3003 North 35th Avenue
Phoenix, Ariz. 85017

Child Welfare Services
Program Development Section-Social Services Division
Department of Human Services
Blue Cross-Blue Shield Building
7th and Gaines Streets
Little Rock, Ark. 77201

Children Social Services Branch
Social Services Division
Department of Health
State Office Building 8
714 P Street
Sacramento, Calif. 95814

Family and Children's Services Section
Title XX Division
Department of Social Services
State Social Services Building
1575 Sherman Street
Denver, Colo. 82203

Department of Children and Youth Services
345 Main Street
Hartford, Conn. 06115

Family and Children's Services
Division of Social Services
Department of Health and Social Services
P.O. Box 309
Wilmington, Del. 19899

Bureau of Family Services
Social Rehabilitation Administration
Department of Human Resources
122 C Street, N.W.
Washington, D.C. 20001

State Advisory Council for Children and Youth
Office of the Governor
State Capital
Honolulu, Hawaii 96813

Bureau of Child Health
Division of Health
Department of Health and Welfare
700 West Jefferson Street
Boise, Idaho 83720

108 / THE HELP BOOK

Department of Children and Family Services
160 North LaSalle
Chicago, Ill. 60601

Child Support Division
Department of Public Welfare
701 State Office Building
Indianapolis, Ind. 46204

Family and Children's Services
Department of Social Services
3619½ Douglas Avenue
Des Moines, Iowa 50319

Division of Services to Children and Youth
Department of Social and Rehabilitation
  Services
Statehouse
Topeka, Kans. 66612

Family and Children's Services
Bureau of Social Services
Department for Human Resources
275 East Main Street
Frankfort, Ky. 40601

Office of Family Services
P.O. Box 44065
Baton Rouge, La. 70804

Office for Children
120 Boylston Street
Boston, Mass. 02116

Bureau of Social Services
Department of Social Services
300 South Capitol Avenue
Lansing, Mich. 48926

Division of Social Services
Bureau of Community Services
Department of Public Welfare
Centennial Office Building
658 Cedar Street
St. Paul, Minn. 55155

Division of Family Services
Department of Social Services
Broadway State Office Building
Jefferson City, Mo. 65101

Child and Youth Development Bureau
Community Services Division
Department of Social and Rehabilitation
  Services
P.O. Box 1723
Helena, Mont. 59601

Center for Children and Youth
Division of Social Services
Department of Public Welfare
301 Centennial Mall, South
Lincoln, Neb. 68509

Welfare Division
Department of Human Resources
251 Jeanell Drive
Capitol Complex
Carson City, Nev. 89701

Child and Family Services
Social and Rehabilitative Services
Department of Health and Welfare
8 Loudon Road
Concord, N.H. 03301

Division of Youth and Family Services
Department of Human Services
Trenton, N.J. 08625

New Mexico Committee on Children and Youth
P.O. Box 26584
Albuquerque, N.M. 87125

Department of Social Services
40 North Pearl Street
Albany, N.Y. 12243

Governor's Advocacy Council on Children and
  Youth
Department of Human Resources
Albemarle Building
325 North Salisbury Street
Raleigh, N.C. 27611

Children's Programs
Department of Institutions, Social, and
  Rehabilitative Services
Dequoyah Memorial Office Building
2400 North Lincoln Boulevard
P.O. Box 25352
Oklahoma City, Okla. 73125

Children Services Division
Department of Human Resources
198 Commercial Street
Salem, Ore. 97310

Bureau of Child Welfare
Office of Children and Youth
Department of Public Welfare
P.O. Box 2675
Harrisburg, Pa. 17120

Child Welfare
Division of Community Services
Department of Social and Rehabilitative
  Services
610 Mount Pleasant Avenue
Providence, R.I. 02908

Division of Individual and Family Services
Department of Social Services
North Tower Complex
1535 Confederate Avenue, Ext.
Columbia, S.C. 29202

Office of Child Development
Office of the Governor
108 Parkway Towers
404 James Robertson Parkway
Nashville, Tenn. 37219

Department of Public Welfare
John H. Reagan State Office Building
Austin, Tex. 78701

Division of Family Services
Department of Social Services
10 Exchange Place
Salt Lake City, Utah 84111

Division of Social Services
Department of Social and Rehabilitation
  Services
Agency of Human Services
81 River Street
Montpelier, Vt. 05602

Commission for Children and Youth
State Office Building
Richmond, Va. 23219

Office of Family, Children, and Adult Services
Bureau of Social Services
Department of Social and Health Services
Olympia, Wash. 98504

Interagency Council for Child Development
  Services
Office of the Governor
Capitol Complex
Charleston, W.Va. 25305

Bureau of Children, Youth and Families
Department of Health and Social Services
1 West Wilson Street
Madison, Wis. 53702

Department of Health and Social Services
Division of Public Assistance
Hathaway Building
Cheyenne, Wyo. 82002

CHILDREARING

The following federal program provides information on parenting and childrearing for youths. (For childrearing in general, see Chapter 42, Parenting.)

Education for Parenthood
National Center for Child Advocacy
Children's Bureau Office of Child Development
U.S. Department of Health, Education, and
  Welfare
P.O. Box 1182
Washington, D.C. 20013

A program to help teen-agers prepare for good parenting by volunteer work with young children as well as educational training about child development and parent roles. The national office provides technical assistance in setting up programs.

LITERATURE: Free reprints of articles on the program; descriptive leaflets.

CHILD/YOUTH PARTICIPATION GROUPS

These national organizations depend upon child/youth active participation through their local chapters, groups, or affiliates. A multitude of projects are offered, from simple companionship and friendship to arts and crafts, tutoring, summer camps, athletics, community service and so forth. Consult your local telephone directory for the nearest branch, or contact the national headquarters for a referral or publications and information.

Big Brothers/Big Sisters of America
2220 Suburban Station Building
Philadelphia, Pa. 19103

Two national organizations founded in 1903, now merged into one, Big Brothers/Big Sisters of America have a combined network of about 400 agencies serving more than 100,000 children throughout the United States. Under the guidance of professional social workers, mature, adult volunteers are matched with children from single-parent homes. The volunteer is expected to see the child about once a week, for four to six hours, for at least one year. The national headquarters makes referrals to your local agency and also answers inquiries about starting a new agency.

LITERATURE: Descriptive booklet on how the programs work.

Boy Scouts of America
North Brunswick, N.J. 08902
(Will be relocating to Texas in July 1979)

Founded in 1910, there are 3.5 million Cub Scouts, Scouts, and Explorers, plus 1.25 million volunteer adults, in 140,000 Cub Scout packs, Scout troops, and Explorer posts. The Scouting program provides for boys and young men and women an effective educational program designed to build desirable character, to train in the responsibilities of participating citizenship, and to develop personal fitness. The national office provides support to 420 local councils through six regions and twenty-nine areas—program development, magazines and literature, uniforms and equipment, operation of six national high adventure bases, and liaison with national chartered organizations using the Scouting program.

LITERATURE: *Boys' Life* ($7.20 for 12 issues a year); *Scouting* (free 6 issues a year for registered adults); *Exploring* (free 6 issues a year for Explorers and Explorer leaders).

Boys' Clubs of America (BCA)
National Headquarters
771 First Avenue
New York, N.Y. 10017

The Boys' Clubs are a prime source of help for youth through the 1,100 member clubs in all fifty states, Puerto Rico, and the U.S. Virgin Islands, and its alumni list reads like a who's who—Joe Dimaggio, O. J. Simpson, George Gershwin, Bill Cosby, Neil Diamond, Sylvester Stallone, Ben Gazzara, and many more. BCA is a national, nonprofit organization annually providing professional adult guidance and supervision to one million young people.

Boys' Clubs are open every day in the afternoon (after school) and evening, when kids need a place of their own to go, a positive alternative to boredom and street life. In addition to the recreational and counseling programs available, there are special projects developed by the national office that have become permanent local additions: Alcohol Abuse Prevention (Project TEAM—Teams Explore Alcohol Moderation); Juvenile Justice and Delinquency Prevention; Education for Family Life (HAK—Help-A-Kid); and Youth Employment (World of Work).

LITERATURE: Reprints from advertisements; fact sheet package; "Why a Boys' Club?"; The

Concerns and Problems of Youth Are Our Concern" (annual report of 1976); "Boys Need Things to Do, a Place to Go, Everyday"; "There Are One Million Boys, in 1,100 Boys' Clubs, 700 Towns"; "A Boy Is a Good Investment."

Childrens Rights Organization
P.O. Box 9494
Marina del Rey, Calif. 90291

(See listing that follows in Legal Rights section.)

Girl Scouts of the U.S.A.
830 Third Avenue
New York, N.Y. 10022

Founded in 1912, there are over 3 million members of this national program to help young girls. There are over 300 local groups, and volunteers and professional workers assist girls in a variety of growth-inspiring experiences, such as leadership, camping, citizenship, health and safety, the arts, community management, and international friendship. Contact your local branch for meeting schedules.

National Commission on Resources for Youth, Inc. (NCRY)
36 West 44th Street
New York, N.Y. 10036

Founded in 1967, this national nonprofit educational organization seeks to expand opportunities for young people to assume responsible and significant roles in their schools and communities. Youth participation is the central concept behind NCRY. Based on the work of some fifty associates around the country, the headquarters is an information clearinghouse on existing programs and encourages the formation of new ones.

NCRY has popularized youth participation projects through its publications and through demonstration projects, such as Youth Tutoring Youth (YTY) and A Day Care Youth Helper. NCRY also provides on-site technical assistance and training to teachers and workers who wish to initiate projects.

LITERATURE: *Resources for Youth Newsletter* (free); publications price list; *What Kids Can Do* ($3.50); YTY programs brochure (free); *Learning and Growing Thru Tutoring* ($3.00).

In addition to the above child/youth participation groups, contact your local branch of the following organizations, which also offer both child and adult participation projects: Young Men's Christian Association (YMCA); Young Women's Christian Association (YWCA); and Young Men's and Young Women's Hebrew Association (YM-YWHA). (See listings of national headquarters in Chapter 40, *Multipurpose Organizations*.)

EDUCATION

For direct assistance in education, contact your local or state department of education. For local agencies, consult your telephone directory. For state agencies, see state listings in Chapter 19, *Education*.

The following national organizations are concerned with the education of children and youths:

American Federation of Teachers (AFT)
11 DuPont Circle, N.W.
Washington, D.C. 20036

Founded in 1916, there are more than 2,100 locals with about 475,000 members of this teachers union, a member of the AFL-CIO.

AFT sponsors an annual convention and has extensive publications.

LITERATURE: *American Teacher*, monthly; *Changing Education*, quarterly.

Association for Childhood Education International (ACEI)
3615 Wisconsin Avenue, N.W.
Washington, D.C. 20016

Information clearinghouse on all education matters related to children and youth, with branches throughout the country. ACEI is also a membership organization of nearly 30,000 (dues: $18.00 a year; $7.50 students) with over thirty committees that hold regional and annual conferences. Files are available to members at no charge.

LITERATURE: *Childhood Education*, published 6 times a year (included in membership); *ACEI Branch Exchange*, membership newsletter; *Children and Drugs* ($2.50); article reprints; free descriptive brochure; extensive publications list.

Council on Interracial Books for Children
1841 Broadway
New York, N.Y. 10023

The council is a nonprofit organization that promotes bias-free (non-racist, non-sexist, non-ageist, non-handicapist, etc.) literature and instructional materials for children in the following ways: 1) by publishing the *Bulletin* eight times a year, which reviews new children's materials for racist, sexist, and other antihuman content and publishes feature articles on related materials; 2) by running a yearly contest for unpublished minority writers of children's literature; 3) by conducting clinics and workshops; 4) by providing consultants and resource specialists in awareness training to educational institutions; and 5) by establishing the Racism and Sexism Resource Center for Educators, which publishes annual reference books, monographs, lesson plans, and audio-visual materials designed to help teachers eliminate racism and sexism and to develop pluralism in education.

LITERATURE: Publications list.

Education Commission of the States
1860 Lincoln Street
Denver, Colo. 80203

A nonprofit organization and information clearinghouse formed in 1966 with forty-five states currently participating with the goal of furthering a working relationship among governors, state legislators, and educators for the improvement of education.

LITERATURE: *Equal Rights for Women in Education, Title X, How It Affects Elementary and Secondary Education* ($3.50); publications list.

Federal Community Education Clearinghouse
Office of Education
6000 Executive Boulevard
Rockville, Md. 20852

This clearinghouse provides information concerning community education to the general public; will answer individual requests; has a registry of community educators and a directory that describes goals, activities, and results of selected projects that the Office of Education has funded; and publishes a quarterly calendar highlighting issues, developments, and events in the education field.

National Association for Gifted Children
217 Gregory Drive
Hot Springs, Ark. 71901

Founded in 1954, this national nonprofit association is dedicated to furthering the education of the gifted child regardless of race, creed, color or sex. Membership is $20.00 and includes a subscription to the journal, *The Gifted Child Quarterly*. A convention is held annually.

LITERATURE: *The Gifted Child Quarterly* ($5.00 each for back issues); fact sheet.

National Association for the Education of Young Children
1834 Connecticut Avenue, N.W.
Washington, D.C. 20009

The association focuses primarily on the provision of educational services and resources of young children through their bimonthly journal, *Young Children*. It holds an annual conference, has over 200 affiliate groups, and sponsors the public education campaign entitled "Week of Young Child." Membership dues range from $15.00 to $40.00.

LITERATURE: Over forty publications plus membership brochures; "Answers About Careers in Early Childhood Education"; "The Essentials for Developing a Good Early Childhood Program."

National Congress of Parents and Teachers (National PTA)
700 North Rush Street
Chicago, Ill. 60611

Headquarters for over 30,000 local groups and 52 state chapters of concerned parents, teachers, and others united to combine school and family efforts on behalf of children; annual conference. (See additional listings for PTA in Chapter 3, *Alcoholism*, and Chapter 42, *Parenting*.)

LITERATURE: Publications list.

National Education Association (NEA)
1201 Sixteenth Street, N.W.
Washington, D.C. 20036

Founded in 1857, there are more than 15 million members in 50 state and 9,000 local groups of this professional organization of elementary and secondary school teachers, college and university professors, and others interested in education. A variety of committees are operated from the national headquarters, such as Teacher's Rights, Educational Finance, and Human Relations. NEA has a variety of professional and general publications.

LITERATURE: *Reporter*, published 8 times yearly; *Today's Education*, quarterly; *Handbook*, an annual directory.

New Schools Exchange
Pettigrew, Ark. 72752

National information clearinghouse on alternative schools for young people.

LITERATURE: *1978 Directory and Resource Guide* ($5.00); *Wall Calendar-Idea Book*; "Bibliography for Alternative Education" ($1.00).

Newspapers in Education (NIE)
American Newspaper Publishers Association Foundation (ANPAF)
P.O. Box 17407
Dulles International Airport
Washington, D.C. 20041

More than 500 daily newspapers and thousands of schools throughout the United States cooperate in the NIE program of using newspapers in schools to supplement text books. Contact your local newspaper (such as the *Chicago Tribune* or *St. Louis Globe Democrat*) to find out what their program is, if none is operating in your local schools; the national office will provide free descriptive literature on the program and article reprints.

U.S. Department of Health, Education, and Welfare
Commissioner of Education
400 Maryland Avenue, S.W.
Washington, D.C. 20202

Contact this federal agency for information or your local regional office for direct services on educational matters.

EMPLOYMENT

Contact your local or regional office of the U.S. Department of Labor for direct help in either finding a job-placement service or information on child labor, minimum-wage laws, and so forth. For more general information, federal assistance is offered through the national headquarters:

U.S. Department of Labor
Director of Information, Publications, and Reports
200 Constitution Avenue, N.W.
Washington, D.C. 20210

Through its ten regional offices and numerous subdivisions, a variety of programs and publications are offered to assist, and inform, youths seeking work. Some of those programs include the Employment Service, which provides special assistance to youths between the ages of sixteen and twenty-two through its cooperative school program; the Summer Employment Program, whereby school youths are referred to private and public summer jobs; and the Bureau of Apprenticeship, whereby on-job training is carried out through supervised programs. Contact your regional office or state labor department office for details on these and other programs as well as minimum-wage and minimum-wage requirements.

LITERATURE: "It's Easy to Hire Teenagers," free leaflet from Employment Standards Administration, Wage and Hour Division; "A Guide to Child Labor Provisions of the Fair Labor Standards Act," bulletin no. 101, Superintendent of Documents, U.S. Government Printing Office, Washington, D.C. 20402 ($.20); "Program highlights" fact sheets; *Occupational Handbook Outlook*, issued annually (approx. $7.00).

For local assistance and laws concerning the employment of children, contact your state Department of Labor. National information clearinghouses on children and work include the following:

JOBS Program
National Alliance of Business (NAB)
1730 K Street, N.W.
Washington, D.C. 20006

Largest national effort to place disadvantaged youths in summer and part-time jobs during the school year. Contact your local NAB for direct assistance.

National Child Labor Committee
145 East 32nd Street
New York, N.Y. 10016

Founded in 1904 and chartered by Congress in 1907, the members of this child labor advocacy organization serve without compensation. Chief concerns are youth employment problems and the education of migrant workers' children.

LITERATURE: *Rite to Passage: The Crisis of Youth's Transition From School to Work* ($2.50); *New Generation*, quarterly ($5.00); *Promises to Keep* ($2.50).

Women's American ORT (Organization for Rehabilitation through Training)
1250 Broadway
New York, N.Y. 10001

Founded in 1880, ORT operates a national vocational training program for Jewish youths, especially in high school, by developing and maintaining high-level vocation education programs.

It aids young people by volunteering to train impoverished youths who lack educational prerequisites. Annual membership dues are $10.00.

LITERATURE: Free descriptive leaflets; reprints of newspaper articles about ORT.

FOOD AND NUTRITION

For direct assistance in obtaining food, consult your local Department of Social Services for the correct referral. Or contact the local branch of such national organizations as The Salvation Army, the American National Red Cross, and the United Way. Contact your local board of health or Bureau of Poison Control in regard to specific child food/health problems. Information on the federal food stamp programs as well as other home and school food assistance is available through your field office of the U.S. Department of Agriculture (see listing below).

The organizations listed below also act as clearinghouses on child food and nutrition problems and programs:

American Home Economics Association
2010 Massachusetts Avenue, N.W.
Washington, D.C. 20036

This national professional association of home economics teachers offers a wide range of pamphlets and booklets on food and nutrition.

The Children's Foundation
1028 Connecticut Avenue, N.W., Suite 1112
Washington, D.C. 20036

Founded in 1969, this national, nonprofit organization is concerned with eliminating hunger and acts as a food rights advocacy group that monitors federal food programs. The foundation maintains liaison to community and parent groups concerned with child food and nutrition.

LITERATURE: Free pamphlets include "How Communities Can Get Extra Food for Mothers and Kids (WIC)," "School Breakfast Survey," "Rise and Shine," "You Have a Right to a Good Breakfast," *Your Rights in the National School Lunch Program, School Breakfast Savings, Fact Sheet on the Child Care Food Program, Umbrella Sponsorship for Family Day Care,* and *Fact Sheet on the Summer Food Program;* other brochures—*Student's School Breakfast Handbook* (50¢); *Feed Kids—It's the Law,* a general food program news monthly ($6.00 yearly); *Whose Children?* ($1.50); send for complete listing. People unable to pay will be sent materials for free.

Food Research and Action Center (FRAC)
200 Eye Street, N.W.
Washington, D.C. 20006

Founded in 1970, this national resource center is dedicated to ending hunger in the United States and is available for legal advice with regard to federally funded food programs.

LITERATURE: "FRAC's Guide to the National School Lunch and Breakfast Programs" ($.75); "FRAC's Guide to the Child Care Food Program" ($.75); "FRAC's Guide to the Food Stamp Program" ($1.00); "Profile of the Federal Food Programs" (free). People unable to pay will be sent all materials for free.

U.S. Department of Agriculture
Food and Nutrition Service
Washington, D.C. 20250

Coloring books, wall charts, pamphlets, and leaflets on food and nutrition written for children are available free or for less than one dollar from the Information Division and from the Office of Communication of the Department of Agriculture. If possible, submit your order to your regional office (listed under "U.S. Government" in your local directory) and include title, series, and number of the publications. A free, complete publications price list is available.

LITERATURE: *From the Information Division:* "Nutrients and Foods for Health" (FNS-95/$.75); "The Good Foods Coloring Book" (PA-912/$.60); "A Daily Food Guide" (FNS-13/$.25); "A Student's Guide to Food Programs of the Food and Nutrition Service" (free); "Food for Youth Study Guide" (FNS-10/$1.70); "Discovering Vegetables" (FNS-127/$.40).

From the Office of Communication: "The Thing the Professor Forgot," about the four basic food groups; "Fred, the Horse Who Likes Bread"; "Mary Mutton and the Meat Group"; "Gussie Goose Introduces the Fruit and Vegetable Group"; and "Meet Molly-Moo."

HANDICAPS

For agencies providing direct help to handicapped children, consult your local or state office of the handicapped (see state listings in Chapter 29, Handicaps). *The following national organizations and one federal agency offer information and/or referrals and help for physically handicapped children and youth:*

CHEAR (Children's Hearing Education and Research)
871 McLean Avenue
Yonkers, N.Y. 10704

CHEAR provides a national information service for children who are hearing impaired and is supported by private contributions.

LITERATURE: Fact sheets; brochure; newsletter.

The National Information Center for the Handicapped
P.O. Box 1492
Washington, D.C. 20013

A project of the U.S. Department of Health, Education, and Welfare that provides a wealth of published material, including a monthly free newsletter, for parents of children with physical, mental, and emotional handicaps. It is also a link to local organizations, whenever possible.

LITERATURE: *Practical Advice to Parents: A Guide to Finding Help for Handicapped Children and Youth; Report from Closer Look,* newsletter.

International Parents' Organization (IPO)
Alexander Graham Bell Association for the Deaf, Inc.
3417 Volta Place, N.W.
Washington, D.C. 20007

Nonprofit organization whose membership includes thousands of parents of hearing-impaired children who work through local groups to broaden all options open to their children.

LITERATURE: Free descriptive leaflets; *The Volta Review;* "Hearing Alert: Look at the Baby!"

John Tracy Clinic
806 West Adams Boulevard
Los Angeles, Calif. 90007

A national, free, one-year correspondence course ($9.50) for parents of preschool deaf and deaf-blind children available in English or Spanish. The clinic is privately funded and was established by Mrs. Spencer Tracy in 1942. Parents may enroll by writing to the above address, including the child's name and age and the family's full name and address.

LITERATURE: Fact sheets.

National Easter Seal Society of Crippled Children and Adults
2023 West Ogden Avenue
Chicago, Ill. 60612

A descriptive listing of the Easter Seal Society appears in Chapter 29, *Handicaps*. The following is their literature specifically related to children.

LITERATURE: Publications price list; "Books and Pamphlets for Parents of Handicapped Children" (L-4/free); "Brain Injury and Learning Disorders in Children" (L-7/free); "Letter to the Parent of a Cerebral Palsied Child" (A-111/$.10); "Understanding Parents' Feelings" (A-187/$.10); "Once Upon A Bicycle" (PR-22/$.10); "Why Did This Have to Happen?" (E-17/$.25); "On Being a Parent of a Handicapped Child" by Benjamin Spock (E-29/$.35); *The Easter Seal Directory of Resident Camps for Persons With Special Health Needs*, 7th ed. (1971) ($1.00).

The National Foundation/March of Dimes
Box 2000
White Plains, N.Y. 10602

A research organization that also provides birth defects information.

LITERATURE: *International Directory of Genetic Services*, 5th ed. (1977); *Facts: 1977*, a booklet; *Be Good to Your Baby: Before It Is Born*, booklet; Annual Report; "All About the March of Dimes," leaflet; "Nutrition and Pregnancy," leaflet; "Preventing Birth Defects Caused by Rubella," leaflet; one-page reprints from the Public Relations Department of articles on birth-related issues; "Family Medical Record," reprinted from *Woman's Day* (1977).

National Society to Prevent Blindness
79 Madison Avenue
New York, N.Y. 10016

A descriptive listing of the society appears in Chapter 29, *Handicaps*. The following is a list of the society's child-related literature:

LITERATURE: "Eye Safety Education for the Young"; "Home Eye Test for Pre-Schoolers"; "Signs of Possible Eye Trouble in Children"; "Your Child's Sight: How You Can Help"; "Play It Safe!"

HEALTH

For direct help in child health, contact your local or state department of health through your telephone directory or see the state listings in Chapter 30, Health; most national health organizations are concerned with both children and youths and adult health problems and diseases; those dealing mainly with child health problems are listed below:

American Academy of Pediatrics
P.O. Box 1034
Evanston, Ill. 60204

A professional organization offering a wide range of publications on child health concerns, such as infancy, diseases, skin care, and allergies. Write for publications price list.

American Association for Maternal and Child Health, Inc.
P.O. Box 965
Los Altos, Calif. 94022

Established in 1919, this membership organization consists of professionals and lay persons and acts as an information clearinghouse on pregnancy and child health matters. Dues range from $3.00 to $20.00

LITERATURE: *American Baby*, a monthly free to members.

American School Health Association (ASHA)
P.O. Box 708
Kent, Ohio 44240

ASHA provides scientific and professional information for school nurses, health educators, dental and medical personnel concerned with health problems of school-age children and programs for school children; also has publications and professional meetings.

The Candlelighters
123 C Street, S.E.
Washington, D.C. 20003

Started in 1970, this self-help program for parents of young children with cancer now has forty-two groups in twenty states. It maintains a list of parents who wish to correspond with others in their "parent-to-parent" correspondence program.

LITERATURE: National newsletter.

Children Before Dogs (Educational Program of Fran Lee Foundation)
15 West 81st Street
New York, N.Y. 10024

Consumer advocate and TV and radio commentator Fran Lee founded this international organization to inform the public about the health hazards animals pose to infants and children. The organization urges responsible pet ownership and strict enforcement of laws already passed to minimize or eliminate these health hazards due to animal feces and bites. Reprints of articles and reports are available plus a T-shirt for a $10.00 contribution. It will answer telephone inquiries and address groups with scientific research and slides.

Juvenile Diabetes Foundation
23 East 26th Street
New York, N.Y. 10010

Supports diabetes research; supplies educational services to schools, hospitals, and all community resources and counseling services to diabetics and their families. There are local chapters throughout the country.

LITERATURE: Fact sheets; *Dimensions in Diabetes*, quarterly newsletter.

National Sudden Infant Death Syndrome Foundation
310 South Michigan Avenue #1904
Chicago, Ill. 60604

Counsels and educates anyone interested in, or affected by, infant deaths; home visits to parents.

LITERATURE: Descriptive leaflets and pamphlets.

Office of Child Development
U.S. Department of Health, Education, and Welfare
P.O. Box 1182
Washington, D.C. 20013

A federal agency concerned with children's health and offering a variety of publications on child health concerns.

LEGAL RIGHTS

For direct help with the legal rights of minors, contact your local bar association or lawyer referral service. (On how to select a lawyer, see Chapter 36, *Legal Services*.) Criminal charges against minors, which are handled in Family Court, are under state jurisdiction. The court will usually appoint an attorney if one is needed and if the parent is unable to afford one. (See also Chapter 33, *Juvenile Delinquency*.)

The following national organizations provide either legal information or act as advocates on behalf of children's legal rights:

The Children's Defense Fund (CDF)
1520 New Hampshire Avenue, N.W.
Washington, D.C. 20036

Founded in 1973, this national privately-funded children's advocacy organization has a staff of lawyers, researchers, and community workers concerned with reform in education, privacy rights, health care, juvenile justice, and child development programs.

LITERATURE: *Doctors and Dollars are Not Enough: How to Improve Health Services for Children and Their Families* (1976).

Childrens Rights Organization
P.O. Box 9494
Marina del Rey, Calif. 90291

Founded in 1973, full membership is open to those under eighteen, associate membership is open to those over eighteen; a donation for either membership is $5.00. The organization is dedicated to eliminating all crimes of age, vesting civil rights in persons under eighteen, and cleaning up juvenile halls, foster homes, etc. Professional counseling services are provided on a fee basis.

LITERATURE: Literature package, including Youth Bill of Rights ($6.00 donation).

Committee on Rights of Children and Families
Section of Individual Rights and
  Responsibilities
American Bar Association
4147 North Greenview
Chicago, Ill. 60613

A national information clearinghouse and research center on children and family rights; disseminates information to local bar associations and members.

Juvenile Rights Project
American Civil Liberties Union
22 East 40th Street
New York, N.Y. 10016

A national information clearinghouse and research center on the legal rights of minors; contact your local branch of the ACLU for direct assistance.

LITERATURE: *Children's Rights Report* newsletter.

Youth Liberation
2007 Washtenaw Avenue
Ann Arbor, Mich. 48104

A national information clearinghouse providing information on the law to young people under eighteen, teachers, social workers, and youth

120 / THE HELP BOOK

advocates; concerned with children's rights; extensive publications.

LITERATURE: *Student and Youth Organizing* by John Schaller and Mark Chesler with Keith Hefner ($1.50 plus $.50 postage and handling); *FPS: A Magazine of Young People's Liberation*, quarterly ($6.00 for 6 issues); *Young People and the Law* ($.75).

MENTAL HEALTH AND MENTAL RETARDATION

For direct assistance and services for mentally troubled or retarded children, contact your local bureaus of mental health, mental retardation, health, or social services.

The national groups listed below offer information and publications from their headquarters or referrals to local branches for direct help. The federal offices below offer free or low-cost publications as well as written referrals to direct services:

American Academy of Child Psychiatry
1424 Sixteenth Street, N.W.
Washington, D.C. 20009

A national membership organization of professionals practicing child psychiatry and offering educational and publication services to the general public. Referrals are made to member child psychiatrists.

Association for Children with Learning Disabilities
4156 Library Road
Pittsburgh, Pa. 15234

This is the only national referral and information service for learning-disabled children, with over 700 local chapters in all states except Wyoming.

LITERATURE: Publications price list; free reprints on hyperactivity, dyslexia, learning disabilities in general, and other disorders.

Clearinghouse of Mental Health Information
National Institute of Mental Health
U.S. Department of Health, Education, and Welfare
5600 Fishers Lane
Rockville, Md. 20857

A federal office offering free or low-cost publications and referrals. Write for information.

Family Service Association of America
44 East 23rd Street
New York, N.Y. 10010

Offers counseling services through its member agencies. See complete listing for the association in Chapter 14, *Counseling*.

The National Association for Retarded Citizens, Inc.
2709 Avenue E East
P.O. Box 6109
Arlington, Tex. 76011

See listing in Chapter 39, *Mental Retardation and Learning Disabilities*.

National Society for Autistic Children
1234 Massachusetts Avenue, N.W.
Washington, D.C. 20005

A national organization of parents, professionals, and interested lay persons who are united to educate the public about the symptoms and problems associated with the autistic child.

LITERATURE: Newsletter.

Office of Mental Retardation Coordination
U.S. Department of Health, Education, and Welfare
Washington, D.C. 20201

A federal office offering free or low-cost publications and written referrals to direct services. Write for information.

ADDITIONAL LITERATURE

Adult guides to children's books in print include *Children's Books in Print* and *Subject Guide to Children's Books in Print*, both updated annually and available in your library reference section. Another useful reference is *Little Miss Muffet Fights Back: Recommended Non-Sexist Books About Girls for Young Readers*, available from The Feminist Book Mart, 162-11 Ninth Avenue, Whitestone, N.Y. 11357 ($1.00) or in the library reference section.

Your best reference guide to children's books for your children will be your children's teachers, the librarians at their schools and the community libraries, and the children themselves. The teachers and libraries will probably have lists for the asking. (See also Additional Literature in Chapter 42, *Parenting*.)

Advocacy for Child Mental Health, edited by Irving N. Berlin, M.D. (1975). Brunner/Mazel, Inc., 19 Union Square West, New York, N.Y. 10003 ($13.50). An anthology of articles by experts on a variety of child/youth concerns, such as the rights of retarded children, poverty, racism, and courts.

All Our Children: The American Family Under Pressure by Kenneth Keniston and the Carnegie Council on Children (1977). Harcourt Brace Jovanovich, 757 Third Avenue, New York, N.Y. 10017 ($10.95). The controversial study of the rapidly evolving family, the positive and negative influences on it, with specific suggestions for change and policy revisions. Covers such areas as the services a family needs from the community and the effect of television on children.

America's Children 1976: A Bicentennial Assessment, prepared under the direction of Virginia Fleming (1976). The National Council of Organizations for Children and Youth, 1910 K Street, N.W., Room 404, Washington, D.C. 20006 ($4.00). A compilation of facts, presented in a clear style, about handicapped children, child abuse and neglect, foster care and adoption, children in poverty, child health problems, changes in the American family structure, and federal programs serving children.

The Black Child by Dr. Phyllis Harrison-Ross and Barbara Wyden (1973). Berkeley Publishing, 200 Madison Avenue, New York, N.Y. 10016 ($1.50). A good reference for black and white parents on child development. Contains some sensitive and important chapters on how black parents can handle racial anger and what white parents might say to avoid giving their children biased views.

The Boys' and Girls' Book About Divorce by Richard A. Gardner, M.D. (1971). Bantam Books, 666 Fifth Avenue, New York, N.Y. 10020 ($1.50). Written for children in a clear, easy style, disputing myths and answering such common questions as "How much time should you spend with your father?"

Child Care Issues for Parents and Society: A Guide to Information Sources by Andrew Garoogian and Rhoda Garoogian (1977). Gale Research Company, Book Tower, Detroit, Mich. 48226 ($18.00). Useful reference book providing brief annotated listings for publications, audiovisual aids, and organizations offering services for all children.

Child Health Encyclopedia: The Complete Guide for Parents by the Boston Children's Medical Center and Richard I. Feinbloom, M.D. (1975). Delacorte Press/Seymour Lawrence, 245 East 47th Street, New York, N.Y. 10017 ($15.00). Comprehensive guide to everything from car safety to lead poisoning with a front page to insert key telephone numbers and information.

Children Today, bimonthly magazine, published by the Children's Bureau, Administration for Children, Youth, and Families, Office of Human Development. Subscriptions from the Superintendent of Documents, U.S. Government Printing Office, Washington, D.C. 20402 ($6.10 a year; $1.00 single issue). Articles on all child-related concerns, such as day care, the effect of television, single-parenting; book reviews; news and reports; letters section.

The Children's Rights Movement: Overcoming the Oppression of Young People, edited by Beatrice and Ronald Gross (1977). Anchor Press/Doubleday, Garden City, N.Y. 11530 ($3.95). An excellent collection of writings by notables and movement pioneers—Larry Cole, Marian Wright Edelman, Barbara Bode, Benjamin Spock, Kenneth Keniston, John Holt, Margaret Mead, Jules Feiffer, and many others. Excellent resource section of literature and activist groups is included.

Death at an Early Age by Jonathan Kozol, with a preface by Dr. Robert Coles (1967). Bantam Books, 666 Fifth Avenue, New York, N.Y. 10019 ($1.50). Aptly subtitled "The Destruction of the Hearts and Minds of Negro Children in the Boston Public Schools."

Experiencing Youth: First-Person Accounts, 2nd ed., by George W. Goethals and Dennis S. Klos (1976). Little, Brown & Co., 34 Beacon Street, Boston, Mass. 02106 ($7.95). Sensitive, honest, and original stories of youth and adolescence written by college freshmen.

Helping Your Child Learn Right From Wrong by Dr. Sidney B. Simon and Sally Wendkos Olds (1976). McGraw-Hill Paperbacks, 1221 Avenue of the Americas, New York, N.Y. 10020 ($2.95). A self-help manual for parents that shows why the 3 M's—moralizing, manipulating, and modeling—should be replaced with gamelike strategies to allow children to develop their own moral values and emotional self-awareness.

A Hospital Story by Sara Bonnett Stein, in cooperation with Gilbert W. Kliman, M.D., photos by Doris Pinney (1974). Walker and Company, 720 Fifth Avenue, New York, N.Y. 10019 ($5.95). Very well done book for children with a more comprehensive text for parents and teachers on the opposite pages.

The Mothers' and Fathers' Medical Encyclopedia by Virginia E. Pomeranz, M.D., and Dodi Schultz (1972). Little, Brown & Company, 34 Beacon Street, Boston, Mass. 02106 ($17.50). Good reference on child health.

The National Children's Directory: An Organizational Directory and Reference Guide for Changing Conditions of Children and Youth, edited by Mary Lee Bundy and Rebecca Glenn Whaley (1977). Urban Information Interpreters, Inc., P.O. Box AH, College Park, Md. 20740 ($39.95). Annotated listing of national and local organizations and groups whose orientation is the improvement of conditions affecting children and youth.

National Directory of Alternative Schools (1976). NASP Program, School of Education, University of Massachusetts, Amherst, Mass. 01002 ($3.75).

A Reader's Guide for Parents of Children With Mental, Physical, or Emotional Disabilities by Coralie B. Moore and Kathryn Gorham Morton (1976). Consumer Information Center, Dept. 011F, Pueblo, Colo. ($3.00). A 144-page bibliography of books on how to deal with a host of disabilities. Disabilities listed include learning disabilities, mental retardation, autism, emotional disturbance, physical handicaps, epilepsy, visual handicaps, hearing impairments, speech and speech handicaps, cleft palate, and multiple handicaps.

The Rights of Children, Harvard Education Review Reprint #9 (1974). Longfellow Hall, 13 Appian Way, Cambridge, Mass. 02138 ($6.50). Special issue, illustrated with photographs, that is a compilation of articles by experts and children's advocates on the foundation of children's rights and the impact of the policies of various social agencies.

Success With Youth Report. Grafton Publications, Inc., 667 Madison Avenue, New York, N.Y. 10021 ($25.00 a year). Monthly newsletter about developments in the youth field.

Taking Care of Your Child: A Parents' Guide to Medical Care by Robert Pantell, M.D., James Fries, M.D., and Donald Vickery, M.D. (1977). Addison-Wesley, Reading, Mass. 01867 ($10.95). Offers suggestions about handling common childhood medical problems and when to apply home treatment versus when to go to a doctor.

Teaching the "Unteachable" by Herbert R. Kohl, introduction by John Holt (1967). New York Review, 250 West 57th Street, New York, N.Y. 10019 ($1.00).

The Widening World of Childhood: Paths Toward Mastery by Lois Barclay Murphy and collaborators (1962). Basic Books, 10 East 53rd Street, New York, N.Y. 10022 ($10.00). Classic work based on observations of thirty-two children from infancy to age twelve. Focuses on coping, defined as a "child's own manner of dealing with pressure and threats, potential or actual."

See also the following related chapters in *The Help Book:*

ADOPTION AND FOSTER CARE
ALCOHOLISM
BATTERED ADULTS
CHILD ABUSE
CHILDBEARING
COUNSELING
COURTS
DRUGS, SMOKING, AND DRUG ABUSE
EDUCATION
FAMILY PLANNING
FINANCIAL ASSISTANCE
FOOD AND NUTRITION
HANDICAPS
HEALTH
JUVENILE DELINQUENCY
KIDNAPPING, MISSING PERSONS, AND RUNAWAYS
MEDIA AND COMMUNICATIONS
MENTAL HEALTH
MENTAL RETARDATION AND LEARNING DISABILITIES
MULTIPURPOSE ORGANIZATIONS
PARENTING
SAFETY
SEX EDUCATION AND THERAPY
SUICIDE PREVENTION
TRANSPORTATION AND TRAVEL

11

CITIZEN ACTION

- Eleven Los Angeles suburbs—including Pasadena, Arcadia, Alhambra and San Gabriel—got together and set up a seismic safety unit to study the potential threat of earthquakes and to evaluate slopes and soils in that region so that landslides could be prevented.
- The Long Island, New York, suburbs of Islip, Babylon, and Huntington, with their combined population of 736,000 are developing a multitown solid-waste disposal plant to be located at a point convenient to all three towns. Islip and Babylon are also sharing a shellfish-management program to transplant clams from polluted to nonpolluted waters.
- When citizens of the Boston suburbs of Medford and Everett wanted to set up a drug-counseling program similar to the one in nearby Malden, they helped Malden obtain state funding so that its program could open branch offices in all of their communities.
- Residents of several Jefferson County suburbs near Denver, Colorado, alarmed at the rate at which their green acres were disappearing, organized Plan Jeffco, a campaign for a half-cent county sales tax to buy up open spaces for parks, hiking trails, and bikeways. The proposal passed a countywide referendum in 1972.

These examples represent the growing trend of suburbs to unite with each other to achieve common goals. But within large cities, citizens are also joining together to take on those problems that public officials are failing to solve. For example, in 1977 when the park system in New York City first felt the financial cutbacks, thousands of urban dwellers of all ages and in all boroughs began cleaning and maintaining the city's 572 parks and 775 neighborhood playgrounds. In Van Cortlandt Park in the Bronx, 1,200 marigolds were planted with money donated by the Citizens Committee for New York City. Not just beautification, but better police protection has been a cause taken up by the citizens—the Central Park Community Council has five mounted auxiliary police posts staffed by sixty unpaid volunteers.

Citizen action today is divided into two distinct camps—citizens doing the tasks that paid civil servants neglect and citizen groups or advocates challenging the accountability of those responsible to the public. In Birmingham, Alabama, a class-action suit was filed by lawyers on behalf of 10,000 resort owners, vacationers, fishermen, and others against a chemical company on the charge that it polluted Gulf of Mexico and river waters. Thousands of citizens are applying pressure to bank executives where it has been learned that the bank was practicing red-lining—reinvesting local investors' money outside of the community, often precipitating neighborhood decay and property depreciation. National organizations such as the National Community Development Association and Public Interest Research Group (PIRG) are seeking to coordinate these local citizen action efforts so that, with proper cause and guidance, you *can* fight City Hall.

If there is an active local citizen group where you live, you should be hearing about it. Citizen action means precisely that—making your voice heard, deciding on the issues you will fight and how you will go about it. Citizen action starts with the tenant association, then the block association; the citizen action group is larger and concerned with broader issues, such as utilities and waste disposal. Until governments become more efficient and less bureaucratic, citizen action is a step toward getting private control back to the people.

One national organization that has been very effective in initiating local citizen action groups is Ralph Nader's Public Interest Research Group (PIRG). The headquarters acts as an information clearinghouse on its local activist group's projects; it also publishes information on citizen action issues in general. Write to:

National PIRG Clearinghouse
1329 E Street, N.W., Suite 1127
Washington, D.C. 20004

Actual organizing is carried out through its local affiliates. The organizers are paid professional staff members; students may help in back-up research and organizing activities. The New Mexico PIRG, for example, has published a "Renter's Guide" and a booklet on "Birth Control and Maternity Information."

The following are operating PIRG Citizen Action Groups (CAG):

Alaska PIRG
Box 1093
630 West 4th Avenue
Anchorage, Alaska 99510

Cal PIRG Berkeley
214 Eshlenden
University of California
Berkeley, Calif. 94720

California CAG
2315 Westwood Boulevard
Los Angeles, Calif. 90064

California CAG
909 12th Street
Sacramento, Calif. 95814

California PIRG
3000 East Street
San Diego, Calif. 92102

Northern Cal PIRG
Box 702
Santa Clara, Calif. 95052

CoPIRG
Box 208
Colorado State University Student Center
Fort Collins, Colorado 80521

Colorado PIRG
University Center, Room 221A
University of Northern Colorado
Greely, Colorado 80631

Connecticut CAG
Box G
130 Washington Street
Hartford, Conn. 06101

Connecticut PIRG
Box 1571
Hartford, Conn. 06101

D.C. PIRG
Box 19542
Washington, D.C. 20036

Florida PIRG
Florida State University
Box 334
Tallahassee, Fla. 32306

Georgia PIRG
201 Washington Street, S.W.
Atlanta, Ga. 30303

Illinois PIRG
Student Center
Southern Illinois University
Carbondale, Ill. 62901

Indiana PIRG
406 North Fess
Bloomington, Ind. 47401

Iowa PIRG
7035 Activities Center
IMU
Iowa City, Iowa 52242

Kentucky PIRG
White Hall, University of Louisville
Louisville, Ky. 40208

Maine PIRG
68 High Street
Portland, Me. 04101

Maryland PIRG
University of Maryland, Room 3110
New Main Dining Hall
College Park, Md. 20742

Massachusetts PIRG
120 Boylston Street, Room 320
Boston, Mass. 02216

Michigan PIRG
Room 590, Hollister Building
106 West Allegan
Lansing, Mich. 48933

Minnesota PIRG
3036 University Avenue, S.E.
Minneapolis, Minn. 55414

Missouri PIRG
Box 8276
St. Louis, Mo. 63156

Nebraska PIRG
Union, Room 205
University of Nebraska
Lincoln, Neb. 68509

New Hampshire PIRG
Box 300
Hanover, N.H. 03755

New Jersey PIRG
32 West Lafayette Street
Trenton, N.J. 08608

New Mexico PIRG
P.O. Box 4564
Albuquerque, N.M. 87106

New York PIRG
5 Beekman Street
New York, N.Y. 10038

North Carolina PIRG
Box 2901
Durham, N.C. 27705

Ohio PIRG
65 South Fourth Street
Columbus, Ohio 43215

Oregon PIRG
Pythian Building
918 S.W. Yamhill Street
Portland, Ore. 97205

Pennsylvania PIRG
Temple University School of Law
Philadelphia, Pa. 19122

Rhode Island PIRG
University of Rhode Island
Memorial Union
Kingston, R.I. 02895

Box 28384
Furman University
Greenville, S.C. 29613

Texas PIRG
Box 237 UC
University of Houston
Houston, Tex. 77004

Utah PIRG
P.O. Box 8752
Salt Lake City, Utah 84108

Washington PIRG
Box 225 FK-10
University of Washington
Seattle, Wash. 98195

Vermont PIRG
26 State Street
Montpelier, Vt. 05601

Virginia PIRG
Campus Center
College of William and Mary
Williamsburg, Va. 23185

West Virginia CAG
1324 Virginia East
Charleston, W.Va. 25301

West Virginia PIRG
S.O.W. Mountainlair
West Virginia University
Morgantown, W.Va. 26506

Ontario PIRG
University of Waterloo
Physics Suite 226
Waterloo, Ontario, Canada N2L 3G1

If you want to start a citizen action group, the following national information clearinghouses and technical resource organizations will provide assistance:

Center for Community Change (CCC)
1000 Wisconsin Avenue, N.W.
Washington, D.C. 20007

Through a series of guides and their monthly newsletter, CCC shows how local citizen action groups have tapped federal sources for funding.

LITERATURE: Bimonthly newsletter ($10.00); guides include *Monitoring Community Development Block Grants; Comprehensive Employment and Training Act (CETA);* and *Economic Development Block Grants Federal Programs Monitor.*

Citizen Action Group
Public Citizen
1346 Connecticut Avenue, N.W. #1209
Washington, D.C. 20036

One of the numerous groups that are part of Ralph Nader's Public Citizen organization, Citizen Action Group supplies information to assist citizens and students in organizing projects to assure greater consumer protection and to effect social change.

LITERATURE: Publications price list.

IFCO (Interreligious Foundation for Community Organization, Inc.)
475 Riverside Drive
New York, N.Y. 10027

A national organization providing free assistance to local community groups who wish to organize to fight oppression and deteriorating living conditions. IFCO holds a National Organizers' Conference attended by community organizations from rural and urban areas around the country. Areas of concern for local organizing groups are racial discrimination, grand jury abuse, sterilization abuse, and poverty. Membership is $25.00; other donations are welcomed.

LITERATURE: *IFCO News* ($1.00 a year); descriptive leaflet.

Institute for Local Self-Reliance
1717 Eighteenth Street, N.W.
Washington, D.C. 20009

Technical consulting on a fee basis to community organizations and municipalities in its areas of expertise: municipal waste management, municipal finance, urban energy resources, urban food production, and community housing.

LITERATURE: *The Self-Reliance Newsletter* bimonthly ($6.00); publications price list.

Mobilization For Survival (MFS)
1213 Race Street
Philadelphia, Pa. 19107

This national organization is a coalition of peace, safe energy, and human needs organizations united around an action program with four goals: zero nuclear weapons, banning nuclear power, stopping the arms race, and funding human needs. It assists direct action projects, demonstrations, teach-ins, and related activities by providing information on issues, organizing guides, speakers, and the names of active groups.

LITERATURE: Free newsletter; resource packet ($5.00); poster ($.30).

National Association of Counties Research Foundation
County Resources Department
Human Resources Center
1735 New York Avenue, N.W.
Washington, D.C. 20006

In addition to providing technical assistance to help coordinate county services with those offered by local community action agencies, NACo has extensive publications providing technical assistance on a variety of community problems and related programs, including community economic development, emergency food and medical services, comprehensive health, drug rehabilitation, and alcoholic counseling and recovery programs.

LITERATURE: *Addressing the Diverse Needs of Rural Counties: Report on the 1974–1975 Rural Human Resources Program* (free); *County News*, by subscription; fact sheets.

National Association of Neighborhoods (NAN)
1901 Que Street, N.W.
Washington, D.C. 20009

Membership organization ($100.00 full organizational; $50.00 special organizational; $15.00 individual) composed of community and neighborhood organizations, city-wide coalitions, and some individuals who have joined together to promote neighborhood involvement in all levels of social and political decision making. Sponsors national meetings and task forces.

LITERATURE: *NAN Bulletin* (monthly); membership fact sheet.

National Community Development Association (NCDA)
1620 Eye Street, N.W. Suite 503
Washington, D.C. 20006

A membership organization of community development directors with committees on citizen participation, housing and economic development, small cities, and human development that is also an information clearinghouse on housing affairs. NCDA has workshops on community development, housing, and economic development and an annual spring conference.

LITERATURE: Publications brochure.

National People's Action (NPA)
1123 West Washington Boulevard
Chicago, Ill. 60607

This loose national coalition of neighborhood residents is a technical resource center as well as an information clearinghouse, providing legislative analysis and coordination of grass-roots lobbying efforts; leadership meetings determine what issues the community organizations will focus on. For example, NPA was an active force in the initiation of government-funded local community anticrime programs.

LITERATURE: Free descriptive leaflet.

Southwest Research and Information Center
P.O. Box 4524
Albuquerque, N.M. 87106

A nonprofit, public interest organization providing scientific and legal assistance to citizen action groups on environmental and social problems utilizing four basic tools: public education, community organizing, environmental research, legal action; extensive government document and periodical collection in their library; conducts news conferences on pertinent New Mexico-based projects; help with consumer-related lawsuits; "at-cost" printing for local action groups; campaigns against radioactive waste disposal in New Mexico.

LITERATURE: Fact sheets; *The Workbook* magazine ($10.00).

There are also training schools around the country for organizers, although their courses are not free. Each of these centers act as information clearinghouse and resource center for community organizations. Consultation and research is also available on a fee basis. Write for their publications price lists as well as a schedule and description of available training seminars and sessions:

National Training and Information Center
 (NTIC)
121 West Superior Street
Chicago, Ill. 60610

Midwest Academy, Inc.
600 West Fullerton Avenue
Chicago, Ill. 60614

New England Training Center for Community
 Organizers
19 Davis Street
Providence, R.I. 02908

The following are the state agencies for community affairs:

Development Office
Office of the Governor
3734 Atlanta Highway
%State Capitol
Montgomery, Ala. 36130

Department of Community and Regional
 Affairs
213 Community Building
Pouch B
Juneau, Alaska 99811

Office of Economic Planning and
 Development
1700 West Washington Street
Phoenix, Ariz. 85007

Department of Local Services
900 First National Bank Building
Little Rock, Ark. 72201

Department of Housing and Community
 Development
921 Tenth Street
Sacramento, Calif. 95814

Division of Local Government
Department of Local Affairs
1313 Sherman Street
Denver, Colo. 80203

Department of Community Affairs
1179 Main Street
Hartford, Conn. 06103

Department of Community Affairs and
  Economic Development
630 State College Road
Dover, Del. 19901

Department of Housing and Community
  Development
1325 G Street, N.W., Room 904
Washington, D.C. 20005

Department of Community Affairs
Howard Building
2571 Executive Center Circle, East
Tallahassee, Fla. 32301

Department of Community Affairs
7 Martin Luther King, Jr. Drive
Atlanta, Ga. 30334

Bureau of State Planning and Community
  Affairs
Division of Budget, Policy Planning, and
  Coordination
Office of the Governor
122 Statehouse
700 West Jefferson Street
Boise, Idaho 83720

Department of Local Government Affairs
303 East Monroe Street
Springfield, Ill. 62706

Community Services Administration
20 North Meridian Street
Indianapolis, Ind. 46204

Division of Municipal Affairs
Office for Planning and Programming
523 East 12th Street
Des Moines, Iowa 50319

Department of Economic and Community
  Development
2525 Riva Road
Annapolis, Md. 21401

Department of Community Affairs
Leverett Saltonstall State Office Building
100 Cambridge Street
Boston, Mass. 02202

Office of Local and Urban Affairs
State Planning Agency
100 Capitol Square Building
550 Cedar Street
St. Paul, Minn.

Mississippi Research and Development Center
3825 Ridgewood Road
Jackson, Miss. 39205

Division of Community Development
Department of Consumer Affairs, Regulation
  and Licensing
Jefferson State Office Building
P.O. Box 118
Jefferson City, Mo. 65101

Department of Community Affairs
1424 Ninth Avenue
Helena, Mont. 59601

Division of Community Affairs
Department of Economic Development
P.O. Box 94666
Lincoln, Neb. 68508

Office of Comprehensive Planning
Office of the Governor
State House Annex
Capitol Street
Concord, N.H. 03301

Department of Community Affairs
363 West State Street
Trenton, N.J. 08625

Division of Community Assistance
Department of Natural Resources and
  Community Development
P.O. Box 27687
Raleigh, N.C. 27611

Community Services Division
State Capitol
Bismarck, N.D. 58505

Department of Economic and Community
  Development
State Office Tower
30 East Broad Street
Columbus, Ohio 43215

Division of Community Affairs and Planning
Department of Economic and Community Affairs
5500 North Western Avenue
Oklahoma City, Okla. 73118

Intergovernmental Relations Division
Executive Department
240 Cottage Street, S.E.
Salem, Ore. 97310

Department of Community Affairs
216 South Office Building
Harrisburg, Pa. 17120

Department of Community Affairs
150 Washington Street
Providence, R.I. 02903

State Planning Bureau
Department of Executive Management
A206 Capitol Building Annex
Pierre, S.D. 57501

Department of Economic and Community Development
1007 Andrew Jackson State Office Building
500 Deaderick Street
Nashville, Tenn. 37219

Department of Community Affairs
P.O. Box 13166, Capitol Station
Austin, Tex. 78711

Department of Community Affairs
110 State Capitol
Salt Lake City, Utah 84114

Agency of Development and Community Affairs
Pavilion Office Building
109 State Street
Montpelier, Vt. 05602

Department of Intergovernmental Affairs
916 Ninth Street Office Building
Richmond, Va. 23219

Office of Community Development
400 Capitol Center Building
Olympia, Wash. 98504

Resource Development Support Division
Office of Federal-State Relations
Office of the Governor
R-150 State Capitol
1800 Kanawha Boulevard, E.
Charleston, W.Va. 25305

Department of Local Affairs and Development
123 West Washington Avenue
Madison, Wis. 53703

Department of Public Assistance and Social Services
361 Hathaway Building
2300 Capitol Avenue
Cheyenne, Wyo. 82002

ADDITIONAL LITERATURE

Action for a Change: A Student's Manual for Public Interest Organizing by Ralph Nader and Donald Ross with Brent English and Joseph Highland (1971). Grossman Publishers, 625 Madison Avenue, New York, N.Y. 10022 ($5.95). This student activism guide tells how to organize and host a student Public Interest Research Group (PIRG). Sample projects, such as retail price comparisons and employment discrimination, are suggested and described.

Action Now! A Citizen's Guide to Better Communities by Richard W. Poston (1976). Southern Illinois University Press, Box 3697, Carbondale, Ill. 62901 ($4.95). The author believes that neighborhood action, no matter what national programs are offered, is the key to democratic self-determinism. He provides guidelines for organizing such committees as Industrial Development, Retail Trade and Services, Housing, Education, and Health.

For the People by Joanne Manning Anderson, introduction by Ralph Nader (1977). Addison-Wesley, Reading, Mass. 01867 ($5.95.) A citizen action/consumer action handbook suggesting projects that groups and individuals may carry out for greater civic initiative. Covers numerous areas including: compiling a consumer's directory of doctors, effecting change in nursing homes, changing the laws, working with the media, and lowering utility bills.

How to Do Leaflets, Newsletters, and Newspapers by Nancy Brigham (1976). The New England Free Press, 60 Union Square, Somerville, Mass. 02143 ($1.25). A low-cost, popular guide to reaching the public for the community organizer.

How to Start Your Own Community Newspaper by John McKinney (March 1977). Meadow Press, P.O. Box 35, Port Jefferson, N.Y. 11777 ($9.95). Simple step-by-step instructions for putting together one of the practical tools of the citizen activist.

How to Publish Community Information on an Impossibly Tight Budget by Vic Pawlak (1976). Do It Now Foundation, Institute for Chemical Survival, P.O. Box 5115, Phoenix, Ariz. 85010 ($ .50). This booklet contains information on graphic and production matters, such as offsetting, layouts, choosing a printer, and mailing.

Lending Policies Exposed: Prime Factor in Neighborhood Decay (1976). National Training & Information Center, 121 West Superior Street, Chicago, Ill. 60610 ($2.00). Through Illinois examples, this booklet documents the need for a national policy that has neighborhood reinvestment as a prime goal.

Neighborhood Power: The New Localism by David Morris and Karl Hess (1975). An Institute for Policy Studies monograph published by Beacon Press, 25 Beacon Street, Boston, Mass. 02108 ($3.95). Suggests how to return political and economic power to the community; guidelines for developing neighborhood awareness. Bibliography and resource sections.

A *Public Citizen's Action Manual* by Donald K. Ross (1973). Grossman Publishers, 625 Madison Avenue, New York, N.Y. 10022 ($1.95). Excellent one-volume guide to citizen action on a variety of consumer and legal issues, including toy safety, sex discrimination in education, forming a citizen's lobby, evaluating government inspection systems, and improving small claims courts. Well-written with ample follow-up addresses and resources.

The Workbook (monthly). P.O. Box 4524, Albuquerque, N. Mex. 87106 ($7.00 students; $10.00 individuals; $20.00 institutions; $1.00 single issues). This newspaper-quality magazine is a first-rate monthly directory for anyone interested in some or all of the areas in *The Help Book*. It provides related articles and address updates. The masthead aptly describes its philosophical base and goals: ". . . a tool for all the people who, in their various ways, are working to provide a world characterized by economic justice; clean air and water and uncontaminated soils; abundant, safe, minimally-polluting energy supplies. . . ." A sample issue will be sent upon request.

See also the following related chapters in *The Help Book:*

ANIMAL RIGHTS
CONSUMER AFFAIRS
CRIME PREVENTION
ENVIRONMENT
**INFORMATION RIGHTS AND
    RESOURCES**
MEDIA AND COMMUNICATIONS
POLITICAL ACTION
VOLUNTEERISM

12

CIVIL RIGHTS AND DISCRIMINATION

In order to protect your rights, to be sure they have not been violated, it is necessary to know exactly what the U.S. Constitution guarantees:

BILL OF RIGHTS

Amendment 1
Congress shall make no law respecting an establishment of religion, or prohibiting the free exercise thereof; or abridging the freedom of speech, or of the press; or the right of the people peaceably to assemble, and to petition the Government for a redress of grievances.

Amendment 2
A well-regulated Militia, being necessary to the security of a free State, the right of the people to keep and bear Arms, shall not be infringed.

Amendment 3
No Soldier shall, in time of peace be quartered in any house, without the consent of the Owner, nor in time of war, but in a manner to be prescribed by law.

Amendment 4
The right of the people to be secure in their persons, houses, papers, and effects, against unreasonable searches and seizures, shall not be violated, and no Warrants shall issue, but upon probable cause, supported by Oath or affirmation, and particularly describing the place to be searched, and the persons or things to be seized.

Amendment 5
No person shall be held to answer for a capital, or otherwise infamous crime, unless on a presentment or indictment of a Grand Jury, except in cases arising in the land or naval forces, or in the Militia, when in actual service in time of War or public danger; nor shall any person be subject for the same offence to be twice put in

jeopardy of life or limb; nor shall be compelled in any criminal case to be a witness against himself, nor be deprived of life, liberty, or property, without due process of law; nor shall private property be taken for public use, without just compensation.

Amendment 6
In all criminal prosecutions, the accused shall enjoy the right to a speedy and public trial, by an impartial jury of the State and district wherein the crime shall have been committed, which district shall have been previously ascertained by law, and to be informed of the nature and cause of the accusation; to be confronted with the witnesses against him; to have compulsory process for obtaining witnesses in his favor, and to have the Assistance of Counsel for his defence.

Amendment 7
In Suits at common law, where the value in controversy shall exceed twenty dollars, the right of trial by jury shall be preserved, and no fact tried by a jury, shall be otherwise re-examined in any Court of the United States, than according to the rules of the common law.

Amendment 8
Excessive bail shall not be required, nor excessive fines imposed, nor cruel and unusual punishments inflicted.

Amendment 9
The enumeration in the Constitution, of certain rights, shall not be construed to deny or disparage others retained by the people.

Amendment 10
The powers not delegated to the United States by the Constitution, nor prohibited by it to the States, are reserved to the States respectively, or to the people.

ADDITIONAL AMENDMENTS

Amendment 13
Section 1. Neither slavery nor involuntary servitude, except as a punishment for crime whereof the party shall have been duly convicted, shall exist within the United States, or any place subject to their jurisdiction.

Amendment 14
Section 1. All persons born or naturalized in the United States, and subject to the jurisdiction thereof, are citizens of the United States and of the State wherein they reside. No State shall make or enforce any law which shall abridge the privileges or immunities of citizens of the United States; nor shall any State deprive any person of life, liberty, or property, without due process of law; nor deny to any person within its jurisdiction the equal protection of the laws.

Amendment 15
Section 1. The right of citizens of the United States to vote shall not be denied or abridged by the United States or by any State on account of race, color, or previous condition of servitude.

Amendment 19
The right of citizens of the United States to vote shall not be denied or abridged by the United States or by any State on account of sex.

CIVIL RIGHTS

Your county or city government probably has an Office of Civil Rights where you can inquire about laws and lodge complaints about infringements on your civil rights or unfair discrimination against you because of race, religion, national origin, sex, age, physical or mental handicaps.

The federal civil rights agency is:

Office of Civil Rights
H.E.W. North Building
330 Independence Avenue, S.W.
Washington, D.C. 20201

This agency enforces civil rights laws. It also protects against discrimination because of race, religion, national origin, sex, age, and physical and mental handicaps, and offers individual counseling.

LITERATURE: *HEW and Civil Rights* (free pamphlet).

The following is a list of national civil rights organizations:

American Civil Liberties Union (ACLU)
22 East 40th Street
New York, N.Y. 10016

Through its forty-nine state affiliates and over 350 chapters, ACLU offers free legal help in selected cases where basic constitutional rights have been violated. Founded in 1920, the ACLU is concerned with these constitutional rights: freedom of expression, due process of law, right to privacy, and equal protection of the laws. Since its founding, some of the best-known issues in which the organization has been involved have been the Scopes trial (the right to teach evolution in public schools); the right of labor to organize; the Sacco-Vanzetti case; and the right of public protest. About 5,000 lawyers around the country do the legal work for ACLU on a volunteer basis, but membership is mainly private citizens (only 7 percent are lawyers). Dues range from limited income ($5.00) to basic ($20.00) to life ($1,000.00). The national office serves as an information clearinghouse on the activities of local affiliates plus rights in general, and also makes referrals to local branches.

LITERATURE: Publications price list; free pamphlets describing the ACLU; "The Privacy Act: How It Affects You, How to Use It"; *Civil Liberties* newsletter (included with membership).

American Association for Affirmative Action
Ball State University
210 Administration Building
Muncie, Ind. 47306

A national professional association, founded in 1975, that fosters the implementation of affirmative action and equal opportunity in employment and in education and sponsors educational programs. Individual membership is $25.00 a year; institutional membership dues are on a scale dependent on the number of employees.

LITERATURE: Descriptive brochure; newsletter.

Association on American Indian Affairs, Inc.
432 Park Avenue South
New York, N.Y. 10016

This national organization, supported by private contributions, provides continuing programs in Indian economic and community development; health, education, and welfare; legal defense; public education; and arts and crafts. It aids Indian tribes in mobilizing federal, state, and private resources for a coordinated attack on the problems of poverty and injustice.

LITERATURE: *Indian Affairs*, newsletter; *Indian Family Defense*, quarterly bulletin; *Indian Natural Resources*, quarterly.

Center for Constitutional Rights (CCR)
853 Broadway
New York, N.Y. 10003

Founded in 1966 by William Kunstler, Benjamin Smith, and Arthur Kinoy, the CCR gets involved in legal battles involving the defense of the constitutional rights of diverse social movement groups and individuals. Beginning with the civil rights movements and school desegregation, up through the war in Vietnam, women's rights, and grand jury abuse, the CCR has taken on numerous issues and cases. It is supported by tax-deductible contributions.

LITERATURE: *CCR—The First Ten Years*; *Pre-Trial Detainees Manual*; "Representation of Women Who Defend Themselves Against Physical or Sexual Assault."

International League for Human Rights
777 United Nations Plaza, Suite 6F
New York, N.Y. 10017

Founded in 1942, the league has established civil liberties groups around the world and now has thirty-eight affiliates, including the ACLU, the NAACP, and the American Jewish Committee. Its concerns are broad, including slavery, genocide, torture, imprisonment without trial, denial of the right to leave one's country, restriction on family reunification, repression of free speech and free press, and racial and religious discrimination. Attention, and success in specific cases, has been brought about by publications bringing notice to specific injustices, sending investigative missions where serious violations are reported, dispatching international judicial observers to trial, conducting direct negotiations with governments, and the support of civil liberties groups around the world. It is a private organization supported by donations.

LITERATURE: Fact sheets; annual report; special reports.

Operation P.U.S.H.
930 East 50th Street
Chicago, Ill. 60615

An outgrowth of the civil rights movement, P.U.S.H. deals with economic/political issues confronting grass-roots, poor, and oppressed persons. It is action-issue oriented and has ongoing programs for education, housing, unemployment, and civil rights.

LITERATURE: *Push for Excellence*, pamphlet.

Project on National Security and Civil Liberties
122 Maryland Avenue, N.E.
Washington, D.C. 20002

A research and educational center with the primary purpose of dealing with official claims of "national security" that have been used to override basic civil liberties. It provides assistance in the use of the federal Freedom of Information Act to obtain documented information about illegal programs of the intelligence bureaucracy.

LITERATURE: Free pamphlets on how to obtain information through the Freedom of Information Act; *First Principles* newsletter on national security and civil liberties ($15.00 a year; $10.00 student/hardship); *Litigation Under the Federal Freedom of Information Act* ($20.00; $6.00 to nonprofit public interest groups).

The following is a list of state agencies for human rights, which formulate and enforce policies to eliminate discrimination because of race, creed, color, national origin, or sex in certain areas of public concern:

Human Rights Commission
Office of the Governor
204 East Fifth
Anchorage, Alaska 99501

Civil Rights Advisory Board
1645 West Jefferson Street
Phoenix, Ariz. 85007

Division of Civil Rights
Department of Regulatory Agencies
State Services Building
1525 Sherman Street
Denver, Colo. 80203

Commission on Human Rights and
  Opportunities
90 Washington Street
Hartford, Conn. 06115

Office of Human Relations
Department of Community Affairs and
  Economic Development
James Williams Service Center
805 River Road
Dover, Del. 19901

Office of Human Rights
Executive Office of the Mayor
District Building
14th and E Streets, N.W.
Washington, D.C. 20004

Commission on Human Relations
Howard Building
2571 Executive Center Circle, East
Tallahassee, Fla. 32301

Office of Human Affairs
Office of the Governor
State Capitol
Atlanta, Ga. 30334

Human Rights Commission
Statehouse
Boise, Idaho 83720

Commission on Human Relations
160 North LaSalle Street
Chicago, Ill. 60601

Civil Rights Commission
311 West Washington Street
Fair Building
Indianapolis, Ind. 46204

Civil Rights Commission
Liberty Building
418 6th Avenue
Des Moines, Iowa 50309

Commission on Civil Rights
535 Kansas Avenue
Topeka, Kans. 66603

Commission on Human Rights
828 Capital Plaza Tower
Frankfort, Ky. 40601

Division of Human Services
530 Lakeland Drive
Baton Rouge, La. 70804

Human Rights Commission
State House
Augusta, Me. 04333

Commission on Human Relations
Metro Plaza at Mondawmin
Baltimore, Md. 21215

Commission Against Discrimination
John W. McCormack State Office Building
1 Ashburton Place
Boston, Mass. 02108

Department of Civil Rights
Stoddard Building
Lansing, Mich. 48933

Department of Human Rights
Bremer Building
7th and Robert Street
St. Paul, Minn. 55101

Commission on Human Rights
Department of Consumer Affairs, Regulation, and Licensing
314 East High Street
Jefferson City, Mo. 65101

Human Rights Division
Department of Labor and Industry
7 West Sixth Avenue
Helena, Mont. 59601

Equal Opportunity Commission
P.O. Box 94934
Lincoln, Neb. 68509

Nevada Equal Rights Commission
215 East Bonanza Road
Las Vegas, Nev. 89158

Commission for Human Rights
66 South Street
Concord, N.H. 03301

Division on Civil Rights
Department of Law and Public Safety
1100 Raymond Boulevard
Newark, N.J. 07102

Human Rights Commission
Bataan Memorial Building
Santa Fe, N.M. 87503

Division of Human Rights
Two World Trade Center
New York, N.Y. 10047

Human Relations Council
Department of Administration
530 North Wilmington Street
Raleigh, N.C. 27604

Ohio Civil Rights Commission
220 South Parsons Avenue
Columbus, Ohio 43215

Human Rights Commission
G-11 Jim Thorpe Office Building
2101 North Lincoln Boulevard
Oklahoma City, Okla. 73105

Bureau of Labor
State Office Building
1400 S.W. 5th Avenue
Portland, Ore. 97201

Human Relations Commission
100 North Cameron Street
Harrisburg, Pa. 17101

Commission for Human Rights
334 Westminster Mall
Providence, R.I. 02903

Human Affairs Commission
1111 Belleview Street
P.O. Box 11300
Columbia, S.C. 29211

Division of Human Rights
Department of Commerce and Consumer Affairs
Capitol Building
Pierre, S.D. 57501

Commission for Human Development
C3-305 Cordell Hull Building
436 6th Avenue, North
Nashville, Tenn. 37219

Governor's Office of Equal Employment Opportunity
202 Sam Houston State Office Building
201 East 14th Street
P.O. Box 12428, Capitol Station
Austin, Tex. 78711

Office of Human Resources
Ninth Street Office Building, 6th Floor
9th and Grace Streets
P.O. Box 1475
Richmond, Va. 23212

Human Rights Commission
Evergreen Plaza Building
Seventh and Capitol Way
Olympia, Wash. 98504

Human Rights Commission
215 Professional Building
1036 Quarrier Street
Charleston W. Va. 25305

Equal Rights Division
Department of Industry, Labor, and Human Relations
201 East Washington Avenue
Madison, Wis. 53702

DISCRIMINATION

Education

Equal Rights for Women in Education
Education Commission of the States
1860 Lincoln, Suite 300
Denver, Colo. 80203

Offers a variety of printed materials on sex discrimination in education geared toward legislatures and departments and state boards of education.

National Center for Quality Integrated Education
NEA Building, Room 403
1201 16th Street, N.W.
Washington, D.C. 20036

Project of the National Conference of Christians and Jews (NCCJ).

Project on Equal Education Rights
National Organization for Women Legal Defense and Education Fund
1029 Vermont Avenue, N.W., Suite 800
Washington, D.C. 20005

This project of NOW is working toward educational equity in individual school systems and elimination of discriminatory treatment of pupils. It is also an information clearinghouse on efforts in this area.

LITERATURE: *PEER Perspective* newsletter.

Project on the Status and Education of Women
Association of American Colleges
1818 R Street, N.W.
Washington, D.C. 20009

Comprehensive information clearinghouse on sex discrimination in education; extensive free and low-cost publications in this area.

LITERATURE: "Federal Laws and Regulations Affecting Sex Discrimination in Educational Institutions" free chart; publications listing; "A Survey of Research Concerns on Women's Issues," booklet.

Employment

Equal Employment Opportunity Commission
2401 E Street, N.W.
Washington, D.C. 20506

A federal agency handling individual charges of employment discrimination. The commission has thirty district offices.

U.S. Department of Labor
Employment Standards Administration
Washington, D.C. 20210

This federal agency oversees abuses of the Equal Pay Act of 1963, which amended the Fair Labor Standards Act, to require that men and women performing equal work must receive equal pay. For more information, contact your local Wage and Hour Division's nearest office list in the U.S. government section of most telephone directories under U.S. Department of Labor, Wage and Hours Division.

LITERATURE: "Equal Pay" leaflet.

Housing

U.S. Department of Housing and Urban Development
451 7th Street, S.W.
Washington, D.C. 20410

This federal agency handles complaints about housing discrimination on account of race, religion, color, sex, or national origin. Complaints are forwarded to regional offices.

National Committee Against Discrimination in Housing (NCDH)
1425 H Street, N.W.
Washington, D.C. 20005

This public interest organization, founded in 1950, is dedicated to achieving open housing and is opposed to any segregation or discrimination of the poor or minority groups. It is an information clearinghouse designed for public education and providing legal information and advice. NCDH holds regional seminars.

LITERATURE: *Trends in Housing.*

Race and Religion

Committee on Elimination of Racial Discrimination
Office of Public Information
United Nations
New York, N.Y. 10017

An eighteen-member body composed of experts serving in their personal capacity was established in 1969; holds yearly international conference.

LITERATURE: Pamphlets, background papers, press releases.

National Association for the Advancement of Colored People (NAACP)
1790 Broadway
New York, N.Y. 10019

Started in 1909, there are now more than 1,500 local chapters of the NAACP; the national headquarters acts as a clearinghouse for the local groups. The goal is equal citizenship rights for all Americans which would be achieved by eliminating all types of segregation and discrimination.

LITERATURE: Pamphlets and leaflets; publications price list; annual report; "Highlights of NAACP History 1909–1974."

NAACP Legal Defense and Educational Fund (LDEF)
Ten Columbus Circle
New York, N.Y. 10019

Founded in 1939, this is the legal arm of the civil rights movement, functioning independently of the NAACP. It represents civil rights groups as well as individual citizens with legitimate civil rights claims and has a 2,000-volume library.

National Urban League
500 East 62nd Street
New York, N.Y. 10021

A national community-service agency with local groups around the country to help blacks and other economically and socially disadvantaged groups in the areas of employment, housing, education, and social welfare.

American Jewish Committee
Institute of Human Relations
165 East 56th Street
New York, N.Y. 10022

Founded in 1906, the committee has more than 100 chapters and units in 600 communities with over 40,000 members. Goals of the organization are to protect the civil and religious rights of Jews here and abroad and to advance the cause of improved human relations for all people.

LITERATURE: Descriptive pamphlets, including "Milestones of the American Jewish Committee."

Anti-Defamation League of B'nai B'rith
315 Lexington Avenue
New York, N.Y. 10016

Works to end discrimination among all religious groups and nationalities. The league has twenty-six regional offices.

National Conference of Christians and Jews (NCCJ)
43 West 57th Street
New York, N.Y. 10019

Founded in 1928, the NCCJ is a nonprofit human relations organization engaged in a nationwide program of intergroup education to eliminate prejudice and discrimination; educational programs include literature and local projects on the police, crime victims, racial discrimination, and desegregation.

LITERATURE: Reprints; "Youth Organized United and Involved"; "Biomedical Ethics"; descriptive brochure.

Sex

Center for Law and Social Policy
Women's Rights Staff
1751 R Street, N.W.
Washington, D.C. 20036

A national organization that handles class action suits against the government for groups of women having the same problems. Fights sex discrimination in education, health, and insurance, providing lawyers for women needing aid.

Institute for Studies in Equality
926 J Street, Suite 1014
Sacramento, Calif. 95814

Information clearinghouse and referral service on all aspects of equality for women.

LITERATURE: Free pamphlets; *Equal Rights Monitor* magazine.

NOW Legal Defense and Education Fund
9 West 57th Street
New York, N.Y. 10019

This is the legal defense and education affiliate of the National Organization for Women, supported by tax-deductible contributions; it is engaged in teaching women what their rights are and, in legal cases, where rights have been violated.

LITERATURE: Descriptive leaflet and fact sheets.

Women's Action Alliance, Inc.
370 Lexington Avenue
New York, N.Y. 10017

Information clearinghouse and resource center for those working against sex discrimination; related projects include Project Share (Support-Hookup-Assistance-Research-Education) and the Non-Sexist Child Development Project. The National Women's Agency Project coordinates 100 national women's groups.

LITERATURE: *Women's Agenda*, monthly; *A Practical Guide to the Women's Movement* ($5.00), excellent listings by category with annotated descriptions.

Women's Equity Action League (WEAL)
National Press Building
Washington, D.C. 20045

Files discrimination complaints against employers on behalf of women working in schools, business, industry, and government.

LITERATURE: *The Equal Rights Amendment for Equal Rights Under the Law* ($.50); chart showing federal laws and regulations prohibiting sex discrimination ($1.25); send for extensive listings and "packets" available.

Women's Rights Program Unit
U.S. Commission on Civil Rights
Washington, D.C. 20425

A federal agency concerned with all aspects of women's civil rights; conducts conferences and serves as an information clearinghouse.

Working Women United Institute
593 Park Avenue
New York, N.Y. 10021

Information clearinghouse on sexual harassment; publishes a newsletter for attorneys.

LITERATURE: Handbook.

ADDITIONAL LITERATURE

The Bill of Rights Today by Thomas I. Emerson (1973). Public Affairs Committee, Inc., 381 Park Avenue South, New York, N.Y. 10016 ($ .50). A concise explanation of the Bill of Rights by a Yale law professor.

Blaming The Victim, revised ed., by William Ryan (1976). Vintage Books, 201 East 50th Street, New York, N.Y. 10022 ($2.45). Civil rights advocate, professor, and researcher Ryan explores why Americans prefer blaming the poor for their poverty than faulting the inequalities in our society. Ryan's classic thesis has implications for all types of victims, not just victims of poverty.

Civil Rights: A Current Guide to the People, Organizations and Events, 2nd edition, edited by Joan Martin Burke (1974). R. R. Bowker, 1180 Avenue of the Americas, New York, N.Y. 10019 ($14.95). A list of civil rights laws in various states as well as a bibliography of groups and persons important in the civil rights movement up to 1974.

Civil Rights Digest. U.S. Commission on Civil Rights, Washington, D.C. 20425 (free). Quarterly magazine with articles by recognized authorities covering a variety of topics, including battered women, the health system, and the economic status of minorities and women.

Guide to Federal Laws and Regulations Prohibiting Sex Discrimination, Clearinghouse Publication No. 46 (July 1976), U.S. Commission on Civil Rights. For sale from Superintendent of Documents, U.S. Government Printing Office, Washington, D.C. 20402.

Higher Education, a WEAL Fund Kit prepared by Carol Parr (Spring 1977). Women's Equity Action League Educational and Legal Defense Fund, 733 Fifteenth Street, N.W., Suite 200, Washington, D.C. 20005 ($4.00). An assortment of printed brochures, leaflets, typescript reports and fact sheets concerning sex discrimination in educational institutions, how to file complaints, plus bibliographic sources.

Lobbying for Freedom by Kenneth P. Norwich (1975). St. Martin's Press, 175 Fifth Avenue, New York, N.Y. 10010 ($3.95). Handbook on how to fight censorship at the state level, including practical tips on how to lobby.

The Nature of Prejudice by Gordon W. Allport, abridged (1958). Doubleday Anchor Books, Garden City, N.Y. 11530 ($1.45). Psychologist Allport, in this classic work, deals with racism and ethnic isolation in an in-depth and multifaceted way. He discusses how prejudices are acquired, why scapegoats have been chosen throughout history, what traits occur because one is ostracized, and whether legislation can curb prejudice.

Peer Perspective (quarterly). NOW Legal Defense and Education Fund, 1029 Vermont Avenue, N.W., Washington, D.C. 20005 (free). Resources and news about implementation of Title IX—federal legislation prohibiting discrimination in education.

Prejudice and Your Child by Kenneth B. Clark (1963). Beacon Press, 25 Beacon Street, Boston, Mass. 02108 ($1.95).

The Pulse of Freedom edited by Alan Reitman (1975). W. W. Norton & Co., 500 Fifth Avenue, New York, N.Y. 10036 ($12.50). The history of civil liberties in the United States from 1920 to the present is traced through six essays.

The Races of Mankind by Ruth Benedict and Gene Weltfish (1943). Public Affairs Committee, 381 Park Avenue South, New York, N.Y. 10016 ($ .50). The authors, distinguished anthropologists, present race from a scientific vantage point in clear, simple language.

The Rights of Americans: What They Are—What They Should Be edited by Norman Dorsen (1971). Vintage Books, 201 East 50th Street, New York, N.Y. 10022 ($3.95). A collection of essays on all types of rights, such as the right to housing, welfare, legal services, protest, publish, privacy, and the rights of students, suspects, juveniles, mental patients, and aliens. Written on the anniversary of the founding of the American Civil Liberties Union (ACLU), each article contains a wealth of legislative and historical information, substantiated by source notes; well edited and a good reference guide.

Simple Justice: The History of Brown vs. Board of Education and Black America's Struggle for Equality by Richard Kluger (1977). Vintage Books/Random House, 201 East 50th Street, New York, N.Y. 10022 ($6.95). A controversial and highly acclaimed study of racial desegregation.

Your Rights, Past and Present by James Haskins (1975). Hawthorn Books, Inc., 260 Madison Avenue, New York, N.Y. 10016 ($5.95). Written for children in grades 7 and up.

See also the following related chapters in *The Help Book:*

COURTS
EDUCATION
EMPLOYMENT
GAY LIBERATION
HANDICAPS
HEALTH
HOUSING
INFORMATION RIGHTS AND RESOURCES
LEGAL SERVICES
MENTAL HEALTH
OFFENDERS AND EX-OFFENDERS
POLITICAL ACTION

13

CONSUMER AFFAIRS

How can you stop the continued sale of an unsafe product, or obtain a replacement for a defective appliance, when profit-making companies seem to have all the power and resources on their sides? Help can be obtained in a number of ways. Sometimes it can be obtained by making just one phone call; in other cases it can be obtained by writing a letter to the manufacturer, by requesting the free assistance of your local or state consumer protection agency or attorney general, by going to the right federal department, or by seeking the aid of a voluntary local or national consumer group.

What are some steps to take in lodging a complaint? The following list can be considered a scale of tactics, from the simplest to the most dramatic. If first, quick methods fail, keep going until you get the action and the results that you are entitled to:*

1. Telephone inquiry.

2. Written complaint to the retailer.

3. Written complaint to the manufacturer.

4. Written complaint to the trade association, Better Business Bureau, or Chamber of Commerce.

5. Written complaints to local or state agencies.

6. Written complaints to federal agencies, such as the Federal Trade Commission (the basic national consumer protection agency, with regional offices), the Food and Drug Administration, or the U.S. Consumer Product Safety Commission (the last for all complaints except foods, drugs, and cosmetics).

7. Legal action (small claims court, hire a lawyer).

8. Written or telephone complaint to voluntary local, statewide, or national consumer organizations.

9. Enlisting the help of the media—newspapers, television, radio.

10. Unconventional tactics, such as sending the defective product directly to the company's president, picketing, or distributing leaflets.

* Based upon chapter 3, "The Strategy of Escalation," by John Dorfman in *A Consumer's Arsenal* (Praeger Publishers, 1976)

Generally, the kinds of consumer complaints discussed in this chapter include: faulty advertising (or not having an item available that was advertised for sale); unsatisfactory performance, quality, or repair; and customer service. More serious consumer problems—consumer fraud or other crimes—should be directed to the consumer affairs bureau of your local district attorney. If that office cannot handle your complaint, it will refer you to the consumer affairs bureau of your state attorney general or the district court of the federal judicial system, whichever is appropriate. (See Chapter 7, *Business Information: Crimes Against Business* or Chapter 17, *Crime Victims and Witnesses: Fraud.*)

GETTING HELP TO RESOLVE YOUR CONSUMER COMPLAINTS

Your first concern is how to get quick, easy, and effective action for your consumer problem. Since all transactions may lead to complaints, keep receipts and good records. For example, a man purchased an electric blender at his local appliance store. The next day, he discovered it was defective. Angry, he put it back in the box and returned to the appliance store. He was amazed that the saleswoman gladly exchanged it for a new, working blender. (The saleswoman was happy to have a satisfied customer who might come back and make another purchase; she would fight with the manufacturer herself.)

Sometimes a consumer's complaint can be handled that simply and amicably, if the consumer takes the time either to go back to the store with the defective product, or at least telephones or writes. The dealer depends on satisfied customers and good will to stay in business.

But what if your right to return a product is denied by the salesperson? Go to the complaint manager. If that fails, go to the president or the manager of the store. Keep complaining until you get what you deserve—in this case, a new blender or a complete refund. If the store in question will not listen to you, go to the manufacturer.

How do you find out who the manufacturer is or what company to write to with your complaint? The easiest way is to look on the product—quite often the address of the corporate headquarters will be listed. If it's not, or if you've lost the outside packaging, you might consult the library for a reference book with names and addresses of all major companies. One book with such listings is *Consumer Sourcebook* (see Additional Literature for further comments on this title), or the *EM Complaint Directory for Consumers*, updated annually, available for $1.25 from Everybody's Money, Box 431B, Madison, Wis. 53701. Or you might consult the *Consumer Complaint Guide* by Joseph Rosenbloom, updated annually, published by Macmillan Information, 866 Third Avenue, New York, N.Y. 10022.

But if the manufacturer fails to provide you with a working, new product, or treats you unsatisfactorily, some industries have founded Consumer Action Panels (CAPs) that will intervene. (This industry-wide self-policing was inspired both by the growing consumer movement and by an awareness that if there wasn't better business-sponsored consumer help, there might be government intervention.) The first CAP was MACAP, the Major Appliance Consumer Action Panel, founded in 1970; other industries and manufacturers have followed suit.

Whenever you contact a CAP, or, for that matter, any time you document a consumer complaint, you should include the following information in your letter (keeping a copy for your files):

- Your name, address, and telephone number.
- Manufacturer's name and address, if known.
- Retailer's name and address.
- Date of purchase.
- Description of the item, including style, color, number, etc.
- A short and clear summary of the problems and the services provided to date, as well as copies of any correspondence, receipts, or notes regarding telephone or in-person discussions about the matter (keep the originals in your own files).

The major CAP programs are:

FICAP (Furniture Industry Consumer
   Advisory Panel)
P.O. Box 951
High Point, N.C. 27261

MACAP (Major Appliance Consumer Action
   Panel)
20 North Wacker Drive
Chicago, Ill. 60606

The following are some other industry-wide business-run consumer complaint services addressing some of the other sources of consumer grievances:

Direct Mail/Marketing Association (DMMA)
Mail Order Action Line
6 East 43rd Street
New York, N.Y. 10017

National Advertising Review Board (NARB)
845 Third Avenue
New York, N.Y. 10022

If you've exhausted this stage of consumer protesting, or if you wish to try to get results through an intermediary, you might consult your local Better Business Bureau. The BBB is part of a national network coordinated through the Council of Better Business Bureaus (CBBB):

Council of Better Business Bureaus
1150 Seventeenth Street, N.W.
Washington, D.C. 20036

Founded in 1970, the CBBB oversees the activities of member Better Business Bureaus (BBBs) around the country. The goals of the CBBB are "to be an effective national self-regulatory force for business, and to demonstrate an active concern for consumers." The approximately 140 local BBBs can provide you with information about a company before you do business with it and also help to resolve a complaint that you might have with a firm. They offer consumer arbitration to resolve buyer-seller disputes and also monitor advertising and selling practices. Speakers are available for educational purposes and provide information on consumer subjects.

BBBs are nonprofit corporations supported entirely by membership dues or subscription sales; if illegal practices are uncovered and the business will not cooperate with the BBB, the business is reported to the appropriate law enforcement agency.

LITERATURE: Publication price list; contact your local bureau for description of available "tip sheets" and "tip pamphlets."

The CBBB periodically issues an updated list of local BBB's, but you can always consult your telephone directory for the current telephone number and address of one near you. There are BBB's in the following places:

ALABAMA: Birmingham, Huntsville, Mobile
ARIZONA: Phoenix, Tucson
ARKANSAS: Little Rock
CALIFORNIA: Bakersfield, Colton, Fresno, Long Beach, Los Angeles, Oakland, Orange, Palm Desert, Sacramento, Salinas, San Francisco, San Jose, San Mateo, Soquel, Stockton, Vallejo
COLORADO: Denver
CONNECTICUT: Bridgeport, Hartford, New Haven
DELAWARE: Milford, Wilmington
DISTRICT OF COLUMBIA: Washington, D.C.
FLORIDA: Fort Lauderdale, Miami, North Naples, West Palm Beach
GEORGIA: Atlanta, Augusta, Columbus, Savannah
HAWAII: Honolulu, Kahului
IDAHO: Boise
ILLINOIS: Chicago, Peoria
INDIANA: Elkhart, Fort Wayne, Gary, Indianapolis, South Bend
IOWA: Des Moines, Sioux City
KANSAS: Topeka, Wichita
KENTUCKY: Lexington, Louisville
LOUISIANA: Baton Rouge, Lafayette, Lake Charles, Monroe, New Orleans, Shreveport

MARYLAND: Baltimore, Bethesda
MASSACHUSETTS: Boston, Hyannis, Lawrence, Springfield, Worcester
MICHIGAN: Detroit, Grand Rapids
MINNESOTA: St. Paul
MISSISSIPPI: Jackson
MISSOURI: Kansas City, St. Louis, Springfield
NEBRASKA: Lincoln, Omaha
NEVADA: Las Vegas, Reno
NEW HAMPSHIRE: Concord
NEW JERSEY: Collingswood, Cranbury, Newark, Paramus, Toms River
NEW MEXICO: Albuquerque, Santa Fe
NEW YORK: Buffalo, Fishkill, New York City, Rochester, Syracuse, Utica, Westbury, White Plains
NORTH CAROLINA: Asheville, Charlotte, Greensboro, Research Triangle Park, Winston-Salem
OHIO: Akron, Canton, Cincinnati, Cleveland, Columbus, Dayton, Toledo, Youngstown
OKLAHOMA: Oklahoma City, Tulsa
OREGON: Portland
PENNSYLVANIA: Bethlehem, Philadelphia, Scranton
RHODE ISLAND: Providence
TENNESSEE: Chattanooga, Knoxville, Memphis, Nashville

148 / THE HELP BOOK

TEXAS: Abilene, Amarillo, Austin, Beaumont, Bryan, Corpus Christi, Dallas, El Paso, Fort Worth, Houston, Lubbock, Midland, San Antonio, Waco
UTAH: Salt Lake City
VIRGINIA: Newport News, Norfolk, Richmond
WASHINGTON: Seattle, Spokane, Tacoma, Yakima
WISCONSIN: Milwaukee
CANADA: National Headquarters for Canadian Bureaus, 76 St. Clair Avenue, West, Toronto, Ontario, Canada M4V 1N2

If you've exhausted all local and national business-sponsored sources of help, as well as the BBB, or if there is none in your community, where do you next try to get assistance? Independent, free help is available from your local district attorney's office or private nongovernmental consumer group. But remember, many operate on shoestring budgets and are staffed by volunteers. It will depend upon the individual group whether it even handles private complaints or only serves as an information clearinghouse and advocacy group. If you cannot find a local group listed in your telephone directory, a state-by-state listing of local groups, periodically updated, is available for $2.00 from:

Consumer Federation of America
State and Local Organizing Project
1012 14th Street, N.W.
Washington, D.C. 20005

Many local groups are affiliates of the national Public Interest Research Group (PIRG); those local listings are provided in Chapter 11, *Citizen Action*.

The media can also be a source of independent free help. Some television stations and newspapers have "action lines" or "action columns," but find out if they will actually handle your request or if it will only be referred somewhere else. Red tape problems are the kinds most frequently resolved through media sources (other than the few cases selected as examples of "consumer action.") But there is a North American consumer grievance network whose effectiveness has been commended. It is:

Call For Action (CFA)
1601 Connecticut Avenue, N.W. Suite 780
Washington, D.C. 20036

Started by Ellen and Peter Straus in 1963 at radio station WMCA in New York City, Call For Action has spread to forty-nine broadcast stations around the country, staffed by more than 2,500 volunteers. CFA is a national, nonprofit, referral and action service available free to any and all with consumer problems. More than 360,000 persons were helped in 1977 by CFA volunteers.

CFA handles many types of grievances—from housing and consumer fraud to difficulties with schools, police, drugs, discrimination, employment, and welfare.

The following is a listing by state of the CFA local affiliates:

WYDE CFA
2112-11th Avenue, S., Suite 410
Birmingham, Ala. 35205

KTAR-TV CFA
5020 N. 20th Street
Phoenix, Ariz. 85016

KTKT CFA
P.O. Box 5585
Tucson, Ariz. 85703

KARK-TV CFA
201 West 3rd Street
Little Rock, Ark. 72201

KFWB CFA
6230 Yucca
Los Angeles, Calif. 90028

KGTV CFA
P.O. Box 81047
San Diego, Calif. 92138

KLZ CFA
2149 South Holly Street
Denver, Colo. 80222

WELI CFA
P.O. Box 85
New Haven, Conn. 06501

WTOP CFA
Broadcast House
4001 Brandywine Street, N.W.
Washington, D.C. 20016

WTLV-TV CFA
Box 1212
Jacksonville, Fla. 32201

WCIX-TV CFA
1111 Brickwell Avenue
Miami, Fla. 33131

WDBO CFA
P.O. Box 158
Orlando, Fla. 32802

WGST CFA
550 Pharr Road, N.E.
P.O. Box 11920
Atlanta, Ga. 30355

WIND CFA
625 N. Michigan Avenue
Chicago, Ill. 60611

WDZ CFA
265 South Park Street
Decatur, Ill. 62523

WRAU-TV CFA
500 N. Stewart St.
Creve Coeur, Ill. 61611

KCMO CFA
4500 Johnson Drive
Shawnee Mission, Kan. 66208

WBAL CFA
3800 Hooper Avenue
Baltimore, Md. 21211

WBZ CFA
1170 Soldiers Field Road
Boston, Mass. 02134

WBSM CFA
P.O. Box J 4105
New Bedford, Mass. 02741

WJR CFA
Fisher Building
Detroit, Mich. 48202

KMOX CFA
One Memorial Drive
St. Louis, Mo. 63102

WOW CFA
11128 John Galt Boulevard
Omaha, Neb. 68137

KOB CFA
P.O. Box 1351
Albuquerque, N.M. 87103

WROW CFA
341 Northern Boulevard
Albany, N.Y. 12204

WBEN Radio/TV CFA
2077 Elmwood Avenue
Buffalo, N.Y. 14207

WMCA CFA
888 Seventh Avenue
New York, N.Y. 10019

WGSM CFA
P.O. Box 740
900 Walt Whitman Road
Long Island, N.Y. 11746

WHEN CFA
P.O. Box 6509
620 Old Liverpool Road
Syracuse, N.Y. 13217

WTLB CFA
Kellog Road
Washington Mills, N.Y. 13479

WRAL-TV CFA
115 East Chapel Hill Street
Durham, N.C. 27701

WRAL-TV CFA
209 S. McDowell
Raleigh, N.C. 27601

WAKR CFA
P.O. Box 1590
Akron, Ohio 44309

WERE CFA
1500 Chester Avenue
Cleveland, Ohio 44114

WFMJ CFA
101 W. Boardman
Youngstown, Ohio 44503

KWTV CFA
7401 N. Kelley
P.O. Box 14159
Oklahoma City, Okla. 73114

WFBG CFA
Hilltop, Logan Valley Boulevard
Altoona, Pa. 16603

WFIL CFA
4100 City Line Avenue
Philadelphia, Pa. 19131

KDKA CFA
One Gateway Center
Pittsburgh, Pa. 15222

WJAR CFA
176 Weybosset Street
Providence, R.I. 02903

WDIA CFA
P.O. Box 12045
Memphis, Tenn. 38112

WBAP CFA
3900 Barnett Street
Fort Worth, Tex. 76102

WWVA CFA
Capitol Music Hall
Wheeling, W.Va. 26003

CFCF CFA
405 Ogilvy Avenue
Montreal, Canada H3N 1M4

CJRN CFA
Pen Centre
St. Catherines, Ontario
Canada

If local consumer help has failed, you could take your complaint to the city or county Office of Consumer Affairs, if one exists. Try the city or county government listings in your telephone directory. Every state has a State Agency for Consumer Affairs (or Consumer Protection) as well. What help might you get from the state agency? It might intervene directly to correct your grievance, send you a packet of information, or just a postcard telling you to go somewhere else for help, or you may not receive a reply at all. But the state agencies are one more place to try for free consumer help. The state agencies for consumer protection have the duty of enforcing legislation intended to protect the consumer from injury by product use or merchandising deceit. A list of the code of fair practices and a list of the other divisions within the department are probably available in booklet form. Other printed materials may also be available.

The state agencies for consumer affairs or consumer protection are:

Department of Consumer Protection
138 Adams Avenue
Montgomery, Ala. 36130

Department of Law
410 State Capitol
Pouch K
Juneau, Alaska 99811

Consumer Protection Division
Office of the Attorney General
Justice Building
Capitol Grounds
Little Rock, Ark. 72201

Department of Consumer Affairs
1020 N Street
Sacramento, Calif. 95814

Consumer Section
Office of the Attorney General
Department of Law
State Services Building, 3rd Floor
1525 Sherman Street
Denver, Colo. 80203

Department of Consumer Protection
105 State Office Building
Hartford, Conn. 06115

Division of Consumer Affairs
Department of Community Affairs and
  Economic Development
800 North French Street
Wilmington, Del. 19801

Office of Consumer Protection
1407 L Street, N.W.
Washington, D.C. 20005

Division of Consumer Services
Department of Agriculture and Consumer
  Services
The Capitol
Tallahassee, Fla. 32304

Consumer Protection Office
Department of Agriculture
309 Agriculture Building
Capitol Square, S.W.
Atlanta, Ga. 30334

Office of Consumer Protection
Office of the Governor
520 Kamamalu Building
250 South King Street
Honolulu, Hawaii 96813

Business Regulation/Consumer Protection
  Section
Office of the Attorney General
Statehouse
700 West Jefferson Street
Boise, Idaho 83720

Consumer Protection Division
Office of the Attorney General
160 North LaSalle Street
Chicago, Ill. 60601

Consumer Protection Division
Office of the Attorney General
219 State House
200 West Washington Street
Indianapolis, Ind. 46204

Consumer Protection Division
Office of the Attorney General
209 East Court Avenue
Des Moines, Iowa 50316

Consumer Protection Division
Office of the Attorney General
State House
10th and Harrison Streets
Topeka, Kans. 66612

Division of Consumer Protection
Department of Law
State National Bank Building, 5th Floor
Frankfort, Ky. 40601

Office of Consumer Protection
P.O. Box 44091
Baton Rouge, La. 70804

Bureau of Consumer Protection
Department of Business Regulation
State House
Augusta, Me. 04333

Division of Consumer Protection
Office of the Attorney General
1 South Calvert Street
Baltimore, Md. 21202

Executive Office of Consumer Affairs
1413 John W. McCormack State Office
  Building
1 Ashburton Place
Boston, Mass. 02108

Consumers' Council
Hollister Building
108 West Allegan Street
Lansing, Mich. 48933

Office of Consumer Services
Department of Commerce
Metro Square Building
7th and Robert Streets
St. Paul, Minn. 55155

Consumer Protection Division
Department of Agriculture and Commerce
1603 Walter Sillers Building
550 High Street
Jackson, Miss. 39202

Office of Consumer Services
Department of Consumer Affairs, Regulation,
  and Licensing
505 Missouri Boulevard
P.O. Box 1157
Jefferson City, Mo. 65101

Consumer Affairs Division
Department of Business Regulation
805 North Main Street
Helena, Mont. 59601

Consumer Protection Division
Attorney General's Office
State Capitol
Lincoln, Neb. 68509

Consumer Affairs Division
Department of Commerce
201 South Fall
Las Vegas, Nev. 89701

Consumer Protection Division
Office of the Attorney General
208 State House Annex
Capitol Street
Concord, N.H. 03301

Division of Consumer Affairs
Department of Law and Public Safety
1100 Raymond Boulevard
Newark, N.J. 07102

Consumer Protection Division
Office of the Attorney General
Bataan Memorial Building
P.O. Box 2246
Santa Fe, N.M. 87501

Consumer Protection Board
Executive Department
99 Washington Avenue
Albany, N.Y. 12210

Consumer Protection Division
Department of Justice
Justice Building
P.O. Box 629
Raleigh, N.C. 27602

Department of State Laboratories and
  Consumer Affairs
26th and Main Streets
Bismarck, N.D. 58505

Division of Consumer Protection
Department of Commerce
Borden Building
180 East Broad Street
Columbus, Ohio 43215

Department of Consumer Affairs
460 Jim Thorpe Office Building
2101 North Lincoln Boulevard
Oklahoma City, Okla. 73105

Consumer Services Division
Department of Commerce
Labor and Industries Building
Capitol Mall
Salem, Ore. 97310

Bureau of Consumer Protection
Department of Justice
301 Market Street
Harrisburg, Pa. 17101

Consumer's Council
365 Broadway
Providence, R.I. 02909

Department of Consumer Affairs
2221 Devine Street
P.O. Box 5757
Columbia, S.C. 29250

Division of Consumer Protection
Department of Commerce and Consumer Affairs
Capitol Building
Pierre, S.D. 57501

Division of Consumer Affairs
Department of Agriculture
Ellington Agricultural Center
Hogan Road
Nashville, Tenn. 37220

Antitrust and Consumer Protection Division
Office of the Attorney General
Supreme Court Building
P.O. Box 12548, Capitol Station
Austin, Tex. 78711

Consumer Protection Division
Office of the Attorney General
236 State Capitol
Salt Lake City, Utah 84114

Consumer Protection Division
Office of the Attorney General
109 State Street
Montpelier, Vt. 05602

Office of Consumer Affairs
Department of Agriculture and Commerce
825 East Broad Street
Richmond, Va. 23219

Consumer Protection
Office of the Attorney General
Dexter Horton Building
Seattle, Wash. 98104

Consumer Protection Division
Department of Agriculture
E-111 State Capitol
1800 Kanawha Boulevard, East
Charleston, W.Va. 25305

Bureau of Consumer Protection
Department of Agriculture, Trade, and Consumer Protection
801 West Badger Road
Madison, Wis. 53702

You might also go to the federal government with your complaint. But will it help you? You can try, but in 1975, fifteen federal agencies received 669,000 complaints.

To amend the consumer snags at the federal level, an independent consumer agency has been proposed. In 1976 a bill advocating the enactment of the necessary legislation passed both the House of Representatives and the Senate, but since it was an election year and both presidents Ford and Nixon were opposed to the agency, it was decided to table the bill until the new president (Jimmy Carter) took office. Unfortunately, the bill has still not been passed.

In the meantime, if you do approach a federal agency with a complaint, try,

154 / THE HELP BOOK

right from the start, to direct it to the correct office or agency. That will speed up handling of your complaint since one major cause for delays is the rerouting of mail. You might also want to try contacting your regional office of the federal agencies listed below since their volume of complaints might be smaller and any follow-up phone calls may prove to be less expensive.

The headings that precede each of the federal consumer offices that follow refer to the popular term for the kind of complaints and information requests that they handle. For all Washington, D.C. addresses, you can obtain the correct telephone number by dialing 202-555-1212; for toll-free numbers, dial 800-555-1212. For Maryland information, dial 301-555-1212. For the few other locations, check the area code directory in Chapter 52, *Telephone Directory*.

Advertising
Director, Bureau of Consumer Protection
Federal Trade Commission
Washington, D.C. 20580

Air Travel/Routes and Service
Director
Office of Consumer Advocate
Civil Aeronautics Board
Washington, D.C. 20423

Alcohol
Chief, Trade and Consumer Affairs Division
Bureau of Alcohol, Tobacco, and Firearms
Department of the Treasury
Washington, D.C. 20226

Alcoholism, Drug Abuse, and Mental Illness
Office of Public Affairs
Alcohol, Drug Abuse, and Mental Health Service
5600 Fishers Lane
Rockville, Md. 20857

Antitrust
Antitrust Division
Justice Department
Washington, D.C. 20530

Auto Safety and Highways
Director, Office of Public and Consumer Affairs
Transportation Department
Washington, D.C. 20590

National Highway Traffic Safety Administration
Washington, D.C. 20590
Toll-free hotline everywhere but Washington, D.C.

Banks
Federal Credit Unions:
  National Credit Union Administration
  Washington, D.C. 20456

Federal Reserve Banks:
  Office of Saver and Consumer Affairs
  Federal Reserve System
  Washington, D.C. 20551

Federally Insured Savings and Loans:
  Office of Housing and Urban Affairs
  Federal Home Loan Bank Board
  Washington, D.C. 20552

National Banks:
  Consumer Affairs
  Office of the Comptroller of the Currency
  Washington, D.C. 20219

State-Chartered Banks:
  Office of Bank Customer Affairs
  Federal Deposit Insurance Corporation
  Washington, D.C. 20429

Boating
Chief, Information and Administrative Staff
U.S. Coast Guard
Washington, D.C. 20590

Bus and Train Travel
Interstate Commerce Commission
Washington, D.C. 20423

Business
Office of the Ombudsman
Department of Commerce
Washington, D.C. 20230

Consumer Affairs
Small Business Administration
1441 L Street, N.W.
Washington, D.C. 20416

Children and Youth
Director of Public Information
Office of Human Development Services
Department of Health, Education, and
  Welfare
Washington, D.C. 20201

Commodity Trading
Consumer Hotline
Commodity Futures Trading Commission
2033 K Street, N.W.
Washington, D.C. 20581
Toll-free hotline in all states but Washington,
  D.C.

Consumer Affairs/Complaints
Director, Office of Consumer Affairs
Department of Health, Education, and
  Welfare
621 Reporters Building
Washington, D.C. 20201
(Serves as a consumer-complaint
  clearinghouse; refers any complaints not
  directly handled to the appropriate federal,
  state, or local offices.)

Copyrights
Copyright Office
Crystal Mall
1921 Jefferson Davis Highway
Arlington, Va. 20559

Credit
Director, Bureau of Consumer Protection
Federal Trade Commission
Washington, D.C. 20850

Crime Insurance
Federal Crime Insurance
Department of Housing and Urban
  Development
P.O. Box 41033
Washington, D.C. 20014
Toll-free hotline in all states but Washington,
  D.C.

Customs
Public Affairs Divisions
U.S. Customs
Washington, D.C. 20229

Drugs and Cosmetics
Consumer Inquiry Section
Food and Drug Administration
5600 Fishers Lane
Rockville, Md. 20857

Education Grants and Loans
Office of Public Affairs
Office of Education
Washington, D.C. 20202

Elderly
Administration on Aging
Washington, D.C. 20201

Employment and Job Training
Employment and Training Administration
Department of Labor
Washington, D.C. 20201

Energy
Director of Consumer Affairs
Department of Energy
Washington, D.C. 20461

Energy Efficiency
Information Office
National Bureau of Standards
Washington, D.C. 20234

Environment
Office of Public Affairs
Environmental Protection Agency
Washington, D.C. 20460

Firearms
Chief, Trade and Consumer Affairs Division
Bureau of Alcohol, Tobacco, and Firearms
Department of the Treasury
Washington, D.C. 20226

Fish Grading
National Marine Fisheries Services
Department of Commerce
Washington, D.C. 20240

Fish and Wildlife
Fish and Wildlife Service
Office of Public Information
Washington, D.C. 20240

Flood Insurance
National Flood Insurance
Department of Housing and Urban Development
Washington, D.C. 20410
Toll-free hotline in all states but Washington, D.C.

Food
Assistant Secretary for Food and Consumer Services
U.S. Department of Agriculture
Washington, D.C. 20250

Consumer Inquiry Section
Food and Drug Administration
5600 Fishers Lane
Rockville, Md. 20857

Fraud
Director, Bureau of Consumer Protection
Federal Trade Commission
Washington, D.C. 20580

Handicapped
Director, Division of Public Information
Office of Human Development Services
U.S. Department of Health, Education, and Welfare
Washington, D.C. 20201

Housing
Assistant Secretary for Neighborhoods
Voluntary Associations and Consumer Protection
U.S. Department of Housing and Urban Development
Washington, D.C. 20410
(Discrimination in housing complaints may be telephoned to the toll-free hotline in all states but Washington, D.C.)

Immigration and Naturalization
Information Services
Immigration and Naturalization Service
425 Eye Street, N.W.
Washington, D.C. 20536

Indian Arts and Crafts
Indian Arts and Crafts Board
Washington, D.C. 20240

Job Safety
Office of Public Affairs
Occupational Safety and Health Administration
Department of Labor
Washington, D.C. 20201

Mail Fraud or Undelivered Merchandise
Chief Postal Inspector
U.S. Postal Service
Washington, D.C. 20260

Mail Service
Consumer Advocate
U.S. Postal Service
Washington, D.C. 20260

Maps
Geological Survey
National Center
Reston, Va. 22092

Medicaid/Medicare
Health Care Financing Administration
U.S. Department of Health, Education, and Welfare
Washington, D.C. 20201

Mental Illness
Office of Public Affairs
Alcohol, Drug Abuse and Mental Health Service
5600 Fishers Lane
Rockville, Md. 20857

Metric Information
Information Office
National Bureau of Standards
Washington, D.C. 20234

Moving
Interstate Commerce Commission
Toll-free hotline in all states but Washington, D.C.

Parks and Recreation
National Forests:
   Forest Service
   U.S. Department of Agriculture
   Washington, D.C. 20250

National Parks and Historic Sites:
   National Park Service
   Washington, D.C. 20204

Recreation Areas:
   Office of Public Affairs
   U.S. Department of the Interior
   Washington, D.C. 20204

Passports
Passport Office
U.S. Department of State
1425 K Street, N.W.
Washington, D.C. 20524

Patents and Trademarks
Commissioner of the Patent Office or Commissioner of the Trademarks Office
U.S. Department of Commerce
Washington, D.C. 20231

Pensions
Office of Communications
Pension Benefit Guaranty Corporation
2020 K Street, N.W.
Washington, D.C. 20006

Labor Management Standards Administration
U.S. Department of Labor
Washington, D.C. 20210

Product Safety
Consumer Product Safety Commission
Consumer Services Branch
Washington, D.C. 20207
Toll-free hotlines

Radio and Television
Consumer Assistance Office
Federal Communications Commission
Washington, D.C. 20554

Runaway Children
1346 Connecticut Avenue, N.W.
Washington, D.C. 20036
National Runaway Hotline; toll-free phones

Solar Heating
National Solar Heating and Cooling Information Center
P.O. Box 1607
Rockville, Md. 20850
Toll-free hotlines

Social Security
Division of Public Inquiries
Social Security Administration
6401 Security Boulevard
Baltimore, Md. 21235

Stocks and Bonds
Consumer Liaison Office
Securities and Exchange Commission
Washington, D.C. 20549

158 / THE HELP BOOK

Taxes
Director, Taxpayer Service Division
Internal Revenue Service
Washington, D.C. 20224
Toll-free hotlines; ask for your state's hotline

Travel Information
U.S. Travel Service
U.S. Department of Commerce
Washington, D.C. 20230
Toll-free hotlines

Venereal Disease
Center for Disease Control
Technical Information Services
Bureau of State Services
Atlanta, Ga. 30333
Toll-free hotlines

Veterans Information
Veterans Administration
810 Vermont Avenue, N.W.
Washington, D.C. 20210
Toll-free hotlines in each state

Wages and Working Conditions
Employment Standards Administration
U.S. Department of Labor
Washington, D.C. 20210

Of all the government consumer-related offices, the following are singled out as providing the most consumer information of general interest:

Office of Consumer Affairs
U.S. Department of Health, Education, and Welfare
621 Reporters Building
Washington, D.C. 20201

Handles individual consumer complaints for all problem areas and also produces a wide range of consumer information: a newsletter ($4.00 a year); the column "Dear Consumer," which is distributed weekly to about 6,000 newspapers; the radio program "Help," which is heard on over 1,000 stations; position papers on consumer matters; publications, including a consumer education bibliography; and conferences.

LITERATURE: *Forming Consumer Organizations* ($.55); *Directory of Federal, State, County, City Government Consumer Offices*, 1977 edition ($1.00); *President's Committee on Consumer Interests, Office of Consumer Affairs, 1969–1977, An Eight-year Report; News for Consumers* (releases); *Guide to Federal Consumer Services* (free; some names and addresses are out of date, but the descriptions of the departments are succinct and clear).

Office of Consumer Inquiries
U.S. Food and Drug Administration (FDA)
U.S. Department of Health, Education, and Welfare
5600 Fishers Lane
Rockville, Md. 20857

The FDA publishes numerous free pamphlets and leaflets on food and drug safety, medical devices, cosmetics, biologics, radiation emission, and veterinary products. (See listing in Chapter 25, *Food and Nutrition*.) Single free copies of the following Consumer Memos are available by writing to the above address:

General
Bibliography
Brochures Available from FDA
Careers in FDA
Enforcing the Food, Drug, and Cosmetic Act
Fair Packaging and Labeling Act
Glazes and Decals on Dinnerware
How You Can Report to FDA
Prices and FDA
Quackery

Foods
Albumin, Sodium Erythorbate, and Lecithin
BHT and BHA as Food Additives
Facts About Food Poisoning
Facts About Meat Tenderizers and Monosodium Glutamate (MSG)
Food Colors (Color Additives)
Food Standards
Metric Measures on Nutrition Labels
The New Look in Food Labels
Nitrates and Nitrites
Nutrition Labeling—Terms You Should Know
Nutrition Labels and U.S. RDA
Safety of Cooking Utensils
Some Questions and Answers About Canned Foods
Some Questions and Answers About Food Additives
Standards for Packaged Nuts
Struvite Crystals and Canned Seafood
Symbols on Food Labels

Drugs
Antibiotics and the Food You Eat
Aspirin
Caffeine
Chloramphenicol
Dimethyl Sulfoxide (DMSO)
HCG and Weight Control
Hexachlorophene
Krebiozen
Laetrile
Self-Medication
Thalidomide
U Series—Dr. Henry Turkel

Devices
An Important Notice for Women Wearing an IUD
Relaxacizor

Cosmetics
Cosmetics
Facts About "Tanning" Products

HOW YOU CAN REPORT TO FDA*

If you come across a food, drug, medical device or cosmetic that you believe may be mislabeled, insanitary, or otherwise harmful, you will perform a public service by reporting it to the Food and Drug Administration.

The information consumers supply to FDA can and often does lead to detection and correction of a violation. Many products have been recalled or removed from the market because of action initiated by consumers.

FDA promptly investigates all consumer complaints. If a hazard is found, the Agency will seek to remedy the situation in accordance with the requirements of the law.

Here are some guidelines to follow in reporting hazards to FDA.

Before You Report

Before you report to FDA about the possible hazards of a product, ask yourself these questions:

- Have I used the product for its intended purpose?
- Did I follow the instructions carefully?
- Did an allergy contribute toward the bad effect?
- Was the product old or outdated when I opened it?

* Reprinted from *FDA Consumer Memo*.

Make sure you've taken all these factors into consideration before you report a possible hazard to FDA. The hazard may lie in improper use of a product rather than in an inherent defect.

If illness or injury has resulted from the use of the product, seek medical assistance at once, then be prepared to give the name, address, and telephone number of the doctor or medical facility consulted.

Where To Report

You may refer your complaint in writing or by phone to the nearest FDA field office or resident inspection station.

FDA has more than 130 offices throughout the United States. You can find the address and phone number of the nearest FDA office in the telephone directory under U.S. Government, Department of Health, Education, and Welfare, Food and Drug Administration.

If you wish, you may write about your complaint directly to FDA headquarters. The address is Food and Drug Administration, 5600 Fishers Lane, Rockville, Maryland 20857. The complaint will reach the correct person.

How To Report

Report your complaint as soon as possible after it occurs. Give your name, and the address and telephone number where you can be contacted.

State clearly what appears to be wrong.

Describe in as much detail as possible the label of the product. Give any code marks that appear on the container. For example, markings on canned foods are usually embossed or stamped on the lid.

Give the name and address of the store where the article was bought, and the date of purchase.

Save whatever remains of the suspect product or the empty container for your doctor's guidance or possible examination by FDA.

Retain any unopened containers of the product you bought at the same time.

Report the suspect product to the manufacturer, packer, or distributor shown on the label, and to the store where you bought it.

FDA has limited jurisdiction over certain consumer products. If you have complaints about any of the following, these are the agencies to inform:

- Suspected false advertising—*Federal Trade Commission.*
- Meat and poultry products—*U.S. Department of Agriculture.*
- Sanitation of restaurants—*local health authorities.*
- Products made and sold exclusively within a State—*local or State Health Department or similar law enforcement agency.*
- Suspected illegal sale of narcotics or dangerous drugs (such as stimulants, depressants, and hallucinogens)—*Drug Enforcement Administration, U.S. Department of Justice.*

- Unsolicited products by mail—*U.S. Postal Service.*
- Accidental poisonings—*Poison Control Centers.*
- Dispensing practices of pharmacists and drug prices—*State Board of Pharmacy.*
- Pesticides, air and water pollution—*Environmental Protection Agency.*
- Hazardous household products and toys—*Consumer Product Safety Commission.*

Office of the Ombudsman Consumer Affairs Division
U.S. Department of Commerce
Washington, D.C. 20230

An information clearinghouse on government reports or publications, and agencies dealing with business-related affairs, including the Bureau of Domestic Commerce of the Domestic and International Business Administration, the National Bureau of Standards, and other departments and bureaus within the U.S. Department of Commerce (see listing in Chapter 7, *Business Information*). The Office of the Ombudsman receives about 10,000 complaints a year from businesspersons and consumers.

LITERATURE: *Situation Report*, bulletins; pamphlets explaining the metric system; consumer booklets, such as "Household Furniture and Appliances: Basic Information Sources"; write for publications list.

Office of Public Information
Federal Trade Commission (FTC)
6th Street and Pennsylvania Avenue, N.W.
Washington, D.C. 20580

The FTC is an independent law enforcement agency charged by Congress with protecting consumers and businesspersons against anticompetitive behavior and unfair and deceptive business practices. Individual complaints should be addressed to its eleven regional field offices. The FTC's Bureau of Consumer Protection investigates and litigates such cases and has a national education program to alert consumers to deceptive trade practices and the role it plays in correcting them.

LITERATURE: "Your FTC: What It Is and What It Does"; "Buyer's Guide" leaflet series—includes "Don't Be Gypped," "Sold Out Supermarket Specials," and "Unordered Merchandise"; list of publications; "FTC News Summaries."

U.S Consumer Product Safety Commission
5401 Westbard Avenue
Washington, D.C. 20207

Toll-free numbers in all states (after-hours answering service). Investigates reports of injuries related to specific products and will refer calls to other agencies if the case does not fall within their area of concern. The commission publishes over 200 free fact sheets, leaflets, pamphlets, and booklets on a variety of safety and consumer concerns, including poisoning, specific chemicals, and utensils (see Chapter 45, *Safety*, for more complete listing).

LITERATURE: Write for publications and audio-visual listings.

NATIONAL CONSUMER INFORMATION SOURCES

There is a wealth of free or inexpensive literature available on all consumer matters from private corporations, national consumer organizations, and the federal government.

Private corporations are often overlooked as an information source. They are most frequently called on to answer inquiries or complaints relating to their specific products, but the larger corporations have consumer information services that write and offer booklets and pamphlets of general interest. For example, Johnson Wax, Consumer Services Center, Racine, Wis. 53403, has a variety of free publications on Johnson Products and such booklets as "Furniture Care," "How to Redecorate Your Room," "A Raft of Crafts," "Rug and Carpet Care," and so forth. You can drop a postcard to any company or business inquiring about their free offerings. Another information source originating in the business community is:

Chamber of Commerce of the United States
1615 H Street, N.W.
Washington, D.C. 20062

This agency publishes a variety of pamphlets and leaflets on consumer concerns, such as *Up With Consumers: A Consumer Redress* ($5.00), which includes the booklets "Consumer Complaint Mediation-Arbitration Programs" and "Handling Customer's Complaint."

The national consumer groups that follow lobby for legislative change and monitor current practices on a variety of consumer-related issues—from food prices to products. Most are not equipped to handle individual complaints but they offer information free or at low cost; write for more specific details to determine which group most closely matches your concerns.

American Council on Consumer Interests (ACCI)
162 Stanley Hall
University of Missouri
Columbia, Mo. 65201

A membership organization ($15.00 a year) that provides consumer education materials through its *Newsletter, The Journal of Consumer Affairs,* and Consumer Education Forum.

LITERATURE: Descriptive brochure.

Center for the Study of Responsive Law
P.O. Box 19367
Washington, D.C. 20036

The center is involved in research and investigative activities related to the protection and advancement of consumer interests but does not answer individual consumer complaints; they do, however, note the numbers of consumer complaints in a certain area. The center has investigated various federal agencies, such as the Food and Drug Administration and the Federal Trade Commission.

LITERATURE: Publications price list.

Consumer's Association
14 Buckingham Street
London WC2N 6DS, England

Publishers of a variety of consumer-oriented magazines, including *The Good Food Guide, Which? Money Which?* and *Drug and Therapeutics Bulletin*. It is supported by sale of publications.

Consumers Education and Protective Association International, Inc. (CEPA)
6048 Ogontz Avenue
Philadelphia, Pa. 19126

Established in 1965, CEPA has more than thirty-three branches following its pioneering self-help method of settling consumer complaints; $6.50 annual membership includes a one-year subscription to *Consumers Voice*.

LITERATURE: Fact sheets.

Consumers' Research Inc.
Bowerstown Road
Washington, N.J. 07882

Publishes *Consumers' Research* Magazine ($10.00 a year) and also makes available reprints of specific articles (minimum charge of $1.00 for each order). Consumers' Research is an independent, nonprofit, scientific, and educational organization supported solely by the consumers who buy its publications; it does not accept advertising.

LITERATURE: List of reprints available.

Consumers Union of United States, Inc.
256 Washington Street
Mount Vernon, N.Y. 10550

A nonprofit organization with nearly 200,000 members throughout the United States that is organized to provide information, education, and counsel about consumer goods and services and the management of family income.

LITERATURE: *Consumer Reports*, monthly ($11.00); *Consumers Union News Digest*, semimonthly ($36.00); reprints of *Consumer Reports* articles.

International Organization of Consumers Unions (IOCU)
9 Emmastraat
The Hague, Netherlands

Founded in 1960, this international organization seeks to promote international cooperation on all aspects of consumer information, education, and protection and acts as a clearinghouse for all consumer affairs information; over 100 consumer organizations in 44 countries are members. IOCU maintains the following committees: Testing; Education; Representation; Development; and Legal. Consumer organizations must meet certain standards to be eligible for membership.

LITERATURE: *Consumers Directory*, updated every two years (including information on some 200 national and local consumer organizations around the world); newsletters and reviews; monographs and special publications.

National Consumers League (NCL)
1028 Connecticut Avenue, N.W.
Washington, D.C. 20036

Founded in 1899, NCL has more than 15,000 members (individuals and organizations). There are two affiliates: Consumers League of New Jersey and Consumers League of Ohio. NCL has fought against child labor, unfair labor laws for women, inhumane working conditions and, more recently, for an end to abuses in the marketplace. Membership fees of $15.00 a year include a subscription to the bimonthly newsletter.

LITERATURE: Publications price list; *Model of Consumer Action* ($ .25); *Consumer Complaint Action Guide* ($ .25).

Public Citizen, Inc.
1346 Connecticut Avenue, N.W.
Washington, D.C. 20036

Founded in 1971, this is Ralph Nader's umbrella organization that supports action groups involved in education, community organization, litigation, research, and lobbying in the public interest with numerous subgroups, including Health Research Group, Tax Reform Research Group, Congress Watch, Public Citizen Litigation Group, Citizen Action Group, and Capital Hill News Service.

Telephone Users Association, Inc.
816 National Press Building
Washington, D.C. 20045

The association represents consumer interests in telephone rate cases. It provides telephone consultation on fighting rate increases before the Federal Communication Commission (FCC).

LITERATURE: *Telephone Tips* ($3.50).

As for federal government agencies, the most efficient way to find out if they publish free or inexpensive fact sheets, leaflets, pamphlets, and booklets of consumer interest is through the Consumer Information Center, established by the General Services Administration of the federal government to act as a federal clearinghouse of publications. Each year they issue four catalogs (one a season). Over 200 government publications are listed representing practically every agency. You can get advice on everything from choosing a nursing home to conserving heat in the winter to how to can fruit. The *Consumer Information Catalog* is free; send a postcard to:

Consumer Information Center
Pueblo, Colo. 81009

When the catalog arrives (it may take from two to five weeks), there will be a place for ordering booklets. (A maximum of twenty free titles are permitted; an unlimited number of low-cost publications may be ordered.) You will also be able to ask to be placed on the mailing list for the next free issue of the catalog.

This one-stop federal consumer information catalog will cut down on paperwork for the individual departments. You should also know that many government publications grew out of consumer requests for such information; therefore, if you feel there should be some published material on some problem, product, or concern, let them know about it.

You can also subscribe to *Consumer News* ($6.00 a year) or the *FDA Consumer* ($10.00 a year) through the Pueblo Center.

ADDITIONAL LITERATURE

The Alert Consumer: A Survival Guide for New Yorkers by Bruce Drake (1976). Newspaperbooks, 800 Third Avenue, New York, N.Y. 10022 ($2.10) or by mail, P.O. Box 34, Norwood, N.J. 07648 ($2.70; make checks payable to the New York News). Although the focus is on New York, the information in this clearly-written book is applicable elsewhere. Chapters include "Liability," "Jury Waiver," "Getting Help—How Government Agencies Work," "Small Claims Courts," and "Consumer Booklets."

Changing Times, monthly magazine. 1729 H Street, N.W., Washington, D.C. 20006 ($9.00 a year). First published in 1947, this popular magazine has many articles covering a wide range of consumer concerns and issues, often with follow-up sources for help and annotated recommended readings. There is no advertising. With each new subscription, you receive a free copy of 99 *New Ideas on Your Money, Job, and Living*.

A Consumer's Arsenal by John Dorfman (1976). Praeger Publishers, Inc., 383 Madison Avenue, New York, N.Y. 10017. ($3.95). An excellent guide by a former editor at *Consumer Reports*. It lists consumer protection, state-by-state, such as where to go with each complaint, from advertising to toys to vocational schools.

Consumer Sourcebook, edited by Paul Wasserman and Jean Morgan (1974). Gale Research Company, Book Tower, Detroit, Mich. 48226 ($35.00). The contents of this useful reference is best described by its subtitle: "A Directory and Guide to Government Organizations; Associations, Centers and Institutes; Media Services;

Company and Trademark Information; and Bibliographic Material Relating to Consumer Topics; Sources of Recourse; and Advisory Information." The bibliography in this 593-page book is annotated, complete with ordering addresses and prices.

Consumer Survival Kit, a series of booklets ($1.00 each) developed through the Consumer Survival Kit television series aired over the Public Broadcasting Service network. Send for a list of publications available from Consumer Survival Kit, P.O. Box 1978, Owings Mills, Md. 21117. A few of the titles in the series are "Weight Control," "How to Complain," "Advertising," and "Tots: Kid Consumer." (These booklets are now available in book form.)

A Guide to Consumer Action by Helen E. Nelson, Liz Allen, and Kit McNally (1978). Consumer Information Center, Department 686F, Pueblo, Colorado 81009 (Single copies free by sending a postcard). This booklet, issued by the Office of Consumers' Education of the U.S. Office of Education, contains valuable guidelines for becoming a better-educated consumer as well as advice on how to organize other consumers.

A Guide to Sources of Consumer Information by Sarah M. Thomas and Bernadine Weddington (1973). Information Resources Press, 2100 M Street, N.W., Washington, D.C. 20037. A good reference divided into two parts—published information and organizations.

Help: The Useful Almanac, edited by Arthur E. Rowse with Joel W. Makower and Ann Rosenthal (1977–78 edition). Distributed by Whirlwind Book Company, 80 Fifth Avenue, New York, N.Y. 10011 ($4.95). A handy directory with much factual information on consumer issues, such as environment, pollution content of the air, food additives, banks, and credit counseling, plus an introductory essay entitled "The Quality of Life."

1001 Valuable Things You Can Get Free, 10th ed., by Mort Weisinger, Bantam Books, Inc. 666 Fifth Avenue, New York, N.Y. 10019 ($1.95). Where you can obtain a wealth of free information, booklets, and products.

See also the following related chapters in *The Help Book:*

AGING
ANIMAL RIGHTS
BUSINESS INFORMATION
CITIZEN ACTION
COURTS
CRIME VICTIMS AND WITNESSES
DRUGS, SMOKING, AND DRUG ABUSE
FOOD AND NUTRITION
HEALTH
MEDIA AND COMMUNICATIONS
PARENTING
POLITICAL ACTION
SAFETY
TRANSPORTATION AND TRAVEL

14

COUNSELING

A family doctor may be able to refer you to a psychological counselor. If that is not possible, another way to find a counselor is to call the local branch of your community mental health association, which usually provides callers with the names of three therapists. However, this might not be the best way, since you will probably not be told anything about the therapists but their names and telephone numbers. Unanswered will be your questions about the therapist's qualifications, training, and therapeutic technique.

But if it is an emergency and you have to talk to "someone"—to give you the time to find a therapist for a longer counseling commitment—you might call a local confidential telephone crisis center, hot line, or crisis intervention service. These services are usually operated independently and privately by a mental health facility or by charitable or religious organizations. (See Chapter 47, *Suicide Prevention*.)

Medical schools with psychiatric residence training programs may also have free or low-cost counseling services as may graduate schools with Ph.D. programs in psychology. Many local women's groups also have peer counseling for stressful situations; contact your nearest group or branch of N.O.W. (National Organization for Women) to find out what services they offer, or for referrals. Other organizations offering counseling through their local branches are: American National Red Cross, YMCA, YWCA, YM-YWHA, and The Salvation Army. (See Chapter 40, *Multipurpose Organizations*.)

What type of counseling do you need? Although practically everyone thinks of "psychiatrist" when someone mentions the need for a therapist, there are several other categories of trained and licensed professionals who provide intensive, one-to-one or group counseling. They include psychologists, social workers, pastoral counselors, psychotherapists, and psychoanalysts. If you feel that talking to a close friend or self-help group does not help you sufficiently and if you have the name of a therapist that you might want to begin treatment with, first request a consultation, so you can evaluate the therapist and decide whether this kind of help is best for you.

What are some of the situations in which counseling might be needed? Any crisis that effects you so severely that your day-to-day functioning is directly impaired: death, or separation (e.g., divorce) from a close member of the family or a loved one; loss of a job; severe illness or impairment; the inability to handle the demands or problems of another person; school problems; suicidal thoughts.

Too often someone behaves stoically when something overwhelming occurs—to the detriment of those around him or her. In the case of the death of one child in a family including several children, for example, Harriet Sarnoff Schiff, author of *The Bereaved Parent*, writes, ". . . I was unable to come up with any situation in which parents had been able to put aside their own mourning to comfort these children" even though the siblings were also grieving. Schiff also noted that many marital problems, such as sexual unhappiness, may be related to a child's death. Since two persons with the same grief cannot support each other, Schiff believes that some outside intervention might relieve the long- and short-term demands placed on the bereaved family.

The decision to seek aid from a self-help group—a free service with counseling by peers—or professional treatment from a social worker, psychiatrist, psychoanalyst, or psychologist should *not* be based solely on money. Many insurance plans will pay $1,000 or more for psychiatric expenses and there are also clinics and mental health facilities that charge no fees or scale their rates. There are also hundreds of self-help books available on how to solve this or that emotional problem. But you should remember, if you are considering "bibliotherapy," that your problem is, in many ways, unique to you and that textbook solutions are, at best, intellectual and not emotional ones.

Services listed in this chapter offer referrals to or direct and immediate intervention—crisis counseling, self-help peer counseling, psychiatric or other professional assistance and treatment. Information resources are listed in Chapter 38, *Mental Health*.

PROFESSIONAL COUNSELING

Once you have decided what kind of counselor you want (art therapist? psychiatric social worker? psychoanalyst? psychologist? psychiatrist? marital counselor?) you might find out the name of a local professional with the specialty you have chosen through the variety of national organizations that provide referrals to member therapists. (These organizations will also direct you to local counseling services, clinics, groups, or training centers.) You can purchase their organizational directories, or check your local or citywide library to see if these directories are available in the reference section. For example, the United Fund or Public Welfare Association directories list all the local counseling services that are member agencies.

The following professional organizations will provide telephone or written referrals to counselors:

The American Association of Marriage and Family Counselors (AAMFC)
225 Yale Avenue
Claremont, Calif. 91711

Telephone or written requests are referred to local member groups, who will then provide the names of three counselors who are members of the AAMFC.

American Association of Pastoral Counselors (AAPC)
3 West 29th Street
New York, N.Y. 10001

Started in 1963, this is a national association of clergy of all faiths who have special counseling training. The association is divided into ten regional groups. An annual directory is available for referrals to approved church-related counseling centers.

LITERATURE: Bimonthly newsletter; *Journal of Pastoral Care*, quarterly.

American Psychiatric Association
1700 Eighteenth Street, N.W.
Washington, D.C. 20009

A professional association of psychiatrists whose main assistance to the public is through its membership directory and publications.

LITERATURE: *Membership Directory* ($8.00 to nonmembers), listing names and addresses of member psychiatrists alphabetically and by location; *Psychiatric News*, monthly newspaper; pamphlets, such as *Careers in Psychiatry*.

American Psychological Association
1200 Seventeenth Street, N.W.
Washington, D.C. 20036

A professional association of psychologists whose main nonmember service is its publications.

LITERATURE: *The APA Membership Register* ($15.00 to nonmembers); *Graduate Studies in Psychology* ($6.00); dozens of additional journals, a monthly newspaper, and other materials.

CONTACT Teleministries USA, Inc.
900 South Arlington Avenue
Harrisburg, Pa. 17109

A national organization with lay counselors throughout the country. In twenty-three states, 104 communities are served through seventy-four fully accredited centers staffed by trained volunteers who provide telephone counseling, information and referral, crisis intervention, and suicide prevention services. Each CONTACT center is operated twenty-four hours a day; in the past three years, an average of more than 10,000 calls per year were responded to by each center. There are at least seventy-five "listeners" at each CONTACT center. Each listener has at least fifty hours of training. The national headquarters will provide referrals to your nearest center, if you cannot find it in your local telephone directory, and also acts as an information clearinghouse on this type of counseling.

LITERATURE: Extensive descriptive brochures; "Directory of Centers and Services," updated periodically; publications price list; films available for small rental fees; booklets, brochures, posters, books.

Family Service Association of America (FSAA)
44 East 23rd Street
New York, N.Y. 10010

Founded in 1911, FSAA has about 300 member agencies located in forty-two states. FSAA's national office sets standards, accredits agencies, and provides consultation and information to help member agencies improve their programs. The national office will make referrals to local accredited agencies. It also publishes books and journals for the professional counselor, such as *Social Casework* and *The Family*.

LITERATURE: *Family Service Highlights*, bimonthly newsletter; *Plays for Living*, a drama/audience discussion package series on contemporary problems; an annually updated directory; *Strength to Families; Annual Report; Programs and Services;* descriptive brochures; publications list.

International Association of Counseling Services
1607 New Hampshire Avenue, N.W.
Washington, D.C. 20009

Information and referrals only through its *Directory of Counseling Services* ($4.50), updated annually, which lists over 400 accredited counseling agencies in the United States. The *Directory* gives basic information on the agencies, plus their fees, staff, and orientation.

National Association of Social Workers (NASW)
Publication Sales Department
1425 H Street, N.W., Suite 600
Washington, D.C. 20005

A professional organization of social workers with more than 55,000 members and over 173 local chapters.

LITERATURE: *Directory of Professional Social Workers* (1978), updated every few years; *Social Work*, journal ($20.00 a year for 6 issues for nonmembers; $4.00 single issue).

National Council on Family Relations
1219 University Avenue Southeast
Minneapolis, Minn. 55414

Provides the public with the names of counselors, but is basically an organization for professionals working with families.

National Marriage Guidance Council
Little Church Street
Rugby, Warwickshire CV21 3AP
England

The national headquarters for marriage counseling centers throughout the United Kingdom, which provide client-centered counseling, educational group work in the schools and with adult groups, and behavioral treatment for sexual disfunctions. Contributions are made at the client's discretion; a listing of councils is available.

As Americans become more able to openly face the emotional consequences of death, counseling centers for widows and widowers are being established in many communities attached to a variety of social service agencies or counseling centers. Check your local directory or Social Service Department to see if there is one in your community. There is no national organization making those referrals, but the following agency is acting as a resource for similar services being started, or now operating, in the United States:

Widows and Widowers Family Service
% Family Service of Westchester
470 Mamaroneck Avenue
White Plains, N.Y. 10605

Professional help for those with phobias, or fears, is also something you must explore at the local level. Two such programs are:

170 / THE HELP BOOK

Terrap, Inc.
1010 Doyle Street
Menlo Park, Calif. 94025

Phobia Self-Help Group
White Plains Hospital
Davis Avenue
White Plains, New York 10606

But there is a national program available for those who are afraid to fly:

Fearful Flyers
Pan American Airways, Inc.
30 South Michigan Avenue
Chicago, Ill. 60603

Fearful Flyers arranges seminars for people with a fear of flying, for a $100.00 fee.

PEER COUNSELING (SELF-HELP GROUPS)

(For specific self-help groups catering to particular problems, see the listings in those chapters—for example, *Alcoholism, Child Abuse, Gambling,* etc.)

The self-help movement is apparent not just by the proliferation of such self-help books as *How to Be Your Own Best Friend* and *I'm Okay, You're Okay,* but by the number of self-help counseling groups for everything from marriage problems to depression and gambling. But groups come and go, and, far more frequently, local chapters disband. However, there is a national clearinghouse on self-help groups:

National Self-Help Clearinghouse
Graduate School and University Center/CUNY
33 West 42nd Street, Room 1227
New York, N.Y. 10036

This clearinghouse publishes a newsletter about self-help groups around the country and also runs workshops and conferences. It is a joint activity of the New Human Services Institute, the Center for Advanced Study in Education, the Graduate School and University Center of the City University of New York, and *Social Policy* magazine. A New York City Self-Help Clearinghouse was established in July 1978.

LITERATURE: *Self-Help Reporter,* free bi-monthly newsletter (except July and August).

The following national self-help organizations have local affiliates throughout the country; the headquarters act as information clearinghouses and will refer you to your nearest local chapter if you cannot find it in your telephone directory:

Divorce Anonymous
P.O. Box 5313
Chicago, Ill. 60680

Started in 1949, this is a nonprofit, nonsectarian all-volunteer organization and information clearinghouse dedicated to helping those with marriage and divorce problems, providing peer counseling and rap sessions. There are individual chapters throughout the United States, based on the principles of the Twelve Steps of Alcoholics Anonymous. There are monthly, educational programs with professional speakers, self-help group meetings, and referrals to local groups.

LITERATURE: Descriptive brochure.

The Compassionate Friends
P.O. Box 3247
Hialeah, Florida 33013

National coordinators for the more than 100 chapters of this self-help counseling network for parents whose children have died. The original organization was founded in 1968 by an Anglican priest, in England. At the once-a-week meetings, parents have rap sessions to aid each other through their grief.

LITERATURE: "No death so sad" (free folder).

Neurotics Anonymous International Liaison, Inc.
Colorado Building
1341 G Street, N.W., Room 426
Washington, D.C. 20005

Founded in 1964, this international self-help organization provides peer counseling at its local branches for all people with mental and emotional problems. It is based on the Twelve Steps concept of Alcoholics Anonymous. Community education is another goal.

LITERATURE: Introductory literature is free to interested people; other literature is available at nominal cost; booklets include *Journal of Mental Health* ($4.00 a year).

Recovery, Inc., The Association of Nervous and Former Mental Patients
116 South Michigan Avenue
Chicago, Ill. 60603

A systematic method of self-help aftercare developed in 1937 by Dr. Abraham A. Low, this self-help organization is operated, managed, supported, and controlled by patients and former patients trained in the Recovery method. Check your telephone directory for your local branch or contact the headquarters for referrals.

LITERATURE: International directory of group meeting information; new inquiries receive descriptive form letter and price list of available publications, cassettes, and books.

Schizophrenics Anonymous International (SA)
Box 913
Saskatoon, Saskatchewan
Canada

This is the headquarters for branches of SA throughout the United States and Canada. It makes referrals to local self-help groups. SA is based on principles similar to Alcoholics Anonymous.

LITERATURE: Descriptive brochures.

The following sampling of local free or sliding scale-fee counseling services, arranged by state, suggests the diversity of sources you might explore (universities, religious groups, police department special units, women's centers, mental health facilities, etc.):

Crisis Center of Jefferson County
3600 Eighth Avenue South
Birmingham, Ala. 35222

Fairbanks Crisis Clinic Foundation
Box 832
Fairbanks, Alaska 99707

Police Crisis Intervention Specialists
Scottsdale Police Department
3739 North Civic Center Plaza
Scottsdale, Ariz. 85251

Soteria Project/MRI
555 Middlefield Road
Palo Alto, Calif. 94301

Widow-Widower Outreach Program
Jewish Family & Children's Service
1600 Scott Street
San Francisco, Calif. 94115

Community Crisis and Information Center
626 Remington Street
Fort Collins, Colo. 80521

Dade Family Therapy
950 E. 56th Street
Hialeah, Fla. 33013

Central Crisis Center
P.O. Box 6393
Jacksonville, Fla. 32205

We Care, Inc.
112 Pasadena Place
Orlando, Fla. 32804

Carroll Crisis Intervention Center
201 Presbyterian Avenue
Carrollton, Ga. 30117

Ravenswood Hospital Community Mental
  Health Center
Widow/Widower Outreach Program
4550 North Winchester
Chicago, Ill. 60640

Crisis Center
112½ East Washington Street
Iowa City, Iowa 52240

Crisis Line
1528 Jackson Avenue
New Orleans, La. 70130

Passage Crisis Center
Alternatives and Counseling Program
Montgomery County Health Department
8500 Colesville Road
Silver Spring, Md. 20910

Washtenaw County Community Mental
  Health Center
2929 Plymouth Road
Ann Arbor, Mich. 48105

SOS Crisis Center
114 North River Street
Ypsilanti, Mich. 48197

Walk-In Counseling Center, Inc.
2421 Chicago Avenue South
Minneapolis, Minn. 55404

Life Crisis Services, Inc.
7438 Forsyth Suite 210
St. Louis, Mo. 63105

Central New Hampshire Community Mental
  Health Services, Inc.
5 Market Lane
Concord, N.H. 03301

O.C.E.A.N., Inc.
Western Community Development Center
R.D. 1, Box 102, Route 527
Jackson, N.J. 08527

Communication—Help Center
Kean College of New Jersey
Morris Avenue
Union, N.J. 07083

Bereavement and Loss Center of New York
170 East 83rd Street
New York, N.Y. 10028

Jewish Board of Family and Children's
  Services
120 West 57th Street
New York, N.Y. 10019

Save A Marriage (SAM)
41 Central Park West
New York, N.Y. 10023

Outside-In Sociomedical Aid Station
1236 S.W. Salmon
Portland, Ore. 97205

Help, Inc.
638 South Street
Philadelphia, Pa. 19147

Tooele County Crisis Center
P.O. Box 429
Tooele, Utah 84074

Connections
2800 North Pershing Drive
Arlington, Va. 22201

Community Service Officers Program
1810 E. Yesler
Seattle, Wash. 98102

TAP Line (Troubles And Problems)
Luther Hospital
310 Chestnut Street
Eau Claire, Wis. 54701

The Dane County Mental Health Center
31 South Henry Street
Madison, Wis. 53703

ADDITIONAL LITERATURE

The books and pamphlets in this section are divided into the following categories: Therapy and Therapeutic Process; Self-Help; Love, Marriage, and Divorce; and Death and Dying.

THERAPY AND THE THERAPEUTIC PROCESS

A Complete Guide to Therapy: From Psychoanalysis to Behavior Modification by Joel Kovel, M.D. (1976). Pantheon Books, 201 East 50th Street, New York, N.Y. 10022 ($3.95). Summarizes the multitude of therapies with a key feature, "Practical Synopsis," a paragraph addressing what kinds of problems are best suited to a particular type of therapy; glossary included.

Consumer's Guide to Mental Health by Brian Mishara and Robert Patterson, M.D. (1977). Times Books, Three Park Avenue, New York, N.Y. 10016 ($9.95).

Crisis: Psychological First Aid for Recovery and Growth by Ann S. Kliman (1978). Holt, Rinehart and Winston, 383 Madison Avenue, New York, N.Y. 10017 ($8.95). Kliman is Director of the Situational Crisis Service of the Center for Preventive Psychiatry in Westchester County, New York, and she has written a sensitive and helpful book based upon the individuals and families in crisis that she has counseled. The author's plea for psychological first aid in such unexpected crises as suicide, illness, death, violent injury, and discovery of handicaps is effectively supported throughout the book. Includes an annotated bibliography.

A Layman's Guide to Psychiatry and Psychoanalysis by Eric Berne, M.D. (1947, 1971). Grove Press, Inc., 196 West Houston Street, New York, N.Y. 10014 ($1.50). Freud in popular, but in-depth, language.

The Psychotherapy Maze: A Consumer's Guide to the Ins and Outs of Therapy by Otto Ehrenberg and Miriam Ehrenberg (1977). Holt, Rinehart and Winston, 383 Madison Avenue, New York, N.Y. 10017 ($3.95). An excellent guide for anyone who is thinking about starting psychotherapy or is already in treatment. It provides basic information on the wide range of orientations available (Freudian, Adlerian, Reikian, etc.) as well as what to expect from therapy, common problems and questions, and when to terminate therapy; bibliography included.

Twelve Therapists: How They Live and Actualize Themselves, edited by Arthur Burton and Associates (1972). Jossey-Bass, Inc., Publishers, 615 Montgomery Street, San Francisco, Calif. 94111. A fascinating collection of autobiographical essays by therapists. Their candid writings help to "humanize" your view of the professional healer.

SELF-HELP

Columnist Ann Landers, who screens hundreds of self-help books to write her syndicated column, named the following dozen books as the best, "on the basis of their content, simplicity of language, and practicality. Each is unclinical and easy to understand."* Check your local library for these titles:

Looking Out for Number One by Robert J. Ringer

Learning to Say Good-by: When a Parent Dies by Eda LeShan

The Trouble Book by Eugene Kennedy

Living With Everyday Problems by Eugene Kennedy

A Marital Therapy Manual by Peter A. Martin, M.D.

The Dance-Away Lover by Daniel Goldstine, Katherine Larner, Shirley Zuckerman, and Hillary Goldstine

*Reprinted from *Bookviews* (September 1977), published by R. R. Bowker Co., a Xerox Company. Copyright © 1977 by Xerox Corporation.

You Can Fight Cancer and Win by Jane E. Brody et al.

Sex After Sixty: A Guide for Men and Women in Their Later Years by Robert Butler and Myrna Lewis

Prison of My Mind by Barbara Field

Peace From Nervous Suffering by Dr. Claire Weekes

You Can Do It by Sen. William Proxmire

What to Do and When—and Why by Marjabelle Young Stewart and Ann Buchwald

How to Cope With Crises by Theodore Irwin (1971). Public Affairs Pamphlets, 381 Park Avenue South, New York, N.Y. 10016 ($.50). Irwin defines what crisis is and what the most severe crises are—serious illness or accident; job loss of the family breadwinner; divorce or separation; being "jilted"; premature birth; death of a loved one; news of a fatal illness; and psychological emergencies of children. The author also offers suggestions on how to help yourself or how others can help you.

Kicking the Fear Habit: Using Your Automatic Orienting Reflex to Unlearn Your Anxieties, Fears and Phobias by Manuel J. Smith (1977). Dial Press, 245 East 47th Street, New York, N.Y. 10017 ($8.95). Covers fear of flying, heights, animals, sex, and crowds with how-to-stop advice, such as using a tape recorder or orienting oneself to bodily touch.

Partners in Coping: Groups for Self and Mutual Help by Elizabeth Ogg (1978). Public Affairs Committee, Inc., 381 Park Avenue South, New York, N.Y. 10016 ($.50). A pamphlet that surveys the self-help movement, with listings of resources and descriptions of sample groups, such as Alcoholics Anonymous and the Delancey Street Foundation.

Passages: Predictable Crises of Adult Life by Gail Sheehy (1976). Bantam Books, Inc., 666 Fifth Avenue, New York, N.Y. 10019 ($2.50). An important book about the traumas of middle years, previously ignored by many writers.

Self-Rescue by John Cantwell Kiley, introduction by William F. Buckley, Jr. (1977). McGraw-Hill Book Company, 1221 Avenue of the Americas, New York, N.Y. 10020 ($7.95). How to get out of a snowbank, survive a tragedy, keep from wounding yourself, avoid suicide, cure an ulcer, be cheerful, have a decent future, trust yourself, and so forth.

Shyness: What It Is, What to Do About It by Philip G. Zimbardo (1977). Addison-Wesley Publishing Company, Inc., Reading, Mass. 01867 ($5.95). Zimbardo, professor of social psychology at Stanford University, studied shyness for five years, an affliction that eight million people are believed to have, and offers suggestions about how to cure shyness as well as how to prevent it.

The Strength in Us: Self-Help Groups in the Modern World by Alfred H. Katz and Eugene I. Bender (1976). New Viewpoints/Franklin Watts, 730 Fifth Avenue, New York, N.Y. 10019 ($6.95). A collection of articles about self-help in general as well as reports on specific self-help groups, such as Recovery, Inc.

The Total Man: The Way to Confidence and Fulfillment by Dan Benson (1977). Tyndale House Publishers, Inc., 336 Gundersen Drive, Wheaton, Ill. 60187 ($3.95). If you can overlook the book's religious overtones and biblical quotations, there is some solid information here for women as well as men on how to avoid becoming "all work and no fun."

LOVE, MARRIAGE, AND DIVORCE

The Art of Loving by Erich Fromm (1974). Harper and Row, 10 East 53rd Street, New York, N.Y. 10022 ($1.50). Still the classic, simple exploration of loving oneself as the first step toward loving someone else.

The Divorce Experience by Morton and Bernice Hunt (1977). McGraw-Hill Book Company, 1221 Avenue of the Americas, New York, N.Y. 10020 ($8.95). A comprehensive book that grew out of Morton Hunt's 1966 study, *The World of*

the Formerly Married. Good epilogue about what divorce really means.

For Better, For Worse: A Feminist Handbook on Marriage and Other Options by Jennifer Baker Fleming and Carolyn Kott Washburne (1977). Charles Scribner's Sons, 597 Fifth Avenue, New York, N.Y. 10017 ($7.95). A collection of practical information on everything from the history of marriage laws, motherhood, and alternative lifestyles to family violence; thorough resource and bibliography sections.

"The Failing Marriage" produced and directed by Alan Summers, M.D., Ph.D. (1977). Transactional Dynamics Institute, P.O. Box 414, Glenside, Pa. 19038. Rental $30; Purchase $300. A twenty-minute color film available in 16mm or ¾" video cassette. Through transactional analysis and replays, a couple's fight is used to demonstrate poor communication techniques.

Intimate Relations by Murray S. Davis (1973). The Free Press, Macmillan Publishing Co., Inc., 866 Third Avenue, New York, N.Y. 10022 ($3.95). A sociologist's descriptions of how people relate to each other, from the coming together of two strangers, to the "do me a favor," "making up," and "breaking up" stages.

Learning to Love Again by Mel Krantzler (1978). T. Y. Crowell, 666 Fifth Avenue, New York, N.Y. 10019 ($7.95). The author of the best-selling *Creative Divorce* in this book offers advice to divorced persons who are ready to find new relationships.

A New Look at Love by Elaine Walster and G. William Walster (1978). Addison-Wesley Publishing Company, Inc., Reading, Mass. 01867 ($5.95). Researchers Walster and Walster explore the difference between passionate and companionate love.

No-Fault Marriage by Marcia Lasswell and Norman M. Lobsenz (1976). Ballantine Books, 201 East 50th Street, New York, N.Y. 10022 ($1.95).

Women in Transition: A Feminist Handbook on Separation and Divorce by Women in Transition, Inc., coordinated by Carolyn Kott Washburne (1975). Charles Scribner's Sons, 597 Fifth Avenue, New York, N.Y. 10017 ($7.95). Comprehensive book to help anyone through the separation-divorce process with chapters on children in transition, how to find legal services, economic problems, and so on. Good bibliographic and resource sections.

DEATH AND DYING

About Dying by Sara Bonnett Stein, in cooperation with Gilbert W. Kliman, M.D., photos by Dick Frank (1974). Walker and Company, 720 Fifth Avenue, New York, N.Y. 10019 ($5.95). A book for children with accompanying text for parents and teachers; a sensitive, touching, and simple explanation of death that explores, from a child's vantage point, some of the traditions and questions surrounding death.

The Bereaved Parent by Harriet Sarnoff-Schiff (1977). Crown Publishers, Inc. One Park Avenue, New York, N.Y. 10017 ($7.95). Meant to give comfort and insight to a parent who has lost a child, this book could apply to anyone who has lost a close relative or friend. Its strength is the author's honesty and personal experience with tragedy.

A Death in the Family by Elizabeth Ogg (1976). Public Affairs Committee, Inc., 381 Park Avenue South, New York, N.Y. 10016 ($.50). A well-written and sensitive pamphlet that should give comfort and useful information to anyone suffering from loss or counseling those who are going through grief.

The Dying Person and the Family by Nancy Doyle (1972). Public Affairs Committee, Inc., 381 Park Avenue South, New York, N.Y. 10016 ($.50). Doyle summarizes the findings of those who have counseled dying patients, such as Kübler-Ross and Saunders.

Help for Your Grief by Arthur Freese (1977). Schocken Books, Inc., 200 Madison Avenue, New York, N.Y. 10016 ($9.95). A popular discussion of the predictable reactions to the death of a loved one by his or her survivors.

Learning to Say Good-by: When a Parent Dies by Eda LeShan, illustrated by Paul Giovanopoulos (1976). Macmillan Publishing Company, Inc., 866 Third Avenue, New York, N.Y. 10022 ($5.95). A book for the whole family to read and discuss, although it is primarily written for bereaved children. Nicely written and illustrated.

On Death and Dying by Elisabeth Kübler-Ross, M.D. (1969). Macmillan Publishing Company, Inc., 866 Third Avenue, New York, N.Y. 10022 ($2.25). The basic work to describe the stages of emotional response to learning someone close is dying as well as what the person who is dying goes through and the post-death traumas. Based on the author's interviews with terminally ill cancer patients, it is uplifting and inspirational.

See also the following related chapters in *The Help Book:*

ADOPTION AND FOSTER CARE
AGING
ALCOHOLISM
ARTS
BATTERED ADULTS
CHILD ABUSE
CHILDBEARING
CHILDREN
CRIME VICTIMS AND WITNESSES
DRUGS, SMOKING, AND DRUG ABUSE
GAMBLING
JUVENILE DELINQUENCY
MENTAL HEALTH
OFFENDERS AND EX-OFFENDERS
SEX EDUCATION AND THERAPY
SUICIDE PREVENTION
ADDITIONAL RESOURCES

15

COURTS

The best time to go to court is when you do not have to—as an educational experience for you and your family. Understanding how the judicial system in the United States operates, or fails to, is a key to building a more effective and representative system. A good way to begin learning about the courts is to volunteer in a court-watching or monitoring project in your area. To find out what court-watching activities there are where you live, contact your local District Attorney's Office, citizen's crime commission, bar association, or those national organizations listed in this chapter's directory for the proper referral.

The most dramatic court encounters are seen on television or found in the real-life experiences of crime victims or those accused, or found guilty, of a crime. But even if none of these extreme real-life situations happens to you, you may find yourself in court for one of the more everyday reasons, such as:

- serving on a jury
- appearing as a witness
- suing someone or defending yourself in a suit
- solving problems such as divorce, child custody or support, adoption, inheritances, or such minor offenses as traffic violations.

The American system of justice is a difficult one to understand because of its dualistic nature—the federal courts and the state courts operate independently—and entire books are necessary to explain the complex differences between the two systems. In addition, since each state has its own criminal code, few generalities can be made. A few popular and more detailed accounts of the court system are suggested in the bibliography at the end of this chapter, and some basic information on two key common experiences—being a juror or appearing as a witness—follows.

When you are called to serve on a jury, you probably will receive a form letter asking you to report to the court clerk's office. You will then fill out a questionnaire and if you are later called to serve—unless you have legitimate and serious extenuating excuses—you are expected to report back to the court for the duration of your jury duty. You either receive a daily fee or, if your employer is paying you during your jury duty, you do not receive a fee or are asked to pass the fee on to your employer.

The process by which potential jurors are questioned is known as the *voir doire*, and it can be harrowing for you if you feel the questions are intended to violate your privacy. But this procedure is a safeguard for both sides to see whether a juror has any biases or previous knowledge that would cause him or her to prejudge that case. Many jurors are also unaware that they are permitted to ask questions at any time during the trial proceedings. Lawyers and judges might not like a juror's interruptions, but it is better to get a point of law or evidence cleared up than to let it go unanswered until the deliberations.

If you are asked to be a witness—or if you volunteer to become a witness or if you are subpoenaed to be one—you will also receive financial compensation for any time you spend as a witness. (This varies from court to court, but some pay transportation, lunch, and a daily fee rate. Expert witnesses may receive very high fees. As in being a juror, if your employer is also paying you, you are generally not allowed to keep both fees.)

The witness is the backbone of our judicial system and a recognition of the poor treatment he or she once received in the courts has led to the establishment of witness information bureaus around the country—attached to district attorneys' offices, police departments, or privately run independent community services. They will answer your questions about your rights and any available compensation that you might be eligible to receive.

Various pamphlets and leaflets are available for witnesses, and many courts have adopted a witness rights card, such as the one below that is distributed in Colorado, to tell the witness exactly what he or she is entitled to:

YOU HAVE THE RIGHT:

- To be free from intimidation.
- To be assisted by your criminal justice agencies.
- To be told about available compensation for court appearances.
- To be told about all available help from Social Service or volunteer agencies.

COURT WATCHING AND WITNESS AID

There are two national programs that will provide direct referrals and information, if you wish to volunteer in the courts:

VIP (Volunteers in Prevention, Prosecution, Probation, Prison, and Parole)
National Council on Crime and Delinquency (NCCD)
200 Washington Square Plaza
Royal Oak, Mich. 48067

A membership fee of $3.00 helps support and promote this one-to-one national court-watching volunteer effort. If there is a program already under way in your area, VIP will advise you of it. If not, they will give you information on how to organize one. Some 2,500 programs are now operating in courts, jails, prisons, and juvenile institutions.

LITERATURE: *VIP Examiner*; descriptive leaflets and booklets.

National Criminal Justice Volunteer Resource Service
University of Alabama
P.O. Box 1935
University, Ala. 35486

Through the University of Alabama, VIP-NCCD, and the W. K. Kellogg Foundation, this national education and training center offers materials to help local volunteers in the courts and in the field of corrections. Audiovisual cassettes are available on loan for fees of less than $7.00.

LITERATURE: Descriptive pamphlets and brochures.

STATE COURTS

Based solely on the number of cases handled each year, the state courts are where most of the legal action is in the United States, but it is the federal courts that get most of the publicity. It is also at the state level that the court system in the United States becomes confusing—even to lawyers. What is legal in California might be illegal in Delaware. In some states, civil and criminal cases are handled in separate courts; in others, they are handled by one court. State systems may also include other local courts, such as the justices of the peace or the small claims courts. But there is one generality—every state has one court as the highest court of appeals, although the name might vary from "Supreme Court" to "Court of Appeals" to "Supreme Court of Errors."

Since no generalities about state civil or criminal law are possible, it is important to know what the laws are *in your own state*. (Youth, for example, are quick to become familiar with differing state drinking laws, but most other legal differences between states are far more complicated.) You cannot obey the law unless you know what it is. Perhaps the trend, observed in some states like New York, of having court decisions and contracts written in conventional English rather than "legalese" will help popularize laws that are now obscure.

For direct assistance on the courts, consult your local telephone directory under "Courts" or a specific court, such as Municipal or Civil or County, Criminal, Family or Domestic Relations, Small Claims Court, etc. (Chicago even has a "Smoker's Court" for those charged with violating a city ordinance prohibiting

180 / THE HELP BOOK

smoking in certain public places.) Although it will save steps if you start at the local level, rather than starting at the state level and working down, each state has an office for court administration. You might consult that office for more general information or local referrals:

The state agencies for court administration are as follows:

Department of Court Management
800 South McDonough Street
Montgomery, Ala. 36130

Alaska Court System
303 K Street
Anchorage, Alaska 99501

Supreme Court
State Capitol
West Wing
Phoenix, Ariz. 85007

Judicial Department
Supreme Court
Justice Building
Capitol Grounds
Little Rock, Ark. 72201

Administrative Office of the Courts
Judicial Council
4200 State Building Annex
455 Golden Gate Avenue
San Francisco, Calif. 94102

Judicial Department
323 State Capitol
200 East Colfax Avenue
Denver, Colo. 80203

Supreme Court
State Library and Supreme Court Building
231 Capitol Avenue
Hartford, Conn. 06115

Administrative Office of the Courts
Supreme Court Building
1112 King Street
Wilmington, Del. 19801

The Clerk of the Superior Court
Superior Court of the District of Columbia
Fifth Street between E and F Streets, N.W.
Washington, D.C. 20001

Supreme Court
Supreme Court Building
Tallahassee, Fla. 32304

Administrative Office of the Courts
84 Peachtree Street
Atlanta, Ga. 30303

Supreme Court
Judiciary Building
417 South King Street
Honolulu, Hawaii 96813

Administrative Office of the Courts
Supreme Court Building
451 West State Street
Boise, Idaho 83720

Administrative Office of the Illinois Courts
℅ Supreme Court Building
118 West Edwards Street
Springfield, Ill. 62706

Judiciary Department
State House
200 West Washington Street
Indianapolis, Ind. 46204

Supreme Court
Capitol Building
1007 East Grand Avenue
Des Moines, Iowa 50319

Supreme Court
State House
10th and Harrison Streets
Topeka, Kans. 66612

Administrative Office of the Courts
Court of Appeals
State Capitol
Frankfort, Ky. 40601

Judicial Council Building
Supreme Court
301 Loyola Avenue
New Orleans, La. 70112

Supreme Judicial Court
Court House
P.O. Box 368
Portland, Me. 04112

Administrative Office of the Courts
Courts of Appeal Building
361 Rowe Boulevard
Annapolis, Md. 21401

Supreme Judicial Court
Court House
55 Pemberton Square
Boston, Mass. 02208

State Court Administrative Office
Law Building
525 West Ottawa Street
Lansing, Mich. 48913

Supreme Court
Capitol Building
Aurora Avenue and Park Street
St. Paul, Minn. 55155

Supreme Court
Supreme Court Building
Jefferson City, Mo. 65101

State Court Administrator
State Capitol
Lincoln, Neb. 68509

Supreme Court
Supreme Court Building
Carson City, Nev. 89701

Supreme Court
Supreme Court Building
Concord, N.H. 03301

Administrative Office of the Courts
State House Annex
Trenton, N.J. 08625

Administrative Office of the Courts
Supreme Court Building
Santa Fe, N.M. 87503

Office of Court Administration
270 Broadway
New York, N.Y. 10007

Administrative Office of the Courts
Justice Building
Raleigh, N.C. 27602

Supreme Court
State Capitol
Bismarck, N.D. 58505

Supreme Court
State Office Tower
30 East Broad Street
Columbus, Ohio 43215

Supreme Court of Oklahoma
1 State Capitol
Lincoln Boulevard
Oklahoma City, Okla. 73105

State Court Administrator
Supreme Court Building
1147 State Street
Salem, Ore. 97310

Court Administrator
1414 Three Penn Center Plaza
15th and Market Streets
Philadelphia, Pa. 19102

Office of the State Court Administrator
Providence County Courthouse
250 Benefit Street
Providence, R.I. 02903

Supreme Court Building
1301 Gervais Street
P.O. Box 11788
Columbia, S.C. 29211

Supreme Court
Capitol Building
Pierre, S.D. 58505

Tennessee Supreme Court
300 Supreme Court Building
401 Seventh Avenue, North
Nashville, Tenn. 37219

Texas Supreme Court
Supreme Court Building
P.O. Box 12248, Capitol Station
Austin, Tex. 78711

Office of the Court Administrator
250 East Broadway, Suite 240
Salt Lake City, Utah 84111

Supreme Court
111 State Street
Montpelier, Vt. 05602

Supreme Court of Virginia
Supreme Court Building
1101 East Broad Street
Richmond, Va. 23219

Administrator for the Courts
Temple of Justice
Olympia, Wash. 98504

Court Administrator
E-404 State Capitol
1800 Kanawha Boulevard, East
Charleston, W.Va. 25305

Administrative Director of Courts
110 E. Main Street
Madison, Wis. 53703

Court Coordinator
Supreme Court Building
Capitol Avenue at 23rd Street
Cheyenne, Wyo. 82002

The following national organization is involved in projects designed to modernize and standardize procedures in the state courts:

National Center for State Courts
300 Newport Avenue
Williamsburg, Va. 23185

An information clearinghouse, but primarily a research center studying the modernization of court operations and the improvement of justice at the state and local levels. It functions as an extension of the state court systems, working for them at their direction.

LITERATURE: *Report*, newsletter: *State Court Journal*, quarterly for those involved in the field of judicial administration; *Facets of the Jury System: A Survey* ($5.50); *Small Claims Courts* ($1.00); send for publications price list.

CIVIL COURT

If civil and criminal matters are divided into two court jurisdictions in your state, it is advisable to know precisely what is available to you locally on the civil level. For example, is there a housing court within civil court where you can bring about a tenant-initiated action? Are you living in one of the thirty states that has a small claims court?

The major difference between a civil and a criminal suit is that in a civil case, the plaintiff (person bringing suit) can be you; in a criminal case, the plaintiff is always the state, not an individual. Some crimes are also civil wrongs and since damages are awarded to persons in civil suits, many victims may decide to sue civilly, whether or not a criminal action was taken by the state. (For example, your "friend" hit you on the head and you had to be hospitalized; therefore you sue him for a civil wrong of assault and battery so that you could use the judgment money to pay medical bills.)

Another major difference between a civil and criminal case is that in a civil case, the jury must usually believe one side more than the other by "a preponderance of evidence." In a criminal case, to be convicted, the defendant must be found guilty "beyond a reasonable doubt," a much harder standard.

Unless you are taking a case to small claims court (where a lawyer is not necessary), you will want to consult an attorney before going into any civil court (see How to Find a Lawyer in Chapter 36, *Legal Services*).

SMALL CLAIMS COURT

Any person who feels that he or she has received unfair treatment from a business or individual can file a suit, without hiring a lawyer, in the small claims court in your area. This court is usually part of the civil division of the municipal court of your county or city. The maximum amount of money involved in small claims cases varies from $100 to $1,000 in property damage cases to slightly higher amounts for unfulfilled contracts, accounts, and notes.

When should you use the small claims court? Only you can decide if it is worth the time and effort involved. (Studies have shown that, after receiving a favorable decision, it is often hard to collect the awarded damages.) But the following examples are typical cases that might be brought to small claims court:

- Your landlord failed to fix a leak in your bedroom, causing you to awake in a bed soaked with water, get a cold, and incur a large doctor's bill.
- You advanced your floor polisher $75.00 for a job he never returned to do.
- You bought a typewriter for $250.00 that does not work, and the company will not repair it or refund your money.
- The dry cleaners ruined your clothing, valued at $50.00, but will not reimburse you.

The procedure for filing a small claims case will vary but generally you must go to the clerk's office and fill out a form stating who it is you wish to sue, why, and for how much. (To avoid later problems, be sure you have the exact name of the person or firm you are suing. If you have doubts, stop at the county clerk's office and check the business filing name of the person or firm you are suing.) After completing the form, you will pay a filing fee (usually less than $10.00) and a notice will be delivered to the person you are filing against (there may be another small fee—less than $10.00—for delivery of the notice.) When your case is called (it may take about a month), the judge will hear both sides of the story. Be sure to bring any evidence and witnesses you have (receipts, damaged clothing, sales tickets) along with you.

If you win your case, you will receive a judgment for the amount of damages listed on your claim plus the fees you paid to bring the case to court. In some states, if the defendant does not pay you within thirty days of receiving notification of the court's decision, you will be allowed to go back to court and sue the defendant for three times the amount of the original award, plus legal costs. If you lose the case, and the defendant had a lawyer, you will be charged court costs. Otherwise, "you just lose the case," as one clerk explained it.

For information on how to file in your area, contact the small claims court or information office of the municipal court through your telephone directory. There may also be descriptive pamphlets on small claims court available through local consumer groups or the Consumer Affairs Bureau of your county or city government. Your local affiliate of the Public Interest Research Group (PIRG) may also be able to help you (see listings in Chapter 11, *Citizen Action*).

FAMILY COURT

What situations will appear in family court? Basically the jurisdiction of family court is all legal matters concerning family life: divorce and annulment, paternity actions, child custody, adoption, delinquency, child neglect, child support, and assault offenses in which victim and offender are members of the same family (although there is a movement to take assault cases out of family court and into criminal court).

In family court, the family court judge acts as both judge and jury, relying heavily on police officer and victim/witness testimony, and investigations by probation and court liaison officers to make a judgment. There are generally four procedures in the family court process: probation intake (which has the discretion to adjust the case and throw it out, if necessary); intake (which is similar to arraignment in adult criminal court); fact-finding hearing; and disposition of the case. The disposition might be ACD (Adjoinment and Contemplation of Dismissal), which usually gives a six-month period to see how the accused performs; probation; placement in a group home, prison, training school, private placement in another type of institution, or with other relatives; a fine; or a dismissal. (For a fuller discussion of juvenile court, see Chapter 33, *Juvenile Delinquency*.)

CRIMINAL COURT

The following federal agencies and national organizations provide information on various aspects of the criminal justice (court) system:

American Bar Association
Circulation Department
1155 East 60th Street
Chicago, Ill. 60637

Offers publications, such as *Modernizing Criminal Justice Through Citizen Power*, on how to improve the criminal justice system. Send for publications price list for additional listings.

American Bar Association
Section on Criminal Justice
1800 M Street, N.W.
Washington, D.C. 20036

General information about citizen involvement to improve the criminal justice system, such as the free pamphlet by Philip B. Singer, *How to Mobilize Citizen Support for Criminal Justice Improvement*. *Criminal Justice* is a newsletter available upon payment of membership dues by qualified persons, including lawyers, law students, and those involved in the criminal justice system.

American Judicature Society
200 West Monroe Street, Suite 1606
Chicago, Ill. 60606

A national clearinghouse for news and developments in the administration of justice.

LITERATURE: *AJS Joint Enterprise,* newsletter available by subscription that includes roundups on citizen activities around the country, new publications, and listings of major meetings and conferences.

Crime and Justice Courses by Newspaper
University Extension
University of California, San Diego
La Jolla, Calif. 92093

A program funded by the National Endowment for the Humanities that offers to newspapers a series of educational articles on crime, law, punishment, and justice. A local community or four-year college or university then cooperates with the newspapers and offers credit for a course based on the articles that the newspaper runs.

LITERATURE: Free descriptive material; *Reader* ($6.95); *Study Guide* ($2.95); *Booklet of Newspaper Articles* ($2.50); audio cassettes ($9.95); *Source Book* ($2.50).

National Criminal Justice Reference Service
Law Enforcement Assistance Administration
U.S. Department of Justice
Washington, D.C. 20530

The service will answer a specialized inquiry on the criminal justice system—courts, corrections, police—by providing a computerized search and print out; registered users will receive information; copies of available documentation on request; onsite library use open to qualified persons.

Search Group, Inc.
National Clearinghouse for Criminal Justice Information Systems
1620 35th Avenue
Sacramento, Calif. 95822

Free technical assistance provided to agencies planning or undertaking transfer of criminal justice information systems; promotion of effective use of national criminal justice resources.

LITERATURE: Newsletter and descriptive brochures.

U.S. Department of Justice
Office of Public Information
Constitution Avenue and 10th Street, N.W.
Washington, D.C. 20530

Will answer inquiries about activities of the Justice Department and its subordinate agencies, such as the Law Enforcement Assistance Administration (LEAA), Drug Enforcement Administration, Bureau of Prisons, and Federal Bureau of Investigation, and about federal criminal and civil cases. Some information requests will be forwarded to other agencies.

LITERATURE: News releases, pamphlets, and other documents; annual reports; yearly *Uniform Crime Reports; Two Hundred Years of American Criminal Justice: An LEAA Bicentennial Study* ($3.00).

FEDERAL COURTS

When someone mentions "federal courts," many people think of the Supreme Court with its nine eminent justices. But the Supreme Court, although it is the highest court (or court of last resort) to which state or federal cases can appeal, is not the only federal court. The federal justice system is also composed of ninety-four U.S. district courts and eleven courts of appeal staffed by about 400 federal judges. Cases must first be argued in these courts before going to the Supreme Court.

What matters will come up in federal district courts? Crimes such as tax evasion, drug dealing, robbery of banks insured by the federal government, conflicts between people in two different states where more than $10,000 is involved, and cases involving a matter of federal civil or criminal law.

The following federal offices provide information on the federal courts, including the Supreme Court:

Administrative Office of the United States Courts
Washington, D.C. 20544

This office answers inquiries on the federal court system and makes referrals to those individual courts when a specific case is not handled directly by the Administrative Office. It is concerned with the administration, operation, budget, and maintenance of the eleven U.S. courts of appeals, ninety-four U.S. district courts, and other special courts. It also administers the Public Defender Program, the Criminal Justice Act, the U.S. magistrates system, the Bankruptcy Act, and the federal probation system.

LITERATURE: *Federal Probation,* free quarterly journal with articles and book reviews; reports and statistical data on the business of the federal courts.

Federal Judicial Center
Dolley Madison House
1520 H Street, N.W.
Washington, D.C. 20005

Created by an act of Congress in 1967, this center's goal is to further the development and adoption of improved judicial administration in the U.S. courts; although court personnel are favored, all requests for information on any judicial administration area will be answered or referred to other sources. The center maintains a 5,000-book library that is available for on-site use or on a limited-loan basis.

LITERATURE: *The Third Branch,* monthly bulletin; annual reports; periodic reports and papers on judicial administration.

Supreme Court of the United States
Office of the Clerk
1st and East Capitol Streets, N.E., Room 17
Washington, D.C. 20543

Answers questions on recent decisions and status of pending cases; acts as a liaison between the Supreme Court, attorneys, and the public. The office maintains a library, but its use is restricted to members of Congress, attorneys for federal agencies, and members admitted to practice before the Supreme Court.

OUT-OF-COURT DISPUTE SETTLEMENTS

Because settling a dispute in a court of law is often time consuming, expensive, and formal, voluntary private solutions are becoming a more common way of handling grievances in civil and minor criminal matters. Two procedures—arbitration and mediation—are followed. In arbitration the parties agree beforehand to accept the arbiter's decision. In mediation there is an agreement to "consider" the mediator's opinion.

The most extensive service for settling disputes out of court is the National Center for Dispute Settlement, run by the American Arbitration Association, with branches in several major cities. Known as the 4-A Program, it seeks to keep lesser complaints from coming to trial. It is, however, strictly voluntary, and if the accused party does not agree to arbitration, the victim may still prosecute the original charge through the courts. The most common grievances handled by the program are neighbors' squabbles and simple assaults and invasion of privacy. A lawyer may be present at the hearings if desired. The mediator at the hearings can only advise the parties to moderate their demands so that they may reach an equitable solution.

In business-related grievances that you do not wish to take to court, you may consult your local Better Business Bureau to find out if they offer a free arbitration service (see listings in Chapter 13, *Consumer Affairs*). Similar problems, as well as landlord-tenant and agency complaints, may be resolved through the intervention of a local Call For Action program. (Consult your local telephone directory or see listings in *Consumer Affairs*.) Many colleges, universities, and law schools are forming "clinics" where volunteers, who have been through a training program, will also act as arbitrators or mediators.

You should also watch for the development of Neighborhood Justice Centers. The U.S. Department of Justice has been running test programs in Los Angeles, Atlanta, and Kansas City, and it seems probable that in the near future they will be administering additional community dispute centers staffed by non-court personnel and run outside the court system. The goal of these centers is to refer certain offenses away from the overcrowded municipal courts and have the disputes resolved through mediation. Since compliance is voluntary, the courts are still another resort if this step fails.

The following national organizations and federal agency provide information on dispute settlement and, through their regional or local offices, have direct services available:

Grassroots Citizen Dispute Resolution Clearinghouse (CDR)
1300 Fifth Avenue
Pittsburgh, Pa. 15219

A program of the Middle Atlantic Region of the American Friends Service Committee, CDR programs provide informal places where people's conflicts may be settled out of court.

CDR programs are being organized by community groups around the country.

LITERATURE: *The Mooter*, quarterly ($5.00); *Citizen Dispute Resolution Organizer's Handbook* ($2.00).

National Center for Dispute Settlement of the American Arbitration Association
1212 Sixteenth Street, N.W.
Washington, D.C. 20036

A national organization with regional offices in Philadelphia, Rochester, Boston, Cleveland, Los Angeles, San Francisco, Seattle, and Jackson, Mississippi, that resolve disputes through arbitration and mediation, including matrimonial and family matters, community disputes, and social problems.

LITERATURE: "A Businessman's Guide to Commercial Arbitration"; "How to Settle Business Disputes Painlessly"; "Family Dispute Services."

Federal Mediation and Conciliation Service
2100 K Street, N.W.
Washington, D.C. 20427

A federal agency established by law to assist in the settlement of labor and management disputes and to prevent or shorten work stoppages. Offices are maintained in eighty cities (see listings under U.S. Government in telephone directories). Federal law requires formal written notices to be filed regarding anticipated contract expirations.

LITERATURE: *Securing Labor-Management Peace Through Mediation* (leaflet).

ADDITIONAL LITERATURE

For popular articles on the courts, consult *The Readers' Guide to Periodical Literature* and the *Social Sciences and Humanities Index*. Also see the *Index to Legal Periodicals*, started in 1908 and covering more than 325 legal periodicals and bar association journals.

Call the Final Witness: The People vs. Darrell R. Mathes As Seen by the Eleventh Juror by Melvyn Bernard Zerman (1977). Harper & Row, 10 East 53rd Street, New York, N.Y. 10022 ($8.95). While serving as a juror on a murder trial, the author kept a private journal. After the defendant's acquittal, Zerman interviewed him, his family, and the defense attorneys. *New York Times* reporter Tom Wicker called this book "one of the most authentic studies of a jury in deliberation that I know about."

Courts by the National Advisory Commission on Criminal Justice Standards and Goals (1973). Superintendent of Documents, U.S. Government Printing Office, Washington, D.C. 20402 ($3.95). A reference book on the courts, part of a six-volume series, that also offers suggestions for improvement.

Courts on Trial by Jerome Frank, with an introduction by Edmond Cahn (1963). Atheneum, 122 East 42nd Street, New York, N.Y. 10017 ($2.95). Well-written philosophical study of the courts "intended for intelligent nonlawyers as well as lawyers." Frank explores the jury system, judges, legal reasoning, legal education, and "the unblindfolding of justice."

The Criminologist, quarterly. American Society of Criminology, 1314 Kinnear Road, Suite 212, Columbus, Ohio 43212 (free to members of the society; $7.00 to nonmembers; $1.50 single copy). Information on conferences, workshops, and newsworthy items concerning the criminal justice community; book reviews; original articles and summaries of research.

Directory of Criminal Justice Information Sources by Kevin E. O'Brien, Guy Boston, and Marvin Marcus (1976). National Institute of Law Enforcement and Criminal Justice, Law Enforcement Assistance Administration. Available from Superintendent of Documents, U.S. Government Printing Office, Washington, D.C. 20402 ($2.35). Annotated listing of private and public criminal justice information sources around the country.

Federal and State Court Systems—A Guide by Fannie J. Klein (1977). Ballinger Publishing Company, 17 Dunster Street, Cambridge, Mass. 02138 ($7.95). Published for The Institute of Judicial Administration, law professor Klein describes the dual court system as well as the state court systems in nine states. Klein also summarizes the history of the petit jury and the development and functions of the grand jury.

How Our Laws Are Made by Charles J. Zinn (1974). Revised and updated by Edward F. Willett. Superintendent of Documents, U.S. Government Printing Office, Washington, D.C. 20402 ($1.05). The best-selling government pamphlet that explains the legislative process.

The Judicial Process, 3rd ed., by Henry J. Abraham (1975). Oxford University Press, 200 Madison Avenue, New York, N.Y. 10016 ($6.50). Good, comprehensive study of the U.S. court system as compared to the courts of England and France; for the more serious reader.

Justice System Journal. Institute for Court Management, 1405 Curtis Street, Suite 1800, Denver, Colo. ($12.00 a year; $18.00 for institutions). Articles reporting on empirical research concerning the development of innovative policies in the justice system, including evaluations of police, prosecutorial, medical, correctional, and defender programs.

The Jury Returns by Louis Nizer (1966). Pocket Books, 666 Fifth Avenue, New York, N.Y. ($1.25). Noted trial lawyer Nizer, also author of *My Life in Court*, presents a good picture of what happens in a court case.

National Employment Listing Service for the Criminal Justice System. Texas Criminal Justice Center, Sam Houston State University, Huntsville, Tex. 77341 ($30.00 a year for institutions; $16.00 for individuals). A monthly booklet announcing employment opportunities around the country for those in the criminal justice community, including professors, court officers, probation and correction officers, law enforcement and administrative personnel.

Sue the Bastards: The Victim's Handbook by Douglas Matthews (1973). Arbor House Publishing Company, Inc., 641 Lexington Avenue, New York, N.Y. 10022 ($2.95).

What Can You Do About Quarreling? by Harry Milt (1965). Public Affairs Pamphlets, 381 Park Avenue South, New York, N.Y. 10016 ($.50). Common sense pamphlet discussing approaches to disputes that might pervent their escalation into court-related conflicts.

What to Do Until the Lawyer Comes by Stephan Landsman, Donald McWherter, and Alan Pfeffer (1977). Anchor Books/Doubleday, Garden City, N.Y. 11530 ($2.95). A well-written popular book on a highly complex subject that simplifies the legal system without too much distortion.

See also the following related chapters in *The Help Book*:

ADOPTION AND FOSTER CARE
AGING
BATTERED ADULTS
BUSINESS INFORMATION
CHILDREN
CIVIL RIGHTS AND DISCRIMINATION
CONSUMER AFFAIRS
CRIME VICTIMS AND WITNESSES
JUVENILE DELINQUENCY
KIDNAPPING, MISSING PERSONS, AND RUNAWAYS
LAW ENFORCEMENT
LEGAL SERVICES
OFFENDERS AND EX-OFFENDERS

16

CRIME PREVENTION

In 1977 daytime burglaries in the city of St. Louis decreased 33 percent. Much of the credit for that improvement goes to a citizens' group called the Women's Crusade Against Crime, which acted on the belief that "much crime results from its increased profitability." One of the ways the Women's Crusade sought to make crime less profitable was Operation Ident(ification). One of the Crusaders told the police department about Operation Ident in the early seventies. Together, they popularized it. In Operation Ident, citizens are instructed to engrave their state drivers license number on their valuables, so that if, say, a stereo or typewriter is stolen and later recovered, the owners can identify and reclaim the item. So effective is Operation Ident that when $1 million worth of stolen property was recovered by the St. Louis police department in October 1977, all but $20,000 worth was returned to its owners.

The "blue label," displayed on home and apartment doors to indicate that the household participates in Operation Ident, also discourages burglars. One burglar, who confessed to eighty-seven successful crimes, admitted that he would always avoid the "blue label" when deciding which homes or apartments to rob.

In addition to Operation Ident, the St. Louis Women's Crusade has been involved in several other crime-prevention programs. The Corrections Committee, for example, concentrates on one-to-one interaction between Crusade volunteers and imprisoned men and women. To reduce recidivism by improving job-related skills, the volunteers have also tutored juveniles and men and women awaiting trial or already serving sentences in jail.

Crime Blockers, another Crusade program, has thousands of participants throughout St. Louis. Together with police community relations officers, the Crusaders recruit and train citizens to be the extra "eyes and ears" of the police. Police officers conduct a one-day session in which they explain how to describe a suspected criminal in a thorough enough way to be useful to the responding police officers. Volunteers are also taught to distinguish a priority call, such as an attempted burglary or assault, from a nuisance call, such as barking dogs or poor sanitation. The civilian Crime Blockers each have a number, and when they call in with a complaint or crime report, the radio dispatcher gives that call priority since the caller has had police department training. The caller's identity is known to only one or two high-ranking officials, so he or she is unafraid of possible reprisals for "informing."

Closely allied to Crime Blockers is the Secret Witness Program, in which witnesses may report crimes anonymously to a hot line staffed by Women's Crusade members. Tips from secret witnesses have helped uncover drug dealings, prostitution rings, and pornography distribution centers.

Thousands of success stories that have proven the Women's Crusade Against Crime's effectiveness as a crime-fighting volunteer effort will probably never make newspaper headlines. A youth jailed for the first time on a minor drug offense, for example, is given counseling so that his first offense may be his last. A fifteen-year-old prostitute is helped to return to her family, and the house of prostitution where she worked is permanently closed down. Senior citizens attend workshops arranged by the Women's Crusade and learn how to avoid being the victims of con games. As the Women's Crusade grows—in numbers as well as in effectiveness—the citizens of St. Louis are finding that their city is a more desirable place in which to live, work, and raise their children.

HOW TO BEGIN A CRIME-FIGHTING CRUSADE

1. Learn about crime and the criminal justice system by talking with officials, observing the courts and the police in operation, and by reading.

2. Set specific objectives and organize your group into subgroups to implement them.

3. Publicize your group's formation and accomplishments through TV and radio stations, newspapers, other organizations, local politicians, government officials, and business leaders.

4. Develop a realistic budget. If funding is not available from private or public foundations and membership dues are insufficient, consider allying yourself with a preexisting organization.

5. Develop proven programs to carry out your crime-reduction goals, such as Operation Ident, Crime Blockers, ex-offender counseling, and crime prevention seminars.

6. Keep a written record of your goals and achievements. Distribute a newsletter to maintain contact with members.

7. Orientation programs for new volunteers should be held at times that allow both working and home-bound members to attend.

OPERATION IDENTIFICATION

Check with your local police department to find out what marking system they follow. (Some use social security numbers, some follow that with a code for the county or state, some use telephone numbers, some use state driver's license numbers.) Engrave that number on all your valuables. You may usually borrow the engraving tool from your local citizens crime prevention group, police department, or other community or legal service participating in this nationwide effort. Then make a list of those valuables, identifying characteristics, and take a photograph—using an instant camera if possible so that there is no negative—and attach it to your list. If jewelry and other items are too small for your number, invent a symbol, use a special pen, and clearly indicate on your record sheet what those items are and how they can be identified. Keep this sheet in a safe, concealed place, but one that will be accessible in case of theft, loss, or fire. The following is a typical example of an entry on your list:

Type of Item	Number Inscribed	Date of Purchase	Description
SONY tape recorder	Social security number-NYC	9/1/78	Model #TC-105 Silver with black leather case; initials **SAV** engraved on lower-right-hand side

The following two national programs, one volunteer and non-profit and the other a business organization, offer information and/or direct help in implementing an operation identification program:

GFWC HANDS UP Program
General Federation of Women's Clubs
1728 N Street, N.W.
Washington, D.C. 20036

This is a national volunteer effort to halt crime carried out on the local level by the thousands of GFWC chapters. Operation Identification is encouraged, as is community awareness of the crime problem and simple advice on how to avoid common personal and property crime.

LITERATURE: *Checklist* pamphlet.

Identifax Nationwide Registry
Director of Marketing
600 Third Avenue
New York, N.Y. 10017

A private company offering one-time lifetime registration coverage of valuables in the event of theft for a fee of $10.00 to individuals. Registrants are provided with an engraving tool and a booklet, "How to Protect Your Home from Burglars."

DIRECT HELP IN PREVENTING CRIME

The nearest source of direct, free help in preventing crime is your local police department or sheriff's office. The community affairs office or the crime prevention unit will have free literature available on crime prevention. They will also talk to you personally, or to any formal or informal citizens group, on all aspects of crime prevention, on how to start a citizen crime commission, on how citizens can help the police in fighting crime, on home security checks, and on how to be a less-likely victim. Some departments are more seasoned and professional at this than others. Some have slide shows, films, and trained lecturers; other will only talk from experience and on-the-job training. On a national level, information and educational materials on crime prevention are available through this law-enforcement related organization:

National Neighborhood Watch Program
National Sheriffs' Association
1250 Connecticut Avenue, N.W.
Washington, D.C. 20036

Started in 1972, this program provides information on burglaries to increase citizen awareness of this kind of crime and of the means by which it can be prevented. Their goals are to train citizens to better secure their homes, apartments, and property and to develop neighborhood action programs whereby neighbors maintain a continuous watch over one another's property and assist the police by reporting suspicious persons and activities. They encourage citizen cooperation with law enforcement agencies by increased reporting of crime.

LITERATURE: *National Neighborhood Watch Program Manual; How to Protect Your Home When You Are Away From Home;* warning decals; door labels, "Member Neighborhood Watch"; telephone stickers.

There are also crime prevention programs being run by such organizations as the Girl Scouts, Boys' Clubs, Boy Scouts of America, YMCA's, YWCA's, and 4-H Clubs. Check your local telephone directory for your nearest chapter to find out what is offered and how you can get involved. College campuses are also starting crime prevention programs. Contact the campus security guards for information or advice in starting one on your campus. Also check if you have a local crime prevention club in your area. Local police departments will also make free home or business security checks.

194 / THE HELP BOOK

Since crime prevention has to be a cooperative effort, knowing about your police department and how you can assist it will be of enormous help to the police—for example, knowing how to describe a suspect. It's not enough to say someone was tall and blonde, not in cities of three million or even in towns of thirty thousand. Charts and training programs are often available to private citizens. A sample suspect identification chart is given below.

A national clearinghouse for many of the crime prevention citizens' commissions is:

National Association of Citizens Crime Commissions
1336 Hickory Street
Waukegan, Ill. 60085

Founded in 1952 by eleven Citizens Crime Commissions, this is a loose-knit organization of about twenty-five member commissions. It is nonpolitical and nonpartisan. Its member groups primarily act as community watch-dogs or monitors keeping an eye on government, courts, law enforcement agencies, and the elected or appointed officers in those three areas to see that they perform their functions effectively, efficiently, and in the best interests of the citizens they serve. The National Association acts as an information clearinghouse to assist fledgling groups interested in organizing; arranges visits to those groups by nearby commissions whenever possible; provides information on the nearest commission and whom to contact; and helps with problems and specific inquiries.

LITERATURE: "How to Organize and Operate a Citizens Crime Commission" ($1.50).

Membership includes the following crime commissions (mostly citywide):

Phoenix Citizens Crime Commission
Phoenix, Ariz.

Tucson Urban Area Crime Commission
Tucson, Ariz.

Burbank Citizens' Crime Prevention
   Committee
Burbank, Calif.

KEEP THIS "SUSPECT IDENTITY CHART" NEAR YOUR TELEPHONE TO ASSIST YOU IN REPORTING CRIME.

SEX_____
RACE_____
HEIGHT_____
WEIGHT_____
COMPLEXION_____
EYES____COLOR____EYEGLASSES
(ALERT____NORMAL____DROOPY)

VISIBLE SCARS, MARKS, TATTOOS

AGE_____

METHOD OF ESCAPE

DIRECTION_____
LICENSE_____
VEHICLE DESCRIPTION

REMARKS

- HAT
- HAIR COLOR—CUT
- BEARD OR MOUSTACHE—SIDEBURN
- SHIRT
- NECKTIE
- JACKET OR COAT
- WEAPON
- RIGHT OR LEFT HANDED
- TROUSERS
- SHOES

Reprinted courtesy of the Crime Prevention Bureau of the Police Department, Mansfield, Ohio.

Delaware Citizens Crime Commission, Inc.
Wilmington, Del.

Crime Commission of Greater Miami
Miami, Fla.

Metropolitan Atlanta Crime Commission, Inc.
Atlanta, Ga.

Chicago Crime Commission
Chicago, Ill.

Lake County Citizens Crime Commission
Waukegan, Ill.

Wichita Crime Commission
Wichita, Kan.

Metropolitan Crime Commission of New
 Orleans
New Orleans, La.

Saginaw Citizens Crime Commission
Saginaw, Mich.

Mississippi Coast Crime Commission
Gulfport, Miss.

Kansas City Crime Commission
Kansas City, Mo.

Citizens Crime Commission of Philadelphia
Philadelphia, Pa.

Law Enforcement Commission of Chatta-
 nooga-Hamilton County
Chattanooga, Tenn.

Citizens Against Crime
Abilene, Tex.

Greater Dallas Crime Commission
Dallas, Tex.

Tarrant County Crime Commission
Fort Worth, Tex.

Citizens Council Against Crime
Seattle, Wash.

In addition to local-level programs, direct assistance in preventing crime is also provided by statewide crime prevention programs. They are administered through a variety of state government offices, including the criminal justice coordinating councils, the state Attorney General's office, and independent private groups. The first four statewide programs were the Florida Help Stop Crime!, started in May 1972, the Illinois Crime Prevention Officers Association, December 1972, and the Minnesota Crime Watch and the Texas statewide crime prevention coordinating program, both established in July 1973.

The following states have statewide crime prevention programs:

Community Education Crime
 Prevention Project
University of Alaska
3211 Providence Center
Criminal Justice Center
Anchorage, Alaska 99504

Arkansas Crime Check
3701 West Roosevelt
P.O. Box 4005
Little Rock, Ark. 72204

Colorado Crime Check
2002 South Colorado Blvd.
Denver, Colo. 80222

Help Stop Crime
Office of the Att. General
The Capitol
Tallahassee, Fla. 32304

GBI State Crime Prevention
 Program
1001 International Blvd
Suite 800
Atlanta, Ga. 30354

Georgia State Patrol
P.O. Box 1456
Atlanta, Ga. 30301

Illinois Law Enforcement Commission
Crime Prevention Specialist
120 South Riverside Plaza
Chicago, Ill. 60606

Indiana Crime Prevention
State Office Bldg R 705
Indianapolis, Ind. 46204

Iowa Bureau of Criminal Investigation
Robert Lucas State Office Bldg.
Des Moines, Iowa 50319

Kentucky Crime Check
Kentucky Dept of Justice
Office of Crime Prevention
625 Comanche Trail
Frankfort, Ky. 40601

Governor's Commission on Law Enforcement & Administration of Justice
Executive Plaza 1
Cockeysville, Md. 21030

Michigan State Police
Crime Prevention Unit
714 South Harrison Rd.
East Lansing, Mich. 48823

Minnesota Crime Watch
Governor's Comm. on Crime Prevention & Control
818 Transportation Building
St. Paul, Minn. 55155

Crime Prevention Program
Governor's Commission on Crime & Delinquence
G.A.A. Plaza
Building #3
169 Manchester Street
Concord, N.H. 03301

Office of Crime and Delinquency Prevention
N.Y. State Bureau of Municipal Police
Executive Park Tower
Stuyvesant Plaza
Albany, N.Y. 12203

North Dakota Crime Watch
Box B
Bismarck, N.D. 58505

Operation Crime Alert
30 East Broad Street
26th floor
Columbus, Ohio 43215

Crime Prevention
Community Relations & Citizen Involvement in Texas
Governor's Office
Criminal Justice Division
411 West 13th Street
Austin, Tex. 78701

Utah Crime Check
255 South Third East
Salt Lake City, Utah 86111

Washington Crime Check
Attorney General's Off.
Dexter Horton Bldg.
Seattle, Wash. 98104

There are also hundreds of local community-based crime prevention groups throughout the country. Check with your community or block association for names and phone numbers or try your telephone directory. One exemplary local program is:

CLASP (Citizens Local Alliance For A Safer Philadelphia)
1405 Locust Street
Philadelphia, Pa. 19102

The emphasis in this group, formed in 1972, is on organizing a block before there is a criminal tragedy; the group seeks to build a support structure on a block and in a neighborhood so that people come to know each other and respond more easily when there is trouble. CLASP has a speakers bureau; provides general crime prevention and crime victim compensation information; and it sponsors the Neighborhood Block Safety Program, Operation Identification, Freon Horns, and the Senior Citizen Crime Prevention Program. Membership is $5.00 for an individual; $10.00 for a block. It is a model program that can serve as an example for other cities.

LITERATURE: Fact sheets—Toward a Safer Philadelphia; Neighborhood Block Safety Program; Hints For Human Safety; Wallets and Handbags—Safety Hints; Senior Citizen's Safety Hints; Operation Identification; Any Block Can.

The following national crime prevention organizations also have local groups throughout the country; they will provide educational materials on crime prevention and on starting a crime-fighting program in your area:

AFL-CIO Labor Participation Program
1101 Fifteenth Street, N.W.
Washington, D.C. 20005

Started in 1971 and coordinated through the National Council on Crime and Delinquency (NCCD), this national program provides direct technical assistance to central labor councils around the country in an effort to get them involved in the development and operation of criminal and juvenile justice projects with individual councils deciding on their own programs. It is also concerned with the development of citizen volunteer corps in crime prevention (NCCD specialists provide technical assistance). Some of the programs include the Community Assistance Program for Ex-Offenders (CAPE) in Des Moines, Iowa, and the Leo Perlis Remotivation Center in Cleveland, Ohio.

LITERATURE: Fact sheets; "Toward a Safer America," pamphlet.

Project offices of the AFL-CIO Labor Participation Program are:

201 South Fifth Street, 2nd floor
Terre Haute, Ind. 47807

1216 West Sycamore
Kokomo, Ind. 46901

2000 Walker
Des Moines, Iowa 50317

6001 Gulf Freeway, Suite C120
Houston, Tex. 77023

Kiwanis International
"Safeguard Against Crime"
101 East Erie Street
Chicago, Ill. 60611

The national headquarters provides educational materials to its local chapters for implementing a "Safeguard Against Crime" educational program for local citizens. Started in 1976, the first phase covered eight basic steps that Kiwanis International recommended for voluntary organizations who wanted to initiate the Safeguard Against Crime program. The second phase is involved with educating children and young people, as well as parents and teachers about those aspects of crime that concern young citizens. The CAQ (Crime Awareness Quotient) is part of the second phase; spot broadcast announcements are available for increasing citizens' CAQ.

LITERATURE: "Safeguard Against Crime: A Project Guide for Voluntary Organizations" ($1.00); "Safeguard Against Crime—II"

($1.00); "Law Enforcement Career Cop Program" (free fact sheets); "What is Your CAQ?" (free fact sheets); posters and flyers for mailing are available at low costs.

National Council on Crime and Delinquency (NCCD)
Continental Plaza
411 Hackensack Avenue
Hackensack, N.J. 07601

A national membership organization of about 60,000 citizens that coordinates crime prevention programs run by its local affiliates. The Hackensack headquarters, which maintains an extensive library, acts as an information clearinghouse on those programs as well as others on juvenile delinquency and crime. Other offices are as follows:

345 Park Avenue
New York, N.Y. 10022

703 Market Street, Room 1707
San Francisco, Calif. 94103

728 West Peachtree Street, N.W.
Atlanta, Ga. 30308

3409 Executive Center Drive, Suite 212
Austin, Tex. 78731

200 Washington Square Plaza
Royal Oak, Mich. 48067

LITERATURE: Booklets: *Citizen Action to Control Crime and Delinquency: Fifty Projects* and *How to Protect Your Home: A Guide to the Home Owner and Apartment Dweller*.

National Exchange Club
Crime Prevention Kit
3050 Central Avenue
Toledo, Ohio 43606

The National Exchange Club is a membership organization with 1,300 local chapters in fifty states whose members are business and professional persons committed to social improvement. "Counter Crime in Your Community" is one of five basic community service programs offered to its membership for local implementation. Public education material is distributed to chapter presidents to help in the yearly National Crime Prevention Week, held during February, which this organization started. Available materials include films-on-loan; daily activities for teachers; public service radio and television announcements; sample speeches; and posters.

LITERATURE: *Personal Crime Prevention Action File* with advice on preventing crime as well as a place to write essential telephone numbers and information (free); *Community Counter Crime Conference Handbook* (free); brochures and fact sheets on the National Exchange Club; Crime Fact Sheet based on the previous year's FBI Uniform Crime Reports; Police Officer-of-the-Month Year Award Program.

U.S. Department of Justice
Federal Bureau of Investigation
Washington, D.C. 20535

The FBI's Crime Resistance Program includes training of their own agents, but the major thrust, as it relates to the general public, is in working with law enforcement agencies, civic organizations, schools, the media, and others to educate and alert people to how they can reduce their vulnerability to crime.

LITERATURE: Extensive free and low-cost pamphlets and leaflets available; write for a listing or sample copies.

Women's Crusade Against Crime (WCAC)
1221 Locust
St. Louis, Mo. 63103

This national organization, with satellite crusades in other cities in Missouri as well as in several other states, has grown from just a few women in 1969 to over 3,000 members. The headquarters acts as an information clearinghouse on crime prevention and also coordinates the activities of its local groups. Local groups are involved in implementing several crime-fighting programs endorsed by WCAC, including Crime Blockers, Operation Ident, Secret Witness, Auto-Identification, and Whistle-STOP. (See introduction to this chapter for details.) Sponsors a yearly national crime prevention conference. Donations are welcomed; other funding comes from government and private sources. Except for a small paid staff, all other participants work on a volunteer basis.

LITERATURE: *The Crusade Courier*, a quarterly newsletter (available by donation); periodic fact sheet updates; booklets available by sending a self-addressed envelope plus $.25—"A Crusade in Action," "Lady Be Careful," "The Sensitive Subject of Rape and How to Handle It," "The St. Louis Woman's Touch in Fighting Crime," "Court Watcher's Guide," and "Save Your $$$$ With Senior Security"; leaflets available by sending a self-addressed, stamped envelope plus $.15—"The Importance of Being a Witness," "Operation Ident," "Crime Blockers," "Secret Witness," "Youth and the Law," and "The Eyes Have It—Be a Court Watcher"; whistles and the leaflet "Blow the Whistle on Crime" ($1.70); shrill alarm ($3.70); invisible ink marking pen ($1.50).

TECHNICAL ASSISTANCE

The following organizations provide technical assistance in crime prevention to community leaders and programs on a fee-paid basis:

ITREC (International Training Research and Evaluation Council)
10500 Sager Avenue, Suite G
Fairfax, Va. 22030

ITREC is active in providing basic and advanced crime prevention planning, management, and evaluation services. It conducts crime prevention seminars and is developing statewide crime prevention programs in New York State. Fees are negotiable.

LITERATURE: Publications price list and brochure.

National Crime Prevention Institute (NCPI)
University of Louisville, Shelby Campus
Louisville, Ky. 40222

Founded in 1971, this crime prevention training institute is a division of the School of Police Administration at the University of Louisville. Training programs are provided at various times of the year at the Louisville campus for community organizations, government administrators, private businesses, citizens, and law enforcement personnel. The two-day to four-week seminars are offered for a variety of fees; send for price list. They also provide on-site technical assistance as well as on-site crime prevention training on a contractual basis. NCPI also functions as an information clearinghouse on all areas of crime prevention through publications, research, topical packages, educational work, and speakers bureaus; conferences are held annually. NCPI Associates was formed for graduates of NCPI training institutes and others engaged in voluntary or paid work in the crime prevention field. Membership dues are $25.00 a year, which include the *Alumni Directory* and a *Hotline* newsletter subscription.

LITERATURE: *The NCPI Alumni Directory* ($10.00); *Hotline* ($10.00); Special Information Packages on a variety of crime prevention programs are available.

INFORMATION CLEARINGHOUSES

The following national and federal organizations provide information on crime prevention:

American Association of Retired Persons
National Retired Teachers Association
1909 K Street, N.W.
Washington, D.C. 20049

This educational program is provided by the National Retired Teachers Association, Action for Independent Maturity, and the American Association of Retired Persons. Free literature is published by the national heaquarters and distributed to its members.

LITERATURE: "Preventing Crime Through Education"; "How to Spot a Con Artist"; "Your Retirement Crime Prevention Guide" ($.20 each).

Center for Community Change
Community Crime Prevention Services
  Project
1000 Wisconsin Avenue, N.W.
Washington, D.C. 20007

The center provides technical assistance services under the LEAA (Law Enforcement Assistance Administration) Community Anti-Crime Program, including a clearinghouse on crime prevention information. It also publishes *Action Line,* a newsletter on up-to-date resource materials and program ideas.

Community Crime Prevention Resource Center
c/o Shanahan Library
Marymount Manhattan College
221 East 71st Street
New York, N.Y. 10021

This reference collection was started in 1978 as part of ACT-ONE (Anti-Crime Through Organized Neighborhood Effort), an L.E.A.A.-funded Community Anti-Crime project. The library staff is unable to handle out-of-town telephone or mail requests, but books, booklets, pamphlets, newspaper and magazine article reprints, and audiovisual materials on crime prevention are available during regular library hours for on-site examination. Organizations around the country are invited to send any free descriptive materials for inclusion in its resources.

National Alliance for Safer Cities
165 East 56th Street
New York, N.Y. 10022

Started in 1970, this is a coalition of sixty-five national organizations plus local alliances representing 32 million members focusing on community crime prevention, victimless crimes, and prison reform. Annual dues are $25.00. The National Alliance arrives at policies and programs but the local autonomous alliances are still free to choose which programs they will implement. It also provides general information on crime prevention and a speakers bureau.

LITERATURE: Reprints ($.25 each) include "Twenty-Two Steps to Safer Neighborhoods," and "The Challenge of Crime"; *Crimes Without Victims* booklet ($1.00).

Office of Community Anti-Crime Program
Law Enforcement Assistance Administration
  (L.E.A.A.)
U.S. Department of Justice
633 Indiana Avenue, N.W.
Washington, D.C. 20531

A federal agency that funds programs and research designed to help curb crime with two major objectives: (1) to improve the criminal justice system's treatment of citizens, particularly crime victims and witnesses; and (2) to educate citizens and to encourage their individual and collective participation in community crime prevention efforts as well as the criminal justice system and correction processes.

LITERATURE: Annual report; description of crime victim-witness programs.

PERSONAL DEFENSE

You can learn personal self-defense—karate, judo, and other martial arts—free or for a very low cost if classes are offered by your local women's group, rape crisis center, victim-witness counseling service, YMCA or YWCA. If you already belong to a health club—private or community-sponsored—check if they have self-defense classes. Of course there are also the private martial arts centers; check your yellow pages for listings.

Another type of self-defense is the bodyguard or private security guard. In addition to local private companies that you can find through your yellow pages, the following national private security and protection companies have branches throughout the country; contact the main office for referrals and free descriptive literature.

Pinkerton's
100 Church Street
New York, N.Y. 10007

Burns International Security Services Inc.
320 Old Briarcliff Road
Briarcliff Manor, N.Y. 10510

Wackenhut Corporation
5 Beekman Place
New York, N.Y. 10017

Or contact:

National Council of Investigation and Security Services
1730 Pennsylvania Avenue, N.W., Suite 1150
Washington, D.C. 20006

A karate class at the Women's Martial Arts Center in New York City (Susan Murdock, Director).

This national membership organization is for those persons or organizations involved in personal security. The council holds conferences and develops standards for its members; they provide public education materials about what investigation and guard companies do. Write for a descriptive brochure.

There are also various crime prevention devices you can buy for yourself or for your home, the most common being locks and burglar alarms. Some hotels are using coded credit card-like systems instead of keys. But the key-in-knob lock offers the least protection against theft. Although you need a key to open it, it can be locked without a key. But even the most unskilled burglar, using a piece of rigid plastic (a credit card, for example) or a pair of pliers, can open such a lock. Police departments recommend that every door have a second lock—a drop-bolt or deadbolt lock with a bolt that is at least one inch long. These second locks, which offer better protection, cost anywhere from $10.00 to $150.00, depending on the type of construction, design, finish, and installation. The lock should be "pick resistant"; a cylinder guard is also a good investment. But remember that if your door is weak or there are noticeable spaces between the door and the frame that would permit use of a crowbar, even the best lock may be useless. (A steel, fire-resistant door is recommended in high crime areas.) Also, although a peephole and a chain lock will not eliminate forced entry while you are away from home, they do give you some control over whom to allow inside.

Good locks cannot prevent all break-ins, but they do discourage amateur burglars. And the more equipment that even an experienced burglar must use to gain entry, the greater the likelihood that evidence to help the police in apprehension of the criminal will be found.

If you're interested in a bulletproof vest, the following companies are just two of many other commercial organizations that will provide information upon request:

Protect Company
4104 Apparel Mart/2300 Stemmons Freeway
Dallas, Tex. 75207

Second Chance Body Armor
P.O. Box 578
Central Lake, Mich. 49622

Police whistles can be ordered from your local crime prevention group, or rape crisis center. Practically every local police or sheriff's department has free brochures and leaflets on making your home safer against burglaries. Try there first, or you can get free literature (*Home Security Alarms* and *Home Security Starts at Your Door*) from the federal government, National Bureau of Standards, U.S. Department of Commerce, by sending a postcard to Consumer Information Center, Pueblo, Colo. 81009.

A good resource on security devices is:

The Complete Book of Locks, Keys, Burglar and Smoke Alarms and Other Security Devices by Eugene A. Sloane (1977). William Morrow and Company, Inc., 105 Madison Avenue, New York, N.Y. 10016 ($12.95 hardcover; $7.95 paperback). The most innovative contribution of this thorough book is the illustrations, which clearly show how certain locks are easily removed by criminals. It explains how to install your own system to save money, includes several chapters on smoke sensors, and even talks about devices that "scramble" telephone calls to assure privacy.

For information on guns, see Chapter 28, *Gun Control*.

ADDITIONAL LITERATURE

The Child's Key to Crime Prevention (1977). Miller Productions, Inc., Educational Materials Division, 800 West Avenue, Box 5584, Austin, Tex. 78763 ($16.00). A teacher's guide for grades kindergarten through six.

Citizen Involvement in Crime Prevention by George J. Washnis (1976). Lexington Books, 125 Spring Street, Lexington, Mass. 02173 ($14.50). A survey of 150 American cities and towns and actual case experiences of crime prevention groups in twenty of them.

Community Crime Prevention, prepared by the National Advisory Commission on Criminal Justice Standards and Goals (1973). Superintendent of Documents, U.S. Government Printing Office, Washington, D.C. 20402 ($3.75). A reference book filled with anticrime suggestions and an analysis of some exemplary programs. It will serve as a much-needed summary and guide for the practicing or would-be crime prevention organization.

Community Crime Prevention Letter, edited by Lawrence Resnick. 123 East 5th Street, Plainfield, N.J. 07060 ($42.00 a year). A monthly information exchange regarding programs in crime prevention, conferences, publications, films, and news in a newsletter format. It is an up-to-date and thorough information bank in this field and is useful for anyone involved with research or implementation of a crime prevention program. Each article and item includes the name of a person to contact, address, and phone number; reader reaction is solicited.

Crime and Youth: A Practical Guide to Crime Prevention by Peter Arnold (1976). Julian Messner, 1230 Avenue of the Americas, New York, N.Y. 10020 ($7.29). Written for the most crime victim-prone group—twelve- to nineteen-year-olds—this informative book on personal crime prevention is based on interviews with two hundred young people.

Crime Control Digest. Washington Crime News Services, 7620 Little River Turnpike, Annandale, Va. 22003 ($98.00 a year). An independent, weekly news summary of government and local law enforcement programs and personnel for criminal justice and police services personnel.

Criminal Justice and the Public. Grafton Publications, Inc., 667 Madison Avenue, New York, N.Y. 10021 ($32.00 a year). A monthly newsletter that excerpts crime statistics around the country with relevance to other communities as well as innovative crime prevention programs that are worth noting.

Crime Prevention: A Practical Look at Deterrence of Crime by Paul Whisenand ($13.95). Holbrook Press, Inc., 470 Atlantic Avenue, Boston, Mass. 02210 ($13.95). A textbook discussing crime prevention by the police, the criminal justice system, and the community.

The Honest Politician's Guide to Crime Controls by Professors Norval Morris and Gordon Hawkins (1970). University of Chicago Press, 5801 Ellis Avenue, Chicago, Ill. 60637 ($3.95). A concise study of crime—its incidence, costs, victims, causes, including organized crime, juvenile delinquency, the police, murder, and rehabilitation.

How to Mobilize Citizen Support for Criminal Justice Improvement: A Guide for Civic and Religious Leaders by Philip B. Singer (1976). American Bar Association Section of Criminal Justice, Circulation Department, 1800 M Street, N.W., Washington, D.C. 20036 (limited number of free copies available). "Crime is everybody's business," begins this pamphlet; it then discusses four major issues: police effectiveness and victim witness assistance; pretrial release and speedy trial; sentencing; and interagency cooperation. The author also suggests ways to plug into existing programs and initiate action.

How You Can Join the War Against Crime and Drug Pushers, presented by The Reader's Digest as a public service. Write to Reprint Editor, Reader's Digest, Pleasantville, N.Y. 10570 (free). A good little booklet that describes two citizen-participation programs—Secret Witness and TIP (Turn In a Pusher)—how they evolved, and how to implement them in your community.

Let's Take Action Against Crime: A Safety Program for Primary Grades (1978). Kiwanis International Foundation, 101 East Erie Street, Chicago, Ill. 60611 ($4.95 prepaid). An innovative book containing an eleven-page teacher's and parent's guide plus sixteen spirit duplicating masters designed to equip children to meet emergency situations and to avoid dangers. It involves the family in practice games, such as "If a Stranger Asks You to Get Into a Car." There are sheets on which the children fill in their answers and draw pictures.

Letter to the President on Crime Control by Norval Morris and Gordon Hawkins (1977). University of Chicago Press, 5801 Ellis Avenue, Chicago, Ill. 60637 ($1.95). A controversial, honest, clear, short proposal on how to implement a realistic and effective crime prevention and control program in the United States.

Marshaling Citizen Power Against Crime. Chamber of Commerce of the United States, 1615 H Street, N.W., Washington, D.C. 20006 ($2.00). A 133-page booklet on why citizen action is necessary, how to go about getting it, and how to apply it toward crime prevention.

A National Strategy to Reduce Crime by the National Advisory Commission on Criminal Justice Standards and Goals (1973). U.S. Government Printing Office, Washington, D.C. 20402 ($2.55). Extensive discussions on how to go about fighting crime with descriptions and discussions of model programs.

Preventing Retail Theft, *Preventing Burglary and Robbery Loss*, and *Preventing Shoplifting Losses*, three free booklets available from the U.S. Small Business Administration, 1441 L Street, N.W., Washington, D.C. 20416.

"Protecting Your Bike From Theft," film clip available from Master Lock Company, 2600 North 32nd Street, Milwaukee, Wis. 53210 (free loan).

Protecting Yourself Against Crime by J. L. Barkas (1978). Public Affairs Committee, 381 Park Avenue South, New York, N.Y. 10016 ($.50). This booklet summarizes crime prevention on the individual, community, and societal levels—what is being done and what should be done. In addition to numerous examples to illustrate each point, follow-up organizations and literature are listed for further information.

Security Letter newsletter. 475 Fifth Avenue, New York, N.Y. 10017 ($75.00 a year in the U.S. and Canada; foreign airmail $15.00 additional everywhere but the Caribbean where it is $10.00 additional). A private newsletter on issues of organizational planning and business security. It has information on crime, crime prevention, and loss prevention with supplements that list security organizations or agencies and other information or resources in detail.

FILMS

(Check with your state Office of Crime Prevention to see if you qualify for loan of any of the films that they may have available for free circulation.)

Learning Corporation of America, 1350 Avenue of the Americas, New York, N.Y. 10019 has several Community Relations Films for teaching about crime prevention. They may be rented or bought. These include: "Mugging—You Can Protect Yourself!" based on a book by Police Officer Liddon R. Griffith; it shows Griffith working with a variety of groups, from senior citizens to children. (Running time: 30–35 minutes; Rental—$50.00; Sale—$395.00); and "Shoplifting: Sharon's Story" shows what happens to a young woman after she is caught stealing from a department store. (Running time: 25 minutes; Rental—$50.00; Sale—$395.00.)

MTI Teleprograms Inc., 4825 North Scott Street, Suite 23, Schiller Park, Ill. 60176, has several excellent films on crime prevention for the general public as well as for educational groups, such as police officers or community organizers. "Not A Weapon Or a Star" (28½ minutes; $50.00 rental; $395.00 sale) shows suburban and urban communities in Illinois organizing to fight crime through block watching, Operation Identification, and other techniques. "Whose Neighborhood Is This?" is a more general film to motivate a community to begin crime prevention efforts; moving interviews with crime victims put the issue on a more personal level. Write for their catalog, which also describes related films on rape prevention, the battered spouse problem, child abuse, and so forth.

See also the following related chapters in *The Help Book:*

AGING
BATTERED ADULTS
BUSINESS INFORMATION
CHILD ABUSE
CITIZEN ACTION
CRIME VICTIMS AND WITNESSES
GUN CONTROL
JUVENILE DELINQUENCY
KIDNAPPING, MISSING PERSONS, AND RUNAWAYS
LAW ENFORCEMENT
OFFENDERS AND EX-OFFENDERS
RAPE AND SEXUAL ASSAULT

17

CRIME VICTIMS AND WITNESSES

In 1977, according to official records, there were 11 million reported victims of major, violent crimes against persons and property—homicide, rape, robbery, serious assault, burglary, larceny-theft, and auto theft. Unofficially, it is estimated that at least 40 million Americans are criminally victimized each year. Crime has become a serious problem in every community, whether it is a rural, urban, or suburban one. For example, in July 1977, a young mother and her seven children were killed in Prospect, Connecticut (population 8,000). In New York City that same year (population 7,500,000) there were 1,557 victims of homicide.

What is being done to help victims of crime and their families? The Commission on Victim Witness Assistance of the National District Attorney's Association has encouraged and supported victim and witness services; more than 150 such units have been established in prosecutors' offices throughout the country. In addition, there are both public and private rape crisis centers, shelters for battered wives, and homes for abused children. Not only is operation of these victim services varied—from district attorneys' offices to police departments, social service agencies, and parole bureaus, from courthouses to private homes—but so are the services offered and the quality of their counseling and information referrals. Although some of these free services are understaffed and under-financed and must rely on undertrained but well-meaning volunteers, they fill a gap where virtually no help previously existed.

What is the government doing to help victims of violent crime? State crime compensation is available in nearly half of the states, but because of a financial means test and numerous other requirements, only a fraction of all crime victims are actually compensated. But state crime compensation is a real step toward greater government responsibility for its own failure to protect its citizens from crime. Those people who do qualify for public funds would be helpless without them, as in the cases of crime victims who become permanently disabled or non-working women with children whose husbands have been murdered. But it is only a step. What is needed for crime victims is more state and federal aid to pay for physical injuries as well as some system to provide reimbursement for property losses. Also there should be a national self-help peer counseling support network, similar to Alcoholics Anonymous. These non-profit, self-supporting local groups would not be an extra financial burden to taxpayers or victims, but would provide a greatly needed outlet for all victims of crime. There is a national self-help organization that provides free self-help counseling for parents whose children have died; many members of the organization are crime victims. Compassionate Friends, with headquarters at P.O. Box 3247, Hialeah, Florida 33013, could be a model for a national Crime Victims Anonymous network.

Larger national efforts, however, are being organized without government funding and on shoestring budgets by those who feel social services for the victim alone are not the answer—they want to change the criminal justice system itself. The biggest group is Crime Victim's Rights Organization, Inc., a group with more than 50,000 members based in New York City. It was started in 1976 by twenty-five-year-old Barry Sudiker, who has a black belt in karate and an M.A. in psychology. "Ninety percent of our membership have not personally been victims," Sudiker explains, "but people are fed up and they want some place to turn to." The group has staged marches with over 4,000 participants; they also rate political candidates with a "muggers rating" and a "victims rating." Their two primary goals are to make elected officials think about the victim, rather than the criminal, and to make crime unprofitable. "I've interviewed muggers who make between $100,000 and $200,000 a year," explains Sudiker, "and they have lawyers on retainer. Crime *does* pay." Victims who are members include parents whose children have been murdered, a woman who has been mugged ten times, and Robert Vialente, a young man blinded from gunshot wounds received from the killer known as "Son of Sam." "Vialente," Sudiker continues, "says he's a member because 'I don't want what happened to me to happen to anyone else.'"

VIOLENT CRIME VICTIMS

Just a few years ago, it would have been possible to list the few dozen local direct services for victims and witnesses in violent crimes—relatives of homicide victims, victims of rape, robbery, and assault. But in the past few years, at least 800 local services have been established and are now operating through various private and publicly supported sources. For example, in Johnston, Rhode Island, public contributions pay for Victim Alert, Inc.; in Philadelphia, Pennsylvania, the bar association runs the Victim Counseling Service. However, most victim and witness helping services are attached either to the district attorney's office and are

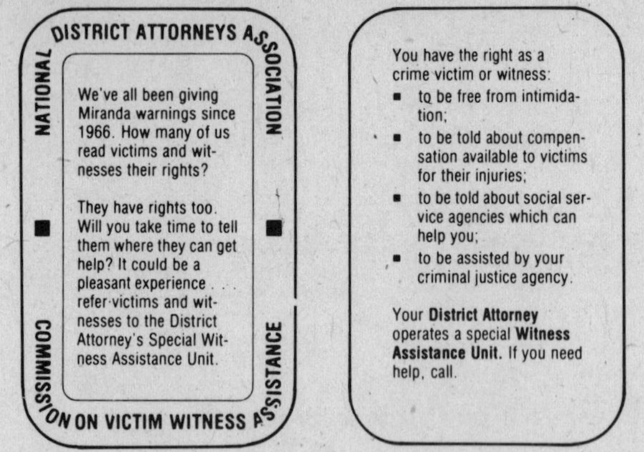

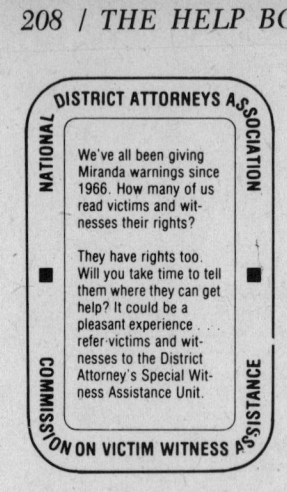

This card is designed to be handed out by police officers to victims who seem to be in need of services furnished by the victims' assistance programs.

located there or in the courthouse building, or are attached to the police department. Other sponsors include probation departments, juvenile courts, charitable organizations, or other social service agencies.

Because of the growing number of victim-witness assistance programs, and the variety of private and public facilities that they are attached to, only a selected list of local services is possible here. Therefore, you should also consult your local telephone directory under "Victim," or call the information office of either the police or probation departments, bar association, juvenile court, district attorney's office, or criminal courthouse to find out about one.

What services do most victim-witness programs provide? Almost all are free; witnesses (including victims who are also witnesses) may even receive a fee for the time they spend testifying if their case goes to trial (see Chapter 15, *Courts*, for further details). Although the range of services offered to victims and witnesses will vary from program to program, the majority provide many of the following services (listed in order of descending frequency):

- Some type of counseling, whether by professional psychiatrists, social workers, or trained lay volunteers.
- Legal information on the rights of the victim; reporting a crime; what a witness is expected to do; eligibility for crime victim compensation or emergency funds.
- Information on the victim's criminal case (did it go to trial? what was the outcome?)
- Escort services through various parts of the victim-witness experience—to the hospital, police station, courts.
- Transportation to and from court.
- Referrals to relevant social and health services (physicians, counselors, emergency shelter, locksmiths, funding).
- Speakers bureau providing the community with speakers on victims, witnesses, and the criminal justice system.

- Training programs for related personnel—physicians, police officers, lawyers, volunteers.
- Self-defense classes.
- Rap sessions.
- Follow-up (to offer continued aid).
- Educational materials (leaflets, booklets, fact sheets, audio-visual materials).

If you cannot find a victim-witness assistance program in your area, the National District Attorneys Association (666 North Lake Shore Drive, Suite 1432, Chicago, Ill. 60611) is compiling those listings and would be able to make a referral to your nearest active program. In addition to continual updating of their membership lists of cooperating victim-witness assistance programs, the association has published a booklet, *The Victim Advocate* (November 1978), which lists, state-by-state, over 150 victim-witness assistance programs, excluding local child abuse and rape victim services.

The following listing of local groups is compiled from a survey by this author as well as entries listed in The Victim Advocate:

Court Coordinator's Project
405 Courthouse
Birmingham, Ala. 35203

Trial Coordinator's Office
Mobile County Courthouse
Mobile, Ala. 36602

Citizen's Participation and Support Project
7012 North 58th Drive
Glendale, Ariz. 85301

Maricopa County Sheriff's Department
120 South First Avenue
Phoenix, Ariz. 85003

Police Crisis Intervention Specialists
Scottsdale Police Department
3739 North Civic Center Plaza
Scottsdale, Ariz. 85251

Victim-Witness Advocate Program
Office of the Pima County Attorney
600 Administration Building
131 West Congress
Tucson, Ariz. 85701

Victim Witness Program
Contra Costa County District Attorney's Office
Eastern-Central Operations
1957-C Parkside Drive
Concord, Calif. 94519

El Cerrito Police Department
Victim Assistance Program
109000 San Pablo Avenue
El Cerrito, Calif. 94530

Fremont Victim Services Program
Police Department
39710 Civic Center Drive
Fremont, Calif. 94538

Victim Assistance Program
Fresno County Probation Department
County Courthouse, 8th floor
Fresno, Calif. 93709

Victim Witness Assistance Program
Fresno County District Attorney's Office
1100 Van Ness Avenue
Fresno, Calif. 93721

The Witness Project
Los Angeles Municipal Court
210 West Temple Street
Los Angeles, Calif. 90012

Victim Witness Assistance Center
District Attorney of the County of Los
  Angeles
210 West Temple Street
Los Angeles, Calif. 90012

Victim Witness Assistance Bureau
District Attorney's Office
1225 Fallon Street, 9th floor
Superior Courthouse
Oakland, Calif. 94612

Victim Advocate's Office
Sacramento Police Department
625 H Street
Sacramento, Calif. 95814

Victim-Witness Assistance Unit
Sacramento County District Attorney
P.O. Box 749
Sacramento, Calif. 95804

District Attorney Information Service
District Attorney's Office
Main Office, Courthouse
202 West Broadway
San Diego, Calif. 92101

Victim/Witness Assistance Program
District Attorney's Office of San Francisco
560 Seventh Street
San Francisco, Calif. 94103

Victims Project
c/o The National Conference of Christians &
  Jews, Inc.
601 North First Street, Room 203
San Jose, Calif. 95112

Victim/Witness Assistance Program
777 North First Street, Suite 620
San Jose, Calif. 95112

District Attorney's Office
Court House Annex
San Luis Obispo, Calif. 93401

Aid to Victims and Witnesses
30 West 39th Avenue
San Mateo, Calif. 94403

S.H.O.P. (Students Helping Other People)
University of Santa Clara
Box 1201
Santa Clara, Calif. 95053

Boulder County District Attorney's Victim
  Witness Assistance Project
6th and Canyon Boulevard
The Justice Center
Boulder, Colo. 80306

Victim Service Bureau
119 North Nevada Street
Colorado Springs Police Department
Colorado Springs, Colo. 80903

SCHT-Special Crime Attack Team
City and County of Denver
Department of Police
Police Building
2195 Decatur Street
Denver, Colo. 80211

Victim Support System
York Street Center
1632 York Street
Denver, Colo. 80207

Victim/Witness Assistance Program
Hall of Justice
Golden, Colo. 80419

Victim Services Unit
Department of Police Service
1 Union Avenue
New Haven, Conn. 06510

Victim Assistance Program
80 Main Street
Putnam, Conn. 06260

Witness Notification Unit
Department of Justice
Wilmington Tower Building
Twelfth and Market Streets
Wilmington, Del. 19899

Victim-Witness Liaison Office
201 S.E. 6th Street, Suites 427–429
Fort Lauderdale, Fla. 33301

Victim Advocate Program
Fort Lauderdale Police Department
1300 West Broward Boulevard
Fort Lauderdale, Fla. 33312

Victim Advocate Program
Duval County Sheriff's Office
1041 South McDuff Avenue
Jacksonville, Fla. 32205

Victims Advocate Program
1515 N.W. 7th Street, Room 112
Miami, Fla. 33125

Project Concern
P.O. Box 2842
St. Petersburg, Fla. 33731

Florida Association of Victim Advocates
(FAVA)
P.O. Box 10092
Tallahassee, Fla. 32302

Palm Beach County Victim/Witness Aid
Program
P.O. Box 107.
West Palm Beach, Fla. 33402

Operation Octopus
Waikiki Improvement Association, Inc.
2222 Kalakaua Avenue, Suite 1410
Honolulu, Hawaii 96815

Victim/Witness Assistance Project
2600 South Carolina Avenue, Room 122
Chicago, Ill. 60608

Victim/Witness Advocate
Public Safety Building
2 South Street
Danville, Ill. 61832

Witness Information Service
Peoria County Courthouse, Room 116
Peoria, Ill. 61602

Prosecutor's Witness and Victim Assistance
Office
Marin County Prosecutor's Office
City-County Building Room 542
Indianapolis, Ind. 46204

Marion County Victim Advocate Program,
Inc.
4602 Thornleigh Drive
Indianapolis, Ind. 46226

Victim Witness Assistance Program
Johnson County Courthouse
P.O. Box 728
Olathe, Kans. 66061

Victim Information Program
Commonwealth's Attorney
Hall of Justice
Louisville, Ky. 40202

Victim/Witness Assistance Bureau
Nineteenth Judicial District
Office of the District Attorney
East Baton Rouge Parish
233 St. Ferdinand Street
Baton Rouge, La. 70801

Witness Assistance Bureau
2700 Tulane Avenue
New Orleans, La. 70119

Witness Victim Assistance Program
District Attorney's Office
142 Federal Street
Portland, Me. 04111

Victim Witness Assistance Program
State's Attorney's Office
Montgomery County
P.O. Box 151
Rockville, Md. 20850

Victim Witness Assistance
State's Attorney's Office
Baltimore County Courthouse
Townson, Md. 21204

Victim Witness Assistance Program
New Suffolk County Court House
Pemberton Square
Boston, Mass. 02108

212 / THE HELP BOOK

Suffolk County District Attorney's Office
Victim/Witness Assistance Project
503B Washington Street
Dorchester, Mass. 02124

Victim Witness Assistance
204 Washtenaw County Building
P.O. Box 48107
Ann Arbor, Mich. 48107

Witness/Victim Assistance Program
190 East Michigan
Battle Creek, Mich. 49014

Victim/Witness Assistance Program
Office of the Wayne County Prosecutor
Frank Murphy Hall of Justice
1441 St. Antoine
Detroit, Mich. 48226

Victim Witness Assistance Program
501 Court House
Duluth, Minn. 55802

Victim Witness Assistance Program
Hennepin County Attorney's Office
C-2000 Government Center
Minneapolis, Minn. 55487

Partners Against Crime
1141 Belt Avenue
St. Louis, Mo. 63112

Aid To Victims of Crime, Inc.
607 North Grand Avenue, Suite 705
St. Louis, Mo. 63103

Clark County District Attorney
Victim/Witness Assistance Center
302 East Carson Avenue, Suite 400
Las Vegas, Nev. 89101

Clark County Juvenile Court Services
Victim's Assistance Program
3401 East Bonanza Road
Las Vegas, Nev. 89101

Victim Witness Assistance Program
Atlantic County Prosecutor's Office
600 Guarantee Trust Building
Atlantic City, N.J. 08401

Victim Witness Assistance Unit
Office of the Prosecutor
Burlington County
49 Rancocas Road
Mt. Holly, N.J. 08060

Victim Service Center
Police Department
20 Park Place
Newark, N.J. 07102

Victim/Witness Assistance Program
District Attorney's Office
Bernalillo County Courthouse
Albuquerque, N.M. 87102

Crime Victim Assistance Unit
215 East 161st Street
Bronx, N.Y. 10451

VOCAL (Victims of Crime Aid League, Inc.)
Bronx Supreme Court
c/o Probation Department
900 Grand Concourse
Bronx, N.Y. 10451

Crime Victim Hotline
Victim/Witness Assistance Project
Vera Institute of Justice
50 Court Street
Brooklyn, N.Y. 11201

The Crime Victim/Witness Aid Bureau
District Attorney of the County of New York
155 Leonard Street
New York, N.Y. 10013

Victim Services Agency, Inc.
2 Lafayette Street
New York, N.Y. 10007

Victim Assistance Program
Public Safety Building
Plaza Level, Room 104
Rochester, N.Y. 14614

Criminal Justice Action Committee
262 East Onondaga Street
Syracuse, N.Y. 13202

Victim/Witness Assistance Center of
 Onondaga County
Onondaga County Civic Center, 12th floor
421 Montgomery Street
Syracuse, N.Y. 13202

Victim-Witness Assistance Unit
Office of the District Attorney
County of Westchester
111 Grove Street
White Plains, N.Y. 10601

Witness Assistance Program
Courthouse
209 South High Street
Akron, Ohio 44308

Victim Witness Program
Furnace Street Mission
P.O. Box 444
Akron, Ohio 44309

State County Victim/Witness Coordination
 Project
Courthouse Annex
P.O. Box 167 D.T. Station
Canton, Ohio 44701

Franklin County Prosecuting Attorney Victim
 Witness Assistance
369 South High Street
Columbus, Ohio 43209

Victim/Witness Division
Montgomery County Prosecutor's Office
41 North Perry Street
Dayton, Ohio 45402

Witness And Victim Education Center
 (W.A.V.E.)
Oklahoma County District Attorney's Office
211 County Office Building
Oklahoma City, Okla. 73102

Multnomah County Victims Assistance
 Program
Multnomah County Courthouse
1201 S.W. 4th
Portland, Ore. 97204

Victim Witness Assistance Unit
Bucks County Court House
Doylestown, Pa. 18901

Erie County Victim/Witness Program
Office of the District Attorney
Erie County Court House
Erie, Pa. 16501

Allegheny County Center for Victims of
 Violent Crimes
810 Walnut Street
McKeesport, Pa. 15037

Victim Service Center
12 West Front Street
Media, Pa. 19063

District Attorney's Victim Witness Unit
2300 Centre Square West
Philadelphia, Pa. 19102

Victim Counseling Service
Philadelphia Bar Association
419 City Hall Annex
Philadelphia, Pa. 19107

Allegheny County Center for Victims of
 Violent Crimes
311 Jones Law Annex
Pittsburgh, Pa. 14219

Victim Alert, Inc.
28 Harding Avenue
Johnston, R.I. 02919

Victims Assistance
C.I.D. Division
Police Department
110 Public Square
Nashville, Tenn. 37201

Citizens for Victims of Crime
c/o The National Conference of Christians and
 Jews, Inc.
4848 Fulton, Suite 212
Houston, Tex. 77027

Victim Witness Assistance Program
Office of the District Attorney
301 San Jacinto
Houston, Tex. 77002

Salt Lake County Attorney's Office
C-220 Metropolitan Hall of Justice
Salt Lake City, Utah 85111

Victim Witness Assistance Program
Davis County Attorney's Office
Courthouse
Farmington, Vt. 84087

Victim/Witness Coordination Program
Commonwealth's Attorney
601 Crawford Street Civic Center
Portsmouth, Va. 23705

Victim Witness Services Program
John Marshall Courts Building
800 East Marshall Street
Richmond, Va. 23219

Victim Witness Coordinator's Office
Office of the Prosecuting Attorney
312 South First Avenue, West
Kelso, Wash. 98626

Victim Assistance Unit
Office of the Prosecuting Attorney
King County Courthouse
516 Third Avenue
Seattle, Wash. 98104

Victim Assistance Project
700 West 12th Street
Vancouver, Wash. 98660

Project Turnaround
821 West State Street
Milwaukee, Wis. 53233

The following national organizations are conducting research, disseminating information, and sponsoring conferences about the needs of victims and witnesses of crime:

American Bar Association
Victims Committee
Section of Criminal Justice
1800 M Street, N.W.
Washington, D.C. 20036

A task force to help lawyers become more aware of the needs of victims and witnesses of crimes. The committee conducts research and its findings are reported at conferences. It also reviews standards for criminal justice with treatment of the victim in mind and proposes recommended revisions.

LITERATURE: Fact sheet of goals.

American Federation of Jewish Fighters, Camp Inmates and Nazi Victims, Inc.
315 Lexington Avenue
New York, N.Y. 10017

The umbrella organization for all Nazi Holocaust survivor organizations in the United States and Canada with an emphasis on distributing Holocaust educational material. Joint projects are conducted with other national Jewish organizations, and the federation is active in furthering the observance of Holocaust and Remembrance Day, commemorating the memory of the 6 million Jews murdered by the Nazis.

LITERATURE: *Martyrdom and Resistance*, bimonthly newsletter; *The Holocaust and Resistance: An Outline of Jewish History in Nazi Occupied Europe (1933–1945)*.

Americans for Effective Law Enforcement (AELE)
4530 Oceanfront Drive
Virginia Beach, Va. 23451

A national, nonprofit, legal organization concerned with the rights of the victims of crime. It maintains a central research library on the legal rights of crime victims involved in lawsuits against perpetrators or third parties who are responsible for victimization. Free research data are available to victims' attorneys.

LITERATURE: Free article reprint—*Victims' Rights Litigation: A Wave of the Future* by Frank Carrington.

Center for Criminal Justice and Social Policy
Marquette University
Milwaukee, Wis. 53233

Conducts research projects on victims of crime.

LITERATURE: "Victims and Witnesses: A Guide for Community Service."

Center for Women Policy Studies
2000 P Street, N.W.
Washington, D.C. 20036

A clearinghouse on physically and sexually abused women and sexually abused children.

LITERATURE: *Response* newsletter.

Crime Victim's Rights Organization, Inc.
100 Church Street
New York, N.Y. 10007

Started in 1976, there are now more than 50,000 members in this national, private advocacy group for crime victims. Their two primary goals are to have elected officials who are for the victim and who support legislation ensuring that *crime does not pay*. It also sponsors marches to bring public attention to the plight of crime victims.

LITERATURE: Free fact sheets.

National Association for Crime Victims Rights Inc.
P.O. Box 16161
Portland, Ore. 97216

Started in 1976, this national, non-profit, private organization is concerned with providing public education about the needs of all crime victims, including law enforcement officers and affected families. They also hope to raise enough money through their membership dues ($15.00/yearly) and a victim's "living memorial" to develop a "victim fund," to give directly to victims and victim service agencies without other funding.

LITERATURE: Flyer; newsletter (free with membership).

National Organization of Victim Assistance, Inc. (NOVA)
Southern Station
Box 9227
Hattiesburg, Miss. 39401

A national organization aimed at unifying scholars, students, professional members of the criminal justice system, volunteers, grass roots organizations, and lay citizens who are committed to the humanization of the criminal justice system through victim advocacy. Membership fee ($10.00 for individuals, $50.00 for agencies) includes a subscription to their newsletter. Annual conference with workshops, panels, and discussions on victim services.

LITERATURE: Flyer; newsletter; membership directory.

CRIME VICTIM COMPENSATION

There is no federal program to compensate victims of violent crimes, but financial aid is available at the state level. Those victims living in states without compensation must rely on their own resources—making claims on health insurance, bringing civil suits for compensation, or requesting aid from charitable organizations. Although all states with publicly funded crime compensation plans are consistent in that they apply only to injuries or disabilities related to *violent* crimes and not to property losses, there is a wide disparity in all other eligibility requirements. For example, state laws vary as to whether the victim has to show financial need, as to the maximum amount of time allowed between the victimization and the reporting of the offense to the compensation board, and in regard to the legal implications of the relationship of the victim to the offender. Therefore, the only way to find out if you qualify for compensation is to write to the headquarters of the crime compensation board in your state (or the state where the victimization occurred, if different), ask if there is an operational plan that applies to your case, and request a brochure and/or application form.

For several years a federal crime victims bill has been introduced and has come close to passage by Congress. Since one feature of the proposed federal plan calls for federal reimbursement of funding twenty-five percent of state victims compensation payments—and the granting of aid to those states without plans who set one up—there will be a major increase in available public compensation when the legislation finally passes. For information on the status of the proposed federal legislation on crime victim compensation—or if you wish to voice your opinion on such a plan—write to:

Committee on the Judiciary
Subcommittee on Criminal Justice
Congress of the United States—House of
   Representatives
Rayburn House Office Building, Room 2137
Washington, D.C. 20515

The following is a list of the state violent crime victim compensation plans:

Department of Health and Social Services
Violent Crimes Compensation Board
Pouch H-02A
Juneau, Alaska 99811

State Board of Control
926 J Street, Suite 300
Sacramento, Calif. 95814

Violent Crimes Compensation Board
800 Delaware Avenue Suite 601
Wilmington, Del. 19801

Crimes Compensation Commission
State of Florida
2562 Executive Center Circle West
Tallahassee, Fla. 32301

Criminal Injuries Compensation Commission
State of Hawaii
Department of Social Services and Housing
P.O. Box 339
Honolulu, Hawaii 96809

Crime Victims Compensation
Clerk, Illinois Court of Claims
Suite 615 Lincoln Tower Plaza
115 West Monroe
Springfield, Ill. 62756

Crime Victims Compensation Board
113 E. Third Street
Frankfort, Ky. 40601

Criminal Injuries Compensation Board
1123 North Eutaw Street, Room 601
Baltimore, Md. 21201

Compensation to Victims of Violent Crimes
Department of the Attorney General
1 Asherburton Place
Boston, Mass. 02108

Crime Victims Compensation Board
P.O. Box 30026
Lansing, Mich. 48909

Crime Victims Reparations Board
Minnesota Department of Public Safety
702 American Center Building
160 East Kellogg Boulevard
St. Paul, Minn. 55101

Violent Crimes Compensation Board
State of New Jersey
Department of Law and Public Safety
1100 Raymond Boulevard, Room 101F
Newark, N.J. 07102

State Board of Examiners
Blasdel Building, Room 205
209 E. Mussee Street
Carson City, Nev. 89701

Crime Victims Compensation Board
State of New York
875 Central Avenue
Albany, N.Y. 11206

Crime Victims Reparations
Workmen's Compensation Bureau
Highway 83 North—Russel Building
Bismarck, N.D. 58505

Victims of Crime Division
Court of Claims of Ohio
30 East Broad Street, 17th floor
Columbus, Ohio 43215

Crime Victims Compensation Board
1920 Paxton Street
Harrisburg, Pa. 17104

Criminal Injuries Compensation Fund
State Board of Claims
450 James Robertson Parkway
Nashville, Tenn. 37219

Division of Crime Victims Compensation
Industrial Commission of Virginia
P.O. Box 1794
Richmond, Va. 23214

Crime Victims Compensation Division
Washington State Department of Labor and Industries
General Administration Building
Olympia, Wash. 98504

Crime Victims Compensation
P.O. Box 7951
Madison, Wis. 53707

Crime Compensation Programs in the Provinces of Canada:

Alberta Crimes Compensation Board
Madison Building, 9919 - 105 Street
Edmonton, Alberta T5K 2E8

Workers Compensation Board
Criminal Injuries Section
5255 Heather Street
Vancouver, British Columbia U5Z 3L8

Criminal Injuries Compensation Board
333 Maryland Street
Winnipeg, Manitoba R3G 1M2

Department of Justice
Centennial Building
Fredricton, New Brunswick E3B 5H1

Criminal Injuries Compensation Board
329 Duckworth Street
St. John's, Newfoundland A1C 1G9

Deputy Attorney General
Halifax, Nova Scotia B3J 2L8

Criminal Injuries Compensation Board
505 University Avenue, 3rd floor
Toronto, Ontario M5G 1X4

Department of Justice
P.O. Box 2000
Charlottetown, Prince Edward Island C1A 7N8

Crime Victim Compensation Department
524, Bourdages
C.P. 1200
Quebec G1K 7E2

Crimes Compensation Board
Legislative Building
Regina, Saskatchewan

218 / THE HELP BOOK

Criminal Injuries Compensation
Government of the Northwest Territories
Yellowknife, N.W.T. XOE 1HO

Government of the Yukon Territory
P.O. Box 2703
Whitehorse, Yukon Y1A 2C6

Crime compensation programs in the United Kingdom:

Criminal Injuries Compensation Board
10–12 Russell Square
London, England WC1B 5EN

Criminal Injuries Compensation Board
Dundonald House
Upper Newtonards Road
Belfast, Northern Ireland BT4 3SU

PROPERTY CRIME VICTIMS

On the local level, victims of nonviolent property crimes—fraud, burglary, auto theft, larceny, etc.—should contact their local police departments and their insurance companies. Other local agencies that can handle complaints of this sort—often mislabeled consumer complaints—are district attorney's offices, offices of the Better Business Bureau, Call For Action offices, and small claims courts. (See listings in Chapter 13, *Consumer Affairs*, and Chapter 15, *Courts*.)

Since fraud is a real crime (even though it's sometimes known as a white-collar crime) your state will have agencies—the state attorney general's office, for instance—with responsibility for investigating such criminal offenses. However, state agencies are often complex in their operations and slow to respond. You may also wish to try Call For Action or your local Better Business Bureau.

Mail fraud is a federal offense; specific complaints or requests for free pamphlets should be directed to:

U.S. Postal Inspection Services
475 L'Enfant Plaza, S.W.
Washington, D.C. 20260

The Postal Inspection Services enforces the Mail Fraud Statute, which was passed when the U.S. mail system was established. In addition to investigating individual complaints about mail fraud, the Postal Inspection Services have an educational fraud prevention program that offers information including free booklets. The Postal Inspection Services also works to increase consumer awareness by publicizing the most widely used and successful mail-order frauds, such as the promotion of fake contests, the sending of unordered merchandise, numerous charity rackets, the sale of fraudulent business directories, fake lab tests, and many kinds of credit card frauds. They also publish the booklet "Mail Fraud Laws Protecting Consumers, Investors, Businessmen, Patients, Students" ($ .20).

Another federal agency providing information about crimes against business is:

U.S. Department of Commerce
Bureau of Domestic Commerce
14th Street and Constitution Avenue, N.W.,
  Room 1104
Washington, D.C. 20230

The bureau provides answers to specific questions as well as referrals to other federal departments. Literature includes news releases to qualified recipients and booklets, such as "The Costs of Crime Against Business," available from the Superintendent of Documents (see Additional Literature at the end of this chapter for annotated listings and ordering instructions).

FEDERAL CRIME INSURANCE

In twenty-three states where consumers are unable to buy low-cost insurance because they live in a high-crime area (or have a business in such an area), the federal government operates a crime insurance program. The following states are currently included in the Federal Crime Insurance Program for residential and/or business robbery and/or burglary insurance:

Alabama, Arkansas, Colorado, Connecticut, Delaware, Florida, Georgia, Illinois, Iowa, Kansas, Maryland, Massachusetts, Minnesota, Missouri, New Jersey, New York, North Carolina, Ohio, Pennsylvania, Rhode Island, Tennessee, Virginia, the District of Columbia, and Puerto Rico.

(See the listing in *Insurance* in Chapter 7, *Business Information*, for more complete details.) Applications and free descriptive booklets are available from:

Federal Crime Insurance
P.O. Box 41033
Washington, D.C. 20014

Toll-free telephone number throughout the United States except Washington, D.C., and Maryland, where you can call collect.

LITERATURE: HUD NEWS description of the Federal Crime Insurance Program, Questions and Answers (periodically updated); application forms; article reprints; descriptive brochure.

RESTITUTION

In some states, especially in the case of property crimes where the criminal has been caught, restitution of stolen goods, money, or property to the victim, in addition to or in lieu of imprisonment, has been established. This system makes it possible for victims to be reimbursed directly for their crime-related losses. Some programs, such as the Minnesota Restitution Center, have been operating since 1972; others, such as a series of four restitution shelters in Georgia, were started more recently. Check with your district attorney's office, juvenile court, or state parole board to find out if a restitution center is operating in your state.

The following is a sampling of restitution programs:

Colorado Crime Victims Restitution Program
Commission on Criminal Justice Standards and Goals
State Centennial Building, 4th floor
1313 Sherman Street
Denver, Colo. 80203

Sole Sanction Restitution Program
Georgia Department of Corrections
Offender Rehabilitation
800 Peachtree Street, N.W., Room 321
Atlanta, Ga. 30308

Maine Criminal Justice Planning and Assistance Agency
295 Water Street
Augusta, Me. 04330

Victim Restitution Programming
Massachusetts Parole Board
100 Cambridge Street
Boston, Mass. 02202

Minnesota Restitution Center
Minnesota Department of Corrections
Metro Square Building
7th & Robert Streets
St. Paul, Minn. 55101

Project Repay
1021 S.W. 4th Street
Multnomah County Courthouse
Portland, Ore. 97204

ADDITIONAL LITERATURE

Considering the Victim: Readings in Restitution and Victim Compensation, edited by Joe Hudson and Burt Galaway (1975). Charles C. Thomas, Publisher, 301-327 East Lawrence Avenue, Springfield, Ill. 62717. An anthology of articles by criminologists, penologists, and sociologists on restitution and compensation, with some early writings by Jeremy Bentham and L. T. Hobhouse.

The Cost of Crimes Against Business by the U.S. Department of Commerce, Domestic and International Business Administration, Bureau of Domestic Commerce (January 1976). Available from the Superintendent of Documents, U.S. Government Printing Office, Washington, D.C. 20402 ($1.60). This booklet contains tables on crimes throughout the United States as well as in thirteen major American cities and describes the most common crimes against business, such as bad checks, counterfeiting, and robbery.

The Crime Victim's Handbook, by Morton Bard and Dawn Sangrey (1979). Basic Books, Inc., 10 East 53rd Street, New York, N.Y. 10022 ($10.00).

Criminal Justice and the Victim, edited by William F. McDonald (1976). Sage Criminal Justice System Annuals, Volume VI, 275 South Beverly

Drive, Beverly Hills, Calif. 92012 ($17.50 hardcover; $7.50 paperback). Twelve original essays about the crime victim's relationship to the criminal justice system that are a good secondary source for criminologists, victimologists, lawyers, and prosecutors.

Crisis: Psychological First Aid for Situational Victims by Ann Kliman (1978). Holt, Rinehart and Winston, 383 Madison Avenue, New York, N.Y. 10017 ($8.95). Kliman, who is Director of the Situational Crisis Service of the Center for Preventive Psychiatry in Westchester County, N.Y., demonstrates through actual cases how to help both victims and survivors recover from loss and unexpected violence. This book is particularly useful for those who will be counseling survivors of homicide or rape victims.

Federal Government Sources on Crimes Against Business. U.S. Department of Commerce, Domestic and International Business Administration, Bureau of Domestic Commerce, Washington, D.C. 20230. This booklet lists the various federal agencies and what publications in this area are available, as well as their price and where to write to obtain them.

Forgotten Victims: An Advocate's Anthology, edited by George Nicholson, Thomas W. Condit, and Stuart Greenbaum (1977). California District Attorneys Association, 555 Capitol Mall, Suite 1545, Sacramento, Calif. 95814 ($5.95). Prepared by the California District Attorneys Association as part of the educational program during California's Forgotten Victims Week in 1977. Articles are by leading victimologists, such as Gilbert Geis and Emilio C. Viano.

Gadfly, P.O. Box 444, Akron, Ohio 44309 (by contribution). A newsletter published every other month by the Victim Assistance Program of the Furnace Street Mission. Contains articles and announcements of activities and conferences.

The Importance of Being a Witness (1975). Women's Crusade Against Crime, 1221 Locust Street, St. Louis, Mo. 63103 ($.35). Leaflet that describes what a witness in a crime might expect to experience as he or she goes through the criminal justice system.

Integrated Services for Victims of Crime: A County Based Approach by Mary E. Baluss (1975). The National Association of Counties Research Information, 1735 New York Avenue, N.W., Washington, D.C. 20006. A description of a sampling of victim programs in Fort Lauderdale, Fla., The Bronx, N.Y., Fresno County Cal., St. Louis, Mo., Sacramento, Cal., that makes a plea for "better organization of existing resources."

Legal Issues in Compensating Victims of Violent Crime (1976). The National Association of Attorney General, Committee on the Office of Attorney General, 3901 Barrett Drive, Raleigh, N.C. 27609 ($3.00). A thorough discussion of such legal issues as the definition of a victim, the method of paying compensation, the time for filing claims, eligibility for compensation, and so forth. Also includes a discussion of the Uniform Crime Victims Reparation Act and the role of the attorney general.

Someone Else's Crisis, produced by The Filmmakers, Inc., for Motorola Teleprograms, Inc., 4825 North Scott Street, Schiller Park, Ill. 60176 (purchase $360.00; rental $50.00). A 16mm color/sound film that is an excellent law enforcement and public education tool describing the ways in which victims are viewed. Incorporates the stop, fade out technique to permit discussions after each film sequence. An excellent manual by psychologist Robert T. Flint accompanies the film, providing developmental and practical information on helping victims of crime.

The Victim and His Criminal: A Study in Functional Responsibility by Stephen Schafer (1968). Random House, Inc. 201 East 50th Street, New York, N.Y. 10022 ($4.95). The late Professor Schafer reviews victimology and the history of the victim's rights. He then describes a study he conducted in victim-offender relationships at a Florida prison.

Victimology: An International Journal, P.O. Box 39045, Washington, D.C. 20016 ($17.50). A scholarly, quarterly journal devoted to studies of victims of crime of all sorts. Contributors include criminologists, rape victim counselors, police officials, and so on. Resource and review section and updates on pertinent conferences are also included.

Victims by J. L. Barkas (1978). Charles Scribner's Sons, 597 Fifth Avenue, New York, N.Y. 10017 ($10.95). Thorough interviews with victims and their families plus extensive research on the history, psychology, and sociology of victims of violent personal and property crimes. " '*Victims*' contains an important message. One solution to the problem of evil is to work for the good. Becoming aware of the needs of America's victims and accepting their reality is certainly a precondition to beginning this work. It's a beginning Barkas' readers will be hard put to ignore" (Jay Becker, *The Washington Post*).

The Victims by Frank G. Carrington (1975). Arlington House Publishers, 165 Huguenot Street, New Rochelle, N.Y. 10801 ($9.95). How the seemingly lenient treatment of offenders has hurt crime victims. Well documented.

Victims & Society by Emilio C. Viano (1976). Visage Press, Inc., 3409 Wisconsin Avenue, N.W., Washington, D.C. 20016 ($8.95). An anthology of scholarly essays, delivered at the International Study Institute on Victimology in Bellagio, Italy, in July 1975, with contributions by Benjamin Mendelsohn, Ezzat A. Fattah, and Lynn A. Curtis.

Victims and Witnesses: Their Experiences With Crime and the Criminal Justice System by Richard D. Knudten, Anthony C. Meade, Mary S. Knudten, William G. Doerner (1977). National Institute of Law Enforcement and Criminal Justice, Law Enforcement Assistance Administration, U.S. Department of Justice. Informative booklet available from the Superintendent of Documents, U.S. Government Printing Office, Washington, D.C. 20402.

See also the following related chapters in *The Help Book:*

**AGING
BATTERED ADULTS
CHILD ABUSE
CONSUMER AFFAIRS
COUNSELING
COURTS
CRIME PREVENTION
FINANCIAL ASSISTANCE
GUN CONTROL
JUVENILE DELINQUENCY
KIDNAPPING, MISSING PERSONS, AND RUNAWAYS
LAW ENFORCEMENT
LEGAL SERVICES
MULTIPURPOSE ORGANIZATIONS
RAPE AND SEXUAL ASSAULT
VOLUNTEERISM**

18

DRUGS, SMOKING, AND DRUG ABUSE

When someone says "drugs" most people immediately think of marijuana, heroin, or sleeping pills. Yet all of the following are drugs*:

- Alcohol
- Marijuana (cannabis)
- Depressants (sedatives; hypnotics)
    Phenobarbital, Pentobarbital, Amobarbital, Secobarbital, Gluthethimide, Chloral hydrate, Paraldehyde
- Hallucinogens
    LSD (lysergic acid diethylamide), mescaline, psilocybin, morning glory seeds
- Narcotics
    Opium, morphine, codeine, heroin, Dialudid, Demeral
- Stimulants
    Amphetamine, Benzedrine, Dexedrine, Ritalin
- Tranquilizers
    Phenothiazines, Chlorpromazine, reserpine, equanil, Librium, Valium

Americans, who once thought that drugs were the answer to depression, nervousness, headaches, colds, lethargy, boredom, obesity, and so forth, are questioning their use more and more. Part of that backlash against the reliance on drugs is due to the "health" or "natural" movement of the 60's and 70's; part of it is due to the media reports on the physical and psychological effects of short-term or long-term use of certain drugs; and part of it is a reaction to the high cost of drugs. After all, if some drugs are not necessary, and even detrimental, why buy them?

Some of the organizations that disseminate information about various kinds

---

* Based on *Drugs and Their Abuse* (1971) by The American National Red Cross.

of drugs are simply concerned that Americans know about their uses, abuses, and the consequences of using them. Other groups are geared toward helping the drug abuser—someone who becomes dependent on increasing dosages of a particular drug. Other organizations are concerned with educating the public on the excessive hold that drugs have developed on our nation. Other groups believe that the use of a particular drug—such as marijuana or laetrile—should be decriminalized and that the user (not society) should be the one who decides if he or she can use it.

Any drug may be pleasurable or dangerous, depending on its type, frequency of use, and the chemistry and health of its user. The significant fact is that millions of Americans choose drugs and living habits that are in opposition to their body's best interest. Unfortunately, the emphasis today is not on educating the public as to what drugs really are, when they are necessary, and the consequences of indulgence or abuse, but instead it is on whether or not a particular drug is legal or lethal. Some manufacturers are so powerful that they have even stopped the removal from the marketplace of certain food additives that have been proven harmful. Other manufacturers have heeded the warnings of researchers and have changed the formulas for their products (hair dyes, for instance) so that harmful ingredients are excluded in their production.

The controversy over smoking is a good example of a conflict between research scientists and industry. It is doubtful that cigarettes will ever be banned—and it is not proven that banning would decrease smoking anyway. But at least the rights of nonsmokers are becoming recognized. For example, it is just in the last few years that smoking has been outlawed in certain public places, such as elevators or specific buildings, or that nonsmoking areas are so designated in restaurants and on trains. These actions were prompted by reports that nonsmokers may develop some of the same health symptoms as smokers if exposed to a smoker's smoke. Unfortunately, all of the health warnings and publicity around the adverse effects of smoking are diminished by the appealing advertisements and images that encourage smoking among the most vulnerable part of the population—teenagers. Recently there has been a rise in smoking, especially among women, and the two forces—better health versus conformity to a previously-endorsed image of the smoker as the rebel and free-thinker—will be at odds for many years to come.

At least an awareness of how drugs permeate every food, cosmetic, and daily habit in American life is the trend today. No longer is taking drugs something positive in and of itself. Help for the drug abuser—like the person addicted to alcohol—has also been recognized as a medical—and not a moral—problem. But the severity of drug addiction should not be minimized. The grave dangers of ODing—namely death—necessitate a concerted attention to the use—and the abuse—of every single drug.

DRUGS

The following federal agencies, national organizations, and industry associations provide information on drugs:

DES Action National
Long Island Jewish-Hillside Medical Center
New Hyde Park, N.Y. 11040

A national organization providing information to the DES-exposed offspring of women who took the hormone DES during pregnancy. Chapters have been formed in California, Michigan, Massachusetts, Oregon, and Washington, D.C.

LITERATURE: Fact sheets; "From One DES Teenager to Another"; DES Newsletter ($15.00 a year).

Cosmetic, Toiletry and Fragrance Association, Inc.
1133 15th Street, N.W.
Washington, D.C. 20005

An industry association that published the CTFA Ingredient Dictionary, recognized as the controlling compendium for nomenclature for cosmetic ingredients. Write for free booklets, such as *Introducing the Cosmetic, Toiletry, and Fragrance Industry Today*.

Do It Now Foundation
Institute for Chemical Survival
P.O. Box 5115
Phoenix, Ariz. 85010

An organization maintaining a 24-hour hotline for reporting "drug ripoffs" and publishing alcohol and drug education materials. Do It Now will send up to three pamphlets free to students or parents (not organizations) on any drug topic.

LITERATURE: *Drug Survival News*, a bimonthly newspaper ($2.50); "Some Little-Known Facts About Drugs & Alcohol," a four-page pamphlet; "Emergency Poison & Overdose Information Chart"; "Megavitamin Therapy and the Drug Wipeout Syndrome"; free catalog.

Environmental Defense Fund
1525 18th Street, N.W.
Washington, D.C. 20036

To find out if a particular hair-coloring product may have any chemicals that are suspected carcinogens, write for the fund's booklet ($.50).

Food and Drug Administration
U.S. Department of Health, Education, and Welfare
Public Health Service
5600 Fishers Lane
Rockville, Md. 20857

If you have a complaint about specific drugs, contact this federal agency. It also has numerous free or low-cost publications about various drugs.

LITERATURE: Pamphlets include "Adverse Reactions to Medicines" and "Aspirin Myocardial Infarction Study"; article reprints include "Laetrile: The Making of a Myth," "The Saccharin Ban," and "Food and Drug Interactions."

Food and Drug Administration Division of Cosmetics Technology
HFF-430
200 C Street, S.W.
Washington, D.C. 20204

Report any adverse effects of a cosmetic to the manufacturer or this division of the FDA. Their Consumer Memo, "Cosmetics," is a free one-page flyer that gives extensive instructions on regulations as well as reporting procedures.

LITERATURE: Pamphlets and leaflets on cosmetics including "If You're Coloring Your Hair" by Jane Heenan and "Cosmetics: We Want You to Know What We Know" ($.25).

Cosmetics*

Beauty is big business in the United States. With confidence that a new shade of nail enamel, an intoxicating scent, or "covering the gray" may lead to romance, social acceptability, job advancement or other elusive goals, Americans spend $5.4 billion a year on cosmetic products.

The Food, Drug, and Cosmetic Act does not require that a cosmetic fulfill all the hopes and dreams that may be encouraged by its advertising. The law does require, however, that a cosmetic be labeled, without false or misleading representations, with informative information about the product, its manufacturer, packer, or distributor, and the quantity of its contents. The law also provides that a cosmetic must be free of substances that may make it injurious, that it be packaged in a safe and non-deceptive container, and that it be produced in a sanitary plant.

The law defines a cosmetic as an article (except soap) intended to be rubbed, poured, sprinkled, sprayed on, introduced into, or otherwise applied to the human body for cleansing, beautifying, promoting attractiveness, or altering the appearance.

If a toilet article is offered to prevent or cure an ailment, or to affect the structure or function of the body, it is a drug as defined by Federal law, even though it may be promoted and sold as a cosmetic. Some examples are products that are claimed to grow hair on bald heads, to remove wrinkles, to cure a skin disease or to treat and prevent dandruff.

Certain other products, such as hormone creams or antibiotic deodorants, are defined as drugs because their ingredients affect the function of the human body. New drug products must be demonstrated to be safe and effective before they can be marketed.

If a cosmetic contains a deleterious substance which may be injurious under the customary conditions of use, it is deemed to be adulterated. Coal-tar hair dyes are exempt from this provision; however, it is known that these hair dyes can cause allergic reactions in some persons. The law requires the label of this kind of hair dye to bear a conspicuous warning that it contains ingredients which may irritate the skin, and to give directions for the user to make a sensitivity test, called a "patch test," before using the product. This is to enable a person to tell whether she will be sensitive to the dye, and to avoid its use if she is.

In addition, the label warns against use of the dye on eyelashes or eyebrows because of the possibility of serious eye injury or blindness.

*FDA Consumer MEMO, March 1974. Reprinted with permission from the U.S. Department of Health, Education, and Welfare, Public Health Service, Food and Drug Administration, Rockville, Maryland.

If the intended use of the article makes it a drug, the label also must give information on composition, directions for use, and warnings, if any are needed, to protect against injury or misuse.

The Food, Drug and Cosmetic Act provides the authority to remove from interstate commerce any cosmetic which is shown to be unsafe, adulterated or misbranded, and any drug which is either unsafe, adulterated, misbranded or ineffective.

Four regulations issued by FDA in 1972 and 1973 will afford consumers greater protection in the cosmetics area.

The first regulation calls for voluntary registration of cosmetics firms and products. As of February 1974, a total of 771 manufacturing establishments out of an estimated 1,000 had registered with FDA. The products marketed by those firms comprise 85 percent of the cosmetic products now being sold.

The second regulation calls for cosmetics companies to submit formula data. As of February 1974, only 50 percent of the market's current formulations had been submitted, by 486 firms.

The third regulation calls on industry to report to FDA any product experiences it learns from consumers. This regulation was published in October 1973.

A fourth regulation, issued by FDA October 17, 1973, under authority of the Fair Packaging and Labeling Act, requires cosmetic ingredients to be listed on the label. This regulation takes effect January 1, 1976.

FDA encourages consumers who are injured by cosmetics or who otherwise have a complaint about cosmetics to report to FDA. The address is:

Food and Drug Administration
Division of Cosmetics Technology
HFF-430
200 C Street, S.W.
Washington, D.C. 20204

Health Research Group (HRG)
2000 P Street, N.W.
Washington, D.C. 20036

An organization financed by Public Citizen, Inc. (one of the Ralph Nader-derived organizations) concerned with removing dangerous drugs and harmful chemicals and cosmetics from the market. It has conducted extensive monitoring of the Food, Drug, and Cosmetic Act and develops scientific data on possible product hazards for presentation to the FDA and the public. HRG supports Congressional legislation requiring explicit drug safety data disclosure before decisions are made about the introduction of a new drug. It also supports state and local Public Interest Research Groups by providing them with detailed information on food, drug, and product hazards.

NORML (National Organization for the Reform of Marijuana Laws)
2317 M Street, N.W.
Washington, D.C. 20037

An information clearinghouse and advocacy group on marijuana. NORML conducts research, makes policy statements, and provides detailed state-by-state information on criminal laws for the possession, sale, or use of marijuana. Membership is $15.00, and includes a subscription to *The Leaflet*, a newsletter.

LITERATURE: *Marijuana: The Facts, Official NORML Policy 1977* and *The Marijuana Issue*.

Office of Cancer Communications
National Cancer Institute
Bethesda, Md. 20014

Provides free publications on smoking and on the hormone DES, such as "Questions and Answers About DES Exposure Before Birth," a nine-page pamphlet, and "Were You or Your Daughter Born After 1940?," a leaflet.

Pharmaceutical Manufacturers Association
1155 Fifteenth Street, N.W.
Washington, D.C. 20005

An industry organization that answers written or telephone inquiries about prescription medicines, diagnostics, and devices. The association will send printed materials and, under appropriate circumstances, will provide free speakers.

LITERATURE: "The Medicine Your Doctor Prescribes—A Guide for Consumers," a twelve-page pamphlet; "Some Substances Used for Non-Prescribed Drugging Effects," folder.

The Proprietary Association
1700 Pennsylvania Avenue, N.W
Washington, D.C. 20006

An association representing manufacturers of non-prescription medicines that will provide information on such drugs.

Student Association for the Study of Hallucinogens (STASH)
118 South Bedford Street
Madison, Wis. 53703

Founded in 1969, the membership of STASH consists of high schools, police departments, researchers, and others with the purpose of translating clinical and professional research into reports and printed matter easily understood by students and the general public. STASH also sponsors seminars and maintains a library on drugs and related journals.

LITERATURE: *Drugs: Information for Crisis Treatment* ($.50); *Drugs of Abuse: An Introduction to Their Actions and Potential Hazards* ($.50); *Journal of Psychedelic Drugs; A Comprehensive Guide to the English Literature on Cannabis* ($5.00 a copy; $20.00 a year); *Directory of Drug Information* (monthly); *Grassroots*.

TOBACCO AND SMOKING

The following federal agencies and national organizations provide information on smoking:

Action on Smoking and Health (ASH)
Room 302
2000 H Street, N.W.
Washington, D.C. 20006

A national organization concerned with protecting the rights of nonsmokers. ASH was behind the 1967 drive that freed up television and radio time for antismoking public service announcements, prompting the ban of cigarette commercials, and later got smoking/no-smoking sections on planes, trains, and buses.

American Cancer Society
777 Third Avenue
New York, N.Y. 10017

Free literature on smoking is available from your local unit or the national headquarters. Local chapters sponsor low-cost (about $10.00) stop-smoking clinics.

LITERATURE: "If You Want to Give Up Cigarettes"; "The I Quit Kit"; "Quit Cigarettes, Live Longer"; "So You Want to Stop"; and others.

American Heart Association
7320 Greenville Avenue
Dallas, Tex. 75231

Provides free leaflets and booklets on the relationship of smoking to heart disease.

American Lung Association
1740 Broadway
New York, N.Y. 10019

Founded in 1904, this national organization provides community education and free literature on smoking.

LITERATURE: "No Smoking" (prepared by and for children); "Me Quit Smoking? How?"; "Me Quit Smoking? Why?"; "Cigarette Smoking: The Facts About Your Lungs"; "How Not to Love Your Kids"; "Q&A of Smoking and Health"; "Smoking and the Two of You"; "Women Are Kicking the Cigarettes: Find Out Why and How"; "Facts and Features for Nonsmokers & Smokers" (all free).

National Clearinghouse for Smoking and Health
U.S. Department of Health, Education, and Welfare
Public Health Service
Bureau of Health Education
Center for Disease Control
Atlanta, Ga. 30333

A federal agency that conducts research and publishes booklets and leaflets on nicotine, tar, and smoking. Single copies are free; multiple copies may be ordered from the U.S. Government Printing Office, Washington, D.C. 20402, or purchased at the government bookstore in your city.

LITERATURE: "Tar and Nicotine Content of Cigarettes"; "If You Must Smoke . . ." ; "Facts: Smoking and Health"; "Chart Book on Smoking, Tobacco, and Health"; "Smoker's Self-Testing Kit"; "Smoking and Health Experiments, Demonstrations, and Exhibits"; "The Smokers Aid to Non-smoking: A Scorecard"; "Teenage Self Test Cigarette Smoking."

Office of Cancer Communications
National Cancer Institute
Bethesda, Md. 20014

Provides free a thirty-two page booklet "Cigarette Smoking Among Teenagers and Young Women."

For direct help in stopping smoking, the following national organizations have local chapters throughout the country:

American Cancer Society, Inc.
777 Third Avenue
New York, N.Y. 10017

Many of the over 2,000 local units sponsor free smoke-ending clinics. Contact your nearest chapter to see if such a program is available or contact the national headquarters for referrals to local chapters.

smokEnders
525 Memorial Parkway
Phillipsburg, N.J. 08865

Founded in 1969 by Jacquelyn Rogers to help her end her twenty-two-year smoking habits, there are now smokEnders chapters in thirty states, Canada, and Norway. There is a tuition fee for the course (which varies throughout the country); contact your nearest branch for details. smokEnders will also answer telephone and written inquiries.

LITERATURE: Booklets include "Matchless" and "Those Who Know About smokEnders." Articles reprints and a quarterly newspaper ($2.00 a year) are also available.

DRUG ABUSE

The following federal agencies and national or international organizations are concerned with and/or provide information on drugs and drug abuse:

Addiction Research Foundation
33 Russell Street
Toronto 4 Ontario
Canada M5S 2S1

Conducts research and publishes information on addiction.

LITERATURE: *The Ethical Pharmaceutical Industry and Some Of Its Economic Aspects*, compiled by David C. Sevigny ($10.00).

Alcohol and Drug Problems Association of North Americas (ADPA)
1101 15th Street, N.W.
Washington, D.C. 2005

ADPA is a non-profit corporation founded by a group of state alcoholism project directors in 1949 "to be responsive to the needs of professionals in the field of alcohol and drug problems." There are five categories of membership in ADPA; fees for individual members are $20.00 a year. There are additional charges (from $1.00 to $5.00) for membership in special interest sections, such as community action, education, social work, poverty programs, and armed services.

Drug Abuse Council, Inc.
1828 L Street, N.W.
Washington, D.C. 20036

Started by four philanthropic corporations, the council supports research in drug-abuse related areas and maintains a 2,000-volume library.

Drug Enforcement Administration (DEA)
1405 I Street, N.W.
Washington, D.C. 20537

Established with the Department of Justice in July 1973, DEA's purpose is to curtail illicit drug traffic and prosecute dealers, whenever cases are discovered. It also regulates the legal trade in narcotic and dangerous drugs. There are fourteen regional offices of the DEA; for further information, contact the Office of Public Affairs at DEA.

Hazelden Foundation
Consultation and Education Services
Box 176
Center City, Minn. 55012

An educational organization that offers low-cost literature on drugs, chemical dependency, and alcohol.

LITERATURE: *Chemical Dependence: Psychological vs. Physiological* ($.10); *Dynamics of Drug Dependency* by Richard O. Heilman, M.D. ($.40); and *Teen Drug Use; What Can Parents Do?* ($.40)

National Clearinghouse for Drug Abuse Information (NCDAI)
11400 Rockville Pike, Room 110
Rockville, Md. 20852

An information clearinghouse established in 1970 and linked to the Alcohol, Drug Abuse, and Mental Health Administration and the National Institute on Drug Abuse (NIDA). Extensive single copies of booklets are provided free; additional copies may be ordered from the Superintendent of Documents, U.S. Government Printing Office, Washington, D.C. 20402. NCDAI also publishes computer printouts of local treatment facilities and will make telephone and written referrals to local direct help.

LITERATURE: *The National Directory of Drug Abuse Treatment Programs* (lists over 3,800 federal, state, local, and privately funded drug abuse treatment facilities); descriptive booklets about services and publications; "Questions and Answers About Drug Abuse."

National Council on Crime and Delinquency
Continental Plaza
411 Hackensack Avenue
Hackensack, N.J. 07601

A national educational and research organization that has low-cost literature on drug abuse and crime. Write for their publications price list.

National Council on Drug Abuse (NCDA)
9 South Michigan Avenue
Chicago, Ill. 60603

Founded in 1971, NCDA consists of lay persons, clinicians, and physicians organized to do research on drug abuse, to disseminate information, and to compile statistics.

LITERATURE: Fact sheets; monthly newsletter.

PACT/NADAP (Business and Labor Joined Against Drug Abuse)
355 Lexington Avenue
New York, N.Y. 10017

A national, nonprofit organization concerned with drug abuse problems that is funded by business and labor to work nationwide in assisting governmental agencies, municipalities, industries, and schools to respond to the problems surrounding illegal drug use. A local grant enables them to find employment for any New York State resident who has a drug history.

Society for the Study of Addiction to Alcohol and Other Drugs
c/o Hon. Treasurer
St. Christopher
52 Hurst Road
Horsham, Sussex, England

Originally founded in 1884, this charitable organization publishes the *British Journal of Addiction* (see Additional Literature), holds special meetings and symposiums, and maintains a library at the Wellcome Foundation, Euston Road, London N.W.1.

DIRECT HELP FOR DRUG ABUSE

Most counties and cities have a Bureau of Substance Abuse, a Bureau of Alcohol and/or Drug Abuse, or a Department of Health that will make referrals to local, direct-help out-clinic and in-patient treatment facilities for persons with drug abuse problems. Many publish leaflets or booklets with that information, such as "Drug and Alcoholism Treatment Centers," available from the city of Detroit. Call or write your appropriate local government agency for a referral.

In addition the Salvation Army, the American National Red Cross, the Young Men's Christian Association, and the Young Women's Christian Association have drug abuse treatment programs at many of their local branches. Check with the nearest affiliate to see if such free help is available. Local mental health clinics and hospitals often have drug abuse treatment programs.

The following national organizations also have local affiliates to help the families of drug abusers or the abusers themselves:

Families Anonymous
P.O. Box 344
Torrance, Calif. 90501

A national organization with branches throughout the United States to provide self-help peer counseling for the relatives and friends of those who have drug use or related behavioral problems. Consult your local directory for your nearest chapter or contact the national headquarters for a referral. Counseling is based on the principles of Alcoholics Anonymous and its family-related program, Al-Anon.

LITERATURE: Directory of meetings; descriptive leaflets.

The Odyssey Institute is a national organization providing direct services and information on drug abuse that has several branches throughout the United States. For information contact them at Odyssey Institute.

Public Information
24 West 12th Street
New York, N.Y. 10011

Educational Services
68 South 6 East
Salt Lake City, Utah 84102

Family Cooperative
61 Lincoln Park
Newark, N.J. 07102

Drug abuse programs (Odyssey Houses) are located in Louisiana, Michigan, New Hampshire, New York, and Utah. Addresses are:

Louisiana Odyssey House
1125 North Tonti Street
New Orleans, La. 70119

Shreveport Odyssey House
Community Involvement Center
609 Milam
Shreveport, La. 71101

Michigan Rubicon Odyssey House
1225 Detroit Street
Flint, Mich. 48503

Re-Entry House
631 Leith Street
Flint, Mich. 48503

Unicorn Gift Gallery
605 South Saginaw Street
Flint, Mich. 48503

Detroit Rubicon Odyssey House
7441 Brush Street
Detroit, Mich. 48224

New Hampshire Odyssey House
Whittier Inn
30 Winnacunnet Road
Hampton, N.H. 03842

Dover Farm Re-Entry House
Longhill Road Extension
Dover, N.H. 03842

Young Adult Treatment Unit
208–210 East 18th Street
New York, N.Y. 10003

Adult Treatment Unit
309–311 East 6th Street
New York, N.Y. 10003

Re-Entry House
24 West 12th Street
New York, N.Y. 10011

Utah Odyssey House
68 South 6th East
Salt Lake City, Utah 84102

Community Involvement Center
Thrift Shop
384 4th Avenue
Salt Lake City, Utah 84102

Practically every state has a government agency for drug abuse. That agency will make referrals to local treatment facilities. Many states, such as Maryland, publish directories of local treatment facilities. They also publish information on drug abuse as well as the current laws related to the use and sale of certain drugs. The National Association of State Drug Abuse Program Coordinators (1612 K Street, N.W., Suite 900, Washington, D.C. 20006) coordinates these agencies.

The following is a list of the state agencies for drug abuse:

Alcoholism and Drug Abuse Division
Department of Mental Health
502 Montgomery Avenue
Montgomery, Ala. 36130

Office of Drug Abuse
Department of Health and Social Services
210 Ferry Way
Anderson-Wilson Building
Juneau, Alaska 99801

Drug Abuse Program
Behavioral Health Services Division
Department of Health Services
1740 West Adams
Phoenix, Ariz. 85007

Office on Alcohol Drug Abuse Prevention
Department of Human Services
1515 West Seventh Street
Little Rock, Ark. 72203

Office of Narcotics and Drug Abuse
915 Capitol Mall
Sacramento, Calif. 95814

Alcohol and Drug Abuse Division
Department of Health
4210 East 11th Avenue
Denver, Colo. 80220

Alcohol and Drug Dependence Programs
Department of Mental Health
90 Washington Street
Hartford, Conn. 06115

Office of Drug Abuse Control
Department of Health and Social Services
3000 Newport Gap Pike
Wilmington, Del. 19808

Substance Abuse Administration
Department of Human Resources
South Potomac Building
613 G Street, N.W.
Washington, D.C. 20001

Drug Abuse Program
Mental Health Program Office
Department of Health and Rehabilitative Services
1323 Winewood Boulevard
Tallahassee, Fla. 32301

Alcohol and Drug Abuse Section
Division of Mental Health
 and Mental Retardation
618 Ponce de Leon Avenue, N.E.
Atlanta, Ga. 30308

Alcohol and Drug Abuse Branch
Department of Health
1250 Punchbowl Street
Honolulu, Hawaii 96813

Bureau of Substance Abuse
Division of Community Rehabilitation
Department of Health and Welfare
State Office Building
700 West State Street
Boise, Idaho 83720

Division of Addiction Services
Department of Mental Health
5 Indiana Square
Indianapolis, Ind. 46204

Iowa Drug Abuse Authority
615 East 14th Street
Des Moines, Iowa 50319

Alcohol and Drug Abuse Section
Department of Social and Rehabilitation
 Services
State Office Building
Topeka, Kans. 66606

Drug Abuse Section
Division for Preventive Services
Bureau for Health Services
Department of Human Resources
Health Building
275 East Main Street
Frankfort, Ky. 40601

Bureau of Substance Abuse
P.O. Box 44215
Baton Rouge, La. 70804

Office of Alcoholism and Drug Abuse
 Prevention
Bureau of Rehabilitation
Department of Human Services
32 Winthrop Street
Augusta, Me. 04330

Drug Abuse Administration
Department of Health and Mental Hygiene
Herbert R. O'Conor State Office Building
201 West Preston Street
Baltimore, Md. 21201

Division of Drug Rehabilitation
Department of Mental Health
190 Portland Street
Boston, Mass. 02114

Office of Substance Abuse Services
Department of Public Health
3500 North Logan Street
Lansing, Mich. 48909

Chemical Dependency Program Division
Department of Public Welfare
658 Cedar Street
St. Paul, Minn. 55155

Division of Alcohol and Drug Abuse
Department of Mental Health
619 Robert E. Lee Building
Jackson, Miss. 39201

Division of Alcoholism and Drug Abuse
Department of Mental Health
2002 Missouri Boulevard
Jefferson City, Mo. 65101

Alcohol and Drug Abuse Division
Adaptive Services Division
Department of Institutions
1539 11th Avenue
Helena, Mont. 59601

Commission on Drugs
State Capitol
1445 K Street
Lincoln, Neb. 68509

Bureau of Alcohol and Drug Abuse
Rehabilitation Division
Department of Human Resources
505 East King Street
Carson City, Nev. 89710

Drug Abuse Coordinator
Office of the Governor
State House
Concord, N.H. 03301

Division of Alcohol, Narcotic,
  and Drug Abuse Control
Department of Health
John Fitch Plaza
Trenton, N.J. 08608

Drug Abuse Section
Department of Health and Environment
725 St. Michael's Drive
Santa Fe, N.M. 87503

Office of Drug Abuse Services
Executive Park South
Albany, N.Y. 12203

Drug Commission
Department of Administration
3800 Barrett Drive
P.O. Box 19324
Raleigh, N.C. 27609

Division of Alcoholism and Drug Abuse
Department of Mental Health and
  Retardation Services
909 Basin Avenue
Bismarck, N.D. 58501

Bureau of Drug Abuse
Department of Mental Health and Mental
  Retardation
1352 State Office Tower
30 East Broad Street
Columbus, Ohio 43215

Drug Abuse Services
Department of Mental Health
408-A North Walnut Street
P.O. Box 53277
Oklahoma City, Okla. 73107

Drug Programs Coordinator
Mental Health Division
Department of Human Resources
2575 Bittern Street, N.E.
Salem, Ore. 97310

Governor's Council on Drug and Alcohol
  Abuse
Riverside Office Building 1
2101 North Front Street
Harrisburg, Pa. 17120

Department of Addiction Services
MM Building
Ramón B. Lopez Avenue
P.O. Box B-Y, Rio Piedras Station
Rio Piedras, P.R. 00928

Drug Abuse Unit
Department of Health
Davis Street
Cranston, R.I. 02908

Commission on Alcohol and Drug Abuse
3700 Forest Drive
Columbia, S.C. 29204

Division of Drugs
Department of Health
Joe Foss Building
Pierre, S.D. 57501

Alcohol and Drug Abuse Section
Department of Mental Health and Mental
  Retardation
501 Union Street
Nashville, Tenn. 37219

Drug Abuse Division
Department of Community Affairs
210 Barton Springs Road
Austin, Tex. 78711

Division of Alcoholism and Drugs
Department of Social Services
554 South 3rd East Street
Salt Lake City, Utah 84102

Alcohol and Drug Abuse Division
Department of Social and Rehabilitation
  Services
Waterbury Complex
State Office Building
Montpelier, Vt. 05602

Substance Abuse Division
Department of Mental Health and Mental Retardation
James Madison Building, 13th Floor
109 Governor Street
Richmond, Va. 23219

Drug Abuse Prevention Office
Office of Community Development
400 Capitol Center Building
410 West 5th Street
Olympia, Wash. 98504

Division on Alcoholism and Drug Abuse
Department of Mental Health
265 State Office Building 3
1800 Washington Street, E.
Charleston, W. Va. 25305

Bureau of Alcoholism and Drug Abuse
Division of Mental Hygiene
Department of Health and Social Services
Wilson Street State Office Building
1 West Wilson Street
Madison, Wis. 53702

Advisory Council on Mental Health, Alcohol Abuse, and Drug Abuse
Hathaway Building
2300 Capitol Avenue
Cheyenne, Wyo. 82002

ADDITIONAL LITERATURE

The A. A. Member and Drug Abuse, rev. ed. (1964). Alcoholics Anonymous World Services, Inc., P.O. Box 459, Grand Central Station, New York, N.Y. 10017. This pamphlet was prepared by a group of doctors in A.A. It shows how certain drugs may hurt or help the alcoholic.

Addiction and Substance Abuse Report. Grafton Publications, Inc., 667 Madison Avenue, New York, N.Y. 10021 ($25.00 a year). Monthly newsletter on drugs, alcohol, tobacco, medicines, and foods.

Anxiety, Conflicts & Chemical Dependency by Daniel J. Anderson, Ph.D., edited by Diane DuCharme (1976). Hazelden, P.O. Box 176, Center City, Minn. 55012 ($ .75). Excerpts from lectures by Dr. Anderson on why people use mood altering drugs.

The British Journal of Addiction to Alcohol and Other Drugs. Subscription Manager, Longman Group Ltd., 43/45 Annandale Street, Edinburgh EH7 5JX, Scotland ($30.00 a year; $8.50 single issue). A publication of the Society for the Study of Addiction to Alcohol and Other Drugs; articles are by experts in the field who are attached to such organizations as the Addiction Research Foundation and psychiatry departments at universities.

Cocaine: A Drug and Its Social Evolution by Lester Grinspoon and James B. Bakalar (1976). Basic Books, 10 East 53rd Street, New York, N.Y. 10022 ($15.00). Includes the history of cocaine as well as a neurophysiological and pharmacological analysis of its effects.

A Consumer's Dictionary of Cosmetic Ingredients by Ruth Winter (1976). Crown Publishers, One Park Avenue, New York, N.Y. 10016 ($4.95). A useful directory, in dictionary form, explaining in clear, simple language the ingredients in cosmetics.

The Consumers Union Report on Smoking and the Public Interest (1963). Consumer Union, 256 Washington Street, Mount Vernon, N.Y. 10550 (Out of print; check your library).

Consumers Union's The Medicine Show, revised and expanded, by the Editors of Consumers Reports (1974). Pantheon Books, 201 East 50th Street, New York, N.Y. 10022 or Consumers Union (see address above) ($3.95). Reports on everything from aspirin to sugar, drugs during pregnancy to the vitamin E "cure."

Cosmetics: The Substances Beneath The Form by Margaret Morrison (1978). U.S. Department of Health, Education, and Welfare, Public

Health Service, Food and Drug Administration, Office of Public Affairs, Washington, D.C. 20857. This updated and revised version of an April 1977 *FDA Consumer* report is a good explanation of recent regulations affecting cosmetics as well as some of the ingredients in cosmetics.

Drugs and Death: The Nonmedical Use of Drugs Related to All Modes of Death, edited by Patricia Ferguson, Thomas Lennox, and Dan J. Lettieri (November 1974). National Institute on Drug Abuse, 11400 Rockville Pike, Rockville, Md. 20852 ($2.25). This research report deals with suicide and homicide as well as all opiate related deaths and such other drug-related deaths in regard to depressants, stimulants, LSD, inhalants, methadone, etc. Its language is rather technical.

Drugs and Their Abuse (1971). American National Red Cross, 17th and D Streets, N.W., Washington, D.C. 20006 (free). Excellent booklet describing the various kinds of drugs—alcohol, marijuana, depressants, hallucinogens, inhalants, narcotics, stimulants, and tranquilizers—and what first aid treatment is called for in cases of abusive use of each. The booklet also tells how to take care of someone who stops breathing (with illustrations).

Drugs and the Public by Norman E. Zinberg and John A. Robertson (1972). Simon and Schuster, 1230 Avenue of the Americas, New York, N.Y. 10020 ($8.95).

Drug Survival News: The Journal of New Ideas in the Chemical Dependency Field (published six times a year). Do It Now Foundation, Institute for Chemical Survival, P.O. Box 5115, Phoenix, Ariz. 85010 ($2.50). Pertinent feature articles and news reports as well as annotated listings of new literature in this field. Projects around the country are also described with follow-up addresses for more information.

Food and Drug Interactions by Phyllis Lehmann (1978). A reprint from the *FDA Consumer Memo* that succinctly explains the hazards of mixing certain medicines with foods and drinks. For a free copy, send a postcard to the Consumer Information Center, Dept. 698F, Pueblo, Colo. 81009.

Painkillers: Their Uses and Dangers by Annabel Hecht (1977). Reprinted from *FDA Consumer*. Send a postcard to the Consumer Information Center (address above). (Free.) A brief discussion of the potential hazards of aspirin and other painkillers.

Journal of Drug Issues, P.O. Box 4021, Tallahassee, Fla. 32303. Quarterly journal ($25.00 a year). Publishes articles by experts in this area on drug abuse and the criminal justice system, drug crisis intervention, the free clinic movement in the United States, and similar articles.

Licit & Illicit Drugs by Edward M. Brecher and the Editors of Consumer Reports (1972). Consumers Union, 256 Washington Street, Mount Vernon, N.Y. 10550 ($4.00). An exhaustive, but fascinating historical and physiological discussion of narcotics, stimulants, depressants, inhalants, hallucinogens, marijuana, caffeine, nicotine, and alcohol. Well-written and documented.

Marihuana Reconsidered by Lester Grinspoon (1971). Harvard University Press, 79 Garden Street, Cambridge, Mass. 02138 ($15.00).

National Directory of Drug Abuse Treatment Programs (1976). National Institute on Drug Abuse, 11400 Rockville Pike, Rockville, Md. 20852. Names, addresses, phone numbers, and brief descriptions of what kind of treatment is offered for 3,800 federal, state, local, and privately funded agencies responsible for providing drug abuse treatment services throughout the United States. Information was compiled through a survey conducted by the National Institute on Drug Abuse as of June 30, 1975; updates are planned.

The New Handbook of Prescription Drugs by Richard Burack, M.D. Ballantine Books, 201 East 50th Street, New York, N.Y. 10022 ($1.50).

The Odyssey House Story: We Mainline Dreams by Judianne Densen-Gerber, J.D., M.D. (1973). Doubleday & Company, Inc., Garden City, N.Y. 11530 ($9.95). A well-written narrative on how Dr. Densen-Gerber, who is also concerned about child abuse, created Odyssey House, a treatment and rehabilitation program for drug abusers.

The People's Pharmacy by Joe Gradedon (1977). Avon Books, 859 Eighth Avenue, New York, N.Y. 10019 ($3.95). Consumer guide to prescription drugs, brand-name medications, and home remedies in a readable style with case histories to support opinions.

Sensual Drugs: Deprivation and Rehabilitation of the Mind by Hardin B. Jones and Helen C. Jones (1977). Cambridge University Press, 32 East 57th Street, New York, N.Y. 10022 ($3.95). Jones, professor of medical physics and physiology at the University of California at Berkeley, and his wife have written a thorough study of the effects of such drugs as alcohol, marijuana, and heroin on the brain and sexual functioning. Extensive bibliography.

The Staff Burn-Out Syndrome by Herbert J. Freudenberger (1975). Drug Abuse Council, Inc., 1825 L Street, N.W., Washington, D.C. 20036. A booklet about what to do when the staff of a hot line, crisis intervention center, runaway house, free clinic, and so on gets "burned out" and how to prevent that from happening.

They Satisfy: The Cigarette in American Life, by Robert Sobel (1978). Anchor Books, Doubleday, Garden City, N.Y. 11530 ($8.95). A well-written history of the rise of smoking in the habits of Americans, traced from the 1880s.

To Parents/About Drugs (1970, 1977). Metropolitan Life Insurance Company, One Madison Avenue, New York, N.Y. 10010 (free). Pamphlet describing the various types of drugs, including a chart with key questions answered and a brief information resource section.

The U.S. Journal of Drug and Alcohol Dependence, 7541 Biscayne Boulevard, Miami, Fla. 33138 ($24.00 organizations; $20.00 individuals; $12.00 students). Monthly journal in newspaper format with articles, legislative information, and reviews of literature.

What About Drugs and Employees? (1975). Kemper Insurance Companies, Long Grove, Ill. 60049 (free booklet). This booklet addresses itself to the problems of drug use within a company, noting that it has to be recognized and treated just as alcoholism is today.

Young Men & Drugs—A Nationwide Survey by the National Institute on Drug Abuse (February 1976). National Institute on Drug Abuse, 11400 Rockville Pike, Rockville, Md. 20852. ($6.75). This is a thorough study of the nonmedical use of psychoactive drugs among young men in the United States, based on interviews with 2,510 men. Tables are included in this technical report.

The following booklets ($.50 per copy) are available from the Public Affairs Committee, Inc., 381 Park Avenue South, New York, N.Y. 10016:

Drugs—Use, Misuse, Abuse by Margaret Hill

Drug Abuse and Your Child by Alice Shiller

El Abuso De Las Drogas—Que Podemos Hacer? ("Drug Abuse—What Can Be Done?") by Jules Saltman

What You Should Know About Drug Abuse by Jules Saltman

Women and Smoking by Jane E. Brody and Richard Engquist

See also the following related chapters in *The Help Book:*

ALCOHOLISM
BATTERED ADULTS
CHILDREN
CONSUMER AFFAIRS
COUNSELING
EMERGENCIES AND DISASTERS
HEALTH
JUVENILE DELINQUENCY
LAW ENFORCEMENT
MENTAL HEALTH
OFFENDERS AND EX-OFFENDERS
PARENTING
SUICIDE PREVENTION

19

EDUCATION

Anyone can talk about the irrelevance of textbooks, but Al Wilson, principal of the Emerson School, an elementary school in Granite City, Illinois, along with a nationwide program known as NIE (Newspaper in Education), offer real improvements. Every teacher in Mr. Wilson's elementary school, from kindergarten through sixth grade, uses the newspaper as a "living textbook." The results: scores from fourth graders showed Emerson students achieving a month closer to their anticipated scores than the average for the district. "At the first PTA meeting this year," Mr. Wilson explains, "one mother whose first-grade child had just transferred to our school said, 'I can't believe what my daughter is coming home talking about. We just talk so much more now.'"

Each morning, for about twenty minutes before school begins, the teachers meet in the lounge and discuss the newspaper while having coffee. They point out articles in that day's *St. Louis Globe-Democrat,* and Mr. Wilson suggests where a particular story might supplement or even replace a textbook reading. "For example, today there is a story on the priest who is president of St. Louis University," says Wilson. "The headline reads, 'Fifty Years As a Jesuit.' Now the sixth grade social studies textbook has a chapter on religion and how the Society of Jesus was formed." The newspaper article will be read by the students in conjunction with the text. But a third grade class read excerpts of an article on population drifts away from the cities that actually contradicted what their formal reader said about population.

The NIE program is administered through the American Newspaper Publishers Association Foundation (ANPAF, P.O. Box 17407, Dulles International Airport, Washington, D.C. 20041). Each newspaper has its own follow-up materials geared to its locality; for example, the *Chicago Tribune* has its own Educational Services Programs based on the ANPAF format. Some of the skills strengthened by the material, offered for every level from kindergarten through eighth grade, are language and reading, social studies, mathematics, consumer education, home economics, health, business and economics, sciences, art, and music. More than 500 daily newspapers and thousands of schools throughout the United States cooperate in the program.

If your child's school is not participating in NIE, you might want to discuss initiating the program at your next PTA meeting. You might also consider a personal family program using the newspaper. There are several resources for that. *Parent Power,* by John Douglas, associate editor of *Science News* magazine, is a 120-page book and 14-part newspaper series available through Newspaper Enterprise Association's (NEA) reader service program. It covers a variety of subjects, from how a parent can help a child learn, to how to meet and work with the child's teacher, to step-by-step instructions on using the newspapers. It is available for $2.00 from NEA, 1200 West Third Street, Cleveland, Ohio 44113. *Let's Play and Learn Together* ($3.50) is available from Newspaper in the Classroom, The Commercial Appeal, 495 Union Avenue, Memphis, Tennessee 38101.

But elementary schools are not the only educational institutions that are undergoing change and innovation. High schools are beginning to be more responsive to their diverse students' needs. For example, more audio-visual teaching materials and high-interest subject matter textbooks written at lower-reading skills levels are being used. In that way, poor readers have greater motivation to improve—and not abandon—reading as an educational tool. Part of the problem is that public education, until late in the nineteenth century, basically consisted of an elementary school education. In less than one hundred years, not just a high school degree but a college degree have become necessary "job credentials." For example, in 1900 only 11 percent of those who were high-school age were actually attending school, but two-thirds of those high school students went on to college. By the late 1960s, 90 per cent of those of high school age were in school. Although in the 1940's only one-third of those who graduated from high school went on to college, since the 1950's there has been a 10 percent annual increase in that rate. Concern is now as great about the college dropout as it was—and still is—for the high school dropout. But is college for everyone? Should high school be a training ground for college or a place where skills are taught that can instantly be translated into jobs? The criticism once aimed at high schools—that they were not training young men and women to obtain jobs—is now being directed at colleges.

In 1976, there were about 11 million persons enrolled in postsecondary educational institutions. But not all were college freshmen who had graduated from high school the previous June. What has changed is the variety of choices—work/study, night school, external degree programs—and the variety of students, such as returning adult women and even older adults changing careers in middle age. Combining school and work is becoming more common for all students who pass the minimum age requirements for employment. Courses aimed at job educating full-time college students are trying to prevent the graduation of disenchanted youths who find they have not been trained for a realistic career. Students with Ph.D. degrees in liberal arts fields are even being retrained by business and nonacademic institutions as teaching and research positions in their chosen fields become almost nonexistent.

The federal agency providing information on all educational matters is the U.S. Office of Education. Write to the agency's national headquarters for a list of available programs and publications:

OE Information Center
U.S. Office of Education
400 Maryland Avenue, S.W.
Washington, D.C. 20202

LOCAL EDUCATIONAL RESOURCES

Postsecondary education, including vocational training, whether for self-improvement, an advanced degree, or job development, is more available now. Course offerings are found at locations ranging from someone's apartment to local university branches and are advertised in daily and special newspapers. Local libraries have developed Learner Advisory Services to help you sort out what courses, programs, or training you might want to pursue. It is a free service. Your high school or college alumni or counseling offices may also have brochures and guidance to direct you through the adult educational maze—from college and graduate school to the professional school or job training. Learning exchanges are agencies that have been established for sharing information. Independent learning groups, such as the Writer Network, a group of twelve writers who decided to meet once a month to share resources and problems, are being started to continue the learning process.

Correspondence courses, tape cassettes, videotapes, and films available for free or small fees are other learning tools. There are also traditional college programs or "open curriculums," where you choose your own program; free universities or "colleges without walls" often have such open curriculums.

STATE AGENCIES FOR EDUCATION

The following is a list of state agencies for education—primary, secondary, and vocational—that will provide information, referrals, set standards, and have educational materials:

Department of Education
State Office Building
Montgomery, Ala. 36130

Department of Education
State Office Building
Pouch F
Juneau, Alaska 99811

Board of Education
1535 West Jefferson
Phoenix, Ariz. 85007

Department of Education
Education Building
Capitol Mall
Little Rock, Ark. 72201

Department of Education
721 Capitol Mall
Sacramento, Calif. 95814

Department of Education
Education Building
201 East Colfax
Denver, Colo. 80203

Department of Education
340 Capitol Avenue
Hartford, Conn. 06101

Department of Public Instruction
Townsend Building
Court Street
Dover, Del. 19901

Board of Education
Presidential Building
415 12th Street, N.W.
Washington, D.C. 20004

Department of Education
The Capitol
Tallahassee, Fla. 32304

Education Authorities
270 Washington Street, S.W.
Atlanta, Ga. 30334

Department of Education
Queen Liliuokalani Building
1390 Miller Street
Honolulu, Hawaii 96813

Department of Education
Len B. Jordan Building
650 West State Street
Boise, Idaho 83720

State Board of Education
100 North First Street
Springfield, Ill. 62777

State Board of Education
229 State House
Indianapolis, Ind. 46204

Department of Public Instruction
Grimes State Office Building
East 14th and Grand Avenue
Des Moines, Iowa 50319

Department of Education
State Education Building
120 East 10th Street
Topeka, Kan. 66612

Department of Education
Capital Plaza Tower
Frankfort, Ky. 40601

Board of Elementary and Secondary Education
Education Building
Baton Rouge, La. 70804

Department of Educational and Cultural Services
Education Building
Augusta, Me. 04333

Department of Education
Baltimore-Washington International Airport
P.O. Box 8717
Baltimore, Md. 21240

State Board of Education
31 St. James Avenue
Boston, Mass. 02116

Department of Education
124 West Allegan Street
Lansing, Mich. 48933

Department of Education
Capitol Square Building
550 Cedar Street
St. Paul, Minn. 55155

Department of Education
501 Walter Sillers Building
550 High Street
Jackson, Miss. 39202

Department of Elementary and Secondary
  Education
Jefferson State Office Building
Jefferson City, Mo. 65101

State Board of Education
33 South Last Chance
Helena, Mont. 59601

Department of Education
P.O. Box 94987
Lincoln, Neb. 68508

Department of Education
400 West King Street
Capitol Complex
Carson City, Nev. 89701

Department of Education
410 State House Annex
Concord, N.H. 03301

Department of Education
225 West State Street
Trenton, N.J. 08625

Department of Education
Education Building
300 Don Gaspar Avenue
Santa Fe, N.M. 87503

Education Department
Washington Avenue
Albany, N.Y. 12234

Department of Public Education
Education Building
100 West Edenton Street
Raleigh, N.C. 27611

Department of Public Instruction
State Capitol
Bismarck, N.D. 58505

Department of Education
Ohio Departments Building
65 South Front Street
Columbus, Ohio 43215

Department of Education
Oliver Hodge Memorial Education Building
2500 North Lincoln Boulevard
Oklahoma City, Okla. 73105

Department of Education
942 Lancaster Drive, N.E.
Salem, Ore. 97310

Department of Education
Education Building
Harrisburg, Pa. 17120

Department of Education
199 Promenade Street
Providence, R.I. 02908

Department of Education
1429 Senate Street
Rutledge Building
Columbia, S.C. 29201

Division of Elementary and Secondary
  Education
Department of Education and Cultural Affairs
Kneip Building
Pierre, S.D. 57501

Department of Education
Cordell Hull Building
436 6th Avenue, North
Nashville, Tenn. 37219

Texas Education Agency
201 East 11th Street
Austin, Tex. 78701

State Board of Education
250 East 500 South Street
Salt Lake City, Utah 84111

Department of Education
State Office Building
120 State Street
Montpelier, Vt. 05602

Department of Education
Ninth Street Office Building
9th and Grace Streets
Richmond, Va. 23219

Superintendent of Public Instruction
Old Capitol Building
Olympia, Wash. 98504

Department of Education
358 State Office Building 6
1900 Washington Street E.
Charleston, W.Va. 25305

Department of Public Instruction
126 Langdon Street
Madison, Wis. 53702

Department of Education
Hathaway Building
2300 Capitol Avenue
Cheyenne, Wyo. 82002

This national organization is an information clearinghouse on alternative schools for young people:

New Schools Exchange
Pettigrew, Ark. 72752

Through its newsletter and annual directory, parents may learn about schools, conferences, and other contact information.

LITERATURE: *1978 Directory & Resource Guide* ($5.00 prepaid); *New Schools Exchange Newsletter* ($1.00 per back issue; write for listing of available issues).

The following is a list of statewide agencies for higher education:*

Alabama Commission on Higher Education
One Court Square
Montgomery, Ala. 36104

Department of Higher Education
1301 West 7th Street
Little Rock, Ark. 72201

California Postsecondary Education
  Commission
1020 12th Street
Sacramento, Calif. 95814

Colorado Commission on Higher Education
1550 Lincoln Street
Denver, Colo. 80203

State Board of Higher Education
340 Capitol Avenue
Hartford, Conn. 06115

Delaware State College
Dover, Del. 19901

District of Columbia Commission on
  Postsecondary Education
1329 E Street, N.W.
Washington, D.C. 20004

Florida Board of Regents
Collins Building
107 West Gaines Street
Tallahassee, Fla. 32304

Board of Regents of the University System of
  Georgia
244 Washington Street, S.W.
Atlanta, Ga. 30334

Hawaii State Postsecondary Education
  Commission
Bachman Hall
2444 Dole Street
Honolulu, Hawaii 96822

State Board of Education and Board of
  Regents of the University of Idaho
650 West State Street
Boise, Idaho 83720

Illinois Board of Higher Education
500 Reisch Building
4 West Old Capitol Square
Springfield, Ill. 62701

* Reprinted with permission of *The Chronicle of Higher Education* (December 12, 1977), p. 8. Copyright © 1977 by Editorial Projects for Education, Inc.

Indiana Commission for Higher Education
143 West Market Street
Indianapolis, Ind. 46204

Iowa State Board of Regents
Grimes State Office Building
Des Moines, Iowa 50319

Board of Regents, State of Kansas
Merchants National Bank Tower
Topeka, Kan. 66612

Council on Higher Education
West Frankfort Office Complex
Frankfort, Ky. 40601

Louisiana Board of Regents
P.O. Box 44362
Baton Rouge, La. 70804

University of Maine
107 Maine Avenue
Bangor, Me. 04401

Maryland State Board for Higher Education
16 Francis Street
Annapolis, Md. 21401

Board of Higher Education
31 Saint James Avenue
Boston, Mass. 02116

State Board of Education
P.O. Box 30008
Lansing, Mich. 48902

Minnesota Higher Education Coordinating Board
Capital Square Building
550 Cedar Street
St. Paul, Minn. 55101

Board of Trustees of State Institutions of Higher Learning
P.O. Box 2336
Jackson, Miss. 39205

Coordinating Board for Higher Education
600 Clark Avenue
Jefferson City, Mo. 65101

Board of Regents of Higher Education
33 South Last Chance Gulch
Helena, Mont. 59601

Nebraska Coordinating Commission for Postsecondary Education
301 Centennial Mall South
Lincoln, Neb. 68509

Board of Regents, University of Nevada System
405 Marsh Avenue
Reno, Nev. 89509

New Hampshire Postsecondary Education Commission
66 South Street
Concord, N.H. 03301

Board of Higher Education
225 West State Street
Trenton, N.J. 08625

Board of Educational Finance
Legislative Executive Building
Santa Fe, N.M. 87503

Regents of the University of the State of New York
State Education Department
Albany, N.Y. 12234

Board of Governors of the University of North Carolina
P.O. Box 2688
Chapel Hill, N.C. 27514

North Dakota State Board of Higher Education
State Capitol Building
Bismarck, N.D. 58505

Ohio Board of Regents
30 East Broad Street
Columbus, Ohio 43215

Oklahoma State Regents for Higher Education
500 Education Building
State Capitol Complex
Oklahoma City, Okla. 73105

Educational Coordinating Commission
495 State Street
Salem, Ore. 97310

State Board of Education
Box 911
Harrisburg, Pa. 17126

Board of Regents for Education
199 Promenade Street
Providence, R.I. 02908

South Carolina Commission on Higher Education
1429 Senate Street
Columbia, S.C. 29201

South Dakota Board of Regents
State Office Building #3
Pierre, S.D. 57501

Tennessee Higher Education Commission
501 Union Building
Nashville, Tenn. 37219

Coordinating Board, Texas College and University System
P.O. Box 12788, Capitol Station
Austin, Tex. 78711

State Board of Regents
807 East South Temple Street
Salt Lake City, Utah 84102

Vermont State Colleges Board of Trustees
322 South Prospect Street
Burlington, Vt. 05401

State Council of Higher Education for Virginia
700 Fidelity Building
Ninth and Main Streets
Richmond, Va. 23219

Council for Postsecondary Education
908 East Fifth Avenue
Olympia, Wash. 98504

West Virginia Board of Regents
950 Kanawha Boulevard East
Charleston, W.Va. 25301

Board of Regents of the University of Wisconsin System
1860 Van Hise Hall
1220 Linden Drive
Madison, Wis. 53706

Wyoming Higher Education Council
New Boyd Building
1720 Carey Avenue
Cheyenne, Wyo. 82002

*The following is a list of statewide agencies for junior (two-year) colleges:**

Alabama State Department of Education
Junior College Branch
817 South Court Street
Montgomery, Ala. 36104

Board of Regents
University of Alaska Statewide System
Fairbanks, Alaska 99701

State Board for Community Colleges
1535 West Jefferson
Phoenix, Ariz. 85007

Department of Higher Education
1301 West 7th Street
Little Rock, Ark. 72201

California Community Colleges
1238 S Street
Sacramento, Calif. 95814

State Board for Community Colleges and Occupational Education
State Services Building
1525 Sherman Street
Denver, Colo. 80203

Regional Community Colleges
1280 Asylum Avenue
Hartford, Conn. 06105

Delaware Technical and Community College
P.O. Box 897
Dover, Del. 19901

*Reprinted with permission of *The Chronicle of Higher Education* (February 6, 1978), p. 8. Copyright © 1978 by Editorial Projects for Education, Inc.

Florida Department of Education
Division of Community Colleges
Collins Building
107 West Gaines Street
Tallahassee, Fla. 32304

Board of Regents of the University System of
  Georgia
244 Washington Street, S.W.
Atlanta, Ga. 30334

University of Hawaii
Bachman Hall
2444 Dole Street
Honolulu, Hawaii 96822

State Board of Education and Board of
  Regents of the University of Idaho
650 West State Street
Boise, Idaho 83720

Illinois Community College Board
518 Iles Park Place
Springfield, Ill. 62718

Indiana Commission for Higher Education
143 West Market Street
Indianapolis, Ind. 46204

Iowa State Board of Public Instruction
Grimes State Office Building
Des Moines, Iowa 50319

State Department of Education
Postsecondary Administration Section,
  Community College Unit
120 East 10th Street
Topeka, Kan. 66612

University of Kentucky
102 Breckinridge Hall
Lexington, Ky. 40506

Louisiana Board of Regents
P.O. Box 44362
Baton Rouge, La. 70804

University of Maine Board of Trustees
107 Maine Avenue
Bangor, Me. 04401

State Board for Community Colleges
16 Francis Street
Annapolis, Md. 21401

Board of Regional Community Colleges
470 Atlantic Avenue
Boston, Mass. 02210

State Board of Education
P.O. Box 30008
Lansing, Mich. 48909

State Board for Community Colleges
550 Cedar Street
St. Paul, Minn. 55101

State Department of Education
Division of Junior Colleges
P.O. Box 771
Jackson, Miss. 39205

Coordinating Board for Higher Education
600 Clark Avenue
Jefferson City, Mo. 65101

Montana Board of Regents of Higher
  Education
33 South Last Chance Gulch
Helena, Mont. 59601

Nebraska Coordinating Commission for
  Postsecondary Education
301 Centennial Mall South
Lincoln, Neb. 68509

Board of Regents, University of Nevada
  System
405 Marsh Avenue
Reno, Nev. 89509

State Department of Education
Division of Postsecondary Education
163 Loudon Road
Concord, N.H. 03301

Department of Higher Education
225 West State Street
Trenton, N.J. 08625

Board of Educational Finance
Legislative Executive Building
Santa Fe, N.M. 87503

State University of New York
99 Washington Avenue
Albany, N.Y. 12246

State Board of Education
Department of Community Colleges
Education Building
Raleigh, N.C. 27611

North Dakota State Board of Higher
    Education
State Capitol Building
Bismarck, N.D. 58505

Ohio Board of Regents
30 East Broad Street
Columbus, Ohio 43215

Oklahoma State Regents for Higher Education
500 Education Building
State Capitol Complex
Oklahoma City, Okla. 73105

Oregon Department of Education
Division of Community Colleges
942 Lancaster Drive, N.E.
Salem, Ore. 97310

Department of Education
Box 911
Harrisburg, Pa. 17126

Rhode Island Junior College State System
400 East Avenue
Warwick, R.I. 02886

State Board for Technical and Comprehensive
    Education
Rutledge Building
1429 Senate Street
Columbia, S.C. 29201

State Board of Regents
State University and Community College
    System of Tennessee
1161 Murfreesboro Road
Nashville, Tenn. 37217

Coordinating Board
Texas College and University System
P.O. Box 12788, Capitol Station
Austin, Tex. 78711

State Board of Regents
807 East South Temple Street
Salt Lake City, Utah 84102

Vermont State Colleges Board of Trustees
322 South Prospect Street
Burlington, Vt. 05401

Community College System
P.O. Box 1558
Richmond, Va. 23212

State Board for Community College Education
319 East 7th Avenue
Olympia, Wash. 98504

West Virginia Board of Regents
950 Kanawha Boulevard East
Charleston, W.Va. 25301

Wisconsin Board of Vocational, Technical and
    Adult Education
4802 Sheboygan Avenue
Madison, Wis. 53702

Community College Commission
1720 Carey Avenue
Cheyenne, Wyo. 82002

ACCREDITATION

For free or low-cost information on courses of study, career descriptions, recognized schools, and advice, contact the agencies in the lists that follow of accrediting agencies in higher education.

The following associations are responsible for institutional accreditation of colleges and universities:*

Middle States Association of Colleges and Schools
Commission on Higher Education
3624 Market Street
Philadelphia, Pa. 19104

Accredits schools in Delaware, District of Columbia, Maryland, New Jersey, New York, Pennsylvania, Canal Zone, Puerto Rico, and the Virgin Islands.

New England Association of Schools and Colleges
Commission on Institutions of Higher Education
131 Middlesex Turnpike
Burlington, Mass. 01803

Accredits schools in Connecticut, Maine, Massachusetts, New Hampshire, Rhode Island, and Vermont.

North Central Association of Colleges and Schools
Commission on Institutions of Higher Education
1221 University Avenue
Boulder, Colo. 80302

Accredits schools in Arizona, Arkansas, Colorado, Illinois, Indiana, Iowa, Kansas, Michigan, Minnesota, Missouri, Nebraska, New Mexico, North Dakota, Ohio, Oklahoma, South Dakota, West Virginia, Wisconsin, and Wyoming.

Northwest Association of Schools and Colleges
Commission on Colleges
3700B University Way, N.E.
Seattle, Wash. 98105

Accredits schools in Alaska, Idaho, Montana, Nevada, Oregon, Utah, and Washington.

Southern Association of Colleges and Schools
Commission on Colleges
795 Peachtree Street, N.E.
Atlanta, Ga. 30308

Accredits schools in Alabama, Florida, Georgia, Kentucky, Louisiana, Mississippi, North Carolina, South Carolina, Tennessee, Texas, and Virginia.

Western Association of Schools and Colleges
Accrediting Commission for Senior Colleges and Universities
Box 9990
Mills College
Oakland, Calif. 94613

Accredits schools in California, Hawaii, American Samoa, Guam, and the Trust Territory of the Pacific.

The following agencies, which are recognized by the U.S. Office of Education, grant accreditation for professional and specialized programs:*

Architecture
National Architectural Accrediting Board
1735 New York Avenue, N.W.
Washington, D.C. 20006

Accredits first professional programs.

Art
National Association of Schools of Art
11250 Roger Bacon Drive
Reston, Va. 22090

Accredits professional schools and programs.

---

*Reprinted with permission of *The Chronicle of Higher Education* (October 3, 1977), pp. 9–10 (based on the U.S. Office of Education and Council on Postsecondary Accreditation with updating by the *Chronicle*). Copyright © 1977 by Editorial Projects for Education, Inc.

Bible College Education
American Association of Bible Colleges
Box 543
Wheaton, Ill. 60187

Accredits three-year institutes and four- and five-year colleges.

Blind and Visually Handicapped Education
National Accreditation Council for Agencies Serving the Blind and Visually Handicapped
79 Madison Avenue
New York, N.Y. 10016

Accredits residential schools for the blind.

Blood Bank Technology
American Medical Association, in cooperation with American Association of Blood Banks
Department of Allied Health Evaluation
535 North Dearborn Street
Chicago, Ill. 60610

Accredits programs for the specialist in blood bank technology.

Business
American Assembly of Collegiate Schools of Business
760 Office Parkway, Suite 50
St. Louis, Mo. 63141

Accredits baccalaureate and graduate degree programs.

Association of Independent Colleges and Schools
Accrediting Commission
1730 M Street, N.W.
Washington, D.C. 20036

Accredits private junior and senior colleges of business and private business schools.

Chiropractic
Council on Chiropractic Education
Commission on Accreditation
1434 East Main Street
Watertown, Wis. 53094

Accredits programs leading to the D.C. degree.

Clinical Pastoral Education
Association for Clinical Pastoral Education
475 Riverside Drive
Room 450
New York, N.Y. 10027

Accredits professional training centers.

Cosmetology
Cosmetology Accrediting Commission
1707 L Street, N.W.
Washington, D.C. 20036

Accredits cosmetology schools and programs.

Cytotechnology
American Medical Association, in cooperation with American Society of Cytology
Department of Allied Health Evaluation
535 North Dearborn Street
Chicago, Ill. 60610

Accredits programs for the cytotechnologist.

Dentistry
American Dental Association
Commission on Accreditation of Dental and
  Auxiliary Programs
211 East Chicago Avenue
Chicago, Ill. 60611

Accredits programs leading to D.D.S. or D.M.D. degrees, advanced specialty and general practice residency programs, and programs in dental hygiene, dental assisting, and dental technology.

Dietetics
American Dietetic Association
Commission on Evaluation of Dietetic
  Education
430 North Michigan Avenue
Chicago, Ill. 60611

Accredits coordinated undergraduate programs in dietetics and dietetic internships.

Engineering
Engineers' Council for Professional Development
345 East 47th Street
New York, N.Y. 10017

Accredits first professional degree programs in engineering and baccalaureate degree programs in engineering technology.

Forestry
Society of American Foresters
5400 Grosvenor Lane
Washington, D.C. 20014

Accredits professional schools.

Funeral Service Education
American Board of Funeral Service Education
201 Columbia Street
Fairmont, W.Va. 26554

Accredits independent schools and college departments.

Health Services Administration
Accrediting Commission on Graduate Education for Health Services Administration
One Dupont Circle
Washington, D.C. 20036

Accredits graduate programs.

Histologic Technology
American Medical Association, in cooperation with National Accrediting Agency for Clinical Laboratory Sciences
Department of Allied Health Evaluation
535 North Dearborn Street
Chicago, Ill. 60610

Accredits programs for the histologic technician.

Home Study Education
National Home Study Council
Accrediting Commission
1601 Eighteenth Street, N.W.
Washington, D.C. 20009

Accredits private home study schools.

Interior Design Education
Foundation for Interior Design Education Research
730 Fifth Avenue
New York, N.Y. 10019

Accredits professional and technical programs.

Journalism
American Council on Education for Journalism
Accrediting Committee
563 Essex Court
Deerfield, Ill. 60015

Accredits professional programs.

Laboratory Assistant Education
American Medical Association, in cooperation with National Accrediting Agency for Clinical Laboratory Sciences
Department of Allied Health Evaluation
535 North Dearborn Street
Chicago, Ill. 60610

Accredits programs for the laboratory assistant.

Landscape Architecture
American Society of Landscape Architects
1750 Old Meadow Road
McLean, Va. 22101

Accredits first professional degree programs.

Law
American Bar Association
Administration Building
Indiana University-Purdue University
355 North Lansing Street
Indianapolis, Ind. 46202

Accredits professional schools.

Librarianship
American Library Association
Committee on Accreditation
50 East Huron Street
Chicago, Ill. 60611

Accredits five-year master's degree programs.

Medical Assistant
Accrediting Bureau of Medical Laboratory Schools
Oak Manor Offices
29089 U.S. 20 West
Elkhart, Ind. 46514

Accredits private medical assistant programs and institutions.

American Medical Association, in cooperation with American Association of Medical Assistants
Department of Allied Health Evaluation
535 North Dearborn Street
Chicago, Ill. 60610

Accredits one- and two-year medical assistant programs.

Medical Laboratory Technician Education
Accrediting Bureau of Medical Laboratory Schools
Oak Manor Offices
29089 U.S. 20 West
Elkhart, Ind. 46514

Accredits technical schools and programs.

American Medical Association, in cooperation with National Accrediting Agency for Clinical Laboratory Sciences
Department of Allied Health Evaluation
535 North Dearborn Street
Chicago, Ill. 60610

Accredits technical programs.

Medical Records Education
American Medical Association, in cooperation with American Medical Record Association
Department of Allied Health Evaluation
535 North Dearborn Street
Chicago, Ill. 60610

Accredits programs for medical record administrators and technicians.

Medical Technology
American Medical Association, in cooperation with National Accrediting Agency for Clinical Laboratory Sciences
353 North Dearborn Street
Chicago, Ill. 60610

Accredits professional programs.

Medicine
Liaison Committee on Medical Education
Department of Undergraduate Evaluation
Council on Medical Education
535 North Dearborn Street
Chicago, Ill. 60610

Accredits programs leading to the M.D. degree. The committee represents the American Medical Association and the Association of American Medical Colleges.

Music
National Association of Schools of Music
11250 Roger Bacon Drive
Reston, Va. 22090

Accredits baccalaureate and graduate programs.

Nuclear Medicine Technology
American Medical Association, in cooperation with Joint Review Committee on Educational Programs in Nuclear Medicine Technology
Department of Allied Health Evaluation
535 North Dearborn Street
Chicago, Ill. 60610

Accredits programs for the nuclear medicine technologist.

Nursing
American Association of Nurse Anesthetists
111 East Wacker Drive
Chicago, Ill. 60601

Accredits professional schools of nurse anesthesia.

National Association for Practical Nurse Education and Service
122 East 42nd Street
New York, N.Y. 10017

Accredits practical nurse programs.

National League for Nursing
10 Columbus Circle
New York, N.Y. 10019

Accredits professional, technical, and practical nurse programs.

Occupational Therapy
American Medical Association, in cooperation with American Occupational Therapy Association
Department of Allied Health Evaluation
535 North Dearborn Street
Chicago, Ill. 60610

Accredits professional programs.

Occupational, Trade, and Technical Education
National Association of Trade and Technical Schools
Accrediting Commission
2021 L Street, N.W.
Washington, D.C. 20036

Accredits private trade and technical schools.

Optometry
American Optometric Association
Council on Optometric Education
7000 Chippewa Street
St. Louis, Mo. 63119

Accredits professional programs.

Osteopathic Medicine
American Osteopathic Association
Office of Education
212 East Ohio Street
Chicago, Ill. 60611

Accredits programs leading to the D.O. degree.

Pharmacy
American Council on Pharmaceutical Education
1 East Wacker Drive
Chicago, Ill. 60601

Accredits professional schools.

Physical Therapy
American Medical Association, in cooperation with American Physical Therapy Association
Department of Allied Health Evaluation
535 North Dearborn Street
Chicago, Ill. 60610

Accredits professional programs.

Physician's Assistant Education
American Medical Association, in cooperation with Joint Review Committee on Educational Programs for Physician's Assistants
Department of Allied Health Evaluation
535 North Dearborn Street
Chicago, Ill. 60610

Accredits programs for the assistant to the primary care physician.

Podiatry
American Podiatry Association
Council on Podiatry Education
20 Chevy Chase Circle, N.W.
Washington, D.C. 20015

Accredits professional and graduate programs and programs for podiatric assistants.

Psychology
American Psychological Association
Office of Accreditation
1200 Seventeenth Street, N.W.
Washington, D.C. 20036

Accredits doctoral and internship programs in clinical and counseling psychology and doctoral programs in school psychology.

254 / THE HELP BOOK

Public Health
Council on Education for Public Health
1015 Eighteenth Street, N.W.
Washington, D.C. 20036

Accredits master's degree programs and graduate professional schools of public health.

Rabbinical and Talmudic Education
Association of Advanced Rabbinical and Talmudic Schools
Accreditation Commission
175 Fifth Avenue
New York, N.Y. 10010

Accredits Rabbinical and Talmudic schools.

Radiologic Technology
American Medical Association, in cooperation with Joint Review Committee on Education in Radiologic Technology
Department of Allied Health Evaluation
535 North Dearborn Street
Chicago, Ill. 60610

Accredits programs for technologists in radiology and radiation therapy.

Respiratory Therapy
American Medical Association, in cooperation with Joint Review Committee for Respiratory Therapy Education
Department of Allied Health Evaluation
535 North Dearborn Street
Chicago, Ill. 60610

Accredits programs for respiratory therapists and respiratory therapy technicians.

Social Work
Council on Social Work Education
Division of Standards and Accreditation
345 East 46th Street
New York, N.Y. 10017

Accredits master's and baccalaureate degree programs.

Speech Pathology and Audiology
American Speech and Hearing Association
Education and Training Board
10801 Rockville Pike
Rockville, Md. 20852

Accredits master's degree programs.

Teacher Education
National Council for Accreditation of Teacher Education
1750 Pennsylvania Avenue, N.W.
Washington, D.C. 20006

Accredits baccalaureate and graduate degree programs.

Theology
Association of Theological Schools in the United States and Canada
P.O. Box 130
Vandalia, Ohio 45377

Accredits graduate professional schools.

Veterinary Medicine
American Veterinary Medical Association
930 North Meacham Road
Schaumburg, Ill. 60196

Accredits programs leading to D.V.M. or V.M.D. degrees.

The following organizations are members of the Council on Postsecondary Accreditation, but are not on the U.S. Office of Education's list of recognized agencies:

Chemistry
American Chemical Society
Committee on Professional Training
1155 Sixteenth Street, N.W.
Washington, D.C. 20036

Accredits undergraduate professional programs.

Construction Education
American Council for Construction Education
1140 Northwest 63rd Street
Oklahoma City, Okla. 73116

Accredits bachelor's degree programs.

Home Economics
American Home Economics Association
Office of Professional Development
2010 Massachusetts Avenue, N.W.
Washington, D.C. 20036

Accredits baccalaureate programs.

Industrial Technology
National Association of Industrial Technology
P.O. Box 627
Charleston, Ill. 61920

Accredits baccalaureate programs.

Law
Association of American Law Schools
One Dupont Circle
Suite 370
Washington, D.C. 20036

Accredits professional schools.

Rehabilitation Counseling
Council on Rehabilitation Education
Rehabilitation Institute
General Classrooms Building
Southern Illinois University
Carbondale, Ill. 62901

Accredits master's degree programs.

NATIONAL ORGANIZATIONS FOR EDUCATION

The following national organizations provide information about colleges and universities or non-traditional college credit and/or programs:

American Association for Higher Education (AAHE)
One Dupont Circle, Suite 780
Washington, D.C. 20036

A national membership organization open to all educators and lay persons concerned with effective American higher education. It also sponsors NEXUS, a telephone referral service that links the caller with knowledgeable persons engaged in almost any area in postsecondary education. AAHE has extensive publications and holds a national conference.

LITERATURE: *College and University Bulletin; Current Issues in Higher Education.*

American Association of Community and Junior Colleges (AACJC)
One Dupont Circle
Washington, D.C. 20036

Founded in 1920, this national organization provides a directory of community and junior colleges ($10.00).

American Association of State Colleges and Universities (AASCU)
One Dupont Circle, Suite 700
Washington, D.C. 20036

A membership organization of 323 state colleges and universities whose activities fall into these areas—government relations; program development; information; and international programs. AASCU has Veterans Information Clearinghouse workshops and conferences and holds an annual meeting.

LITERATURE: Free descriptive leaflet; *MEMO: To the President,* newsletter ($7.00); publications price list; *International Study Centers* (free); *Low Tuition Factbook* ($.50); *Public Aid to Private and Proprietary Institutions* (free); *Recommendations for National Action Affecting Higher Education* (free); *The Case for Educational Support* (free).

Association of American Colleges (AAC)
1818 R Street, N.W.
Washington, D.C. 20009

Founded in 1915, AAC is a national association with more than 600 two- and four-year colleges graduate, and professional schools as members. In addition to publications, programs are sponsored in more than a dozen cities across the country.

LITERATURE: *Liberal Education* (quarterly); *Update* (monthly); *Forum; Trend Reports; Dialogues.*

Association of American Publishers, Inc. (AAP)
AAP Student Service
One Park Avenue
New York, N.Y. 10016

The AAP Student Service was developed by AAP to help students improve their basic reading, writing, and study skills. Booklets for students and college faculty are available.

LITERATURE: (One copy of the following 5 booklets is free; orders for multiple booklets, minimum of 100 booklets, is $7.00)—*How to Build Your Writing Skills; How to Get the Most Out of Your Textbooks; How to Prepare for Examinations; How to Improve Your Reading Skills;* and *What Nonprint Materials Can Do for You in College Teaching.*

CLEP (College-Level Examination Program)
College Board Publications Orders
P.O. Box 2815
Princeton, N.J. 08540

CLEP administers tests in over forty-five subject areas equal to introductory college courses and accepted for credit by many colleges and universities, instead of taking formal classes. There is a $20.00 testing fee for each examination. Write for an application and for the location of the testing center nearest to you.

LITERATURE: *CLEP May Be for You,* descriptive booklet (free).

Educational Resources Information Center (ERIC)
Clearinghouse on Higher Education
One Dupont Circle, Suite 630
Washington, D.C. 20036

George Washington University, under contract with the National Institute of Education, maintains the ERIC Clearinghouse on Higher Education (ERIC/HE), collecting, screening, indexing, and abstracting journals and other related publications on higher education for inclusion in two ERIC bibliographic publications, *Resources in Education* and *Current Index to Journals in Education.*

National University Extension Association
One Dupont Circle, Suite 360
Washington, D.C. 20036

A national organization started in 1915 whose members are universities, colleges, and related organizations and their professional staffs who are dedicated to lifelong learning and public service. The association sponsors a number of publications of interest for the general public and professionals in the field of continuing education.

LITERATURE: Publications price list; *The Guide to Independent Study* ($2.00); newsletter ($27.50); handbook and directory ($25.00).

Office of New Degree Programs
College Entrance Examination Board
888 Seventh Avenue
New York, N.Y. 10019

An organization providing information about innovative programs in higher education.

On-the-job training, or apprenticeships, are sponsored by many local, state, and federally sponsored businesses and organizations. Studying alongside a recognized expert, rather than in a formal institutional educational setting, is one of the oldest forms of education.

The following organizations will refer you to a local apprenticeship program in your field and also provide free or low-cost information on apprenticeships:

Bureau of Apprenticeship and Training
Manpower Administration
U.S. Department of Labor
Washington, D.C. 20213

LITERATURE: Numerous program pamphlets are offered, including *Jobs for Which Apprenticeships Are Available; Apprenticeship; Apprentice Training: Sure Way to a Skilled Craft; Apprenticeship: Past and Present; The National Apprenticeship Program.*

Council of National Organizations for Adult Education
819 Eighteenth Street, N.W.
Washington, D.C. 20006

The membership of this national organization are those associations that offer training programs. The council will provide information on programs that are available in your field.

The following national organizations offer information and educational materials on all types of adult education, including nontraditional innovative programs such as learning exchanges:

Adult Education Association of the United States of America (AEA)
810 Eighteenth Street, N.W., Suite 500
Washington, D.C. 20006

An information clearinghouse and research center on adult education for educators in all areas.

LITERATURE: Descriptive leaflet and publications price list; *Lifelong Learning: The Adult Years* ($18.00 per year); *Adult Education* ($15.00 per year).

Campus-Free College
1239 G Street, N.W.
Washington, D.C. 20005

The College provides a nationwide listing of persons who have been through non-traditional adult education and will offer advice.

Division of Adult Education Programs
U.S. Department of Health, Education, and Welfare
400 Maryland Avenue, S.W.
Washington, D.C. 20202

Through its regional offices or the national headquarters, information is available on adult education programs.

LITERATURE: Write for list of periodicals and literature available for free or a small charge.

Free University Network (FUN)
1221 Thurston
Manhattan, Kan. 66502

FUN publishes a directory of free universities around the country ($1.00) and is itself a free learners' network. For those who would like to start a community education program in their town, write for *How to Start a Free University* ($1.00).

Institute of Lifetime Learning
NRTA/AARP
1909 K Street, N.W.
Washington, D.C. 20049

This national organization of retired persons has branches in major cities throughout the United States. The national headquarters will refer you to your nearest location. If you find the right course, you can register by paying a small membership fee.

The Learning Exchange
P.O. Box 920
Evanston, Ill. 60204

A telephone listing and referral service for educational and recreational subjects that is designed to place individuals in touch with one another to teach, learn, or share a common interest. Associate membership is $15.00.

LITERATURE: *The Learning Exchange News*, quarterly newsletter; *The Learning Exchange Catalog*; "The Learning Exchange: An Alternative in Adult Education" (free with membership).

National Education Association (NEA)
Division of Adult Education Service
1201 16th Street, N.W.
Washington, D.C. 20036

Contact your nearest local NEA office to find out what adult education services and literature they have available to help you.

WOMEN AND EDUCATION

The following national organizations have special programs for women pursuing higher education and women's studies curriculum:

American Association of University Women
2401 Virginia Avenue, N.W.
Washington, D.C. 20037

Founded in 1882, the association has about 200,000 members plus 800 colleges and universities around the country. It is open to women who have a bachelor's, or higher, degree. The association provides educational and informational services, awards for advanced study, research and project grants for AAUW members, and the Recognition Award to Young Scholars (women under 35 years of age). It has extensive publications, sponsors AAUW Educational Foundation, and has local branches throughout the United States. Membership dues are $8.50.

LITERATURE: *Educational Financial Aids* ($1.00); *Tool Catalog* ($6.50); ERA aprons ($4.25); *AAUW Journal* ($4.00; free to members).

Business and Professional Women's Foundation
2012 Massachusetts Avenue, N.W.
Washington, D.C. 20036

The foundation sponsors management seminars around the country (usually for about a $25.00 fee) for strengthening skills in communicating, coordinating, and delegating for administrative assistants, executive secretaries, and supervisors; send for brochure. It also has a special library for women's issue books and a biographical file on important women and on women who are succeeding in fields previously predominated by men.

The Feminist Press
Box 334
Old Westbury, N.Y. 11568

The press's education services include a resource library, speaker services, and courses. Write for a publications list.

National Advisory Council on Women's Educational Programs
1832 M Street, N.W., Rm. 821
Washington, D.C. 20036

Established in 1974 under the Women's Educational Equity Act, the council was appointed by the President to advise and recommend federal policies affecting equitable women's education. It has communications offices, legislative analysis, evaluation of women's studies programs, promotion of equal education (especially for rural girls and women), and a review of HEW's education division.

LITERATURE: Descriptive leaflet.

Office of Women in Higher Education
American Council on Education
One Dupont Circle
Washington, D.C. 20036

Established in 1973 to strengthen the position of women in academic life—as deans, administrators, and college presidents. The office conducts research into the precise number of women in such positions and publishes reports and materials.

LITERATURE: *Institutional Self-Evaluation: The Title IX Requirement* ($1.50).

Project on the Status and Education of Women
Association of American Colleges
1818 R Street, N.W.
Washington, D.C. 20009

An information clearinghouse that works with institutions, government agencies, and other associations and programs affecting women in higher education. Reprints are available covering financial aid for women in education, sexual harassment, related reading lists, and so forth.

WEECN (Women's Educational Equity Communications Network)
Far West Laboratory
1855 Folsom Street
San Francisco, Calif. 94103

Established in 1977 and supported by the U.S. Office of Education, WEECN is an information service and communication system related to women's educational equity. It also compiles bibliographies on non-sexist educational materials, has guidance and counseling, and makes referrals.

LITERATURE: Free descriptive leaflet; write about being placed on their mailing list for their newsletter and notification of available publications.

ADDITIONAL LITERATURE

Adult and Continuing Education Today. Today Publications & News Service, Inc., National Press Building, Washington, D.C. 20045 ($32.00 prepaid). Biweekly newsletter with legislative updates and news items based upon hundreds of transcripts, press releases, scholarly papers, articles, and government documents. Workshops, on-the-job training, and innovative educational techniques are some of the topics covered.

The Chronicle of Higher Education, 1717 Massachusetts Avenue, N.W., Washington, D.C. 20036 ($25.00). Monthly journal with information on innovative college-level programs as well as news articles and job openings for instructors and teachers.

The College Handbook, 16th ed., edited by Susan F. Watts. College Board Publications Orders, Box 2815, Princeton, N.J. 08540 ($8.95). The latest information on more than 2,000 colleges and universities including admission requirements, costs, curriculum, and financial aid. It is a companion volume to *The College Handbook Index of Majors*, listing more than 350 fields of study offered by colleges ($6.95).

College Planning/Search Book. American College Testing Program, P.O. Box 808, Iowa City, Iowa 52240 ($5.00). Checklists and worksheets help high-school students, parents, and counselors choose from the more than 2,700 two-year and four-year colleges.

Continuing Education Programs and Services for Women by the Women's Bureau, U.S. Department of Labor, Pamphlet 10 (1973). Available from the Superintendent of Documents, U.S. Government Printing Office, Washington, D.C. 20402 ($.70). This booklet reports on 450 programs specifically geared to the educational needs of adult women. A background chapter explores the reasons behind the return to college and the need to revise college programs with the unique problems and assets of the returning adult woman in mind.

Directory of Accredited Home Study Schools. National Home Study Council, 1601 18th Street, N.W., Washington, D.C. 20009. Free directory.

Directory of Accredited Private Trade and Technical Schools. National Association of Trade and Technical Schools, 2021 L Street, N.W., Washington, D.C. 20036. Free directory.

Get Credit For What You Know (1974). Women's Bureau, Employment Standards Administration, U.S. Department of Labor, Washington, D.C. 20210. (For sale from the Superintendent of Documents, U.S. Government Printing Office, Washington, D.C. 20402, $.70). A leaflet describing how to get credit from non-school sources, such as on-the-job training, TV, etc.

Getting Skilled by Tom Herbert and John Coyne (1976). E. P. Dutton, 2 Park Avenue, New York, N.Y. 10016 ($4.95). A guide and listing of private and technical schools.

The Graduate (published annually). 13-30 Corporation, 505 Market Street, Knoxville, Tenn. 37902 ($2.00). Magazine-format handbook for graduating college and university students with articles on how to independently continue learning, employment outlooks, how to find a job, starting your own business, getting into professional schools, and more.

The Guide to Career Education by Muriel Lederer (1975). Quadrangle Books, 3 Park Avenue, New York, N.Y. 10016. Comprehensive sourcebook to 200 types of jobs that do not require a college education. It lists apprenticeships, community- and industry-based training programs, and government-sponsored opportunities.

A Guide to Sources of Educational Information by Marda L. Woodbury (1976). Information Resources Press, 2100 M Street, N.W., Washington, D.C. 20037 ($25.00 + $1.85 postage and handling). Invaluable annotated resource and research reference book for anyone working in or interested in education or finding hidden information sources. It also includes nonprint education sources (films, cassettes, etc.).

Guidelines for Students Rights and Responsibilities. The University of the State of New York, The State Education Department, Albany, N.Y. 12234. Check to see if your state education department publishes a similar booklet for students' rights and responsibilities in your state. This booklet published by the University of the State of New York is an excellent discussion of student government, press, inquiry and expression as well as whether a board of education may impose limitations on dress and the availability of student records.

Higher/Wider: A Report on Open Learning Education by Ronald Gross. Office of Reports, The Ford Foundation, 320 East 43rd Street, New York, N.Y. 10017 (free). Booklet on non-traditional education opportunities in your community for you to discover.

I Can Be Anything: Careers and Colleges for Young Women, rev. ed., by Joyce Slayton Mitchell (1978). College Board Publications Orders, P.O. Box 2815, Princeton, N.J. 08541 ($7.95). A detailed discussion of over 100 careers.

The Lifelong Learner by Ronald Gross (1977). Simon and Schuster, 1230 Avenue of the Americas, New York, N.Y. 10020 ($8.95). The pleasant, informative tone of the book is illustrated in the first sentence: "You are already something of a lifelong learner, or you wouldn't have started reading this book." Exactly. If you are a lifelong learner, this is a book you need for your reference shelf after you've digested its wisdom. It has valuable resource sections and an annotated bibliography.

Look Out For Yourself! Helpful Hints For Selecting a School or College (1977). U.S. Department of Health, Education, and Welfare, Office of the Assistant Secretary for Education, Washington, D.C. 20202. A pamphlet presented in question-and-answer format with suggestions on sources of financial aid, some of the terminology in higher education, and a list of information sources.

Lovejoy's College Guide. Lovejoy's College Guide, Inc., 2 Drummond Place, Red Bank, N.J. 07701 ($4.95). Help for the high school student in deciding which college to attend; it contains detailed descriptions of course and department offerings, costs, and follow-up addresses.

National Directory of External Degree Programs by Alfred W. Munzert, Ph.D. (1977). Hawthorn Books, 260 Madison Avenue, New York, N.Y. 10016 ($4.95). In addition to listing available external degree programs by state, an introductory section explains some of the proficiency examinations, correspondence study, and credit for life experience programs.

"New Routes to a College Degree: *New York* Handbook to Nontraditional College Education in New York and New Jersey" by Pat Thaler and Sonya Shapiro. *New York* Magazine, Department H, 755 Seventh Avenue, New York, N.Y. 10017 ($1.00). Ten-page directory to specific schools that also includes a brief "key to educational jargon" and first-person essays by those who have gotten nontraditional degrees.

The New York Times Guide to Continuing Education in America, prepared by the College Entrance Examination Board, Frances Coombs Thomson, editor (1972). Quadrangle Books, 3 Park Avenue, New York, N.Y. 10016 ($4.95). A comprehensive book on this subject, arranged by state with complete addresses and lengthy descriptions.

Peer Perspective. Published by the Project on Equal Education Rights, a project of the NOW Legal Defense and Education Fund, 1029 Vermont Avenue, N.W., Washington, D.C. 20005 (free). This newsletter is concerned with what progress is being made under federal law that prohibits sex discrimination in education. Annotated resources, with ordering instructions, are included as well as legislative updates. Write for their publications price list for other related materials.

Profiles of American Colleges. Barron's Educational Series, Inc., 113 Crossways Park Drive, Woodbury, N.Y. 11797 ($6.95). A directory for the potential student that describes college costs and curricula.

Tips on Home Study Schools. Council of Better Business Bureaus, 1150 17th Street, N.W., Washington, D.C. 20036 (free). This pamphlet in the BBB's Consumer Information Series describes what home study is, the type that is available, accreditation, and a consumer check list.

The Weekend Education Source Book by Wilbur Cross (1976). Harper's Magazine Press, 10 East 53rd Street, New York, N.Y. 10022 ($6.95). A directory of fifty information sources and some 320 centers providing adult education classes or resources.

The following booklets ($.50 per copy) are available from the Public Affairs Committee, Inc., 381 Park Avenue South, New York, N.Y. 10016:

Helping the Slow Learner (#405)
How to Help Your Child in School (#381)
New Paths to Learning: College Education for Adults (#546)

See also the following related chapters in *The Help Book:*

AGING
ARTS
BUSINESS INFORMATION
CHILDREN
CIVIL RIGHTS AND DISCRIMINATION
EMPLOYMENT
FINANCIAL ASSISTANCE
HANDICAPS
INFORMATION RIGHTS AND
   RESOURCES
MEDIA AND COMMUNICATIONS
PARENTING
VETERANS

20

EMERGENCIES AND DISASTERS

Since most natural disasters (tornadoes, hurricanes, fires, earthquakes, blackouts, snowstorms) or medical emergencies (heart attacks, choking, cessation of breathing, wounds) come with little or no warning, BE PREPARED is the best advice. The tools, information, and supplies necessary to deal with an emergency or disaster need not be elaborate or expensive, but they have to be readily available. Information can often minimize risks and reduce the time elapsing from the actual event until the arrival of help. A personal almanac, such as the one that follows, and some basic equipment, can maximize the chances for a person's or a family's survival ability whether in an urban apartment, a suburban home, a car, or a rural cabin.

Make copies of the form or "almanac" that follows and then fill one out for yourself and one for each member of your family. Place copies of these almanacs in your residence or business. Up-to-date photographs are helpful in case a child or an adult is missing; this will save time hunting through albums and also insure that the likeness is a current one. Write in pencil or make copies of the blank record to be used later, since vital information may change from time to time.

For certain information—such as blood type, allergies, and inoculations—do not guess. If you are unsure, have a test rerun, find old records, or call your physicians so that the information contained in your almanac is accurate and readily usable.

Keep one copy of this almanac in an accessible place. An abbreviated version with just a few crucial numbers is also included. That form should be placed by the telephone. Parents should be careful to have a list of vital numbers available for babysitters; someone, perhaps a neighbor, should be listed for contacting in case the parents cannot be reached.

A PERSONAL ALMANAC

NAME _____ DATE OF BIRTH _____

[Insert photo]

Individual or Family (or Office Staff) Photograph

EMERGENCY TELEPHONE NUMBERS

Fire Department _____

Police Emergency Number _____

Local Police Precinct _____ (Telephone) _____

Ambulance Service _____ (Telephone) _____

Nearest Hospital _____ (Telephone) _____

Physicians

Family Physician Name _____ (Office) _____ (Home) _____

Psychiatrist Name _____ (Office) _____ (Home) _____

 or Mental Health Clinic _____

Dentist Name _____ (Office) _____ (Home) _____

Poison Control _____

Suicide Prevention _____

Crime Victims Assistance _____

Next of kin Name _____ Relationship _____

 (Home) _____ (Office) _____

Nextdoor Neighbor _____ (Home) _____ (Office) _____

OTHER INFORMATION SERVICES

Lawyer Name _____
Legal Aid _____
Health Department _____
Consumer Complaints _____
Local Medical Association _____
Local Bar Association _____
Local information service _____
Local branch of the federal information center _____

HEALTH, ACCIDENT, AND CRIME INSURANCE BASIC INFORMATION

Social Security Number _____
Automobile Registration # _____ Type of Car _____ Year _____
Driver's license # _____ Expiration date _____
Health Insurance Policy (Company) _____ # _____
Crime Insurance Policy (Company) _____
Fire Insurance Policy (Company) _____
Homeowners Policy (Company) _____

PERSONAL RECORDS

Credit Cards Type _____ # _____ To report loss _____
           Type _____ # _____ To report loss _____
Checking Account Number _____ Bank & Telephone _____
Savings Account Number _____ Bank & Telephone _____
                        _____ Bank & Telephone _____

MEDICAL HISTORY AND RECORD

Blood Type _____ Rh _____

Any known allergies _____

_____

Any conditions that should be known (diabetes, hemophilia, etc.) _____

_____

_____

Weight _____ Height _____

Any distinguishing scars or birthmarks _____

Major Operations

  Date _____ Type _____ Surgeon _____

  Date _____ Type _____ Surgeon _____

Place this list, or a facsimile, by the telephone:

IMPORTANT TELEPHONE NUMBERS

Fire Emergency _____

Police Emergency Number _____

Local Police Precinct _____

Ambulance Service _____

Nearest Hospital _____

Family Physician   office/home _____

Poison Control _____

Crisis Intervention Counseling _____

Nextdoor Neighbor _____

Parents at work   Father _____

               Mother _____

Children's Schools _____

  Teacher _____

EMERGENCIES

Every four seconds there is a medical emergency in this country. How quickly help is available to the victim may determine life or death. Local

Emergency Medical Services (EMS) vary greatly from community to community. They vary in quality, in who administers the assistance, in how many persons or vehicles are available, and in how quickly help arrives. But even the few minutes that it takes the most efficient and trained medical emergency team to appear might be crucial. Therefore, one or all members of a family should have a working knowledge of basic first aid, including such lifesaving techniques as CPR (cardiopulmonary resuscitation) and what to do in case of heart attack, severe bleeding, choking, snake bites, and major burns.

Free CPR courses are given by many branches of the American National Red Cross, the American Heart Association, and such community service organizations as the Knights of Columbus. General first aid training is also offered at little or no cost by your local health department, fire or police departments, hospital emergency center, local chapters of the American National Red Cross, certain labor departments, insurance companies, and public and private schools.

BASIC FIRST AID SUPPLIES CHECKLIST

You may buy a readymade first aid kit, or you may make up your own, storing the supplies in a plastic or metal case. (Even a commercial kit should be checked, and, if necessary, supplies added.) Check off those supplies that you have and purchase the missing ones. Recheck your kit periodically, to make sure products are still intact—for example, alcohol and peroxide are likely to dry up, thermometers may break, gauze may no longer be sterile.

SUPPLIES	CHECK IF ON HAND	SUPPLIES	CHECK IF ON HAND
Burn ointment	_____	Antiseptic soap or cleanser	_____
Ammonia inhalants	_____	Peroxide	_____
Baking soda	_____	Adhesive bandages (Bandaids)	_____
Epsom salts	_____	Adhesive tape	_____
Boric acid	_____	Oral thermometer	_____
Bicarbonate of soda	_____	Rectal thermometer	_____
Petroleum jelly		Pharmacist-prepared universal	
Sterile absorbent cotton	_____	antidote for poisons	_____
Sterile cotton swabs	_____	Scissors	_____
Sterile eye pads	_____	Tweezers	_____
Sterile gauze pads	_____	Flashlight	_____
Sterile gauze roll (2 inches wide)	_____	Hot water bottle	_____
		Eye cup	_____
Rubbing alcohol	_____		

EMERGENCIES AND DISASTERS / 267

Keep another basic first aid kit in your car that includes splints, a blanket, sterile gauze dressings and adhesive tapes of varying sizes, sterile absorbent cotton, scissors, petroleum jelly, burn ointment, and a flashlight.

HOME OR OFFICE SURVIVAL CHECKLIST

SUPPLIES	CHECK IF ON HAND	SUPPLIES	CHECK IF ON HAND
Fire extinguisher	____	Blanket	____
Smoke detector	____	Emergency lighting (battery-powered units that plug into 110-volt outlets and begin working when lights go out)	____
Battery-operated flashlight in working condition	____		
Checked-out and complete first aid kit	____	Extra batteries	____
Long-burning candles	____	Crime-resistant door and window locks that prevent opening windows more than a few inches	____
Matches	____		
Completed Personal Almanac	____		
First aid book	____	Escape rope or other approved ladder	____
Battery-operated radio	____		
Citizens band radio	____		
Canned foods (that do not require cooking) and bottled water for three days	____		

Certain life-threatening situations, such as impaired breathing, heart failure, severe bleeding, or shock, will require immediate treatment. As necessary, emergency help should be given in this order:

1. Clear the air passage
2. Restore breathing and heartbeat
3. Stop bleeding
4. Treat for shock

Please note, however, that these emergency measures are *not* intended to substitute for either trained medical assistance or even for treatment by a person who has passed approved courses in first aid. Instead they are guidelines to be familiar with if no other alternative is practical and someone's life is possibly in the balance. Remember, if at all possible, it is always best to enlist the help of qualified medical personnel immediately.

The following are some first aid and emergency care methods that you should be familiar with:

BLEEDING*

Signs/Symptoms
Blood coming from an artery, vein, or capillary.

a. Artery—spurting blood, bright red in color

b. Vein—continuous flow of blood, dark red in color

c. Capillary—blood oozing from a wound

First Aid Treatment
1. Cover wound with the cleanest cloth immediately available or with your bare hand and apply direct pressure on the wound. Most bleeding can be stopped in this way.

2. Elevate the arm or leg as you apply pressure (if there is no broken bone).

3. Digital pressure at a pressure point is used if it is necessary to control bleeding from an arterial wound (bright red blood spurting from it). Apply your fingers to the appropriate pressure point—a point where the main artery supplying blood to the wound is located. Hold pressure point tightly for about 5 minutes or until bleeding stops. The three pressure points in the head and neck should only be used as a last resort if there is a skull fracture and direct pressure can't be used. If direct pressure can be used, it will stop bleeding on the head in about 95 percent of the injuries.

4. A tourniquet should be applied to an arm or leg only as a last resort when all other methods fail. A tourniquet is applied between the wound and the point at which the limb is attached to the body, as close to the wound as possible but never over a wound or fracture. Make sure it is applied tightly enough to stop bleeding completely.

In the case of an improvised tourniquet, the material should be wrapped twice around the extremity and half knotted. Place a stick or similar object on the half knot and tie a full knot. Twist the stick to tighten the tourniquet only until the bleeding stops—no more. Secure the stick or level in place with the loose ends of the tourniquet, another strip of cloth, or other improvised material.

Once the tourniquet is put in place, do not loosen it. Mark a "T" on the victim's forehead and get him to a medical facility as soon as possible. Only a doctor loosens or removes a tourniquet.

Note: A tourniquet can be improvised from a strap, belt, handkerchiefs, necktie, cravat bandage, etc. Never use wire, cord, or anything that will cut into the flesh.

INTERNAL BLEEDING

Signs/Symptoms
1. Cold and clammy skin

2. A weak and rapid pulse

3. Eyes dull and pupils enlarged

4. Possible thirst

5. Nausea and vomiting

6. Pain in affected area

First Aid Treatment
1. Treat victim for shock.

2. Anticipate that victim may vomit, give nothing by mouth.

3. Get the victim to professional medical help as quickly and safely as possible.

---

*The following sections on bleeding and shock are reprinted with permission from *First Aid Safety Manual No. 3* by Linda H. Byers and Marilyn Hutchison, M.D., © 1976, U.S. Department of Labor, Mine Safety and Health Administration, pages 15–20.

SHOCK

Shock may accompany any serious injury: blood loss, breathing impairment, heart failure, burns. Shock can kill—treat as soon as possible and continue until medical aid is available.

Signs/Symptoms
1. Shallow breathing
2. Rapid and weak pulse
3. Nausea, collapse, vomiting
4. Shivering
5. Pale, moist skin
6. Mental confusion
7. Drooping eyelids, dilated pupils

First Aid Treatment
1. Establish and maintain an open airway.
2. Control bleeding.
3. Keep victim lying down.

EXCEPTION: Head and chest injuries, heart attack, stroke, sunstroke. If no spine injury, victim may be more comfortable and breathe better in a semi-reclining position. If in doubt, keep the victim flat.

4. Elevate the feet unless injury would be aggravated by this position.
5. Maintain normal body temperature. Place blankets under and over victim.
6. Give nothing by mouth, especially stimulants or alcoholic beverages.
7. Always treat shock in all serious injuries and watch for it in minor injuries, too.

FIRST AID FOR EYE EMERGENCIES*

Specks in the Eye

DO lift upper eyelid outward and down over the lower lid.

DO let tears wash out speck or particle.

DO —if it doesn't wash out—keep eye closed, bandage lightly and see a doctor.

DO NOT rub the eye.

Blows to the Eye

DO apply cold compresses immediately, for 15 minutes; again each hour as needed to reduce pain and swelling.

DO —in case of discoloration or "black eye," which could mean internal damage to the eye—see a doctor.

Cuts and Punctures of Eye or Eyelid

DO bandage lightly and see a doctor at once.

DO NOT wash out eye with water.

DO NOT try to remove an object stuck in the eye.

Chemical Burns

Eye damage from chemical burns may be extremely serious, as from alkalis or caustic

*Reprinted with permission of the National Society to Prevent Blindness.

acids; or less severe, as from chemical "irritants."

In all cases of eye contact with chemicals:

DO flood the eye with water immediately, continuously and gently, for at least 15 minutes. Hold head under faucet and pour water into the eye using any clean container. Keep eye open as widely as possible during flooding.

DO NOT use an eye cup.

DO NOT bandage the eye.

SPRAY CANS are an increasing source of chemical eye injury, compounded by the force of contact. Whether containing caustics or "irritants," they must be carefully used and kept away from children.

TRAFFIC EMERGENCIES*

Auto Accident

Move the vehicles well off the road or out of the traffic flow, if possible, and turn off the ignition.

Help the injured, but don't move them unless they are in danger of further injury from fire or traffic.

Administer only as much first aid as you are qualified to do.

Use flares or warning devices to warn oncoming traffic. **Warning:** Do not light flares near spilled gasoline. Place one 10 feet back of the rear of the vehicle, another 300 feet behind and a third 100 feet ahead of the scene.

Notify the police and send for an ambulance if one is needed.

Write down the license number of the cars involved. Get the names and addresses of other drivers as well as any witnesses.

If you are first at the scene of an accident, park well ahead of the vehicles, account for all occupants, size up the situation, and decide the order of action.

Brake Failure

Pump the brake pedal. You may regain some pressure. If this doesn't help, shift to a lower gear, so engine compression can help slow the car, and apply the parking brake.

If you are traveling down a steep incline when the brakes fail, and you can't reduce speed by downshifting and using the parking brake, drive into heavy brush or snow, or sideswipe a guardrail, sandbank or even parked cars. Avoid a head-on collision at all costs.

Tire Blowout

Don't slam on the brakes. Apply careful pressure on the brake pedal and keep a firm grip on the wheel.

If it's a front tire, the car may pull to the side of the blowout. A rear tire may cause the car to fishtail. Don't oversteer.

When the car is under control and speed reduced, pull onto the road shoulder and look for a level spot on which to change the tire. Switch on your flasher signals and position flares to warn oncoming cars.

* Reprinted with permission from *The Pocket Emergency Handbook*, © 1975 The National Safety Council, pages 12–13.

WHEN BREATHING STOPS

IF A VICTIM APPEARS TO BE UNCONSCIOUS — TAP VICTIM ON THE SHOULDER AND SHOUT, "ARE YOU OKAY?"

IF THERE IS NO RESPONSE — TILT THE VICTIM'S HEAD, CHIN POINTING UP. Place one hand under the victim's neck and gently lift. At the same time, push with the other hand on the victim's forehead. This will move the tongue away from the back of the throat to open the airway.

IMMEDIATELY LOOK, LISTEN, AND FEEL FOR AIR.
While maintaining the backward head tilt position, place your cheek and ear close to the victim's mouth and nose. Look for the chest to rise and fall while you listen and feel for the return of air. Check for about 5 seconds.

IF THE VICTIM IS NOT BREATHING — GIVE FOUR QUICK BREATHS.
Maintain the backward head tilt, pinch the victim's nose with the hand that is on the victim's forehead to prevent leakage of air, open your mouth wide, take a deep breath, seal your mouth around the victim's mouth, and blow into the victim's mouth with four quick but full breaths just as fast as you can. When blowing, use only enough time between breaths to lift your head slightly for better inhalation. For an infant, give gentle puffs and blow through the mouth *and* nose and do not tilt the head back as far as for an adult.

If you do not get an air exchange when you blow, it may help to reposition the head and try again.
AGAIN, LOOK, LISTEN, AND FEEL FOR AIR EXCHANGE.

IF THERE IS STILL NO BREATHING — CHANGE RATE TO ONE BREATH EVERY 5 SECONDS FOR AN ADULT.

FOR AN INFANT, GIVE ONE GENTLE PUFF EVERY 3 SECONDS.

MOUTH-TO-NOSE METHOD — The mouth-to-nose method can be used with the sequence described above instead of the mouth-to-mouth method. Maintain the backward head-tilt position with the hand on the victim's forehead. Remove the hand from under the neck and close the victim's mouth. Blow into the victim's nose. Open the victim's mouth for the look, listen, and feel step.

For more information about these and other life-saving techniques, contact your Red Cross chapter for training.

AMERICAN RED CROSS   **ARTIFICIAL RESPIRATION**

Reprinted with permission from the American Red Cross poster "Artificial Respiration" (revised April 1978).

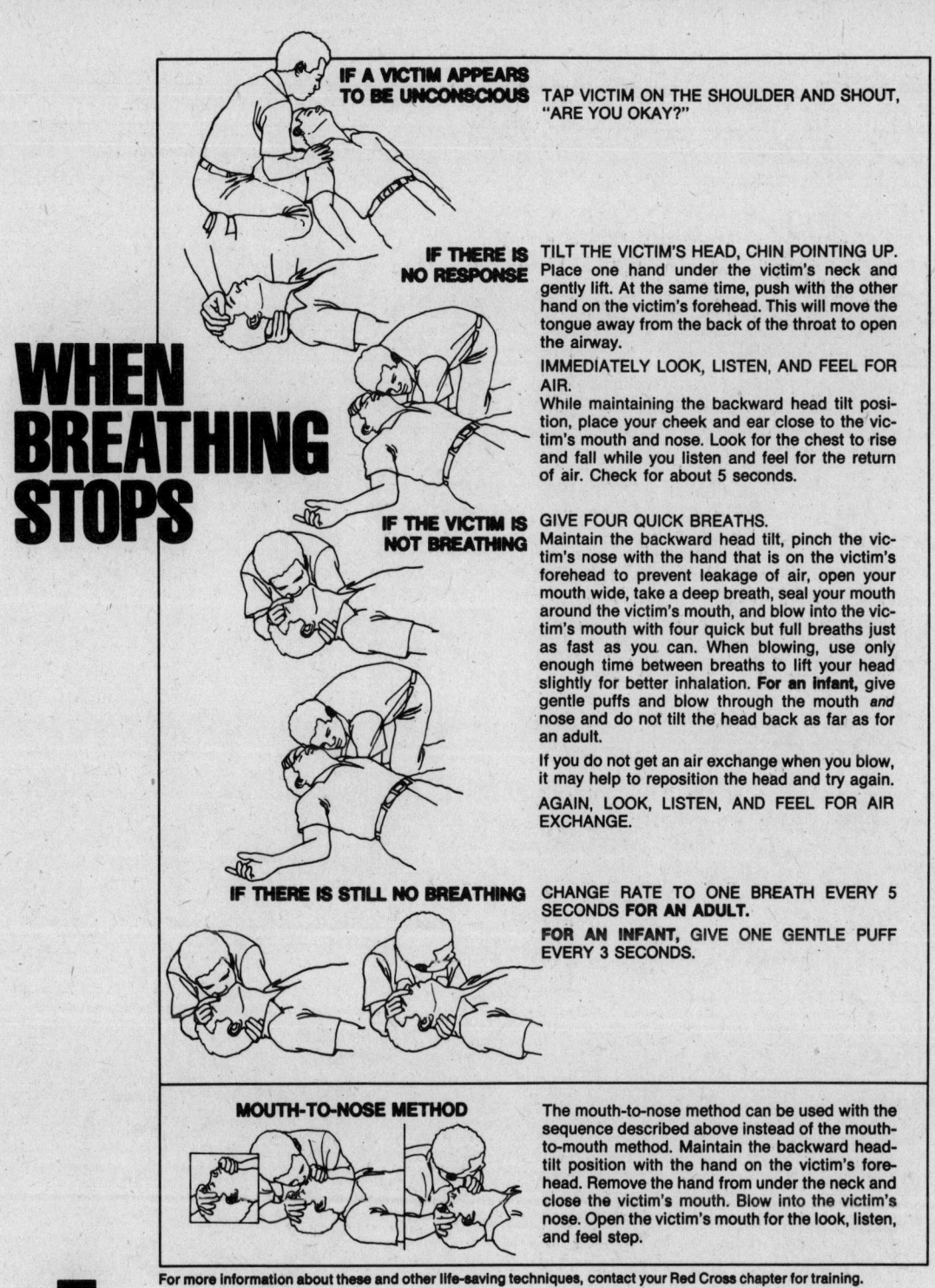

A person choking on food will die in 4 minutes – you can save a life using the HEIMLICH MANEUVER*

Food-choking is caused by a piece of food lodging in the throat creating a blockage of the airway, making it impossible for the victim to breathe or speak. The victim will die of strangulation in four minutes if you do not act to save him.

Using the Heimlich Maneuver* (described in the accompanying diagrams), you exert pressure that forces the diaphragm upward, compresses the air in the lungs, and expels the object blocking the breathing passage.

The victim should see a physician immediately after the rescue. Performing the Maneuver* could result in injury to the victim. However, he will survive only if his airway is quickly cleared.

If no help is at hand, victims should attempt to perform the Heimlich Maneuver* on themselves by pressing their own fist upward into the abdomen as described.

WHAT TO LOOK FOR
The victim of food-choking:

1. Can Not Speak or Breathe.

2. Turns Blue.

Heimlich Sign: Hand to neck signals: "I am choking!"

3. Collapses.

HEIMLICH MANEUVER*

RESCUER STANDING
Victim standing or sitting

- ☐ Stand behind the victim and wrap your arms around his waist.
- ☐ Place your fist thumb side against the victim's abdomen, slightly above the navel and below the rib cage.
- ☐ Grasp your fist with your other hand and press into the victim's abdomen with a **quick upward thrust**.
- ☐ Repeat several times if necessary.

When the victim is sitting, the rescuer stands behind the victim's chair and performs the maneuver in the same manner.

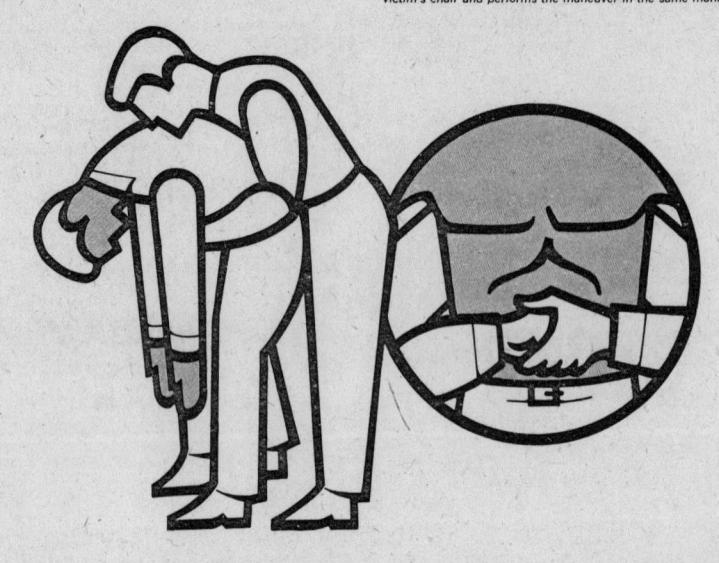

OR

RESCUER KNEELING
Victim lying face up

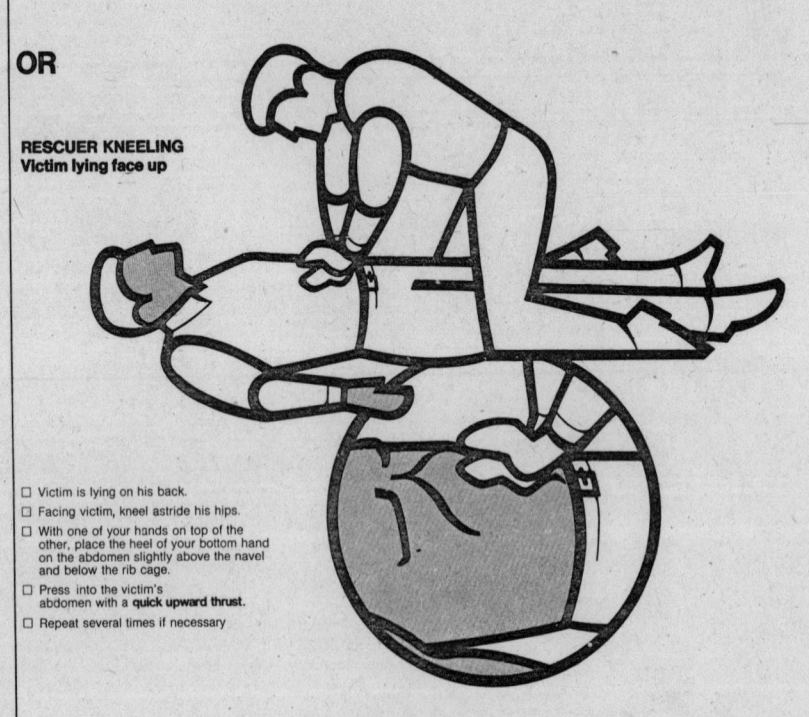

- ☐ Victim is lying on his back.
- ☐ Facing victim, kneel astride his hips.
- ☐ With one of your hands on top of the other, place the heel of your bottom hand on the abdomen slightly above the navel and below the rib cage.
- ☐ Press into the victim's abdomen with a **quick upward thrust**.
- ☐ Repeat several times if necessary

*T.M. PENDING

Reprinted with permission of EDUMED, INC., Box 52, Cincinnati, Ohio 45201 © 1976 and Dr. Henry J. Heimlich. Posters, flyers, teaching slides, and t-shirts on the Heimlich Maneuver are now available. For information, send a stamped, self-addressed envelope to EDUMED, INC., Box 52, Cincinnati, Ohio 45201.

How to tell you're having a heart attack.

A heart attack usually doesn't happen suddenly.
Your body has an early warning system.
Knowing these signs could save your life.

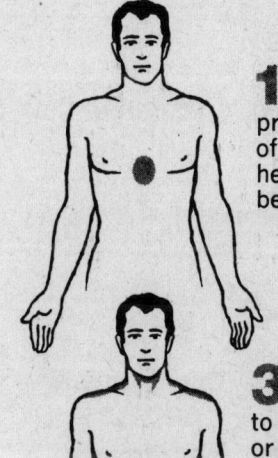

1. One of the first signs is pressure or pain in the middle of the chest. That's where your heart is, not on the left as many believe.

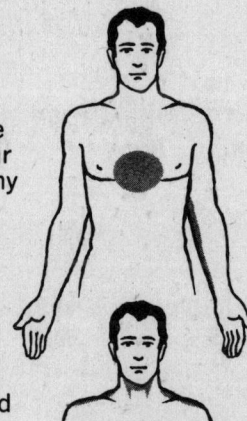

2. This pain can get worse and spread through the whole chest as well as down the left arm.

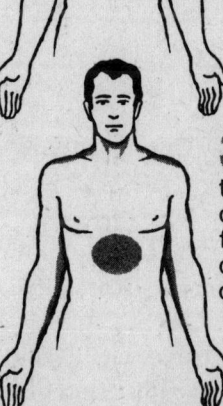

3. The pain may also spread to both arms, shoulders, neck or jaw. A sensation of pressure, fullness or squeezing may occur in the abdomen, and is often mistaken for indigestion.

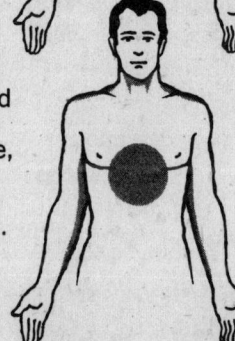

4. Pain may occur in any one or a combination of these areas at the same time. It could even go away and return later. Many times, sweating, nausea, vomiting or shortness of breath may come with the pain.

What to do.

At the first sign of any of these symptoms, call your doctor. If you can't reach your doctor immediately, go to the nearest hospital emergency room at once and ask for prompt treatment.

**Listen to your heart.
It may not warn you again.**

Please fill in.

Doctor's Phone:

Address of Nearest Hospital Emergency Room:

Reprinted with permission of the New York Heart Association.

The following national organizations will provide free or low-cost educational training booklets and leaflets on first aid:

American Academy of Pediatrics
P.O. Box 1034
Evanston, Ill. 60204

American Medical Association
Department of Health Education
535 North Dearborn Street
Chicago, Ill. 60610

American National Red Cross
17th and D Streets, N.W.
Washington, D.C. 20006

National Safety Council
444 North Michigan Avenue
Chicago, Ill. 60611

Pyramid Films (P.O. Box 1048, Santa Monica, Calif. 90406) rents or sells 16mm emergency films; free descriptive brochures are available upon request. Films include: *Bleeding: What to Do* (16 minutes; color; sale $250.00, rental $25.00); *Burn Emergency* (24 minutes; color; sale $350.00, rental $35.00); *New Breath of Life* (20 minutes; color; sale $300.00, rental $30.00); *New Pulse of Life* (CPR—cardiopulmonary resuscitation) (30 minutes; color; sale $350.00, rental $30.00); *Water: Friend or Foe* (23 minutes; color; sale $325.00, rental $30.00).

The following federal and national organizations are involved in helping communities upgrade their EMS services. For further information, contact:

ACT Foundation
Basking Ridge, N.J. 07920

Founded in 1971, ACT Foundation is a nonprofit organization promoting improved emergency medical care in the United States. It is supported by several leading pharmaceutical manufacturers and currently provides information and technical assistance to communities engaged in the same upgrading processes. It also has a public education program.

LITERATURE: EMS Action newsletter (free); order card for free loan films, such as "A Life in your Hands"; *Pre-Hospital Emergency Care: The Life-Saver; ACT Foundation— What It Is and What It Does;* public service TV announcements; position papers, journal articles; "Saving Lives with Pre-Hospital Emergency Care"; "What You Can Do to Help Develop an Effective Emergency Medical Services System in Your Area; heart attack emergency help card.

U.S. Department of Transportation
National Highway Traffic Safety
  Administration
Washington, D.C. 20590

A series of National Training Courses have been developed for Emergency Medical Technicians—paramedics, ambulance drivers, dispatchers, and crash injury management for traffic law enforcement officers. Contact your state's Emergency Medical Service Agency or the Governor's Representative for Highway Safety at your state capital (see listings in Chapter 45, *Safety*) for further information.

LITERATURE: Brochures are available on each program from the above address; teaching aids may be purchased from the Superintendent of Documents, U.S. Government Printing Office, Washington, D.C. 20402.

To help report highway and medical emergencies directly to emergency services, the National Emergency Aid Radio Program (NEAR) has been started to provide organized emergency communication on Citizen's Band (CB) radio. The following states and territories had established or were organizing NEAR programs by January 1978: Alabama, Alaska, Arkansas, California, Florida, Georgia, Hawaii, Idaho, Illinois, Kentucky, Louisiana, Maryland, Nevada, New Mexico, Oklahoma, Oregon, Pennsylvania, South Carolina, Tennessee, Texas, Virginia, Washington, American Samoa, and Guam. For further information on these programs, or to inquire how to start one, contact your state Department of Highway Safety. (See listings for those state agencies in Chapter 45, *Safety*).

The U.S. Department of Transportation has written a booklet that tells how to report highway and medical emergencies through NEAR: *Citizens Band Monitor Guide*. It's available by sending $.80 to Consumer Information Center, Dept. 019F, Pueblo, Colo. 81009.

If you have any medical conditions that are vital to any emergency treatment you might receive, you should register with:

Medic Alert Foundation
P.O. Box 1009
Turlock, California 95380

An international program with a unique system of emergency medical identification designed to speak for individuals with special medical conditions when they cannot communicate in an emergency. Bracelets or necklaces are made that bear the insignia of the medical profession and the words "Medic Alert" in red engraved with specific problem(s) (diabetes, allergic to penicillin, etc.) of the wearer. The onetime basic lifetime membership fee is the cost of the emblem ($7.00–$28.00).

If you are going to be traveling outside your country or city, you might consider learning about emergency medical services registered with:

Intermedic
777 Third Avenue
New York, N.Y. 10017

An international program with participating physicians throughout the world. English-speaking doctors in 170 cities in 89 countries participate under a system of set fees. Yearly membership fees are $6.00 for an individual, $10.00 for a family and include a copy of the *Directory of Participating Physicians*.

POISONING

There are more than 3,000 fatal poisonings yearly; over 200 children die. Another 250,000 survive because of immediate medical attention. All these accidents and deaths are preventable. Keep these poisons* locked up and far out of the reach of children:

---

* Based on *Poison Perils in the Home*, National Safety Council, 1973.

Kitchen Products That Can Kill
Detergent
Drain cleaner
Scouring powder
Oven cleaner
Furniture polish
Floor wax
Metal polish
Wax remover
Wall cleaner
Ammonia
Floor cleaner
Toilet bowl cleaner
Food extracts

Bathroom Poisoners
Aspirin
Prescription drugs
Rubbing alcohol
Liniment
Laxatives
Tinctures
Boric acid

Also Be Wary of:
Shampoo
Hair spray
Bowl cleaner
After shave lotion
Hair tonic

In the Bedroom
Hair spray
Cologne
Nail polish
Polish remover
Face cream
Astringent
Depilatory

Utility Areas Poisoners
Solvents
Turpentine
Paint and varnish
Paint thinner
Pesticides and herbicides
Auto waxes and polishes
Dyes
Charcoal starter
Drain opener
Lye
Glues
Rat and ant poison
Gasoline
Kerosene
Bleach

Check if your county or city has a Poison Control Center. You may easily find out what its telephone number is by calling the local telephone operator or looking in your phone book. Most are 24-hour operations. This is the place to start if there is a poisoning emergency; they give advice about what to do. There are more than 600 poison control centers in the United States; the New York City center, which received 48,000 calls in 1976, is the largest. The Poison Information Center in Philadelphia handled 35,000 calls in 1976. At a poison control center, thousands of index cards contain information on drugs and their antidotes.

CONTAMINATED FOOD*

If you find that a food you bought is contaminated, you will be doing a public service by reporting it to the federal government.

Many legal actions taken by the government are based on information supplied by consumers.

* Reprinted with permission from "Facts About Food Poisoning," *FDA Consumer Memo* (December 1975).

Not all complaints will lead to legal action. But each will be investigated.

If you find a food that is contaminated, call the nearest office of the Food and Drug Administration. You can look it up in the phone book under United States Department of Health, Education, and Welfare.

Be prepared to describe the problem and provide the name of the store in which you bought the food and any codes that appear on the label or container. Also report the problem to the store in which you bought the food, and its manufacturer, packer, or distributor.

This national center provides backup assistance to local poison control emergency programs:

National Clearinghouse for Poison Control Centers
5401 Westbard Avenue
Bethesda, Md. 20016

For information about poisoning and poison prevention, contact these national organizations:

American Association of Poison Control Centers
Committee on Educational Activities
c/o Academy of Medicine
Cleveland Poison Information Center
10525 Carnegie Avenue
Cleveland, Ohio 44106

This national organization offers a wide range of educational materials, such as captioned slide shows, filmstrips, activity books for children, posters, pamphlets, and checklists.

LITERATURE: Home Checklist flyer (free); *Poison Isn't Kid Stuff* (free); *When Times Get Hot and You're Under Stress* (free); publications/audio-visual price list.

National Poison Center Network
Children's Hospital of Pittsburgh
125 DeSoto Street
Pittsburgh, Pa. 15213

This national network serves about 90 million Americans with regional and satellite centers that have 24-hour-a-day staff coverage; each center must meet definite standards. The national center is dedicated to public education about preventive measures—and emergency ones—in case of poisoning.

LITERATURE: "Mr. Yuk" stickers (for labeling household poisons with room for the number of your local poison control center) available with a self-addressed stamped envelope; "Under 5 Understanding Cards: A New Approach to Teaching Poison Prevention"; other free or low-cost leaflets and pamphlets.

National Safety Council
444 North Michigan Avenue
Chicago, Ill. 60611

Numerous free or low-cost pamphlets on poisoning as well as on-going information on poison dangers through its quarterly popular magazine, *Family Safety*.

U.S. Consumer Product Safety Commission
Washington, D.C. 20207

Although the Food and Drug Administration does publish some fact sheets about various types of food poisoning, the Consumer Product Safety Commission is the main information source on preventing poisoning.

278 / THE HELP BOOK

LITERATURE: *Publications, Radio, Films, Slides, Fact Sheets, T.V.*, a free booklet listing the extensive number of publications and audiovisual training aids (geared for the general public) that may be ordered, including *Together We Can Reduce Injury, Wake Up!*

Smoke Detectors Can Save Your Life If . . . ; Take a Close Look: The CPSC Openness Policy; Hazards of Flammable Liquids; Guide to Fabric Flammability; and *Gasoline is Made to Explode.*

FIRST AID FOR POISONING

EYE CONTACT OR SKIN CONTACT:
Flush thoroughly with water for at least 15 minutes.

POISONOUS GASES — Remove victim from fume exposure. In so doing be sure to minimize your exposure to the fumes. If patient is not breathing, start artificial respiration immediately. Do not stop until victim is breathing or help arrives.

CALL YOUR POISON CENTER OR PHYSICIAN PROMPTLY.

SWALLOWED POISONS:

If patient is unconscious or having symptoms of poisoning:
— Transport to nearest medical facility. (If you drive, have someone else attend the patient.)
— Bring with you container(s) of the substance(s) involved.
— If vomiting occurred, bring the vomitus.

If patient is conscious:
— Get medical advice promptly.
— Dilute the poison by giving patient at least one 8 oz. glass of water.
— Induce vomiting (only on medical advice) BUT NOT IF patient is: unconscious or in a coma
   having seizures
   the swallowed poison is a corrosive such as drain cleaner, lye, acid. In this case give liquids.

To induce vomiting (only on medical advice):
— Give one (1) tablespoonful (one-half ounce) of Syrup of Ipecac (for patient one year or older) followed by one 8 oz. glass water. If vomiting does not occur in 15 minutes the dose may be repeated only once. Place patient in spanking position when vomiting begins.

If patient has swallowed kerosene, gasoline or other petroleum distillate, the physician or poison center may advise vomiting. Do so only if directed.

CALL FOR HELP PROMPTLY

Poison Control Center Phone _____   Rescue Squad Phone _____

Physician's Home Phone _____   Physician's Office Phone _____

BE SURE TO HAVE 1 OZ. SYRUP OF IPECAC IN YOUR HOME
(To be used only on medical advice)

Printed as a public service for the American Association of Poison Control Centers
by PLOUGH, INC., Memphis, TN 38151

11/77

Reprinted with permission of the American Association of Poison Control Centers and Plough, Inc., Memphis, Tenn. 38151.

To complain about improperly labeled household products, or to bring pressure on the manufacturers for more accurate and complete information about dangers, contents, and accidental poisoning help, contact your city and state health departments, state legislators, the U.S. Department of Health, Education, and Welfare (Food and Drug Administration), the Consumer Product Safety Commission, and the Department of Agriculture.

NATURAL DISASTERS

Direct help is available from your local fire and police departments, volunteer citizens corps, health bureau, and through the following national organization's local participating branches:

American National Red Cross
Disaster Relief Program
17th and D Streets, N.W.
Washington, D.C. 20006

REGIONAL OFFICES: Eastern Area Office
615 North St. Asaph Street
Alexandria, Va. 22314

Midwestern Area Office
10195 Corporate Square
St. Louis, Mo. 63132

Southeastern Area Office
1955 Monroe Drive, N.E.
Atlanta, Ga. 30324

Western Area Office
P.O. Box 3673
San Francisco, Calif. 94119

The Red Cross provides free emergency assistance in the form of fixed or mobile feeding stations, clothing, shelter, first aid, or provision of other basic needs in all natural disasters. It also makes referrals to disaster loan or grant programs for the victims and maintains disaster action teams.

LITERATURE: *Disaster Relief Program* (brochure) and *Your Community Could Have a Disaster*, with a chart on how the government and Red Cross interact to help victims (both free).

Mennonite Disaster Service
21 South Twelfth Street
Akron, Pa. 17501

Founded in 1950, this transnational disaster relief organization (United States, Canada, Central America, and the Caribbean) was recognized by the Disaster Relief Act of 1974 to help victims of natural disasters, such as earthquakes, floods, hurricanes, tornadoes, and wind storms. They assist in clean up, temporary and permanent repairs, and long-term reconstruction for the elderly, handicapped, widowed, low-income, poverty, and disadvantaged minorities.

LITERATURE: Quarterly newsletter; mid-month bulletin.

The Salvation Army
National Public Affairs Office
1025 Fifteenth Street, N.W.
Washington, D.C. 20005

To meet the needs of victims of natural and man-made disasters, your local office of the Salvation Army offers individual and family counseling, and casework services; registration and identification of victims; missing persons services; medical assistance; temporary shelter, mass feeding, mobile feeding, collection of donated goods for victims, and clothing distribution; furniture, food, commodities, and bedding distribution; services to emergency workers; and referrals.

LITERATURE: Brochures, including "When Disaster Strikes and Rebirth," *Action! The Salvation Army Manual for Emergency Disaster Service* (1972).

The following federal agencies provide information on and/or assistance in disasters:

Federal Disaster Assistance Administration (FDAA)
U.S. Department of Housing and Urban Development
451 Seventh Street, S.W.
Washington, D.C. 20410

Coordinates all government agency disaster programs; administers the Disaster Relief Fund; conducts disaster research and programs in disaster relief and recovery and readiness determination. It is best to inquire on the local level about aid available to victims of major disasters. However, questions will be answered about what programs someone might be eligible for from the Washington, D.C. headquarters. A 24-hour disaster operation center is operated from Washington, D.C., but most calls are from public officials, Congressional representatives, and even the White House to determine the status of a disaster-struck area. Local residents should first contact their local representatives to find out that information.

LITERATURE: *Digest of Federal Disaster Assistance Programs* (available for $2.05 from the Superintendent of Documents, U.S. Government Printing Office, Washington, D.C. 20402), detailed information on federal assistance available in all kinds of emergencies with listings of FDAA regional offices and state disaster offices; fact sheet (July 1, 1974); "Public Law 93-288—An Act" (Disaster Relief Act Amendments of 1974); *Federal Register* (May 28, 1975), "Federal Disaster Assistance Administration."

Disaster Assistance and Emergency Mental Health Section
U.S. Department of Health, Education, and Welfare
National Institute of Mental Health
5600 Fishers Lane
Rockville, Md. 20857

Established in 1974, this section of HEW is aimed at helping community mental health and/or service organizations to respond to the mental health needs of the victims of major disasters. This section stimulates, plans, and develops research, training, and service projects in mental health disaster assistance and other areas related to mental health crises. Technical assistance and consultations are provided to state and local organizations with relevant information disseminated nationwide. They have a referrals program for counselors, physicians, lawyers, and other social services, including emergency shelters and in-service training programs for hospital personnel and mental health workers, including psychiatrists.

LITERATURE: Descriptive brochure.

Internal Revenue Service
1111 Constitution Avenue N.W.
Washington, D.C. 20224

To find out about immediate tax relief available to those who have been victims of emergency or disaster problems, call your local Internal Revenue Service, listed in your telephone directory. If you live in an area that is presidentially designated as an emergency or disaster, write "Disaster Area Loss" at the top of your income tax return. (Or you could claim the losses on the next year's return.)

FIRES

More than 80 percent of the serious fires that claim in excess of 12,000 lives a year in the United States occur in the home while the family is asleep. To reduce a family's vulnerability to fire, the home smoke detector has been invented. Its cost ranges from about $10.00 to $60.00 for each unit. To find out where you can buy one in your area, look in your Yellow Pages under "Fire Protection Equipment" or "Fire Alarms."

FIRE EMERGENCIES*

Steps to Take When Fire Strikes

1. Have an escape plan that the whole family knows about. Try out and perfect the escape routes and practice emergency evacuation with the entire family at least once a year.

2. If fire strikes, don't panic, keep calm. Follow your evacuation plan and make certain everyone is safely out.

3. Call the Fire Department. Learn the location of the nearest fire alarm box and make sure each member of the family knows it too. When reporting a fire: speak slowly and plainly; give address or location; tell extent of fire; and then wait for questions.

Escape Rules

1. Get close to the floor.

2. Take short breaths—and cover face with wet cloth.

3. Keep away from excessive heat, smoke. Feel doors—if hot, don't open.

4. Never leave doors, windows open. This spreads fire.

5. Have an outside gathering point. Is everyone out?

6. Don't re-enter burning building except to save a life.

The following national organizations have numerous free or low-cost materials about fire safety, including smoke detectors:

National Fire Protection Association (NFPA)
470 Atlantic Avenue
Boston, Mass. 02210

NFPA is a public education program, that includes television commercials ("Learn Not to Burn"), Fire Prevention Week, Project EDITH (Exit Drills In The Home), and Spring Clean-Up. It develops codes and standards with NFPA membership either accepting or rejecting proposals at national meetings held twice a year in different cities; local, state, and federal governments have adopted many of those codes and standards as laws. NFPA provides technical assistance, including the largest collection of fire information, with some 17,000 volumes. Membership dues are $40.00 and include the *Fire Journal and Fire News* (newsletter).

LITERATURE: Single free copies of pamphlets if accompanied by self-addressed, stamped business envelope; *Facts about Fire* (fact sheet); news features; publications and visual aids catalog; *Fire Technology Quarterly* ($100.00 a year); *Fire Command Monthly* ($6.00 for members; $8.00 for nonmembers);

---

*Reprinted with permission of Marsh & McLennan, Inc., 1221 Avenue of the Americas, New York, N.Y. 10020.

pamphlets include: "Can Your Roof Burn?" "Home Fire Detection," "Library of Films for Rental and Selected Features For Sale," "Dynamite!," "Mobile Home Fire Check," "Fire, Electricity, and Your Home," "In a Fire Seconds Count," and "This is How Most Fire Extinguishers Work."

National Safety Council
444 North Michigan Avenue
Chicago, Ill. 60611

An information clearinghouse with educational programs in all safety matters, including child safety, fire protection, poisoning, transportation safety, and so forth.

LITERATURE: Free booklets include *All About Fire* and *Detection: First Step in Fire Protection*.

ADDITIONAL LITERATURE

EMERGENCIES

American Medical Association First Aid Manual (1977, 1971). Order Department OP-015, American Medical Association, 535 North Dearborn Street, Chicago, Ill. 60610 ($.30). Useful, illustrated booklet for your home or office library.

Child Safety Is No Accident: A Parent's Handbook of Emergencies by Jay M. Arena, M.D., and Miriam Bachar (1978). Duke University Press, Box 6697, College Station, Durham, N.C. 27708 ($10.95).

Dr. Taylor's Self-Help Medical Guide by Robert B. Taylor, M.D. (1977). Arlington House Publishers, 165 Huguenot Street, New Rochelle, N.Y. 10801 ($9.95). A lively, entertaining, and well-written collection of information on various ailments, listed under their common and medical names. It is not intended as a how-to-treat-yourself medical guide, although some may try to use it that way.

Emergency Medical Guide, 3rd ed., by John Henderson, M.D. (1973). McGraw-Hill Book Company, 1221 Avenue of the Americas, New York, N.Y. 10020 ($12.50). Unlike *A Sigh of Relief* (see below), this is a reference book, since the format does not suggest instant answers. It is a layperson's guide to be read and studied to help understand and avoid the most common or even baffling medical problems.

Family Emergency Almanac (1961). National Safety Council, 444 North Michigan Avenue, Chicago, Ill. 60611 (Stock No. 599.66). A 32-page booklet written with the cooperation of the American Medical Association that covers most common hazards and risk situations facing a family. A colorful, illustrated, and welcome addition to the household, including "How to Call For Help" and an "Emergency Telephone Numbers" page to be filled in.

First Aid, Safety Manual No. 3 by Linda H. Byers and Marilyn Hutchinson, M.D., published by the Mining Enforcement and Safety Administration, U.S. Department of the Interior. Order from Consumer Information Center, Dept. 120E, Pueblo, Colo. 81009 ($ .80). Clear, simple, comprehensive first aid guide for injuries from fractures to snake bites, with line drawings marked with red arrows for key instructions. This is an instant, fast, convenient, all-purpose guide for everyone to have on hand.

The Pocket Emergency Handbook (1975). National Safety Council, 444 North Michigan Avenue, Chicago, Ill. 60611. A 28-page booklet, with a place for emergency numbers, covering medical, traffic, home, and recreation emergencies.

A Sigh of Relief: The First-Aid Handbook for Childhood Emergencies by Martin I. Green (1977). Bantam Books, 666 Fifth Avenue, New York, N.Y. 10019 ($6.95). A primer for parents on the dozens of life-threatening emergency situations that they may have to handle. The drawings are clear and very graphic; the clarity and straightforwardness of the book, which even shows the drugs that children commonly use, may help prevent or alleviate tragedies.

POISONING

"Facts About Food Poisoning," *FDA Consumer Memo* (rev. December 1975), U.S. Department of Agriculture, Washington, D.C. 20250 or U.S. Department of Health, Education, and Welfare, Public Health Service, Food and Drug Administration, 5600 Fishers Lane, Rockville, Md. 20857 (free). A 4-page leaflet on the four common causes of food poisoning—Salmonella, Clostridium perfringens, Staphylococcus, and Clostridium botulinium.

Home Poisons: The Dangerous Trails. National Safety Council, 444 North Michigan Avenue, Chicago, Ill. 60611 (free leaflet).

Poison Perils in the Home. National Safety Council, 444 North Michigan Avenue, Chicago, Ill. 60611 (free booklet).

Protecting Your Family From Accidental Poisoning by Arthur S. Freese (1971). Public Affairs Pamphlets, 381 Park Avenue South, New York, N.Y. 10016 ($ .50). Concise booklet with information on various types of chemical and food poisoning with advice on emergency help procedures.

"Protecting Your Family From Foodborne Illness." Food and Drug Administration, HFG-20, 5600 Fishers Lane, Rockville, Md. 20857 (free single copies).

"Salmonella and Food Poisoning." Food and Drug Administration, HFG-20, 5600 Fishers Lane, Rockville, Md. 20857 (free single copies).

The U.S. Consumer Product Safety Commission, Washington, D.C. 20207, provides the following free literature: "Carbon Monoxide," Fact Sheet No. 13 (rev. May 1975); "Lead Paint Poisoning," Fact Sheet No. 14 (rev. May 1975); *Poison Prevention Packaging: What Pharmacists Should Know;* and *Take a Tip From Safety Sadies: Poison-Proof Your Home*.

DISASTERS

Beginners Guide to Family Preparedness by Rosalie Mason (1978). Horizon Publishers and Distributors, P.O. Box 490, Bountiful, Utah 84010 ($3.95). Household information on food storage, needed medical supplies, candles, clothing, and so on.

The Great International Disaster Book by James Cornell (1976). Charles Scribner's Sons, 597 Fifth Avenue, New York, N.Y. 10017 ($12.50). Some fascinating statistics on natural and manmade disasters, plus a presentation of the stages of reaction to a disaster as well as some practical advice on what to do to protect yourself if a disaster threatens from a volcano, hurricane, tornado, avalanche, and so forth. The second half of the book is a compilation of disaster horror stories through the ages.

"National Disaster Survival Test," *Survival Bulletin* (1977). National Safety Council, 444 North Michigan Avenue, Chicago, Ill. 60611 (free). On May 1, 1977, NBC-TV introduced the basic techniques of survival through their Survival Test. This bulletin is a photographic essay highlighting the key points in the program, such as what to do in a flash flood, earthquake, fire, or if you get sunstroke, frostbite, and much more.

FIRE

Children's Fire Safety Lessons (1976). Kemper Insurance Companies, Long Grove, Ill. 60049 (free). Eight safety lessons, written for children, and illustrated with attractive drawings as a teaching aid about fire prevention for the classroom or at home. It includes the "Children's Fire Safety Song," which is sung to the tune of "Mary Had a Little Lamb."

Fire Safety in the Home: A Security Guide for You and Your Family (1976). National Fire Association, 470 Atlantic Avenue, Boston, Mass. 02210 ($6.95, No. SPP-40). A comprehensive discussion of every exterior and interior part of your home, reevaluated for fire prevention, plus

284 / THE HELP BOOK

information on automatic fire and smoke warning systems, arranging a home inspection by the fire department, and a good home checklist.

Protect Your Home From Fire (1975). Kemper Insurance Companies, Long Grove, Ill. 60049 (free). A home inspection checklist to fireproof your residence, with a few basic facts on fire burns, damage, and fire-related deaths.

Smoke Detectors: What They Are and How They Work (1976). U.S. Department of Commerce, National Bureau of Standards, Washington, D.C. 20230. Illustrated leaflet.

See also the following related chapters in *The Help Book:*

ALCOHOLISM
BATTERED ADULTS
BUSINESS INFORMATION
CHILD ABUSE
CRIME VICTIMS AND WITNESSES
DRUGS, SMOKING, AND DRUG ABUSE
FINANCIAL ASSISTANCE
HANDICAPS
HEALTH
MENTAL HEALTH
MULTIPURPOSE ORGANIZATIONS
SAFETY
SUICIDE PREVENTION
TRANSPORTATION AND TRAVEL

21

EMPLOYMENT

In the past ten years, many changes in the traditional employment area have made the world of work a concern to all Americans. For example, more and more women have entered or reentered the job market. The mandatory retirement age for people working in certain jobs has been raised from sixty-five to seventy, thereby keeping more Americans at work. Flextime, part time, job-sharing, and shorter work weeks have been adopted by more and more companies. Changing careers at midstream is becoming more of the rule than the exception. Financial pressures are forcing seasonal employees, such as teachers or waiters, to find second jobs during their vacation months. The high cost of schooling has forced many students, from the elementary school level through graduate school, to have one or even two part-time or full-time jobs. Therefore skills such as developing a résumé or looking for a job must be learned and relearned.

How is job sharing, just one of the newer trends, working out for some of its advocates? How do you go about finding a shared job?

- At a department store in New Jersey, two women share a job in public relations. Ann Reed and Marilyn Pfaltz, who started out coauthoring cookbooks, worked out such an effective partnership that they persuaded the store to let them split one full-time job.
- At the Federal Reserve Bank of Boston several years ago, Carol Schwartz Greenwald worked half-days as assistant vice-president and economist in partnership with Stephen McNees, a full-time economist. (They both have moved into different positions.)

Traditionally, women who wanted to return to a career have had two choices: a full-time job, possibly necessitating a family upheaval; or a part-time position, generally at the lowest level and without fringe benefits. But now, more and more women (and men) are pairing up with another person and persuading employers to let them handle one full-time job (or its equivalent) between the two of them. They devise their own arrangement for sharing the work load, the paycheck, and the fringe benefits. For example, a married couple in Iowa share a 40-hour week and an annual salary of $11,000 so that they may take turns caring for their two children.

Job pairing, though a distinct newer trend in employment, is still in its infancy. "Theoretically it's a highly workable idea," says Felice N. Schwartz, president of Catalyst, a nationwide organization devoted to expanding career opportunities for women. Catalyst has already set up two successful pilot projects in which women shared jobs as social workers and teachers. Now it is trying to get the concept going full-force in business.

The hardest hurdle is persuading an employer that two can do the job as competently as one. The Iowa couple searched for a year before they found an employer who was open to this novel arrangement; and although they are "very happy this way," they find it difficult to live on their joint small salary. "We eat very little," the husband says. But Carol Greenwald, who started out with the Federal Reserve as a full-time employee, proved so indispensable that the bank actually encouraged a shared arrangement when she was about to have her first child.

What it takes to nail down a buddy-system position is a carefully planned campaign to show a prospective employer how the details can be worked out and what the advantage will be to him or her. Keep in mind that you are trying to accommodate yourself to a job already in existence, not one that an employer will create especially for you. So don't start by figuring out how you and your best friend can sell yourselves as one package.

Instead, isolate the type of job you alone can do and draw up your own résumé. Then look for someone else whose skills match or are compatible with yours. Two women who had majored in art history and had held separate museum jobs were able to talk a major east coast art museum into letting them split one assistant curatorship. Two others, former college friends with library certificates, persuaded a high school in New Jersey to hire them both as one full-time librarian.

Decide in advance how you will share your schedule and how you will communicate with each other so that the two of you can act as one. "The main objection of the store manager," recalls Marilyn Pfaltz, "was how we would 'pass the baton.'" Marilyn was able to explain that it would not be a problem. From their long association as a writing team, she and Ann Reed had already developed a congenial communications system. Now in nightly telephone conversations, they fill each other in on what happened at the office.

Go to the initial interview alone. Sell yourself first, and then present the concept of job pairing. The interviewer will raise certain basic objections. Respond with the proven advantages of job pairing: no absenteeism or unproductive days because you and your partner can fill in for each other; complementary skills and a doubled source of energy for the price of one employee. Explain that fringe benefits need not cost the company more than they would for one employee. Most job pairs pro-rate their benefits by the amount of time each spends at work. Other benefits can be combined or eliminated. A two-week vacation could be restructured so that each partner gets one week.

A detailed guide to reentering the employment market on the buddy system can be found in a booklet, *Your Job Campaign*, available for $1.75 from Catalyst, 14 East 60th Street, New York, N.Y. 10022.

FINDING A JOB

Job-hunting can be one of the most important steps that you take, and also one of the most devastating. Whether you are looking for your first job, reentering the job market, or changing jobs or even careers, help is available in how to prepare a résumé, how to conduct yourself during interviews, and how to discover more job opportunities.

One starting point for free expert advice is your public library. Not only will this specialized library program tell you about available reference books and directories, it may also have actual job opportunities—daily newspaper ads, state or federal job openings, compilations of "Help Wanted" ads in hundreds of trade and professional journals and magazines not easily accessible on your own or in one place. Services vary from library to library, so you might want to call ahead to find out if an appointment is necessary. Another place, if you are a student or even an alumni, is the college employment or career information service. Some, such as the Placement Service Library and the Counseling Service Career Information Library of Lehigh University in Bethlehem, Pennsylvania, have compiled annotated job-hunter's bibliographies. Since the usefulness of such a listing is that the identifying library code numbers are matched to their particular collection, it is best to find out what published guidebooks are available from your library—the one you will actively use in your job hunting.

If you already know the field or type of job you are interested in, you might find out if there is a local branch of the national professional or trade association that pertains to that field or job in your community; speak to someone there about job listings or printed information sheets. They may also know if a national listing, by state, is published in your field. These monthly employment listings, however, are often purchased on a subscription basis. One such subscription listing service is the *National Employment Listing in Criminal Justice*, Texas Criminal Justice Center of Sam Houston State University, Huntsville, Texas 77341 ($16.00 a year).

Many free or low-cost career counseling services are available through your local branch of these national organizations: National Organization for Women

(N.O.W.), Young Men's Christian Association (YWCA), Young Women's Christian Association (YWCA), B'nai B'rith, American Association of University Women (AAUW), National Federation of Business and Professional Women's Clubs, and so forth. Don't overlook classes or workshops offered by your high school, college, university, or trade, professional, and graduate schools in job finding. They may also have a job placement service with which it would be worthwhile registering. (If possible, get a personal interview with the placement officer.) Even after you obtain a job, remember to send updated or revised résumés to placement services to maintain contacts if and when you go looking again. For commercial career counseling assistance, look under "Job Placement" or "Career Counseling" in the phone book.

In addition, each state has a state employment service for free assistance in job hunting. Most state employment services do not make referrals to private agencies where the placement of the individual would result in a fee being charged. The employment or job service may be within the employment security commission, which may also cover unemployment compensation, finance and services. Some states also have job service improvement programs to find out how the state would better serve employer/employee needs. For example, in the state of Mississippi, this resulted in PRO (Professional Resource Office), which acts as a statewide résumé clearinghouse for professional, technical, and managerial applicants. Some states also give priority attention to veterans and preferential treatment to disabled veterans looking for jobs.

The following are the state agencies for labor:

Department of Labor
Administrative Building
64 North Union Street
Montgomery, Ala. 36130

Department of Labor
Sealaska Plaza, 3rd floor
P.O. Box 1149
Juneau, Alaska 99811

Labor Department
Industrial Commission
Commerce Building
1601 West Jefferson
Phoenix, Ariz. 85007

Department of Labor
Capitol Hill Building
4th and High Streets
Little Rock, Ark. 72201

Department of Industrial Relations
State Building Annex
455 Golden Gate Avenue
P.O. Box 603
San Francisco, Calif. 94101

Division of Labor
Department of Labor and Employment
1210 Sherman Street
Denver, Colo. 80203

Department of Labor
200 Folly Brook Boulevard
Wethersfield, Conn. 06109

Department of Labor
801 West Street
Wilmington, Del. 19801

Department of Manpower
600 Employment Security Building
500 C Street, N.W.
Washington, D.C. 20001

Division of Labor
Department of Commerce
510 Collins Building
Tallahassee, Fla. 32304

Department of Labor
Labor Building, Room 288
Atlanta, Ga. 30334

Department of Labor and Industrial Relations
825 Mililani Street
Honolulu, Hawaii 96813

Department of Labor and Industrial Services
317 Main Street
Boise, Idaho 83720

Department of Labor
Alzina Building
100 North First Street
Springfield, Ill. 62706

Division of Labor
1013 State Office Building
Indianapolis, Ind. 46204

Bureau of Labor
East 7th and Court Avenue
Des Moines, Iowa 50309

Department of Human Resources
401 Topeka Boulevard
Topeka, Kans. 66603

Department of Labor
Capital Plaza Tower
Frankfort, Ky. 40601

Department of Labor
P.O. Box 44094
Baton Rouge, La. 70804

Bureau of Labor
Department of Manpower Affairs
State Office Building
Augusta, Me. 04333

Labor and Industry Division
Department of Licensing and Regulation
203 East Baltimore Street
Baltimore, Md. 21202

Department of Labor and Industries
100 Cambridge Street
Boston, Mass. 02202

Department of Labor
Leonard Plaza Building
Lansing, Mich. 48909

Department of Labor and Industry
Space Center Building
444 Lafayette Road
St. Paul, Minn. 55155

Employment Security Commission
1520 West Capitol Street
Jackson, Miss. 39209

Department of Labor and Industrial Relations
421 East Dunklin Street
Jefferson City. Mo. 65101

Department of Labor and Industry
Employment Security Building
Lockey and Roberts
Helena, Mont. 59601

Department of Labor
P.O. Box 94600
Lincoln, Neb. 68509

Office of the Labor Commissioner
601 Kinkead Building
505 East King Street
Capitol Complex
Carson City, Nev. 89710

Department of Labor
1 Pillsbury Street
Concord, N.H. 03301

Department of Labor and Industry
John Fitch Plaza
Trenton, N.J. 08625

Labor and Industrial Bureau
Employment Services Division
Kennedy Hall
College of Santa Fe
Santa Fe, N.M. 87503

Department of Labor
State Campus, Building 12
Albany, N.Y. 12240

Department of Labor
4 West Edenton Street
Raleigh, N.C. 27601

Department of Labor
State Capitol
Bismarck, N.D. 58505

Department of Administrative Services
30 East Broad Street
Columbus, Ohio 43215

Department of Labor
118 State Capitol
Lincoln Boulevard
Oklahoma City, Okla. 73105

Bureau of Labor
State Office Building
1400 S.W. 5th Avenue
Portland, Ore. 97201

Department of Labor and Industry
Labor and Industry Building
Harrisburg, Pa. 17120

Department of Labor
220 Elmwood Avenue
Providence, R.I. 02907

Labor Department
Landmark Center
3600 Forest Drive
Columbia, S.C. 29211

Division of Labor and Management
Department of Labor
Capitol Plaza Office Building
Pierre, S.D. 57501

Department of Labor
501 Union Street
Nashville, Tenn. 37219

Department of Labor and Standards
P.O. Box 12157, Capitol Station
Austin, Tex. 78711

Office of Labor and Training
1331 South State
Salt Lake City, Utah 84115

Department of Labor and Industry
120 State Street
Montpelier, Vt. 05602

Employment Commission
P.O. Box 1358
Richmond, Va. 23211

Department of Labor and Industries
General Administration Building, Third Floor
Olympia, Wash. 98504

Department of Labor
B451 State Office Building 6
1900 Washington Street East
Charleston, W.Va. 25305

Department of Industry, Labor, and Human Relations
201 East Washington Avenue
Madison, Wis. 53702

Department of Labor and Statistics
Barrett Building
2301 Central Avenue
Cheyenne, Wyo. 82002

The U.S. Civil Service Commission, which had been in existence since 1883, was dissolved in December 1978. It had been concerned with federal employment, hiring evaluations, appeals from adverse actions, health and life insurance, and a retirement system for public-service employees. As part of President Carter's reorganization plan, a new agency, the Office of Personnel Management, took its place in January 1979. Contact the Washington, D.C., headquarters for further information as to the functions of this new agency and for any free or low-cost descriptive publications.

The following agencies, through their national, regional, and field offices, provide information on federal laws regarding employment, as well as educational publications on work:

Equal Employment Opportunity Commission (EEOC)
2401 E Street, N.W.
Washington, D.C. 20506

Information clearinghouse on employment.

LITERATURE: *Mission*, monthly newsletter.

U.S. Department of Labor
Office of Information, Publication, and Reports
Washington, D.C. 20210

The various subdepartments of the Department of Labor are coordinated through the Office of Information and Consumer Affairs, Employment Standards Administration, Washington, D.C. 20210. They provide a variety of publications on the rights of workers as well as the resources available in the Department of Labor.

The Wage and Hour Division oversees the wage and hour law that covers most jobs in the United States. Any violations are investigated, in confidence, by the government. Contact your local Wage and Hour Division of the U.S. Department of Labor to request an employment information form. Leaflets are available from your local office, or the national one, as well as a publications list. Some leaflets are "Federal Wage Hour Laws: What's In Them for You?," "The Wage and Hour Representative is Here," and "A Message to Young Workers About the Fair Labor Standards Act."

The Bureau of Labor Statistics publishes data on employment as well as occasional materials of interest to the general public, such as *Jobs for Which Junior College, Technical Institute, or Other Specialized Training is Usually Required*. Other programs of the U.S. Department of Labor, such as those benefiting workers and the unemployed, are available.

Employment Standards Administration
Office of Information and Consumer Affairs
U.S. Department of Labor
Washington, D.C. 20210

Publishes a variety of factsheets, posters, and pamphlets describing rights and resources in various parts of the Labor Department's Employment Standards Administration programs. These programs involve minimum wage, child labor, wage garnishment, equal pay, worker's compensation, and benefits in hiring minorities, women, veterans, and handicapped persons on federal contract work.

The following national organizations provide low-cost job-finding assistance in the form of direct help, as well as extensive publications directed toward the specific needs of job applicants:

B'nai B'rith Career and Counseling Services
1640 Rhode Island Avenue, N.W.
Washington, D.C. 20036

A national clearinghouse on career opportunities that provides direct services for career counseling through twenty regional offices. Write for catalog price list.

National Institute of Career Planning
521 Fifth Avenue
New York, N.Y. 10017

The institute offers career planning advice, seminars, workshops, a list of publications, and 70-hour cassettes.

LITERATURE: *College Job Market Fact Sheet; The Career Game.*

National Personnel Associates (NPA)
Executive Director
Waters Building, Suite 300-D
Grand Rapids, Mich. 49503

Founded in 1956 and now composed of 188 independently owned, professional level placement firms, NPA functions as a cooperative network of these agencies and is a vehicle for the exchange among its members of applicant résumés and company job orders. During 1966 the member agencies completed nearly 35,500 placements of technical, administrative, and marketing personnel. Affiliate offices work primarily on an employer-paid fee basis and intensely promote their national and international capabilities via NPA. It also places national advertising in leading financial newspapers and technical periodicals.

Vocations for Social Change
353 Broadway
Cambridge, Mass. 02139

A resource center that provides counseling, work discussion groups, an unemployment law project, workshops, and a labor information project.

LITERATURE: *Work Liberation*, a pamphlet series including four-page essays on such topics as "Towards a New Definition of Work" and "Alternative Workplaces: Collectives and Cooperatives" ($1.25); *Boston People's Yellow Pages—1976* ($2.50); *Getting Together a People's Yellow Pages* ($1.00); *No Bosses Here: A Manual on Working Collectively* ($3.00); free publications list and descriptive brochure.

For information on health careers, contact this national organization:

National Health Council
P.O. Box 40
Radio City Station
New York, N.Y. 10019

The council publishes an excellent free booklet, *200 Ways to Put Your Talent to Work in the Health Field.* Some of the careers require only months of training after high school; others require several years.

LITERATURE: A *Guide to Health Careers for Minorities, Women, Rural Youth* (free).

For more information on a specialized job area, contact the following national associations and societies (unless otherwise indicated, organizations provide general career information only; + indicates that an organization may also provide a list of training schools, * indicates that an organization may also provide financial aid information):**

Alliance for Engineering in Medicine & Biology +
4405 East-West Highway, Suite 404
Bethesda, Md. 20014

American Academy of Family Physicians +*
1740 West 92nd Street
Kansas City, Mo. 64114

**Reprinted with permission of *200 Ways to Put Your Talent to Work in the Health Field*, rev. ed. 1977, National Health Council, Inc.

American Academy of Health Administration +*
P.O. Box 5518
I-30 at Summerhill Road
Texarkana, Tex. 75503

American Academy of Pediatrics +
1801 Hinman Avenue
Evanston, Ill. 60204

American Academy of Physician's Assistants +*
2341 Jefferson Davis Highway, Suite 700
Arlington, Va. 22202

American Art Therapy Association +
c/o Intermanagement
One Cedar Boulevard
Pittsburgh, Pa. 15228

American Association for Clinical Chemistry +*
1725 K Street, N.W., Suite 1402
Washington, D.C. 20006

American Association for Music Therapy +
Education Building
35 West 4th Street
New York, N.Y. 10003

American Association for Rehabilitation Therapy +
Box 93
North Little Rock, Ark. 72116

American Association for Respiratory Therapy +*
7411 Hines Place, Suite 101
Dallas, Tex. 75235

American Association of Anatomists
Department of Anatomy
University of Arkansas Medical Center
4301 W. Markham Street
Little Rock, Ark. 72204

American Association of Blood Banks +
1828 L Street, N.W., Suite 608
Washington, D.C. 20036

American Association of Colleges of Pharmacy +*
4630 Montgomery Avenue, Suite 201
Bethesda, Md. 20014

American Association of Dental Schools +*
1625 Massachusetts Avenue, N.W.
Washington, D.C. 20036

American Association of Medical Assistants +*
1 East Wacker Drive, Suite 1510
Chicago, Ill. 60601

American Association of Nurse Anesthetists +*
111 East Wacker Drive, Suite 929
Chicago, Ill. 60601

American Association of Occupational Health Nurses
79 Madison Avenue
New York, N.Y. 10016

American Association of Ophthalmology
1100 Seventeenth Street, N.W.
Washington, D.C. 20036

American Association of Orthodontists +
7477 Delmar Boulevard
St. Louis, Mo. 63130

American Cardiology Technologist's Association
Box 3425
Temple, Tex. 76501

American College of Hospital Administrators +*
840 North Lake Shore Drive
Chicago, Ill. 60611

American College of Nurse-Midwives +
1000 Vermont Avenue, N.W., Suite 1210
Washington, D.C. 20005

American College of Nursing Home Administrators +
4650 East-West Highway
Washington, D.C. 20014

American College of Obstetricians and Gynecologists*
1 East Wacker Drive
Chicago, Ill. 60601

294 / THE HELP BOOK

American College of Radiology
20 North Wacker Drive, Suite 2920
Chicago, Ill. 60606

American College of Surgeons +*
55 East Erie Street
Chicago, Ill. 60611

American Corrective Therapy Association +*
6622 Spring Hollow Road
San Antonio, Tex. 78249

American Dance Therapy Association +
2000 Century Plaza, Suite 230
Columbia, Md. 21044

American Dental Assistants Association +*
211 East Chicago Avenue, Suite 1230
Chicago, Ill. 60611

American Dental Association +*
211 East Chicago Avenue
Chicago, Ill. 60611

American Dental Hygienists' Association +*
211 East Chicago Avenue, Suite 1616
Chicago, Ill. 60611

American Dietetic Association +*
430 North Michigan Avenue
Chicago, Ill. 60611

American Foundation for the Blind +*
15 West Sixteenth Street
New York, N.Y. 10011

American Health Care Association
1200 Fifteenth Street, N.W.
Washington, D.C. 20005

American Home Economics Association +*
2010 Massachusetts Avenue, N.W.
Washington, D.C. 20036

American Hospital Association
840 North Lake Shore Drive
Chicago, Ill. 60611

American Industrial Hygiene Association +
66 South Miller Road
Akron, Ohio 44313

American Institute of Biological Sciences
1401 Wilson Boulevard
Arlington, Va. 22209

American Medical Association +*
Department of Health Manpower
535 North Dearborn Street
Chicago, Ill. 60610

American Medical Record Association +*
875 North Michigan Avenue, Suite 1850
Chicago, Ill. 60611

American Medical Technologists +*
710 Higgins Road
Park Ridge, Ill. 60068

American Medical Writers' Association
5272 River Road, Suite 290
Bethesda, Md. 20014

American Occupational Therapy
  Association +*
6000 Executive Building
Rockville, Md. 20852

American Optometric Association +*
243 North Lindbergh Boulevard
St. Louis, Mo. 63141

American Orthoptic Council +
555 University Avenue
Toronto, Ontario M5G, 1X8, Canada

American Orthotic and Prosthetic
  Association +
1444 N. Street, N.W.
Washington, D.C. 20005

American Osteopathic Association +*
212 East Ohio Street
Chicago, Ill. 60611

American Physical Therapy Association +*
1156 Fifteenth Street, N.W., Suite 500
Washington, D.C. 20005

American Podiatry Association +
20 Chevy Chase Circle, N.W.
Washington, D.C. 20015

American Psychiatric Association +
1200 Seventeenth Street, N.W.
Washington, D.C. 20036

American School Health Association +
Box 708
Kent, Ohio 44240

American Society for Medical
   Technologists +*
5555 West Loop South, Suite 200
Bellaire, Tex. 77401

American Society for Pharmacology and
   Experimental Therapeutics
9650 Rockville Pike
Bethesda, Md. 20014

American Society of Clinical Pathologists
P.O. Box 4872
Chicago, Ill. 60612

American Society of Cytology +*
Health Sciences Center, Jefferson University
130 S. 9th Street, Suite 1006
Philadelphia, Pa. 19107

American Society of Electroencephalographic
   Technologists +
2997 Moon Lake Drive
West Bloomfield, Mich. 48033

American Society of Radiologic Technologists
500 N. Michigan Avenue, Suite 836
Chicago, Ill. 60611

American Society of Safety Engineers +
850 Busse Highway
Park Ridge, Ill. 60068

American Society of Ultrasound Technical
   Specialists +
Box 1976, University of Kansas Medical
   Center
Kansas City, Kans. 64103

American Speech and Hearing Association +*
9030 Old Georgetown Road
Washington, D.C. 20014

American Statistical Association
806 15th Street, N.W., Suite 640
Washington, D.C. 20005

American Veterinary Medical Association +
930 North Meacham Road
Schaumberg, Ill. 60196

Association for the Advancement of Health
   Education +
1201 Sixteenth Street, N.W.
Washington, D.C. 20036

Association of Medical Illustrators +
6650 Northwest Highway
Chicago, Ill. 60631

Association of Medical Rehabilitation Directors
   and Coordinators
3830 Linklea Drive
Houston, Tex. 77025

Association of Operating Room Nurses +
10170 East Mississippi Avenue
Denver, Colo. 80231

Association of Operating Room Technicians +
1100 W. Littleton Boulevard, Suite 201
Littleton, Colo. 80120

Association of Schools for Public Health +
1825 K Street, N.W., Suite 707
Washington, D.C. 20006

Association of University Programs in Health
   Administration +*
One Dupont Circle, Suite 420
Washington, D.C. 20036

Biological Photographic Association +*
P.O. Box 1057
Rochester, Minn. 55901

Biomedical Engineering Society +
P.O. Box 2399
Culver City, Calif. 90230

Council on Social Work Education +
345 East 46th Street
New York, N.Y. 10017

Environmental Management Association +
1701 Drew Street
Clearwater, Fla. 33515

Health Sciences Communications
   Association +
P.O. Box 79
Millbrae, Calif. 94030

Hospital Financial Management Association
666 North Lake Shore Drive, Suite 245
Chicago, Ill. 60611

Institute of Food Technologists*
221 North LaSalle Street
Chicago, Ill. 60641

International Fabricare Institute +
Box 940
Joliet, Ill. 60434

Joint Commission on Allied Health Personnel
   in Opthalmology +
1575 University Avenue
St. Paul, Minn. 55104

Maternity Center Association + *
919 North Michigan Avenue, Suite 3208
Chicago, Ill. 60611

National Association for Hearing and Speech
   Action
814 Thayer Avenue
Silver Spring, Md. 20910

National Association for Mental Health
1800 N. Kent Street
Arlington, Va. 22209

National Association for Music Therapy + *
Box 610
Lawrence, Kan. 66044

National Association for Practical Nurse
   Education and Service + *
122 East 42nd Street
New York, N.Y. 10017

National Association of Dental Laboratories + *
3801 Mount Vernon Avenue
Alexandria, Va. 22305

National Association of Human Services
   Technologists +
1127 11th Street, Main Floor
Sacramento, Calif. 95814

National Association of Science Writers
Box H
Sea Cliff, N.Y. 11579

National Association of Social Workers *
1425 H Street, N.W., Suite 600
Washington, D.C. 20005

National Athletic Trainers Association + *
3315 South Street
Lafayette, Ind. 47904

National Council for Homemaker-Home Aide
   Services + *
67 Irving Place
New York, N.Y. 10003

National Easter Seal Society for Crippled
   Children and Adults
2023 W. Ogden Avenue
Chicago, Ill. 60612

National Environmental Health Association
1600 Pennsylvania Avenue
Denver, Colo. 80203

National Executive Housekeepers
   Association + *
Business and Professional Building
414 Second Avenue
Gallipolis, Ohio 45631

National Federation of Licensed Practical
   Nurses *
250 West 57th Street, Room 1511
New York, N.Y. 10019

National League for Nursing + *
10 Columbus Circle
New York, N.Y. 10019

National Male Nurse Association + *
2309 State Street
Saginaw, Mich. 48602

National Rehabilitation Counselling
   Association + *
155 K Street, N.W., Suite 1110
Washington, D.C. 20005

National Student Nurses Association *
10 Columbus Circle, Room 2330
New York, N.Y. 10019

National Therapeutic Recreation Society + *
1601 North Kent Street
Arlington, Va. 22209

Opticians Association of America +
1250 Connecticut Avenue, N.W.
Washington, D.C. 20036

Society for Public Health Educators +
693 Sutter Street
San Francisco, Calif. 94102

Society of Nuclear Medicine +
475 Park Avenue South
New York, N.Y. 10016

Technical Education Research Center +
44 Brattle Street
Cambridge, Mass. 02138

U.S. Dept. of Health, Education, and
  Welfare, PHS, HRA
Bureau of Health Manpower*
9000 Rockville Pike
Bethesda, Md. 20014

U.S. Dept. of Transportation
Emergency Medical Services Branch
N-42-13
Washington, D.C. 20540

The growing trend toward alternative, non-"nine-to-five," job opportunities—job sharing, flextime, three- or four-day work weeks—is the concern of these national organizations:

Bureau of Policies and Standards
U.S. Civil Service Commission
1900 E Street, N.W.
Washington, D.C. 20415

This federal bureau has information on flextime or part-time employment in the public sector.

New Ways to Work
457 Kingsley Avenue
Palo Alto, Calif. 94301

An information clearinghouse on innovative work patterns and places, such as job sharing and collective ownership and management arrangements, that provides vocational counseling services, consults with work organizations to try to promote more flexible patterns, and sponsors community education and publications programs. Written requests are preferred.

LITERATURE: Reprints; *A Booklet of General Information About Job Sharing*; *The People's Guide to a Community Work Center: How to Start One and Run It Cooperatively* by Sidney Brown (1977).

Women's Equity Action League (WEAL)
733 Fifteenth Street, N.W., Suite 200
Washington, D.C. 20005

Founded in 1968, WEAL is a nationwide membership organization dedicated to improving the social, economic, and legal status of all women through education, legislation, and litigation.

LITERATURE: *A Guide to Alternative Employment Opportunities*, March 1977 (1.00); write for a listing of original materials on alternative work patterns.

Work in America Institute, Inc.
700 White Plains Road
Scarsdale, N.Y. 10583

An independent, nonprofit organization that brings together representatives from management, labor, and government to discuss such common concerns as alternative work schedules.

LITERATURE: *Alternative Work Patterns: Changing Approaches to Work Scheduling* by David Robison, 1976 ($5.00); *World of Work Report*, monthly ($18.00 a year).

RETIREMENT

Information about retirement—pensions, second careers, mandatory retirement policies—are handled through these national organizations:

298 / THE HELP BOOK

Gray Panthers
National Headquarters
3700 Chestnut Street
Philadelphia, Pa. 19104

Contact your local chapter for information; see complete listing in Chapter 2, *Aging*.

National Retired Teachers Association/ American Association of Retired Persons (NRTA/AARP)
1909 K Street, N.W.
Washington, D.C. 20049

Contact your local chapter for assistance; see complete listing in Chapter 2, *Aging*.

Pension Rights Center
1346 Connecticut Avenue, N.W., #1019
Washington, D.C. 20036

A public interest group organized to protect and promote the rights of persons who look to pension plans for a secure retirement income. It informs individuals about their rights under the Employee Retirement Act of 1974, represents their interests before the government agencies charged with implementing the law, conducts studies, serves as an information clearinghouse on pensions, and publishes fact sheets; it does not handle law suits.

LITERATURE: *Pension Facts 1* lists four pension myths and provides answers; *You and Your Pension* by Ralph Nader and Kate Blackwell ($1.65); send a self-addressed stamped envelope for fact sheets.

UNIONS

Basic information on union activities is provided through the field offices of the following federal agency:

National Labor Relations Board (NLRB)
1717 Pennsylvania Avenue, N.W.
Washington, D.C. 20570

Field offices throughout the United States in most major cities provide information and services for working men and women, employers, and unions. The NLRB was established to enforce the National Labor Relations Act, namely that "employees shall have the right to self-organization, to form, join, or assist a labor organization . . . and shall also have the right to refrain from any or all such activities." The NLRB also oversees union elections.

LITERATURE: "Information for Voters in Labor Board Elections," free descriptive leaflet on the rights of employees and employers; *Jurisdictional Guide*.

The following are the major unions in the United States; contact the headquarters for detailed information on entry requirements, dues, benefits, etc., or for a referral to your nearest local affiliate:

American Federation of Labor—Congress of
 Industrial Organization (AFL-CIO)
815 Sixteenth Street, N.W.
Washington, D.C. 20006

American Federation of State, County, and
 Municipal Employees (AFSCME)
1625 L Street, N.W.
Washington, D.C. 20005

United Automobile, Aerospace and
  Agricultural Implement Workers of America
  (Ind) (UAW)
8000 East Jefferson Avenue
Detroit, Mich. 48214

United Brotherhood of Carpenters and Joiners
  of America (CJA)
101 Constitution Avenue, N.W.
Washington, D.C. 20001

Amalgamated Clothing and Textile Workers of
  America (ACTWA)
15 Union Square
New York, N.Y. 10003

Communication Workers of America (CWA)
1925 K Street, N.W.
Washington, D.C. 20006

International Brotherhood of Electrical
  Workers (IBEW)
1125 Fifteenth Street, N.W.
Washington, D.C. 20005

International Union of Electrical, Radio and
  Machine Workers (IUE)
1126 Sixteenth Street, N.W.
Washington, D.C. 20036

American Federation of Government
  Employees (AFGE)
1325 Massachusetts Avenue, N.W.
Washington, D.C. 20005

Hotel and Restaurant Employees and
  Bartenders International Union (HREU)
120 East Fourth Street
Cincinnati, Ohio 45202

Laborers International Union of North
  America (LIUNA)
905 Sixteenth Street, N.W.
Washington, D.C. 20006

International Ladies Garment Workers Unions
  (ILGWU)
1710 Broadway
New York, N.Y. 10019

National Association of Letter Carriers of the
  U.S.A. (NALC)
100 Indiana Avenue, N.W.
Washington, D.C. 20001

International Association of Machinists and
  Aerospace Workers (IAM)
1300 Connecticut Avenue, N.W.
Washington, D.C. 20036

Meat Cutters and Butcher Workmen of North
  America Amalgamated (AMC & BW)
2800 North Sheridan Road
Chicago, Ill. 60657

United Mine Workers of America (UMW)
900 Fifteenth Street, N.W.
Washington, D.C. 20005

National Education Association (Ind) (NEA)
1201 Sixteenth Street, N.W.
Washington, D.C. 20036

International Union of Operating Engineers
  (IUOE)
1125 Seventeenth Street, N.W.
Washington, D.C. 20036

International Brotherhood of Painters and
  Allied Trades (PAT)
United Unions Building
1750 New York Avenue, N.W.
Washington, D.C. 20006

United Paperworkers International Union
  (UPIU)
163-03 Horace Harding Expressway
Flushing, N.Y. 11365

United Association of Journeymen and
  Apprentices of the Plumbing and Pipefitting
  Industry of the United States and Canada
  (PPF)
901 Massachusetts Avenue, N.W.
Washington, D.C. 20001

American Postal Workers Union (APFWU)
817 Fourteenth Street, N.W.
Washington, D.C. 20005

Brotherhood of Railway, Airline and
Steamship Clerks, Freight Handlers,
Express and Station Employees (BRACK)
6300 River Road
Rosemont, Ill. 60018

Retail Clerks International Association (RCIA)
Suffridge Building
1775 K Street, N.W.
Washington, D.C. 20006

United Rubber, Cork, Linoleum and Plastic
Workers of America (URW)
87 South High Street
Akron, Ohio 44308

Service Employees' International Union
(SEIU)
2020 K Street, N.W.
Washington, D.C. 20006

United Steelworkers of America (USWA)
Five Gateway Center
Pittsburgh, Pa. 15222

American Federation of Teachers (AFT)
11 Dupont Circle, N.W.
Washington, D.C. 20036

International Brotherhood of Teamsters,
Chauffeurs, Warehousemen and Helpers of
America (Ind) (IBT)
25 Louisiana Avenue, N.W.
Washington, D.C. 20001

United Transportation Union (UTU)
1460 Detroit Avenue
Cleveland, Ohio 44107

WOMEN AND WORK

Federal agencies concerned with working women include:

Women's Bureau
Employment Standards Administration
U.S. Department of Labor
Washington, D.C. 20210

Develops policies and programs to promote the welfare of women in the labor force; encourages better use of women power; offers information and assistance to state and community leaders and to other nations regarding women and work; provides speakers; has extensive free publications; provides technical assistance to those preparing conferences or projects related to women workers; serves as an information clearinghouse on working women; and makes referrals to local agencies for direct services.

LITERATURE: *Minority Women Workers: A Statistical Overview; A Guide to Seeking Funds from CETA: A Booklet to Assist Individuals and Organizations to Learn How to Apply for CETA Monies; Women Workers Today; Mature Women Workers: A Profile; The Women's Bureau: 55 Years of Partnership with Women; A Working Woman's Guide to Her Job Rights; Publications of the Women's Bureau.*

Women's Bureau
U.S. Department of Labor
Branch of Labor Force Research
Room 1322
Washington, D.C. 20036

Offers information on job opportunities.

The following national women's organizations are concerned with working women:

Business and Professional Women's Foundation
2012 Massachusetts Avenue, N.W.
Washington, D.C. 20036

See listing in Chapter 7, *Business Information.*

Catalyst
14 East 60th Street
New York, N.Y. 10022

See entry in Additional Literature under "Working Women."

Martha Movement
P.O. Box 283
Burke, Va. 22015

A national organization funded by membership dues ($5.00 a year) and contributions to give recognition and status to homemakers. It is not an antifeminist protest or a lobbying organization, but addresses itself to the needs of the 63 million women over eighteen who identify themselves as homemakers even though some work outside the home and some are widowed or divorced.

LITERATURE: Newsletter, *Martha Matters;* fact sheets; brochure.

National Committee on Household Employment (NCHE)
7705 Georgia Avenue, N.W., Suite 208
Washington, D.C. 20012

A private, nonprofit membership organization that seeks to improve the status, image, and working conditions for the 1.5 to 3 million private household employees; women constitute 97 percent of all workers in that occupation. There are more than forty-one chartered affiliates in twenty-five states with about 10,000 household workers as members.

LITERATURE: Fact sheets; *NCHE News,* newsletter; leaflets.

National Organization for Women (NOW)
5 South Wabash, Suite 1615
Chicago, Ill. 60603

Many of the 800 local chapters of NOW throughout the country offer employment seminars, workshops, and job referral services.

Project on the Status of Education of Women
Association of American Colleges
1818 R Street, N.W.
Washington, D.C. 20009

The project will help women locate women's centers for local job information.

LITERATURE: Fact sheets.

Working Women United Institute
593 Park Avenue
New York, N.Y. 10021

Founded in 1975, this national organization acts as a clearinghouse of information on working women as well as a direct service providing legal and general information, communication education, rap sessions, and a speaker's bureau.

Young Women's Christian Association (YWCA) and Young Women's Hebrew Association (YWHA)

Contact your local branch for employment/career services. See complete listings for national headquarters in Chapter 40, *Multipurpose Organizations.*

Local independent women's work groups have been started throughout the United States to provide help specifically to women in both job counseling and job placement and for women who are already employed; a sampling of local groups follows:

Career Counseling
Career Planning Center, Inc.
1623 South La Cienega Boulevard
Los Angeles, Calif. 90035

National Organization for Women
New York Chapter
47 East 19th Street
New York, N.Y. 10003

Options for Women, Inc.
8419 Germantown Avenue
Philadelphia, Pa. 19118

There are now a number of advocacy groups for working women. Although these groups are basically citywide, they publish newsletters and other materials that can be mailed nationwide. They include the following:

Cleveland Women Working (CWW)
1258 Euclid Avenue
Cleveland, Ohio 44115

A membership organization for women office workers concerned with problems on the job. CWW provides equal employment rights counseling and sponsors forums and special events.

LITERATURE: Bimonthly newsletter; "Resolution on Equal Rights for Working Women" ($15.00); "Working Women's Guide to Greater Cleveland."

9 to 5 Organization for Women Office Workers
140 Clarendon Street
Boston, Mass. 02116

This membership organization (dues on a sliding scale depending on income) also offers their newsletter for $2.00 ($3.00 out of state.) In addition to the Women Office Workers Bill of Rights, 9 to 5 sponsors meetings and pressures companies to change unfair policies. Write for more details on the reports and studies that they have published.

Women Employed (WE)
37 South Wabash Avenue
Chicago, Ill. 60603

A Chicago Loop working women's action group to end discrimination. Membership dues range from $5.00 to $15.00. Discrimination counseling service for Chicago area women, for which there is a fee, is available.

Women Office Workers (WOW)
680 Lexington Avenue
New York, N.Y. 10022

Since its beginnings, WOW has sought to gain better working conditions for women office workers by issuing a Bill of Rights and gaining governmental recognition of Women Office Workers' Week. Conferences are planned throughout the year and membership ($5.00 yearly) includes a subscription to their newsletter.

Women Organized for Employment
127 Montgomery Street
San Francisco, Calif. 94104

A direct-action pressure group of working women organized to fight against job discrimination and for equal pay, job posting, and promotions for women. It works with other groups around the country on affirmative action laws.

WORKER'S COMPENSATION

Each state offers worker's compensation to eligible employees who are either injured on the job or develop occupation-related diseases. The amount of the award for which an individual is eligible varies from state to state, but the federal government has set as a goal not less than two-thirds of the claimant's average weekly wage as well as automatic cost of living adjustments. You should always consider whether an employer is covered by workmen's compensation before you take a job and be careful about signing any waivers that absolve an employer of any responsibility if you sustain job-related injuries. If the legitimacy of your claim is in question, your case will probably be decided by a Workmen's Compensation Review Board. Compensation to workers includes such benefits as medical care, weekly disability payments, death benefits to dependents, and rehabilitation to reduce the disability and allow an injured worker to return to work as soon as possible.

The following are the state agencies for workmen's compensation. They provide information and referrals to your nearest district office:

Workmen's Compensation Division
Department of Industrial Relations
649 Monroe Street
Montgomery, Ala. 36104

Workmen's Compensation Division
Department of Labor
Sealaska Plaza, 3rd floor
P.O. Box 1149
Juneau, Alaska 99811

Compensation Fund
1616 West Adams Street
Phoenix, Ariz. 85007

Workmen's Compensation Commission
Social and Rehabilitative Services Department
Justice Building
Little Rock, Ark. 72201

Division of Industrial Accidents
Workers' Compensation Appeals Board
455 Golden Gate Avenue
San Francisco, Calif. 94102

Division of Labor
Department of Labor and Employment
1210 Sherman Street
Denver, Colo. 80203

Workmen's Compensation Commission
295 Treadwell Street
Hamden, Conn. 06514

Industrial Accident Board
Department of Labor
618 North Union Street
Wilmington, Del. 19805

Bureau of Workmen's Compensation
Division of Labor
Department of Commerce
501 Collins Building
Tallahassee, Fla. 32304

Board of Workmen's Compensation
Labor Building, Room 476
Atlanta, Ga. 30334

Disability Compensation Division
Department of Labor and Industrial Relations
825 Mililani Street
Honolulu, Hawaii 96813

Industrial Commission
317 Main Street
Boise, Idaho 83720

Illinois Industrial Commission
160 North LaSalle Street
Chicago, Ill. 61601

Industrial Board
601 State Office Building
Indianapolis, Ind. 46204

Workers' Compensation Division
Capitol Building
Des Moines, Iowa 50319

Division of Workers' Compensation
Department of Human Resources
401 Topeka Boulevard
Topeka, Kans. 66603

Workmen's Compensation Board
Department of Labor
Capital Plaza Tower
Frankfort, Ky. 40601

Industrial Accident Commission
State Office Building
Augusta, Me. 04333

Workmen's Compensation Commission
108 East Lexington Street
Baltimore, Md. 21202

Division of Industrial Accidents
Leverett Saltonstall State Office Building
100 Cambridge Street
Boston, Mass. 02202

Bureau of Workers' Disability Compensation
Department of Labor
309 North Washington Square
Lansing, Mich. 48909

Workers' Compensation Division
Department of Labor and Industry
Space Center Building
444 Lafayette Road
St. Paul, Minn. 55155

Workmen's Compensation Commission
Room 1404, Sillers Building
Jackson, Miss. 39205

Division of Workmen's Compensation
Department of Labor and Industrial Relations
722 Jefferson Street
Jefferson City, Mo. 65101

Workers' Compensation Division
Department of Labor and Industry
815 Front Street
Helena, Mont. 59601

Workmen's Compensation Court
State Capitol
Lincoln, Neb. 68509

Nevada Industrial Commission
NIC Building
515 East Musser Street
Carson City, Nev. 89714

Department of Labor
Workmen's Compensation Division
1 Pillsbury Street
Concord, N.H. 03301

Division of Worker Compensation
Department of Labor and Industry
John Fitch Plaza
Trenton, N.J. 08625

Workmen's Compensation
Labor and Industrial Bureau
Employment Services Division
College of Santa Fe
Santa Fe, N.M. 87503

Workmen's Compensation Board
Department of Labor
Building 12, State Campus
Albany, N.Y. 12240

Industrial Commission
Eastgate Office Center
4000 Old Wake Forest Road
Raleigh, N.C. 27611

Workmen's Compensation Bureau
Russel Building
Highway 83 North
Bismarck, N.D. 58501

Department of Worker's Compensation
246 North High Street
Columbus, Ohio 43215

Industrial Court
Jim Thorpe Office Building
2101 North Lincoln Boulevard
Oklahoma City, Okla. 73105

Workmen's Compensation Board
Labor and Industries Building
Capitol Mall
Salem, Ore. 97310

Bureau of Occupational Injury and Disease
  Compensation
Department of Labor and Industry
1647 Labor and Industry Building
Harrisburg, Pa. 17120

Division of Workmen's Compensation
Department of Labor
25 Canal Street
Providence, R.I. 02903

Industrial Commission
1800 St. Julian Place
Columbia, S.C. 29204

Division of Labor and Management Relations
Department of Labor
Capitol Plaza Office Building
Pierre, S.D. 57501

Workmen's Compensation Division
Department of Labor
501 Union Street
Nashville, Tenn. 37219

Industrial Accident Board
P.O. Box 12757, Capitol Station
Austin, Tex. 78711

Workmen's Compensation
Industrial Commission
350 East 5th South
Salt Lake City, Utah 84111

Department of Labor and Industry
120 State Street
Montpelier, Vt. 05602

Industrial Commission
Blanton Building
1220 Bank Street
Richmond, Va. 23219

Bureau of Industrial Insurance Appeals
Capitol Center Building
410 West Fifth Street
Olympia, Wash. 98504

Workmen's Compensation Fund
307 State Office Building 4
112 California Avenue
Charleston, W.Va. 25305

Division of Workmen's Compensation
Department of Industry, Labor, and Human
  Relations
152 General Executive Facility 1
201 East Washington Avenue
P.O. Box 7901
Madison, Wis. 53707

Worker's Compensation Division
Office of the State Treasurer
2305 Carey Avenue
Cheyenne, Wyo. 82001

ADDITIONAL LITERATURE

FINDING A JOB

Careers Today by Gene R. Hawes, Mark Hawes, and Christine Fleming (1977). New American Library, Plume Books, 1301 Avenue of the Americas, New York, N.Y. 10019 ($3.95). Descriptions and follow-up addresses for more than 150 jobs that require two years, or less, training. It describes expected income, job hunting (where and how), and further information resources.

Dress for Success by John T. Molloy (1975). Peter H. Wyden, 747 Third Avenue, New York, N.Y. 10017. The best-seller on how to dress to get the job results that you want.

Go Hire Yourself an Employer by Richard K. Irish (1973). Anchor/Doubleday Books, Garden City, N.Y. 11530.

The Graduate: A Handbook for Leaving School (published annually). 13-30 Corporation, 505 Market Street, Knoxville, Tenn. 37902 ($2.00). Useful, well-written how-to articles on job hunting.

The Hidden Job Market by Tom Jackson and Davidyne Maykas (1976). Quadrangle Books, Three Park Avenue, New York, N.Y. 10017

306 / THE HELP BOOK

($12.00). A very popular guide developed by Jackson, who is a frequent college guest lecturer.

How to Get a Job . . . Fifty Essential Questions and Answers About Future Employment for College and University Students (1977). Manager, Corporate Programs, Armco Steel Corporation, Middletown, Ohio 45043 (free). This booklet covers such areas as career and interview preparation, the follow-up interview, and transition to employment.

Merchandising Your Job Talents, U.S. Department of Labor (1978). Consumer Information Center, Department 021F, Pueblo, Colo. 81009 ($1.20). This booklet helps you do a self-appraisal as preparation for writing a résumé or filling out job applications.

Occupation Outlook Handbook (updated annually). Bureau of Statistics, Department of Labor, Superintendent of Documents, U.S. Government Printing Office, Washington, D.C. 20402 ($8.75). Thousands of jobs are described along with their employment outlook and necessary training; follow-up addresses are provided for further information.

What Color Is Your Parachute? A Practical Manual for Job-Hunters and Career-Changers by Richard Nelson Bolles (1978). Ten Speed Press, P.O. Box 7123, Berkeley, Calif. 94707 ($5.95 + $.50 postage and handling). A popular guide providing information on everything from obtaining free job-hunting help to identifying the man or woman who has the power to hire you. This edition features "The Quick-Job-Hunting Map," a chapter to help you identify your skills, where you want to use those skills, and how to get hired in a suitable related job.

"You Can Be More Than You Are." Careers, P.O. Box 111, Washington, D.C. (free). A record and booklet about technical opportunities now available in the United States.

Arco Publishing Company, Inc., 219 Park Avenue South, New York, N.Y. 10003, publishes the *Complete Guide to U.S. Civil Service Jobs* as well as individual, large format, softcover books on each type of job and the civil service tests required for employment. Send for a free catalog and price list.

WORKING WOMEN

Career Options Series. Catalyst, Box H-6, 14 East 60th Street, New York, N.Y. 10022 ($1.95). Self-guidance publications describing opportunities for undergraduate women in ten traditionally male-dominated fields: government and politics, industrial management, finance, engineering, retail management, accounting, sales, restaurant management, insurance, and banking. The series includes two workbooks—*Planning for Career Options* and *Launching Your Career*.

Everything a Woman Needs to Know to Get Paid What She's Worth by Caroline Bird (1973). David McKay, 750 Third Avenue, New York, N.Y. 10017 ($8.95).

The Executive Woman, 1 Dag Hammarskjold Plaza, New York, N.Y. 10017 ($24.00). Offers referrals to women looking for women's business services, professional workshops, courses, occasional job openings, dinners for women to get together and make contacts.

The Good Housekeeping Woman's Almanac by the editors of the *World Almanac* (1977). Newspaper Enterprise Association, Inc., 230 Park Avenue, New York, N.Y. 10017 ($3.95). See especially Chapter 8, "Workers." Other chapters, such as "Artists," "Literary Women," and "Stateswomen," also deal with pertinent job-related information.

I'm Madly in Love With Electricity and Other Comments About Their Work by Women in Science and Engineering by Nancy Kreinberg (1977). Lawrence Hall of Science, University of California, Berkeley, Calif. 94720, Attention: Careers ($1.00). A booklet based on questionnaires completed by 160 women in the San Francisco Bay Area. Photographs.

The Managerial Woman by Margaret Hennig and Anne Jardim (1977). Anchor Press/Doubleday, Garden City, N.Y. 11530 ($7.95). Popular executive advice book.

Ms Magazine, 370 Lexington Avenue, New York, N.Y. 10017 ($1.00 an issue/$10.00 a year). Popular monthly magazine with articles on work.

New Life Options: The Working Woman's Resource Book by Rosalind K. Loring and Herbert A. Otto (1976). McGraw-Hill Book Company, 1221 Avenue of the Americas, New York, N.Y. 10020 ($10.95). A collection of essays on various aspects of the working woman's life from job hunting to volunteer services to living alone to the new world of retirement. Includes annotated bibliographies and additional resources for follow-up inquiries.

The Résumé Preparation Manual—For the Individual Woman (1978). Catalyst, Box H-6, 14 East 60th Street, New York, N.Y. 10022 ($3.50). A step-by-step workbook to help women determine essential first steps, such as job targets, developing a personal biography, analyzing achievements and problem-solving skills.

Woman's Almanac, compiled and edited by Kathryn Pualsen and Ryan A. Kuhn (1976). J. B. Lippincott Company, East Washington Square, Philadelphia, Pa. 19105 ($6.95). See especially the section, "Working," pages 272–322.

The Woman's Dress for Success Book by John T. Molloy (1977). Follett Publishing Company, 1010 West Washington Boulevard, Chicago, Ill. 60607 ($9.95).

WORKING IN GENERAL

Choosing a Union. Vocations for Social Change/WCH, 353 Broadway, Cambridge, Mass. 02139 ($.25).

Four Days, Forty Hours and Other Forms of the Rearranged Workweek, edited by Riva Poor, foreword by Paul A. Samuelson (1970, 1973). New American Library, P.O. Box 999, Bergenfield, N.J. 07621 ($1.95). A profile of four-day firms with a selected bibliography on the workweek.

Hoffa and the Teamsters: A Study of Union Power by Ralph and Estelle James (1965). D. Van Nostrand Company, 450 West 33rd Street, New York, N.Y. 10001 ($6.95). The Jameses were allowed to follow Hoffa around and the result is a book both historically significant and fascinating to read.

The Retirement Threat by Tony Lamb and Dave Duffy (1977). J. P. Tarcher, Inc. 9110 Sunset Boulevard, Los Angeles, Calif. 90069 ($7.95). Intended for persons in their forties and older. Expert Tony Lamb, who is seventy-three, talks about retirement, his senior activism, and how to avoid retirement crises. He provides valuable and extensive directory listings.

Working by Studs Terkel (1972, 1974). Avon Books, 959 Eighth Avenue, New York, N.Y. 10019 ($2.25). Interviews with workers in all fields and disciplines by a veteran journalist and radio commentator.

Working For Yourself by Geof Hewitt (1978). Rodale Press Inc., Organic Park, Emmaus, Pa. 18049 ($6.95). Thirty-five self-employed persons of varying occupations explore the pros and cons, how-to's and how-not-to's of self-employment.

Work Liberation. Vocations for Social Change/WCH, 353 Broadway, Cambridge, Mass. 02139 ($1.25). Nine pamphlets highlighting work and social change issues, including "Towards a Worker's Bill of Rights," "The New U.S. Class Structure," "Workplace Change," and "Towards a New Definition of Work."

You and Your Pension by Ralph Nader and Kate Blackwell (1973). Grossman Publishers, 625 Madison Avenue, New York, N.Y. 10022 ($1.65). A key resource on how to avoid being one of the millions of people who expect pensions but never get them.

Your Rights as a Worker (1978). Vocations for Social Change/WCH, 353 Broadway, Cambridge, Mass. 02139 ($2.00).

Youth and Minority Unemployment by Walter E. Williams (1977). Hoover Institution Press Studies Series, Stanford University, Stanford, Calif. 94305 ($2.00). A 44-page monograph on the reasons for youth and minority unemployment and some policy recommendations.

See also the following related chapters in *The Help Book:*

AGING
ARTS
BUSINESS INFORMATION
CIVIL RIGHTS AND DISCRIMINATION
EDUCATION
FINANCIAL ASSISTANCE
HANDICAPS
INFORMATION RIGHTS AND RESOURCES
VOLUNTEERISM

22

ENVIRONMENT

To complain about an environmental violation in your community, contact the specific city- or county-related office—e.g., Air Pollution Control, Department of Environmental Service, Solid Waste Removal, Energy, Water Pollution. To find out more about state environmental regulations as well as general information, call or write your local bureau or contact the state agency listed on the various subcategories or environmental concerns that follow.

The following federal agencies may offer some help:

Office of Consumer Affairs/Special Impact
Federal Energy Administration (FEA)
Washington, D.C. 20461

FEA has limited jurisdiction to solve individual consumer complaints and will do so only if the problem involves the violation of a federal statute; otherwise, FEA will refer the complainant to another agency or private group for assistance.

U.S. Environmental Protection Agency (EPA)
Office of Public Affairs
401 M Street, S.W.
Washington, D.C. 20460

The EPA accepts complaints about legislation or national regulations. It is an information clearinghouse on all aspects of pollution—its effects on your health, what you can do about it, what causes it. There are fifteen environmental control programs unified into a single independent agency with integrated programs to improve air and water quality, solid waste management, the use of pesticides, and levels of radiation and noise.

LITERATURE: Publications list of free literature; brochures and leaflets include *EPA Protecting Our Environment; Model Noise Control Ordinance; Our Endangered World; Clean Air: The Breath of Life.*

EPA REGIONAL OFFICES

Each regional office has a public affairs director who can provide assistance and materials to individuals and groups seeking to work on environmental problems.

EPA, San Francisco, Calif. 94111: Covers Arizona, California, Hawaii, Nevada, American Samoa, Guam, Trust Territories of the Pacific, Wake Island.

EPA, Denver, Colo. 80203: Covers Colorado, Montana, North Dakota, South Dakota, Utah, Wyoming.

EPA, Atlanta, Ga. 30309: Covers Alabama, Florida, Georgia, Kentucky, Mississippi, North Carolina, South Carolina, Tennessee.

EPA, Chicago, Ill. 60606: Covers Illinois, Indiana, Michigan, Minnesota, Ohio, Wisconsin.

EPA, Boston, Mass. 02203: Covers Connecticut, Maine, Massachusetts, New Hampshire, Rhode Island, Vermont.

EPA, Kansas City, Mo. 64108: Covers Iowa, Kansas, Missouri, Nebraska.

EPA, New York, N.Y. 10007: Covers New Jersey, New York, Puerto Rico, Virgin Islands.

EPA, Philadelphia, Pa. 19106: Covers Delaware, Maryland, Pennsylvania, Virginia, West Virginia, Washington, D.C.

EPA, Dallas, Tex. 75201: Covers Arkansas, Louisiana, New Mexico, Oklahoma, Texas.

EPA, Seattle, Wash. 98101: Covers Alaska, Idaho, Oregon, Washington.

The following national organizations act as educational and informational clearinghouses on several environmental issues:

Center for Environmental Education, Inc.
2100 M Street, N.W.
Washington, D.C. 20037

The center publishes a magazine, *Environmental Education Report*, and administers the Whale Protection Fund.

The Conservation Foundation (CF)
1717 Massachusetts Avenue, N.W.
Washington, D.C. 20036

CF conducts research, education, and information activities in the area of the environment; it is not a membership organization.

LITERATURE: Monthly newsletter; write for publication list of reprints, reports, pamphlets, studies, and books. *Business and Environment: Toward Common Ground* ($10.00); *Environmentalists and Developers: Can They Agree on Anything?* ($2.00); *Paying for Pollution: Water Quality and Effluent Changes* ($4.00); *The Conservation Foundation Letter* ($10.00/yearly).

Environmental Action, Inc. (EA)
1346 Connecticut Avenue, N.W., Suite 731
Washington, D.C. 20036

EA was founded after Earth Day in 1970; it is a lobbying group that lobbies on national legislation and federal regulation on such environmental issues as water pollution, energy conservation, and utility rate reform.

Environmental Defense Fund (EDF)
40 East 54th Street
New York, N.Y. 10022

Founded in 1967, EDF is a nationwide organization of scientists, lawyers, and economists working toward public interest protection in environmental quality, energy, health, and consumer welfare. Bringing about the banning of DDT pesticide in the United States was one of its well-known accomplishments.

LITERATURE: Newsletter.

Friends of the Earth (FOE)
124 Spear Street
San Francisco, Calif. 94105

A national information clearinghouse, lobbying organization, and publisher with chapters throughout the United States, that is concerned with environmental issues; FOE has numerous educational materials and books.

LITERATURE: *Not Man Apart*, biweekly ($25.00 a year) "The Energy and Environment Bibliography," compiled by Betty Warren (April 1977; $2.00); *Sun!* ($2.95); *Progress: As If Survival Mattered* ($6.95); FOE Books Catalogue.

Institute for Local Self-Reliance
1717 Eighteenth Street, N.W.
Washington, D.C. 20009

The institute conducts projects in urban energy resources and municipal waste management.

The National Wildlife Federation (NWF)
1412 Sixteenth Street, N.W.
Washington, D.C. 20036

NWF is a nonprofit, publicly supported conservation education organization with over 3.5 million members in all fifty states and the U.S. territories. Check your local telephone directory for the address and phone number of your state affiliate. Members receive numerous free publications; nonmembers may purchase them. Some of their publications include *National Wildlife*, a bimonthly conservation magazine, *Conservation Report*, and the *Conservation Directory* (see Additional Literature), a valuable listing of government agencies, people, and organizations active in the conservation-environmental field. NWF also sponsors National Wildlife Week each year.

Sierra Club
530 Bush Street
San Francisco, Calif. 94108

Information on environmental issues is available through the Office of Information. Sierra Club is a membership organization ($20.00 yearly).

LITERATURE: Free pamphlets; magazines available by subscription or as part of membership dues; *Sierra Club Bulletin* ($1.00 each issue or included in membership dues).

Many state environmental conservation agencies are "super agencies" with numerous departments and agencies within that agency covering fish and wildlife, environmental protection, parks and recreation, forests, and water resources. Audiovisual materials and low-cost booklets are generally available; referrals are made to appropriate agencies for further information.

The following are the state agencies for environmental affairs:

Environmental Health Administration
381 State Office Building
Montgomery, Ala. 36130

Department of Environmental Conservation
3220 Hospital Drive
Pouch O
Juneau, Alaska 99811

Division of Environmental Health Services
Department of Health Services
1740 West Adams Street
Phoenix, Ariz. 85007

Department of Pollution Control and Ecology
8001 National Drive
Little Rock, Ark. 72209

Resources Agency
Resources Building
1416 9th Street
Sacramento, Calif. 95814

Office of the Governor
127 State Capitol
200 East Colfax Avenue
Denver, Colo. 80203

Department of Environmental Protection
117 State Office Building
Hartford, Conn. 06115

Division of Environmental Control
Department of Natural Resources and
 Environmental Control
Tatnall Building
Capitol Complex
Dover, Del. 19901

Department of Environmental Services
Presidential Building
415 12th Street, N.W.
Washington, D.C. 20004

Department of Environmental Regulation
Montgomery Building
2562 Executive Center Circle, East
Tallahassee, Fla. 32301

Environmental Protection Division
Department of Natural Resources
270 Washington Street, S.W.
Atlanta, Ga. 30334

Office of Environmental Quality Control
Office of the Governor
State Capitol
Honolulu, Hawaii 96813

Division of Environment
Department of Health and Welfare
700 West State
Boise, Idaho 83720

Environmental Protection Agency
2200 Churchill Road
Springfield, Ill. 62706

Environmental Management Board
1330 West Michigan Street
Indianapolis, Ind. 46202

Department of Environmental Quality
3920 Delaware Avenue
Des Moines, Iowa 50313

Division of Environment
Department of Health and Environment
Forbes Field
Topeka, Kans. 66620

Bureau of Environmental Quality
Department for Natural Resources and
 Environmental Protection
Capital Plaza Tower
Frankfort, Ky. 40601

Division of Health and Environmental Quality
P.O. Box 60630
Baton Rouge, La. 70160

Department of Environmental Protection
State House
Augusta, Me. 04333

Maryland Environmental Service
Department of Natural Resources
60 West Street
Annapolis, Md. 21401

Executive Office of Environmental Affairs
100 Cambridge Street
Boston, Mass. 02202

Department of Natural Resources
Stevens T. Mason Building
Lansing, Mich. 48926

Environmental Planning Division
State Planning Agency
100 Capitol Square Building
550 Cedar Street
St. Paul, Minn. 55101

Air and Water Pollution Control Commission
1100 Robert E. Lee Building
Jackson, Miss. 39201

Division of Environmental Quality
Department of Natural Resources
2010 Missouri Boulevard
Jefferson City, Mo. 65101

Environmental Sciences Division
Department of Health and Environmental
 Sciences
Board of Health Building
Helena, Mont. 59601

Department of Environmental Control
P.O. Box 94877
Lincoln, Neb. 68509

State Environmental Commission
113 Nye Building
201 South Fall Street
Capitol Complex
Carson City, Nev. 89710

Department of Environmental Protection
P.O. Box 1390
Trenton, N.J. 08625

Environmental Improvement Division
Health and Environment Department
Crown Building
725 St. Michael's Drive
Santa Fe, N.M. 87503

Department of Environmental Conservation
50 Wolf Road
Albany, N.Y. 12233

Division of Environmental Management
Department of Natural Resources and
  Community Development
P.O. Box 27687
Raleigh, N.C. 27611

Environmental Control Services
Department of Health
Capitol
Bismarck, N.D. 58505

Environmental Protection Agency
361 East Broad Street
Columbus, Ohio 43216

Department of Pollution Control
N.E. 10th and Stonewall Streets
Oklahoma City, Okla. 73105

Department of Environmental Quality
522 S.W. Fifth
Portland, Ore. 97201

Department of Environmental Resources
Evangelical Press Building
3rd and Reily Streets
Harrisburg, Pa. 17120

Environmental Health and Safety
Department of Health and Environmental
  Control
R. J. Aycock Building
2600 Bull Street
Columbia, S.C. 29201

Department of Environmental Protection
Joe Foss Building
Pierre, S.D. 57501

Department of Public Health
349 Cordell Hull Building
436 6th Avenue, North
Nashville, Tenn. 37219

Environmental Protection Division
Office of the Attorney General
Supreme Court Building
P.O. Box 12548, Capitol Station
Austin, Tex. 78711

Bureau of Environmental Health
Division of Health
Department of Social Services
44 Medical Drive
Salt Lake City, Utah 84112

Agency of Environmental Conservation
% State Office Building
Montpelier, Vt. 05602

Council on the Environment
Office of the Governor
Ninth Street Office Building
9th and Grace Streets
Richmond, Va. 23219

Department of Ecology
Olympia, Wash. 98504

Department of Natural Resources
669 State Office Building 3
1800 Washington Street, E.
Charleston, W. Va. 25305

Department of Natural Resources
1408, 4619 University Avenue
Madison, Wis. 53705

Department of Environmental Quality
Hathaway Building
Cheyenne, Wyo. 82002

314 / THE HELP BOOK

The chart on pages 315–316 lists whether or not each state has a pervasive plan for water, air, or noise pollution, the agency that supervises that plan, and maximum penalties for violations.

AIR POLLUTION

To complain about an air-pollution problem in your own area, call the local bureau of air pollution control (usually a part of your county or city Board or Bureau of Health). Although local and state agencies are responsible for implementing and carrying out air pollution control, the Environmental Protection Agency may step in, in certain instances.

*If All Else Fails**

While the Clean Air Act gives the states the main responsibility for bringing the air we breathe to healthful and safe levels, the act also provides that EPA may take action if the states do not. For example:

EPA may, after a thirty-day notice, issue an administrative order or take civil action against anyone violating the requirements of an implementation plan. Criminal penalties for knowing violations range up to $25,000 a day and one year in prison for the first offense, and up to $50,000 a day and two years in prison for subsequent violations.

EPA may enforce all or part of a state plan if a state is not willing or able to do so.

And EPA may seek emergency court action to stop pollution if an air pollution episode threatens "imminent and substantial endangerment" to public health.

The EPA also publishes numerous booklets on air pollution control, including "Don't Leave It All to the Experts: The Citizen's Role in Environmental Decision Making"; "Pollution and Your Health"; "Clean Air: It's Up to You, Too"; "Clean Air: The Breath of Life."

The following federal agencies and national organizations are concerned with air pollution, its control and its effects on individuals and the environment:

American Lung Association
1740 Broadway
New York, N.Y. 10019

This national organization, through its local chapters, publishes and distributes numerous free leaflets, booklets, and research papers on the health effects of air pollution. Contact your local association, or write to the national headquarters for information.

LITERATURE: "Air Pollution: The Facts About Your Lungs," leaflet; *Controlling Air Pollution*, booklet; *Air Pollution Primer; Photochemical Oxident: Health Effects Report; Sulphur Oxides/Particulars, Health Effects*

---

* Reprinted from *Clean Air. It's Up to You, Too* (March 1973), U.S. Environmental Protection Agency, Washington, D.C.

	WATER POLLUTION			AIR POLLUTION			NOISE
	PERVASIVE PLAN	SUPERVISING BODY	MAXIMUM PENALTIES	PERVASIVE PLAN	SUPERVISING BODY	MAXIMUM PENALTIES	NOISE POLLUTION LAWS
ALABAMA	YES	Dept. of Health; Water Improvement Commission	Cease & Desist Orders	YES	Dept. of Health; Air Pollution Control Comm.	$10,000/violation/day; 1 yr. jail	NO
ALASKA	YES	Dept. of Environmental Conservation	$25,000/violation; 1 yr. in jail	YES	Dept. of Environmental Conservation	$25,000/violation; 1 yr. in jail	NO
ARIZONA	YES	Dept. of Health; Water Quality Control Council	Injunction; 1 yr. jail	YES	Dept. of Health; Div. of Air Pollution Control	$5,000/day	NO
ARKANSAS	YES	State Pollution Control Commission	$1,000/day + 30 days jail	YES	State Pollution Control Commission	$1,000/day; 30 days jail	NO
CALIFORNIA	YES	State Water Quality Control Board; Local Water Quality Control Boards	6 mos. jail & injunction	YES	State Air Resources Board; Local Air Pollution Control Districts	$6,000/day	YES
COLORADO	YES	Dept. of Health; Water Pollution Control Comm.	Injunctions	YES	Dept. of Health; Air Pollution Control Comm.	None stated except injunctions	YES
CONNECTICUT	YES	Dept. of Environmental Protection	$1,000/day	YES	Dept. of Environmental Protection	$5,000/week	YES
DELAWARE	YES	Dept. of Natural Resources & Environmental Control	$500/violation	YES	Dept. of Natural Resources & Environmental Control	$500/violation	NO
D.C.	YES	Federal Statutes and Agencies Apply	$1,000; 3 yrs. jail	YES	Dept. of Environmental Services	$300/day; 90 days jail	NO
FLORIDA	YES	Air & Water Pollution Control Board	$5,000/violation	YES	Air & Water Pollution Control Board	$5,000/violation	NO
GEORGIA	YES	Dept. of Natural Resources Div. of Environmental Protection	$1,000/violation & $500/day	YES	Dept. of Natural Resources Div. of Environmental Protection	$1,000/violation & $500/day	NO
HAWAII	YES	Dept. of Health	$2,500/violation/day	YES	Dept. of Health	$2,500/violation/day	YES
IDAHO	YES	State Board of Health	None stated	YES	State Board of Health	None stated	NO
ILLINOIS	YES[2]	Illinois Inst. for Environmental Quality Control Bd., Environmental Protection Agency	$10,000 + $1,000/day	YES[2]	Illinois Inst. for Environmental Quality Control Bd., Environmental Protection Agency	$10,000 + $1,000/day	YES
INDIANA	YES	Indiana Environmental Mgt. Bd., Stream Pollution Control Board	$10,000/violation & $1000/day	YES	Indiana Environmental Mgt. Bd., Air Pollution Control Board	$10,000/violation & $1000 day	NO
IOWA	YES	Dept. of Environmental Quality; Water Quality Commission	$500/day	YES	Dept. of Environmental Quality; Air Quality Commission	$500/day	NO
KANSAS	YES	State Board of Health	$1000/violation/day	YES	State Board of Health	$1000/violation/day	NO
KENTUCKY	YES	Dept. of Environmental Protection	$1000/violation/day; 1 yr. jail	YES	Dept. of Environmental Protection	$1000/violation/day; 1 yr. jail	YES
LOUISIANA	YES	La. Stream Control Comm.	$10,000/violation/day	YES	La. Air Control Comm.	$2000/violation/day	NO
MAINE	YES	Board of Environmental Protection	Fine & jail[8] sentence	YES	Board of Environmental Protection	Fine & jail[8] sentence	NO
MARYLAND	YES	Dept. of Water Resources	$10,000/violation/day	YES	Dept. of Health; Div. of Air Quality Control	$10,000/violation/day	NO
MASSACHUSETTS	YES	Water Resources Comm. Div. of Water Pollution	$1000/violation/day	YES	Commission of Public Health	$500/violation/day[1]	YES
MICHIGAN	YES	Dept. of Natural Resources Water Resources Comm.	$500/violation/day	YES	State Dept. of Health Air Pollution Control Commission	$500/violation & $100/day	NO
MINNESOTA	YES	Pollution Control Agency	Fine & jail[8] sentence	YES	Pollution Control Agency	Fine & jail[8] sentence	YES
MISSISSIPPI	YES	State Air & Water Pollution Control Comm.	$3000/violation/day	YES	State Air & Water Pollution Control Comm.	$3000/violation/day	NO
MISSOURI	YES	Water Pollution Board	$500/violation/day; 90 days jail	YES	Air Conservation Board	$200/violation/day	NO
MONTANA	YES[2,3]	Dept. of Health & Environmental Sciences	$1000/violation/day	YES[2,3]	Dept. of Health & Environmental Sciences	$1000/violation/day	NO

ENVIRONMENT / 315

| | WATER POLLUTION ||| AIR POLLUTION ||| NOISE |
	PERVASIVE PLAN	SUPERVISING BODY	MAXIMUM PENALTIES	PERVASIVE PLAN	SUPERVISING BODY	MAXIMUM PENALTIES	NOISE POLLUTION LAWS
NEBRASKA	YES	Dept. of Environmental Control	$500/violation & $10/day	YES	Dept. of Environmental Control	$500/violation & $10/day	NO
NEVADA	YES	State Water Pollution Control Agency	$2500/violation/day	YES	State Air Pollution Control Agency	$5000/violation/day	NO
NEW HAMPSHIRE	NO	NONE	NONE	NO	NONE	NONE	NO
NEW JERSEY	YES	Dept. of Environmental Protection	$3000/violation/day	YES	Dept. of Environmental Protection	$2500/violation/day	NO
NEW MEXICO	YES	Environmental Improvement Agency	NONE	YES	Environmental Improvement Agency	$1000/violation/day	NO
NEW YORK	YES	Dept. of Environmental Conservation	NONE	YES (weak)	Dept. of Environmental Conservation	Fine or jail after abatement order	
NORTH CAROLINA	YES	Dept. of Conservation & Development[4]	NONE	YES	Dept. of Conservation & Development[4]	NONE	NO
NORTH DAKOTA	NO	NONE	NONE	NO	NONE	NONE	YES
OHIO	YES	State Dept. of Health; Water Pollution Control Board	$500/violation/day	YES	Air Pollution Control Board	$10,000/violation/day	NO
OKLAHOMA	YES	Oklahoma Water Resources Board; State Dept. of Pollution Control	$500/violation	YES	State Dept. of Health; State Dept. of Pollution Control	Misd. fine & jail[8] sentence	NO
OREGON	YES	Dept. of Environmental Quality	Misd. fine & jail[8] sentence	YES	Dept. of Environmental Quality	Misd. fine & jail[8] sentence	NO
PENNSYLVANIA	YES	Dept. of Environmental Resources	Misd. fine & jail[6] sentence	YES	Dept. of Environmental Resources	Misd. fine & jail[5] sentence	NO
RHODE ISLAND	YES	Dept. of Natural Resources	$500 and/or 30 days/violation	YES	Director of Dept. of Health	$500 and/or 30 days/violation	NO
SOUTH CAROLINA	YES	Pollution Control Authority	$5000 and/or 2 yrs./violation/day	YES	Pollution Control Authority	$5000/and/or 2 yrs./violation/day	NO
SOUTH DAKOTA	YES	Committee on Water Pollution	$100 and/or 1 yr./violation/day	YES	Air Pollution Commission	$500/violation/day	NO
TENNESSEE	YES	Tenn. Water Quality Control Board	$10,000 and/or 2 yrs./violation/day	YES	Air Pollution Control Bd.	$1000/violation/day	NO
TEXAS	YES	Water Quality Board	$1000/violation/day	YES	Air Control Board	$1000/violation/day	NO
UTAH	YES	Div. of Health; Committee on Water Pollution	Misd. fine & jail[8] sentence	YES	Div. of Health, Committee on Air Conservation	$1000/violation/day	NO
VERMONT	YES	Agency of Environmental Conservation; Dept. of Water Resources	Misd. fine & jail[8] sentence	YES	Agency of Environmental Conservation & Board of Health	Misd. fine & jail[8] sentence	NO
VIRGINIA	YES	State Water Control Board	$5000 and/or 1 yr./violation/day	YES	State Air Pollution Board	$1000/violation/day	NO
WASHINGTON	YES	Dept. of Ecology; Water Pollution Control Comm.	$100/violation/day	YES	Dept. of Ecology; Air Pollution Control Authority	$1000/violation; 1 yr. in jail; $250/day	NO
WEST VIRGINIA	YES	State Water Resources Bd.	Fine and/or jail sentence[8]	YES	Air Pollution Control Comm.	$1000/violation/day	NO
WISCONSIN	YES	Dept. of Natural Resources	$5000/violation/day	YES	Dept. of Natural Resources	$5000/violation/day	NO
WYOMING	YES	Dept. of Health & Social Services; Div. of Health & Medical Services	$200 and/or 6 mos./violation/day	YES	Dept. of Health & Social Services; Air Resources Council	$750/violation/week	NO

[1] For the second conviction; the maximum penalty for the first offense is $100/violation/day.
[2] State Constitutional Amendment gives all citizens the right to a healthful environment and gives all citizens the right to sue to protect environment.
[3] Environmental Quality Council provides for interdepartmental planning.
[4] Advisory only.
[5] Misdemeanor after third offense.
[6] Misdemeanor after second offense.
[7] For dumping oil in state waters the fine is $20,000.00.
[8] The source material for this chart, Martindale-Hubbell Digest of American Laws, Volume 5, 1973, did not list the exact amount of maximum fines and penalties; it only listed violations of pollution laws as punishable by fine and/or jail sentence.
*Pollution chart reprinted from *Legal First Aid*, © 1973, 1974, 1975 by Henry Shain. Reprinted by permission of Harper & Row, Publishers, Inc.

Report; write for publications list that includes films available for loan.

National Clean Air Coalition
620 C Street, N.W.
Washington, D.C. 20003

A national organization composed of environmental, health, and government watchdog groups and unions lobbying for effective Clean Air Act amendments. The coalition provides updates and bulletins on legislation.

National Clearinghouse for Mental Health Information
National Institute of Mental Health
U.S. Department of Health, Education, and Welfare
5600 Fishers Lane
Rockville, Md. 20857

Publishes a booklet, *Pollution: Its Impact on Mental Health, A Literature Survey and Review of Research,* available for $.45 from the Superintendent of Documents, U.S. Government Printing Office, Washington, D.C. 20402.

Small Business Administration
Washington, D.C. 20416

Publishes a free booklet, *Reducing Air Pollution in Industry* by James A. Commins (February 1973), Management Aids No. 217.

Reprinted with permission of the American Lung Association from the *American Lung Association Bulletin* (March 1975).

The following are the state agencies for air pollution control and information:

Air Pollution Control Commission
381 State Office Building
Montgomery, Ala. 36130

Department of Environmental Conservation
3220 Hospital Drive
Pouch O
Juneau, Alaska 99811

Air Pollution Control Hearing Board
1740 West Adams Street
Phoenix, Ariz. 85007

Air Pollution Division
Department of Pollution Control and Ecology
8001 National Drive
Little Rock, Ark. 72209

Air Resources Board
P.O. Box 2815
Sacramento, Calif. 95812

Air Pollution Control Division
Department of Health
4210 East 11th Avenue
Denver, Colo. 80220

Air Compliance
Division of Environmental Quality
Department of Environmental Protection
161 State Office Building
Hartford, Conn. 06115

Air Resources Section
Division of Environmental Control
Department of Natural Resources and
　Environmental Control
Tatnall Building
Capitol Complex
Dover, Del. 19901

Bureau of Air and Water Quality Control
Environmental Health Administration
Department of Environmental Services
5010 Overlook Avenue, S.W.
Room 201
Washington, D.C. 20032

Division of Environmental Programs
Department of Environmental Regulation
Montgomery Building
2562 Executive Center Circle, East
Tallahassee, Fla. 32301

Air Protection Branch
Environmental Protection Division
Department of Natural Resources
270 Washington Street, S.W.
Atlanta, Ga. 30334

Environmental Protection and Health Services
　Division
Department of Health
1250 Punchbowl Street
Honolulu, Hawaii 96813

Air Quality Bureau
Division of Environment
Department of Health and Welfare
700 West State Street
Boise, Idaho 83720

Division of Air Pollution Control
Environmental Protection Agency
2200 Churchill Road
Springfield, Ill. 62706

Division of Air Pollution Control
Bureau of Engineering
Board of Health
1330 West Michigan Street
Indianapolis, Ind. 46202

Air Quality Management Division
Department of Environmental Quality
3920 Delaware Avenue
Des Moines, Iowa 50313

Bureau of Air Quality and Occupational
　Health
Division of Environment
Department of Health and Environment
Forbes Field
Topeka, Kans. 66620

Air Pollution Control Division
Bureau of Environmental Protection
Department of Natural Resources and
　Environmental Protection
Capital Plaza Tower
Frankfort, Ky. 40601

Air Control Commission
P.O. Box 60630
New Orleans, La. 70160

Bureau of Air Quality Control
Department of Environmental Protection
State House
Augusta, Me. 04333

Bureau of Air Quality and Noise Control
Environmental Health Administration
Department of Health and Mental Hygiene
201 West Preston Street
Baltimore, Md. 21203

Division of Air Quality Control
Department of Environmental Quality
　Engineering
600 Washington Street
Boston, Mass. 02111

Air Pollution Control Commission
Department of Natural Resources
P.O. Box 30028
Lansing, Mich. 48909

Division of Air Quality
Pollution Control Agency
1935 West County Road, 82
Roseville, Minn. 55113

Air and Water Pollution Control Commission
1100 Robert E. Lee Building
Jackson, Miss. 39201

Air Conservation Commission
Division of Environmental Quality
Department of Natural Resources
2010 Missouri Boulevard
Jefferson City, Mo. 65101

Air Quality Bureau
Environmental Sciences Division
Department of Health and Environmental
  Sciences
224 Cogswell Building
Helena, Mont. 59601

Division of Air Pollution Control
Department of Environmental Control
P.O. Box 94877
Lincoln, Neb. 68509

Environmental Protection
Department of Human Resources
Nye Building
201 South Fall Street
Capitol Complex
Carson City, Nev. 89710

Air Pollution Control Agency
Division of Public Health Services
Department of Health and Welfare
8 Loudon Road
Concord, N.H. 03301

Clean Air Council
Division of Environmental Quality
Department of Environmental Protection
P.O. Box 1390
Trenton, N.J. 08625

Air Quality Division
Environmental Improvement Agency
Health and Environment Department
Crown Building
725 St. Michaels Drive
Santa Fe, N.M. 87503

Division of Air Resources
Department of Environmental Conservation
50 Wolf Road
Albany, N.Y. 12233

Air Quality Section
Division of Environmental Management
Department of Natural Resources and
  Community Development
P.O. Box 27687
Raleigh, N.C. 27611

Division of Environmental Engineering
Department of Health
1200 Missouri Avenue
Bismarck, N.D. 58505

Office of Air Pollution Control
Environmental Protection Agency
361 East Broad Street
Columbus, Ohio 43216

Air Quality Service
Environmental Health Service
Department of Health
P.O. Box 53551
Oklahoma City, Okla. 73105

Environmental Quality Commission
522 S.W. Fifth
Portland, Ore. 97201

Bureau of Air Quality and Noise Control
Department of Environmental Resources
Fulton Building
Harrisburg, Pa. 17120

Division of Air Pollution Control
Department of Health
83 Park Street
Providence, R.I. 02903

Bureau of Air Quality Control
Environmental Quality Control Division
Department of Health and Environmental
  Control
R. J. Aycock Building
2600 Bull Street
Columbia, S.C. 29201

320 / THE HELP BOOK

Division of Air Quality and Solid Waste
Department of Environmental Protection
Joe Foss Building
Pierre, S.D. 57501

Air Pollution Control Division
Bureau of Environmental Health Services
Department of Public Health
256 Capitol Hill Building
301 7th Avenue, North
Nashville, Tenn. 37219

Air Control Board
8520 Shoal Creek Boulevard
Austin, Tex. 78758

Air Conservation Committee
72 East 4th South, Suite 305
Salt Lake City, Utah 84012

Air Pollution and Solid Waste Division
Agency of Environmental Conservation
7 School Street
Montpelier, Vt. 05602

State Air Pollution Control Board
1106 Ninth Street Office Building
Richmond, Va. 23219

Office of Air Programs
Department of Ecology
Olympia, Wash. 98504

Air Pollution Control Commission
1558 Washington Street, East
Charleston, W.Va. 25311

Bureau of Air Management
Division of Environmental Standards
Department of Natural Resources
4610 University Avenue
Madison, Wis. 53702

Air Quality Division
Department of Environmental Quality
Hathaway Building
Cheyenne, Wyo. 82002

ENERGY

The following federal agencies and national organizations publish information and/or act as advocacy groups on energy issues:

American Association for the Advancement of Science (AAAS)
1776 Massachusetts Avenue, N.W.
Washington, D.C. 20036

Send for their publications price list for books, article reprints, and audiocassettes dealing with energy.

American Public Power Association
2600 Virginia Avenue, N.W.
Washington, D.C. 20037

A national trade association of municipal and other publicly owned electric utilities that has energy-related publications for sale.

LITERATURE: *Energy Conservation Guidebook* ($50.00); *Public Power*, bimonthly ($8.50 a year; January–February Directory Issue $5.00).

American Wind Energy Association (AWEA)
S4468 CR 31
Bristol, Ind. 46507

A national information clearinghouse to further the application and use of wind energy. Membership dues are $25.00 a year.

LITERATURE: Quarterly newsletter.

Consumer Information Center
General Services Administration
Washington, D.C. 20405

Free energy-related publications that are available are *Energy Saving Through Automatic*

Thermostat Controls; Solar Energy and Your Home; Checking Your Utility Bills; Tips for Energy Savers. Low-cost publications are *Gasoline: More Miles Per Gallon* ($ .35); *Buying Solar* ($1.85).

Council on Economic Priorities (CEP)
84 Fifth Avenue
New York, N.Y. 10011

1666 Union Street
San Francisco, Calif. 94123

A national nonprofit organization "established to disseminate unbiased and detailed information on the practices of U.S. corporations," with energy and environment as two key issues they are researching. Annual dues are $15.00, unemployed and retired persons $7.50; members receive newsletters and a complimentary copy of *The Pollution Audit: A Guide for 50 Industrials for Responsible Investors*.

LITERATURE: CEP Newsletters; energy publications price list.

Energy Project
Center for Science in the Public Interest
1757 S Street, N.W.
Washington, D.C. 20009

An information clearinghouse and nonprofit consumer research organization concerned with increasing the consumer's role in energy decisions.

LITERATURE: *People & Energy* newsletter ($10.00); *A Citizen's Oil Factbook* ($2.00); *The Contrasumers: A Citizen's Guide to Resource Conservation* ($3.50).

Environmental Action Reprint Service (EARS)
2239 East Colfax
Denver, Colo. 80206

Started in 1973, this independent nonprofit organization is supported by sales of energy and environment-related literature from their catalog and occasional donations. Solar, alternative energy, and nuclear power information are the focal point of the books, article reprints, posters, bumper stickers, T-shirts, and label pins offered for sale. They also maintain free libraries on solar energy and nuclear power as well as a bookstore in the Denver area.

LITERATURE: *Energy Catalog*.

National Solar Heating and Cooling Information Center
P.O. Box 1607
Rockville, Md. 20850

An information clearinghouse on solar heating with numerous free publications, as well as films, exhibits, and a speaker's bureau.

LITERATURE: "Reading List for Solar Energy"; *Solar Energy in Your Home;* lists of builders, architects, and distributors.

Office of Energy Conservation
Federal Energy Administration
Washington, D.C. 20461

This federal agency is responsible for developing and carrying out a variety of programs designed to encourage and assist various sectors of the United States society and economy to conserve energy.

LITERATURE: Many free publications are available, such as *How to Save Money by Insulating Your Home; Energy Reporter*.

Residential Utility Consumer Action (RUCAG)
Public Interest Research Group (PIRG)
P.O. Box 19312
Washington, D.C. 20036

A Ralph Nader–based group concerned with increasing citizen involvement in the areas of utilities and energy. It is also an information clearinghouse supported by contributions and in the process of establishing local branches throughout the country.

LITERATURE: "RUCAG: A Consumer's Check-Off to Fight Utility Rip-Offs" (*Public Citizen*, 1975).

Public Resource Center
1747 Connecticut Avenue, N.W.
Washington, D.C. 20009

Started in May 1977, the research and educational purposes of this organization are twofold: community federalism—"the linking of communities across this land in struggle for justice and liberation," and political ecology—"the bringing together of citizen power, economic democracy, and decent respect for the integrity of the biosphere."

LITERATURE: *The Elements*, published eleven times a year ($7.00).

U.S. Department of Agriculture
Publications Division
Office of Communication
Washington, D.C. 20250

Free pertinent energy publications include *A Guide to Energy Savings for the Poultry Producer; A Guide to Energy Savings for the Orchard Grower; A Guide to Energy Savings for the Daily Farmer; Solar Heating for Milking Parlors; A Guide to Energy Savings for the Field Crops Producer; and A Guide to Energy Savings for the Vegetable Producers*.

U.S. Department of Commerce
National Technical Information Service
Washington, D.C. 20004

Free single copies of pamphlets are available on various aspects of promoting greater energy efficiency in the business sector.

LITERATURE: *An Inexpensive Economical Solar Heating System for Homes*; send for complete listing.

U.S. Department of Housing and Urban Development (HUD)
Publications and Information Division
451 Seventh Street, N.W.
Washington, D.C. 20410

In cooperation with the Department of Energy, HUD is publishing energy-conserving literature in a public education program.

LITERATURE: *Residential Energy From the Sun; Solar Energy in Your Home;* and *Solar Hot Water and Your Home* (all free).

The following are the state agencies for energy:

Energy Management Board
Development Office
3734 Atlanta Highway
Montgomery, Ala. 36109

Division of Energy and Power
Department of Commerce and Economic
  Development
MacKay Building
338 Denali Street
Anchorage, Alaska 99501

Minerals and Energy Division
Land Department
1624 West Adams Street
Phoenix, Ariz. 85007

State Office of Energy
960 Plaza West Building
Lee and McKinley
Little Rock, Ark. 72203

Energy Resources Conservation and
  Development Commission
1111 Howe Avenue
Sacramento, Calif. 95825

Office of Energy Conservation
1600 Downing
Denver, Colo. 80218

Department of Planning and Energy Policy
20 Grand Street
Hartford, Conn. 06115

Office of Emergency Preparedness
The Municipal Center
301 C Street, N.W.
Washington, D.C. 20001

State Energy Office
Department of Administration
Carlton Building
Tallahassee, Fla. 32304

State Energy Office
7 Martin Luther King, Jr., Drive, S.W.
Atlanta, Ga. 30334

Energy Office
Department of Planning and Economic
  Development
Kamamalu Building
250 South King Street
Honolulu, Hawaii 96813

Office of Energy
Executive Office of the Governor
Northeast Corner Basement
Statehouse
Boise, Idaho 83720

Energy Resources Commission
612 South Second Street
Springfield, Ill. 62706

Energy Group
Department of Commerce
336 State House
Indianapolis, Ind. 46204

Energy Policy Council
215 East Seventh
Des Moines, Iowa 50319

Energy Office
503 Kansas Avenue, Room 241
Topeka, Kans. 66603

Department of Energy
Capital Plaza Tower
Frankfort, Ky. 40601

Energy Division
Department of Natural Resources
P.O. Box 44396
Baton Rouge, La. 70804

Office of Energy Policy
Executive Department
Statehouse
Annapolis, Md. 21404

Energy Policy Office
Executive Office of Consumer Affairs
73 Tremont Street
Boston, Mass. 02108

Energy Agency
740 American Center Building
150 East Kellogg Boulevard
St. Paul, Minn. 55101

Energy Office
Office of the Governor
Woolfolk State Office Building
501 North West Street
Jackson, Miss. 39201

Missouri Energy Council
Department of Natural Resources
1014 Madison Street
Jefferson City, Mo. 65101

Energy Planning Division
Department of Natural Resources and
  Conservation
25 South Ewing
St. John's Hospital Building
Helena, Mont. 59601

Nevada Bureau of Mines and Geology
University of Nevada
Reno, Nev. 89557

Energy Council
Executive Department
3 Capitol Street
Concord, N.H. 03301

Department of Energy
1100 Raymond Boulevard
Newark, N.J. 07102

Energy and Minerals Department
113 Washington Avenue
Santa Fe, N.M. 87501

324 / THE HELP BOOK

State Energy Office
Executive Department
Swan Street Building, Core 1, Floor 2
Empire State Plaza
Albany, N.Y. 12223

Energy Division
Department of Military and Veteran's Affairs
215 East Lane Street
Raleigh, N.C. 27611

Office of Energy Management and
 Conservation
1533 North Twelfth Street
Bismarck, N.D. 58501

Ohio Energy and Resource Development
 Agency
State Office Tower
30 East Broad Street
P.O. Box 1001 (43216)
Columbus, Ohio 43215

Department of Energy
4400 North Lincoln Boulevard, Suite 251
Oklahoma City, Okla. 73105

Department of Energy
528 Cottage Street, N.E.
Salem, Ore. 97310

Governor's Energy Council
Third and State Street
905 Payne-Shoemaker Building
Harrisburg, Pa. 17120

Governor's Energy Office
80 Dean Street
Providence, R.I. 02909

Energy Management Office
Edgar A. Brown Building
1205 Pendleton Street
Columbia, S.C. 29201

Office of Energy Policy
Capitol Building
Pierre, S.D. 57501

Tennessee Energy Office
250 Capitol Hill Building
301 7th Avenue, North
Nashville, Tenn. 37219

Governor's Energy Advisory Council
7703 North Lamar Boulevard
Austin, Tex. 78752

Energy Conservation and Development
 Council
Salt Lake City, Utah 84114

Energy Office
109 State Street
Montpelier, Vt. 05602

Virginia Energy Office
823 East Main Street, Room 300
Richmond, Va. 23219

Energy Office
1000 South Cherry Street
Olympia, Wash. 98504

Fuel and Energy Office
Governor's Office of Economic and
 Community Development
1262½ Greenbrier Street
Charleston, W. Va. 25311

Energy Conservation Coordinator
Capitol Hill Building
320 West 25th
Cheyenne, Wyo. 82002

NUCLEAR ENERGY

The following national organizations are particularly concerned with nuclear energy:

Committee for Nuclear Responsibility, Inc. (CNR)
P.O. Box 332
Yachats, Ore. 97498

A national educational organization and information clearinghouse on nuclear and solar energy and advocacy group endorsing a nuclear

A protestor is hauled away during a demonstration against the construction of a nuclear plant in New Hampshire. *Wide World Photos, Inc.*

power plant moratorium. It is supported by tax-deductible contributions.

LITERATURE: "Common Sense" flyer; "We Can Not Solve the Energy Problem by Creating a Radiation Problem"; send for extensive publications list of articles, technical reports, etc.

Critical Mass: The Citizens' Movement for Safe and Efficient Energy
P.O. Box 1538
Washington, D.C. 20013

A national citizens' network primarily concerned with nuclear energy.

LITERATURE: *Critical Mass* newspaper ($7.50 individuals; $37.50 libraries and government); *Citizens' Guide to Nuclear Power* ($5.00).

Environmental Action Foundation (EAF)
724 Dupont Circle Building
Washington, D.C. 20036

Nuclear energy is one of the key concerns of this national tax-exempt research and citizen education organization formed as an outgrowth of Earth Day in 1970.

LITERATURE: *Countdown To a Nuclear Moratorium,* edited by Richard Munson ($3.00); *Nuclear Power: The Bargain We Can't Afford* by Richard Morgan ($3.50); *The Power Line*, monthly ($15.00 regular; $7.50 citizen groups; $35.00 profit-making businesses); *Nuclear Economics Information Packet* ($2.50); *The Case for a Nuclear Moratorium* ($1.50); *Environmental Action* magazine ($15.00).

Mobilization for Survival
1213 Race Street
Philadelphia, Pa. 19107

Citizens group opposed to nuclear power. (See complete listing in Chapter 11, *Citizen Action*.)

SANE (A Citizens' Organization for a Sane World)
318 Massachusetts Avenue, N.E.
Washington, D.C. 20002

A national membership educational organization ($15.00 a year; $5.00 senior citizens, students, GIs, and low income) opposed to nuclear energy.

LITERATURE: "Welcome to the (Nuclear) Club" ($.05).

Task Force Against Nuclear Pollution
P.O. Box 1817
Washington, D.C. 20013

A national organizing effort of citizens to stop nuclear power and to begin major efforts in solar power and energy efficiency; supported by private contributions.

LITERATURE: *Progress Report* newsletters; *Clean Energy Petition*.

LAND CONSERVATION

For local information on land conservation, beautification, or regulations, contact your county or city department of planning or conservation or the local information office to find out the correct department to contact. For example, the planning department may have published information, or will answer telephone inquiries about how to select, plant, and care for trees and plants to beautify your area as well as ordinances and fees for such activities. One such booklet, *Trees for New York City*, is available for $1.00 from the New York Department of City Planning, Map Sales, Room 1616, 2 Lafayette Street, New York, N.Y. 10007. Prepared in cooperation with the New York Botanical Garden, it tells where to write to get a planter or a sidewalk cut permit and the type and care of certain trees.

Another local source of help in such land matters as planting a community vegetable or flower garden would be your neighborhood block association, citizen action group, or horticulture society.

The following federal agencies and national organizations are concerned with land conservation or beautification and provide information or conduct research:

Backyard Wildlife Habitat Program
National Wildlife Federation
1412 Sixteenth Avenue, N.W.
Washington, D.C. 20036

A free "Backyard Kit" is available for those who are interested in providing water, cover, and reproductive areas for wildlife by planting trees and shrubs, and installing birdbaths, feeders, and so on. Write for more information and an application for certification.

Gardens For All, Inc.
National Association for Gardening
Bay and Harbor Roads
P.O. Box 371A
Shelburne, Vt. 05482

Founded in 1972, this national information clearinghouse of gardening provides educational materials for those who use their own property as well as the renewed community gardening movements (which really started in the United

States at the turn of the century). They will provide local referrals to those projects and persons active in this area.

LITERATURE: Mimeographed reports, such as "Community Gardening Attracting Millions"; booklets, including *Guide to Community Garden Organization, Community Gardening,* and *A Guide Through the Vegetable Garden* ($.50); *How to Start a School Gardening Program* by Peter J. Wotowiec, Supervisor of Horticultural Educational, Cleveland, Ohio, Public Schools ($10.00 per manual; $5.00 per companion pieces with lesson plans for various grade levels).

Hunger Action Center
The Evergreen State College
Olympia, Wash. 98505

The center's booklet *Community Garden Handbook* (February 1976) provides a thorough analysis of the Seattle P-Patch Program as an example for other communities; there is general information that would also be applicable in most other similar gardening ventures. Be sure to enclose a reply label and stamps with your request.

Keep America Beautiful, Inc. (KAB)
99 Park Avenue
New York, N.Y. 10016

Founded in 1953, this national organization of companies and trade associations is an educational public service group dedicated to environmental improvement. It sponsors Clean Community System (CCS) to reduce litter by improving attitudes toward waste handling, and works through thirty state affiliates and some 4,000 local groups.

LITERATURE: "You Take the First Step," flyer; "Suggestions for Preventing Littering at Bicentennial Events"; *KAB Reports* (quarterly newsletter); "Keep America Beautiful . . . More Than a Slogan."

Soil Conservation Society of America (SCSA)
7515 N.E. Ankeny Road
Ankeny, Iowa 50021

Founded in 1941, this national organization has 155 local groups. Its members are working in fields related to the conservation, use, and management of natural resources. Related educational materials are available.

LITERATURE: *Journal of Soil and Water Conservation,* bimonthly; booklets; glossary of soil and water conservation terms.

U.S. Department of Agriculture
Agricultural Research Service
14th and Independence Streets
Washington, D.C. 20250

Publishes bulletins concerning house and garden activities.

U.S. Department of Agriculture
Forest Service
P.O. Box 2417
Washington, D.C. 20013

The Forest Service manages the national forests and grasslands and cooperates with state and private forest owners. Contact them about conservation and the use of the country's forests and land resources.

LITERATURE: *What the Forest Service Does.*

U.S. Geological Survey
National Center
Reston, Va. 22092

The Geological Survey is involved in the solid earth sciences and conducts studies and investigations of energy, mineral, and water resources of the United States. It prepares topographic and special purpose maps, and supervises mineral, oil, and gas operations on all federal lands.

LITERATURE: *The United States Geological Survey; Sources of Information and Services of the USGS; Popular Publications of the USGS; Motion Picture Film Services of the USGS.*

SOLID WASTE MANAGEMENT (AND RECYCLING)

Waste disposal concerns include the use of recycled paper, solid waste disposal, recycled canned products, bottles, and so forth. To find out what public or private recycling plants are active in your area, and what their collection schedule is, contact your city or county solid waste disposal bureau, usually within the environmental control, health, or pollution control departments. The EPA provides information about federal legislation and availability of federal funding in solid and hazardous waste management. For information write to Office of Solid Waste, U.S. Environmental Protection Agency, 401 M Street, S.W., Washington, D.C. 20460.

The following national organizations provide information on waste disposal:

Committee of Tin Mill Products Producers
American Iron and Steel Institute
1000 Sixteenth Street, N.W.
Washington, D.C. 20036

Provides information on steel can recycling systems around the country as well as how to get one started in your area if none is available.

LITERATURE: *Progress Report on Recycling* (free).

Institute of Scrap Iron and Steel, Inc.
1627 K Street, N.W.
Washington, D.C. 20006

Founded in 1928 by the ferrous scrap processing industry, this national organization has over 1,500 member firms with chapters throughout the United States. The headquarters provides information on the ferrous scrap industry, recycling, and conservation of materials.

LITERATURE: "It's Our Choice" audiovisual program available on free loan; *Phoenix Quarterly*, free magazine; *Mines Above Ground*, free folder; *Facts*, statistical yearbook ($2.00); *Specifications for Iron and Steel Scrap*, booklet ($.50).

Paper Stock Conservation Committee
American Paper Institute, Inc.
260 Madison Avenue
New York, N.Y. 10016

Public education is the primary purpose of this organization, whose membership includes the leading paper manufacturers in the country. Materials such as recycled buttons, doorknob hangers, and posters are available at cost to help promote paper drives in your community.

LITERATURE: *How to Recycle Waste Paper*, booklet explaining how to organize and promote a campaign in your community (free).

Solid Waste Project
The National Association of Counties (NACo)
1735 New York Avenue, N.W.
Washington, D.C. 20006

The Solid Waste Project operates on a grant from the Environmental Protection Agency, "Technical Assistance for Counties in Solid Waste Management." They are assisting the EPA Office of Solid Waste in implementing legislation and satisfying public participation and technical assistance mandates.

Contact the following major manufacturers to find about out about their recycling activities:

Can Manufacturers Institute
1625 Massachusetts Avenue, N.W.
Washington, D.C. 20036

National Canners Association
1133 20th Street, N.W.
Washington, D.C. 20036

National Soft Drink Association
1101 16th Street, N.W.
Washington, D.C. 20036

United States Brewers Association, Inc.
1750 K Street, N.W.
Washington, D.C. 20006

WATER POLLUTION

For complaints or information on the local level, follow the same procedures for air pollution, directing your call or inquiry to the water pollution control department or the proper person within the Environmental Protection Agency or the Department of Health.

On the state level, for information, regulations, and local referrals, contact your state agency given later in this chapter.

These federal agencies and national organizations are concerned with clean water and/or provide information on water resources:

Clean Water Action Project
P.O. Box 19312
Washington, D.C. 20036

A national, citizens lobbying organization for clean and safe drinking water and strong water pollution control.

LITERATURE: "Citizens' Manual for Clean Water Act Hearings" ($5.00); *Clean Water Action News*, bimonthly ($15.00 a year).

Environmental Action (EA)
1346 Connecticut Avenue, N.W.
Washington, D.C. 20036

EA has educational materials on water pollution and will also refer you to local water coalitions in your area that you might want to join.

LITERATURE: "Water Pollution," flyer.

Sierra Club
530 Bush Street
San Francisco, Calif. 94108

Water resources is one of the many environmental committees of this national group, which has 300 regional groups. The Sierra Club office at 330 Pennsylvania Avenue, S.E., Washington, D.C. 20003 is part of the steering committee for the Clean Water Campaign and provides educational materials on water pollution.

LITERATURE: *National News Report*, weekly; *Sierra Club Bulletin*, monthly.

U.S. Environmental Protection Agency (EPA)
Office of Public Affairs
Washington, D.C. 20460

The EPA offers educational publications on water quality and water pollution.

LITERATURE: *Building For Clean Water: Federal Grants Lend a Hand* and *A Drop to Drink: A Report on the Quality of Our Drinking Water*.

Water Information Center (WIC)
7 High Street
Huntington, N.Y. 11743

Publishes reference volumes on water resources.

LITERATURE: *Sources of Information in Water Resources* ($23.50); *Water Newsletter*, semi-monthly ($48.00); *Water Publications of State Agencies*, 2 volumes ($49.50); *Water Policies for the Future* ($25.00); *Water Atlas of the United States* ($40.00).

Water Quality Association
477 East Butterfield Road
Lombard, Ill. 60148

Provides information on water problems and their treatment; supported by membership dues.

LITERATURE: Send for publications price list; "Easy-to-Use Guide to Sodium in Food, Medicine, and Water" by Richard Weickart ($ .50).

Water Resources Scientific Information Center
Office of Water Research and Technology
U.S. Department of the Interior
18th and C Streets, N.W.
Washington, D.C. 20240

Since 1966 the center has disseminated scientific and technical information in the water resources area. It maintains an information retrieval network service in ten related fields. Upon request, a catalog of publications and bibliographies will be sent.

The following are the state agencies for water pollution control:

Water Programs
Department of Environmental Conservation
3220 Hospital Drive
Pouch O
Juneau, Alaska 99811

Bureau of Water Quality Control
Division of Environmental Health Services
Department of Health Services
1740 West Adams
Phoenix, Ariz. 85007

Water Pollution Division
Department of Pollution Control and Ecology
8001 National Drive
Little Rock, Ark. 72209

Water Resources Control Board
P.O. Box 100
Sacramento, Calif. 95801

Water Quality Control Division
Department of Health
4210 East 11th Avenue
Denver, Colo. 80220

Water Compliance and Hazardous Substances
Division of Environmental Quality
Department of Environmental Protection
161 State Office Building
Hartford, Conn. 06115

Division of Environmental Control
Department of Natural Resources and
  Environmental Control
Tatnall Building
Capitol Complex
Dover, Del. 19901

Bureau of Air and Water Quality Control
Environmental Health Administration
Department of Environmental Services
North Potomac Building
614 H Street, N.W.
Washington, D.C. 20001

Bureau of Water Resources
Department of Environmental Regulation
206 Turner Building
2562 Executive Center Circle East
Tallahassee, Fla. 32301

Water Protection Branch
Environmental Protection Division
Department of Natural Resources
270 Washington Street, S.W.
Atlanta, Ga. 30334

Environmental Protection and Health Services
  Division
Department of Health
1250 Punchbowl Street
Honolulu, Hawaii 96813

Bureau of Water Quality
Division of Environment
Department of Health and Welfare
700 West State
Boise, Idaho 83720

Division of Water Pollution Control
Environmental Protection Agency
2200 Churchill Road
Springfield, Ill. 62706

Division of Water Pollution Control
Bureau of Engineering
Board of Health
1330 West Michigan Street
Indianapolis, Ind. 46202

Water Quality Management Division
Department of Environmental Quality
3920 Delaware Avenue
Des Moines, Iowa 50313

Bureau of Water Quality
Division of Environment
Department of Health and Environment
Forbes Field
Topeka, Kans. 66620

Division of Water Quality
Bureau of Environmental Protection
Department for Natural Resources and
   Environmental Protection
Capitol Plaza Tower
Frankfort, Ky. 40601

Water Pollution Control
Department of Natural Resources
Stream Control Commission
P.O. Box 44396
Baton Rouge, La. 70804

Bureau of Water Quality Control
Department of Environmental Protection
State House
Augusta, Me. 04333

Environmental Health Administration
Department of Health and Mental Hygiene
P.O. Box 13387
Baltimore, Md. 21203

Water Pollution Control Division
Department of Environmental Quality
   Engineering
110 Tremont Street
Boston, Mass. 02108

Water Resources Commission
Department of Natural Resources
P.O. Box 30028
Lansing, Mich. 48909

Water Quality Division
Pollution Control Agency
1935 West County Road, 82
Roseville, Minn. 55113

Air and Water Pollution Control Commission
1100 Robert E. Lee Building
Jackson, Miss. 39201

Clean Water Commission
Division of Environmental Quality
Department of Natural Resources
2010 Missouri Boulevard
Jefferson City, Mo. 65101

Water Quality Bureau
Environmental Sciences Division
Department of Health and Environmental
   Sciences
555 Fuller Street
Helena, Mont. 59601

Division of Water Pollution Control
Department of Environmental Control
P.O. Box 94877
Lincoln, Neb. 68509

Environmental Protection
Department of Human Resources
Nye Building
201 South Fall Street
Capitol Complex
Carson City, Nev. 89710

Water Supply and Pollution Control
   Commission
Prescott Park
105 Loudon Road
Concord, N.H. 03301

332 / THE HELP BOOK

Division of Water Resources
Department of Environmental Protection
P.O. Box 2809
Trenton, N.J. 08625

Water Pollution Control Division
Environmental Improvement Agency
Health and Environment Department
Crown Building
725 St. Michael's Drive
Santa Fe, N.M. 87503

Division of Pure Waters
Department of Environmental Conservation
50 Wolf Road
Albany, N.Y. 12233

Water Quality Section
Division of Environmental Management
Department of Natural Resources and
 Community Development
P.O. Box 27687
Raleigh, N.C. 27611

Division of Water Supply and Pollution
 Control
Department of Health
1200 Missouri Avenue
Bismarck, N.D. 58505

Office of Wastewater Pollution
 Control
Environmental Protection Agency
361 East Broad Street
Columbus, Ohio 43215

Water Resources Board
Jim Thorpe Office Building
2101 North Lincoln Boulevard
Oklahoma City, Okla. 73105

Environmental Quality Commission
522 S.W. Fifth
Portland, Ore. 97201

Bureau of Water Quality Management
Department of Environmental Resources
Fulton Building
Harrisburg, Pa. 17120

Division of Water Pollution Control
Department of Environmental Affairs
83 Park Street
Providence, R.I. 02903

Bureau of Waste Water and Stream Quality
 Control
Environmental Quality Control Division
Department of Health and Environmental
 Control
R. J. Aycock Building
2600 Bull Street
Columbia, S.C. 29201

Water Quality Program
Department of Environmental Protection
Joe Foss Building
Pierre, S.D. 57501

Water Hygiene Program
Department of Environmental Protection
Joe Foss Building
Pierre, S.D. 57501

Division of Water Quality Control
Bureau of Environmental Health Services
Department of Public Health
621 Cordell Hull Building
436 6th Avenue, North
Nashville, Tenn. 37219

Water Quality Board
Stephen F. Austin State Office Building
Austin, Tex. 78711

Committee on Water Pollution
Division of Health
Department of Social Services
44 Medical Drive
Salt Lake City, Utah 84112

Department of Water Resources
Agency of Environmental Conservation
State Office Building
120 State Street
Montpelier, Vt. 05602

State Water Control Board
2111 North Hamilton Street
Richmond, Va. 23230

Water Quality Control
Health Services Division
Office of Environmental Health
  Programs
Building #4, Airdustrial Park
Olympia, Wash. 98504

Bureau of Water Quality
Division of Environmental Standards
Department of Natural Resources
4610 University Avenue
Madison, Wis. 53702

Water Quality Division
Department of Environmental Quality
Hathaway Building
Cheyenne, Wyo. 82002

ADDITIONAL LITERATURE

ENVIRONMENT IN GENERAL

Becoming an Environmentalist: Or How I Learned to Stop Worrying and Love the Energy Crisis by Barbara Hershey Clark (1976). Cottonwood Publishing Company, P.O. Box 1222, Walla Walla, Wash. 99362 ($1.95). A step-by-step description of how the author transformed her house so that "each room was a model of environmental purity." A light, enjoyable booklet with an appendix of food recipes.

Environment Action Bulletin (biweekly). 33 East Minor, Emmaus, Pa. 18049 ($10.00 a year).

How to Plan an Environmental Conference: A Technique for Developing Citizen Leadership (1972). League of Women Voters Education Fund, 1730 M Street, N.W., Washington, D.C. 20036, Publication No. 695 (free booklet). Subtitled "A Technique for Developing Citizen Leadership," this booklet is based on the experience of the League of Women Voters Education Fund, 1965–71, when land and water use seminars were held in various cities around the country.

Mother Earth News (monthly). P.O. Box 70, Hendersonville, N.C. 28739 ($8.00 a year). Products and feature articles to facilitate a "back to nature" existence.

Rainbook: Resource for Appropriate Technology by the editors of *Rain* (1977). Schocken Books, 200 Madison Avenue, New York, N.Y. 10016 ($7.95). An annotated directory written in a chatty, casual style; good resource on the environment. Topics covered include: energy, waste recycling, agriculture, transportation, communications, economics, community building, health, and appropriate technology. Illustrated.

Association Films, 866 Third Avenue, New York, N.Y. 10022, loans or sells films for numerous organizations, including the following with environmental concerns: Sierra Club, Friends of Animals, Environmental Defense Fund, and so forth. Send for their free catalog.

ENERGY

Alternate Sources of Energy (quarterly). Route 2, Box 90-A, Milaca, Minn. 56353 ($5.00 a year).

"A Citizen's Handbook on Solar Energy," rev. ed., by Anita Gunn (1977). Public Interest Research Group, P.O. Box 19312, Washington, D.C. 20036 ($3.50 individuals; $15.00 businesses and institutions; all orders prepaid). A basic introduction to solar energy.

"An Energy Source Directory," compiled for *Library Journal* by Neal-Schuman Publishers, Inc. (January 1, 1978, issue, pages 26–79). Annotated listing of more than 600 sources of print and nonprint information.

Energy Sources 77/78. Enercom, 909 17th Street, Suite 601, Denver, Colo. 80202 ($10.95). Published by Enercom, a private company, in cooperation with the Traders Association, this is an anthology of articles by experts on water, conservation, wind, oil, gas, and statistical data, and on possible solutions in solving the country's energy problems.

Green Mountain Post Films, P.O. Box 177, Montague, Mass. 01351. Send for their illustrated catalogue describing films that are available for rental loan or for purchase on nuclear energy. Titles include "The Last Resort," "Lovejoy's Nuclear War," and "Sentenced to Success."

Rain—Journal of Appropriate Technology (10 issues per year). 2270 N.W. Irving, Portland, Ore. 97210 ($10.00 a year; $5.00 a year for those with incomes of less than $5,000; some back issues available for $1.00 each). A monthly listing of annotated publications and pertinent organizations; feature articles.

"Save Energy: Save Money!" by Sandra and Eugene Eccli (December 1974). National Center for Community Action, Network Services: Energy, 1711 Connecticut Avenue, N.W., Washington, D.C. 20009 (free booklet).

Solar Age Magazine. Church Hill, Harrisville, N.H. 03450 ($20.00 a year).

Solar Age Catalog by SolarVision, Inc. (1977). Cheshire Books, Harrisville, N.H. 03450 ($8.50). A directory with articles, advertised products, manufacturer addresses; illustrated.

Solar Utilization News (SUN) (monthly), c/o Alternate Energy Institute, P.O. Box 3100, Estes Park, Colo. 80517 ($8.00 a year individuals; $15.00 for institutions). A magazine published by the Alternate Energy Institute highlighting publications, seminars, and selected new patents in this field.

Synerjy: A Directory of Energy Alternatives (published twice a year). P.O. Box 4790, Grand Central Station, New York, N.Y. 10017 ($9.00 a year individuals; $18.00 institutions). Typescript listing of more than 2,000 publications, major articles, conferences, research associations, manufacturers, and facilities.

Wind Power Digest (quarterly), c/o Jester Press, 54468 CR 31, Bristol, Ind. 46507 ($6.00 a year; $2.00 per copy). Articles and photographs on wind power.

NATURAL RESOURCES AND WEATHER

The Campaign for Cleaner Air by Marvin Zeldin (1973). Public Affairs Pamphlets, 381 Park Avenue South, New York, N.Y. 10016. Pamphlet No. 494 ($.50). Concise, well-written introduction to the Clean Air Act, the hazards of pollution, and suggestions for control.

Cleansing Our Waters by Gladwin Hill (1973). Public Affairs Committee, 381 Park Avenue South, New York, N.Y. 10016 ($.50). This booklet describes the size of the water pollution problem, some suggested and ongoing remedies, the 1972 water pollution control act, and what citizens can do to influence legislators on this issue.

Climates of Hunger by Reid A. Bryson and Thomas J. Murray (1977). The University of Wisconsin Press, Box 1379, Madison, Wis. 53701. An explanation of how climate works and changes and what might be expected in the future.

Conservation Directory, edited by Fran Mitchell (published annually). National Wildlife Foundation, 1412 Sixteenth Street, N.W., Washington, D.C. 20036 ($3.00). Annotated listings of more than 1,600 organizations and 9,500 individuals; the most comprehensive national guide to natural resource use and management. Includes audiovisual materials.

The Green Revolution (published ten times per year). C/o The School of Living, Heathcote Center, Route 1, Box 129, Freelance, Md. 21053 ($6.00 a year).

Plant a Tree by Michael Weiner (1975). Macmillan Publishing Company, Inc., 866 Third Avenue, New York, N.Y. 10022 ($6.95). Manual for planting and maintaining trees in all types of settings—rural, urban, and suburban.

SOLID WASTE DISPOSAL

A Citizens' Solid Waste Management Project: Mission 5000 by the U.S. Environmental Protection Agency (1972). Available from the Superintendent of Documents, U.S. Government Printing Office, Washington, D.C. 20402 ($.50). Describes Mission 5000, whose purpose is to eliminate open dumps and replace them with environmentally sound, nonpolluting waste disposal methods.

Hazardous Wastes by the U.S. Environmental Protection Agency (1975). Available from the Superintendent of Documents, U.S. Government Printing Office, Washington, D.C. 20402 ($.85). A booklet defining hazardous wastes—where they come from and what can be done. Illustrated with color photographs.

Garbage in America: Approaches to Recycling by Neil Seldman (1975). Institute for Local Self-Reliance, 1717 18th Street, N.W., Washington, D.C. 20009 ($2.25).

The National Buyer's Guide to Recycled Paper, compiled by Sally Dane (1973). Environmental Educators, Inc., 1621 Connecticut Avenue, N.W., Washington, D.C. 20009 ($4.00). Information on how and where to buy recycled paper supplies for printing.

Recycle: In Search of New Policies for Resource Recovery (1972). League of Women Voters of the United States, 1730 M Street, N.W., Washington, D.C. 20036 ($.75). Introductory booklet on recycling—what it is, what individuals and communities can do to encourage it; resource section.

See also the following related chapters in *The Help Book:*

ANIMAL RIGHTS
CITIZEN ACTION
CONSUMER AFFAIRS
HEALTH
POLITICAL ACTION

23

FAMILY PLANNING

The first step toward family planning is for girls and boys, women and men, to understand how menstruation works. With that information, the details of conception and contraception are more comprehensible.

Normal Menstrual Cycle*

DAY 1. Menstrual period begins.

DAY 5. An egg in a follicle (pocket, sac) in one of your ovaries has begun to ripen to maturity. The egg starts developing in response to a hormonal message (FSH) from your pituitary gland, which in turn has been triggered indirectly by the low level of *estrogen* (an ovarian hormone) at the time of your period.

DAYS 5–14. The follicle in which the egg is developing makes first a little, then more and more *estrogen:*

    1. *Estrogen* stimulates the lining of your uterus to get thicker in preparation for pregnancy.

    2. As *estrogen* increases, it slows down and then cuts off FSH.

DAY 14. Ovulation: *estrogen* peak and a spurt of *progesterone* occurring during days 12–13 indirectly trigger ovulation. Ripe egg is released from ovary, starts 4-day trip down fallopian tube to uterus. Fertilization by sperm from the man must occur in first 24 hours.

DAYS 14–26. The ruptured follicle, now called *corpus luteum* ("yellow body"), makes two hormones for about 12 days:

    Estrogen continues.

    Progesterone increases and peaks about day 22:

    1. makes your cervical mucus (plug of mucus in cervix) thick and dry, a barrier to sperm;

---

* From *Our Bodies, Ourselves*, copyright © 1971, 1973, 1976 by the Boston Women's Health Collective, Inc. Reprinted by permission of Simon & Schuster, a division of Gulf & Western Corporation.

2. stimulates the glands in lining of your uterus to secrete a sugary substance and further thickens the lining.

DAYS 26–27–28. If pregnancy did not occur, *corpus luteum's* manufacture of *estrogen* and *progesterone*, slows down to a very low level. The lining of your uterus, which needs the stimulation and support of these hormones, starts to disintegrate.

DAY 29–DAY 1. Menstrual period begins. Low level of *estrogen* (see Day 26) will begin indirectly to stimulate pituitary's egg-development hormone (FSH) to start a new cycle.

Although no birth control method is 100 percent effective (since women have been known to forget to take a pill and diaphragms can tear), some birth control methods are reasonably reliable. At the present time, the following birth control methods are available (check with your doctor, gynecologist, or local family planning center for a thorough description of their effectiveness, safety and side effects, and costs):

- Diaphragm used with spermicidal jelly or cream
- Birth control pills
- IUD (intrauterine device): coil, loop, and shield
- Condom (rubber, prophylactic, "safe")
- Foam—aerosol vaginal spermicide
- Spermicidal jellies and creams for use without a diaphragm
- Natural family planning, such as the rhythm, abstention, or withdrawal (*coitus interruptus*)
- The "morning-after" pill

But how effective are the most commonly used contraceptive methods? The following chart highlights that information, although effectiveness should not be the only consideration when deciding on a birth control plan (other factors include health risks, personal habits, cost, and so forth):

Failure Rates of Birth Control Methods*

Birth control pill (combination pill)	0.5** (theoretically 0 if no pills are forgotten)
IUD	1.5–8
Condom	10–15
Diaphragm	10–15
Vaginal contraceptives	15–25
Rhythm method	15–30
Withdrawal	20–30

*Reprinted from *Birth Control Handbook*, 12th edition (1975), Montreal Health Press, Inc.
**The above rates should be read as "pregnancies in 100 women using the . . . method for 1 year."

Although the best way to plan when to have children is to use effective, safe, and uninhibiting methods of birth control, we are far from that ideal. Mistakes happen, and for many people abortion is one way to correct such accidents. But no matter how young the fetus, abortion is a traumatic and decisive event for practically all women who go through with it (and probably for just as many men). It should be adopted as a carefully-considered recourse *only* when seen as the lesser of two undesirable alternatives.

Martha, who is now thirty, talks of the abortion she had when she was nineteen:

> I was about a month along. I feel very foolish that it ever happened. When I got pregnant, I had only known him for about four months. I knew I didn't ever want to marry him. I had to tell him that I was pregnant. I needed the money. Abortion was illegal then; it cost three hundred dollars. After a lot of effort on my part, he gave me the whole amount.
>
> I know I was very upset. Even now I really do regret what I did, but I found out the guy had been on some very heavy drugs when I got pregnant—LSD for one—so I've always felt the baby wouldn't have been right anyway. Destroying a life is a very big thing to do and it made me decide a lot more things. I wish there were less drastic ways to learn than from traumatic events, but people will make these mistakes, especially in a society where sex is substituted for love because there is so little physical affection. Especially when you're young and you feel let down because of lack of love, so you do things that only later you realize were based on the wrong feelings.
>
> About two years later, I met my husband. I told him about the abortion right before we got married. Of course he was very upset. But I'm glad I told him, because it might always have come back to me. When I do get pregnant, the doctor might ask me if I ever was pregnant before and then it might come out. It seemed better to tell him when we were happy so he could absorb the impact more easily.

To avoid unwanted pregnancies, growing numbers of women and men are permanently altering their childbearing capacities. Such operations as vasectomies or the tying of the fallopian tubes are gaining acceptance, although there are opponents who call such surgery unnatural and irreversible.

Yet a 1975 survey based on a sample of 3,403 persons revealed that sterilization is even more widely used than the pill. Jane E. Brody, reporting in the *New York Times* ("Pill Use Rivaled By Sterilization, Survey Indicates," July 22, 1977), stated that "approximately 6.8 million married couples of childbearing age had chosen contraceptive sterilization (and an additional 1.1 million were sterilized for medical reasons), as against 7.1 million couples who were using the pill to prevent unwanted births."

At the present time, all birth control methods have their limitations. Either they are not completely reliable or, like the pill, they have grave short- and long-term effects on the woman and perhaps even the children that might be born.

BIRTH CONTROL

For direct help in family planning (methods of birth control—the diaphragm, IUD, the pill, foam, condom, voluntary sterilization) or, as a last resort, abortion, contact your local county or city department of health, medical society, school, university, hospital services, women's center, or a clinic sponsored by Planned Parenthood.

International Planned Parenthood Federation
18-20 Lower Regent Street
London SW1 4PW England

U.S. Headquarters:
Planned Parenthood Federation of America, Inc.
810 Seventh Avenue
New York, N.Y. 10019

Canadian Headquarters:
Planned Parenthood Federation of Canada
1226 A Wellington Street
Ottawa, Ontario K1Y 3A1

The Planned Parenthood Federation of America, Inc. is the U.S. member of the seventy-nine-nation International Planned Parenthood Federation, which provides family planning services, guidance, or referral in medically supervised clinics that offer direct services, including abortion, contraception devices, pregnancy testing, infertility therapy, and voluntary sterilization. There are over 700 clinics servicing more than one million persons in the United States every year with more than 20,000 volunteers working in 200 communities in 42 states. If you cannot find a Planned Parenthood clinic near you by looking in your local telephone directory or calling information, the national headquarters will make referrals; they also publish a periodically updated directory, *Planned Parenthood Affiliates & Chapters*. Other programs include the Association of Planned Parenthood Physicians, the Youth and Student Affairs Program, and the Justice Fund to "serve as a fund for the neediest: assisting women who seek abortions." The national headquarters also acts as an educational center, publishing dozens of pamphlets that are usually also available from the local affiliates.

LITERATURE: Free booklets and leaflets including: *We Are Planned Parenthood; Planned Parenthood Profile; Modern Methods of Birth Control; Foam Fact Sheets, Diaphragms and How They Work; The Safe Period; You and the Pill; The Condom; Birth Control: All the Methods That Work and the Ones That Don't; Nearly Every Woman Gets It* [*vaginal infection*]; *All About Vasectomy; Sterilization for Women;* and *Voluntary Sterilization for Men and Women*.

The following national organizations provide referrals for birth control direct help as well as information:

Association for Voluntary Sterilization, Inc.
708 Third Avenue
New York, N.Y. 10017

An information clearinghouse for men and women on sterilization as an alternative means of birth control; if requested, a referral will be made to a doctor who will perform the operation; speakers available.

LITERATURE: Free leaflet; pamphlets include *Questions and Answers on Voluntary Sterilization for Men and Women* and *Your Right to Know—Your Right to Choose.*

Birthright Inc. (U.S.A.)
62 Hunter Street
Woodbury, N.J. 08096

An alternative to abortion with childbearing clinics and adoption assistance throughout the world. See complete listing in Chapter 9, *Childbearing.*

Ladies Center of South Florida, Inc.
12550 Biscayne Boulevard
North Miami, Fla. 33181

A nonprofit medical and birth control center for adolescents that accepts women of all ages; there is a staff gynecologist, registered nurse, and therapist and a conducive atmosphere for teens. The center contacts schools and will send literature upon request. Welcomes telephone inquiries from around the country through its 24-hour hotline and toll-free number.

LITERATURE: Descriptive brochures; fact sheets.

Resource Center
The American College of Obstetricians and Gynecologists (ACOG)
One East Wacker Drive
Chicago, Ill. 60601

In addition to referrals to Fellows of the College, ACOG provides printed materials on women's health, including family planning and abortion.

LITERATURE: *Seminar in Family Planning*, rev. ed., 1974 ($5.00); "What's Sure Besides the Pill?" (R-5); "Abortion" (R-18); "Important Facts About the Pill" (R-39); "Health Care After Abortion" (R-35); "Birth Control for Men: A Discussion of Vasectomy" (R-28).

Zero Population Growth, Inc.
1346 Connecticut Avenue, N.W.
Washington, D.C. 20036

This group has free referral services for most birth control procedures, including abortions, sterilization, counseling services, VD testing, menstrual extraction, and basic gynecological care. Consult your local phone book for the nearest branch. For more extensive information, referrals are made to the local Planned Parenthood or its national headquarters.

LITERATURE: Leaflets on contraception.

The following federal agencies are information sources on family planning:

Maternal and Child Health Service
Public Health Service
U.S. Department of Health, Education, and Welfare
5600 Fishers Lane
Rockville, Md. 20857

National Center for Family Planning Services
Health Services and Mental Health Administration
U.S. Department of Health, Education, and Welfare
5600 Fishers Lane
Rockville, Md. 20857

National Institute of Child Health and Human Development
Office of Research Reporting
National Institutes of Health
Bethesda, Md. 20014

The Fertility Regulation and Contraceptive Safety Program includes evaluation of currently available methods of contraception and research into the development of newer, better, and safer methods. Eighty percent of the institute's budget for this and its other programs goes to outside scientists in grants and contracts.

U.S. Department of Health, Education, and Welfare
Public Health Service
Food and Drug Administration
5600 Fishers Lane
Rockville, Md. 20857

Publishes pertinent reports on contraceptive devices for the general public.

LITERATURE: "An Important Notice for Women Wearing an IUD," DHEW Publication No. (FDA) 75-4004; "Women and the Pill," *FDA Consumer Memos* (April and May 1976).

The following organizations are educational resources on family planning:

Alan Guttmacher Institute (AGI)
515 Madison Avenue
New York, N.Y. 10022

Founded in 1968 as a part of Planned Parenthood Federation of America Inc., AGI is now an independent research institute in the field of fertility regulation. It is also an educational center that publishes papers, books, and periodicals in this field and promotes the development of sound public policies on birth control.

LITERATURE: Four periodicals by subscription—*Family Planning Perspectives* (bimonthly); *Planned Parenthood Washington Memo* (biweekly); *Family Planning/Population Reporter* (bimonthly); *International Family Planning Digest* (quarterly).

National Organization for Non-Parents (NON)
806 Reisterstown Road
Baltimore, Md. 21208

Founded in 1972, NON is an educational organization that seeks "to make the childfree lifestyle a realistic and socially accepted and respected option and to eliminate pronatalist social and economic discrimination."

LITERATURE: Extensive article and newspaper reprints; brochures and pamphlets available include *Am I Parent Material?* and "Want a Baby?" by Mary R. Felsheker, from *Bride's; Annual Report; Parenthood Is Optional or Is It?;* newsletter, which lists chapters, affiliates, and contacts throughout the world (single copies of pamphlets free).

The Population Council
One Dag Hammarskjold Plaza
New York, N.Y. 10017

Founded in 1952, this independent, nonprofit organization conducts multidisciplinary research and provides technical and professional services in the broad field of population. Its work is international in scope. The council has a complete staff of about 190 with associates on assignments in sixteen countries. It consists of the Center for Biomedical Research, Center for Policy Studies, International Programs Division, and Program Support and Services Division, which contains the Publications and Information Office.

LITERATURE: Journals issued free to professionals in the population field include *Studies in Family Planning* (monthly) and *Population and Development Review* (quarterly); back issues and bulk copies are charged on a cost basis. Pamphlets and annual reports are distributed free. Monographs, handbooks, and fact books are published and distributed free to libraries of population institutions in the developing countries of Asia, Africa, and Latin America; these books are sold in the developed world by Key Book Service, Inc., 425 Asylum Street, Bridgeport, Conn. 06610.

SIECUS (Sex Information and Education Council of the United States)
137 North Franklin Street
Hempstead, N.Y. 11550

Provides educational materials on human sexuality, including contraception. See complete listing in Chapter 46, *Sex, Education and Therapy*.

ABORTION

For direct help in abortion, contact your nearest abortion counseling center, which should provide you with information on abortion and abortion alternatives—adoption or keeping the baby, or, if you decide to go ahead with it, referrals to free or private clinics or physicians, such as Planned Parenthood or a community service. (Refer back to the section in this chapter on birth control since abortion should be the last resort when contraception has failed.)

The following organizations provide information on abortion:

American Family Planning Association
149 Lewis Road
Havertown, Pa. 19083

This hotline takes calls from all over the United States and makes referrals to the nearest abortion clinic. It will handle six-week to twenty-four week pregnancies and helps in placing unwanted infants in adoption.

Catholics For a Free Choice
201 Massachusetts Avenue, N.E. #312
Washington, D.C. 20002

A national organization supported by private fees of $5.00 and up that believes "that it is an individual woman's right to make decisions regarding contraception and abortion in accordance with her own conscience. [They] oppose any efforts to deny this right and lobby at the federal and state levels in opposition to any type of legislation which would eliminate or restrict these rights."

LITERATURE: *Conscience*, mailed monthly to members; free descriptive leaflet.

National Abortion Federation
110 East 59th Street, Suite 1019
New York, N.Y. 10022

Provides brochures dealing with the legal, moral, medical, and social problems of abortion and a consumer brochure on how to choose an abortion facility; sponsors a national conference.

LITERATURE: *Update* newsletter; pamphlets; *How to Choose an Abortion Facility* (booklet).

National Abortion Rights Action League (NARAL)
825 Fifteenth Street, N.W.
Washington, D.C. 20005

NARAL is the only national membership and lobby organization formed for the single purpose of keeping abortion legal. It has affiliates in most states and hundreds of volunteers coordinating political action networks.

LITERATURE: Brochures; *Abortion Q & A; Abortion—NARAL IS Protection the Right to Choose; 900,000 Women Receive Legal Medically Safe Abortions in 1974;* public opinion polls.

National Right to Life Committee, Inc.
529 Fourteenth St. N.W., #341
Washington, D.C. 20045

Assists 1,400 chapters in their quest to overturn the Supreme Court decision of 1973 by obtaining a human life amendment to the U.S. Constitution.

LITERATURE: *National Right to Life Report*, monthly newsletter; fact sheets; *The U.S. Supreme Court Has Ruled It's Legal to Kill a Baby;* publications lists.

Religious Coalition for Abortion Rights
100 Maryland Avenue, N.E.
Washington, D.C. 20002

A legislative action group to encourage and coordinate support for safeguarding the legal option of abortion; membership consists of representative Jewish and Christian groups. It has a twofold purpose: (1) to educate the general public on the views held by the religious organizations in their coalitions; (2) to stimulate citizen action in opposition to proposed legislation which would infringe on the constitutional right of choice regarding abortion.

LITERATURE: Fact sheets; *Abortion Rights History 1973–77; Summary and Status of Abortion Rights Legislation—95th Congress*, "We Affirm . . . Excerpts From Statements About Abortion Rights as Expressed by National Religious Organizations"; "Judaism and Abortion"; publications price list for fact sheets and other information (prices range from $.05 to $2.50 for "Study Packet on Abortion).

Reproductive Freedom Project
American Civil Liberties Foundation (ACLU)
22 East 40th Street
New York, N.Y. 10016

The project has published the *Abortion Clinic Directory.*

ADDITIONAL LITERATURE

BIRTH CONTROL

The Birth Control Book by Howard I. Shapiro, M.D. (1977). St. Martin's Press, 175 Fifth Avenue, New York, N.Y. 10010 ($10.00). A comprehensive discussion of all birth control methods with dozens of illustrations and photographs. Shapiro is candid and thoughtfully comments on specific commercial products, not just general principles.

Birth Control Handbook, 12th ed., edited by the members of the Montreal Health Press (November 1974). Montreal Health Press, P.O. Box 1000, Station G., Montreal, Quebec H2W 2N1, Canada (free; $.35 for postage and handling). Excellent, comprehensive booklet with photographs and illustrations about the various methods of birth control—how they work, side effects, effectiveness, and so forth.

Birth Control in America: The Career of Margaret Sanger by David Kennedy (1970). Yale University Press, 92A Yale Station, New Haven, Conn. 06520 ($4.95).

Contraceptive Technology, 9th ed. (1978–1979), by Robert A. Hatcher, M.D., Felicia Guest, Pamela Stratton, and Angela H. Wright (1978). Irvington Publishers, Inc., 551 Fifth Avenue, New York, N.Y. 10017 ($2.95). Thorough, clear discussion of all available birth-control methods.

Contraception: Comparing the Options by the Food and Drug Administration (FDA), U.S. Department of Health, Education, and Welfare (1978). Consumer Information Center, Department 692F, Pueblo, Colo. 81009 (free). This booklet, in chart form, describes the most popular types of contraceptives—their effectiveness, advantages and disadvantages, side effects, health factors to consider, and any long-term effects on the ability to have children.

The Doctor's Case Against the Pill by Barbara Seaman (1970). Avon Books, 959 Eighth Avenue, New York, N.Y. 10019 ($.95). Based on the reports and comments of more than 100 medical specialists, this book alerts American women and doctors to the grave potential health hazards of the birth control pill.

The Joy of Birth Control by Stephanie Mills (1975). Emory University, Family Planning Program, Atlanta, Ga. Send orders to Box 26069, 80 Butler Street, S.E., Atlanta, Ga. 30303 ($1.25). With the assistance of the physicians on the staff of Emory University's family planning program, this booklet presents the basics of fertilization and contraception in language that would be especially appealing to teenage girls. Each method is illustrated with drawings and photos. Question-and-answer interviews with men and women working in the birth control field enliven the booklet even more.

Our Bodies, Ourselves: A Book by and for Women, revised and expanded, by the Boston Women's Health Book Collective (1976). Simon & Schuster, 1230 Avenue of the Americas, New York, N.Y. 10020 ($4.95; $1.20 each plus shipping costs for 12 or more copies to clinics and other health counseling services). See especially Chapter 10, "Birth Control," and Chapter 11, "Abortion."

Pregnancy, Birth and Family Planning by Alan Guttmacher, M.D. (1973). Signet Books, New American Library, 1301 Avenue of the Americas, New York, N.Y. 10019.

Seeking the Balance of Care (1975). The Emko Company, St. Louis, Mo. 63143 ($.50). From four general principles in a caring relationship—confirm, acknowledge, reinforce, and equalize—this booklet goes on to discuss sexuality in a relationship as well as the contraceptive foam method, manufactured by the booklet's author.

Sex & Birth Control for Men: The View from Our Side by Tom Zorabedian (1975). Grady Memorial Hospital, Materials Section, Family Planning Program, Box 26069, Atlanta, Ga. 30303 ($.50). This illustrated booklet discusses anatomy, sexual relations, childbirth, birth control, abortion, venereal disease, rape, homosexuality, and men's liberation.

Three Essays on Population by Thomas Malthus, Julian Huxley, and Frederick Osborn (1960). Mentor Books, New American Library, 1301 Avenue of the Americas, New York, N.Y. 10019 ($.50). Classic perspectives on the future dangers of overpopulation including Reverend Malthus's 1824 discussion of how, if unchecked, the population would geometrically progress and double every twenty-five years.

Voluntary Sterilization by Elizabeth Ogg (1974). Public Affairs Pamphlets, 381 Park Avenue South, New York, N.Y. 10016. Pamphlet No. 507 ($.50). Explains the surgical procedures, the costs, and some of the psychological, social, and ethical questions involved in male and female sterilization.

Woman's Body: An Owner's Manual by the Diagram Group (1977). Paddington Press, 95 Madison Avenue, New York, N.Y. 10016 ($6.95). Contains amply illustrated sections on contraception and abortion.

Woman's Body, Woman's Right: A Social History of Birth Control in America by Linda Gordon (1976). Penguin Books, 625 Madison Avenue, New York, N.Y. 10022 ($3.95).

Women and the Crisis in Sex Hormones by Dr. Gideon and Barbara Seaman (1977). Rawson Associates, 630 Third Avenue, New York, N.Y. 10017. See especially the chapters entitled "Recovering from the Pill" and "The Queen of Contraception" (about the diaphragm).

ABORTION

Abortion—In Necessity and Sorrow: Life and Death in an Abortion Hospital by Magda Denes (1977). Basic Books, Inc., 10 East 53rd Street, New York, N.Y. 10022 ($10.00). Written by a psychologist who is also the married mother of two sons. Denes writes, "Abortion is an abomination unless it is experienced as a human event of great sorrow and terrible necessity."

"Abortion in America" by Frank Donegan (August 1977). *Viva* magazine, pages 91–100. Article, plus state-by-state synopsis of abortion availability and prices.

Abortion: Public Issue, Private Decision by Harriet F. Pilpel, Ruth Jane Zuckerman, and Elizabeth Ogg (1975). Public Affairs Pamphlets, 381 Park Avenue South, New York, N.Y. 10016.

Pamphlet No. 527 ($.50). Provides a brief survey of the Jan. 22, 1973, Supreme Court ruling on abortion and the private decisions it did not decide, as well as the medical perspective on abortion techniques, women's health and safety, and the religious viewpoints.

Crimes Without Victims: Deviant Behavior and Public Policy (Abortion, Homosexuality, Drug Addiction) by Edwin M. Schur (1965). Prentice-Hall, Inc., Englewood Cliffs, N.J. 07632. A sociologist explores abortion—for the doctor, the woman, and law enforcement—in the days before it became legal.

"Letter to a Child Never Born" by Oriana Fallaci (May 1977), excerpt in *Viva* magazine from a book by the same title published by Simon & Schuster, 1230 Avenue of the Americas, New York, N.Y. 10020. Moving personal account of abortion by a famous Italian journalist.

What Now? Under 18 and Pregnant by Linda Carroll, Diane LaBelle, Valerie Wooldridge, and Laurie Zarkowsky (1976). Origins, Inc., 140 Washington Street, Salem, Mass. 01970 ($3.00). These four women, who were ages 15 to 18 and CETA youth workers when this 37-page booklet was written, interviewed adolescent women who had had babies or had undergone abortions or miscarriages.

See also the following related chapters in *The Help Book:*

ADOPTION AND FOSTER CARE
CHILDBEARING
CHILDREN
HEALTH
LEGAL SERVICES
MENTAL HEALTH
MULTIPURPOSE ORGANIZATIONS
PARENTING
RAPE AND SEXUAL ASSAULT
SEX EDUCATION AND THERAPY

24

FINANCIAL ASSISTANCE

All sources offering financial aid require that the recipients meet certain specifications. For example, the federal government usually requires that someone who receives financial aid prove a certain need as reflected in his or her previous or projected income level. Other groups, such as those listed in the chapters covering the arts, crime victim compensation, and veterans, require need as well as membership in a relevant subgroup. The groups listed in this chapter are generally open to all needy persons, regardless of color, race, age, sex, or religion.

But there are many persons and groups who need financial assistance—on a short-term or extended basis—who do not meet the "impoverished" standards set by either local, state, or federal governments. Students, for example, may claim financial independence from their parents but schools may not recognize that status—no matter what the student's age—and require parental financial information in order to decide eligibility for tuition and living cost grants or stipends. Many persons may resist applying for government-sponsored financial assistance programs because they find the red tape or the required disclosure of information undesirable. Certain housing developments, for instance, require submission of income tax returns for three years prior to the application as well as complete income disclosure during the entire residency period.

What financial aid sources are left if the "red tape" of government turns you off? You can turn to the private sector: to individuals, foundations, and corporations. How do you go about getting money from a corporation, whether you are an individual, a school, or an organization?

One man who not only knows the answers but has been successfully raising funds for thirteen years is Dennis O'Brien, the founder and director of Logos School, a high school in St. Louis for emotionally disturbed adolescents. In 1976 alone, O'Brien raised over $300,000 completely from private sources and without a professional fund raiser on his staff. It's not easy; O'Brien finds it takes six to eight written or telephone inquiries to get one financial award. But it's worth it. "With corporations," says O'Brien, "our retention rate is eighty-eight percent. That means those corporations who give once, tend to give again. And they give more the second time. For example, the average first time gift is $122, but last year the average corporation gift was $468. It takes a long time to get initial grants from corporations, but it's a way to build a base, as we have done." O'Brien recommends keeping good records and also developing a newsletter or some interesting format of telling a story that also publicizes your needs to the people that you are approaching for funds. They can also read about the good that you do with their money as motivation for giving to your cause.

Where do you start? Listed below is a beginning—the top thirty-three foundations in the United States:

Name†	Year Established	Headquarters	Assets (at market, 1968)
Ford Foundation	1936	New York	$3,661,000,000
Rockefeller Foundation	1913	New York	890,000,000
Duke Endowment	1924	New York	629,000,000
Lilly Endowment	1937	Indianapolis	579,000,000
Pew Memorial Trust	1948	Philadelphia	437,000,000
W.K. Kellogg Foundation	1930	Battle Creek	435,000,000
Charles Stewart Mott Foundation	1926	Flint	413,000,000
Nemours Foundation*	1936	Jacksonville	400,000,000
Kresge Foundation	1924	Detroit	353,000,000
John A. Hartford Foundation	1929	New York	352,000,000
Carnegie Corporation of New York	1911	New York	334,000,000
Alfred P. Sloan Foundation	1934	New York	329,000,000
Andrew W. Mellon Foundation**	1969	New York	273,000,000
Longwood Foundation	1937	Wilmington	226,000,000
Rockefeller Brothers Fund	1940	New York	222,000,000
Houston Endowment	1937	Houston	214,000,000
Moody Foundation	1942	Galveston	191,000,000
Danforth Foundation	1927	St. Louis	173,000,000
Emily & Ernest Woodruff Foundation	1938	Atlanta	167,000,000
Richard King Mellon Foundation	1947	Pittsburgh	162,000,000
Sarah Mellon Scaife Foundation	1941	Pittsburgh	145,000,000
Commonwealth Fund	1918	New York	142,000,000
Irvine Foundation	1937	San Francisco	119,000,000
Haas Community Fund***	1945	Philadelphia	115,000,000
Brown Foundation Inc.	1951	Houston	108,000,000

Name	Year Established	Headquarters	Assets (at market, 1968)
Edwin H. and Helen M. Land Foundation	1961	Cambridge	$ 107,000,000
Henry J. Kaiser Family Foundation	1948	Oakland	106,000,000
Sid W. Richardson Foundation	1947	Fort Worth	106,000,000
Surdna Foundation	1917	Yonkers	105,000,000
Vincent Astor Foundation	1948	New York	103,000,000
Charles F. Kettering Foundation	1927	Dayton	103,000,000
Max C. Fleischmann Foundation	1952	Reno	102,000,000
A. G. Bush Foundation	1953	St. Paul	100,000,000

* Beneficiary of Alfred I. duPont Estate, which owns bulk of assets listed.
** Created out of merger of Old Dominion Foundation and Avalon Foundation, established in 1941 and 1940 respectively.
*** Formerly the Phoebe Waterman Foundation.
† From *The Big Foundations* by Maxwell S. Stewart, based on the *Twentieth Century Fund Study* by Waldemar A. Nielsen. Reprinted with permission of Columbia University Press and the Public Affairs Committee, Inc. Public Affairs Pamphlets (November 1973).

In addition, you can find out all the names and addresses and assets of foundations and corporations, as well as the directors' names, in the annually updated Dun and Bradstreet directories. (Check with your local public library to see if they keep a copy, or check an affiliate of a foundation office in your area for a copy.) These directories are massive in size; they can also be rented. Another resource is the IRS microfiche cards of 990 SR forms—since foundations are responsible to the public, information on their assets is open to everyone. There are also directories of foundations at your local libraries. In addition, foundation centers, such as the Foundation Center in New York, with branches throughout the United States, and the Grantsmanship Center in California (see annotated entries that follow) provide further resources, extensive libraries, and how-to advice in this growing field of financial assistance.

When you need financial assistance, the place to start is at the local level, with the county or city social services agency (Division of Social Services, Department of Welfare) or the local branch of such multipurpose, charitable organizations as The Salvation Army, YMCA/YWCA, YMHA/YWHA, American National Red Cross, and so forth.

In the past ten years, there has been a proliferation of local People's Yellow Pages, as they are called, directories compiled to explain social services in the area. Financial assistance is one of the needs covered. One example is *The Los Angeles People's Yellow Pages*, which is subtitled "A Directory of Social Change

Resources, Low Cost Non-Ripoff Services, and Good Things in L.A. County"; it is updated annually, as are most of the People's Yellow Pages. These types of private, nonprofit information sources, together with the free government offerings, are a good starting point for exploring what your community really offers to someone in need. Check your local bookstore to see if such a directory exists. A useful booklet, *Putting Together a People's Yellow Pages,* is available for $.50 from Vocations for Social Change, 353 Broadway, Cambridge, Mass., 02139.

In addition to directories, some communities have independent help for the needy, such as Everything for Everybody in New York City, which offers free meals, clothes, and shelter in emergency situations. They also publish a monthly newspaper ($5.00 a year) with all sorts of tips on free services around the city. Some of the social service hot-lines in your city or county may supply you with similar free emergency centers.

In addition to borrowing money from your friends, the bank, or other well-known options, here are some examples of innovative sources of financial assistance or emergency funds:

- In order to finance a vacation trip, a teacher signed up ten other people and received his own air fare and accommodations free.
- A writer made a list of the supplies that were necessary to physically complete a manuscript—typewriter ribbons, correction fluid, and paper—and then wrote personal letters to the presidents of the companies that manufactured those products. Within a month she had received the needed supplies from all of them.
- Housesitting, plant care, and animal-sitting services can be exchanged for temporary or long-term free rent, room, and board.
- Garage sales.
- Setting up a film society in your community and charging admission fees. (You can rent such classics as *The Bridge on the River Kwai* or *Suspicion* for less than $100.00, if they are shown to less than 300 people.)

If you've lost your job, contact your state unemployment insurance department to see if you are eligible for benefits and what they will be. (See Chapter 21, *Employment,* for job hunting aids.) If you are out of work because of a job-related injury, find out if you are eligible for workers' compensation. (See Chapter 21, *Employment,* for further information and a listing of the state agencies for workers' compensation.) For general financial assistance, as well as information on related free services offered in your state (health care, food stamps, aid to families with dependent children), contact your state Department of Public Aid, Public Welfare, or Social Services.

The following are the state agencies for welfare:

Bureau of Public Assistance
Office of Program Administration
Department of Pensions and Security
Administrative Building
64 North Union Street
Montgomery, Ala. 36130

Division of Public Assistance
Department of Health and Social Services
318 Alaska Office Building
Pouch H-07
Juneau, Alaska 99811

Department of Economic Security
1717 West Jefferson Street
Phoenix, Ariz. 85007

Department of Human Services
Division of Social Services
P.O. Box 1437
Little Rock, Ark. 72203

Department of Benefit Payments
744 P Street
Sacramento, Calif. 95814

Department of Social Services
State Social Services Building
1575 Sherman Street
Denver, Colo. 80203

Department of Social Services
110 Bartholomew Avenue
Hartford, Conn. 06115

Division of Social Services
Department of Health and Social Services
P.O. Box 309
Wilmington, Del. 19899

Public Assistance Administration
500 First Street, N.W.
Washington, D.C. 20001

Division of Social and Economic Services
Department of Health and Rehabilitative
  Services
1323 Winewood Boulevard
Tallahassee, Fla. 32301

Division of Benefits Payments
Department of Human Resources
47 Trinity Avenue, S.W.
Atlanta, Ga. 30334

Public Welfare Division
Department of Social Services and Housing
1390 Miller Street
Honolulu, Hawaii 96813

Division of Welfare
Department of Health and Welfare
700 West State
Boise, Idaho 83720

Department of Public Aid
316 South Second Street
Springfield, Ill. 62762

Department of Public Welfare
701 State Office Building
Indianapolis, Ind. 46204

Bureau of Benefit Payments
Division of Community Services
Department of Social Services
Hoover Building
Des Moines, Iowa 50319

Division of Social Services
Department of Social and Rehabilitation
  Services
State Office Building
Topeka, Kans. 66612

Bureau for Social Insurance
Department for Human Resources
275 East Main Street
Frankfort, Ky. 40601

Office of Family Services
P.O. Box 44065
Baton Rouge, La. 70804

Bureau of Social Welfare
Department of Human Services
221 State Street
Augusta, Me. 04333

Department of Human Resources
1100 North Eutaw Street
Baltimore, Md. 21201

Department of Public Welfare
600 Washington Street
Boston, Mass. 02111

Department of Social Services
300 South Capitol Avenue
Lansing, Mich. 48926

Department of Public Welfare
Centennial Office Building
658 Cedar Street
St. Paul, Minn. 55155

Department of Public Welfare
600 Dale Building
2906 North State Street
P.O. Box 4321, Fondren Station
Jackson, Miss. 39216

Division of Family Services
Department of Social Services
Broadway State Office Building
Jefferson City, Mo. 65101

Economic Assistance Division
Department of Social and Rehabilitation
  Services
SRS Building
111 Sanders
Helena, Mont. 59601

Department of Public Welfare
301 Centennial Mall South
Lincoln, Neb. 68509

Welfare Division
Department of Human Resources
251 Jeanell Drive
Capitol Complex
Carson City, Nev. 89701

Division of Welfare
Department of Health and Welfare
8 Loudon Road
Concord, N.H. 03301

Division of Public Welfare
Department of Human Services
State Office Building
Trenton, N.J. 08625

Income Support Division, Human Services
  Department
301 PERA Building
Santa Fe, N.M. 87503

Department of Social Services
1450 Western Avenue
Albany, N.Y. 12243

Division of Social Services
Department of Human Resources
Albemarle Building
325 North Salisbury Street
Raleigh, N.C. 27611

Economic Opportunity and Community
  Action Agency
State Capitol
Bismarck, N.D. 58505

Department of Public Welfare
30 East Broad Street
Columbus, Ohio 43215

Department of Institutions, Social, and
  Rehabilitative Services
Sequoyah Memorial Office Building
2400 North Lincoln Boulevard
Oklahoma City, Okla. 73125

Public Welfare Division
Department of Human Resources
400 Public Service Building
Capitol Mall
Salem, Ore. 97310

Department of Public Welfare
P.O. Box 2675
Harrisburg, Pa. 17120

Assistance Payments
Division of Management Services
Department of Social and Rehabilitative
  Services
Aime J. Forand Building
600 New London Avenue
Cranston, R.I. 02905

Bureau of Public and Medical Assistance
Department of Social Services
North Tower Complex
1531 Confederate Avenue Extension
P.O. Box 1520
Columbus, S.C. 29202

Department of Social Services
Kneip Building
Pierre, S.D. 57501

Department of Human Services
410 State Office Building
Charlotte Avenue
Nashville, Tenn. 37219

Department of Public Welfare
John H. Regan State Office Building
Austin, Tex. 78701

Office of Assistance Payments Administration
Department of Social Services
231 East 4th South Street
Salt Lake City, Utah 84111

Department of Social Welfare
Agency of Human Services
87 Main Street
Montpelier, Vt. 05602

Department of Welfare
8007 Discovery Drive
Richmond, Va. 23288

Office of Information and Adjustment
Department of Social and Health Services
Olympia, Wash. 98504

Welfare Department
617 State Office Building 6
Charleston, W.Va. 25305

Division of Family Services
Department of Health and Social Services
1 West Wilson Street
Madison, Wis. 53702

Department of Health and Social Services
Hathaway Building
Cheyenne, Wyo. 82002

The following national educational institutions provide information for those seeking financial assistance from private and public organizations:

Foundation Center
888 Seventh Avenue
New York, N.Y. 10019

Founded in 1956, the Foundation Center is an independent, nonprofit, educational organization with more than forty regional offices throughout the country. It collects, analyzes, and disseminates information about philanthropic foundations and the grants that they award. Their library, with directories, is open to the public; telephone reference services are only available to members ($200.00 a year).

LITERATURE: Free descriptive brochures; *Finding Foundation Facts: A Guide to Information Sources* ($3.00); *Foundation News*, bimonthly ($20.00 a year); *The Foundation Center Source Book* (2 volumes, $175.00 each); and *The Foundation Directory* ($35.00 plus $1.00 postage and shipping).

The Grantsmanship Center
1015 West Olympic Boulevard
Los Angeles, Calif. 90015

A nonprofit, educational institution providing three basic services to other private nonprofit and government organizations: (1) small training workshops for up to twenty-two participants that are held around the country on how to locate and approach grant sources, write proposals and plan programs (tuition $325.00); (2) bimonthly publication of the *Grantsmanship Center News* (subscription $15.00 a year) on proposal writing and program planning, government funding, foundation and corporate funding, and management of nonprofit organizations; and (3) reprint service of articles that have been in past issues of the *News* ($.75–$1.25 each, special bulk rates).

LITERATURE: Publications price list; fact sheet; sample copy of *News* available upon request; free brochures.

The following federal agencies provide financial assistance through their field or regional offices; the national headquarters will provide general background information on eligibility requirements:

Aid to Families with Dependent Children (AFDC)
Assistance Payments Administration
U.S. Department of Health, Education, and Welfare
Washington, D.C. 20201

This is the nation's major cash assistance program—over 11 million persons received payments in October 1977.

Public Services Administration (PSA)
HEW South Building
330 C Street, S.W.
Washington, D.C. 20201

PSA deals with state social service agencies to carry out Title 20 of the Social Securities Act, providing assistance that is neither cash payment nor medical with five goals: (1) economic self-sufficiency; (2) personal self-care; (3) protection of children or vulnerable adults from abuse, neglect, or exploitation; (4) reductions or avoidance of housing persons in institutions by providing services in the local community; (5) arranging for appropriate institutionalization when it is the best alternative. Examples of assistance are emergency home and child care services; day care for children and adults; adoption; case management; chore services; and day care for emotionally disturbed children.

Social Security Administration
U.S. Department of Health, Education and Welfare
6401 Security Boulevard
Baltimore, Md. 21235

More than 1,300 local offices of the Social Security Administration are located in principal cities and towns throughout the United States. Trained personnel assist in filing claims for retirement, survivor benefits, and disability insurance. Medicare health insurance is available for low-income families or individuals. The service also includes a supplemental security income program.

LITERATURE: *What You Have to Know About SSI; Social Security Information for Young Families; A Brief Explanation of Medicare; Your Social Security; If You Become Disabled; A Woman's Guide to Social Security.*

ARTS

Apply to your state council on the arts or the federal National Endowment for the Arts (addresses and descriptions appear in Chapter 5, *Arts*) to find out what grants, fellowships, and awards are available. The major trade magazines in each of the arts—*Writer's Digest, The Writer, Art News, Performing Arts Review*, etc.—usually list prizes, free summer- or winter-residence camps or colonies, and other available awards. Private art organizations are another financial aid information source. For example, *Grants and Awards Available to American Writers* is updated annually and is available from PEN American Center, 47 Fifth Avenue, New York, N.Y. 10010 ($3.00).

Private art organizations are also a source of immediate financial aid. For example, the Authors League Fund (234 West 44th Street, New York, N.Y. 10036) makes interest-free loans to professional, published authors in need of help on account of misfortune, illness, or some temporary emergency. If you are a professional, published writer who needs this type of assistance, as distinct from a grant (they cannot subsidize writers while they work on their writing), you can send for an application blank. When you complete the application and return it, it will be considered by their committee, which acts on requests. (Consult the directories listed in Additional Literature in Chapter 5, *Arts*, for listings of other art organizations for you to contact for emergency funds.)

Although private patronage of the arts is not as common as in the days of Renaissance Italy, some endowed individuals do finance needy, promising artists on a one-to-one basis. How you would approach such a person—or even locate him or her—would require advice as fundamental (or as complicated) as how to find a new friendship. But it is another option to consider as you create a list of alternative funding possibilities for your artistic work.

EDUCATION

Certain schools, such as Antioch College in Yellow Springs, Ohio, include work experience in their college curriculum; students are paid anywhere from the minimum wage on up for off-campus employment. You might want to consider such a program since it offsets steep tuition and room-and-board costs. In addition to educational assistance from private foundations, such as the John Simon Guggenheim Memorial Foundation, you might consider applying to a college or university group, such as the American Association of University Women, Educational Foundation (2401 Virginia Avenue, N.W., Washington, D.C., 20037), or writing for booklets that describe available fellowships, published by such organizations as the Social Science Research Council (605 Third Avenue, New York, N.Y. 10016), the Institute of International Education (809 United Nations Plaza, New York, N.Y. 10017), and the National Academy of Sciences (2101 Constitution Avenue, N.W., Washington, D.C., 20418).

The following federal agency, through its regional offices, has applications for financial assistance in postsecondary education:

Office of Education
Department of Health, Education, and Welfare
7th and D Street, S.W.
Washington, D.C. 20202

Supports five programs for anyone enrolled or accepted for enrollment in an approved postsecondary educational institution (college, university, vocational or technical school, or hospital school of nursing): Basic Educational Opportunity Grants, Supplemental Educational Opportunity Grants, College Work-Study, National Direct Student Loans, and Guaranteed Student Loans.

LITERATURE: Free fact sheets.

FINANCIAL ASSISTANCE / 355

The following is a listing of the regional offices of Guaranteed Student Loans of the U.S. Department of Health, Education, and Welfare; address your inquiry to the Assistant Regional Commissioner, Office of Education, HEW, Guaranteed Student Loan Program, at the addresses given below:

Region I*
P.O. Box 8370
Boston, Mass. 02114

Region II
26 Federal Plaza, Suite 402
New York, N.Y. 10007

Region III
P.O. Box 13716
3535 Market Street
Philadelphia, Pa. 19101

Region IV
50 Seventh Street, N.E., Room 513
Atlanta, Ga. 30323

Region V
P.O. Box 8422
Chicago, Ill. 60680

Region VI
1200 Main Tower Building, 15th Floor
Dallas, Tex. 75202

Region VII
601 East 12th Street
Kansas City, Mo. 64106

Region VIII
11037 Federal Building
19th and Stout Streets
Denver, Colo. 80202

Region IX
50 United Nations Plaza
San Francisco, Calif. 94102

Region X
Arcade Plaza Building
1321 Second Avenue, M.S. 1512
Seattle, Wash. 98101

(For additional financial aid advice in educational matters, consult the books and directories listed at the end of this chapter in Additional Literature. Further general information on education is available in Chapter 19, *Education*, and Chapter 10, *Children*.)

FOOD

For information on self-supporting food cooperatives, see Chapter 25, *Food and Nutrition*. Emergency food is available through your local branch of The Salvation Army; for other emergency food sources, see Chapter 20, *Emergencies and Disasters*.

The main federal contribution in food emergencies are food stamps and school lunch programs:

Food Stamp Program
U.S. Department of Agriculture
Food and Nutrition Service (FNS)
500 12th Street, S.W., #650
Washington, D.C. 20250

Applications for food stamps are available from the Food Stamp Certification Office in your county. Once you submit it, there will be an interview and you will be notified if you are eligible for food stamps within thirty days. Other

*If you are unsure what region you live in, check with your local Federal Information Center, your local telephone directory, or see the listings in Chapter 32, *Information Rights and Resources*.

programs include: Child Nutrition Division's School Lunch Program, Summer Feeding Program, Child Care Food Program, School Breakfast Program; and the Special Supplemental Food Division's WIC (Women, Infants, and Children) Program.

LITERATURE: *The Food Stamp Program; Shopping With Food Stamps* (free).

HEALTH

Free or low-cost medical help is available through your local department of health, publicly operated hospitals, free health clinics, and so forth. For state health departments, see the listings in Chapter 30, *Health*. For general information on obtaining insurance, see Chapter 7, *Business Information*.

Medicare is for anyone age 65 or older, rich or poor. It also covers certain kinds of needy and low-income people, including the blind, disabled, members of families with dependent children, and, in some states (at the state's expense), other needy and low-income people. Medicare is an insurance program. To apply for Medicare, go to your Social Security office.

Medicaid is an assistance program that pays medical bills for eligible people from federal, state, and local taxes. Since states design their own Medicaid programs within federal guidelines, medicaid varies from state to state. To find out where to apply for Medicaid, call your welfare office.

For information on the federal Medicaid/Medicare programs, and the eligibility requirements, contact:

Social Security Administration
U.S. Department of Health, Education, and Welfare
6401 Security Boulevard
Baltimore, Md. 21235

Your regional or field office will refer you to the organization in your state which has been selected by the Social Security Administration to handle medical insurance claims. The national headquarters publishes educational booklets for the general public on Medicare and Medicaid.

LITERATURE: *Your Medicare Handbook; Medicare Coverage in a Skilled Nursing Facilty; A Brief Explanation of Medicare; Medicaid/Medicare—Which is Which?* (all free).

ADDITIONAL LITERATURE

Directory of Special Programs for Minority Group Members edited by Willis L. Johnson (1975). Garrett Park Press, Garrett Park, Md. 20766 ($8.50). This annotated directory includes career information services, employment skills banks, financial aid sources with an additional section on employment assistance services for women.

A series of related booklets by Michele S. Wilson is available for $2.00 each from the same address: *Financial Aid for Minority Students in Education; Financial Aid for Minority Students in Law; Financial Aid for Minority Students in*

Business; and *Financial Aid for Minority Students in Journalism/Communications.*

The Doctoral Dissertation Grant Program (1975). U.S. Department of Labor, Employment and Training Administration, Washington, D.C. 20213 (free leaflet). Those who have completed all requirements for the Ph.D. except the dissertation, or those who will have the requirements completed when the grant starts, are eligible to apply for a variety of grants.

Don't Miss Out: The Ambitious Student's Guide to Scholarships and Loans. Octameron Associates, P.O. Box 3437, Alexandria, Va. 22302 ($1.50 including postage and handling). This helpful student financial guide is updated each August for the school year starting in September. It is organized in the same way a student would approach the question of financial aid—the family's contribution, the estimated college costs, and ways to add to your resources. Descriptions, as well as addresses to write to for further information and applications, are included.

"Educational Financial Aid Sources for Women." Prepared by the Clairol Loving Care Scholarship Program, 345 Park Avenue, 5th floor, New York, N.Y. 10022 (free). Leaflet describing a variety of scholarships for women as well as selected additional reference materials.

Financial Aid Guide for College by Elizabeth Suchar, Director, Financial Aid Service, College Scholarship Service, with Phyllis Harris. Simon & Schuster, 1230 Avenue of the Americas, New York, N.Y. 10020 ($5.95).

Financial Aids for Higher Education (updated periodically). William C. Brown Company Publishers, 2460 Kerper Boulevard, Dubuque, Iowa 52001 ($14.95).

The Foundation Directory, 5th edition, edited by Marianna O. Lewis. Columbia University Press, 136 South Broadway, Irvington, N.Y. 10533 ($30.00). In addition to this extensive resource on private philanthropy, an updated list of private foundations is sent to purchasers every six months. Over two thousand listings are annotated with address, date of incorporation, purposes and activities, financial data, and names of trustees and officers. The prime audience for this resource is the grant seeker, especially organizations.

The Grantsletter (published monthly), 48 West 21st Street, New York, N.Y. 10010 (Subscriptions $36.00; $3.00 per single issue). "Funding Information for Professionals in the Sciences and Social Sciences," containing articles such as "Making and Using Contacts"; "Information Base" on foundations with amounts of money available, addresses and phone numbers, types of research being funded; and "Sponsored Project Development." Each issue contains short news items on various private and government agencies and foundations and their possible granting availability.

The Grants Register 1977–79. St. Martin's Press, Reference Department, 175 Fifth Avenue, New York, N.Y. 10010 ($25.00). A detailed listing of awards and prizes.

Guide to Financial Aid for Students and Parents. Simon & Schuster, Reference, Technical, and Review Book Division, 1230 Avenue of the Americas, New York, N.Y. 10020 ($4.95).

Meeting College Costs. College Entrance Examination Board, Box CSS-10, 888 Seventh Avenue, New York, N.Y. 10019 (free; enclose self-addressed stamped envelope). This booklet will help you determine your need and eligibility for student financial aid, as well as how to apply for it.

National Directory of Arts Supported by Private Foundations. Washington International Arts Letters, P.O. Box 9005, Washington, D.C. 20003 ($45.00). Lists more than 1,200 private foundations and the recipients of their grants.

1978 National Directory of Summer Internships for Undergraduate College Students, compiled by Mary Elizabeth Updike and Mark Edward Rivera and sponsored by the Career Planning Offices of Bryn Mawr and Haverford colleges.

Directory of Summer Internships, Career Planning Office, Haverford College, Haverford, Pa. 19041 ($8.50 including postage and handling). A nationwide listing of summer internships for undergraduates in various fields, including the arts, education, communication, health, government, business, finance, and industry. It is updated periodically and a good resource for students, career advisers, and prospective employers.

Scholarships, Fellowships, and Loans, Vol. 6, edited by S. Norman Feingold and Marie Feingold (1977; updated periodically). Bellman Publishing Company, P.O. Box 164, Arlington, Mass. 02174 ($17.00). Dr. S. Norman Feingold, National Director of B'nai B'rith Career and Counseling Services, and Marie Feingold, who is a practicing certified rehabilitation counselor, describe available financial assistance through the Vocational Goals Index, for quickly pointing out major qualifications and eligibility requirements for specific awards. Educational aid is described for all levels of study—undergraduate, master's degree, doctorate, post-doctorate, professionals, vocational-technical, and non-degree study. Each annotation explains where to apply, what the qualifications are, the amount of the award, and other information.

Stalking the Large Green Giant: A Fund Raising Manual for Youth Serving Agencies by Ingrid Utech (1976). National Youth Work Alliance, 1346 Connecticut Avenue, N.W., Washington, D.C. 20036. These suggestions on fundraising strategies and funding opportunities (local, state, and federal government; general revenue sharing; foundations; other private sources) are geared to youth service programs, but may be applied to other social needs. A good annotated bibliography is also included.

Student Aid Annual (updated annually). Chronicle Guidance Publications, Inc., P.O. Box 271, Moravia, N.Y. 13118 ($12.00). Financial aid programs are described that noncollegiate organizations, independent and AFL-CIO affiliated labor unions, and federal and state governments offer undergraduate, graduate, and postgraduate students.

Student Expenses at Postsecondary Institutions 1978–79 by Elizabeth W. Suchar, Stephen H. Ivens, Edmund C. Jacobson (updated annually). College Board Publication Orders, P.O. Box 2815, Princeton, N.J. 08541 ($4.00). An annual directory of average costs and expenses at about 2,800 colleges and universities to help parents and students figure out approximate expenses.

Your Legal Guide to Unemployment Insurance by Peter J. Honigsberg (1975). Golden Rain Press, P.O. Box 2087, Berkeley, Calif. 94702 ($3.35). Honigsberg, who is a member of the New York Bar, explains how unemployment insurance works, how to determine your eligibility, and how to go about filing the necessary forms, and, if necessary, requesting an appeal if your claim has been denied.

See also the following related chapters in *The Help Book:*

**ARTS
BUSINESS INFORMATION
CHILDREN
CRIME VICTIMS AND WITNESSES
EDUCATION
EMERGENCIES AND DISASTERS
EMPLOYMENT
INFORMATION RIGHTS AND
  RESOURCES
MULTIPURPOSE ORGANIZATIONS
VETERANS
VOLUNTEERISM**

25

FOOD AND NUTRITION

By now few Americans need to be told that too much food, or the wrong kind of food, is aesthetically and physically bad for you. But does all the concern about nutrition have a positive influence on America's eating habits, life expectancy, or incidence of heart disease and obesity? The facts indicate that America's preoccupation with good nutrition is very superficial. Looking for easy answers to their bad eating habits, over 70 million overweight Americans spend more than $10 billion a year on diet industry foods, gimmicks, pills, and schemes. What is the problem? One nutritionist has said, "In general, it is not the quality of food supply but the kinds of food we eat. Our choices are not nutritional choices, but instead are governed by the constant barrage of advertising and the speed of supermarket turnover."

Groups such as the National PTA (Parent-Teachers Association) and ACT (Action for Children's Television) are trying to combat the poor eating habits they believe the media has instilled in America's children. What size clothes the next generation wears may indicate the success of current nutrition reeducation programs.

How can you avoid junk food and harmful chemical additives? "Organically grown" foods are not considered *the* answer any longer since many fall short in nutrition and their prices are often beyond the reach of most Americans. How do you balance your diet? How do you make sure you're getting enough protein, minerals and vitamins? A basic understanding of good nutrition—and even experts admit our scientific knowledge of this field is far from complete—is a first step. Continuing the old, non-nutritional eating habits just makes you fatter and primed for an early heart attack. You might also buy and keep handy a reliable pocket guide to calories, proteins, and other important food information, available at most pharmacies, bookstores, or supermarket check-out counters. The information contained in the following charts—Good Sources of Vitamins, Good Sources of the Critical Minerals,

Sample Menus for Adults, and Desirable Weights*—can serve as an introductory guide to good eating.

GOOD SOURCES OF VITAMINS

These are just a few of the many important functions of the vitamins. Since vitamins are involved in the most basic, vital, life processes it is easy to understand why severe deficiencies in specific vitamins over prolonged periods may result in a variety of symptoms such as night blindness and certain skin lesions, or even full-blown deficiency diseases like rickets, scurvy, and others.

VITAMIN A: Liver, egg yolk, deep yellow and dark green leafy vegetables, tomatoes, liver sausage, butter, margarine, and cheese made from whole milk.

VITAMIN D: Liver, egg yoke, liver sausage, and foods fortified with vitamin D—such as fresh "Vitamin D Milk" and evaporated milk. (Direct sunlight also produces vitamin D in the skin of exposed persons. Growing children and expectant and nursing mothers require 400 international units of vitamin D per day and at these stages in life supplementation with vitamin D preparations might be prescribed by the physician.)

THIAMINE (Vitamin B_1): Pork, organ meats such as liver, heart and kidney, whole grain or enriched breads and cereals, peas and beans, nuts and eggs. (Also distributed in smaller quantities in many meats and vegetables.)

RIBOFLAVIN (Vitamin B_2): Organ meats like liver, heart, kidney and tongue, liver sausage, milk, cheese, meats, eggs, green leafy vegetables, enriched breads and cereals, and dried beans. (Also distributed in smaller quantities in other foods.)

NIACIN: Liver, meats, fish, whole grain or enriched breads and cereals, dried peas and beans, nuts and peanut butter.

PYRIDOXINE (Vitamin B_6): Organ meats such as liver and kidney, meats and fish, whole grain cereals, soybeans, tomatoes, peanuts and peanut butter, and corn.

PANTOTHENIC ACID: Organ meats, egg yolk, meats and fish, soybeans, peanuts and peanut butter, broccoli, cauliflower, sweet potatoes, peas, cabbage, potatoes, and whole grain products.

FOLIC ACID: Organ meats such as liver and kidney, asparagus, turnips, spinach, kale, broccoli, corn, cabbage, lettuce, potatoes, and nuts.

VITAMIN B_{12}: Liver and kidney, lean meats and fish, oysters, hard cheese, and milk.

ASCORBIC ACID (Vitamin C): Citrus fruits (oranges, grapefruit, lemons) and their juices, strawberries, cantaloupes, raw or little-cooked vegetables—particularly green peppers, cauliflower, broccoli, kale, brussels sprouts, cabbage, tomatoes, and potatoes.

GOOD SOURCES OF THE CRITICAL MINERALS

CALCIUM: Milk and cheese particularly; also ice cream, shellfish, canned sardines and salmon (with bones), egg yolk, soybeans, and green vegetables.

IRON: Liver, heart, kidney, liver sausage, shellfish, lean meats, egg yolk, soybeans, dried beans and lentils, dried fruits, nuts, whole grain or enriched cereals and cereal products.

IODINE: Iodized salt, seafoods.

FLUORINE: If not naturally present in the local water supply, fluoridated water containing one part per million of fluorine.

---

*The four charts are reprinted with permission from *Facts About Nutrition* (revised 1973), U.S. Department of Health, Education, and Welfare, Public Health Service, National Institutes of Health.

OTHER ESSENTIAL MINERALS: Sodium, potassium, phosphorus, sulfur, chlorine, magnesium, manganese, copper, zinc, cobalt, and possibly molybdenum and selenium.

A well-balanced diet, especially one which contains adequate amounts of protein foods (such as represented by the sample meal plan that follows) usually provides all the essential minerals in sufficient quantity to satisfy the body's requirements.

SAMPLE MENUS FOR ADULTS

Light and Inexpensive

BREAKFAST
Enriched cereal with glass of milk and sugar
Orange or orange juice
Enriched or whole grain toast with enriched margarine and jelly
Beverage

LUNCH
Egg sandwich
Sliced tomatoes
Cottage cheese
Beverage

DINNER
Fruit in season
Beef stew (or hamburger steak and potatoes)
Green vegetable or mixed green salad
Bread with margarine or butter
Pudding
Beverage

BEDTIME SNACK
Fruit and cookies (or cheese and crackers)

Hearty and Elaborate

BREAKFAST
Enriched cereal with glass of milk and sugar
Grapefruit sections
2 eggs
Ham or sausage
Enriched or whole grain toast with butter and marmalade
Beverage

LUNCH
Tomato soup
Chicken pie
Grated carrot-raisin salad
Biscuits and butter
Beverage

DINNER
Canned peaches
Pineapple-cottage cheese salad
Lamb chops
Baked potato
Broccoli spears, mustard sauce
Hot breads and butter
Ice cream
Beverage

BEDTIME SNACK
Chocolate milk and crackers (or cheese and crackers)

DESIRABLE WEIGHTS

WOMEN—Age 25 and Over
For girls between 18 and 25, subtract 1 pound for each year under 25

HEIGHT (WITH SHOES ON) 2-INCH HEELS FEET INCHES	SMALL FRAME	MEDIUM FRAME	LARGE FRAME
4 10	92–98	96–107	104–119
4 11	94–101	98–110	106–122
5 0	96–104	101–113	109–125
5 1	99–107	104–116	112–128
5 2	102–110	107–119	115–131
5 3	105–113	110–122	118–134
5 4	108–116	113–126	121–138
5 5	111–119	116–130	125–142
5 6	114–123	120–135	129–146
5 7	118–127	124–139	133–150
5 8	122–131	128–143	137–154
5 9	126–135	132–147	141–158
5 10	130–140	136–151	145–163
5 11	134–144	140–155	149–168
6 0	138–148	144–159	153–173

MEN—Age 25 and Over
Weight in pounds according to frame (in indoor clothing)

HEIGHT (WITH SHOES ON) 1-INCH HEELS FEET INCHES	SMALL FRAME	MEDIUM FRAME	LARGE FRAME
5 2	112–120	118–129	126–141
5 3	115–123	121–133	129–144
5 4	118–126	124–136	132–148
5 5	121–129	127–139	135–152
5 6	124–133	130–143	138–156
5 7	128–137	134–147	142–161
5 8	132–141	138–152	147–166
5 9	136–145	142–156	151–170
5 10	140–150	146–160	155–174
5 11	144–154	150–165	159–179
6 0	148–158	154–170	164–184
6 1	152–162	158–175	168–189
6 2	156–167	162–180	173–194
6 3	160–171	167–185	178–199
6 4	164–175	172–190	182–204

If you have a complaint about a restaurant, contact your local health authorities.

If you have a complaint about a particular food, contact the manufacturer or producer and also your regional or field office of the Food and Drug Administration (FDA) of the U.S. Department of Health, Education, and Welfare.

If you want information about food, diet, or nutrition, contact your local department of health or department of food and nutrition listed in your telephone directory.

If you want to apply for Food Stamps, contact your regional office of the U.S. Department of Agriculture (see Chapter 24, *Financial Assistance*).

Such multipurpose organizations as The Salvation Army, the American National Red Cross, religious centers, and so forth may have emergency food resources. Check with your nearest local branch.

Another local source of help is your consumer organization. (See Chapter 13, *Consumer Affairs*, if you cannot find a local group in your telephone directory.)

State agencies for food will usually provide some or all of the following services: publication of information on food values and safety, vitamins, and fad diets; consultation for community or other state agencies; nutritional education for other public agencies, consumer groups, students, and researchers; radio programs; recorded telephone messages on various nutritional problems; literature.

The following are the state agencies for food:

Food and Drug Administration
474 South Court Street
Montgomery, Ala. 36104

Division of Public Health
Department of Health and Social Services
503 Alaska Office Building
Pouch H-06
Juneau, Alaska 99811

Sanitarian Services
Bureau of Community Health Services
Department of Health
4815 West Markham Street
Little Rock, Ark. 72201

Food and Drug Section
Environmental Health Services Branch
Department of Health
State Office Building 8
714 P Street
Sacramento, Calif. 95814

Milk, Food, and Drug Section
Engineering and Sanitation Division
Department of Health
4210 East 11th Avenue
Denver, Colo. 80220

Food Division
Department of Consumer Protection
105 State Office Building
165 Capitol Avenue
Hartford, Conn. 06115

Office of Institutional and General Sanitation
Division of Public Health
Department of Health and Social Services
Jesse S. Cooper Memorial Building
Dover, Del. 19901

Bureau of Consumer Health Services
Environmental Health Administration
Department of Environmental Services
415 Twelfth Street, N.W.
Washington, D.C. 20004

Food Guides and Standards Bureau
Division of Inspection
Department of Agriculture and Consumer Services
The Capitol
Tallahassee, Fla. 32304

Food and Drug Branch
Environmental Protection and Health Services
Department of Health
1250 Punchbowl Street
Honolulu, Hawaii 96813

Bureau of Environmental Health
Division of Environment
Department of Health and Welfare
700 West State Street
Boise, Idaho 83720

Division of Food and Drugs
Department of Public Health
535 West Jefferson Street
Springfield, Ill. 62702

Bureau of Food and Drugs
Board of Health
1330 West Michigan Street
Indianapolis, Ind. 46202

Food Products Control
Regulatory Division
Department of Agriculture
Wallace Building
Des Moines, Iowa 50319

Bureau of Food and Drugs
Division of Health
Department of Health and Environment
Forbes Field
Topeka, Kans. 66620

Consumer Health Protection
Bureau for Health Services
Department for Human Resources
275 East Main Street
Frankfort, Ky. 40601

Food and Drugs Division of Health Services and Environmental Quality
P.O. Box 60630
New Orleans, La. 70160

Inspections Division
Department of Agriculture
State House
Augusta, Me. 04333

Bureau of Food and Drugs
Environmental Health Administration
Department of Health and Mental Hygiene
201 West Preston Street
Baltimore, Md. 21201

Division of Food and Drugs
Department of Public Health
305 South Street
Boston, Mass. 02130

Consumer Protection Bureau
Division of Food Inspection
Department of Agriculture
Lewis Cass Building
Lansing, Mich. 48913

Food, Meat, and Poultry Division
Department of Agriculture
State Office Building
Wabasha Street
St. Paul, Minn. 55155

Consumer Protection Division
Department of Agriculture and Commerce
1601 Walter Sillers Building
Jackson, Miss. 39202

Division of Health
Department of Social Services
Broadway State Office Building
Jefferson City, Mo. 65101

Food and Consumer Safety Bureau
Department of Health and Environmental
 Sciences
Board of Health Building
Helena, Mont. 59601

College of Home Economics
University of Nebraska
Lincoln, Neb. 68588

Consumer Protection Service
Division of Public Health
Department of Health and Welfare
Hazen Drive
Concord, N.H. 03301

Division of Food Control
Department of Agriculture and Markets
State Campus, Building 8
Albany, N.Y. 12235

Food and Drug Protection Office of
 Consumer Services
Department of Agriculture
Raleigh, N.C. 27611

State Laboratories Department and
 Consumer Affairs Agency
2635 East Main Avenue
Bismarck, N.D. 58505

Division of Foods, Dairies, and Drugs
Department of Agriculture
Ohio Departments Building
65 South Front Street
Columbus, Ohio 43215

Consumer Protection Service
Department of Health
N.E. 10th and Stonewall Streets
Oklahoma City, Okla. 73105

Food and Dairy Division
Department of Agriculture
Agriculture Building
635 Capitol Street, N.E.
Salem, Ore. 97310

Bureau of Foods and Chemistry
Department of Agriculture
Agriculture Building
2301 North Cameron Street
Harrisburg, Pa. 17120

Division of Food Protection and
 Sanitation
Health Department
75 Davis Street
Providence, R.I. 02903

Division of Food Protection
Medical Care and Health Regulations
Department of Health and Environmental
 Control
R. J. Aycock Building
2600 Bull Street
Columbia, S.C. 29201

Department of Health
Joe Foss Building
Pierre, S.D. 57501

Division of Food and Drugs
Department of Agriculture
Elington Agricultural Center
Hogan Road
Nashville, Tenn. 37220

Division of Food and Drugs
Environmental and Consumer Health
 Protection
Department of Health Resources
1100 West 49th Street
Austin, Tex. 78756

Department of Agriculture
147 North 200 West
Salt Lake City, Utah 84103

Department of Agriculture and Consumer Services
P.O. Box 1163
Richmond, Va. 23209

Dairy and Food Division
Department of Agriculture
406 General Administration Building
Olympia, Wash. 98504

Food and General Sanitation
Department of Health
554 State Office Building
Charleston, W.Va. 25305

Department of Agriculture, Trade, and Consumer Protection
801 West Badger Road
Madison, Wis. 53702

Division of Food and Drug
Department of Agriculture
2219 Carey Avenue
Cheyenne, Wyo. 82002

The following federal agencies and national organizations provide information on food and nutrition:

American Dietetic Association (ADA)
430 North Michigan Avenue
Chicago, Ill. 60611

Founded in 1917, this national organization has fifty-two state groups. Its membership consists of dieticians who meet ADA requirements and are employed in a variety of school, industry, and miscellaneous settings. ADA provides career guidance in the dietician area and is involved in a public education program.

LITERATURE: *Journal of the American Dietetic Association* and "Food Facts Talk Back" ($.75).

Community Nutrition Institute
1910 K Street, N.W.
Washington, D.C. 20006

An information clearinghouse on food and nutrition.

LITERATURE: *CN WEEKLY Report* ($25.00 a year).

Consumers' Research, Inc.
Bowerstown Road
Washington, N.J. 07882

Information resource through *Consumers' Research* Magazine (see complete listing in Chapter 13, *Consumer Affairs*).

LITERATURE: Reprints available postpaid on various food and nutrition topics, such as *Food and Nutrition* ($.50); *Ice Cream* ($.20); *Feeding the Family Dog* ($.20); *Fat in the Diet* ($.20) *The Food You Eat (Chemical Additives)* ($.20); send for complete listing. (Minimum charge of $1.00 per order.)

Council on Food and Nutrition
American Medical Association
535 North Dearborn Street
Chicago, Ill. 60610

Publishes low-cost leaflets and pamphlets on a variety of food-related topics.

Food and Nutrition Information and Educational Materials Center (FNIC)
National Agricultural Library (NAL)
U.S. Department of Agriculture
10301 Baltimore Boulevard
Beltsville, Md. 20705

Publishes a catalog and audiovisual guide to their food, nutrition, and agriculture library holdings.

Food and Nutrition Board (FNB)
National Academy of Sciences-National
  Research Council
2101 Constitution Avenue, N.W.
Washington, D.C. 20418

Founded in 1940, the FNB issues the "Recommended Dietary Allowances," publishes other nutrition information, and maintains a library.

LITERATURE: Descriptive booklet, publications price list.

Nutrition Action Project
Center for Science in the Public Interest
1757 S Street, N.W.
Washington, D.C. 20009

Investigates and seeks to correct problems related to food and health; does not answer individual inquiries.

LITERATURE: *Nutrition Action* ($10.00 a year); *Nutrition Scoreboard: Your Guide to Better Eating* by Michael Jacobson, Ph.D. ($2.50); school food action guide packet; publications price list; books for educators, parents, and the general public.

The Nutrition Foundation
Office of Education and Public Affairs
888 Seventeenth Street, N.W., Suite 300
Washington, D.C. 20006

Founded in 1941, this national organization is sponsored by companies within the food and related industries. It sponsors workshops, produces publications in the nutrition area, and holds an annual meeting.

LITERATURE: *Nutrition Reviews,* monthly ($15.00); *Present Knowledge in Nutrition;* monographs; *Index of Nutrition Education Materials* (1977) ($8.75); publications price list; free single copies of the following booklets—*Renaissance of Nutrition Education; Guidelines for a National Nutrition Policy; Food Science and Technology; Through a Glass Darkly; Selected Nutrition Reference Texts for Physicians and Dentists; Guidelines for Eradication of Vitamin A Deficiency; Xerophthalmia; Choosing Foods to Fit Your Life; Your Diet: Health Is in the Balance;* and *Obesity.*

U.S. Department of Agriculture
Food and Nutrition Service
Washington, D.C. 20250

Contact your regional office with any complaints about meat and poultry products. It also publishes a variety of free or low-cost pamphlets and booklets for children and adults on various food and nutrition topics. Send for their publications catalog.

U.S. Department of Commerce
Consumer Goods and Services Division
Bureau of Domestic Commerce
Room 1104
Washington, D.C. 20203

Publishes a variety of free and low-cost booklets and fact sheets on various foods and condiments.

U.S. Department of Health, Education, and Welfare
Food and Drug Administration
Office of Public Affairs
5600 Fishers Lane
Rockville, Md. 20857

Publishes numerous free pamphlets and leaflets on food and drug safety, medical devices, cosmetics, biologics, radiation-emitting and veterinary products. Comments on particular cosmetics, foods, cooking appliances, or drugs are solicited from the general public in response to (or suggested for inclusion in) the *Federal Register.* Send five copies to the Hearing Clerk, at the above address.

LITERATURE: *A Consumer Guide to FDA* (free); publications list; *FDA Consumer Memos.*

Practically every food manufacturer offers free or low-cost food and nutrition information, both general material or geared to their specific products. (Often the back of packages will give the details of special booklets or offers; if not, at least the address will be listed and you might write to the Consumer Information or Public Affairs Office at that address.)

The following are a few major business-sponsored organizations providing free or low-cost food and nutrition information:

Armour and Company
Public Relations Department
Phoenix, Ariz. 85077

Provides information on meat.

Best Foods, a Division of CPC International Inc.
Englewood Cliffs, N.J. 07632

Offers numerous free recipe and educational pamphlets related to various food products that they manufacture. For a free list of available materials, send a postcard to: Dept. LL-HB, Box 307, Coventry, Conn. 07632.

Home Advisory Service
Dannon Milk Products
22-11 38th Avenue
Long Island City, N.Y. 11101

Provides information on yogurt.

International Apple Institute
2430 Pennsylvania Avenue, N.W.
Washington, D.C. 20037

Offers an apple map and directory to help you locate "pick of your own" operations near you and a poster illustrating the twelve major commercial varieties of apples ($1.00).

National Cheese Institute (NCI)
110 North Franklin Street
Chicago, Ill. 60606

Founded in 1927, the manufacturers, processors, assemblers, and distributors of cheese or cheese products belong to this organization, which also acts as an information clearinghouse on the cheese industry.

National Peanut Council
Communications Division
111 East Wacker Drive, Suite 600
Chicago, Ill. 60601

Information clearinghouse on peanuts.

LITERATURE: *Peanut Facts; Peanuts Pack Protein Power;* fact sheets; *The Great Fun & Goober Fact Folder!*

OVEREATING

"Any sound diet will work, as long as you stick to it," says Dr. Albert Ellis, noted author and psychologist. "The sad truth is that 90 percent of all persons who lose thirty pounds or more gain it back within five years."

Is it hopeless? Not if you understand *why* you overeat and systematically work at changing your behavior. At the Institute for Rational Living in New York

City, Dr. Ellis conducts workshops in the problems of overweight to explain the way cognitive behavior therapy can be applied to overeating.

"At the root of all weight problems are what I call *magical beliefs*," says Dr. Ellis. "That is, nutty ideas that a person maintains as an excuse for his or her self-defeating behavior. The first step to losing weight is recognizing your magical beliefs." Although the list is endless, these are some of the most common ones:

- My husband (wife) only likes me when I'm thin and it shouldn't be that way. I'll show him (her)!
- It isn't fair that my children can eat all they want and I have to deprive myself.
- It's unfair that *I* should have to stick to a diet.
- Eating is the *only* way that I can deal with anxiety.
- I've been overweight so long, I *have* to continue to be fat.
- I'm worthless and worthless people can't achieve anything so I *can't* lose weight.

What is your magical belief? Write it down. Then ask yourself these four questions:

- What am I telling myself?
- Is it really true?
- Where is the evidence?
- What's the worst that could happen if I lost weight?

For the next two weeks, spend ten minutes each day analyzing your nutty idea. After you've effectively knocked that idea out of your head, begin working on another one. But what will give you the incentive? A daily plan of reward and penalty. If you succeed, give yourself an immediate reward: going to see a new movie or making a long distance phone call to an old friend. Use anything *except* food. What if you slip one day? Take a negative penalty: clean the bathroom or wash the kitchen floor. Some couples find it helpful to make their spouse administer the negative penalties.

"The rewards and penalties had better be immediate because people are driven by pleasure," says Dr. Ellis. "Since depression is another big reason for overeating, small progressive steps are reinforcing."

While you are working on your magical belief, begin a medically approved diet that seems to suit your personality, whether you count calories or adhere to planned meals. Then, on a *daily* basis, administer reinforcements for your dieting. Success means what happened that particular day—don't punish yourself tomorrow for today's cheating.

If you are eager to try to put Dr. Ellis's suggestions into practice, answer this important question: Do I secretly believe that just by reading this introduction

I will begin to lose weight? If your answer is "yes," spend ten minutes analyzing that magical belief.

The following organizations have self-help groups throughout the United States for help with the problem of overeating, overweight, and obesity; the national headquarters of each one will refer you to your nearest local affiliate and also offer published information:

Correspondence Weight Reduction
240 South Swall Drive
Beverly Hills, Calif. 90211

An educational program by mail for weight reduction and weight maintenance through behavioral changes, developed by a psychologist and professor at a southern California university; it is a three-month, thirteen-lesson course ($375.00).

LITERATURE: Explanatory letter; pamphlet; journal reprints.

National Association to Aid Fat Americans, Inc. (NAAFA)
P.O. Box 745
Westbury, N.Y. 11745

NAAFA was founded in 1969 to fight discrimination against fat people in various areas including employment, fashion, insurance, medicine, social acceptance, advertising, and the media. NAAFA is a nonprofit, tax-exempt organization supported by its membership dues ($5.00 for students; $10.00, regular; sliding scale fees for seniors and the unemployed) and has more than eighteen local chapters. In addition to the bimonthly *Newsletter*, there is a pen pal and dating program and a book service.

LITERATURE: "For the Overweight Teenager"; free fact sheets.

Overeaters Anonymous
World Service Office
2190 190th Street
Torrance, Calif. 90504

Free self-help groups in all fifty states for compulsive overeaters, with no weigh-ins, modeled after Alcoholics Anonymous. Started in Los Angeles, there are now about 3,300 local groups.

LITERATURE: *A Program of Recovery for Compulsive Overeaters; Questions and Answers; The Tools of Recovery; Just for Today; Good Nutrition: A Vital Ingredient of Abstinence.*

Weight Watchers International, Inc. (WWII)
800 Community Drive
Manhasset, N.Y. 11030

Since Jean Nidetch founded WWII in 1963, there have been more than 9 million enrollments in Weight Watchers classes. There are about 12,000 classes held on a weekly basis throughout the world. Most are coed, but some are for men only and others are for only teenagers. Before starting the Weight Watchers program, prospective members are urged to consult a physician; a certificate of good health is usually required. You must be at least ten pounds overweight to be able to join. At weekly meetings, members are "weighed in" and losses (or gains) are noted on that person's weekly attendance book. There is a small fee for each weekly class (varying from $2.00 to $4.50, depending on where in the country you are a member). A lecturer who has successfully lost weight and is a graduate of the training program leads each class. Since WWII began, the program has become less rigid (allowing such items as spaghetti and potatoes) and uses a behavior modification approach that changing eating habits is as important as the foods that are eaten. The company has expanded into other areas, such as prepackaged foods, the monthly *Weight Watchers Magazine*, cookbooks, WW recipe cards, sleepaway camps, and restaurants. Contact your local Weight Watchers organization, listed in the telephone directory, for an up-to-date meeting schedule and fees.

LITERATURE: Free article reprints; *Nutrition, Weight Control and You!*, free booklet.

HUNGER AND MALNUTRITION

These local organizations, through their national newsletters and publications, are seeking innovative solutions to the problems of hunger and malnutrition:

Anorexia Nervosa Aid Society, Inc.
101 Cedar Lane
Teaneck, N.J. 07666

An information clearinghouse and self-help program for those suffering from anorexia nervosa—a condition of severe emaciation through self-induced starvation—and for their families. (See complete listing in Chapter 30, *Health*.)

FRAC (Food Research and Action Center)
20011 Eye Street, N.W.
Washington, D.C. 20006

This is a private, nonprofit public interest law firm and advocacy center working with poor and low-income persons to end hunger and malnutrition in the United States. FRAC offers legal assistance, organizing aid, training, and information to poor people and those serving them.

LITERATURE: *FRAC's Guide to the National School and Breakfast Programs* ($.75); *School's Out . . . Let's Eat* ($1.00); *FRAC's Profile of Federal Food Programs* (free); *FRAC's Guide to Child Care Food Program* ($.75); *FRAC's Guide to the Food Stamp Program* ($1.00).

Friends of the Third World, Inc.
428 East Berry Street
Fort Wayne, Ind. 46802

The Friends concentrate on economic injustice issues and personal problems relating to them. It has a resource center for groups doing direct personal services, markets handicrafts made by low-income persons, provides advice and assistance to families, cooperatives, and individuals who cannot hold regular jobs because of a lack of training, personal problems, and so on. The New World Media Project provides factual and organizing information on health, housing, aging, women, consumerism, and unemployment.

LITERATURE: Fact sheets.

Hunger Action Center
Evergreen State College
Olympia, Wash. 98505

The center seeks innovative solutions to the problems of hunger and malnutrition through public education, citizen action, and self-development projects. It provides assistance to the elderly who need to eat well on small budgets, to farmer's markets, and to food cooperatives; and general information.

LITERATURE: Free leaflets and brochures, including *Plant Some Seed Money*; *Food Taxes Are Hard to Swallow*; *Seed Money*; monthly newsletter; *Farmers Market Organizers Handbook*.

FOOD COOPERATIVES

To find out how to start a food cooperative, or if one of the over 2,000 food cooperatives currently operating in the United States and Canada is near you, send for this directory:

Food Co-op Directory, 6th edition (1977). 106 Girard S.E., Albuquerque, N.M. 87106 ($1.50 for individuals; $3.00 for businesses, institutions, and government agencies). There are over 2,000 food coops listed in this catalog of the U.S. and Canadian Food Co-op Movement; resource groups and regional newsletters are also noted in annotated form; some advertising is included, but all related to coops; good reference and resource in this key food alternative movement.

VEGETARIANISM

A strange phenomenon now current might be labeled "steak guilt." That delicious piece of red meat, once the object of status and palatable joy, is now a controversial subject. There are even suggestions from such diverse groups as the American Heart Association and the Episcopal Diocese of New York to decrease our meat consumption by as much as one-third. Economist Lester Brown and nutritionist Jean Mayer point out that we might then place the grain fed to the livestock directly into the mouths of the starving people overseas.

It is evident that the United States is at a dietary crossroads. Economic and scientific evidence seem to advocate a vegetarian diet; tradition and industry endorse a livestock economy. We export and encourage a grain diet in underdeveloped nations, but stress the opposite in our own. What is necessary before we take the ultimate step—the switch to production, distribution, and consumption of a high-protein grain diet?

The role of culture in determining the American way of eating should be kept in mind. Resistance to change is clearly ideological, not economic or nutritional. Americans are renowned for technological prowess. One example of that prowess is the richness of the food placed on the American dinner table. Another example is a high-lysine corn developed by Purdue University scientists. That corn, along with a vitamin supplement, can provide an adequate daily diet for an adult. The discovery of high-lysine corn is as revolutionary an "invention" as the light bulb, but in spite of machinery and antibiotics that speed the journey from food source to linen table, we continue to resist strongly the introduction of innovative products.

As long as Americans can afford to buy meat, most will do so. Along with the car, the television, or the house in suburbia, that thick slab of steak surrounded by potatoes, string beans, and finished with a slice of applie pie, *is* prosperity. These are the elements of American wealth that we *know* will not be found on the table of a rice-field worker in Vietnam or a dirt-path lean-to of an Indian laborer. Those people are living on grain. They are growing up on low-protein diets. Why should they rejoice at our shipments of high-protein hybrid plants when we ourselves shun such unappealing dietary experiments? In a nation where annual beef consumption almost doubled from 1950 to 1972—now totaling about 109 pounds per person—is it reasonable to advocate plant protein, on the one hand, while carving a roast with the other?

If we sincerely believe that a radical change in dietary habits should take place, reeducation should commence in elementary school, where the concepts of "basic foods" and "balanced diet" are introduced. What is now said about the soybean, peanut, or almond? If we keep in mind that diet is a cultural phenomenon, the facts will not be clouded. To argue about change from only an economical and nutritional standpoint leads inevitably to a stalemate.

Information on non-animal diets (vegetarianism) is available from these national organizations; they may also direct you to the local vegetarian organization in your area:

"Are you a hunter or a food gatherer?"

Drawing by Koren; ©1975 The New Yorker Magazine, Inc.

American Natural Hygiene Society (ANHS)
1920 Irving Park Boulevard
Chicago, Ill. 60613

ANHS provides educational materials on vegetarianism and natural healing; it also holds an annual convention.

LITERATURE: Publications price list.

American Vegan Society
Box H
Malaga, N.J. 08328

A national organization that sponsors conferences and publishes a wide range of related materials devoted to educating people about a vegan diet—a vegetarian diet that does not include any dairy products whatsoever.

LITERATURE: Publications price list.

American Vegetarian, Inc.
Fruitarian Network
P.O. Box 4333
Washington, D.C. 20012

These national organizations have vegetarian action kits available. They also provide recipes, animal liberation information, and public awareness materials, such as buttons, bumper stickers, and T-shirts.

LITERATURE: *Vegetarian Action* news.

Millennium Guild
40 Central Park South
New York, N.Y. 10019

Founded in 1916, this national organization, despite its rather small membership, has had a tremendous impact on spreading information about vegetarianism; donations are welcomed.

LITERATURE: Numerous booklets and leaflets.

North American Vegetarian Society (NAVS)
501 Old Harding Highway
Malaga, N.J. 08328

NAVS coordinates activities of all local vegetarian groups throughout North America; holds an annual convention; and supplies educational materials.

LITERATURE: *Vegetarian Voice*, bimonthly ($6.00 a year); publications price list.

Vegetarian Activist Collective
616 Sixth Street
Brooklyn, N.Y. 11215

Founded in 1972, this is a national, nonprofit, vegetarian activist organization acting as an information clearinghouse on animals and vegetarianism.

LITERATURE: Vegetarian Activist packet ($3.00); Vegetarian Feminist packet ($3.00); posters ($1.50); T-shirts ($3.50); buttons ($.35 each)—"Respect Animals, Don't Eat Them!" (enclose self-addressed stamped envelope with button orders).

Vegetarian Association of America
100 Gregory Avenue
West Orange, N.J. 07052

Membership organization ($10.00 a year) providing information.

LITERATURE: Membership includes subscriptions to *Vegetarian Living, Special Members Only Supplement,* and *Special Family Living Supplement.*

Vegetarian Information Service
P.O. Box 5888
Washington, D.C. 20014

An information network that publishes news highlights and educational materials for vegetarians.

Vegetarian Society Ltd.
Parkdale, Dunham Road
Altrincham, Cheshire, England

Founded in 1848, this international society is a leading information clearinghouse on vegetarianism.

LITERATURE: Free descriptive pamphlets and brochures (enclose an International Reply Coupon for postage); *The Vegetarian*, monthly newspaper (£2.00 yearly subscription); publications price list.

The following are just three of the dozens of local vegetarian groups that are offering information, cultural and social activities, and publications:

San Francisco Vegetarian Society, Inc.
1450 Broadway, No. 4
San Francisco, Calif. 94109

An educational organization offering monthly lectures, cooking demonstrations, recreational events such as picnics and dining out, newsletters, and a supply of meatless menus on request; $8.00 yearly dues.

LITERATURE: Cookbooks and literature for sale; monthly newsletter summarizing guest lecturers and news in the field.

Southern California Vegetarians (SCV)
P.O. Box 5688
Santa Monica, Calif. 90405

A nonprofit, membership organization ($10.00 a year), SCV members receive *Check That Chick! Evidence on Meat Consumption as a Cause of Cancer and Other Diseases*, a book ($2.00 for nonmembers), membership in the North American Vegetarian Society (includes the newspaper *Vegetarian Voice*), a bumper sticker, and a collection of vegetarian recipes.

LITERATURE: Descriptive flyers (send large, self-addressed, stamped envelope).

Vegetarian Society of the District of Columbia, Inc.
P.O. Box 4328
Washington, D.C. 20012

A vegetarian society and information clearinghouse that has been in existence for about fifty years.

LITERATURE: Newsletter; calendar of events.

ADDITIONAL LITERATURE

FOOD AND NUTRITION

Animal Machines: An Exposé of "Factory Farming" and Its Danger to the Public by Ruth Harrison, with a foreword by Rachel Carson (1966). Ballantine Books, 201 East 50th Street, New York, N.Y. 10022 (currently out of print; check your local library). As revolutionary a book as Carson's *Silent Spring*, Harrison exposes the fact that some farms are not a natural haven anymore. Instead, animals are drugged, force fed, and subjected to crowded conditions.

Books for Cooks: A Bibliography of Cookery, edited by Marguerite Patten (1976). R. R. Bowker, 1180 Avenue of the Americas, New York, N.Y. 10019 ($19.95). A 526-page book containing annotated summaries of 1,700 cookbooks.

Brand Name Guide to Sugar by Ira L. Shannon (1977). Nelson-Hall, Inc., Publishers, 325 West Jackson Boulevard, Chicago, Ill. 60606 ($1.95). A guide to the sucrose content of over 1,000 common foods and beverages.

Cheese Varieties and Descriptions, Dairy Products Laboratory, Agricultural Research Service (1953, rev. 1969). Available from Superintendent of Documents, U.S. Government Printing Office, Washington, D.C. 20402 ($1.50 postpaid). A directory of hundreds of cheeses with two-paragraph descriptions of their contents and origins.

The City People's Book of Raising Food by Helga and William Olkowski (1975). Rodale Press Inc., Book Division, Emmaus, Pa. 18049 ($4.95). A how-to book for those who want to be food self-sufficient, even in the city—whether on the balcony, rooftop, or windowsill.

The Complete Food Handbook by Roger P. Doyle and James L. Redding (1976). Grove Press, Inc., 196 West Houston Street, New York, N.Y. 10014 ($2.45). A nontechnical and readable guide to the basics of food—dairy products, fruits and vegetables, cereals, sweets, nutritional supplements, and so forth.

Composition of Foods: Raw, Processed, Prepared by Bernice K. Watt and Annabel L. Merrill with the assistance of Rebecca K. Pecot, Catherine F. Adams, Martha Louise Orr, and Donald F. Miller. Agriculture Handbook No. 8, Consumer and Food Economics Research Division, U.S. Department of Agriculture (1963). Available from the Superintendent of Documents, U.S. Government Printing Office, Washington, D.C. 20402 ($2.35). *The* comprehensive listing of foods with their protein, vitamin, carbohydrate, fat, refuse, and food energy contents.

A Consumer's Dictionary of Food Additives by Ruth Winter (1972). Crown Publishers, Inc., 419 Park Avenue South, New York, N.Y. 10016 ($5.95). Arranged in alphabetical order, each additive is described in popular language as to its origin, appearance, tastes, uses, and whether it is toxic or beneficial.

Consumer's Guide to Food Additives by Carole Coughlin and Patricia Forman (1977). Consumer Education, Dept. of Consumer Affairs, 80 Lafayette Street, New York, N.Y. 10013 ($.35). A listing of food additives, what they are, where they come from, and if they are harmful or not.

Eating in America: Dietary Goals for the United States. Report of the Select Committee on Nutrition and Human Needs, U.S. Senate, foreword by Sen. George McGovern (1977). MIT Press, Massachusetts Institute of Technology, Cambridge, Mass. 02142 ($1.95). A comprehensive study, developed by a branch of the federal government, on risk factors in the American diet.

Facts About Nutrition, U.S. Department of Health, Education, and Welfare (rev. 1973). Available from Superintendent of Documents, U.S. Government Printing Office, Washington, D.C. 20402 ($.55). A booklet on basic, good nutrition.

Farmers Market Organizer's Handbook by Hunger Action Center (February 1976). Olympia, Wash. 98505 (free). The politically and economically significant reemergence of Farmers Markets in the state of Washington is encouraged by this useful booklet; information is applicable in all states.

Food and Nutrition (bimonthly). Food and Nutrition Service, U.S. Department of Agriculture, Washington, D.C. 20250 ($3.00; single copies, $.50). Interviews with government employees connected with the food services, articles on nutrition education and school lunch programs; photographs.

Food in History by Reay Tannahill (1974). Stein and Day Publishers, Scarborough House, Briarcliff Manor, N.Y. 10510 ($4.95). A survey of food from prehistory to modern times, illustrated with maps, drawings, and photos.

Food is More than Just Something to Eat, prepared by U.S. Department of Agriculture and U.S. Department of Health, Education, and Welfare in cooperation with the Grocery Manufacturers of America and the Advertising Council. Available from the Office of Information, Department of Agriculture, Administration Building, Room 402A, Washington, D.C. 20250 (free). A color-illustrated booklet that describes the major nutrients and where to find them, as well as the food needs of various age groups—from infancy through the later years.

Future Food: Alternate Protein for the Year 2000 by Barbara Ford (1978). William Morrow, 105 Madison Avenue, New York, N.Y. 10016 ($4.50). A report by a former *Science Digest* senior editor on current new food source projects, such as utilizing cotton and tobacco (protein-rich plants) and enhancing the taste of soybeans.

Health Foods: Facts and Fakes by Sidney Margolius (1973, 1977). Public Affairs Pamphlets, 381 Park Avenue South, New York, N.Y. (Pamphlet No. 494, $.50). A booklet excerpting Margolius's book of the same title. It contains a brief history of the health food movement with an evaluation of some of its basic food preferences—blackstrap molasses, honey, wheat germ, and so on.

Joy of Cooking by Irma S. Rombauer and Marion Rombauer Becker (1931, 1964). Signet, c/o New American Library, 1301 Avenue of the Americas, New York, N.Y. 10019 ($3.95 paper). More than a cookbook, this comprehensive book is a mini-encyclopedia on foods and food preparation.

The Supermarket Handbook: Access to Whole Foods by Nikki and David Goldbeck (1974). NAL Plume, Harper & Row, 10 East 53rd Street, New York, N.Y. 10022 ($4.95). A good popular food guide.

OVEREATING

Facts About Obesity. U.S. Department of Health, Education, and Welfare, Public Health Service. Available from Superintendent of Documents, U.S. Government Printing Office, Washington, D.C. 20402. This booklet provides an overview of the obesity problem—what causes it, its consequences, various treatment methods, and its prevention.

Fasting: The Ultimate Diet by Alan Cott, M.D. (1975). Bantam Books, Inc., 666 Fifth Avenue, New York, N.Y. 10019 ($1.75). A controversial book that endorses this centuries-old method of losing weight. Cott explains why fasting, in most cases, is permissible; he also provides menu guides for after the fast.

Fat Chance: A Look at Weight Control, Consumer Survival Kit (1975). Maryland Center for Public Broadcasting, Owings Mills, Md. 21117 ($1.00). A booklet anthologizing other pamphlets and reports on weight control published by insurance companies, medical associations, and journals.

Fat Is a Feminist Issue: An Anti-Diet Guide to Permanent Weight Loss by Susie Orbach (1978). Paddington Press, 95 Madison Avenue, New York, N.Y. 10016 ($8.95). Orbach, who has led self-help compulsive eaters groups, shares the motivations for overeating that other women have told her about. In addition to case histories, Orbach provides step-by-step instructions on how to start your own CE (Compulsive Eaters) group.

Four Steps to Weight Control (1969). Metropolitan Life Insurance Company, One Madison Avenue, New York, N.Y. 10010 (free). Basic booklet in popular language with common-sense advice about watching your weight, with calorie-counting menus and tables.

Obesity by George Christakis, M.D., and Robert K. Plumb. The Nutrition Foundation, Office of Education and Public Affairs, 888 Seventeenth Street, N.W., Suite 300, Washington, D.C. 20006 (single copies free). A clear, common-sense booklet about overweight with tables of normal weights and heights as well as a complete diet based on the New York City Health Department's recommendations.

The Overweight Society by Peter Wyden (1966). Pocket Books, 1230 Avenue of the Americas, New York, N.Y. 10020. One of the earliest books on the "dietmania" fads and crazes of Americans, putting it into a quasi-sociological perspective.

HUNGER

By Bread Alone by Lester R. Brown with Erik P. Eckholm (1974). Praeger Publishers, 200 Park Avenue, New York, N.Y. 10017 ($8.95). A scholarly treatment of famine in human history, the green revolution, nonconventional food sources, and hunger.

Food First: Beyond the Myth of Scarcity by Frances Moore Lappé and Joseph Collins with Cary Fowler (1977). Houghton Mifflin Company, 1 Beacon Street, Boston, Mass. 02107 ($10.95).

Food for the World's Hungry by Maxwell S. Stewart. Public Affairs Pamphlets, 381 Park Avenue South, New York, N.Y. 10016 (Pamphlet No. 511, $.50).

Hunger in America by Maxwell S. Stewart. Public Affairs Pamphlets, 381 Park Avenue South, New York, N.Y. 10016 (Pamphlet No. 457A, $.50). A concise introduction to hunger—what causes it, what can be done—and some comments on malnutrition.

Is the World Facing Starvation? Prepared by the Office of Communication, U.S. Department of Agriculture, Washington, D.C. 20250 (April 1975). This clearly written booklet explains the myths and truths about malnutrition, food supplies and production, and hunger in the format of a twenty-eight question-and-answer, true-and-false "test," with answers at the back of the booklet.

VEGETARIANISM

The Celebrity Vegetarian Cookbook by J. L. Barkas (1975, 1978). Arco Publishing Company, Inc., 219 Park Avenue South, New York, N.Y. 10003 ($2.50). Recipes for soups, salads, main dishes, vegetables, beverages, and desserts presented with interviews with their celebrated inventors—Irving Wallace, Bob Cummings, Yehudi Menuhin, Shelley Winters, and many others; photos and illustrations.

Diet for a Small Planet by Frances Moore Lappé (1975). Friends of the Earth, Ballantine Books, 201 East 50th Street, New York, N.Y. 10022 ($1.95). The classic, popular introduction to non-meat protein sources and how to combine them for nutritious, low-cost meals.

Eating for Life by Nathaniel Altman, introduction by Geoffrey Hodson (1977). Theosophical Publishing House, 306 West Geneva Road, Wheaton, Ill. 60187 ($3.25). A concise plea for vegetarianism.

Laurel's Kitchen: A Handbook for Vegetarian Cookery and Nutrition by Laurel Robertson, Carol Flinders, and Bronwen Godfrey (1978). Bantam Books, Inc., 666 Fifth Avenue, New York, N.Y. 10019 ($3.95). Over 400 tested recipes as well as writing on vegetarianism as a way of life.

The Vegetable Passion: A History of the Vegetarian State of Mind by J. L. Barkas (1975). Charles Scribner's Sons, 597 Fifth Avenue, New York, N.Y. 10017 (out of print; check your local library). From earliest Greco-Roman times to the present (and including anthropological arguments and roots), the doctrine of vegetarianism is presented as a philosophical (not just culinary) concept with an involved social history. Movements, such as the Doukhobours in Russia and Canada, as well as vegetarian practitioners—Shelley, Shaw, Gandhi, Hitler—are described and analyzed.

The Vegetarian Epicure and *The Vegetarian Epicure Book Two* by Anna Thomas (1972, 1978 respectively). Alfred A. Knopf, 201 East 50th Street, New York, N.Y. 10022 ($6.95 each). Two popular cookbooks for the practicing or would-be vegetarian; illustrated.

"The Vegetarian Unit," National Health's Picture Poster Program (1977). National Health Systems, P.O. Box 1501, Ann Arbor, Mich. 48106 ($3.00). (Ask for poster #309). This colorful two-sided poster has, on the front, a chart of protein sources, fruits, vegetables, dairy foods, fats and oils, grains, starches, sugar for vegetarians and, on the back, a text discussion, "A Look at Vegetarianism." Lawrence Power, M.D. was the consultant physician.

Vegetarian Times (bimonthly magazine). 101 Park Avenue, Suite 1838, New York, N.Y. 10017 ($1.50 single copy; $9.00 a year). Features articles, advertisements, activity updates, reader letter columns, and book club. (In the beginning of 1979, *Vegetarian Times* merged with *Vegetarian World*, a periodical that had published independently for five years.)

Worthington Foods, Worthington, Ohio 43085, a division of Miles Laboratories, Inc., manufactures non-meat vegetable protein foods and has a variety of informational leaflets, pamphlets, and recipes. Sample free titles include: "A Food Plan for Fitness," "Facts and Recipes: Soymeal," "Meatless Menu Planning for Diabetic and Weight Control Programs," and "Vegetable Protein Foods—What Are They? Why Are They Important?"

See also the following related chapters in *The Help Book*:

AGING
ALCOHOLISM
ANIMAL RIGHTS
CHILDBEARING
CHILDREN
CONSUMER AFFAIRS

26

GAMBLING

Answer the twenty questions that follow: *

1. Do you lose time from work because of gambling?
2. Is gambling making your home life unhappy?
3. Is gambling affecting your reputation?
4. Have you ever felt remorse after gambling?
5. Do you ever gamble to get money with which to pay debts or to otherwise solve financial problems?
6. Does gambling cause a decrease in your ambition or efficiency?
7. After losing do you feel you must return as soon as possible and win back your losses?
8. After a win, do you have a strong urge to return and win more?
9. Do you often gamble until your last dollar is gone?
10. Do you ever borrow to finance your gambling?
11. Have you ever sold anything to finance gambling?
12. Are you reluctant to use "gambling money" for normal expenditures?
13. Does gambling make you careless about the welfare of your family?
14. Do you ever gamble longer than you had planned?
15. Do you ever gamble to escape worry or trouble?
16. Have you ever committed, or considered committing, an illegal act to finance your gambling?
17. Does gambling cause you difficulty sleeping?
18. Do arguments, disappointments, or frustrations give you an urge to gamble?
19. Do you have an urge to celebrate any good fortune by spending a few hours gambling?
20. Have you ever considered self-destruction because of your gambling?

* Reprinted with permission of Gamblers Anonymous National Headquarters.

Gamblers Anonymous considers a "yes" response to any seven of the above questions a sign that you have a gambling problem.

The life of the gambler has been romanticized in novels, TV shows, and in movies, but the reality is far from romantic. Compulsive gamblers—not those who occasionally play bingo at church but those unable to stop—feel as driven and as hopeless as alcoholics, compulsive eaters, and drug addicts. Unfortunately, there are not that many services to help compulsive gamblers. A gambler may sometimes resort to embezzlement, thievery, and lying to gain the needed gambling funds. And the gambler's family also suffers. Many prison inmates in part attribute their imprisonment to their compulsion to gamble. Bankruptcy, suicide, depression, and alienation are just some of the results provoked by compulsive gambling or the frustration it arouses as a seemingly insoluable problem.

Most Americans are content to buy an occasional lottery ticket or spend an afternoon once a year at the racetrack, more for recreation than because of an addiction. How many addicted gamblers are there in the United States? Gamblers Anonymous (GA) estimates at least 6 million; about 50 million citizens regularly gamble to the tune of $100 billion a year. The withdrawal symptoms from true gambling addiction resemble those of other addictions—diarrhea, severe headaches, restlessness, and shakiness. Some theorists, such as Dr. Robert L. Custer, link gambling to deep-rooted sexual guilt rather than enjoyment. Whatever the number of compulsive gamblers and however severe their problem, gamblers need as much help and support as other addicts in coping with their affliction.

The two self-help groups for gamblers and their families, friends, and children that follow are both based on the principles of Alcoholics Anonymous (see listing in Chapter 3, *Alcoholism*, for a more comprehensive discussion of AA's basic twelve-step philosophy). All these groups have local chapters throughout the United States and provide the direct service of self-help peer counseling at once-a-week meetings; if you cannot find a listing in your local telephone directory, the national headquarters will help you locate your nearest branch. They also have some literature about the organization as well as reprints of related articles.

Gamblers Anonymous (GA)
National Headquarters
P.O. Box 17173
Los Angeles, Calif. 90017

GA started in Los Angeles one Friday the thirteenth in 1957. Since then the GA movement has grown to more than 250 chapters with an estimated 5,000 members. All services are free; no outside contributions are solicited; and there is no publicity department; talks are confidential. Like Alcoholics Anonymous, telephone therapy after meetings is encouraged; sessions start in a similar fashion with the gambler announcing his or her name followed by the declaration, "I am a compulsive gambler." Gamblers Anonymous also has some prison groups. They are located at: Rahway, New Jersey; Green Haven, New York; Caldwell County Jail, New Jersey; Rikers Island, New York City; Jackson, Michigan; Chino, California, and others. So far there are no groups for women prisoners.

LITERATURE: *Gamblers Anonymous*, booklet for members; meeting schedules (supplied by local chapters).

GAM-ANON
P.O. Box 4549
Downey, Calif. 90241

A self-help group modeled after Alcoholics Anonymous' Al-Anon for the spouses, friends, and parents of the gambler. It has telephone therapy, weekly confidential rap sessions, an annual convention, and tries to keep the focus on "me" and not the gambler or the gambler's compulsion.

LITERATURE: *Gam Anews* monthly.

ADDITIONAL LITERATURE

Compulsive Gamblers: Observations on Action and Abstinence by Jay Livingston (1974). Harper Torchbooks, 10 East 53rd Street, New York, N.Y. 10022 ($3.45). A brief survey of the literature on compulsive gambling, a discussion of the personality of gamblers, and through anonymous case histories, how Gamblers Anonymous works.

Esquire's Book of Gambling, edited by David Newman and the editors of Esquire (1962). Harper and Row Publishers, Inc., 10 East 53rd Street, New York, N.Y. 10022.

Fools Die by Mario Puzo (1978). G. P. Putnam's Sons, 200 Madison Avenue, New York, N.Y. 10016 ($12.50). According to Gordon L. Williams, senior editor of *Business Week,* "the best scenes in the book deal with the casino life of Las Vegas and the bizarre world of the compulsive gambler."

The Gambler's Bedside Book, edited by John K. Hutchens (1977). Taplinger Publishing Company, Inc., 200 Park Avenue South, New York, N.Y. 10003 ($12.95). An anthology of writings on and by gamblers—mostly the lighter side of the habit.

"The Gambler Who Must" by Steve Cady. *Reader's Digest* (February 1975), pages 185–188 (condensed from *New York Times Magazine*). A concise report on how doctors are beginning to see gambling as a disease, like alcoholism and drug addiction, with a brief view of how GA works.

"Gambling: The Newest Growth Industry" special report in *Business Week,* June 26, 1978, pp. 110–29. For information on reprints, write Reprint Department, Princeton Road, Hightstown, N.J. 08520. This article covers the increase in state legalization of betting, the economics of this new industry, gambling stocks, and an essay on why legalization is spreading so fast. Illustrated with photographs and charts.

"The Invisible Addiction: Compulsive Gambling." *Fortune News* (January 1975), 229 Park Avenue South, New York, N.Y. 10003 ($.25 per single copy). This issue of this national newspaper to inmate, ex-offenders, and concerned citizens draws attention to the relationship between gambling addiction and crime.

Playboy's Illustrated Treasury of Gambling by David Carroll (1977). Crown Publishers, Inc., One Park Avenue, New York, N.Y. 10016 ($19.95). This illustrated book deals with "everything you want to know about every game of chance and how to play it to win" rather than the addiction to gambling.

The Psychology of Gambling by Edmund Bergler (1970). International Universities Press, 315 Fifth Avenue, New York, N.Y. 10016 ($3.45). Bergler probes the unconscious motivations in compulsive gambling. Chapters include: "Excerpts from case histories of analytically cured gamblers," "The mysterious thrill in gambling," and "Typology of gamblers."

The following audio-text tape cassettes are available for purchase by educational institutions only (or may be in the collection of your local library). They are distributed by the Center for Cassette Studies, 8110 Webb Avenue, North Hollywood, Calif. 91605:

The Pathology of Gambling, 60 minutes, CBC127 ($15.95)

Portrait Of A Gambler, 30 minutes, CBC743 ($12.95)

The Gambler, highlights from Dostoevsky's short story, 27 minutes, 319 ($16.95)

The Gambling Secrets of Nick the Greek, a discussion by Ted Thackrey of his book of the same title, 27 minutes, 8325 ($9.95).

See also the following related chapters in *The Help Book:*

ALCOHOLISM
COUNSELING
FINANCIAL ASSISTANCE
LEGAL SERVICES
MENTAL HEALTH
MULTIPURPOSE ORGANIZATIONS
SUICIDE PREVENTION

— 27

GAY LIBERATION

Until four years ago, sodomy was a crime in every state; since then eighteen states repealed such laws. Although their policy is now being reviewed, the U.S. armed forces still disqualify homosexuals from being part of the military; many are discharged each year because of proven or suspected homosexuality. Erasing the legal penalties for homosexuality will be a first step, but, as with racial desegregation, it will be a long time before attitudes are completely changed. The gay lib movement has stirred, threatened, and confused even more persons than the women's liberation movement. Those opposing rights for homosexuals may harbor fantasies that the male-female couple, the family, and marriage itself—"the backbone of America"—are at stake in their fight.

Although a Gallup Poll released in July 1977 showed that 56 percent of the 1,513 adults surveyed believed homosexuals should have equal job rights, they strongly disapproved of gays holding jobs in the clergy or teaching in elementary schools. Only two major religious denominations have so far taken homosexuals into their clergy—the United Church of Christ and the Episcopal Church. To protest discrimination in churches, more than 20,000 gays have set up about 100 congregations across the United States in a new church, the Universal Fellowship of Metropolitan Community Churches.

A legal step backward for the nation's estimated 10 to 20 million homosexuals, and the one to reach national prominence, was when the voters of Miami and Dade County, Florida, on June 7, 1977, repealed by a two-to-one margin an ordinance that had protected homosexuals from discrimination in employment, public accommodations, and housing. To offset that action, there are groups like the Gay Task Force of the American Civil Liberties Union with offices throughout the country (see listing in Chapter 12, *Civil Rights and Discrimination*), as well as the National Gay Task Force, which is trying to get congressional approval for a national antidiscrimination law. Certain politicians, such as Mayor Edward Koch of

New York City, have proposed that job discrimination of homosexuals in city jobs be outlawed. Mayor Koch's decree was followed by mixed reactions from the police and fire departments, and other city agencies. But in November 1978 the gay rights bill was defeated by the New York City Council for the fourth time in seven years.

Protest marches against gay discrimination have been staged in San Francisco—such as the march by 40,000 in June 1977—and at the United Nations—a march by 500 in August 1977. In April 1976 *New York Times* columnist Anthony Lewis wrote this reaction to the Supreme Court decision to uphold a Virginia law that makes homosexual conduct a crime (although abortion was declared legal): "In the private homosexual situation, there is no direct injury to any third party, much less to potential life. The asserted state interest is in maintaining a particular moral or social climate. Can that be as weighty as the value of potential life in the abortion case? . . . Another possibility is that the prevailing Justices simply feel more distaste for homosexual acts than for abortion, or regard them as less socially justifiable. Such feelings may be appropriate for legislators or moralists, but should they determine the outcome of constitutional lawsuits?"

The following is the "Position Statement on Homosexuality and Civil Rights"* made by the American Psychiatric Association:

This statement was approved by the Board of Trustees of the American Psychiatric Association at its December 14–15, 1973, meeting, upon recommendation of the Council on Professions and Associations. It was prepared by Robert L. Spitzer, M.D., with the approval of the Task Force on Nomenclature and Statistics. The Assembly of District Branches endorsed the statement at its meeting on November 2–4, 1973.

Whereas homosexuality per se implies no impairment in judgment, stability, reliability, or general social or vocational capabilities, therefore, be it resolved that the American Psychiatric Association deplores all public and private discrimination against homosexuals in such areas as employment, housing, public accommodation, and licensing, and declares that no burden of proof of such judgment, capacity, or reliability shall be placed upon homosexuals greater than that imposed on any other persons. Further, the American Psychiatric Association supports and urges the enactment of civil rights legislation at the local, state, and federal level that would offer homosexual citizens the same protections now guaranteed to others on the basis of race, creed, color, etc. Further, the American Psychiatric Association supports and urges the repeal of all discriminatory legislation singling out homosexual acts by consenting adults in private.

(The American Psychiatric Association is, of course, aware that many persons in addition to homosexuals are irrationally denied their civil rights on the basis of

---

*Reprinted with permission from the *American Journal of Psychiatry*, vol. 131, no. 4, page 497, copyright © 1974 the American Psychiatric Association.

pejorative connotations derived from diagnostic or descriptive terminology used in psychiatry and deplores all such discrimination. This resolution singles out discrimination against homosexuals only because of the pervasive discriminatory acts directed against this group and the arbitrary and discriminatory laws directed against homosexual behavior.)

For direct local help, look in the telephone directory under "Gay" or "Homosexual" for services, or consult the *Directory of Homosexual Organizations and Publications,* an annotated directory updated every two years and available from the Homosexual Information Center, 6715 Hollywood Boulevard, Los Angeles, Calif., 90028 ($3.00). You could also telephone the center for a phone referral to your nearest gay service.

There are now hundreds of gay services operating throughout the country, and a sampling follows. These listings show a wide range of available help:

Gay Community Services Center
1213 North Highland Avenue
Hollywoood, Calif. 90038

Started in 1972, the center has trained peer counselors that primarily serve gay men and women, but will help all people with the following resources: legal, medical, and general information; 24-hour hotline; emergency housing and food; rap sessions; speakers bureau; drug and alcohol dependency counseling; venereal disease diagnosis and treatment; lesbian resources; employment services; and referrals.

LITERATURE: Brochure.

Gay News and Events (Gay Newsline)
P.O. Box 1003
Chicago, Ill. 60690

Started in November 1973, this phone service receives over 1,500 phone calls each day, and provides recorded announcements of activities in the Chicago area of interest to the gay community (although about 25 percent of the calls are from out-of-state). It is not sponsored by commercial businesses but by the founder and with listener assistance. Calls from listeners for counseling are handled on a different phone number; referrals are made to gay agencies in Chicago.

West Side Discussion Group (WSDG)
P.O. Box 611
Old Chelsea Station, N.Y. 10011

Started in 1956, weekly discussions are held for men and women and for women only, often with prominent guest speakers. WSDG is an apolitical group with group therapy sessions led by a professional therapist; its facilities are used for meetings of Alcoholics Anonymous and Overeaters Anonymous; and social dances for gay men and women are held each month. A donation of $2.00 is requested at weekly discussions.

LITERATURE: *The West Sider,* monthly newsletter (mailed free for a six-month period to those who have requested it after attending their discussions and renewable in person; others may pay a $3.00 annual subscription fee); one-page flyers on upcoming events.

The following national organizations provide educational materials and information on homosexuality:

Daughters of Bilitis
330 Grove
San Francisco, Calif. 94102

A national communications network for lesbians offering referrals to other gay groups and activities throughout the country. Social events, crisis counseling, legal advice, and lesbian rap groups are offered in the San Francisco Bay Area. National or local membership is $3.00 a year.

LITERATURE: Newsletter.

Gay Alcoholics Anonymous Central Office
1322 North Van Ness Avenue
Los Angeles, Calif. 90028

Headquarters will refer you to the nearest Gay AA group in your area or other gay counseling centers and community programs that offer help to gays battling alcoholism.

Homosexual Community Counseling Center, Inc. (HCCC)
30 East 60th Street
New York, N.Y. 10022

Started in 1970, HCCC is a direct counseling service with sliding scale fees.

LITERATURE: *Homosexual Counseling Journal*, quarterly ($10.00 to individuals; $15.00 to institutions).

Homosexual Information Center, Inc.
6715 Hollywood Boulevard, #210
Los Angeles, Calif. 90028

Founded in 1968, this national information clearinghouse is aimed at the general public as well as the gay community. Its publishing activities include its annotated directory, updated every two years, newsletters, and bibliographies. It maintains the Archives of the Homosexual Movement, a library and resource center; educational and local referrals are made for counseling services. Media appearances and speakers bureau are available.

LITERATURE: Free descriptive brochures; publications price list; "A Selected Bibliography of Homosexuality, 1974" ($.35); *HCI Newsletter* (free with self-addressed stamped envelope, but contributions are welcomed); *Seeds of the American Sexual Revolution* ($3.00); reprints of various magazine articles.

National Gay Student Center (NGSC)
2115 S Street, N.W.
Washington, D.C. 20008

Founded in 1971, NGSC is an information clearinghouse on homosexuality for college students. It has a speakers bureau; resources, including gay studies; course outlines; seminars; a library; and statistical information.

LITERATURE: *Gays on Campus* ($3.00); *Interchange*, quarterly ($5.00 institutions; $3.00 donation individuals); *Gay Bookstores and Mail-Order Services*, directory ($.50); *Gay Studies Syllabi* ($2.00 institutions; $1.00 individuals); *Changes in Gay Student Rights* ($.35).

National Gay Task Force (NGTF)
80 Fifth Avenue
New York, N.Y. 10011

Started in 1973, NGTF is a clearinghouse for the gay movement, promoting gay civil rights legislation and a fair and accurate image of lesbians and gay men in the media. Basic membership fee is $15.00 per year. Packets of information are available to organizers seeking passage of local and state gay rights legislation.

LITERATURE: *It's Time*, newsletter ($.25 a copy; free with membership); *Gay Civil Rights Support Packet* ($2.28); *Gay Teachers Support Packet* ($1.28); *Gay Parents Support Packet*

($1.14); *Our Right To Love: A Lesbian Resource Book*, edited by Ginny Vida ($12.95).

The Outreach Foundation
102 Charles Street, Suite 433
Boston, Mass. 02114

A national organization started in 1976 to provide a counseling referral service for crossdressers, crossgenderists, and transsexuals. It has workshops, symposia for professionals, a speakers bureau to university groups, support services, and reprint publications on these subjects. It is concerned with crossdressing, general role and identification, and human sexuality.

LITERATURE: Quarterly newsletter; leaflets and brochures.

Task Force on Gay Liberation
American Library Association (Social
 Responsibilities Round Table)
P.O. Box 2383
Philadelphia, Pa. 19103

Affiliated with the American Library Association but not a branch of it, this national, privately funded group was started in 1970. They work toward getting more and better gay materials into libraries and out to readers and to eliminate discrimination against gay people as librarians and as library users. By mail and by phone, they will recommend particular materials for distinct purposes and audiences and make referrals to other gay groups and services. Contributions are accepted.

LITERATURE: Flyer; "Can Young Gays Find Happiness in YA Books?" by Frances Hanckel and John Cunningham ($.50 prepaid); "A Gay Bibliography," its most popular publication, updated periodically ($.50 prepaid).

ADDITIONAL LITERATURE

"Books on Homosexuality: A Current Checklist" by Daisy Maryles and Robert Dahlin. *Publishers Weekly* (August 8, 1977), pages 50–52. Annotated descriptions of sixty new titles from thirty-nine publishing firms.

Christopher Street (monthly magazine). Room 417, 250 West 57th Street, New York, N.Y. 10019 ($1.50 an issue). Each issue is filled with nonfiction, fiction, poetry, and cartoons relevant to the gay rights movement.

Gay Chicago News (free weekly for the Chicago area). P.O. Box 785, Chicago, Ill. 60690.

"Gay Clout." *New York* magazine (August 29, 1977), vol. 10, number 35. Articles include "Gay Power" by Clarke Taylor; "Ten Lives" by Louise Bernikow; "The Genius of Gaiety: Social Jesters in a Pompous World" by T. George Harris; and "Style Power" by Suzanne Slesin.

Gay News newspaper. 1A Normand Gardens, Greyhound Road, London W14 9SB, England (U.S. and Canadian subscriptions: $14.00 for 13 issues surface mail, $20.00 airmail; $1.00 for single issues). Called the "World's Largest Circulation Newspaper for Homosexuals," this newspaper highlights news events with a bearing or relationship to gay liberation and homosexual rights. International in scope, it is attempting to develop a worldwide gay community.

Gay Source: A Catalog for Men, compiled, written, and edited by Dennis Sanders with the assistance of Michael Emory (1977). Coward, McCann & Geoghegan, Inc., 200 Madison Avenue, New York, N.Y. 10016 ($6.95). Interspersed with twenty-eight feature articles are listings of local gay hotlines and information services plus gay-oriented magazines, film rentals, poetry publishing, journals, hotels, guest houses and theater resources; illustrated.

Gay: What You Should Know About Homosexuality by Morton Hunt (1977). Farrar, Straus & Giroux, Inc., 19 Union Square West, New York, N.Y. 10003 ($7.95). For ages 12 and up, Hunt shows that homosexuals are not just one type of person—"The only thing that is true of all homosexuals is that they are sexually attracted to people of their own sex." He disputes the other "truisms" in clear, non-hysterical prose, written for the young, but even adults will find much sense and information in this heterosexual's explanation of homosexuality.

GayYellow Pages: National Edition (Fall 1977). Renaissance House, P.O. Box 292, Village Station, New York, N.Y. 10014 ($5.00; Canada, $6.00). Updated annually, this international and state-by-state directory covers baths, bars, businesses, churches, organizations, accommodations, and publications. It also includes an application for a free listing; illustrated.

Homosexuality in Our Society by Elizabeth Ogg (1972). Public Affairs Pamphlets, 381 Park Avenue South, New York, N.Y. 10016 (Pamphlet No. 484, $.50). A popular exploration of the myths and stereotypes surrounding homosexuality with a section entitled, "Some Thoughts for Parents"; suggested readings.

The Homosexual Matrix by C. A. Tripp (1976). Signet Books, New American Library, 1301 Avenue of the Americas, New York, N.Y. 10019 ($2.25). An examination of how homosexuality effects such social institutions as religion, politics, and the military.

The Joy of Gay Sex by Charles Silverstein, Ph.D., and Edmund White (1977). Crown Publishers, Inc., One Park Avenue, New York, N.Y. 10016 ($12.95). Modeled after Alex Comfort's *The Joy of Sex*, Silverstein's book is made up of short, illustrated essays arranged alphabetically under such categories as "Androgyny" and "Wrestling."

The Joy of Lesbian Sex by Bertha Harris and Emily Sisley, Ph.D. (1977). Crown Publishers, Inc., One Park Avenue, New York, N.Y. 10016 ($12.95). A companion volume to *The Joy of Gay Sex*.

Our Right to Love: A Lesbian Resource Book, produced in cooperation with women of the National Gay Task Force and edited by Ginny Vida (1978). Prentice-Hall Publishers, Englewood Cliffs, N.J. 07632 ($12.95). In addition to essays and fifty pages of photographs, this book offers practical help in finding health services, counseling, and bookstores, as well as how to start a lesbian organization.

The Rights of Gay People by E. Carrington Boggan (1975). Avon Books, 959 Eighth Avenue, New York, N.Y. 10019 ($1.75). One of the handbooks in a series produced under the supervision of the American Civil Liberties Union.

Society and the Healthy Homosexual by Dr. George Weinberg (1973). Anchor Books, Doubleday & Co., Inc., Garden City, N.Y. 11530 ($1.95). Weinberg proposes a difference between a homosexual person and someone who is gay. Gay means that a person is "free of shame, guilt, regret over the fact that one is homosexual."

Twenty Questions About Homosexuality: A Political Primer. Gay Activists Alliance, P.O. Box 2, Village Station, New York, N.Y. 10014 ($1.00). Clear, concise booklet answering the most frequent questions about homosexuality, including "Who is a homosexual?," "Can a person change his or her sexual orientation?," and "How many homosexuals are there?" The booklet tries to be informative, rather than preachy; one-page bibliography.

The Lambda Book Club, P.O. Box 248, Belvidere, N.J. 07823. With a one-time membership fee of $10.00, members receive a subscription to the bimonthly *Lambda Bookletter* and discounts on all ordered books.

See also the following related chapters in *The Help Book:*

**CIVIL RIGHTS AND DISCRIMINATION
INFORMATION RIGHTS AND
  RESOURCES
LEGAL SERVICES
POLITICAL ACTION**

28

GUN CONTROL

Nelson T. Shields is now chairman and president of the National Council to Control Handguns; he has a token salary. His wife, Jeanne, is also a volunteer in the office. Their son Nick's death sadly demonstrated the seriousness of guns, particularly handguns, in the possession of the wrong people.

Before tragedy struck our family, I was very non-political; probably like the average citizen. I read the papers thoroughly and did a lot of talking at home, but never got involved much in politics or issues. But then, in April 1974, my son Nick was murdered in the streets of San Francisco in the so-called Zebra killings of that city. It was a random slaying. He was the last of fourteen murder victims; there were twenty-two attempted slayings of which fourteen succeeded. Now how does somebody react to that?

My son was twenty-three at the time. He loved skiing and lacrosse. He was a very sensitive and sweet person. He wrote a lot of poetry. He loved the outdoors. The summer before, he had taken a trip up to the Arctic with five other boys and they canoed five hundred miles through a river complex just short of the Arctic Circle. That was his idea of a summer vacation.

Right after something like this happens, you obviously do a lot of thinking, and very confused thinking, I might add. I started asking myself right away, "What do I do? Do I just go back to work as a marketing executive, go to the next cocktail party and play tennis at the club, as if nothing had happened?" And my reaction was "no," even though everybody told me to cool down; don't do anything rash. So I continued working for the company for the next year. During that time, I went to my congressman and other sources to get educated on the gun-control issues.

I stayed with my company, studying at home and on vacation, till the end of the year. Then I took a leave of absence at the beginning of '75. I had spent twenty-six years at a business career earning money and living the good life and maybe now it was time that I devoted time to doing something more fundamental. I came down to Washington and sat in on the gun control hearings that were going on in

Congress at the time. It was then I discovered the organization that I am now with, the National Council to Control Handguns.

What are some of the statistics about firearms in America today?

- A U.S. Bureau of Alcohol, Tobacco, and Firearms study of guns used in street crimes found that inexpensive, small caliber, short barreled handguns (the "Saturday Night Special") were most frequently used to commit crimes, and that pawnshops or loan-type businesses were their main sellers.
- About 63 persons are killed every day in the United States by a handgun.
- According to the U.S. Conference on Mayors Handgun Control Staff, "ownership of handguns by private citizens for self-protection against crime appears to provide more of a psychological belief in safety than actual deterrence to criminal behavior."
- It is estimated that there are about 50 million privately owned handguns in the United States.
- Sixty-three percent of the 19,120 murders in 1977 were committed through the use of firearms.
- In 1972 London, which has strict gun control laws and a population twelve times greater than Boston, had two handgun murders; Boston had forty-three.

The most frequently cited constitutional justification for owning a gun is the Second Amendment, which states: "A well regulated militia being necessary to the security of a free state, the right of the people to keep and bear arms shall not be infringed." Although to many people this means each individual has the right to bear arms, the U.S. Supreme Court, on four separate occasions, has rejected this interpretation. The court has interpreted this amendment to mean that the federal government cannot interfere with the maintenance of a state militia.

But the battle rages—with hunters, gun manufacturers, and hobbyists leading the pro-gun lobby; crime victims, liberals, and conscientious objectors leading the anti-gun lobby. The pro-gun side has millions of dollars in support funds for lobbying in the legislatures; the anti-gun side has meager funds but dedicated anti-gun spokespersons.

What do you do if you or someone you know want to get rid of a firearm? The National Coalition to Ban Handguns offers this advice if you want to dispose of an unwanted handgun. First, call your local police department and find out how they dispose of guns. (Only give it to them if they melt down unwanted guns; if they sell them to private citizens, the purpose of giving away the gun is defeated by recycling it back into the community.) If you decide not to give it to the local police, call your local U.S. Bureau of Alcohol, Tobacco, and Firearms office (see listing below) to have a government official take the gun. Remember, in all instances, call first; someone will probably come to pick up the gun. (It is a criminal offense in most places to carry a firearm on one's person or in a vehicle.)

To make your opinion about the need for more rigid gun laws heard by Congress, write your congressman or senator, c/o House Office Building, Washington, D.C. 20515 or Senate Office Building, Washington, D.C. 20010.

Since gun laws vary from state-to-state, consult your local police department for information, or the regional office of this federal agency:

Help ATF Disarm the Criminal

INFORMATION WANTED
ON VIOLATORS OF THE GUN CONTROL ACT OF 1968

PERSONS POSSESSING FIREARMS WHO ARE INVOLVED IN CRIMINAL ACTIVITY

PERSONS POSSESSING FIREARMS WHO HAVE BEEN CONVICTED OF SERIOUS CRIMES

PERSONS ILLEGALLY DEALING IN WEAPONS

PERSONS ILLEGALLY POSSESSING GANGSTER TYPE WEAPONS
SUCH AS
MACHINE GUNS
SAWED-OFF SHOTGUNS & RIFLES
BOMBS
SILENCERS FOR WEAPONS

NOTIFY:
BUREAU OF ALCOHOL, TOBACCO AND FIREARMS
Department of the Treasury

Bureau of Alcohol, Tobacco, and Firearms (ATF)
U.S. Department of the Treasury
Washington, D.C. 20226

This federal agency is responsible for reducing the misuse of firearms and explosives and for assisting other federal, state, and local law enforcement agencies in reducing crime and violence. ATF regulates four major industries—alcohol, firearms, explosives, and tobacco—and also serves as an information clearinghouse.

LITERATURE: *ATF Newsreleases* to members of the press, media, law enforcement, and interested groups and individuals; fact sheets; *ATF Project Identification: A Study of Handguns Used in Crime* (1976); Annual Report; *Identification of Firearms Within the Purview of the National Firearms Act* (January 1975); *Gun Control Act: Questions and Answers* ($.45); *ATF Concentrated Urban Enforcement: Explosives Incidents 1977 Semi-Annual Report; Your Guide to Explosives Regulation—1976;* and *Your 1977 Guide to Firearms Regulation.*

ATF REGIONAL OFFICES

<u>Central Region</u> (Indiana, Kentucky, Michigan, Ohio, and West Virginia)
Federal Building
550 Main Street
Cincinnati, Ohio 45202

<u>Mid-Atlantic Region</u> (Delaware, Maryland, New Jersey, Pennsylvania, Viriginia, District of Columbia)
2 Penn Center Plaza
Philadelphia, Pa. 19102

Midwest Region (Illinois, Iowa, Kansas, Minnesota, Missouri, Nebraska, North Dakota, South Dakota, Wisconsin)
35 East Wacker Drive
Chicago, Ill. 60601

North Atlantic Region (Connecticut, Maine, Massachusetts, New Hampshire, New York, Rhode Island, Vermont, Puerto Rico)
P.O. Box 15
Church Street Station
New York, N.Y. 10008

Southeast Region (Alabama, Florida, Georgia, Mississippi, North Carolina, South Carolina, Tennessee)
P.O. Box 2009
Atlanta, Ga. 30301

Southwest Region (Arkansas, Colorado, Louisiana, New Mexico, Oklahoma, Texas)
1114 Commerce Street
Dallas, Tex. 75202

Western Region (Alaska, Arizona, California, Hawaii, Idaho, Montana, Nevada, Oregon, Utah, Washington)
525 Market Street
San Francisco, Calif. 94105

The following national organizations are actively involved in educating the public about the dangers of owning and using guns:

Handgun Control, Inc.
810 Eighteenth Street, N.W.
Washington, D.C. 20006

A nonprofit, nonpartisan public interest membership organization ($15.00 a year) devoting all its time and financial resources to lobbying on or for legislative efforts at controlling handguns. Sponsors "The Victims of Handgun Violence" project.

LITERATURE: Fact sheets; leaflets; *NCCH's Washington Report Legislative Alerts* (with membership); background information on congressmen and senators.

Handgun Control Staff
U.S. Conference of Mayors
1620 Eye Street, N.W.
Washington, D.C. 20006

This separate unit of the U.S. Conference of Mayors (see listing in Chapter 40, *Multipurpose Organizations*) is a national clearinghouse on handgun control whose purposes include educating the public about the problems and methods of control of handguns. Periodic national forums on handgun control are held, and technical assistance is offered through training seminars in such topics as fund raising, community organizing, and public relations, with many publications designed for the independently run handgun control local project.

LITERATURE: *Organizing for Handgun Control: A Citizen's Manual* ($3.00; see Additional Literature); *Handgun Control Issues and Alternatives* ($3.00); *How Well Does the Handgun Protect You and Your Family?* by Matthew G. Yeager with Joseph D. Alviani and Nancy Loving ($2.00); *Targeting in on Handgun Control*, bimonthly newsletter (free); five posters ($2.00); publications price list; free descriptive leaflets.

National Coalition to Ban Handguns
100 Maryland Avenue, N.E.
Washington, D.C. 20002

This organization is an information clearinghouse on handguns. It also lobbies in Congress for handgun legislation.

LITERATURE: Free pamphlets are "What It Is and What It Does" and "Twenty Questions and Answers"; reprints of pertinent articles; fact sheets on gun victims; *Handgun Control News* (quarterly).

National Council for a Responsible Firearms Policy
1028 Connecticut Avenue, N.W.
Washington, D.C. 20036

Founded in 1967, this national organization works toward strict government regulation of the possession, acquisition, and transfer of usable guns; they are involved in stimulating greater public awareness of the dangers and special responsibilities of private gun ownership.

LITERATURE: Background material on council position in the form of article reprints and fact sheets.

The following national organizations are opposed to gun control:

Citizens Committee for the Right to Keep and Bear Arms
Capitol Hill Office
600 Pennsylvania Avenue, S.E., Suite 205
Washington, D.C. 20003

A nonprofit anti-gun control corporation proporting a membership of 150,000 that includes many politicians.

LITERATURE: *Point Blank* magazine ($10.00 a year).

National Rifle Association of America (NRA)
1600 Rhode Island Avenue, N.W.
Washington, D.C. 20036

An anti-gun control lobby promoting the advantages and legal reasons for allowing the ownership of arms. NRA maintains the Institute for Legislative Action.

LITERATURE: Free leaflets; fact sheets; *The American Rifleman*, monthly ($10.00).

National Shooting Sports Foundation, Inc. (NSSF)
1075 Post Road
Riverside, Conn. 06878

A public relations organization whose purpose is to promote a better understanding of the shooting sports. NSSF is opposed to firearm registration or bans, as exemplified in their pamphlet, "Gun Laws Don't Reduce Crime."

LITERATURE: "Gun Registration: Costly Experiment or Crime Cure?"; "Firearms Prohibition"; "The Great American Gun War" by Bruce Briggs; plus many pamphlets on sport-related subjects.

The following is a sampling of state and local gun-control citizen groups around the country; please enclose a self-addressed stamped envelope with all information requests:

Northern California Coalition for Handgun Control
523 F Street
Davis, Calif. 95616

Southern California Coalition for Handgun Control, Inc.
8455 Beverly Boulevard
Los Angeles, Calif. 90048

Maryland Committee for Handgun Control
P.O. Box 4526
Baltimore, Md. 21212

Reduction of Homicide Through Education
P.O. Box 36472
Grosse Point Station, Mich. 48234

Missouri Committee for Firearms Safety
7207 Pershing Avenue
University City, Mo. 63130

Gun Control Federation of Greater Cleveland, Inc.
P.O. Box 20299
Cleveland, Ohio 44120

Central Pennsylvania Handgun Project
315 Peiffer Street
Harrisburg, Pa. 17102

Tennesseans for Handgun Control, Inc.
P.O. Box 40451
Nashville, Tenn. 37204

ADDITIONAL LITERATURE

Do Mandatory Prison Sentences of Handgun Offenders Curb Violent Crime? by Matthew G. Yeager (1976). Handgun Control Staff, U.S. Conference of Mayors, 1620 Eye Street, N.W. Washington, D.C. 20006 ($2.00). This booklet analyzes the pros and cons of mandatory minimum prison sentences and probes the impact of such sentencing on the gun-using offenders.

Gun Control: One Way to Save Lives by Irvin Block. Public Affairs Pamphlets, 381 Park Avenue South, New York, N.Y. 10016 (Pamphlet No. 536, $.50). A popular booklet summarizing the facts about gun ownership and some of the reasons for gun control. Contains charts and a resource section on pro and con organizations.

Gun Law: A Study of Violence in the Wild West by Joseph G. Rosa and Robin May (1977). Contemporary Books, Inc., 180 North Michigan Avenue, Chicago, Ill. 60601 ($5.95). Photos and text document a grim past.

The Gun Owner's Political Action Manual by Alan Gottlieb (1976). Green Hill Publishers, Inc., P.O. Box 738, Ottawa, Ill. 61350 ($1.95). Lists organizations, publications, and pro-con stance of congressmen on the gun control issue.

"Guns." *Fortune News* (December 1975). The Fortune Society, 229 Park Avenue South, New York, N.Y. 10003 ($.25). This issue includes "Ex-Cons Talk About Use of Guns," "Twenty Questions on Handguns," and editorials and pertinent feature articles.

Organizing for Handgun Control: A Citizen's Manual by Nancy Loving, Stephen Holden, Joseph Alviani, Patricia Beaulieu, Michael Berkey, Judy Homberg, and Hugh Mields (1977). Handgun Control Staff, U.S. Conference of Mayors, 1620 Eye Street, N.W., Washington, D.C. 20006 ($3.00). A comprehensive, 154-page booklet providing step-by-step instructions on how to stimulate citizens to become involved in the fight for handgun control. Contains background information on the problem as well as actual organizing techniques—fund raising, recruiting, influencing the legislature, opposition tactics, a directory of pro and con organizations, advertising, and a bibliography. A good resource for anyone who wants to do something on the local level.

People vs. Handguns: The Campaign to Ban Handguns in Massachusetts by Judith Vandell Holmberg and Michael Clancy (1977). Handgun Control Staff, U.S. Conference of Mayors, 1620 Eye Street, N.W., Washington, D.C. 20006 ($2.00). On November 2, 1976, by a margin of two to one, the citizens of Massachusetts voted *no* to a referendum question that would have banned the private possession of handguns in that state. This booklet explains the legislative and political history of the referendum and its chief proponent, *People* vs. *Handguns*.

The Saturday Night Special by Robert Sherrill (1975). Penguin Books, Inc., 72 Fifth Avenue, New York, N.Y. 10011 ($2.75). The subtitle of this classic work describes its comprehensiveness: "The Saturday Night Special and Other Guns With Which Americans Won the West, Protected Bootleg Franchises, Slew Wildlife, Robbed Countless Banks, Shot Husbands Purposely and by Mistake, and Killed Presidents—Together With the Debate over Continuing Same."

Self-Defense. National Coalition to Ban Handguns, 100 Maryland Avenue, N.E., Washington, D.C. 20002 ($.25). Ten-page pamphlet explaining the dangers of using handguns for self-defense and suggesting alternative means.

"Ten Life-Saving Tips on Handgun Safety" by U.S. Conference of Mayors. Available from National Coalition to Ban Handguns, 100 Maryland Avenue, N.E., Washington, D.C. 20002. A color poster directed at making gun owners aware of the dangers of owning a handgun.

Weapons for the World, Update: The U.S. Corporate Role in International Arms Transfers by Steven Lydenberg (1977). Council on Economic Priorities, CEP Report R7-3, 84 Fifth Avenue, New York, N.Y. 10011 ($1.00). A booklet discussing the foreign policy implications of increased weapons sales to developing countries.

See also the following related chapters in *The Help Book:*

CITIZEN ACTION
CIVIL RIGHTS AND DISCRIMINATION
CRIME PREVENTION
CRIME VICTIMS AND WITNESSES
EMERGENCIES AND DISASTERS
HANDICAPS
POLITICAL ACTION
VETERANS

29

HANDICAPS

It is a startling fact that until twenty years ago there were virtually no rehabilitative services for the handicapped. If persons with incapacitating physical problems did not die from neglect, they were placed out of sight. An increase in social services is one healthy change. Another is the growth of activist groups, many led by Vietnam veterans maimed in combat. Further evidence of change is that more and more television programs carry subtitles or use sign language so that the deaf can follow them. Another trend is toward the greater accessibility of all buildings to those in wheelchairs.

What does a handicapped person desire above all else when meeting a nonhandicapped person for the first time? "That the person underneath is seen, not the handicap," says one speech therapist at a New York hospital rehabilitation center. "People immediately attribute to the handicapped person a whole lot of stereotyped behavior related to the handicap. If you've got cleft palate speech, you're immediately seen as mentally retarded. If you're a stutterer, you're thought of as very nervous because of all the comedy that's gone on about the stutterer. Cerebral palsy—remember all the jokes you've heard? People are so frightened of disability and handicaps as a whole. They feel vulnerable. They have not come to terms with their own vulnerability. If a handicapped individual is in an institution, fine, but don't tell me about it and don't let me see him in the street."

Thus, while more organizations and resources exist than ever before for aiding the handicapped, there is still an inordinate amount of fear and prejudice to overcome. An attractive, thirty-year-old woman shares what being handicapped has meant in her life:

> I have been disabled since I was a very young child. Polio. The disability was very much a part of my life growing up. I was in an integrated school; I was not in classes for the disabled, but a good deal of my time was spent with other disabled

children in recreation centers and I went to summer camps for disabled children. But all this time, I was ignoring the fact that I was disabled. Until I was about eighteen or nineteen. I think then the fact that I was disabled hit me hard, as I think it would most people going through adolescence.

But it was only eight years ago, when I came to work at an institute for the handicapped, that what I call my Handicapped Renaissance began. It was a very peculiar feeling. I went through eighty million stages in a very short period of time. A lot of anger and a lot of guilt and finally I started to externalize it and said to myself, "God damn it. There's got to be people somewhere who are not sitting back and taking a lot of this shit." And that's when I came in contact with Disabled in Action [an activist group].

Like that woman, many disabled people *are* starting to fight against the daily discrimination in education, housing, and employment. Aided by the passage of Section 504 of the National Rehabilitation Act of 1973, only signed in 1978, there is now legal recourse against discrimination for example, if a blind person is denied housing because he or she may be a fire hazard, or if someone in a wheelchair is not able to take chemistry or biology classes because the laboratories are not designed to permit his or her access. But many disabled people do not know about Section 504, or the lawsuits at the national level that are challenging those who are reluctant to enforce it. Disabled people must have their basic civil rights. Only with a widespread upgrading of the quality of life will there be a change in attitudes toward the handicapped. If the general population sees handicapped persons living independently and working at their jobs, prejudices will gradually be reduced.

If you have been discriminated against because of a handicap, you have 180 days from the date of the alleged discriminatory act to file a written complaint. Complaints should be sent to:

Employment Standards Administration
Office of Federal Contract Compliance
 (OFCCP)
Third Street and Constitution Avenues, N.W.
Washington, D.C. 20210

Or send the complaint to the OFCCP regional office, listed in most telephone directories under U.S. Government, Department of Labor.

Additional legal assistance is available at the local level by contacting a Legal Services Corporation office in your community (see Chapter 36, *Legal Services*, for additional information). They should know about legal recourse in handicapped discrimination cases. If not, you or your lawyer should contact this national organization for information or referrals:

The National Center for Law and the Handicapped, Inc. (NCLH)
1235 North Eddy Street
South Bend, Ind. 46617

Established in 1972, NCLH has been jointly funded by the Bureau of Education for the Handicapped, Office of Education, and by the Developmental Disabilities Office, Office of Human Development of the U.S. Department of Health, Education, and Welfare. NCLH provides direct legal intervention in selected cases as well as indirect help through consultations with attorneys, organizations, or individuals considering or involved in litigation. NCLH publishes *Amicus*, a bimonthly journal (subscriptions $10.00 a year for individuals; $12.00 for libraries and organizations) and has a publications list of annotated bibliographies and attorney directories that may be ordered.

For free direct local help for the physically handicapped or disabled, contact your city or county Office of Rehabilitation, a separate agency or one within the Department of Health. They may provide you with referrals to hospitals or institutes that offer physical or speech therapy, employment placement or counseling, and information.

The following are just four of the thousands of local services available; they are a sampling of what you might expect, or look for, in seeking direct help:

Federation of the Handicapped
211 West 14th Street
New York, N.Y. 10011

A nonprofit, nonsectarian agency that provides extensive services for the severely disabled including the Trip Program, which helps groups of disabled persons to travel. Although most participants come from New York City and other parts of New York State, many also come from nearby states. There is also a Group Work and Recreation Program ($2.00 annual membership fee); a medical and psychiatric consultation service; a placement program; an internship training program for professional rehabilitation workers; and homebound learning programs.

LITERATURE: Fact sheets.

J.O.B. (Just One Break)
373 Park Avenue South
New York, N.Y. 10016

Since it began in 1949, this free, employment agency for qualified disabled men and women has placed more than 10,000 persons; it is also a research center on employment of the handicapped.

LITERATURE: Free descriptive pamphlets and monthly listing of qualified handicapped persons who are available for employment.

Rehabilitation and Research Center
Institute for the Crippled and Disabled (ICD)
340 East 24th Street
New York, N.Y. 10010

The center provides services for the physically, emotionally, and economically handicapped, including vocational evaluation, counseling, and training; occupational and physical therapy; social work; psychological testing; psychiatric evaluation and treatment; medical evaluation and treatment; sensory feedback therapy; remedial education; reality orientation and attitude therapy; and the Speech and Hearing Institute. ICD is a public charity serving all the handicapped regardless of race, color, religion, or ability to pay. It was founded in 1917 by Jeremiah Milbank and is affiliated with New York University.

LITERATURE: Speech and hearing leaflet; ICD fact sheet; quarterly newsletter; annual report (all free).

Rehabilitation Institute of Chicago
345 East Superior Street
Chicago, Ill. 60611

A private, not-for-profit hospital for physically disabled children and adults with comprehensive programs of patient care, including physical therapy, occupational therapy, speech therapy, and vocational rehabilitation. It is designated federally as the Research and Training Center in Rehabilitation Medicine in the Midwest, and as the Midwest Regional Spinal Cord Injury Care System.

LITERATURE: Descriptive leaflets and brochures.

Most states have a department or governor's committee on the handicapped; some have separate employment for the handicapped offices or ones within the Department of Labor. For general referrals and information, contact the state agency for the handicapped listed below. Many states publish free directories of local services for the handicapped; other have referral services, informational pamphlets, leaflets, and booklets, vocational rehabilitation, newsletters, and special projects on barrier-free design, housing, education, transportation, recreation, and civil rights.

The following are the state agencies for the handicapped:

Vocational Rehabilitation Service
2048 West Fairview Avenue
Montgomery, Ala. 36104

Governor's Committee on Employment of the Handicapped
1400 West Washington
Phoenix, Ariz. 85007

Division of Rehabilitation Services
Department of Human Services
1401 Brookwood Drive
Little Rock, Ark. 72203

Department of Rehabilitation
830 K Street Mall
Sacramento, Calif. 95814

Governor's Committee on Employment of the Handicapped
200 Folly Brook Boulevard
Wethersfield, Conn. 06109

Division of Vocational Rehabilitation
Department of Labor
State Office Building
820 North French Street
Wilmington, Del. 19801

Services to the Handicapped and Disabled Division
Department of Human Resources
122 C Street, N.W.
Washington, D.C. 20001

Commission on Employment of the Handicapped
Office of the Governor
603 Kamamalu Building
250 South King Street
Honolulu, Hawaii 96813

Department of Public Aid
316 South Second Street
Springfield, Ill. 62762

Commission for the Handicapped
State Board of Health
Health Building
1330 West Michigan Street
Indianapolis, Ind. 46206

Governor's Committee on Employment of the
  Handicapped
Grimes State Office Building
Des Moines, Iowa 50319

Advisory Committee on Employment of the
  Handicapped
120 South State Office Building
10th and Topeka Avenue
Topeka, Kans. 66612

Bureau of the Handicapped
530 Lakeland Street
Baton Rouge, La. 70804

Governor's Committee on Employment of
  the Handicapped
32 Winthrop Street
Augusta, Me. 04330

Governor's Committee to Promote
  Employment of the Handicapped
2100 Guilford Avenue
Baltimore, Md. 21218

Massachusetts Rehabilitation Commission
296 Boylston Street
Boston, Mass. 02116

Commission on Employment of the
  Handicapped
7150 Harris Drive
Lansing, Mich. 48909

Council on the Handicapped
208 Metro Square Building
7th and Roberts Streets
St. Paul, Minn. 55155

Department of Institutions
1539 Eleventh Avenue
Helena, Mont. 59601

Governor's Committee on the Employment of
  the Handicapped
Department of Labor
550 South Sixteenth Street
Lincoln, Neb. 68509

Rehabilitation Division
Department of Human Resources
Governor's Committee on the Handicapped
505 East King Street
Carson City, Nev. 89710

Governor's Commission for the Handicapped
Executive Department
Office of the Governor
State House
Concord, N.H. 03301

New Jersey Governor's Committee on
  Employment of the Handicapped
Labor and Industry Building, Room 1005
Trenton, N.J. 08625

Committee on Concerns of the
  Handicapped
811 St. Michael's Drive
Santa Fe, N.M. 87503

Vocational Rehabilitation Services
Department of Human Resources
620 North West Street
Raleigh, N.C. 27611

Division of Vocational Rehabilitation
1407 Twenty-fourth Avenue, South
Grand Forks, N.D. 58201

Governor's Committee on Employment of the
  Handicapped
Will Rogers Memorial Office Building
2401 North Lincoln Boulevard
Oklahoma City, Okla. 73105

Governor's Committee on Employment of the
  Handicapped
Office of the Governor
208 Employment Building
875 Union Street, N.E.
Salem, Ore. 97310

Social and Rehabilitation Services
600 New London Avenue
Cranston, R.I. 02905

Vocational Rehabilitation Department
301 Landmark Center
3600 Forest Drive
Columbia, S.C. 29204

Texas Rehabilitation Commission
7745 Chevy Chase Drive
Austin, Tex. 78752

Governor's Committee on Employment of the Handicapped
250 East 500 Street
Salt Lake City, Utah 84111

Governor's Committee on Employment of the Handicapped
% State Office Building
Montpelier, Vt. 05602

Department of Rehabilitative Services
P.O. Box 11045
Richmond, Va. 23230

Division of Vocation Rehabilitation
P and G Building
2019 Washington Street, E.
Charleston, W. Va. 25305

Division of Vocational Rehabilitation
Department of Health and Social Services
720 Wilson Street State Office Building
1 West Wilson Street
Madison, Wis. 53702

Governor's Committee on Employment of the Handicapped
Department of Health and Social Services
Hathaway Building
Cheyenne, Wyo. 82002

The following federal agencies and national organizations are concerned with the civil rights and the needs of all physically handicapped persons; they also provide information on and for the handicapped:

American Coalition of Citizens With Disabilities, Inc. (ACCD)
1346 Connecticut Avenue, N.W.
Washington, D.C. 20036

A membership organization ($5.00 a year) that was founded in 1974 by 150 persons who felt that the 36 million disabled Americans—physically, mentally, or emotionally—should unite to share their problems and disseminate information. Many national handicap organizations are members, and a Delegate Assembly is held each year.

LITERATURE: *The Coalition*, information newsletter; *ACCD Action*.

Clearinghouse on the Handicapped
Office for Handicapped Individuals
U.S. Department of Health, Education, and Welfare
200 Independence Avenue, S.W., Room 338D
Washington, D.C. 20201

Provides information for handicapped individuals as well as referrals to organizations that will assist them. It also has a directory of 300 national level information providers, as well as local and state resources.

LITERATURE: Descriptive leaflet; newsletter; publications list.

Closer Look
P.O. Box 1492
Washington, D.C. 20013

This national information center for the handicapped helps the parents of children who have physical, mental, or emotional handicaps by providing advice on educational programs and referrals to other special services and resources. It is a public education program that distributes reading material and provides, whenever possible, listings of local organizations. Written inquiries are preferred.

LITERATURE: *Report From Closer Look*, free newsletter; *Practical Advice to Parents: A Guide to Finding Help for Handicapped Children and Youth*, free booklet.

Disability Rights Center, Inc.
1346 Connecticut Avenue, Room 1124
Washington, D.C. 20036

A research center and general advocacy program to insure compliance by national agencies with Section 504 of the Rehabilitation Act. The center reports on medical devices and equipment available to the disabled.

LITERATURE: Fact sheets.

Goodwill Industries of America (GIA)
9200 Wisconsin Avenue
Washington, D.C. 20014

Founded in 1902, this national organization has 165 member Goodwills in principal cities of the United States. The local agencies of GIA are mainly concerned with providing training, counseling, evaluation, employment, placement, and other rehabilitation services to those who are disabled and handicapped. Its annual national conference is held in late June or early July.

LITERATURE: Monthly newsletter available to members only.

Indoor Sports Club Inc.
1145 Highland Street
Napoleon, Ohio 43545

A national social and educational club for the disabled and a public education program.

LITERATURE: *National Hookup* ($2.50).

The National Arts & The Handicapped Information Service
(ARTS)
Box 2040
Grand Central Station, N.Y. 10017

This is a joint project of the National Endowment for the Arts and Educational Facilities Laboratories. Publications are available on architectural accessibility, arts for the blind and visually impaired, new facilities and programs, and annotated bibliographies of written and audiovisual materials. Some publications are free; others may be ordered.

LITERATURE: *Technical Assistance, Information Centers & Consultants; Arts Education for Disabled Students; New Programs & Facilities* (all free).

National Congress of Organizations of the Physically Handicapped (NCOPH), Inc.
1627 Deborah Avenue
Rockford, Ill. 61103

Started in 1958, NCOPH's membership is comprised of 200 organizations concerned with physically handicapped persons. NCOPH acts as an information clearinghouse. It provides to its membership a liaison to professional groups and assistance with their programs. One committee is L.I.F.E. (Living Independence for Everyone).

LITERATURE: Annual *Roster of Organizations* ($5.00); *Bulletin*, quarterly ($2.00 a year); annual publications list.

National Council for Homemaker-Home Health Aide Services, Inc.
67 Irving Place, 6th Floor
New York, N.Y. 10003

A national standard-setting and leadership organization for homemaker-health aide services throughout the United States that makes referrals. There are less than 45,000 homemaker home health aides in the United States, although it is estimated that 300,000 are needed.

LITERATURE: Leaflets; *News;* annual report.

National Rehabilitation Association (NRA)
1522 K Street, N.W.
Washington, D.C. 20005

Started in 1925, this is the national headquarters for seventy local groups of professionals

402 / THE HELP BOOK

(physicians, counselors, therapists, vocational specialists) and laypersons concerned about the rehabilitation of the physically and mentally handicapped and the socially disadvantaged. Annual conventions are held.

LITERATURE: *Journal of Rehabilitation*, quarterly ($20.00 a year); *Newsletter*, available to members only.

Rehabilitation International U.S.A. (RIUSA)
20 West 40th Street
New York, N.Y. 10018

A national information clearinghouse and referral service, founded in 1971, to help disabled individuals and to educate rehabilitation professionals in the United States and abroad. RIUSA is the only world organization dedicated to all the disabled. It provides an international information service to the U.S. rehabilitation community and works to mobilize U.S. support of international rehabilitation projects.

RIUSA is a nonprofit, voluntary national agency, one of sixty-two national rehabilitation organizations in the Rehabilitation International world network.

LITERATURE: *Rehabilitation/WORLD*, quarterly ($15.00); *International Rehabilitation Review* ($15.00); *International Rehabilitation Film Review Catalogue* ($2.00).

United Cerebral Palsy Association, Inc.
66 East 34th Street
New York, N.Y. 10016

A national network of voluntary community agencies serving children and adults who have cerebral palsy (a birth injury that may be characterized by paralysis or weak limbs), as well as their families. The headquarters also provides information on other handicaps.

LITERATURE: Free descriptive leaflets; annual report.

For employment assistance, contact your local city, county, or state employment office, rehabilitation services department, or employment for the handicapped department; the following federal agency acts as an information clearinghouse on employment for the handicapped:

President's Committee on Employment of the Handicapped
Washington, D.C. 20210

Free single copies of *Careers for the Homebound* and *Housing and Handicapped People* are available.

BUILDING ACCESS

The following national organization serves as a clearinghouse on creating a barrier-free environment for all physically handicapped persons:

National Center for a Barrier Free Environment
8401 Connecticut Avenue
Washington, D.C. 20015

Founded in 1974 by ten national private and public organizations, this information clearinghouse on barrier-free design topics is a membership organization ($10.00 for individuals; organizations on a sliding scale). Membership includes a subscription to their bimonthly newsletter, *Report*.

LITERATURE: Sample newsletter sent upon request; list of publications.

Decals and signs with the international symbol of access* are available from these manufacturers:

Ability Building Center, Inc.
1500 First Avenue N.E.
Rochester, Minn. 55901

C.A.P.H., Inc.
P.O. Box 22552
Sacramento, Calif. 98522

Mid Michigan Stamps and Signs, Inc.
P.O. Box 2277
400 North Larch Street
Lansing, Mich. 48912

Jersey Cape Diagnostic, Training and
 Opportunity Center, Inc.
P.O. Box 31
Ocean View, N.J. 08230

Pict-O Signs
P.O. Box 372
Amsterdam, N.Y. 12010

President's Committee on Employment of the
 Handicapped
Washington, D.C. 20210
(indoor decals only)

Screen Art
2331 Tacoma Avenue South
Tacoma, Wash. 98402

Seton Name Plate Corporation
592 Boulevard
New Haven, Conn. 06505

Tacoma Rubber Stamp
919 Market Street
Tacoma, Wash. 98402

Vermont Governor's Committee on
 Employment of the Handicapped
81 River Street
Montpelier, Vt. 05602

TRAVEL

For state-by-state listings of both accessibility and guidebooks for the handicapped who are traveling within that area (or to it), a comprehensive guide is *Access to the World: A Travel Guide for the Handicapped* by Louise Weiss (1977), available from Chatham Square Press, 401 Broadway, New York, N.Y. 10013 ($7.95) or at your local library. Weiss's book is very extensive, covering au-

---

*Reprinted with permission of the National Center for a Barrier Free Environment.

tomobiles, recreational vehicles, buses, trains, ships, air travel, hotels, motels, travel agents, and organizations. Booklets, books, and other information sources are listed along with ordering information and prices. Another resource is *A List of Guidebooks For Handicapped Travelers*, compiled by The Women's Committee, The President's Committee on Employment of the Handicapped, Washington, D.C. 20210 (4th edition, September 1975). Guides to practically every American city and major foreign cities are listed with addresses to write to obtain a copy.

The following national organizations provide information for those handicapped persons who wish to travel:

Accent on Information, Inc.
P.O. Box 700
Bloomington, Ill. 61701

This information retrieval system costs $6.00 for the use of the computer plus $.25 for each photocopied page; ask for a specific category, such as Travel and Touring.

LITERATURE: *Accent on Living* ($3.50 a year).

Mobility International
Colombo Street
London SE1 8DP, England

Provides information on international contacts and travel facilities for the handicapped. It is also developing a European travel directory for the handicapped.

Society for the Advancement of Travel for the Handicapped (SATH)
26 Court Street
Brooklyn, N.Y. 11242

A travel-industry membership organization acting as an information clearinghouse and referral service for all related travel-industry needs for travel for the handicapped, senior citizens, and the mentally retarded.

LITERATURE: Newsletter (free to members); guidebooks.

HELP FOR THE BLIND

The following national organizations provide information and/or services for the blind:

American Foundation for the Blind (AFB)
15 West 16th Street
New York, N.Y. 10011

AFB provides information, public education, and talking books; has a consultation and development program; conducts research; explains government regulations; and has an aids and appliances sales program.

LITERATURE: *Films about Blindness; This is AFB; Reading is for Everyone; Aid and Appliances for the Blind and Visually Impaired.*

Choice Magazine Listening
Department 4
14 Maple Street
Port Washington, N.Y. 11050

This free service for those unable to read standard print because of visual or physical impairment is made possible through the Lucerna Fund. Every other month, 8-rpm-speed phonograph records containing eight hours of unabridged articles, fiction, and poetry are sent to subscribers free. Subscribers may keep the records. If you do not have the necessary talking-book player, you can get one on free permanent loan from the Regional Libraries of the Library of Congress, Division for the Blind and Physically Handicapped (see entry below). Choice Magazine Listening will even send you the forms to facilitate your borrowing the record player.

Selections they anthologize are from such publications as *Atlantic, Esquire, Playboy,* and *The New York Times Magazine*. At the beginning of each record is a verbal description of the titles, authors, and lengths of the material.

To become a free subscriber, write for their introductory packet, which contains a postpaid reservation card.

LITERATURE: Free fact sheets, flyers, and reply forms.

Division for the Blind and Physically Handicapped
Library of Congress
1291 Taylor Street, N.W.
Washington, D.C. 20542

Provides a free library service of recorded and Braille reading material to persons who are unable to read standard print because of visual or physical impairment. The service is provided to eligible persons through a network of more than 150 regional and subregional libraries throughout the United States; contact your local library or write to the Reference Division at the above address for a referral.

You may borrow for free a Talking Book Machine, which plays 8 and 16 rpm disc recordings; a cassette machine that has a playback of $1^7/_8$ lps and $15/_{16}$ lps; and Braille books. Write for further information or application forms.

LITERATURE: Flyers; list of participating libraries by state with addresses; *News*, bimonthly newsletter; publications list (all free).

Jewish Braille Institute of America
110 East 30th Street
New York, N.Y. 10016

Publishes the *Jewish Braille Review*, Hebrew Braille Bible, Braille books in Hebrew and English, and talking books in Hebrew, Yiddish and English, including elementary and secondary level textbooks. The institute maintains a circulating Braille, tape, and large-type library, and promotes Hebrew education and religious instruction.

National Accreditation Council for Agencies Serving the Blind and Visually Handicapped (NAC)
79 Madison Avenue
New York, N.Y. 10016

Started in 1966, NAC is a national organization that has developed standards for special agencies and schools for blind and visually handicapped people and has a list of accredited agencies. It is supported by contributions, grants, and dues. Through the development and public recognition of those schools and services that are deemed accredited, NAC hopes to protect handicapped people and the funds expended for them.

LITERATURE: "Ten Steps to Accreditation" fact sheet; *The Standard-Bearer*, newsletter.

National Federation of the Blind (NFB)
218 Randolph Hotel
Des Moines, Iowa 50309

This national federation of more than 350 local and 50 state organizations of blind people promotes legislation to improve every aspect of a blind person's life—at work and socially. In addition to the evaluation of programs for the blind that are in operation, they support scholarly research in this area and publish the results. The NFB has a public education program that includes National White Cane Week, and holds an annual convention.

LITERATURE: *Braille Monitor*, monthly ($15.00, or without cost where there is need); list of other publications and article reprints.

HELP FOR THE CRIPPLED

The following national organizations provide information for crippled children and adults:

Disabled American Veterans (DAV)
3725 Alexandria Pike
Cold Spring, Ky. 41076

Founded in 1921, there are 2,200 local chapters of this national organization for veterans with wartime, service-connected disabilities and ailments. DAV, through its National Service Offices in more than sixty cities, provides free legal counseling and assistance in processing veterans' claims for benefits and disability compensation. Other programs include: National Officer Training Program, Employment, Fund Raising, and Disaster Relief. DAV offers scholarships to children of financially needy disabled veterans.

LITERATURE: *National Service Newsletter*, monthly (free); *National Employment Newsletter*, monthly (free); *DAV Magazine*, monthly ($4.00 a year); *National Legislative Newsletter*, monthly (free).

National Easter Seal Society for Crippled Children and Adults
2023 West Ogden Avenue
Chicago, Ill. 60612

Founded in Elyria, Ohio, in 1919, this nationwide program coordinates treatment, education, and research on handicapped conditions in fifty states, Washington, D.C., and Puerto Rico and makes referrals to local services.

LITERATURE: Descriptive leaflets and brochures; publications list; *Home Safety Round-Up: A Family Checklist; Help Your Baby to a Happy Smile*.

National Paraplegia Foundation (NPF)
333 North Michigan Avenue
Chicago, Ill. 60601

The national headquarters coordinates programs in promotion of research and treatment and local chapters help individual paraplegics and quadriplegics reach their personal goals. Also interested in elimination of barriers and preservation and extension of rights of disabled people.

LITERATURE: *Paraplegia Life* magazine, bi-monthly, $6.00; publications list available.

Paralyzed Veterans of America (PVA)
4330 East–West Highway, Suite 300
Washington, D.C. 20014

Started in 1946, this is a national organization with twenty-eight regional groups to help paralyzed veterans obtain increased benefits, such as ones from the Veterans Administration. PVA promotes wheelchair sports in a variety of activities and conducts an employment program. It is also active in proposing legislation to give public housing to paraplegics and eliminating architectural barriers.

LITERATURE: *Paraplegia News*, monthly; booklets; leaflets.

HELP FOR THE DEAF AND HARD-OF-HEARING

The following national organizations provide help for the deaf and hard-of-hearing:

Alexander Graham Bell Association for the Deaf, Inc.
3417 Volta Place, N.W.
Washington, D.C. 20007

Committed to the broadening of educational, vocational, and personal opportunities for hearing impaired persons, this national organization has three affiliate programs—American Organization for the Education of the Hearing Impaired (AOEHI); International Parents' Organization (IPO); and Oral Deaf Adults Section (ODAS). It publishes educational leaflets; sponsors conferences and conventions; provides books by mail from a lending library; and has the Children's Rights Committee and Hearing Alert information service. Membership dues are $20.00 a year.

LITERATURE: Free descriptive leaflet; *Volta Review* ($10.80 yearly); *Newsounds* ($3.45).

John Tracy Clinic
806 West Adams Boulevard
Los Angeles, Calif. 90007

Founded in 1942 by Mrs. Spencer Tracy, this is a free correspondence course for parents of preschool age deaf children and another course for parents of deaf-blind children. Both courses are available in English and Spanish.

LITERATURE: Free fact sheets and courses.

Mental Health Program for the Deaf
Department of Health, Education, and Welfare
National Institute of Mental Health
Saint Elizabeth's Hospital
2700 Martin Luther King, Jr. Avenue, S.E.
Washington, D.C. 20032

Inpatient and outpatient mental health services to deaf people, plus psychological evaluations and individual, group, couples, and family counseling.

LITERATURE: Fact sheets with bibliography.

National Association of the Deaf
814 Thayer Avenue
Silver Spring, Md. 20910

The association provides information and referral services for deaf persons and persons interested in deafness and published materials on such special materials as flashing vibrator clocks and toys and games for people with impaired hearing. It also serves as an advocate agency of and for deaf persons.

LITERATURE: List of publications and other available materials; descriptive brochure.

Speech and Hearing Institute
ICD Rehabilitation and Research Center
(Institute for the Crippled and Disabled)
340 East 24th Street
New York, N.Y. 10010

The institute provides evaluation and rehabilitation to persons with any of the full range of communication disorders; specialty services, include laryngectomee rehabilitation, stuttering therapy, vocal rehabilitation for professional voice users, language development, and rehabilitation for aphasic patients; and a counseling staff specializing in communicatively handicapped persons.

LITERATURE: Free speech and hearing leaflet.

HELP FOR MUTES AND SPEECH-IMPAIRED PEOPLE

The following national organizations are concerned with those who cannot speak or who have speech impediments:

American Laryngological, Rhinological and Otological Society (ALROS)
(The Triological Society)
c/o Ann R. Holm, Administrative Assistant
2954 Dorman Road
Broomall, Pa. 19008

Founded in 1895, this professional society of ear, nose and throat specialists publishes the newsletter *Triologistics*.

International Association of Laryngectomees (IAL)
c/o American Cancer Society
777 Third Avenue
New York, N.Y. 10017

Founded in 1952, there are about 260 local groups to assist persons who have had their larynx removed due to cancer. There is the Voice Rehabilitation Institute for training esophageal voice and safety and first aid information.

LITERATURE: Annual directory; pamphlets and reprints on laryngectomees, esophageal voice, and rehabilitation; *IAL News*, bimonthly.

ADDITIONAL LITERATURE

About Handicaps by Sara Bonnett Stein, in cooperation with Gilbert W. Kliman, M.D., photographs by Dick Frank (1974). Walker and Company, 720 Fifth Avenue, New York, N.Y. 10019 ($5.95). Explains handicaps to children.

Access: The Guide to a Better Life For Disabled Americans by Lilly Bruck (1978). Random House, 201 East 50th Street, New York, N.Y. 10022 ($12.95 hardcover; $5.95 paperback). A consumer guide to services, government agencies, and publications pertaining to and for the handicapped. A complete directory covering travel, health care, employment, and dozens of other topics.

Access to the World: A Travel Guide for the Handicapped by Louise Weiss (1977). Chatham Square Press, 401 Broadway, New York, N.Y. 10013; distributed by Contemporary Books, Inc., 180 North Michigan Avenue, Chicago, Ill. 60601 ($7.95). A comprehensive resource on travel.

Cerebral Palsy: More Hope Than Ever by Jacqueline Seaver (1975). Public Affairs Pamphlets, 381 Park Avenue South, New York, N.Y. 10016 ($.50). It is estimated that 15,000 babies are born each year with cerebral palsy. Seaver writes about the scope of the problem, what cerebral palsy is, available help, and organizations that are helping its victims.

Directory Of Organizations Interested in the Handicapped (1976). Committee For the Handicapped, People to People Program, Suite 610, LaSalle Building, Connecticut Avenue and L Street, Washington, D.C. 20036. An annotated directory of hundreds of organizations that assist the handicapped. Many of the entries are for such specialized groups as the Academy of Dentistry for the Handicapped, American Printing House for the Blind, Inc., and World Rehabilitation Fund, Inc.

Help for the Handicapped Child by Florence Weiner (1973). McGraw-Hill Book Company, 1221 Avenue of the Americas, New York, N.Y. 10020 (out of print; consult your library). Although some of the follow-up directory entries are slightly dated, Weiner's basic descriptions of the types of handicaps that afflict children are well done and contain valuable basic information.

If You Become Disabled (January 1977). Social Security Administration, U.S. Department of Health, Education, and Welfare, Baltimore, Md. 21235 ($.40). A booklet explaining disability benefits under social security.

Independent Living: New Goal for Disabled Persons by Irving R. Dickman (1975). Public Affairs Pamphlets, 381 Park Avenue South, New York, N.Y. 10016 ($.50). A discussion of some of the alternatives to institutionalization.

Mainstream (monthly magazine), Advocate of San Diego County's Able-Disabled, 861 Sixth Avenue, Suite 610, San Diego, Calif. 92101 ($.50 an issue; $5.00 a year). Feature articles and practical information.

My Second Twenty Years by Richard P. Brickner (1976). Basic Books, 10 East 53rd Street, New York, N.Y. 10022 ($7.95). A moving autobiography that begins "In May of 1953, a few days after my twentieth birthday, I broke my neck in an automobile accident and lay for a while, precariously, on the farthest rim of existence." The rest of the book describes how the author, forever confined to a wheelchair, sought to recreate, or create, a new life for himself.

National Park Guide for the Handicapped by the National Park Service, U.S. Department of the Interior. Superintendent of Documents, U.S. Government Printing Office, Washington, D.C. 20402 ($.40; minimum mail order $1.00).

We're Pleased That You Are Interested in Making the Arts Accessible to Everyone . . . by Educational Facilities Laboratories, Inc., 850 Third Avenue, New York, N.Y. 10022 (free). Orders to: ARTS, Box 2040, Grand Central Station, New York, N.Y. 10017. A booklet describing arts programs, resources, and facilities that have been designed to overcome architectural barriers to the arts for children, the elderly, and the handicapped.

See also the following related chapters in *The Help Book:*

ADOPTION AND FOSTER CARE
AGING
CHILDBEARING
CHILDREN
CIVIL RIGHTS AND DISCRIMINATION
CRIME VICTIMS AND WITNESSES
EDUCATION
EMERGENCIES AND DISASTERS
EMPLOYMENT
FINANCIAL ASSISTANCE
HEALTH
MENTAL HEALTH
MENTAL RETARDATION AND LEARNING DISABILITIES
MULTIPURPOSE ORGANIZATIONS
TRANSPORTATION AND TRAVEL
VETERANS

30

HEALTH

More than ever before, direct help and information is available on all kinds of health conditions, from allergies, cancer, cataracts, and hypoglycemia to heart disease, multiple sclerosis, psoriasis, and VD. But as scientific knowledge and treatment improve so does the layperson's responsibility to care for himself—to know as much as possible to prevent certain conditions or to get help as soon as problems or diseases arise. Early diagnosis and treatment increase the chances of a complete recovery and also minimize the risk of complications or even death.

Self-care does not mean that the average person has to obtain a medical degree to learn enough for optimum health. But self-care does necessitate that every person take a more active role in achieving and maintaining a fit body. Begin by asking yourself the following questions:

YOUR HEALTH IQ FACTOR*

	Yes	No	Sometimes
1. Do you have a thorough physical checkup, including blood tests, once a year?	___	___	___
2. Do you have your eyes examined by an ophthalmologist once a year?	___	___	___
3. Do you have your teeth checked by a dentist once a year?	___	___	___
4. Do you eat a balanced and varied diet that is nutritionally sound?	___	___	___
5. Do you weigh the ideal number of pounds for your height and body frame? (See charts in Chapter 25, *Food and Nutrition,* if you are unsure of what your weight should be.)	___	___	___

*This "test" is intended for educational purposes only. Do not act upon any of these suggestions without first consulting your physician.

	Yes	No	Some-times
6. Do you follow a regular, twenty-minute exercise program three to four days a week?	___	___	___
7. Are you a nonsmoker?	___	___	___
8. Do you limit the amount of alcohol, coffee, tea, drugs, and refined sugar that you consume?	___	___	___
9. Do you have good sleeping habits?	___	___	___
10. Are you able to function without drugs for either anxiety or sleep?	___	___	___
11. Do you have a family physician or internist that you are pleased with?	___	___	___
12. Do you know the names of several specialists whom you could call on if you had a medical emergency?	___	___	___
13. Do you have medical insurance?	___	___	___
14. Is your insurance adequate for you and/or your family?	___	___	___
15. Are you taking care of any allergies, medical conditions, or permanent handicaps that you have?	___	___	___
16. Have you gotten help for any emotional problems that are making you feel depressed, anxious, or under stress?	___	___	___
17. Do you take a vacation at least once a year?	___	___	___
18. Do you feel that you are in good health?	___	___	___

If you are a woman:

19. Do you have a thorough check-up by a gynecologist once a year?	___	___	___
20. Do you examine your breasts at the same time each month?	___	___	___

If you answered *no* or *sometimes* to any of the previous twenty questions (especially to numbers 1 through 10), your health IQ needs improvement. Now is the time to change those habits and seek out the help and information that will give you an excellent physical IQ score.

A family doctor can be crucial to the budget of your family, as well as to its health. Regular checkups and consultations with your family doctor *before* going to an expensive specialist may help you avoid spending hundreds of dollars. Since it is best to stay with the same family physician (so that he or she has the benefit of a continuing knowledge of your medical and health condition), choose your physician carefully. A referral based on the recommendations of trusted friends is still the best way to find a family doctor; if you do not know anyone who could or would make such a suggestion, contact your local medical society, which will provide several names of physicians from which you may choose.

If you trust and respect your family physician, he or she will probably be the best referral source if you should need a specialist. Published references at your local library that also might be useful are *The Directory of Medical Specialists* and the *Membership Directory of the American Medical Association*.

In recognition of the "certain amount of risk and discomfort associated with all surgery," the Health Care Financing Administration of the U.S. Department of Health, Education, and Welfare is sponsoring a voluntary Second Opinion campaign when non-emergency surgery is suggested. In addition to offering a patient the reassurance from a second opinion that the surgery is necessary, another physician will advise you on the risks and benefits of an operation as well as any alternatives to surgery. Some opponents to the program contend that it is just another way for the medical establishment to get additional patient fees. However, the numerous cases of favored action based on a second opinion dispute that belief. Here, for example, are two actual cases of the second opinion at work. The first case involves a woman who developed nodules on her vocal chords. The first specialist, although noting the delicacy of the operation, suggested removing the nodules. The second specialist advised the patient to refrain from speaking for a month. The patient followed the second opinion; the problem never recurred. In another case, the first surgeon advised against surgery on a rectal ailment. But the patient sought a second opinion, had surgery, and resolved the condition. For further information, write: Department of Health, Education, and Welfare, Health Care Financing Administration, Office of Public Affairs, Room 5215, Mary E. Switzer Building, Washington, D.C. 20201. A free leaflet, "Facing Surgery? Why Not Get a Second Opinion?" is available.

To complain about your doctor, see if your nearest citizen action group, such as a branch of PIRG, has suggestions or publishes information like the NYPIRG Wiseguide #8, *How To Complain About Your Doctor* ($.25), available from NYPIRG, 5 Beekman Street, New York, N.Y. 10038. Or contact your local medical association. (See also Chapter 13, *Consumer Affairs*.)

Your state health department will make referrals to private and public hospitals or medical societies; they also publish free or low-cost pamphlets and booklets about a variety of health problems and health concerns, such as how to pick a nursing home, meeting hospital costs, what is cancer, how to avoid heart problems, and so forth.

The following are the state health agencies:

Department of Public Health
State Office Building
501 Dexter Avenue
Montgomery, Ala. 36130

Division of Public Health
Department of Health and Social Services
503 Alaska Office Building
Pouch H-06
Juneau, Alaska 99811

Department of Health Services
1740 West Adams Street
Phoenix, Ariz. 85007

Department of Health
4815 West Markham Street
Little Rock, Ark. 72201

Department of Health
714 P Street
Sacramento, Calif. 95814

Department of Health
4210 East 11th Avenue
Denver, Colo. 80220

Department of Health
79 Elm Street
Hartford, Conn. 06115

Division of Public Health
Department of Health and Social Services
Jesse S. Cooper Memorial Building
Dover, Del. 19901

Community Health and Hospitals
  Administration
Department of Human Resources
1875 Connecticut Avenue, N.W.
Washington, D.C. 20009

Health Program Office
Department of Health and Rehabilitative
  Services
1323 Winewood Boulevard
Tallahassee, Fla. 32301

Division of Physical Health
Department of Human Resources
47 Trinity Avenue, S.W.
Atlanta, Ga. 30334

Department of Health
Kinau Hale
1250 Punchbowl Street
Honolulu, Hawaii 96813

Division of Health
Department of Health and Welfare
State Office Building
700 West State Street
Boise, Idaho 83720

Department of Public Health
525 West Jefferson Street
Springfield, Ill. 62706

Board of Health
1330 West Michigan Street
Indianapolis, Ind. 46206

Department of Health
Robert Lucas State Office Building
East 12th and Walnut Streets
Des Moines, Iowa 50319

Department of Health and Environment
Forbes Field
Topeka, Kans. 66620

Bureau for Health Services
Department for Human Resources
275 East Main Street
Frankfort, Ky. 40601

Division of Health Services and
  Environmental Quality
P.O. Box 60630
New Orleans, La. 70160

Bureau of Health
Department of Human Services
State House
Augusta, Me. 04333

Department of Health and Mental Hygiene
201 West Preston Street
Baltimore, Md. 21201

Department of Public Health
39 Boylston Street
Boston, Mass. 02116

Department of Public Health
3500 North Logan Street
Lansing, Mich. 48914

Department of Health
717 Delaware Street, S.E.
Minneapolis, Minn. 55440

Mississippi State Board of Health
Underwood Building
Jackson, Miss. 39205

Division of Health
Department of Social Services
Broadway State Office Building
Jefferson City, Mo. 65101

Department of Health and Environmental
  Sciences
200 W. F. Cogswell Building
Helena, Mont. 59601

Department of Health
301 Centennial Mall South
Lincoln, Neb. 68508

Health Division
Department of Human Resources
505 East King Street
Carson City, Nev. 89710

Department of Health and Welfare
8 Loudon Road
Concord, N.H. 03301

Department of Health
John Fitch Plaza
Trenton, N.J. 08625

Health Services Division
Department of Health and Social Services
Crown State Office Building
725 St. Michael's Drive
Santa Fe, N.M. 87503

Department of Health
Tower Building
Empire State Plaza
Albany, N.Y. 12237

Division of Health Services
Department of Human Resources
Cooper Memorial Health Building
225 North McDowell Street
Raleigh, N.C. 27602

Department of Health
State Capitol
Bismarck, N.D. 58505

Department of Health
450 East Town Street
Columbus, Ohio 43215

Department of Health
N.E. 10th and Stonewall Streets
P.O. Box 53551
Oklahoma City, Okla. 73105

Health Division
Department of Human Resources
Portland, Ore. 97201

Department of Health
802 Health and Welfare Building
Harrisburg, Pa. 17120

Department of Health
75 Davis Street
Providence, R.I. 02908

Department of Health and Environmental
  Control
R. J. Aycock Building
2600 Bull Street
Columbia, S.C. 29201

Department of Health
Joe Foss Building
Pierre, S.D. 57501

Department of Health Resources
1100 West 49th Street
Austin, Tex. 78756

Department of Public Health
Cordell Hull Building
436 6th Avenue, N.
Nashville, Tenn. 37219

Division of Health
Department of Social Services
44 Medical Drive
Salt Lake City, Utah 84112

Department of Health
60 Main Street
Burlington, Vt. 05401

Department of Health
James Madison Building
Richmond, Va. 23219

Health Services Division
Department of Social and Health Services
Mail Stop 444
Olympia, Wash. 98504

Department of Health
535 State Office Building 3
Charleston, W.Va. 25305

Division of Health
Department of Health and Social Services
663, 1 West Wilson Street
Madison, Wis. 53702

Department of Health and Social Services
Hathaway Building
2300 Capitol Avenue
Cheyenne, Wyo. 82002

The following organizations provide information on a variety of health issues:

American Medical Association (AMA)
535 North Dearborn Street
Chicago, Ill. 60610

AMA is a federation of 52 state and territorial and 2,000 local county medical societies. They do not recommend physicians; they suggest contacting your local medical society or hospital for referrals. AMA publishes numerous educational materials for the professional and the layperson.

LITERATURE: Write for their extensive publications price list; some pamphlets offered include *When to Call or See Your Physician* ($.20), *Surgery* ($.20), *Allergies* ($.15), *Peptic Ulcer* ($.25), *Tetanus* ($.20), and *Blood Tests* ($.25).

Center for Medical Consumers
237 Thompson Street
New York, N.Y. 10012

A free library established in January 1976 to help citizens take responsibility for their own health with consumer-related books, medical texts and medical journals. The center has an article clipping file, but no staff or facility to research phone or written inquiries. A $5.00 donation will provide *Health Facts*, a one-page annotated bibliography on health-related books issued six to ten times a year. The center also operates a Tel-Med free tape telephone information library.

Health Policy Advisory Center
17 Murray Street
New York, N.Y. 10007

Library and files on health issues available to the public. Health/PAC publishes a bimonthly *Bulletin* and special reports on timely health care issues.

Tel-Med, Inc.
P.O. Box 22700
Cooley Drive
Colton, Calif. 92324

Tel-Med offers more than 300 tapes, averaging three-to-five minutes, on a variety of subjects, such as venereal disease, sex education, alcoholism, drug abuse, breast cancer, medical costs, and vaginitis. Local areas write specific scripts for tapes on such topics as "How to Choose a Doctor in Your County" (reflected by #5000 series). There are ninety programs throughout the country. Write to Tel-Med if you do not find a listing for a local telephone contact in your area. They will send the telephone number of your closest Tel-Med tape library. To use this cassette facility, call a participating Tel-Med system and ask to hear a specific tape. Your only cost is the telephone call.

LITERATURE: Information on how to implement a local Tel-Med Program; brochures; Tel-Med monthly newsletter.

World Health Organization (WHO)
Headquarters: 1211 Geneva 27, Switzerland
U.S. Office: Pan American Sanitary Bureau
525 Twenty-third Street, N.W.
Washington, D.C. 20037

An international organization founded in 1948 within the United Nations system to protect and promote world health by distributing information on outbreaks of communicable diseases, providing International Health Regulations, collecting information on drugs and passing it on to other countries, keeping health statistics, and providing public education and medical literature for up-to-date reports on the international health field.

LITERATURE: Descriptive brochure; *Health for All By the Year 2000*; catalogue of publications; *World Health* magazine ($1.60 per copy).

U.S. Department of Health, Education, and Welfare (HEW)
330 Independence Avenue, S.W.
Washington, D.C. 20201

HEW and its various agencies are the federal government's main health resource centers. HEW's Public Health Service includes these agencies:

National Institutes of Health
Bethesda, Md. 20014

Center for Disease Control
Atlanta, Ga. 30333

Health Care Financing Administration
Washington, D.C. 20201

Health Resources Administration
5600 Fishers Lane
Rockville, Md. 20857

Health Services Administration
5600 Fishers Lane
Rockville, Md. 20857

Food and Drug Administration
5600 Fishers Lane
Rockville, Md. 20857

Alcohol, Drug Abuse, and Mental Health Administration
5600 Fishers Lane
Rockville, Md. 20857

Write to the Director of Public Information at the appropriate agency for a list of free and low-cost publications.

LITERATURE: *This Is HEW*.

REGIONAL OFFICES OF HEW

Region I*
John F. Kennedy Federal Building
Government Center
Boston, Mass. 02203

Region II
Federal Building
26 Federal Plaza
New York, N.Y. 10007

Region III
3535 Market Street
Philadelphia, Pa. 19101

Region IV
50 Seventh Street, N.E.
Atlanta, Ga. 30323

Region V
300 South Wacker Drive
Chicago, Ill. 60606

Region VI
1114 Commerce Street
Dallas, Tex. 75202

Region VII
Federal Office Building
601 East 12th Street
Kansas City, Mo. 64106

Region VIII
Federal Office Building
19th and Stout Street
Denver, Colo. 80202

Region IX
Federal Office Building
50 Fulton Street
San Francisco, Calif. 94102

Region X
Arcade Building
1321 Second Avenue
Seattle, Wash. 98101

Health research is the concern of the following private organizations:

Health Research Group
2000 P Street, N.W.
Washington, D.C. 20036

A Ralph Nader organization with these main goals: occupational safety; health; food and drug legislation; and health care delivery involving the consumer. The group also publishes consumer guides.

LITERATURE: Send for publication price list of books and reports on health-care delivery, hospitals, drugs, food, etc.

The Living Bank
P.O. Box 6725
Houston, Tex.

A nonprofit service organization started in 1968 that helps people who wish to make provisions to donate a part or all parts of their bodies after their deaths for medical research, transplantation, or anatomical studies.

LITERATURE: Brochure.

National Association of Community Health Centers (NACHC)
1625 Eye Street, N.W.
Washington, D.C. 20006

An advocacy agency for 800 health centers across the country providing educational, research and technical assistance.

LITERATURE: *Clearinghouse News*, newsletter; *NACHC Objectives, Organization, Scope, Structure, and Program Activities*, booklet.

---

*If you are unsure of your region, see listings by state in Chapter 31, *Housing*, and under "HUD Field Offices."

National Commission on Confidentiality of Health Records, Inc. (NCCHR)
1211 Connecticut Avenue, N.W., Suite 504
Washington, D.C. 20036

Founded in June 1976 by seventeen health professional and related organizations, the commission is an information clearinghouse on health record confidentiality problems. NCCHR investigates consumer complaints, comments on proposed legislation, conducts conferences and seminars on specific problems and researches and prepares model laws and guidelines for clinics and others who use health information. Membership dues are $18.00 for affiliates, $30.00 for organizations.

LITERATURE: *Your Health Records* (free); *Health Records and Confidentiality: Annotated Bibliography with Abstracts* ($4.95); NCCHR newsletter ($18.00 a year).

The following national public and private agencies or organizations provide information to the public on specific health problems; they are listed alphabetically from Allergy to Venereal Disease:

Allergies

Allergy Foundation of America
801 Second Avenue
New York, N.Y. 10017

Publishes educational materials on allergies ($.25–$.50) including the free leaflets *Allergic Diseases* and *Answers to Some Questions About Allergy.*

National Institute of Allergy and Infectious Diseases
U.S. Department of Health, Education, and Welfare
Public Health Service
National Institutes of Health
Bethesda, Md. 20014

Publishes a series of pamphlets on allergies, including *Drug Allergy, Dust Allergy, Insect Allergy, Mold Allergy, Poison Ivy Allergy,* and *Pollen Allergy.*

Arthritis

The Arthritis Foundation
3400 Peachtree Road, N.E.
Atlanta, Ga. 30326

An information clearinghouse that provides referrals on arthritis; local affiliates are located throughout the United States.

LITERATURE: *Arthritis: The Basic Facts;* fact sheets, patient booklets, article reprints.

National Institute of Arthritis, Metabolism, and Digestive Diseases
National Institutes of Health
Bethesda, Md. 20014

An information clearinghouse.

LITERATURE: *Some Frequently Asked Questions About Ileitis and Colitis; Peptic Ulcer; Gout; Cystic Fibrosis; Osoriasis; Osteoporosis; Digestive Diseases.*

ADDITIONAL ARTHRITIS LITERATURE

If You Become Disabled (1976). U.S. Department of Health, Education, and Welfare, Social Security Administration, 6401 Security Boulevard, Baltimore, Md. 21235 (free leaflet).

How to Cope With Arthritis, prepared by U.S. Department of Health, Education, and Welfare and available from Consumer Information Center, Department 045F, Pueblo, Colo. 81009 ($.60).

Birth Defects

National Foundation–March of Dimes
Public Education Department
Box 2000
White Plains, N.Y. 10602

Maintains free diagnostic, treatment, and birth defect prevention centers. Write for a list of free and low-cost publications that are available.

National Genetics Foundation
9 West 57th Street
New York, N.Y. 10019

Information clearinghouse on genetic counseling and birth defects.

Spina Bifida Association of America
343 South Dearborn, Room 319
Chicago, Ill. 60604

An information exchange with literature on spina bifida; local groups provide direct services, self-help and emotional support to families, tutoring, summer camps, and referrals.

LITERATURE: Brochures; history of birth defects; publication list.

National Tay-Sachs & Allied Diseases Association, Inc.
122 East 42nd Street
New York, N.Y. 10017

Information on these diseases, tests for detection, and treatment.

Blood

For direct help in getting blood, contact your local blood bank or hospital; programs are sponsored by the following national organizations, which also have some general literature available:

American Association of Blood Banks (AABB)
1828 L Street, N.W.
Washington, D.C. 20036

AABB sponsors the National Clearinghouse Program and National Rare Donor File. You can donate at your local hospital but get credit at the more than 1,900 hospitals and community blood banks that cooperate in the program.

LITERATURE: *Questions and Answers About Blood and Blood Banking* (1976).

The American National Red Cross Blood Program
17th and D Streets, N.W.
Washington, D.C. 20006

For direct assistance in donating or receiving blood, contact your local branch of the American National Red Cross. Educational materials are available from the national headquarters.

LITERATURE: *The Story of Blood; Some Facts About Blood*, wallet-size printed card; leaflets.

Hodgkin's Disease and Lymphoma Organization
518 Wingate Drive
East Meadow, N.Y. 11554

Information for the general public on these diseases.

Leukemia Society of America, Inc.
211 East 43rd Street
New York, N.Y. 10017

The Leukemia Society is a national voluntary health agency with chapters in fifty-one cities that is dedicated to seeking the control and eventual cure of leukemia and allied diseases of the blood-forming organs, such as Hodgkin's disease. The agency depends solely on contributions from the public, business—commercial interests, and wills and bequests to support its programs of research, patient assistance, and professional/public education.

LITERATURE: Descriptive leaflets; annual report.

National Hemophilia Foundation (NHF)
25 West 39th Street
New York, N.Y. 10018

Through its fifty-five local chapters, NHF offers support groups for parents of this country's more than 100,000 hemophiliacs. Through its information and educational services, literature is available for the layperson or professional.

LITERATURE: Chapter roster; *Hemofax* newsletter; list of publications; *What You Should Know About Hemophilia* and *The Hemophilic Child in School.*

National High Blood Pressure Education Program
High Blood Pressure Information Center
120/80 National Institutes of Health
Bethesda, Md. 20014

This federal program serves as a national clearinghouse for information on various aspects of hypertension control; assists in locating speakers and other sources of educational materials and audiovisual aids; and has many publications, including some in Spanish.

LITERATURE: Leaflets; publications order form; "What Every Woman Should Know About High Blood Pressure"; fact sheets; *Month-Book* (May 1977).

National Sickle Cell Disease Research Foundation, Inc.
521 Fifth Avenue
New York, N.Y. 10017

Information is available on sickle cell disease.

ADDITIONAL BLOOD LITERATURE

Watch Your Blood Pressure! by Theodore Irwin (rev. ed. 1976). Public Affairs Pamphlets, 381 Park Avenue South, New York, N.Y. 10016 ($.50).

Cancer

American Cancer Society (ACS)
National Headquarters
777 Third Avenue
New York, N.Y. 10017

ACS is a national organization with 2,915 local units that has the threefold purpose of research, education, and direct service aimed at the control and elimination of cancer. Service and rehabilitation programs include information and counseling, transportation, sick room supplies and comfort items. Volunteers visit to assist in rehabilitation of laryngectomy, mastectomy, and ostomy patients. Other patient assistance programs, specific to each local division, are also available.

LITERATURE: *Your Health Is Your Business*, descriptive booklet; numerous other publications.

Reach to Recovery
American Cancer Society, Inc.
777 Third Avenue
New York, N.Y. 10017

Reach to Recovery is a rehabilitative program for women who have had breast-cancer surgery, designed to meet with their physical, psychological, and cosmetic needs. Trained volunteers (former breast cancer patients) make bedside visits bringing information about rehabilitative exercises, exercise equipment, and a temporary breast form. Other services include teaching the exercises and providing information to the family.

LITERATURE: "What Is Reach to Recovery?" (leaflet).

The Candlelighters
123 C Street, S.E.
Washington, D.C. 20003

Self-help group for families of children and adolescents with cancer started in Washington, D.C., in 1970. There are now 100 groups in

> **If you won't read these 7 signals of cancer... You probably have the 8th.**
>
> 1. Change in bowel or bladder habits.
> 2. A sore that does not heal.
> 3. Unusual bleeding or discharge.
> 4. Thickening or lump in breast or elsewhere.
> 5. Indigestion or difficulty in swallowing.
> 6. Obvious change in wart or mole.
> 7. Nagging cough or hoarseness.
>
> 8. A fear of cancer that can prevent you from detecting cancer at an early stage. A stage when it is highly curable. Everyone's afraid of cancer, but don't let it scare you to death.
>
> American Cancer Society

Reprinted with permission of the American Cancer Society.

forty-one states throughout the United States. The headquarters maintains a list of parents who wish to correspond with each other for the "parent-to-parent" writing program.

LITERATURE: *National Newsletter Quarterly*; bibliography.

Make Today Count, Inc.
Box 303
Tama Building, Suite 514
Burlington, Iowa 52601

A national organization with 117 chapters in the United States, Germany, and Canada for persons with life-threatening illnesses, such as cancer, and for their spouses and families, physicians, nurses, and other health-care persons. Chapters meet once or twice each month as a support group. Seminars are held to help bring together the health-care teams and patients to establish communications and to promote openness and honesty.

LITERATURE: Newsletter ($10.00 a year); assorted brochures; article reprints.

National Cancer Institute (NCI)
Office of Cancer Communications
Building 31, Room 10A21
National Institutes of Health
Bethesda, Md. 20014

Sponsors Can-Dial, a toll-free, seven-day, free telephone service with fifty tapes, from one to twenty minutes, on all aspects of cancer, including "Childhood Cancer" and "What is Cancer?" Can-Dial is operated by comprehensive cancer centers throughout the country along with the National Cancer Institute. You may also contact the Cancer Information Service, toll-free number twenty-four hours a day, seven days a week, for free referral to local cancer treatment and examination.

ADDITIONAL CANCER LITERATURE

Breast Self Examination, National Cancer Institute, National Institutes of Health, 5600 Fishers Lane, Rockville, Md. 20857. Free booklet with drawings and easy-to-follow steps to regular breast self-examination. Send postcard to Dept. 574G, Consumer Information Center, Pueblo, Colo. 81009.

Treating Cancer, Office of Cancer Communications, National Cancer Program. Available from Consumer Information Center, Department 662F, Pueblo, Colo. 81009 (free). Booklet summarizing the current ways to treat cancer—surgery, radiation, chemotherapy. Includes a glossary and a list of references.

Single copies of the following publications are available free from the Office of Cancer

Communications, National Cancer Institute, Bethesda, Md. 20014:

Cancer Rates and Risks. A paperback describing cancer trends in the United States and other countries.

Cancer Questions and Answers About Rates and Risks. A simplified version of the above title.

Cancer: What to Know, What to Do About It. Gives basic facts and figures as well as information about signs and treatment of cancer.

Progress Against Pamphlets. Individual pamphlets discussing symptoms, diagnosis, and treatment of the following cancers: bladder; bone; breast; colon and rectum; larynx; lung; mouth; prostate; skin; stomach; uterus; Hodgkin's Disease; and leukemias, lymphomas, and multiple myeloma.

Drugs vs. Cancer. Information on the present status of cancer chemotherapy; a list of drugs now in use is included.

Progress Against Leukemia Research Report. Summarizes present knowledge concerning the causes and treatment of leukemia and indicates the directions in which current research is going.

Research on Malignant Diseases of the Brain. A discussion of the increased research effort directed at brain tumors.

Cystic Fibrosis

National Cystic Fibrosis Research Foundation
3379 Peachtree Road, N.E.
Atlanta, Ga. 30326

Publishes a directory of diagnosis and treatment clinics.

Dental Concerns

American Dental Association
Bureau of Health Education
211 East Chicago Avenue
Chicago, Ill. 60611

Professional association that also has free and low-cost booklets and leaflets on dental issues aimed at the general public.

National Institute of Dental Research
National Institutes of Health
U.S. Public Health Service
Building 31
Bethesda, Md. 20014

Conducts research on dental caries; infomation is available on fluoridation in water as a cavities-reducing procedure.

ADDITIONAL DENTAL LITERATURE

The Complete Family Guide to Dental Health by Jacob Himber, D.D.S. (1977). McGraw-Hill Book Company, Inc., 1221 Avenue of the Americas, New York, N.Y. 10020 ($7.95).

How to Become a Wise Dental Consumer, American Dental Association, 211 East Chicago Avenue, Department C, Chicago, Ill. 60611 (free).

How to Save Your Teeth and Your Money by Melvin Denholtz, D.D.S., and Elaine Denholtz (1977). Van Nostrand Reinhold Company, 450 West 33rd Street, New York, N.Y. 10001 ($8.95).

Diabetes

American Diabetes Association, Inc.
600 Fifth Avenue
New York, N.Y. 10020

The association provides patient education and research programs into the causes, cure, and prevention of diabetes and better treatment methods.

LITERATURE: *Forecast,* bimonthly; extensive leaflets and booklets for diabetics, their families, and health educators.

Juvenile Diabetes Foundation
23 East 26th Street
New York, N.Y. 10010

National organization with local chapters around the country providing information and direct help to those with juvenile diabetes and their parents.

LITERATURE: Newsletter; leaflets and fact sheets.

ADDITIONAL DIABETES LITERATURE

Don't Be Afraid of Diabetes: A Handbook for Diabetics (1977) and *Vacationing With Diabetes, Not From Diabetes* (1976), both by Stanley Mirsky, M.D. E.R. Squibb & Sons, Inc., P.O. Box 4000, Princeton, N.J. 08540 (free booklets).

Digestive Diseases

American Digestive Disease Society
420 Lexington Avenue
New York, N.Y. 10017

Voluntary health agency concerned about 25 million victims of digestive disease.

LITERATURE: Leaflets on gall bladder problems, pancreatitis, hiatal hernia, irritable bowel, peptic ulcer, and diverticulosis.

Digestive Diseases Information Center
6410 Rockledge Drive
Bethesda, Md. 20034

Information clearinghouse established in 1978. Publications include a bimonthly memo and fact sheets.

National Foundation for Ileitis and Colitis, Inc.
295 Madison Avenue
New York, N.Y. 10017

Information clearinghouse to professionals and the general public on these intestinal afflictions; supports research into the causes, treatment, and cure of ileitis and colitis. There are regional groups.

National Institute of Arthritis, Metabolism and Digestive Diseases
National Institutes of Health
Bethesda, Md. 20014

Conducts research and publishes educational materials for the general public, including *Peptic Ulcer* and *Digestive Diseases—Recent Research Advances, Future Opportunities and Needs*.

United Ostomy Association
1111 Wilshire Boulevard
Los Angeles, Calif. 90017

Information clearinghouse and self-help group with more than 32,000 members in 475 chapters in North America; members have had ostomy surgery, where the bowel or bladder is altered to create a surgical opening due to a variety of reasons.

Eating Disorders

Anorexia Nervosa Aid Society, Inc.
101 Cedar Lane
Teaneck, N.J. 07666

Local organization that is seeking to form a national organization aimed at helping those afflicted with anorexia nervosa, a condition whereby a person refuses to eat. Sponsors self-help groups for parents, anorexics, and provides information, counseling, referrals, a speakers bureau and conducts research. Membership is $10.00 a year for individuals; $25.00 for a family.

Self-help groups for overweightness or obesity are available from the following national organizations (see Chapter 25, *Food and Nutrition*, for annotated descriptions):

National Association to Aid Fat Americans, Inc. (NAAFA)
P.O. Box 745
Westbury, N.Y. 11745

Overeaters Anonymous (OA)
World Service Office
2190 190th Street
Torrance, Calif. 90504

Weight Watchers International, Inc.
800 Community Drive
Manhasset, N.Y. 11030

ADDITIONAL LITERATURE ON EATING DISORDERS

Eating Disorders: Obesity, Anorexia, Nervosa, and the Person Within by Hilde Bruch, M.D. (1973). Basic Books, Inc., 10 East 53rd Street, New York, N.Y. 10022 ($16.50). This is a comprehensive work concerned with those "individuals who misuse the eating function in their efforts to solve or camouflage problems of living that to them appear otherwise insoluble." Bruch covers historical, sociocultural, and biological bases of eating disorders including the history of the concept of anorexia nervosa and the treatment of the person with an eating disorder.

Epilepsy

Epilepsy Foundation of America
1828 L Street, N.W., Suite 406
Washington, D.C. 20036

National headquarters for about 100 local chapters with literature, information, booklets, and *National Spokesman* newsletter. Direct services are provided by local chapters.

National Epilepsy League (NEL)
6 North Michigan Avenue
Chicago, Ill. 60602

Since epileptics are on medication for life, the league provides a pharmacy service at greatly reduced rate. Annual membership is $1.00. It also has an insurance program that includes all members of the family, including life insurance for epileptics, a referral service, literature, and a film library.

LITERATURE: Leaflets and fact sheets.

Exercise

American Alliance for Health, Physical Education and Recreation (AAHPER)
1201 Sixteenth Street, N.W.
Washington, D.C. 20036

Founded in 1885, there are fifty-four state groups, six regional groups, and seven national associations in this national professional organization for students preparing and educators practicing in the fields of physical education, dance, health, safety education, recreation, outdoor education, and athletics. It publishes professional and educational materials on health, education, exercise, sex education, and safety.

LITERATURE: Quarterly journals.

National Jogging Association
1910 K Street, N.W.
Washington, D.C. 20006

Educational organization supported by membership dues ($15.00 a year), which includes a subscription to *The Jogger* (eight times a year) and a copy of *Guidelines to Successful Jogging*.

ADDITIONAL EXERCISE LITERATURE

Successful Jogging, President's Council on Physical Fitness and Health and the National Jogging Association (1977). Available from Consumer Information Center, Department 641E, Pueblo, Colo. 81009 (free booklet). Includes a general schedule for a basic twelve-week jogging program and how to adjust it because of injury or illness.

Eyes

American Optometric Association (AOA)
7000 Chippewa Street
St. Louis, Mo. 63119

A national organization representing a membership of more than 20,000 optometrists, with a public information program on aspects of vision care.

LITERATURE: Send a self-addressed stamped envelope to receive free sample copies of inexpensive pamphlets, including *Are You Seeing Straight About Optometric Fees; A Consumer's Guide to Optometric Care; Information Resource List;* and *What Is An Optometrist?*

National Eye Institute
National Institutes of Health
Building 31
Bethesda, Md. 20014

Conducts research into eye-related disorders.

National Retinitis Pigmentosa Foundation (NRPF)
Rolling Park Building
8331 Mindale Circle
Baltimore, Md. 21207

Founded in 1971, this national organization serves as an information clearinghouse on RP, an inherited, degenerative disease in children, which may result in blindness by the age of thirty. In addition to coordinating research and available help for RP victims, NRPF funds related research and sponsors an annual workshop.

LITERATURE: Quarterly newsletter.

National Society to Prevent Blindness, Inc.
79 Madison Avenue
New York, N.Y. 10016

Provides free single copies of pamphlets on many aspects of eye health and eye safety, including "The Aging Eye: Facts on Eye Care for Older Persons"; "Your Child's Sight: How You Can Help"; "Your Eyes . . . For a lifetime of sight"; and "20 Questions on Eye Safety"; send for publications and films catalog.

ADDITIONAL EYE LITERATURE

"*Soft Contact Lenses,*" by Margaret Morrison, reprinted from *FDR Consumer* (July/August 1976), U.S. Department of Health, Education, and Welfare, Public Health Service, Food and Drug Administration, Office of Public Affairs, Washington, D.C. 20201. Illustrated two-page article with basic information on soft contact lenses.

"Glaucoma" (1976), typescript available from Lederle Laboratories, A Division of American Cyanamid Company, Pearl River, N.Y. 10965.

Foot Care

American Podiatry Association
20 Chevy Chase Circle, N.W.
Washington, D.C. 20015

This professional society of foot specialists maintains a library and has 52 state groups; foot health literature is available.

Gynecological Concerns

American College of Obstetricians and Gynecologists
One East Wacker Drive
Chicago, Ill. 60601

Publishes numerous leaflets, pamphlets, and booklets on gynecological concerns, such as vaginitis, uterine tumors, and hysterectomy. Send for publications price list.

Feminist Women's Health Center
1112 S. Crenshaw Boulevard
Los Angeles, Calif. 90019

Local groups: 1017 Thomasville Road
Tallahassee, Fla. 32303

429 South Sycamore
Santa Ana, Calif. 92707

2445 West Eight Mile Road
Detroit, Mich. 48203

Women working for women—in medical areas involved with reproduction, abortion, and gynecology in general. There is also an educational program and self-help clinic.

LITERATURE: Descriptive brochures; fact sheets; "Abortion In a Clinic Setting," leaflet; publications flyer; *Report*, annual newspaper.

Health Right, Inc.–Women's Health Forum
175 Fifth Avenue
New York, N.Y. 10010

Publishes and distributes literature and has classes and workshops on patient advocacy and women's health.

LITERATURE: Pamphlets include *Infections of the Vagina*, *Menopause*, and *The Gynecological Check-Up*; *Healthright*, quarterly Newspaper; fact sheets.

Hearing

American Speech and Hearing Association
9030 Old Georgetown Road
Washington, D.C. 20014

(For other organizations helping those with impaired hearing, see Chapter 29, *Handicaps*.)

Heart Conditions

American Heart Association
7320 Greenville Avenue
Dallas, Tex. 75231

American Heart Association offices are located in all states, in Puerto Rico, and in most towns and cities of the United States. Requests for help should be directed to the nearest office rather than to the national center. Local offices can provide quicker assistance and with greater accuracy because programs vary from place to place and from time to time, depending on local needs. Information and referral services are provided by all offices. Other community service programs include: diet and nutrition counseling; blood pressure screening; cardiopulmonary resuscitation CPR training; smoking withdrawal clinics; information on emergency medical services, stress-testing facilities, exercise programs, and stroke rehabilitation programs.

Make Today Count, Inc.
(See listing under *Cancer*.)

National Heart & Lung Institute
U.S. Department of Health, Education, and Welfare
National Institutes of Health
9000 Rockville Pike
Bethesda, Md. 20014

Conducts research and publishes educational materials, such as *Varicose Veins*, a leaflet; *The Human Heart: A Living Pump*, a booklet; annual reports; lists of publications; and special photocopied reports, such as *A Handbook of Heart Terms* and others.

Mended Hearts, Inc.
721 Huntington Avenue
Boston, Mass. 02115

National organization of recovered heart surgery patients with eighty-seven chapters in thirty states, Canada, and Argentina. Through the local chapters, volunteers visit patients in the hospital before and after surgery, as well as in-person or telephone communication upon returning home. Although the main purpose of the volunteers is visiting the surgery patient, as needed, families are also provided with companionship. The national headquarters is an information clearinghouse only.

LITERATURE: "Heart to Heart from the Mended Hearts, Inc."; "What Is the Mended Hearts, Inc.?"

Huntington's Disease

Committee to Combat Huntington's Disease
250 West 57th Street
New York, N.Y. 10019

The committee provides public education, promotion, research, genetic counseling, patient services, and referrals.

LITERATURE: Free leaflets and booklets; newsletter; *The Impact of Genetics; Huntington's Disease.*

Hypoglycemia

Adrenal Metabolic Research Society of the Hypoglycemia Foundation, Inc.
153 Pawling Avenue
Troy, N.Y. 12180

Founded in 1956, this is a professional organization of physicians and paramedical investigators concerned with hypoglycemia (low blood sugar). It is not a membership organization, but general information on hypoglycemia, a physician referral service, and a 2,000-volume library on endocrinology are available.

LITERATURE: *Homeostasis Quarterly*, newsletter; booklets.

Infectious Diseases

National Institute of Allergy and Infectious Diseases
Public Health Service
National Institutes of Health
Bethesda, Md. 20014

Conducts research in infectious diseases and publishes popular educational materials on hepatitis, flu, and so forth.

Infertility

American Fertility Society
1608 Thirteenth Avenue South
Birmingham, Ala. 35205

Provides help in locating an infertility specialist by making referrals to someone in your area. Enclose a self-addressed stamped envelope with your request.

Resolve, Inc.
P.O. Box 474
Belmont, Mass. 02178

Headquarters for this self-help support group for infertile people, with local chapters throughout the United States.

Kidney Disease

Kidney Disease Control Program
5600 Fishers Lane
Rockville, Md. 20857

Federal government program that maintains a list of services.

National Association of Patients on Hemodialysis and Transplantation (NAPHT)
505 Northern Boulevard
Great Neck, N.Y. 11021

Information clearinghouse that will make referrals to the 21 local NAPHT chapters throughout the country. Membership includes persons on hemodialysis and with kidney transplants, their families and friends, and professionals. NAPHT is concerned with public education about these conditions and promoting a donor program.

LITERATURE: *NAPHT News* ($8.50 a year); free leaflet, brochures, and pamphlets.

National Kidney Foundation
116 East 27th Street
New York, N.Y. 10016

The foundation provides organ donor information and educational material on various kidney diseases, including a newsletter, annual report, and a warning signs card.

Multiple Sclerosis

National Multiple Sclerosis Society
205 East 42nd Street
New York, N.Y. 10017

A research organization that services and treats patients through local chapters throughout the United States. It handles newly-diagnosed and long-term patients and will send literature, on request.

ADDITIONAL MULTIPLE SCLEROSIS LITERATURE

But You Look So Well! by John R. Ginther, Ph.D. (1978). Nelson-Hall Publishers, 325 West Jackson Boulevard, Chicago, Ill. 60606 ($10.95). The personal account of the symptoms and treatment of MS and how the disease affected the author and his family.

Muscular Dystrophy

Muscular Dystrophy Association
810 Seventh Avenue
New York, N.Y. 10019

A nonprofit national organization with local chapters throughout the United States conducting research, raising funds for research and special projects, and providing public education materials.

LITERATURE: Leaflets on a variety of related medical problems, including myasthenia gravis, muscular dystrophy, the cpk test for the detection of female carriers of duchenne muscular dystrophy, amyotrophic lateral sclerosis, and others.

Myasthenia Gravis

Myasthenia Gravis Foundation
230 Park Avenue
New York, N.Y. 10017

There are 52 state groups to this research, educational, and victim support organization. Publishes pamphlets and a quarterly national newsletter; lay and professional films are also available upon request.

Parkinson's Disease

American Parkinson Disease Association
147 East 50th Street
New York, N.Y. 10022

Provides counseling and public information related to Parkinson's Disease.

LITERATURE: *A Manual for Patients with Parkinson's Disease* (free).

Psoriasis

National Psoriasis Foundation
6415 S.W. Canyon Court
Portland, Ore. 97221

Information clearinghouse on psoriasis skin disease.

LITERATURE: *National Psoriasis Foundation*, quarterly bulletin; fact sheets.

Psoriasis Research Association, Inc.
107 Vista Del Grande
San Carlos, Calif. 94070

Provides research grants to qualified medical personnel in the field of the little-understood ailment of psoriasis; news bulletins; correspondence to patients and doctors; computer processing of case history questionnaire data plus registry of patient-volunteers; interchange of research reports with groups in Europe and England; and an annual meeting each May in San Mateo, California.

LITERATURE: Fact sheets; *News*.

Respiratory and Lung Conditions

American Lung Association (ALA)
1740 Broadway
New York, N.Y. 10019

ALA maintains a local chapter in each state; the national headquarters coordinates public education and general information. It is concerned with tuberculosis, numerous lung diseases, air pollution, and smoking. Extensive publications, including free pamphlets, leaflets, booklets, and films for loan are available.

LITERATURE: *The Respiratory System*, free chart; publications list.

Children's Asthma Research and Hospital
Denver, Colo. 80204

(See Chapter 18, *Drugs, Smoking, and Drug Abuse* for groups related to smoking.)

Skin

American Academy of Dermatology
2250 N.W. Flanders Street
Portland, Ore. 97210

This is a professional society for those medical doctors who specialize in diseases of the skin.

Sleep Disorders

American Narcolepsy Association, Inc.
P.O. Box 5846
Stanford, Calif. 94305

Information clearinghouse on narcolepsy; mail is answered by volunteers; membership dues are $12.00 a year.

LITERATURE: Fact sheets.

Better Sleep Council
1270 Avenue of the Americas
New York, N.Y. 10010

An information clearinghouse on sleep disorders, such as insomnia, which maintains a list of clinics and sleep laboratories to aid someone with these problems. Tips on how to aid sleep, provided by the council, were published in "Beauty & Sleep" by Robin Tracy, *Ambiance Magazine*, January 1979, pages 35 and 102.

ADDITIONAL SLEEP DISORDER LITERATURE

"Consumer Fact Sheet: Insomnia," free from Public Health Service, Alcohol, Drug Abuse, and Mental Health Administration, National Institute of Mental Health, 5600 Fishers Lane, Rockville, Md. 20857.

Venereal Disease

Most counties and cities have a bureau of venereal disease control within the Department of Health. Contact it for direct help—referrals to clinics and physicians—and for general information.

American Social Health Association
260 Sheridan Avenue, Suite 307
Palo Alto, Calif. 94306

This nonprofit research and development corporation is working on the VD problem and provides free single copies of booklets or leaflets on VD, such as "Some Questions and Answers About V.D.," "About Herpes," and "About Penicillin Resistant Gonorrhea." They also have films on VD with student and teacher's guides.

Montreal Health Press
P.O. Box 1000 Station G
Montreal, Quebec
Canada H2W 2N1

Publishes an excellent free illustrated booklet, *VD Handbook*, describing gonorrhea, syphilis, non-gonococcal urethritis, vaginitis, and other related diseases—how you get them, what they are, what treatments are available.

National Operation Venus Program
1213 Clover Street
Philadelphia, Pa. 19107

National toll-free hotline providing information on venereal disease as well as referrals to local treatment facilities.

Ortho Pharmaceutical Corporation
Raritan, N.J. 08869

Publishes and distributes the free leaflet, *VD: A Fact of Life*.

U.S. Department of Health, Education, and Welfare
Public Health Service
Center for Disease Control
Venereal Disease Control Division
Atlanta, Ga. 30333

Free publications available; VD information clearinghouse and research.

LITERATURE: *Directory of Venereal Disease Research; VD Fact Sheet* (1975); article reprints; "Recommended Treatment Schedules for Syphilis 1976."

ADDITIONAL LITERATURE

AHA Guide to the Health Care Field (published annually). American Hospital Association, 840 Lake Shore Drive, Chicago, Ill. 60611 (1978 edition $30.00 to AHA personnel and institutional members; $37.50 to others). This directory includes lists of hospitals in the United States with selected statistical data, AHA members, international, national, and regional organizations in the health care field, state health care organizations and agencies, and accredited educational programs for thirty different health care occupations.

The Book of Health, 3rd edition, compiled and edited by Randolph Lee Clark, M.D., and Russell W. Cumley, Ph.D. (1977). Harcourt Brace Jovanovich, 757 Third Avenue, New York, N.Y. 10017 ($8.95 paperback). A comprehensive family medical guide based on the contributions of 270 specialists. Includes descriptions of body functions, diseases, and recent treatment developments.

The Consumer's Guide to Successful Surgery by Seymour Isenberg, M.D., and L. M. Elting, M.D. (1976). St. Martin's Press, 175 Fifth Avenue, New York, N.Y. 10010 ($10.00 postpaid).

Facts About Medical and Dental Practitioners, U.S. Department of Health, Education, and Welfare, Public Health Service, Health Resources Administration. Available from the Superintendent of Documents, U.S. Government Printing Office, Washington, D.C. 20402 ($.40). Booklet providing simple, clear descriptions of the various specialists, such as opthalmologists and optometrists, pedodontists and prosthodontists.

Family Health (monthly). 149 Fifth Avenue, New York, N.Y. 10010 ($12.00 a year). Popular health magazine; regular features include "Ask the Dentist," "Ask the Vet," "Diet Menu of the Month," and "Health Matters" monthly roundup.

Get the Life That's Coming to You (1977). Blue Cross/Blue Shield of Greater New York, P.O. Box 345, Grand Central Station, New York, N.Y. 10017 (free booklet). The "Seven-Part Life Package" advocates eating a good breakfast, three square meals a day, exercise, seven to eight hours of sleep, keeping weight normal, drinking in moderation or not at all, and no smoking.

Gray's Anatomy (1974). The Illustrated Running Press Edition of Henry Gray's 1901 Anatomy, Descriptive and Surgical. Running Press, 38 South Nineteenth Street, Philadelphia, Pa. 19103 ($8.95 plus $.25 postage). One of the numerous current available editions of Gray's classic text; a good reference to have on hand.

Health Law Newsletter (monthly). National Health Law Program, 2401 Main Street, Santa Monica, Calif. 90405 (free). Distributed to legal services clients and attorneys and to health providers and consumers who wish to learn about health-related problems of the poor.

How to Be Your Own Doctor (Sometimes) by Keith W. Sehnert, M.D., with Howard Eisenberg (1975). Grosset and Dunlap, Inc., Box 941, Madison Square Station, New York, N.Y. 10010 ($10.70 postpaid).

How to Survive Being Alive: Stress Points and Your Health by Donald L. Dudley, M.D., and Elton Welke (1977). Doubleday and Company, Inc., Garden City, N.Y. 11550 ($6.95). How to avoid stress and improve coping behaviors, such as emotional responses, personal and unconscious habits.

Journal of Medical Ethics (quarterly). Society for the Study of Medical Ethics, Tavistock House North, Tavistock Square, London WC1H 9LG, England ($25.00 for U.S. and overseas).

Man's Body: An Owner's Manual by the Diagram Group (1977). Paddington Press, distributed by Grosset and Dunlap, 51 Madison Avenue, New York, N.Y. 10010 ($6.95). An illustrated, popular medical and health guide to understanding one's body.

Medical and Health Information Directory, edited by Anthony T. Kruzas (1977). Gale Research Company, Book Tower, Detroit, Mich. 48226 ($48.00). A 680-page annotated guide to state, national, and international organizations, government agencies, educational institutions, hospitals, journals, newsletters, publishers, research centers, computer data banks, libraries, and much more.

Medical Self-Care: Access to Medical Tools, edited by Tom Ferguson, M.D. (quarterly). P.O. Box 717, Inverness, Calif. 94937 ($7.00 a year; $2.00 single copies and sample issue). Annotated and illustrated reviews of popular medical books and sources for hard-to-get medical equipment. Articles cover the spectrum of health care issues; excellent publication with thoughtful, informative reviews.

The Merck Manual of Diagnosis and Therapy, 13th edition, edited by Robert Berkow (1977). Merck & Co., Inc., P.O. Box 2000, Rahway, N.J. 07065 ($9.75). A home medical reference, but not a substitute for treatment; a "read along with your physician" for the inquisitive patient.

Modern Home Medical Adviser, edited by Morris Fishbein, M.D. (1969). Doubleday and Company, Inc., Garden City, N.Y. 11550 ($9.95). A popular lay guide to health and medicine. Illustrated.

Our Bodies, Ourselves: A Book By and For Women by the Boston Women's Health Collective (1976). Simon and Schuster, 1230 Avenue of the Americas, New York, N.Y. 10020 ($4.95). The best-selling guide to all medical information and health concerns of a woman—from menstruation to birth control—amply illustrated with charts, drawings, and photographs.

"Patient Brochure and Self-Help Manual," by Walt Stoll, M.D., 412 North Broadway, Lexington, Ky. 40505 ($1.00 postpaid).

"A Patient's Bill of Rights." American Hospital Association, 840 North Lake Shore Drive, Chicago, Ill. 60611 (free document).

The People's Hospital Book by Ronald Gots, M.D., Ph.D. and Arthur Kaufman, M.D. (1978). Crown Publishers, One Park Avenue, New York, N.Y. 10016 ($8.95). A book for the consumer on how to judge a doctor's capabilities, pick the best hospital, and understand hospital procedures.

Personal Health Appraisal by Walter D. Sorochan (1976). John Wiley and Sons, Inc., One Wiley Drive, Somerset, N.J. 08873 ($7.50). A variety of scales and inventories for self-analysis in the areas of health status, mental health, chronic diseases, nutrition, physical fitness, recreation, family living, and so on. Although intended for the college student, it will help anyone become more aware of their present state of health and to assess their health habits, behavior, and lifestyle.

The Rights of Hospital Patients by George J. Annas, American Civil Liberties Union Handbook (1975). Avon Books, 959 Eighth Avenue, New York, N.Y. 10019 ($1.75).

Seizing Our Bodies: The Politics of Women's Health Care, edited and with an introduction by Claudia Dreifus (1978). Vintage Books, Inc., 201 East 50th Street, New York, N.Y. 10022 ($4.95). A collection of articles on birth control, hysterectomy, and menopause, by Barbara Seaman, Ellen Frankfort, Adrienne Rich, and others.

"A Self-Health Bibliography," compiled by Milton Huber, Ph.D. (1976). University of Wisconsin-Milwaukee, P.O. Box 413, Milwaukee, Wis. 53201 ($.50). Annotated bibliography of books and medical journal articles on self-help for healthful living.

Take Care of Yourself: A Consumer's Guide to Medical Care by Donald M. Vickery, M.D., and James F. Fries, M.D. (1976). Addison-Wesley, Reading, Mass. 01867 ($9.95 postpaid). Descriptions of sixty-eight common medical problems plus consumer-oriented chapters, such as choosing a doctor and reducing your drug bills.

Talk Back to Your Doctor: How to Demand (and Recognize) High Quality Health Care by Arthur Levin, M.D. (1976). Doubleday and Company, Inc., Garden City, N.Y. 11550 ($7.95).

The Well Body Book by Mike Samuels, M.D., and Hal Bennett (1973). Random House, 201 East 50th Street, New York, N.Y. 10022 ($7.75).

Wellness Inventory by John Travis, M.D. Barbara McNeill/Wellness Inventory, Wellness Resource Center, 42 Miller Avenue, Mill Valley, Calif. 94941 ($.50 plus stamped self-addressed envelope). Self-scoring questionnaire of 100 items on your eating, stress, smoking, drinking, and inactivity that can help you evaluate what aspects of your life need changing.

The Whole Health Catalogue: How to Stay Well Cheaper by Shirley Linde (1977). Rawson Associates Publishers, 630 Third Avenue, New York, N.Y. 10017 ($12.95 hardcover, $6.95 paperback). Linde, who coauthored Dr. Atkins' *Super-Energy Diet,* has put together a popular guide to such universal health problems as "How to Stop the Killing Habits So You Can Live Your Longest," "How to Raise a Better Child," and "Do-It-Yourself Emergency Techniques." Lively reading and a good general reference.

The World Almanac *Whole Health Guide* by David Hendin (1977). New American Library, Plume Books, 1301 Avenue of the Americas, New York, N.Y. 10019 ($4.95). Newspaper columnist Hendin covers a wide range of health and medical care topics—from getting lab-test results to buying health insurance—in a lively, informative style. Follow-up addresses for further information are also provided.

Woman's Body: An Owner's Manual by The Diagram Group (1977). Paddington Press, distributed by Grosset and Dunlap, 51 Madison Avenue, New York, N.Y. 10010 ($6.95). An illustrated popular explanation of the functions of the body.

Your Body and How It Works by J. D. Ratcliff (1975). Reader's Digest Press/The Dial Press, 245 East 47th Street, New York, N.Y. 10017 ($8.95). Based on the popular *Reader's Digest* series, "I am Joe's [ear] [cell] [throat]," this comprehensible approach has a lot of basic information to offer.

Your Body and How It Works by American Medical Association, Department of Health Education. Orders to AMA, OP-176, Box 821, Monroe, Wis. 53566 ($1.50). Illustrated booklet about all parts of the body aimed at the six-to-nine-year-olds.

Lederle Laboratories, Pearl River, N.Y. 10965, publishes a variety of fact sheets on various medical and health problems, such as immunization, and tuberculosis.

See also the following related chapters in *The Help Book:*

AGING
ALCOHOLISM
CHILDBEARING
CHILDREN
CONSUMER AFFAIRS
COUNSELING
DRUGS, SMOKING, AND DRUG ABUSE
EMERGENCIES AND DISASTERS
ENVIRONMENT
FAMILY PLANNING
FOOD AND NUTRITION
HANDICAPS
MENTAL HEALTH
MULTIPURPOSE ORGANIZATIONS
PARENTING
SAFETY
SEX EDUCATION AND THERAPY
TRANSPORTATION AND TRAVEL

31

HOUSING

City, suburbs, or country? Urban or rural? In the 1960s, the choice seemed to be largely an economic one—if you were wealthy, you could live in the city and have a place in the country. If you were middle class, you moved to the less-fashionable but safe suburbs. If you were poor, you were forced to stay in the deteriorating areas of the city.

The 1970s, though, have seen a rebirth of the cities and a reevaluation of the suburbs. Psychologists, such as Columbia University's Professor Jonathan Freedman, promote the city as a reasonable place to live. In *Crowding and Behavior: The Psychology of High-Density Living*, Freedman showed that high-density living need not cause distress, and can also be beneficial. Freedman concluded:

1. There is no relationship between crowding and pathology.
2. There is no evidence that crowding causes either stress or arousal.
3. In high density areas, important social and intellectual stimulation is provided by other people.

So as the crime rate in the suburbs goes up, along with the cost of commuting to the city—for employment and culture—more and more middle-class persons are trying to buy apartments or houses in the cities and keep areas attractive to avoid the exodus–slum pattern. What has stood in their way is often the ability to get mortgage money (loans) from local banks. One citizen action group in New York, NYPIRG (New York Public Interest Research Group, Inc.) studied the amount of money reinvested by local banks in the community. Brooklyn College students spent over a year examining 10,000 mortgage applications and for the first time were able to document a pattern of redlining—the refusal to grant monies to local homeowners and the investment of local money in other states. NYPIRG then started organizing the community, placing pressure on the banks to reverse their redlining policies. The results? Articles began appearing in which people praised

Brooklyn banks for beginning to aid their communities and in which "greenlining, not redlining" was advocated. Studies were published to help the lay public learn how to stop the dreaded decay of their cities, such as *A Consumer Guide to Bank Mortgage Disclosure Statements* by Richard W. Golden or *Take the Money and Run! Redlining in Brooklyn* (available from NYPIRG; see listing in Chapter 11, *Citizen Action*).

This anti-redlining movement isn't occurring just in New York—in St. Louis, realtor Adolph K. Feinberg, his wife Virginia, and the Women for City Living found the same situation in the central west end of the city and fought it. Now abandoned luxury apartment buildings and decaying one-family houses are slated for redevelopment, not leveling.

Ultimately, the consumer must determine how cities, suburbs, and rural areas will look in the years to come. The division of country areas into too many small housing plots and developments undertaken without the necessary increase in services for new tenants are just some of the situations that are the direct responsibility of the people, who will suffer most if their communities, rural or urban, are destroyed.

For local direct help in housing, contact your county, city housing department. They should have information on financial assistance, including loans, subsidies, and grants for community renewal and low- and middle-income housing. They should also have technical assistance information for housing development. Or contact a private, nonprofit, citizen action group in your area concerned with housing. (See the listings for local branches of PIRG in Chapter 11, *Citizen Action*.) Other free local sources of information on your rights as a tenant may be your state assemblyman or your local chapter of the League of Women Voters. You might also call the continuing education department of your nearest college or university, or have the latest bulletin sent to you, to see if they offer any courses on buying or renovating a house or brownstone, or on financing, construction, and so forth. Check with your local public library for any forthcoming free lectures on these and related housing topics. Citizen action and housing committee groups will often offer single lectures or courses. Often they are free, but reservations may have to be made in advance.

Throughout the country, private, nonprofit independent housing agencies have sprung up to preserve and redevelop neighborhoods. For example, Action-Housing, Inc. (Two Gateway Center, Pittsburgh, Pennsylvania 15222) is concerned with research into housing in Allegheny County, community education, rehabilitation, and urban development. Organizations, such as U-HAB-Urban Homesteading Assistance Board in New York City, have been active in helping low- and moderate-income families rehabilitate abandoned housing, thereby encouraging economic development and neighborhood preservation. In Brentwood, Maryland, the Neighborhood Uniting Project was formed to reverse the trend of older neighborhoods deteriorating while newer parts of the county were vitalized by growth spurts. A coalition of more than 140 citizen associations, PTAs, church groups, block clubs, and other organizations combined to carry out a conscientious program in home repairs and renovations. Other examples of local groups that have been formed to improve housing and develop neighborhoods include the Community Development Clearinghouse in Montpelier, Vermont, and the Peoples Housing Network, Inc. (PHN) in New York City. PHN is a statewide grass roots organization with offices in Manhattan, Utica, Schenectady, and Syracuse. It publishes *Network*, a bimonthly magazine about housing issues such as co-ops, redlining, evictions, tenant fights, neighborhood restoration and organization.

If your community does not have a housing development program, you might consider organizing one. Two information sources for such efforts are the following national private clearinghouses:

The Midwest Academy, Inc.
600 West Fullerton Avenue
Chicago, Ill. 60614

An information clearinghouse on community organizing that also offers, for a fee, training workshops for leaders and organizers.

LITERATURE: *People Before Property: A Real Estate Primer and Research Guide* (Urban Planning Aid, 1972, $6.00); *Organizing in the Urban Crisis* by Steve Max (1976, $1.00); *What Is An Organizer?* by Rich Rothstein ($.60); *Why Organize* by Steve Max ($.50).

National Training and Information Center
1123 West Washington Boulevard
Chicago, Ill. 60607

This resource center for community organizations has training sessions, publications, videotape productions, and research and consultation (on sliding scale fees) for neighborhood residents focusing on community issues, including housing.

LITERATURE: *Disclosure*, ten issues a year ($10.00 for individuals; $15.00 for institutions); *Lending Policies Exposed: Prime Factor in Neighborhood Decay* ($2.00); *Neighborhoods First: From the '70s Into the '80s* ($3.00).

You might also contact your nearest office of your state's division of housing and community renewal, listed in the white pages under the state government listing for **Housing**. That agency usually administers the building and housing codes and will supply information about all regulations as well as financial and technical assistance for community development. Your state housing department or housing development agency may also have a housing counseling program as well as rental housing loan programs. They may also publish a housing journal, and the annual report will have detailed accounts of other services offered to you.

The following federal agency provides information on those federal programs that provide assistance for housing and the development of communities:

U.S. Department of Housing and Urban Development (HUD)
451 Seventh Street, S.W.
Washington, D.C. 20410

Direct your inquiries to the nearest regional or area office (see listings below) or to the headquarters at the above address. Some of the programs, and consumer functions, of HUD include the Federal Crime Insurance Program (see Chapter 7, *Business Information*), Flood Insurance (see Chapter 7, *Business Information*), and Emergency Homeowners Relief. HUD also investigates complaints of discrimination in housing, provides sound technical basis for planning and design of housing under the Minimum Property Standards, programs Housing Assistance by insuring mortgages to finance construction or home improvement, provides mortgage insurance through Mortgage Credit Assistance for Homeownership, Interstate Land Sales Registration, Real Estate Settlement Procedures, and Structural Defects Repairs. This last program provides federal reimbursement, in specific cases, for faulty repairs in certain HUD-insured houses in older, declining urban neighborhoods.

LITERATURE: Address inquiries to the Public Service Center, Room B-258, at the above headquarters address; ask for a list of publications.

HUD FIELD OFFICES

Region I: Maine, Vermont, New Hampshire, Massachusetts, Connecticut, Rhode Island.
John F. Kennedy Federal Building
Boston, Mass. 02203

Region II: New York, New Jersey, Puerto Rico, Virgin Islands.
26 Federal Plaza
New York, N.Y. 10007

Region III: Delaware, Maryland, District of Columbia, Pennsylvania, Virginia, West Virginia.
6th and Walnut Streets
Philadelphia, Pa. 19106

Region IV: North Carolina, Kentucky, South Carolina, Tennessee, Georgia, Mississippi, Alabama, Florida.
1371 Peachtree Street, N.E.
Atlanta, Ga. 30309

Region V: Minnesota, Wisconsin, Michigan, Illinois, Indiana, Ohio.
300 South Wacker Drive
Chicago, Ill. 60606

Region VI: New Mexico, Oklahoma, Arkansas, Louisiana, Texas.
Federal Office Building
Dallas, Tex. 75202

Region VII: Iowa, Nebraska, Kansas, Missouri.
Federal Office Building
911 Walnut Street
Kansas City, Mo. 64106

Region VIII: Montana, North Dakota, South Dakota, Wyoming, Utah, Colorado.
Executive Tower
1405 Curtis Street
Denver, Colo. 80202

Region IX: California, Nevada, Arizona, Hawaii.
450 Golden Gate Avenue
San Francisco, Calif. 94102

Region X: Washington, Oregon, Idaho, Alaska.
Arcade Plaza Alaska Building
1321 Second Avenue
Seattle, Wash. 98101

The following national organizations will provide information on housing, neighborhood redevelopment, and related subjects:

National Center for Urban Ethnic Affairs (NCUEA)
1521 Sixteenth Street, N.W.
Washington, D.C. 20036

Founded in 1970, NCUEA serves as an information clearinghouse providing technical assistance and support activities for urban neighborhoods and organizations interested in helping to revitalize those neighborhoods. NCUEA is affiliated with the United States Catholic Conference.

LITERATURE: "Bibliography of Ethnic Heritage Studies Program Materials"; *Capacity Building in City Government for Neighborhood Revitalization* by Chester D. Haskell and Arthur J. Naparstek (1977).

National Community Development Association (NCDA)
1620 I Street, N.W., Suite 503
Washington, D.C. 20006

Since 1970, this membership organization has been affiliated with the National League of Cities (NLC) and the U.S. Conference of Mayors (USCM). Annual meetings are held each spring in Washington, D.C. Housing and community development are prime NCDA areas of concern.

LITERATURE: *A Guide to Preparing Housing Assistance Plans* ($3.50); *A Guide to Meeting Citizen Participation Requirements for Community Development* ($5.00).

National Land for People (NLP)
1759 Fulton, Room 11
Fresno, Calif. 93721

A national organization doing research and litigation to enforce the Reclamation Law, which will open large tracks of land wherever the U.S. Bureau of Reclamation has irrigation projects. Membership ($5.00 for low-income individuals; $10.00 regular) includes a subscription to NLP's newsletter.

LITERATURE: Descriptive folder (free); "This Land Belongs to You and Me" poster ($3.00); button ($.50 each); "Discover America" slide show (rental $25.00; purchase $100.00); "Who Owns the Land," a nationwide survey of land ownership and manipulations ($.50).

National Peoples Action
121 West Superior Street
Chicago, Ill. 60610

Founded in 1972, this organization is comprised of neighborhood residents throughout the country. NPA coordinates grass-roots lobbying efforts and analyzes pending legislation. They write testimony and also act as an information clearinghouse on such topics as housing, home mortgages, and neighborhood redevelopment. (See listing in Chapter 11, *Citizen Action*.)

National Rural Center (NRC)
1828 L Street, N.W.
Washington, D.C. 20036

Started in 1976, this national organization acts as an information clearinghouse for rural Americans. It is concerned with development and economic enhancement in the areas of legal services, education, housing, community economic development, health, and transportation.

LITERATURE: *Director of Rural Organizations* (limited copies available for free; second copy $2.00); periodic rural health newsletter; brochures and activities report on request.

Rural Housing Alliance/Rural America
1346 Connecticut Avenue, N.W.
Washington, D.C. 20036

Founded in 1967, this national nonprofit membership organization is an information clearinghouse and advocacy group that seeks equity for rural people in federal and state assistance programs. Membership dues are $5.00 for families with incomes below $10,000; $15.00 for others. Rural Housing Alliance, the housing program of Rural America, offers assistance to local groups seeking to improve housing and related facilities in rural areas.

LITERATURE: *The RHA Reporter* ($10.00 a year); *Self-Help Housing Handbook* ($12.50); *Rural America: A Voice for Small Town and Rural People*, monthly newspaper; ($10.00 a year; free to members); "Toward a Platform for Rural America" ($2.50); "The Urban Crisis Begins Here," leaflet; "What Is the Rural Housing Alliance?" brochure; publications price list.

The National Trust for Historic Preservation
740–748 Jackson Place, N.W.
Washington, D.C. 20006

A nonprofit, charitable, and educational organization chartered by Congress to encourage Americans to preserve districts, sites, buildings, structures, and objects that are central to American history. Members ($5.00 student; $15.00 active, numerous other categories, sliding scale) may visit designated National Trust Historic Houses throughout the country without charge.

LITERATURE: *Preservation News* ($1.60 a year or included in membership); *Historic Preservation* ($3.00 a year or included in membership).

Small Towns Institute (STI)
P.O. Box 517
Ellensburg, Wash. 98926

A national nonprofit organization that acts as an information clearinghouse on life in small towns and rural communities. Membership dues ($15.00 for individuals) includes subscription to *Small Town*.

LITERATURE: *Small Town*, monthly magazine; *Planning*, booklet; descriptive brochure.

United Nations Centre for Housing, Building and Planning (CHBP)
United Nations
New York, N.Y. 10017

One of the major units of the Department of Economic and Social Affairs of the United Nations Secretariat. CHBP's major objective is to assist member states, particularly developing countries, in the formulation of policies and programs for human settlements planning, development, and management. Its overall work program comprises six substantive topics: settlement policies and strategies; settlement planning; housing and upgrading of slums, squatter and rural settlements; development of the building sector; institutions and management; and exchange of information.

LITERATURE: *World Human Settlements Survey*, a quinquiennial global analytical and comparative report on world human settlements conditions and trends, published in English, French, and Spanish ($9.00); *Human Settlements*, a quarterly newsletter containing articles on research, technical cooperation projects, newsbriefs, abstracts of related United Nations publications and conferences (free); *Cumulative List of United Nations Documents and Publications in the Field of Housing, Building, and Planning, June 1975*, published every five years and updated yearly (free).

The following national organization is concerned with housing discrimination complaints:

National Committee Against Discrimination in Housing (NCDH)
1425 H Street, N.W.
Washington, D.C. 20005

Founded in 1950, this public interest organization is dedicated to open housing and opposed to segregation or discrimination against the poor or minority groups. NCDH acts as an information clearinghouse and public education resource center and provides legal information services, advice, and regional seminars.

LITERATURE: *Trends in Housing*, bimonthly ($5.00 a year).

For other resources on complaints about discrimination in housing, see Chapter 12, *Civil Rights and Discrimination*.

ADDITIONAL LITERATURE

Crowding and Behavior: The Psychology of High-Density Living by Jonathan Freedman (1975). Viking Press, 625 Madison Avenue, New York, N.Y. 10022 ($7.95). Freedman contends that high-density housing need not be a negative influence on behavior.

Doing It! Practical Alternatives for Humanizing City Life (bimonthly). P.O. Box 303, Worthington, Ohio 43085 ($10.00 a year; $12.00 outside the U.S.). Counterculture grass roots magazine on new innovative housing programs, health care, learning, communes, food, neighborhood governments, and so forth.

Fixing Up Your Home: What To Do and How to Finance It by U.S. Department of Housing and Urban Development (1977). Send a postcard to the Consumer Information Center, Department 666F, Pueblo, Colo. 81009 (free). This leaflet, which lists the HUD area offices and FHA insuring offices, gives some pointers on using a contractor and obtaining a loan.

The Future of Large, Older American Cities to the Year 2000 by Anthony Downs (1977). Available from *Discourses*, Department of Political Science, Room 601, Loyola University, 820 North Michigan Avenue, Chicago, Ill. 60611 ($1.00).

"House-Buying For the Unmarried: The Legal and Emotional Ties That Bind" by Susan Wilder in *Working Woman*, December 1977 (pages 67–69). Wilder recommends the following references for anyone interested in buying a house: *The Realities of Buying a Home* (National Gypsum Company, Buffalo, N.Y. 14202, $1.00); *Settlement Costs, A HUD Guide*, published by the U.S. Department of Housing and Urban Development, June 1976 (distributed by The Mortgage Bankers Association of America, 1125 15th Street, N.W., Washington, D.C. 20005); and "Buying a House? How to Deal with Closing Costs" (*Consumer Reports*, Orangeburg, N.J. 10762, August 1975, $1.00).

House Construction—How to Reduce Costs by the U.S. Department of Agriculture (1978). Consumer Information Center, Dept. 49G, Pueblo, Colo. 81009 ($.80). Money-saving tips on economical designs and floor plans to follow as well as how to avoid high maintenance or replacement costs.

ISR Newsletter (quarterly). Institute For Social Research, The University of Michigan, P.O. Box 1248, Ann Arbor, Mich. 48106 (free). Articles in this newsletter, which includes the Survey Research Center, Research Center For Group Dynamics, Center for Research on Utilization of Scientific Knowledge, and Center for Political Studies, often pertain to housing issues. See, for example, the Autumn 1977 issue with a report on a rental housing study.

Network: The Magazine of the Housing Movement. Peoples Housing Network, Inc., 29 East 22nd Street, New York, N.Y. 10010 ($3.00 a year for six issues). Premier issue included such articles as "State Study Confirms Redlining," "A Trash Plant in Your Backyard?," and "Public Housing Tenants Gain in Schenectady."

Reviving an Inner City Community by Ed Marciniak (1977). Available from *Discourses*, Department of Political Science, Room 601, Loyola University, 820 North Michigan Avenue, Chicago, Ill. 60611 ($2.95). Marciniak, President of the Institute of Urban Life, reports on urban change in East Humboldt Park in Chicago— how the working class residents together tried to reverse the urban decay process by hiring their own planner and reshaping their community.

Selecting and Financing a Home by the U.S. Department of Agriculture (1978). Orders to Consumer Information Center, Department 091F, Pueblo, Colo. 81009 ($1.10). Answers such questions as whether to rent or to buy, how much to spend, how to shop for a mortgage, and what insurance to purchase.

Small Town (monthly). Small Towns Institute, P.O. Box 517, Ellensburg, Wash. 98926 (sample copy sent free on request; $15.00 membership includes subscription). Magazine for membership of Small Towns Institute that does not accept paid advertisements; it publishes articles and reviews on conferences, organizations, and issues pertinent to small communities.

Super Tenant: New York City Tenant Handbook—Your Legal Rights and How to Use Them by John M. Striker and Andrew O. Shapiro (1978). Holt, Rinehart, and Winston, 383 Madison Avenue, New York, N.Y. 10017 ($4.95). Deals with such issues as how to compute your maximum legal rent, winning the right to sublet, suing your landlord in small claims court, and tightening building security.

The Tenant Survival Book by Emily Jane Goodman (1972). Bobbs-Merrill Company, Inc., 4300 W. 62nd Street, Indianapolis, Ind. 46206 ($3.95).

See also the following related chapters in *The Help Book:*

AGING
ARTS
BATTERED ADULTS
BUSINESS INFORMATION
CITIZEN ACTION
CIVIL RIGHTS AND DISCRIMINATION
CONSUMER AFFAIRS
FINANCIAL ASSISTANCE
MULTIPURPOSE ORGANIZATIONS
POLITICAL ACTION

32

INFORMATION RIGHTS AND RESOURCES

If you are able to master the art of how to uncover information and do research, you will be way ahead in a world that is ever-changing because of an explosion of facts and data. Keeping up with the latest developments in your career—whether it is auto mechanics, child care, chemistry, or cooking—may have practical benefits in terms of job advancement. Sometimes the volume of new research and publications—reports, newsletters, magazines, journals, pamphlets, booklets, films, and books—overwhelms rather than inspires. With free time often at a premium, you may want to amass your own basic information resources so that trips to the library or the bookstore are focused on difficult-to-find (or new) materials. How do you start creating a personalized, inexpensive office or home information bank? By initiating or expanding a home or office reference library; by knowing what county, city, state, federal, and private free information services can provide or can refer you to by way of other organizations or agencies for additional literature or practical guidelines; or by learning what your rights to documents are under the Freedom of Information Act (FOIA). These are just some of the topics covered in this chapter.

A home or office library may be the fastest way to answer your everyday questions, such as spellings of proper names or words, thumbnail sketches on authors you may be reading, grammar rules to aid in writing letters, or a quotation to liven up a speech that you might have to give at your company or in a civic community meeting. Your home or office library might contain the following basic references:

- dictionary
- thesaurus
- book of familiar quotations
- world atlas

- world almanac
- general encyclopedia
- first-aid manual
- home-repair guide
- writing or grammar text

The next place for gathering information is your local public or college library. (Check with the college or university in your community to see if you are allowed to use their collections on a reference or a circulating basis.) Some schools may require you to purchase a library card in order to borrow books. Most local libraries will answer questions over the phone—about particular books or other information sources—and have numerous special services, in addition to their magazine, book, film, and record collections. A librarian may be your best research tool so consider introducing yourself to the librarian and letting him or her know your information needs.

An article about better utilization of your local public library, "Questions, Anyone?" written by Carolyn Additon Anthony and reprinted from *American Education* magazine by the U.S. Department of Health, Education, and Welfare, is offered free from the Consumer Information Center, Pueblo, Colo. 81009. It also has a state-by-state listing of library agencies for further information. Anthony highlights basic reference books in a variety of subject areas—retirement and consumer complaints, for instance.

For further information on libraries, contact the following organizations:

American Library Association (ALA)
Public Information Office
50 East Huron Street
Chicago, Ill. 60611

Founded in 1876, ALA has fifty-six chapters throughout the country. Its main activity is the development of standards and guidelines for all types of libraries and library services and the accreditation of library education programs. It has an extensive professionals education program and a general public education program that includes booklets, audiovisual aids, and pamphlets related to library science and services. Each year, ALA sponsors National Library Week and two conferences for professionals.

LITERATURE: Free fact sheet.

Office of Libraries and Learning Resources
U.S. Office of Education
7th and D Streets, S.W.
Washington, D.C. 20202

Under the Library Services and Construction Act (LSCA), numerous projects are annually funded. A report by Ann Erteschik, *Library Programs Worth Knowing About*, describes programs in thirty-four states. A complimentary copy of the report will be sent on request as long as the supply lasts.

Another local source of free information is the travel bureau in your own city. Since their information has to be updated constantly, they can be a key re-

444 / THE HELP BOOK

source on places to visit, events, local maps, listings of hotels, restaurants, and basic services. Consult your telephone directory for county, city, or state government listings under "Convention and Visitors Bureau" or "Tourism." The tourist bureau is also a prime business or service organization to aid in community improvement programs, such as crime prevention plans or beautification.

Some mayors' offices have information centers as well. For example, the Mayor's Office for Information and Service in Philadelphia provides professional counseling and a full range of services including emergency housing, food, and funds; legal, crime compensation, medical, and general information; training of police, medical, and psychiatric personnel; and much more. They also have a variety of city publications available. Check your local telephone directory to see if your county or city has a mayor's office for information.

If you need information about state services and programs, contact the information office at your state capitol at the following addresses:

State Capitol
Montgomery, Ala. 36130

State Capitol
120 Fourth Street
Juneau, Alaska 99811

State Capitol
1700 West Washington Street
Phoenix, Ariz. 85007

State Capitol
5th and Woodland
Little Rock, Ark. 72201

State Capitol
10th and L Streets
Sacramento, Calif. 95814

State Capitol
200 East Colfax Avenue
Denver, Colo. 80203

State Capitol
210 Capitol Avenue
Hartford, Conn. 06115

State Capitol
Dover, Del. 19901

District Building
14th and E Streets, N.W.
Washington, D.C. 20004

The Capitol
Tallahassee, Fla. 32304

State Capitol
Capitol Square, S.W.
Atlanta, Ga. 30334

State Capitol
415 South Beretania Street
Honolulu, Hawaii 96813

Statehouse
700 West Jefferson Street
Boise, Idaho 83720

State Capitol
Springfield, Ill. 62706

State House
200 West Washington Street
Indianapolis, Ind. 46204

Capitol Building
107 East Grand Avenue
Des Moines, Iowa 50319

State House
10th and Harrison Streets
Topeka, Kans. 66612

State Capitol
Frankfort, Ky. 40601

State Capitol
900 Riverside North
Baton Rouge, La. 70804

State House
Augusta, Me. 04330

State House
State Circle
Annapolis, Md. 21404

State House
Beacon Street
Boston, Mass. 02133

Capitol Building
Lansing, Mich. 48933

State Capitol
Aurora Avenue and Park Street
St. Paul, Minn. 55155

New Capitol Building
Jackson, Miss. 39205

State Capitol
Jefferson City, Mo. 65101

Capitol Building
Helena, Mont. 59601

State Capitol
1445 K Street
Lincoln, Neb. 68509

State Capitol
Carson City, Nev. 89701

State House
107 North Main Street
Concord, N.H. 03301

State House
Trenton, N.J. 08625

State Capitol
Santa Fe, N.M. 87501

State Capitol
Albany, N.Y. 12224

State Capitol
Raleigh, N.C. 27611

State Capitol
Bismarck, N.D. 58505

State House
Broad and High Streets
Columbus, Ohio 43215

State Capitol
2302 Lincoln Boulevard
Oklahoma City, Okla. 73105

State Capitol
Salem, Ore. 97310

Main Capitol Building
Harrisburg, Pa. 17120

State House
82 Smith Street
Providence, R.I. 02903

State House
Columbia, S.C. 29211

Capitol Building
Pierre, S.D. 57501

State Capitol
Nashville, Tenn. 37219

State Capitol
Austin, Tex. 78711

State Capitol
Salt Lake City, Utah 84114

State House
State Street
Montpelier, Vt. 05602

State Capitol
Capitol Square
Richmond, Va. 23219

State Capitol
Olympia, Wash. 98504

State Capitol
1800 Kanawha Boulevard, East
Charleston, W.Va. 25305

State Capitol
Capitol Square
Madison, Wis. 53702

State Capitol
Capitol Avenue at 24th Street
Cheyenne, Wyo. 82001

446 / THE HELP BOOK

If you need information on any of the programs or services of the federal government, visit, telephone, or write the nearest Federal Information Center (FIC) in your area. They will search their own resources, or provide the proper referral, so you can get the answers or publications that you need. A free pamphlet, updated periodically, listing the local FICs, may be picked up at your nearest FIC office or from FIC, General Services Administration, Washington, D.C. 20405.

FEDERAL INFORMATION CENTERS*

Alabama
Birmingham
Toll-free tieline to Atlanta, Ga.

Mobile
Toll-free tieline to New Orleans, La.

Arizona
Federal Building
230 North First Avenue
Phoenix, Ariz. 85025

Tucson
Toll-free tieline to Phoenix, Ariz.

Arkansas
Little Rock
Toll-free tieline to Memphis, Tenn.

California
Federal Building
300 North Los Angeles Street
Los Angeles, Calif. 90012

Federal Building and U.S. Courthouse
650 Capitol Mall
Sacramento, Calif. 95814

Federal Building
880 Front Street
San Diego, Calif. 92188

Federal Building and U.S. Courthouse
450 Golden Gate Avenue
San Francisco, Calif. 94102

San Jose
Toll-free tieline to San Francisco, Calif.

Santa Ana
Toll-free tieline to Los Angeles, Calif.

Colorado
Colorado Springs
Toll-free tieline to Denver, Colo.

Federal Building
1961 Stout Street
Denver, Colo. 80294

Pueblo
Toll-free tieline to Denver, Colo.

Connecticut
Hartford
Toll-free tieline to New York, N.Y.

New Haven
Toll-free tieline to New York, N.Y.

District of Columbia
Seventh and D Streets, S.W., Room 5716
Washington, D.C. 20407

Florida
Fort Lauderdale
Toll-free tieline to Miami, Fla.

Jacksonville
Toll-free tieline to St. Petersburg, Fla.

Federal Building
51 Southwest First Avenue
Miami, Fla. 33130

Orlando
Toll-free tieline to St. Petersburg, Fla.

* Adapted from *Federal Information Centers* (March 1978). To find out the area codes to dial information to get current phone numbers, see Chapter 52, *Telephone Directory*.

St. Petersburg
William C. Cramer Federal Building
144 First Avenue South
St. Petersburg, Fla. 33701

Tampa
Toll-free tieline to St. Petersburg, Fla.

West Palm Beach
Toll-free tieline to Miami, Fla.

Georgia
Federal Building
275 Peachtree Street, N.E.
Atlanta, Ga. 30303

Hawaii
P.O. Box 50091
300 Ala Moana Boulevard
Honolulu, Hawaii 96850

Illinois
Everett McKinley Dirksen Building
219 South Dearborn Street
Chicago, Ill. 60604

Indiana
Federal Building
575 North Pennsylvania
Indianapolis, Ind. 64204

Iowa
Des Moines
Toll-free tieline to Omaha, Neb.

Kansas
Topeka
Toll-free tieline to Kansas City, Mo.

Wichita
Toll-free tieline to Kansas City, Mo.

Kentucky
Federal Building
600 Federal Place
Louisville, Ky. 40202

Louisiana
Federal Building
701 Loyola Avenue, Room 1210
New Orleans, La. 70113

Maryland
Federal Building
31 Hopkins Plaza
Baltimore, Md. 21201

Massachusetts
J.F.K. Federal Building
Cambridge Street
Lobby, 1st Floor
Boston, Mass. 02203

Michigan
McNamara Federal Building
477 Michigan Avenue
Detroit, Mich. 48226

Minnesota
Federal Building and U.S. Courthouse
110 South Fourth Street
Minneapolis, Minn. 55401

Missouri
Federal Building
601 East Twelfth Street
Kansas City, Mo. 64106

St. Joseph
Toll-free tieline to Kansas City, Mo.

Federal Building
1520 Market Street
St. Louis, Mo. 63103

Nebraska
Federal Building and U.S. Post Office and Courthouse
215 North 17th Street
Omaha, Neb. 68102

New Jersey
Federal Building
970 Broad Street
Newark, N.J. 07102

Trenton
Toll-free tieline to Newark, N.J.

New Mexico
Federal Building and U.S. Courthouse
500 Gold Avenue, S.W.
Albuquerque, N.M. 87101

Santa Fe
Toll-free tieline to Albuquerque, N.M.

New York
Albany
Toll-free tieline to New York, N.Y.

Federal Building
111 West Huron Street
Buffalo, N.Y. 14202

Federal Building
26 Federal Plaza, Lobby
New York, N.Y. 10007

Rochester
Toll-free tieline to Buffalo, N.Y.

Syracuse
Toll-free tieline to Buffalo, N.Y.

North Carolina
Charlotte
Toll-free tieline to Atlanta, Ga.

Ohio
Akron
Toll-free tieline to Cleveland, Ohio

Federal Building
550 Main Street
Cincinnati, Ohio 45202

Federal Building
1240 East Ninth Street
Cleveland, Ohio 44199

Columbus
Toll-free tieline to Cincinnati, Ohio

Dayton
Toll-free tieline to Cincinnati, Ohio

Toledo
Toll-free tieline to Cleveland, Ohio

Oklahoma
U.S. Post Office and Courthouse
201 Northwest 3rd Street
Oklahoma City, Okla. 73102

Tulsa
Toll-free tieline to Oklahoma City, Okla.

Oregon
Federal Building
1220 Southwest Third Avenue
Portland, Ore. 97204

Pennsylvania
Allentown/Bethlehem
Toll-free tieline to Philadelphia, Pa.

Federal Building
600 Arch Street
Philadelphia, Pa. 19106

Federal Building
1000 Liberty Avenue
Pittsburgh, Pa. 15222

Scranton
Toll-free tieline to Philadelphia, Pa.

Rhode Island
Providence
Toll-free tieline to Boston, Mass.

Tennessee
Chattanooga
Toll-free tieline to Memphis, Tenn.

Clifford Davis Federal Building
167 North Main Street
Memphis, Tenn. 38103

Nashville
Toll-free tieline to Memphis, Tenn.

Texas
Austin
Toll-free tieline to Houston, Tex.

Dallas
Toll-free tieline to Fort Worth, Tex.

Fritz Garland Lanham Federal Building
819 Taylor Street
Fort Worth, Tex. 76102

Federal Building and U.S. Courthouse
515 Rusk Avenue
Houston, Tex. 77002

San Antonio
Toll-free tieline to Houston, Tex.

Utah
Ogden
Toll-free tieline to Salt Lake City, Utah

Federal Building
125 South State Street
Salt Lake City, Utah 84138

Virginia
Stanwick Building
3661 East Virginia Beach Boulevard
Norfolk, Va. 23502

Washington
Federal Building
915 Second Avenue
Seattle, Wash. 98174

Tacoma
Toll-free tieline to Seattle, Wash.

Wisconsin
Milwaukee
Toll-free tieline to Chicago, Ill.

For additional federal information, find out where your nearest Federal Depository library is in order to save time and effort that might be spent by writing or going to a federal department's regional or Washington, D.C. office. These depositories maintain selected government documents, such as census data, study reports, and congressional journals, and the public may have free use of this material. You may obtain a list of all depository libraries in the United States by writing to Superintendent of Documents, U.S. Government Printing Office, Washington, D.C. 20402.

The following are additional federal and national information sources:

Alliance of Information and Referral Services (AIRS)
5020 North 20th Street, Suite 201
Phoenix, Ariz. 85061

A national coordinating organization for information and referral specialists.

LITERATURE: Newsletter.

Center for Information on America
Washington, Conn. 06793

A research and information organization that publishes material on areas of importance to citizens, such as unemployment and population.

Gale Reader Service Bureau
Gale Research Company
Book Tower
Detroit, Mich. 48226

A free service for readers of the *Encyclopedia of Associations* (see description in Additional Literature section of Chapter 51, *Additional Resources*) whose information needs are not met by that book or its supplement, *New Associations and Projects*, recognizing that the service's staff may possess information about certain groups that has not been published.

National Referral Center
Library of Congress
Washington, D.C. 20540

This federal center compiles information on government resources and makes this service available free of charge.

National Technical Information Service (NTIS)
5285 Port Royal Road
Springfield, Va. 22161

Operated by the U.S. Department of Commerce, this central source for the public sale of government-sponsored research, development, and engineering reports and other analyses prepared by federal agencies must charge for its services since it is sustained by the sales, not government funds. Send for their free catalogue of available materials and more details on NTIS's operation.

Population Reference Bureau, Inc.
1337 Connecticut Avenue, N.W.
Washington, D.C. 20036

Established in 1929, this educational organization studies, analyzes, and reports on population and related concerns, such as population movement, growth, and the effect of people on their environment. Membership fees are $20.00 and up.

LITERATURE: Population bulletins; *Intercom*, monthly newsletter; *World Population Data Sheet*; PRB Reports.

Science for the People
897 Main Street
Cambridge, Mass. 02139

This organization has chapters throughout the United States involved with a variety of issues, from sociobiology, genetics, and nuclear power to energy, agriculture, nutrition, health care, economics, and recombinant DNA. Branches are located in Ann Arbor, Mich., Berkeley, Calif., Amherst, Mass., New York City, San Francisco, Calif., Santa Cruz, Calif., St. Louis, Mo., Stony Brook, N.Y., Tallahassee, Fla., and Urbana, Ill. Members are scientists, teachers, technicians, and lay people interested in demystifying science and technology and exposing the social and political ramifications of certain kinds of research. It opposes sexism, racism, and elitism and works toward building a science that is oriented toward people's needs rather than profit.

LITERATURE: Publications list; *Science for the People* magazine ($1.00); *Resources for Teachers* ($.25); *Toward a Science for the People* ($.50).

Southwest Research and Information Center
P.O. Box 4524
Albuquerque, N.M. 87106

An information clearinghouse of organizations and publications of primary interest to the lay person who wants to stay on top of new and offbeat resources. *The Workbook*, a monthly magazine available by subscription, contains annotated entries for organizations and publications; feature articles on related subjects are also included. (See complete listing in Chapter 11, *Citizen Action*.)

FREEDOM OF INFORMATION ACT (FOIA)

One of the most significant issues in recent years in the area of information is the possession by the government on various levels of dossiers or information on private citizens; equally important is the public's right to know and gain access to these and other government documents. Through the FOIA, many government actions have come to light, such as the involvement of one government agency in a twenty-five-year campaign to control the human mind with drugs or of the training of local policemen as burglars. These are just two examples of government actions revealed under the "right to know" or the Freedom of Information Act (FOIA), enacted in 1967 and amended in 1974.

Before the passage of FOIA, government agencies withheld records from the public for numerous legal reasons. Now any private citizen, newspaper, corporation, or interest group can file a request under the FOIA asking for any document for which they give a "reasonable," but necessarily a precise, description. Congressional and the federal court documents are excluded from the act; there are also nine other exemptions, including "properly classified national defense or foreign policy information," "trade secrets and commercial or financial information obtained from a person and privileged or confidential," "certain bank records," "oil well data," personnel, medical, and other private files, and law enforcement investigatory material.

There is no way of knowing exactly how many requests are made each year under the FOIA because government agencies are only required to report the number of requests that are denied. Using that information, and other factors, the *New York Times*, in an August 1977 article, "U.S. Information Act: Difficulties Despite Successes," estimated that there were about 150,000 requests in 1976 and that in 42 percent of the cases, part of the information requested was released. It also noted that the Justice Department said that the amount of time devoted to FOIA and related requests rose from 120,000 man-hours in 1975 to more than 600,000 man-hours in 1976.

But the FOIA, obviously a step forward, must be scrutinized for possible abuses or invasions of privacy. For example, Professor Arthur R. Miller, in his book *The Assault on Privacy* (1972), reports on a case where an employer charged with unfair labor practices by his employees requested under the FOIA the testimony that his employees had given during the investigation. His application was rejected. To try to protect the citizen's privacy, which is "directly affected by the collection, maintenance, use, and dissemination of personal information by Federal agencies" the Privacy Act of 1974 was passed.

Fortunately there are some excellent national organizations to provide the private citizen or interest group with information and advice on how to file under the FOIA and how to protect oneself from related invasions of privacy into government-gathered personal information. Ralph Nader's Freedom of Information Clearinghouse in Washington, D.C., conducts research and also answers hundreds of individual questions each week on the FOIA. The American Civil Liberties Union, through its local and state branches, also publishes related material for the lay person and answers specific requests.

Check with your local citizen action group, such as PIRG (Public Interest Research Group), to see if they publish an inexpensive guidebook to getting public records in your county or city.

The following national organizations provide information and advice on getting information and/or personal records:

452 / THE HELP BOOK

American Civil Liberties Union (ACLU)
22 East 40th Street
New York, N.Y. 10016

Contact your state ACLU affiliate for answers to specific questions; the national headquarters conducts research and publishes general information in this area.

LITERATURE: *Your Right to Government Information: How to Use the FOIA* ($.25).

Freedom of Information Center
University of Missouri
Box 858
Columbia, Mo. 65201

An information clearinghouse on the FOIA; subscriptions are $12.00 for individuals; $24.00 for organizations. The center publishes monthly reports, a bimonthly digest, occasional opinion papers, and the FOI Foundation Series.

Freedom of Information Clearinghouse
P.O. Box 19367
Washington, D.C. 20036

Established in 1972 as part of Ralph Nader's Center for the Study of Responsive Law to give citizens, public interest groups, and members of the press legal and technical help in effectively using the laws that grant a right of access to government-held information.

LITERATURE: *The Freedom of Information Act: What It Is and How to Use It* (free).

Project on National Security and Civil Liberties
122 Maryland Avenue, N.E.
Washington, D.C. 20002

A project of the American Civil Liberties Foundation, started in 1975, to encourage Americans to take advantage of the Freedom of Information Act.

LITERATURE: *Litigation Under the Amended Federal Freedom of Information Act* ($6.00 to nonprofit public interest organizations, law students, and law school faculties; $20.00 to libraries, institutions, government agencies, and attorneys).

Reporters Committee for Freedom of the Press
1750 Pennsylvania Avenue, N.W., Room 112
Washington, D.C. 20006

The News Media & The Law, a magazine published eight times a year, is available to those who become sponsors of the Reporters Committee by sending a tax-deductible contribution of $15.00. Through their Legal Defense and Research Fund, single copies are available of *How to Use the New 1974 FOI Act*.

ADDITIONAL LITERATURE

Many of the reference books listed below are either very expensive or updated too often to make personal ownership feasible. But others may be useful additions to your home or office library. This listing may also serve as a guide to more effective use of your library as an information source.

American Library Directory, 30th edition, edited by Jacques Cattell Press (1976–1977). R. R. Bowker Company, 1180 Avenue of the Americas, New York, N.Y. 10036 ($47.50). Lists more than 25,000 libraries in the United States and 2,000 in Canada.

Art Index (quarterly). H. W. Wilson Company, 950 University Avenue, Bronx, N.Y. 10452. Since 1929, this magazine has indexed articles that appear in about 150 periodicals.

The Assault on Privacy: Computers, Data Banks, and Dossiers by Arthur R. Miller (1971). New American Library, 1301 Avenue of the Americas, New York, N.Y. 10019 ($1.50). Professor Miller describes the impact of information practices on our civil liberties, including ways to control the input, output, and storage of computerized information.

Bartlett's Familiar Quotations by John Bartlett, 14th edition edited by Emily Morison Beck

(1968). Little, Brown and Company, Inc., 34 Beacon Street, Boston, Mass. 02106 ($15.00). Arranged chronologically by the year of the work or the author, excerpts from the Bible, Shakespeare, Whitman, Mao Tse-Tung, and hundreds more are presented. Indexed.

Bicentennial Statistics, reprinted from *Pocket Data Book, USA 1976* by U.S. Bureau of the Census, U.S. Department of Commerce. Available from Superintendent of Documents, U.S. Government Printing Office, Washington, D.C. 20402 ($.90). Handy manual with statistics from 1630 to 1976 and historical information.

Books in Print. R. R. Bowker Company, 1180 Avenue of the Americas, New York, N.Y. 10036. Published annually in the fall—two volumes by title, two volumes by author, and two volumes by subject. Bowker also publishes *Books in Print Supplement*, published annually in the spring and *Paperbound Books in Print*, published twice a year; write for a catalog that lists Bowker's extensive publications. This is the best guide for checking prices, publishers, and new editions of most available in-print books in the United States.

Business Periodicals Index (monthly, except July). H. W. Wilson Company, 950 University Avenue, Bronx, N.Y. 10452. Since 1958, an index of about 250 periodicals. For the period 1913–1958, consult the *Industrial Arts Index*, which this title replaced.

Columbia Encyclopedia, 1975 edition. Columbia University Press, 562 West 113th Street, New York, N.Y. 10025. Since the first edition of this one-volume encyclopedia appeared in 1935, it has been a standard work for the home library, providing succinct but basic information on people, places, and events throughout history.

Dictionary Buying Guide: A Consumer Guide to General English-Language Wordbooks in Print, edited by Kenneth F. Kister (1977). R. R. Bowker Order Department, P.O. Box 1807, Ann Arbor, Mich. 48106 ($15.95).

The Dictionary of Misinformation, edited by Tom Burnam (1977). Ballantine Books, 201 E. 50th Street, New York, N.Y. 10022 ($1.95).

Directory Information Service: A Reference Periodical Covering Business and Industrial Directories, Professional and Scientific Rosters, and Other Lists and Guides of All Kinds (three issues a year). Gale Research Company, Book Tower, Detroit, Mich. 48226 ($36.00). Organized by subject—business, industry, labor—with extensive annotations for each directory, such as address, number of entries, circulation, frequency, and price.

Directory of Special Libraries and Information Centers, 4th edition, edited by Margaret L. Young (1977). Gale Research Company, Book Tower, Detroit, Mich. 48226 ($179.00). More than 13,000 entries in three volumes, arranged alphabetically and by geographic location.

Education Index (monthly except July and August). H. W. Wilson Company, 950 University Avenue, Bronx, N.Y. 10452. Since 1929, it has indexed more than 240 education periodicals.

Encyclopaedia Britannica. 425 North Michigan Avenue, Chicago, Ill. 60611. One of the best-known multivolume general knowledge encyclopedias.

Encyclopedia Buying Guide: A Consumer Guide to General Encyclopedias in Print, 2nd edition, by Kenneth F. Kister (1978). R. R. Bowker Order Department, P.O. Box 1807, Ann Arbor, Mich. 43105 ($17.50). Examines more than thirty-five encyclopedias, including *World Book Encyclopedia, Columbia Encyclopedia,* and *Encyclopedia Americana*.

Facts on File (weekly). 119 West 57th Street, New York, N.Y. 10019 ($270.00 a year). Weekly news service in looseleaf format that is available in most libraries.

Finding Facts Fast by Alden Todd (1972). William Morrow & Company, Inc., 105 Madison Avenue, New York, N.Y. 10016 ($5.95). Todd, who has taught a course in research techniques and fact-finding since 1966, shares his time-saving knowledge in this compact, useful book.

Fundamental Reference Sources by Frances Neal Cheney (1971). American Library Association, 50 East Huron Street, Chicago, Ill. 60611 ($9.95).

Getting Involved With Your Own Computer: A Guide for Beginners by Leslie Solomon and Stanley Veit (1977). Ridley Enslow Publishers, 60 Crescent Place, Box 301, Short Hills, N.J. 07078 ($5.95). A basic guide to what makes computers work and how to use, and choose, a personal computer.

Government Manual, updated annually, Office of the Federal Register, National Archives and Records Service. Available from Superintendent of Documents, U.S. Government Printing Office, Washington, D.C. 20402 ($6.50). In addition to department-by-department listings, there is an introductory section on the Freedom of Information Act and the Privacy Act of 1974 and how to keep up with government publications. The rest of this 800-page guide gives the history, structure, names, addresses, and functions of all government agencies.

Great Treasury of Western Thought: A Compendium of Important Statements on Man and His Institutions by the Great Thinkers in Western History, edited by Mortimer Adler and Charles Van Doren (1977). R. R. Bowker Order Department, P.O. Box 1807, Ann Arbor, Mich. 48106 ($29.95).

Guide to Alternative Periodicals, compiled and edited by Don Carnahan. Sanspark Press, Box 91, Greenleaf, Ore. 97445 ($3.00 prepaid; $4.00 if billed). Periodicals arranged by subject, with an emphasis on non-mass market newsstand publications.

Guide to Reference Books, 9th edition, by Eugene P. Sheehy (1976). American Library Association, 50 East Huron Street, Chicago, Ill. 60611 ($30.00).

Guinness Book of World Records edited by Norris McWhirter (updated annually). Sterling Publishing Company, Inc., 2 Park Avenue, New York, N.Y. 10016 ($7.95).

International Encyclopedia of Statistics, edited by William H. Kruskal and Judith M. Tanur (1978). Macmillan Professional and Library Services, 100B Brown Street, Riverside, N.J. 08075 ($100.00).

International Encyclopedia of the Social Sciences, 8 volumes. Macmillan Professional and Library Services, 100B Brown Street, Riverside, N.J. 08075 ($200.00).

Library Journal (semimonthly, except monthly in July and August). 1180 Avenue of the Americas, New York, N.Y. 10036 ($19.00 a year; $1.35 single issue). Reviews thousands of books each year and also has major articles and news of forthcoming events of interest to librarians and researchers.

Literary Market Place (LMP) With Names and Numbers: The Directory of American Book Publishing (updated annually). R. R. Bowker Company, 1180 Avenue of the Americas, New York, N.Y. 10036 ($30.00). The "bible" of the publishing industry, listing all U.S. publishers with their key personnel, television and radio stations, newspapers, and agents.

Marquis Who's Who, 200 East Ohio Street, Chicago, Ill. 60611. Publishes *Who's Who in Finance and Industry*, *Who's Who in Religion*, and other people directories. Write for catalog.

The Modern Researcher, 3rd edition, by Jacques Barzun and Henry F. Graff (1977). Harcourt Brace Jovanovich, 757 Third Avenue, New York, N.Y. 10017 ($7.95). Excellent theoretical and practical guide to research, nonfiction writing, and bibliographic formats. Points are illustrated with quotations; list of further readings included.

National Directory of Newsletters and Reporting Services, 2nd edition, edited by Robert C.

Thomas. Gale Research Company, Book Tower, Detroit, Mich. 48226 ($36.00).

The New Periodicals Index (twice a year). The Mediaworks, P.O. Box 4494, Boulder, Colo. 80306 ($25.00). Reference book intended to fill in the gaps left by *Readers' Guide to Periodical Literature*.

The New Roget's Thesaurus in Dictionary Form, edited by Norman Lewis (1977). Berkley Publishing Corporation, 200 Madison Avenue, New York, N.Y. 10016 ($1.50). Based on C. O. Sylvester Mawson's alphabetical arrangement of the famous Roget system of word classification.

New York Times Guide to Reference Materials by Mona McCormick (1971). Popular Library, 600 Third Avenue, New York, N.Y. 10016 ($1.50). Helpful guidebook divided into types of reference materials (almanacs, dictionaries, etc.) and subject areas (geography, sports, music). Brief facsimiles of major resources enables more effective use of them.

Oxford Dictionary of Quotations, 2nd edition (1953). Oxford University Press, 200 Madison Avenue, New York, N.Y. 10016 ($26.00). Quotations arranged alphabetically, by the name of the author.

The People's Almanac by David Wallechinsky and Irving Wallace (1975). Doubleday & Company, Inc., Garden City, N.Y. 11530 ($7.95). This 1,481-page paperback touches on everything from "Health and Well-Being" and "The Family" to "Famous Gays" and "Rape Control Fails to Halt Increased Rape Rate."

Periodicals Index. Tallahassee Science for the People, Progressive Technology Company, P.O. Box 20049, Tallahassee, Fla. 32304

Publishers Weekly: The Book Industry Journal (weekly). R. R. Bowker Company, 1180 Avenue of the Americas, New York, N.Y. 10036 ($30.00 a year; $2.00 single issues). Reviews thousands of forthcoming hardcover and paperback books. *PW* also contains media and forthcoming events announcements, feature articles, highlights of copyright law revisions, and author and publisher profiles.

The Quotable Woman (1800–1975) compiled and edited by Elaine Partnow (1977). Corwin Books, 1 Century Plaza, 2029 Century Park East, Los Angeles, Calif. 90067 ($20.00). Indexed by subject and author, this is an encyclopedia of excerpted comments by such notable women as Sylvia Townsend Warner, Marie Curie, and Harriet Tubman.

The Random House Encyclopedia, edited by James Mitchell and Jess Stein (1977). Random House, Inc., 201 East 50th Street, New York, N.Y. 10022 ($69.95). A one-volume illustrated reference of nearly 3,000 pages that can be read by all age groups.

The Reader's Encyclopedia, 2nd edition, by William Rose Benet (1965). T. Y. Crowell, 10 East 53rd Street, New York, N.Y. 10022 ($12.50).

Readers' Guide to Periodical Literature (semimonthly except July and August; bound annually). H. W. Wilson Company, 950 University Avenue, Bronx, N.Y. 10452. Since 1900 *Readers' Guide* has been indexing articles that appear in about 160 general and nontechnical periodicals.

Reference Books: A Brief Guide, 8th edition, compiled by Mary Neill Barton and Marion V. Bell (1977). Enoch Pratt Free Library, 400 Cathedral Street, Baltimore, Md. 21201 ($1.25).

Social Sciences and Humanities Index (quarterly). H. W. Wilson Company, 950 University Avenue, Bronx, N.Y. 10452. Indexes articles in 205 periodicals since 1965, when it replaced the *International Index* (1907–1965).

Statistics Sources: A Subject Guide to Data on Industrial, Business, Social, Educational, Financial, and Other Topics for the U.S. and Internationally, 5th edition, edited by Paul Wasserman and Jacqueline Bernero (1977). Gale

Research Company, Book Tower, Detroit, Mich. 48226 ($58.00).

Synopsis of the Law of Libel and the Right of Privacy by Bruce W. Sanford (1977). NEA, P.O. Box 91428, Cleveland, Ohio. 44101 ($1.25). Originally published for Scripps-Howard's reporters and editors, this edition is now available for those in the communications industry as well as journalists, lawyers, and lay persons.

Webster's Big Seven Collegiate Dictionary, rev. edition (1976). G. & C. Merriam Company, 4 Federal Street, Springfield, Mass. 01101 ($10.95).

Webster's New Dictionary of Synonyms (1973). G. & C. Merriam Company, 4 Federal Street, Springfield, Mass. 01101 ($7.95).

Webster's Third New International Dictionary, Unabridged. G. & C. Merriam Company, 4 Federal Street, Springfield, Mass. 01101 ($59.95).

Who's Who 1978–79 (1978). St. Martin's Press, Reference Department, 175 Fifth Avenue, New York, N.Y. 10010 ($67.50). More than 28,000 entries in this listing of outstanding men and women throughout the world in its 130th year of publication. (Also publishes the six-volume *Who Was Who.*)

Who's Who Among Black Americans (1978). Department CHE, 3202 Doolittle Drive, Northbrook, Ill. 60062 ($49.95).

The World Almanac and Book of Facts (updated annually). Newspaper Enterprise Association, Inc., 230 Park Avenue, New York, N.Y. 10017 ($3.25). One of the leading one-volume information guides. A photocopied version of the 1868 edition is available for $2.95.

World Statistics in Brief (1977). United Nations, Room LX-2300, New York, N.Y. 10017 ($3.95). Presents key data on countries as well as on general topics like population, manufacturing, education, and agriculture.

See also the following related chapters in *The Help Book:*

ADOPTION AND FOSTER CARE
BUSINESS INFORMATION
CITIZEN ACTION
CIVIL RIGHTS AND DISCRIMINATION
EDUCATION
FINANCIAL ASSISTANCE
HEALTH
MEDIA AND COMMUNICATIONS
TRANSPORTATION AND TRAVEL
TELEPHONE DIRECTORY
ADDITIONAL RESOURCES

33

JUVENILE DELINQUENCY

They run away. They steal. They burglarize. They murder. They become lifetime criminals. They get straightened out. They take drugs. They deal in heroin. They band together. They strike alone.

Juvenile delinquency includes all these things. It also includes this particular story, told to the author by a nineteen-year-old freshman at a midwestern university:

It started when I was thirteen. My family was broken apart by my parents' separation. During that time I was in eighth grade and I had started associating with a lot of people who were getting involved with crime or drugs and other negative things. The big problem was just having something to do. First I got involved with drugs. I don't think I ever missed any drug. I had everything from speed to heroin.

We lived in a project and it was organized as far as crime was concerned. Say for instance if a couple of guys wanted to stick some place up, they would lend people guns. All of us stuck together and if you wanted to commit a crime then everyone else was supporting you. It was sort of like organized crime but on a small basis, just within the building.

This is what happened. Me and a couple of—well, they used to be my friends, they grew up with me—we got together during Christmas time. It's not that we needed the money, it was just that drugs were involved and we wanted them for pleasure, just for pleasure.

We went to a tavern. I walked in first and went all the way to the back. When we first came in the gun was all ready to fire. One of us was standing in the middle and the other one was standing by the door. We all told everyone, "This is a stickup. Put your hands against the wall. Don't nobody move." Two of us had the people against the wall while the other person was trying to get the money.

There was one of us standing by the record player and there was a man standing there. He was trying to punch the little buttons they have on the coin machine for the record player. He didn't see us come in and he wasn't paying any attention because the record was going and he couldn't hear anything. But then he saw us and he turned around and tried to grab the gun and the guy standing by him. At the same time the guy shot him. The guy fell to the floor and he started groaning. One of my friends panicked and ran out and the other one went out right after him. I was in there by myself and I could have been killed or anything could have happened.

Well, the thing about it was, I had to go past him because he's laying right in front of the door and he's just groaning, and what's going through my mind is, man, I'm involved in this and this man is laying there and he's dying and I was a part of this.

The police didn't come because no one called them and you couldn't hear the shot outside because they had two doors and each door deadens the sound. So I just walked outside and then from there on you could go down this alley that leads right to the building we lived in.

So it was a quick getaway and no one knew about it, and no one could identify me or the persons that were with me. I went home and gave the gun back. From then on police were looking for whoever done it but they didn't have any evidence. They caught up with us because the person that was supposed to be given the money gave himself up, and from there it led to me.

My sentence wasn't an amount of years because I was a juvenile then. I was nothing but thirteen years old. They charged me with armed robbery and murder but they said I was an accessory to it and a lot of other factors were involved. I was sent to a reformatory in Illinois and I was seen by a psychiatrist; after that I was going to therapy once a week. All the therapist did was to try to find what in my life was connected to me committing the crime and try to better me.

After I went to see this doctor again he said, "Well, you're ready to go," and when I went before the parole board they said, "No, you're not ready to go," so I had to spend something like six more months after I had finished something like four months in the institution.

I wanted to go to college, get my education, come out and be able to talk to different people that are involved in crime and are in prison. I try to talk to them and convince them that this is not the way to go. I try to make myself an example.

For help with a troubled or delinquent juvenile, contact your local police department, bureau of community or youth affairs, or city or county youth programs for direct assistance—counseling, activities, advice, referrals. Check with multipurpose national organizations that may have programs for juvenile delinquents at your local branch, such as the Salvation Army, YMCA/YWCA, YMHA/YWHA, Big Brothers/Big Sisters of America, Boy Scouts of America, Girl Scouts of America. (See listings in Chapter 10, *Children* or Chapter 40, *Multipurpose*

Organizations.) Free counseling—by therapists or social workers—may be available through your local mental health department (see Chapter 12, *Counseling*).

If an arrest has been made, but the crime is not a violent one, your local criminal justice program may have a victim-juvenile offender restitution program, whereby repayment or service to the victim (or a third party) may be an alternative to confinement in an institution. For example, the Victims Program of the Juvenile Bureau of the District Court of Tulsa, Oklahoma, brings together the victim and the juvenile offender. In addition to arranging for restitution to the victim, juveniles are given supportive counseling and jobs, such as working in schools, libraries, nursing homes, and the zoo, at minimum wage, to repay victims.

Other direct services to help juvenile offenders are operated independently from the criminal justice system. For example, SAJA, or Special Approaches in Juvenile Assistance (1743 Eighteenth Street, N.W., Washington, D.C. 20009), provides temporary and long-term residence and counseling for people between the ages of eleven and seventeen. A twenty-four-hour telephone counseling service, plus family counseling and publications are other forms of help offered to the troubled youth and his or her family. *SAJA Quarterly* ($15.00 a year contribution is asked) reports on the political, legal, social, and economic issues affecting young people, especially those labeled "juvenile offenders." Write for a sample issue, enclosing a self-addressed envelope, if you are interested in what they are all about or starting a similar program and newsletter in your community.

Other sources of local help for the juvenile offender are after-school programs run by the schools or volunteer police programs, such as the well-known Police Athletic League, Catholic Big Brothers of New York, Inc., or the following:

Education to Action Project
AFL-CIO Department of Community Services
815 Sixteenth Street, N.W.
Washington, D.C. 20006

In cooperation with the National Council on Crime and Delinquency (NCCD) this program is "specifically designed to divert children from a life of crime" and to educate the public about local juvenile justice facilities and operations. Started in 1969 at the one-day Institute on the Criminal Justice System held in Terre Haute, Indiana, it has been implemented in many other communities, including Akron, Ohio and Kokomo, Indiana.

There are thousands of programs for juvenile offenders; it would be impossible to list them all here. Two key sources to those local alternatives are:

International Halfway House Association
2525 Victory Parkway, Suite 101
Cincinnati, Ohio 45206

A nonprofit professional association with fifty state chapters to provide training, education, and information to those interested in residential treatment for the socially stigmatized—corrections, alcohol, drug, group homes, and mental health. They have regional workshops, a national directory with more than 3,500 listings, national institutes, and an annual conference. The association will answer written or telephone inquiries and make referrals to residential treatment services. Membership dues are $10.00 individual, $5.00 student, $50.00 agency.

LITERATURE: Flyer; *IHHA News*; *Directory of Halfway Houses and Group Homes for Troubled Children*, published annually (free).

Volunteer Programs in Prevention and Diversion, 2nd edition, by Timothy Fautsko and Ivan H. Scheier (1975). National Information Center on Volunteerism, P.O. Box 4179, Boulder, Colo. 80302. Lists local programs along with evaluations, such as Rebound Program (Kansas City, Mo.) and Keep a Child in School, Inc. (South Charleston, W. Va.). It also lists several national resource organizations and has an annotated bibliography.

The federal government provides referral information and conducts research on juvenile delinquency programs through the following agency:

Office of Juvenile Justice and Delinquency Prevention
U.S. Department of Justice
Law Enforcement Assistance Administration
633 Indiana Avenue, N.W., Room 442
Washington, D.C. 20531

An office designed to help states, localities, and public and private agencies develop and conduct effective delinquency prevention programs and to divert more juveniles from the juvenile justice process. It coordinates federal delinquency programs; provides for grants and other funds for action in the juvenile justice field; conducts research and evaluates existing programs; and provides technical assistance to agencies.

LITERATURE: *The Serious Juvenile Offender* (1978).

The following national organizations provide helpful literature on the problem of juvenile delinquency; write for a list of available publications:

Children's Defense Fund (CDF)
1520 New Hampshire Avenue, N.W.
Washington, D.C. 20036

A membership organization concerned with the rights of children, including the operation of juvenile courts.

Juvenile Rights Project
American Civil Liberties Union Foundation
22 East 40th Street
New York, N.Y. 10016

Publishes the *Children's Rights Report* ($15.00 a year for ten issues), which devotes much of its attention to juvenile delinquency. For example, the December 1977–January 1978 edition contained the results of a national survey, "Are State Legislatures 'Getting Tough' With Teenage Delinquents?"

National Association of Counties (NACo)
Criminal Justice Program
1735 New York Avenue, N.W.
Washington, D.C. 20006

A membership organization that provides information to local and county governments on juvenile justice and community-based corrections.

National Center for Youth Law
693 Mission Street
San Francisco, Calif. 94105

3701 Lindell Boulevard
St. Louis, Mo. 63108

A legal services support center that provides expertise in juvenile law to local legal services and defender programs. The National Center does not normally work directly with indigent juveniles and parents involved in juvenile court proceedings.

LITERATURE: *Children in Jails* ($3.00); *The Juvenile Court* by Piersma, Ganousis, and Kramer ($4.00); *Law and Tactics in Juvenile Cases*, 3rd edition ($30.00).

National Council of Juvenile Court Judges
P.O. Box 8978
Reno, Nev. 89507

A membership organization whose main goal is the improvement of the country's juvenile justice system.

LITERATURE: *Juvenile Justice* (quarterly); *Juvenile Court Digest* (monthly).

National Council on Crime and Delinquency
Continental Plaza
411 Hackensack Avenue
Hackensack, N.J. 07601

A membership organization of concerned laypersons, criminal justice personnel, and educators that sponsors projects to aid in the reduction of crime and the prevention of delinquency and also acts as an information clearinghouse in the juvenile justice/delinquency area. Maintains an extensive library.

LITERATURE: *Crime & Delinquency*, quarterly ($10.00 a year subscription; free with $15.00 membership in NCCD); *Journal of Research in Crime and Delinquency*, two issues a year ($10.00 a year subscription; $5.00 single copies); send for publications price list for low-cost pamphlets and reports in the juvenile delinquency area.

National Youth Work Alliance (NYWA)
1346 Connecticut Avenue, N.W.
Washington, D.C. 20009

A nonprofit organization concerned with youth advocacy that has a Juvenile Justice Project. (See complete listing in Chapter 34, *Kidnapping, Missing Persons, and Runaways*.)

The following state agencies coordinate youth services for the prevention of juvenile delinquency and crime; they also provide help and financial aid to those municipalities that want to start youth programs and make referrals to training schools, youth centers, youth camps, and urban homes:

Department of Youth Services
Mt. Meigs Campus
Montgomery, Ala. 36057

Division of Corrections
Department of Health and Social Services
129 Alaska Office Building
Pouch H-03
Juneau, Alaska 99811

Department of Corrections
1601 West Jefferson Street
Phoenix, Ariz. 85007

Division of Youth Services
Department of Human Services
1320 C Brookwood Drive
Little Rock, Ark. 72203

Department of the Youth Authority
4241 Williamsborough Drive
Sacramento, Calif. 95823

Division of Youth Services
Department of Institutions
4150 South Lowell Boulevard
Denver, Colo. 80236

Department of Children and Youth Services
345 Main Street
Hartford, Conn. 06115

Community Based Services Juvenile
  Correction
Department of Correction
821 Franklin Street
Wilmington, Del. 19806

Juvenile Delinquency Services
Social Rehabilitation Administration
122 C Street, N.W.
Washington, D.C. 20001

Youth Services Program Office
Department of Health and Rehabilitative
  Services
1323 Winewood Boulevard
Tallahassee, Fla. 32301

Division of Youth Services
Department of Human Resources
618 Ponce de Leon Avenue, N.E.
Atlanta, Ga. 30308

State Law Enforcement and Juvenile
  Delinquency Planning Agency
Office of the Governor
412 Kamamalu Building
250 South King Street
Honolulu, Hawaii 96813

Youth Rehabilitation Services
Division of Welfare
Department of Health and Welfare
700 West State Street
Boise, Idaho 83720

Division of Juvenile Institution and Field
  Services
Department of Corrections
P.O. Box 246
St. Charles, Ill. 60174

Youth Authority
Department of Correction
804 State Office Building
Indianapolis, Ind. 46204

Bureau of Child Advocacy
Division of Community Services
Department of Social Services
Hoover Building
Des Moines, Iowa 50319

Division of Children, Youth and Others
Department of Social and Rehabilitation
  Services
State Office Building
Topeka, Kans. 66612

Juvenile Delinquency Section
Executive Office of Staff Services
Department of Justice
209 St. Clair Street
Frankfort, Ky. 40601

Office of Youth Services
P.O. Box 44141
Baton Rouge, La. 70804

Bureau of Corrections
Department of Mental Health and Corrections
411 State Office Building
Augusta, Me. 04333

Juvenile Services Administration
Department of Health and Mental Hygiene
201 West Preston Street
Baltimore, Md. 21201

Department of Youth Services
294 Washington Street
Boston, Mass. 02108

Office of Children and Youth Services
Bureau of Social Services
Department of Social Services
300 South Capitol Avenue
Lansing, Mich. 48926

Juvenile Programs/Department of Corrections
430 Metro Square Building
7th and Robert Streets
St. Paul, Minn. 55101

Department of Youth Services
407 Woolfolk State Office Building
Jackson, Miss. 39201

Division of Youth Services
Department of Social Services
402 Dix Road
Jefferson City, Mo. 65101

Department of Institutions
1539 Eleventh Avenue
Helena, Mont. 59601

Youth Service Agency
Department of Human Resources
600 Kinkead Building
505 East King Street
Capitol Complex
Carson City, Nev. 89710

Governor's Commission on Crime and
 Delinquency
169 Manchester Street
Concord, N.H. 03301

Department of Human Services
State Office Building
135 West Hanover Street
Trenton, N.J. 08625

New Mexico Committee on Children and
 Youth
P.O. Box 26584
Albuquerque, N.M. 87125

New Mexico Boys' School
Department of Corrections
P.O. Box 38
Springer, N.M. 87747

Division for Youth
84 Holland Avenue
Albany, N.Y. 12208

Division of Youth Services
P.O. Box 21487
Raleigh, N.C. 29221

Community Services Division
Social Service Board
State Capitol
Bismarck, N.D. 58505

Youth Commission
35 East Gay Street
Columbus, Ohio 43215

Department of Institutions, Social, and
 Rehabilitative Services
Sequoyah Memorial Office Building
2400 North Lincoln Boulevard
P.O. Box 25352
Oklahoma City, Okla. 73125

Juvenile Corrections Services
Department of Human Resources
2450 Strong Road
Salem, Ore. 97310

Office of Youth Services and Correction
 Education
Executive House
2nd and Chestnut Streets
Harrisburg, Pa. 17101

Department of Corrections
250 Benefit Street
Providence, R.I. 02903

Division of Youth Services
P.O. Box 21487
Columbia, S.C. 29221

Office of Youth Services
South Dakota Supreme Court
Pierre, S.D. 57501

Youth Services Division
Department of Correction
First American Center
326 Union Street
Nashville, Tenn. 37219

Texas Youth Council
P.O. Box 9999
Austin, Tex. 78766

Juvenile Court
339 South 6th East Street
Salt Lake City, Utah 84102

Department of Corrections
79 River Street
Montpelier, Vt. 05602

Division of Youth Services
Department of Corrections
22 East Cary Street
Richmond, Va. 23219

Division of Juvenile Rehabilitation
Department of Social and Health Services
Mail Stop OB-42J
Olympia, Wash. 98504

Department of Corrections
714 State Office Building 3
1800 Washington Street, East
Charleston, W.Va. 25305

Juvenile Delinquency
Room 1000 Wilson Street State Office
   Building
1 West Wilson Street
Madison, Wis. 53702

Planning Committee on Criminal
   Administration
Barrett Building, 4th Floor
2301 Central Avenue
Cheyenne, Wyo. 82002

ADDITIONAL LITERATURE

Children Who Kill by Lucy Freeman and Dr. Wilfred C. Hulse (1962). Berkley Publishing Corporation, 200 Madison Avenue, New York, N.Y. 10016. Case histories of child murderers.

Children Without Justice by Edward Wakin, foreword by William O. Douglas (1975). The National Council of Jewish Women, 15 East 26th Street, New York, N.Y. 10010 ($2.00). Based on research gathered by 3,000 council volunteers in thirty-four states, with sections on arrest, detention homes, courts, probation, and reforms and remedies. It emphasizes the importance of treatment rather than punishment, and concludes that the system of juvenile justice is failing the young.

Children's Rights Report, Juvenile Rights Project of the American Civil Liberties Union Foundation, 22 East 40th Street, New York, N.Y. 10016 ($2.00 an issue; 10 issues a year; $15.00 yearly subscription). Legislative updates, essays, critiques of the juvenile justice system. Issues have included national surveys and position reports on indeterminate sentencing of juveniles.

Delinquency and Rehabilitation Report, % Grafton Publications, Inc., 667 Madison Avenue, New York, N.Y. 10021. Newsletter.

Directory of Halfway Houses and Group Homes for Troubled Children (updated annually). P.O. Box 4021, Tallahassee, Fla. 32303 (free). Provides a comprehensive, current reference for organizations and individuals seeking information on community based programs. It is designed to aid in the development of viable and realistic alternatives to conventional correctional care for troubled and troubling youth.

The Hard Core Juvenile Offender by Raymond L. Manella (1977). National Council of Juvenile Court Judges, P.O. Box 8978, Reno, Nev. 89597. Defines the hard core or hyper-aggressive delinquent and examines current methods of dealing with hard core juvenile offenders.

Justice for Our Children: An Examination of Juvenile Delinquency Rehabilitation Programs by Dennis Romig (1978). Lexington Books, 125 Spring Street, Lexington, Mass. 02173 ($18.00). Examines the literature as well as the basic approaches to the rehabilitation of juveniles now used—behavior modification, group counseling, family therapy, diversion, vocational and work programs, residential programs, and others.

Juvenile Delinquency: A Basic Manual for County Officials edited by Aurora Gallagher (1976). National Association of Counties Research Foundation, 1735 New York Avenue, N.W., Washington, D.C. 20006. Booklet with facts about juvenile delinquency, brief analyses of a few diverse programs, helpful appendices on Supreme Court decisions affecting juveniles, and a glossary of terms.

Juvenile Justice and Injustice by Margaret O. Hyde (1977). Franklin Watts, Inc., 730 Fifth Avenue, New York, N.Y. 10019 ($6.90). Written for grades 7 and up, the book discusses who is a delinquent, gangs, juvenile justice, wanderers, wastrels, muggers, and others in juvenile court, with helpful resources and a list of state planning agencies.

Juvenile Justice Digest (twice monthly). Washington Crime News Services, 7620 Little River Turnpike, Annandale, Va. 22003 ($60.00 a year). Summary of news and program information in the juvenile delinquency prevention field.

Juvenile Victimization: The Institutional Paradox by Clemens Bartollas, Stuart J. Miller, and Simon Dinitz (1976). Halsted Press, John Wiley & Sons, 605 Third Avenue, New York, N.Y. 10016 ($17.50). ". . . vividly informs the reader about the ways in which juvenile inmates victimize each other . . ." (*Social Work*).

National Register of Volunteer Jobs in Court Settings (1967). National Information Center on Volunteers in Courts, P.O. Box 2150, Boulder, Colo. 80302 ($3.00).

A Nation of Lords: The Autobiography of the Vice Lords by David Dawley (1973). Doubleday-Anchor Original, Doubleday and Company, Garden City, N.Y. 11530 ($1.95). Dawley tells how he helped the Vice Lords of Chicago develop from a street gang to a street corporation.

Serving Youth as Volunteers by Ivan H. Scheier, Ph.D., and Judith Lake Berry (1972). National Information Center on Volunteerism, Inc., P.O. Box 4179, Boulder, Colo. 80302. A booklet for the concerned citizen on how to do something about juvenile delinquency by active volunteer involvement.

Supreme Court Decisions and Juvenile Justice by Noah Weinstein (1973). National Council of Juvenile Court Judges, P.O. Box 8978, Reno, Nev. 89507.

The Violent Gang, revised edition, by Lewis Yablonsky (1970). Penguin Books, Inc., 7110 Ambassador Road, Baltimore, Md. 21207 ($1.95). A vivid account and analysis of a gang killing of an innocent fifteen-year-old non-gang youth.

Volunteer Programs in Prevention and Diversion by Timothy F. Fautsko and Ivan H. Scheier (1975). National Information Center on Volunteerism, P.O. Box 4179, Boulder, Colo. 80302. Directory developed from a mailing to 293 programs that divides programs into a variety of approaches, lists basic details, and has extensive descriptions, evaluations, annotated bibliography, and a follow-up resource section.

Weeping in the Playtime of Others by Kenneth Wooden (1976). McGraw-Hill Book Company, 1221 Avenue of the Americas, New York, N.Y. 10020 ($3.95). An exposé of America's incarcerated children—status offenders, the interstate commerce of children, *parens patriae*, the juvenile incarceration structure, and runaways. Bibliography.

Films

"I Live in Prison " (1976). Learning Corporation of America, 1350 Avenue of the Americas, New York, N.Y. 10019 (sale, $350.00; rental, $35.00). Three convicts, members of Prison Preventers, tell their stories to a group and answer questions from that audience, led by actor George Peppard. One inmate is serving a life sentence for armed robbery and murder; another has been in and out of prison since age ten for armed robberies committed to support his drug habit; and the third, beginning at age nine, mugged people.

Juvenile Justice Series. MTI Teleprograms, Inc. 4825 North Scott Street, Schiller Park, Ill. 60176 (sale, $1,395; rental, $50.00 for each film). Four films in a worthwhile teaching series: "Delinquency: Street Violence"; "Delinquency: The Process Begins"; "Delinquency: The Chronic Offender"; "Delinquency: Prevention and Treatment." All four films are documentaries using actual interviews with delinquents, victims, and administrators. Two study guides are available for use with the films: *Instructor's Manual: Issues in Juvenile Delinquency* ($4.95) and *Historical Overview and Critical Assessment of Juvenile Justice System* ($1.75).

"The Shopping Bag Lady," starring Mildred Dunnock, written and directed by Bert Salzman (sale, $295.00; rental, $25.00). A 21-

minute sensitive film about the cruel treatment of a Central Park shopping bag lady by a few adolescents until Emily, age fourteen, discovers the shopping bag lady has a history. Learning about this older woman helps Emily appreciate her own grandmother, whose habits she had hated.

See also the following related chapters in *The Help Book:*

**ALCOHOLISM
CHILD ABUSE
CHILDREN
COUNSELING
COURTS
CRIME PREVENTION
CRIME VICTIMS AND WITNESSES
DRUGS, SMOKING, AND DRUG ABUSE
KIDNAPPING, MISSING PERSONS, AND RUNAWAYS
LAW ENFORCEMENT
LEGAL SERVICES
MENTAL HEALTH
MULTIPURPOSE ORGANIZATIONS
OFFENDERS AND EX-OFFENDERS
PARENTING
VOLUNTEERISM**

34

KIDNAPPING, MISSING PERSONS, AND RUNAWAYS

KIDNAPPING

Unlike the missing person or runaway—who may be absent by his or her own choice—the kidnapped individual has been the victim of a crime. In such a situation, the local police should be contacted immediately for direct help and, possibly, the Federal Bureau of Investigation or a private investigator (see Chapter 17, *Crime Victims and Witnesses*, and Chapter 35, *Law Enforcement*). Kidnapping is mainly handled at the local level, but with the increase in worldwide terrorism, an international research unit has been set up, the Committee on a Convention Against Taking of Hostages (Public Inquiries Unit, Office of Public Information, United Nations, New York, N.Y. 10017). It issues press releases describing their conferences. Companies are also adding training programs for their employees on how to handle a hostage situation. Other companies are adding kidnapping to their insurance coverage. One company provided cast insurance for anyone kidnapped during preproduction or filming of a movie. Police departments are developing experts in hostage-negotiating, as they warn the press to "stay out of hostage negotiations."

It is estimated that there are as many as 100,000 victims a year of another form of kidnapping—"childsnatching" or "child stealing," the taking of a child or children by his/her or their noncustodial parents. This is still a "gray" area of the law since the 1934 Lindbergh Law exempted the taking of a child by his or her own parents from the definition of the crime of kidnapping. Little legal recourse is available to the parent whose child is "stolen" and his or her identity or whereabouts is concealed temporarily or forever.

The following national organizations and federal agencies provide information and suggestions to those parents whose children have been taken by their noncustodial parents:

Children's Rights, Inc.
3443 Seventeenth Street, N.W.
Washington, D.C. 20010

Counseling, referrals, and a crisis hotline are available to parents whose former spouses have taken their children. Children's Rights advocates changing the law so that parental stealing of children is a federal offense; it serviced approximately 1,500 victims in 1977.

LITERATURE: Fact sheets; *Our Greatest Resource—Our Children,* quarterly newsletter; *Children's Rights, Inc., Chapter Guide.*

Committee on the Judiciary
Congress of the United States
House of Representatives
Washington, D.C. 20515

A bill that would allow the Justice Department and the FBI to become involved in the investigation of child-snatching by noncustodial parents has failed to pass Congress. The subcommittee to which these bills have been referred reports that they received about six letters a week on the subject during July of 1977; they are investigating other approaches to the problem, besides federal legislation, such as the Uniform Child Custody Jurisdiction Act, drafted by the National Conference of Commissioners on Uniform State Laws in 1968, and adopted by Arizona, California, Colorado, Delaware, Hawaii, Iowa, Maryland, Massachusetts, Michigan, North Dakota, Oregon, Pennsylvania, Wisconsin, and Wyoming. That law says, among other things, that in the interest of the child all parties are bound by a custody decree of the state that has exercised jurisdiction. Copies of the act may be secured from West Publishing Company—Uniform Laws, annotated.

The subcommittee is also encouraging the Parent Finder Service of the U.S. Department of Health, Education, and Welfare to broaden their activities to finding a parent who has absconded with a child.

Anyone who wishes a copy of the proposed kidnapping/childsnatching bill should write to the Committee on the Judiciary. Then, if they support the bill, they should address a letter, stating that, to the committee, who will make that support, or disagreement, known to the appropriate body.

LITERATURE: Copies of any of the hearings regarding the proposed bill may be ordered free from Judiciary Committee, Publications Office, B-3708 RHOB, Washington, D.C. 20515. Copies of the bills themselves may be received free from the Document Room, House of Representatives, Washington, D.C. 20515.

Legal Division
Passport Office
1425 K Street, N.W.
Washington, D.C. 20415

The Passport Office states the following:

"If you have been awarded custody of your child (children) or if you have a restraining order from a court which forbids the departure of your child from this country, and if you fear that the other parent may try to snatch your child and take him or her out of the country, you should immediately submit to the Passport Office a certified copy of the court order awarding you legal custody or restraining the removal of your child from the country and a written request to the Passport Office to deny passport services to your child.

"If the Passport Office receives your notification before any passport has been issued, the Passport Office will deny issuance of a passport to your child should the other parent apply on the child's behalf. At the same time, the Passport Office will notify you that a passport application was submitted. The Passport Office will be able to provide this service until the child reaches the age of majority (eighteen). However, the Passport Office is unable to deny issuance of a passport if the application is made abroad.

"There is one warning—if a passport is issued it may not be revoked and the other parent may retain it until it expires.

"This service is strictly an accommodation. Other than this, there is little the Passport Office can do to prevent childsnatching, although between fifteen to twenty-five new inquiries are received from parents each week about this problem."

United Parents of Absconded Children
Wolf Run Road, Box 127-A
Cuba, N.Y. 14727

Parent victims of "child-stealing" (who, preferably, have court-ordered custody) are given counseling and general information on their legal rights and are referred to other agencies. Established in January 1975, United Parents serviced 300 victims in 1975.

LITERATURE: Copies of pertinent articles; fact sheet.

MISSING PERSONS

Most missing persons are eighteen years old or younger, elderly or senile, or they have a history of mental disturbance. Each city or town will have a different definition for when they consider a person missing long enough to warrant their intervention, but basically the first place to start the search is on the local level. Except in extenuating circumstances where a private investigator or the Federal Bureau of Investigation is initially notified (kidnapping across state lines or where there are specific reasons not to get the local police involved), the missing persons bureau of your local police department will begin the search. In 1976, of the 16,797 persons that were reported missing in New York City, nearly 13,000 were young runaways who returned home within a few days. Since the majority of missing persons turn up within twenty-four to forty-eight hours, most missing persons bureaus will not start a search until after that amount of time has elapsed, unless any of the following circumstances are involved: a child is believed missing; a person who is mentally or physically ill enough to require hospitalization is missing; a person is missing who is a possible drowning victim; a person who has expressed an intention to commit suicide is missing; or someone is missing without any apparent reason under circumstances that could indicate foul play. Local governments will not usually investigate the missing person for whom a warrant has been issued or who is wanted for the commission of a crime or anyone over eighteen who has voluntarily left home because of domestic, financial, or similar reasons.

Because the rules of the missing persons bureau might prevent an immediate search for a particular person missing, you might want to consider hiring a private investigator as soon as possible. That, unfortunately, can be an expensive step since a good private eye in a large city will get $200-to-$300 a day, plus expenses. But if cost does not deter you, how do you go about finding outside assistance to precede or supplement the local police department's detective assigned to the case? Where do you go for help? You could look in the telephone directory under detective agencies or ask the police department to recommend someone, since many retired detectives go into private work. You could also contact this national organization for a referral to a member detective agency in your area:

National Council of Investigation and Security Services (NCISS)
1730 Pennsylvania Avenue, N.W., Suite 1150
Washington, D.C. 20006

Started in 1975, there are sixteen state chapters of this national organization. Its members are persons, partnerships, or corporations that operate as a private contract service in the investigation or guard and patrol business within the United States and who comply with the Council's Code of Ethics and Standards of Conduct.

LITERATURE: *NCISS Report*, monthly newsletter; free descriptive brochure.

RUNAWAYS

It is estimated that every year between 600,000 and 1 million children run away from home in the United States. Why do they run away? Many are fleeing intolerable home situations—sexually abusive fathers, physically abusive parents or siblings, alcoholic parents, emotional neglect, and so forth. Or there may be problems at school, with a boy friend or girl friend, or with a peer group or gang. What all these youngsters have in common is that they are troubled; running away seems the only solution. Their backgrounds vary widely from the very rich to the middle-class to the very poor. Runaways are getting younger every year; the average age has dropped from sixteen to fourteen years old.

If runaways are driven to flight because of negative treatment at home, rarely do they find it any different "in the street," especially if they become involved in the criminal justice system or the social services department. Until the recent growth of national runaway hotlines and free shelters, runaways were incarcerated as if they had committed crimes. But running away—a so-called *status offense*—is still handled inconsistently by incarceration, innovation, or denial of the problem or the children involved. Unfortunately, it usually takes a tragedy—such as the 1967 East Village murder of an eighteen-year-old Greenwich, Connecticut, runaway or the 1973 homosexual mass slayings of twenty-one runaways in Houston, Texas—for the public to become aware of the vulnerability of the runaway and his or her needs for shelter, counseling, and understanding.

Thousands of shelters have been established around the country to provide emergency or long-term housing, food, and counseling for runaways. There are directories that list those local services. What they offer varies widely.

The following local services give an idea of the type of facilities that ideally could be found:

Casa de los Amigos
2640 Bachman Boulevard
Dallas, Tex. 75220

A short-term residential counseling program for runaway young people providing a "breathing space" for up to thirteen young people for up to thirty days. There are family-style living arrangements; individual, group, and family counseling services; nonresidential confidential counseling; referrals; weekly volunteer training sessions; self-defense classes; in-service program for counselors and psychotherapists; rap sessions; follow-ups on ex-residents; and a job bank program. Two hundred fifty runaways were provided with services in 1976.

LITERATURE: Fact sheet; *Our Newsletter*, monthly with writings by residents and information.

Voyage House, Inc.
Suite 1600, 1700 Market Street
Philadelphia, Pa. 19103

"*Change-of-address slip.*"

In 1971, Voyage House was organized as a private, nonprofit corporation to provide aid and assistance to runaway youths and their families. More than three hundred youths and families are assisted at the Counseling Center; the Voyage Outreach Programs aid hundreds more. There is a twenty-four-hour emergency hotline; shelter is available to thirty dependent, neglected and homeless youths. A tutoring program is sponsored through the Community Voyage School. The staff has provided assistance to many public and private child-care agencies and organizations in Philadelphia as well as other parts of the country, traditionally without charge.

For direct help if you are a runaway, contact either of the following national, free, telephone hotline and counseling services:

National Runaway Switchboard
2210 North Halsted
Chicago, Ill. 60614
Toll-free, 24-hour hot line: 800-621-4000
In Illinois: 800-972-6004

Trained volunteers will provide referrals and information for runaway youths around the country and will also serve as a neutral channel through which runaways can make some type of contact with their families. It is run by Metro-Help, a referral, information, and crisis intervention service in the Chicago area since 1971.

LITERATURE: Fact sheet; annual report.

Operation Peace of Mind (OPM)
P.O. Box 52896
Houston, Tex. 77052
Toll-free, 24-hour number: 800-231-6946
In Texas: 800-392-3352

Funded through the Texas governor's office, this telephone service was started after the Houston mass murders in which so many runaway juveniles were found dead. OPM acts as a liaison between parents and children and is completely confidential. Children call in and leave some kind of message for their parents; trained volunteers call the parent; and runaways are encouraged to call back and ask for a return message from their families. Referrals are made to pertinent local social services around the country.

LITERATURE: Free brochure available from First Lady's Volunteer Program, Office of the Governor, 411 West 13th Street, Austin, Tex. 78701.

For information about runaway shelters and related matters, contact:

National Youth Work Alliance (NYWA)
1346 Connecticut Avenue, N.W.
Washington, D.C. 20016

Founded in 1973, this nonprofit organization is dedicated to the development of a variety of social services for youth, particularly those which include youth participation in the design and provision of services. It offers training and technical assistance to youth services staff; free advice; on-site or extensive services for a negotiated fee; youth advocacy; technical assistance to forty runaway programs in the eastern United States; Juvenile Justice Project; developing and staffing the National Network of Runaway and Youth Services, which currently has a membership of more than ninety-three runaway centers; public education; youth-related conferences; consultations; Youth Alternatives Clearinghouse; and a library.

LITERATURE: *Runaways and Runaway Centers, A Bibliography* (free); *Youth Alternatives*, monthly newsletter ($10.00); *National Directory of Runaway Centers* (February 1976, $4.00).

ADDITIONAL LITERATURE

"A Cool-Headed Cop Who Saves Hostages" by Barbara Gelb, in the *New York Times Magazine* (Apr. 17, 1977), pages 30–33, 87–91. A profile of Frank Boly and his squad as well as a chart of the "ABC's of Negotiating."

Criminal Investigation: Basic Perspectives, 2nd edition, by Paul Weston and Kenneth M. Wells (1974). Prentice-Hall, Inc., Englewood Cliffs, N.J. 07632 ($12.95). A textbook geared to police officers but with some interesting historical material for the layperson and practical information for the amateur detective.

Hearing Before the Subcommittee on Crime of the Committee on the Judiciary, Amendments to the Federal Kidnapping Statute, Committee, House of Representatives, 93rd Congress, 2nd Session on H.R. 4191 and H.R. 8722 (February 27 and April 10, 1974), Serial No. 38. Available from Superintendent of Documents, U.S. Government Printing Office, Washington, D.C. 20402. Background on existing and suggested changes in kidnapping laws to protect children from absconsion by noncustodial parents.

Hostage Negotiation For Police. Motorola Teleprograms, Inc., 4825 North Scott Street, Suite 23, Schiller Park, Ill. 60176 (sale, $750.00; weekly rental, $125.00). A fifty-one-minute, 16mm sound/color film on hostage negotiating that would be pertinent to these audiences: law enforcement personnel, government officials, criminal justice students, security executives, and corrections personnel.

Hostage: You Could be Involved! Av-Com Law Enforcement Media, 3075 Alta Laguna Boulevard, Laguna Beach, Calif. 92651 (sale, $150.00; ten-day preview fee, $25.00, applied to purchase). A 35mm slide-audio cassette presentation of the types of hostages taken and what you could do if in that situation. It is suitable for crime prevention seminars sponsored by law enforcement organizations, banks, or community organizations.

Kids on the Run: The Stories of Seven Teenage Runaways by James R. Berry (1978). Four Winds Press, 50 West 44th Street, New York, N.Y. 10036 ($5.95). Written for ages twelve and up, this is a question-and-answer interview format book on runaways.

National Directory of Runaway Programs (1976). National Youth Work Alliance, 1346 Connecticut Avenue, N.W. Washington, D.C. 20016 ($4.00). State-by-state directory listing each program, mailing address, and sponsoring agent as well as what the facilities are, house rules, services offered, and number of runaways helped each year.

On the Run, produced by Richter McBride. Motorola Teleprograms, Inc., 4825 North Scott Street, Schiller Park, Ill. 60176 (sale, $395.00; rental, $50.00). An excellent 27-minute documentary film about runaways that deals with the reasons youths run away and some of the programs available to help them.

Perspectives on Runaway Youth: A Special Report by Ken Libertoff (1976). Massachusetts Committee on Children and Youth, 14 Beacon Street, Suite 706, Boston, Mass. 02108 (free). Discusses Margaret Saltonstall's 1973 publication *Runaways and Street Children in Massachusetts;* outlines "Recent Developments" regarding runaway youths, such as the National Network and Project Place (Boston).

The Runaway Response System: A Team Approach to Brief Family Therapy by Richard Carson, Raymond Rivera, and David Stewart (1975). Youth in Crisis, Inc., 6737 West 34th Street, Berwyn, Ill. ($2.00). A study of adolescent runaways referred to Youth in Crisis, a service bureau in Cook County; it is a typescript for the student or a program director.

Runaways by Anna Kosof, with an introduction by Sen. Birch Bayh (1977). Franklin Watts, Inc., 730 Fifth Avenue, New York, N.Y. 10019 ($6.90). Of the one million young people who run away each year, 188,000 are arrested for that offense. This book has profiles of the runaways and their parents and is written for grades 7 and up.

The Youngest Outlaws: Runaways in America by Arnold P. Rubin, introduction by Sen. Birch Bayh (1976). Julian Messner, 1230 Avenue of the Americas, New York, N.Y. 10020 ($6.29). Runaway case studies and information on getting help.

See also the following related chapters in *The Help Book:*

ADOPTION AND FOSTER CARE
ALCOHOLISM
BATTERED ADULTS
CHILD ABUSE
CHILDREN
COUNSELING
COURTS
CRIME PREVENTION
CRIME VICTIMS AND WITNESSES
JUVENILE DELINQUENCY
LAW ENFORCEMENT
LEGAL SERVICES
PARENTING
RAPE AND SEXUAL ASSAULT
SUICIDE PREVENTION

35

LAW ENFORCEMENT

There are more than 400,000 local and state police and sheriffs in the more than 13,000 law enforcement agencies throughout the United States. The Kojaks, Serpicos, and Starsky and Hutches are the exceptions; most police officers are average people who do an above-average job. Two police officers share their backgrounds and some of their views:

> I became a policeman because it offered me more job security and better opportunities for advancement. I was then twenty-five and working in a bank. My father was an influence in my going for a city job—I had also applied to the fire department. I had an uncle who was a retired cop.
>
> I pride myself in treating people as I find them. I do feel threatened by a potential psycho, someone you can't reason with, someone who's under the influence of alcohol, whether he's the president of a corporation or the local bum. I feel that in the area of having to regulate noncriminal behavior—traffic and summons work—that it can become burdensome and frustrating. People resent being controlled in those areas, and they ask you why you're not out fighting crime. Fortunately, other agencies are starting to pick up our functions in those areas.
>
> The whole criminal justice system needs renovating. I wouldn't know where to start. There's very little coordination and cooperation between the court and the police. I'm sure this has a lot to do with the work load. If we can cut down the amount of people who come into the system, and at least concentrate on recidivists and those who commit the more serious crimes, we'd probably be better off. At least we'd make a dent in the system, rather than trying to attack the whole system at one time.

For free information about your police department, call or write the public information officer at your local precinct. He or she will either answer your ques-

WE'VE BEEN ASKED
About Making a "Citizen's Arrest"

Security guards, shopkeepers and ordinary citizens often consider making a "citizen's arrest" when they see a person they suspect of a crime. This is especially true during the Christmas season, when shoplifting escalates. Just what is a citizen's arrest?

It is the action of someone without law-enforcement powers holding another person in custody in the belief that the suspect has violated a law.

Can you detain a fellow citizen for any suspected infraction?

The laws vary from State to State. Generally, in felony cases, or serious crimes, you must have what a judge would consider reasonable grounds for believing that the person you are arresting committed the offense. This usually means seeing the crime or having reliable information that the suspect was involved.

How about lesser crimes?

Usually, misdemeanors must be committed in your presence to justify a citizen's arrest. As for traffic offenses and violations of city law, authorities encourage witnesses to report lawbreakers, but citizen's arrests are frequently not permitted. Check with your local prosecutor.

Can force be used?

Policemen warn that citizens make arrests at their own risk. "In a one-on-one situation, a criminal is likely to resist with force, because if he beats you he's probably home free," says Richard S. Brooks, an attorney for the Washington, D.C., police.

How long can a suspect legally be held in custody by a citizen?

Most States require you to call police as soon as possible after making a citizen's arrest. Some have time limits, such as 30 minutes or an hour.

When you turn over to authorities a person you have arrested, is your responsibility ended?

You are likely to be a key witness. Your presence may be required at the police station, before a grand jury, or at a trial or any other court action necessary to prosecute the matter. Don't make an arrest if you aren't willing to follow up, police say.

Do you take any risks in making a citizen's arrest?

Definitely. If a crime hasn't been committed or the person you detained was not involved, you could face a damage suit for "false imprisonment" or even kidnaping. If you use what a judge or jury later says is force not justified by the circumstances, you could lose a civil or criminal-assault case.

Suppose you're positive that the arrest is legally valid?

You are probably safe, but that may not stop your target from suing you if he is later acquitted for technical reasons or even if he is convicted. You will likely win the case, but only after going to the trouble and considerable expense of defending yourself.

Do law-enforcement authorities encourage citizen's arrests?

Yes, but only when a citizen knows the law, is not putting himself in great physical danger, and is aware of the pitfalls. If you believe that the suspect can be identified and arrested later by police, concentrate on recalling details of the incident and don't worry about making an arrest.

Do security guards or merchants have greater arrest powers than do private citizens?

Security guards frequently are deputized to act during their working hours as if they were policemen. This way, they usually have more powers to make arrests for crimes they did not witness. And nearly all States have laws allowing shopkeepers and their employes to stop and question persons they suspect of shoplifting.

Do retailers take the same risks as do all other citizens making arrests?

Usually not. Most States give merchants immunity from civil or criminal charges that could arise out of detention of shoplifting suspects. But the laws protect only merchants who act in a "reasonable manner." In practice, this means that tangible or circumstantial evidence is needed to back up an arrest—not merely a suspicion that a customer stole an item.

Citizens who make arrests risk injuries, lawsuits.

Does the power to make a citizen's arrest include the authority to search a person for evidence of a crime?

The shoplifting laws generally allow merchants to search suspects for goods believed to be stolen. In other situations, the law varies among the States. When an arrest is lawful, evidence from a "reasonable" search is usually admissible in court. Several States have even endorsed the principle that private citizens may seize evidence in cases in which police would have to obtain a warrant.

Do law-enforcement officers themselves ever make a citizen's arrest?

Federal agents and State police often do it when they see a violation of a law they're not empowered to enforce. Experts estimate that, including local policemen away from home, more than 1 million officials are eligible to use citizen's-arrest authority.

Are ordinary citizens increasingly using their arrest powers?

No one knows. But experts point to an increase in citizen crime-fighting activities. Says M. Cherif Bassiouni, a law professor at De Paul University: "There is a growing number of people who are becoming increasingly active in self-protection and the protection of others." He expects the number of persons making a citizen's arrest to rise accordingly.

*Reprinted with permission from U.S. News & World Report, Dec. 12, 1977, page 56, copyright © 1977 U.S. News & World Report, Inc.

476 / THE HELP BOOK

tions on the phone or send you descriptive materials on the police department, crime prevention, and how citizens can help the police.

Your local precinct may also be able to refer you to the headquarters for the auxiliary police organization, if there is one in your community. These unarmed but trained men and women voluntarily patrol suburban and urban streets on foot or in private cars. They may wear special uniforms, carry walkie-talkies, or use nightsticks. But since dress, procedures, schedules, qualifications, training programs, and law-enforcement tools vary with each force, consult your civilian police department for specific details. In New York City, for example, there is a Minute Men organization of civilian Radio Taxi patrols whereby cab drivers aid the police at the rate of over 2,000 calls a year. Participating in your area's auxiliary police force may be a gratifying way to personally help in the reduction and prevention of crime in your community.

The following are the state agencies for police, which will provide direct help and information:

Department of Public Safety
500 Dexter Avenue
Montgomery, Ala. 36104

Division of State Troopers
Department of Public Safety
P.O. Box 6188 Annex
Anchorage, Alaska 99502

Department of Public Safety
2010 West Encanto Boulevard
Phoenix, Ariz. 85005

State Police
Department of Public Safety
3703 West Roosevelt Road
Little Rock, Ark. 72214

State Police
Department of General Services
1025 P Street
Sacramento, Calif. 95814

State Patrol
Department of Highways
4201 East Arkansas Avenue
Denver, Colo. 80222

State Police Department
100 Washington Street
Hartford, Conn. 06106

Division of State Police
Department of Public Safety
State Police Headquarters
Route 13
Dover, Del. 19901

Metropolitan Police Department
Municipal Center
300 Indiana Avenue, N.W.
Washington, D.C. 20001

Department of Criminal Law Enforcement
408 North Adams Street
P.O. Box 1489
Tallahassee, Fla. 32302

State Patrol
Department of Public Safety
959 East Confederate Avenue, S.E.
Atlanta, Ga. 30316

State Police
Department of Law Enforcement
3311 West State Street
Boise, Idaho 83731

State Police
Department of Law Enforcement
State Armory
Springfield, Ill. 62706

State Police Department
301 State Office Building
Indianapolis, Ind. 46204

State Patrol
Department of Public Safety
Robert Lucas State Office Building
East 12th and Walnut Streets
Des Moines, Iowa 50319

Highway Patrol
Townsite Plaza
Building 2, Suite 130
200 East Sixth
Topeka, Kans. 66603

State Police
Department of Justice
State Office Building
Frankfort, Ky. 40601

Law Enforcement Commission
1885 Wooddale Boulevard
Baton Rouge, La. 70806

Department of Public Safety
36 Hospital Street
Augusta, Me. 04333

State Police
Department of Public Safety and Correctional
   Services
State Police Headquarters
Pikesville, Md. 21208

Division of State Police
Department of Public Safety
1010 Commonwealth Avenue
Boston, Mass. 02215

Department of State Police
714 South Harrison Road
East Lansing, Mich. 48823

State Patrol Division
Department of Public Safety
107 East State Highway Building
St. Paul, Minn. 55155

Highway Patrol
1900 Woodrow Wilson Drive, Highway 51
   North
Jackson, Miss. 39216

Missouri State Highway Patrol
Department of Public Safety
1510 East Elm Street
Jefferson City, Mo. 65101

Highway Patrol Bureau
Motor Vehicles Division
Department of Justice
1014 National Avenue
Helena, Mont. 59601

State Patrol
14th and Burnham Streets
P.O. Box 94637
Lincoln, Neb. 68509

Highway Patrol
Department of Motor Vehicles
555 Wright Way
Carson City, Nev. 89701

Division of State Police
Department of Safety
James H. Hayes Building
Hazen Drive
Concord, N.H. 03301

Division of State Police
Department of Law and Public Safety
River Road, Route 29
West Trenton, N.J. 08625

State Police
Albuquerque Highway
P.O. Box 1628
Santa Fe, N.M. 87503

Division of State Police
State Campus, Building 22
Albany, N.Y. 12226

Division of Highway Patrol
Department of Crime Control and Public
   Safety
P.O. Box 27682
Raleigh, N.C. 27611

Highway Patrol
State Capitol
Bismarck, N.D. 58505

Highway Patrol
Department of Highway Safety
240 South Parsons Avenue
Columbus, Ohio 43215

Highway Patrol
Department of Public Safety
3600 North Eastern Avenue
Oklahoma City, Okla. 73111

Department of State Police
107 Public Service Building
Salem, Ore. 97310

State Police
P.O. Box 277
Harrisburg, Pa. 17120

State Police
Scituate, R.I. 02857

Law Enforcement Division
Highway Department
1100 Senate Street
P.O. Box 191
Columbia, S.C. 29202

Division of Highway Patrol
Department of Public Safety
Public Safety Building
118 West Capitol Avenue
Pierre, S.D. 57501

Department of Safety
Andrew Jackson State Office Building
500 Deaderick Street
Nashville, Tenn. 37219

Department of Public Safety
5805 North Lamar Boulevard
P.O. Box 4087
Austin, Tex. 78773

Highway Patrol
Department of Public Safety
304 State Office Building
Salt Lake City, Utah 84114

Vermont State Police
Department of Public Safety
26 Terrace Street
Montpelier, Vt. 05602

Department of State Police
P.O. Box 27472
Richmond, Va. 23210

State Patrol
General Administration Building
Mail Stop AX-12
Olympia, Wash. 98504

Department of Public Safety
E-146 State Capitol
1800 Kanawha Boulevard, East
Charleston, W. Va. 25305

State Patrol and Enforcement Bureau
Division of Motor Vehicles
Department of Transportation
Hill Farms State Office Building
4802 Sheboygan Avenue
Madison, Wis. 53702

Highway Patrol
Highway Department
Highway Building
Central Avenue and I-25
Cheyenne, Wyo. 82002

The following federal agencies are concerned with law enforcement and public education:

Federal Bureau of Investigation (FBI)
Pennsylvania Avenue between 9th and 10th Streets, N.W.
Washington, D.C. 20535

Founded in 1908, the FBI currently employs more than 19,000 persons of which more than 8,600 are special agents. There are fifty-nine field offices throughout the United States. The primary function of the FBI and its agents is to investigate violations of certain federal statutes and to aid in the elimination of organized crime. The FBI gathers crime data from local reporting police departments and publishes it throughout the year and in the annual *Uniform Crime Reports.*

LITERATURE: General information about the FBI available free on request, including the booklet 99 *Facts About the FBI; Crime Resistance; Cooperation: The Backbone of Effective Law Enforcement; National Crime Information Center; The FBI Laboratory; Fingerprint Identification.*

U.S. Department of Justice
Public Information
Law Enforcement Assistance Administration (LEAA)
633 Indiana Avenue, N.W.
Washington, D.C. 20531

A clearinghouse of information and research findings in all matters concerning law enforcement and the criminal justice system.

LITERATURE: Fact sheets; publications price list.

The following national associations for law enforcement personnel also provide information for the general public:

American Academy for Professional Law Enforcement
444 West 56th Street, Suite 2312
New York, N.Y. 10019

Sponsors seminars and a yearly national conference on police and the criminal justice system. Affiliated with John Jay College of Criminal Justice, City University of New York, a leading educator in police and criminal justice issues.

American Law Enforcement Officers Association
4005 Plaza Towers
New Orleans, La. 70113

An association of those working in the criminal justice system, including private security firms. It has fifty state affiliates, provides research and general data on law enforcement, and has an awards program. Active membership dues are $15.00 a year.

LITERATURE: Descriptive leaflet; *Police Times* magazine.

American Police Academy
Headquarters Building
2000 P Street, N.W., Room 615
Washington, D.C. 20036

The academy offers home-study training for police, firefighters, security personnel, and those wishing to enter or advance their careers. It also has occasional workshops for public safety personnel who are employed and conducts research projects in the area of crime prevention. Membership dues are $12.00 a year. Courses are offered in arson, private investigation, security, and narcotics and drugs.

LITERATURE: Descriptive brochure; *Academy Bulletin* (free with membership).

International Association of Chiefs of Police (IACP)
11 Firstfield Road
Gaithersburg, Md. 20760

Established in 1893, this leading police association has more than 10,000 members representing sixty-three nations. It is a clearinghouse for identification records, with the Police Weapons Center, which monitors police casualties; conferences; seminars; a traffic safety program; and public information.

LITERATURE: *The Police Chief,* monthly; *Police Yearbook; Journal of Police Science and Administration; Advancing the Art of Police*

Science Around the World, free booklet; publications list.

INTERPOL (International Criminal Police Organization)
Secretariat General
26, rue Armengaud
92210 Saint-Cloud, Paris, France

An international organization with member countries; victims should inquire at their local police stations and, if necessary, the police will contact the Interpol National Central Bureau. It holds conferences and maintains statistical information.

National Police Officers Association of America (NPOAA)
14600 South Tamiami Trail
Venice, Fla. 33595

Established in 1955, there are fifty-two state and territorial groups in this national membership organization. NPOAA maintains the Police Hall of Fame and Museum and a small library, both open to the public.

LITERATURE: *Enforcement Journal,* quarterly.

National Sheriffs' Association (NSA)
1250 Connecticut Avenue, N.W.
Washington, D.C. 20036

Founded in 1940, NSA provides consulting services to local law enforcement officials and general information about criminal justice to the public and has national programs in training and crime prevention, such as "Neighborhood Watch Program." (See further description in Chapter 16, *Crime Prevention.*)

Police Foundation
1909 K Street, N.W., Suite 400
Washington, D.C. 20006

The foundation conducts research and has extensive publications on law enforcement. Send for their publications price list.

ADDITIONAL LITERATURE

Behind the Shield: The Police in Urban Society by Arthur Niederhoffer (1969). Anchor Books/Doubleday, Garden City, N.Y. 11530 ($2.50). Sociologist and retired policeman Niederhoffer explores the social and psychological dynamics behind the men and women who become police officers.

Chief! by Albert A. Seeman and Peter Hellman (1974). Avon Books, 959 Eighth Avenue, New York, N.Y. 10019 ($1.95). Memoirs of former New York City Chief of Detectives Seeman, including the famous Johnson-Genovese, Colombo, and Gallo cases.

City Police by Jonathan Rubinstein (1977). Ballantine Books, 201 East 50th Street, New York, N.Y. 10022 ($1.95). Police reporter Rubinstein entered the police academy of Philadelphia, graduated, and joined a patrol. This book describes how he perceived the functions, problems, and daily situations encountered by law enforcement officers.

Crime in the United States: Uniform Crime Reports (updated annually). Federal Bureau of Investigation. For sale from the Superintendent of Documents, U.S. Government Printing Office, Washington, D.C. 20402. The official crime statistics gathered from cooperating law enforcement bureaus around the country with the emphasis on murder, rape, robbery, aggravated assault, larceny-theft, auto theft, and burglary. Also includes statistical profiles of arrested offenders and law enforcement officers killed or injured while on duty.

Dealing With Death. Motorola Teleprograms, Inc., 4825 N. Scott Street, Suite 23, Schiller Park, Ill. 60176 (sale, $360.00; one-week rental, $50 applicable toward purchase). A 20-minute film based on 200 hours of direct ride-along experience with the Minneapolis Police Department. This is a sensitive exploration of the impact of the police officer's work on the officer and his/her family.

Enforcement Journal: The Official Police Review Journal of the National Police Officers Association of America and the National Police Reserve Officers Association (quarterly). 14600 South Tamiami Trail, Venice, Fla. 33595 ($6.00 a year; $1.50 single copies). Feature articles, new-product reports, advertisements, conference announcements.

Good Cops/Bad Cops: Memoirs of a Police Psychiatrist by Edward E. Shev, M.D., and Jeremy Joan Hewes (1977). San Francisco Book Company, Inc., 2311 Fillmore Street, San Francisco, Calif. 94115 ($8.95). Shev in a clear, readable style stresses the necessity of screening out police applicants who are prejudiced or moral zealots.

The One Hundred Hats of Officer Jones. New York City Police Foundation, One State Street Plaza, New York, N.Y. 10004 (free). Booklet with brief descriptions of what the police officer does as well as citizen programs to help reduce crime. (Check with your county, city, or state police department to see if they provide a similar pamphlet geared to your community.)

The Onion Field by Joseph Wambaugh (1974). Dell Publishing Company, 1 Dag Hammarskjöld Plaza, New York, N.Y. 10017 ($1.75). Nonfiction account of a crime by a former policeman whose other books include *The Blue Knight, The New Centurions,* and *The Choirboys.*

The Police Chief: The Professional Voice of Law Enforcement (monthly). International Association of Chiefs of Police, 11 Firstfield Road, Gaithersburg, Md. 20760 ($12.00 a year; $2.00 single copies; $2.50 back issues). Articles of interest to law enforcement personnel as well as anyone working in the criminal justice area; issues often revolve around a theme, such as "Crime Against the Elderly."

Police Magazine (bimonthly). 801 Second Avenue, New York, N.Y. 10017 ($12.00 a year). Feature articles on police activities and related topics, such as the police wife, and regular columns, including "Roll Call" and "Viewpoint."

Thinking About Crime by James Q. Wilson (1977). Vintage Books, Random House, 201 East 50th Street, New York, N.Y. 10022 ($1.95). See especially chapter 5, "The Police and Crime," and chapter 6, "The Police and the Community."

Your Law Enforcement Officer and You. Av-Com Law Enforcement Media, 3075 Alta Laguna Boulevard, Laguna Beach, Calif. 92651 ($50.00 purchase; $5.00 ten-day review). A 35mm slide-tape cassette presentation suitable for law enforcement officers and community organizations as an educational tool.

See also the following related chapters in *The Help Book:*

AGING
BATTERED ADULTS
CHILD ABUSE
COURTS
CRIME PREVENTION
CRIME VICTIMS AND WITNESSES
DRUGS, SMOKING, AND DRUG ABUSE
EMERGENCIES AND DISASTERS
GUN CONTROL
JUVENILE DELINQUENCY
KIDNAPPING, MISSING PERSONS, AND RUNAWAYS
LEGAL SERVICES

36

LEGAL SERVICES

People seeking legal help generally fall into three categories: those unable to pay; those able to pay moderate fees; and those able to pay any amount. People in the last category either already have their own lawyer or can hire any recommended attorney. It is persons in the first and second categories that need the most help finding an attorney.

For Those Unable to Pay

There are about 850 legal services and defender programs in the United States for those who cannot pay an attorney. Usually these services handle only civil cases, but they sometimes handle misdemeanor criminal charges as well. Your income must be below a certain level to be eligible for this free service.

Look up "Legal Aid" in your white pages or contact the following national organizations for a local referral:

Legal Services Corporation
733 Fifteenth Street, N.W.
Washington, D.C. 20005

There are maximum income levels for the number of persons in a family to be eligible for assistance. (For example, no more than $4,000 a year for a one-member family.) Referrals are made to local participating legal services. The corporation works with the NLADA directory (see following listing).

National Legal Aid and Defender Association (NLADA)
2100 M Street, N.W., Suite 601
Washington, D.C. 20037

A private, nonprofit national organization and information clearinghouse organized in 1911 devoting its resources to the support and development of quality legal assistance for the poor; membership includes about 6,000 attorneys, 3,500 individuals, and about 850 legal services and defender programs around the country. NLADA has extensive publications, including the *NLADA Directory of Legal Aid and Defender Services* ($5.00). This directory contains state-by-state listings of law school clinics, lawyer referral services, legal assistance for the Armed Forces, and other special programs.

LITERATURE: Free leaflets, including *You Can't Take Justice for Granted;* annual report; *Washington Memo and Briefcase* ($15.00 a year to nonmembers).

Pretrial Services Resource Center
1010 Vermont Avenue, N.W., Suite 200
Washington, D.C. 20005

This organization publishes a national directory of pretrial services agencies that is periodically updated; it makes referrals for individuals and program administrators and maintains a library.

LITERATURE: *Pretrial Reporter*, newsletter; *Directory of Pretrial Services Agencies* ($2.50).

For information on poverty law in general, contact:

Legal Services Corporation
National Clearinghouse for Legal Services
500 North Michigan Avenue, Suite 1940
Chicago, Ill. 60611

The clearinghouse has a library service and publishes the monthly *Clearinghouse Review*, which is free to attorneys working full time in programs funded by the Office of Economic Opportunity Legal Services; the monthly is $10.00 to VISTA volunteers and prison law libraries, $20.00 to other libraries and government agencies, and $25.00 to all others.

LITERATURE: Descriptive leaflet; publications price list.

If you are accused of a crime, the right to an attorney is guaranteed by the Sixth Amendment. If you cannot afford to hire a lawyer, even if you are employed, the state or federal government will provide one for you. Although the accused cannot request a specific public defender, someone who is dissatisfied with court-appointed counsel may hire private counsel.

Contact the following state agencies for the public defender for further information or referrals:

Office of the Governor
333 K Street
Anchorage, Alaska 99501

State Public Defender
445 Capitol Mall
Sacramento, Calif. 95814

State Public Defender
718 State Social Services Building
Denver, Colo. 80203

Public Defender Services Commission
83½ Lafayette Street
Hartford, Conn. 06106

Public Defenders Office
101 Court Street
Dover, Del. 19901

Public Defender Service
Judiciary Building
601 Indiana Avenue, N.W.
Washington, D.C. 20004

Office of the Public Defender
Office of the Governor
200 North Vineyard Boulevard, Suite 200
Honolulu, Hawaii 96817

484 / THE HELP BOOK

State Appellate Defender
300 East Monroe Street
Springfield, Ill. 62706

Public Defender
501 State Office Building
Indianapolis, Ind. 46204

Public Defender
State Office Building Annex
Frankfort, Ky. 40601

Louisiana Indigent Defender Board
American Place, Sixteenth Floor
Baton Rouge, La. 70821

Public Defender System
800 Equitable Building
Calvert and Fayette Streets
Baltimore, Md. 21202

Public Defender
University of Minnesota Law School
Minneapolis, Minn. 55455

Office of the Public Defender
Department of the Public Advocate
P.O. Box 141
Trenton, N.J. 08625

Public Defender
215 West San Francisco Street
Santa Fe, N.M. 87503

Office of the Public Defender
Mill Creek Office Park
555 Thirteenth N.E.
Salem, Ore. 97310

Public Defender
250 Benefit Street
Providence, R.I. 02903

Public Defender
South Dakota Supreme Court
Pierre, S.D. 57501

Defender General
43 State Street
Montpelier, Vt. 05602

Public Defender Board
123 West Washington Avenue
Madison, Wis. 53702

For Those Able to Pay Moderate Fees

In 1937 the American Bar Association initiated a service that would meet the legal needs of this group of Americans. It is called the Lawyer Referral Service (LRS) and it is administered through the local bar association. There are more than 250 cities operating active referral services. Basically, the LRS offers an initial consultation at a very modest fixed fee. A client may thus know in advance what costs the legal work may involve. Consult your local directory under "Lawyer Referral Service" or ask your local bar association for more details.

The following national association will also provide more information and referrals:

Standing Committee on Lawyer Referral Service
American Bar Association
1155 East 60th Street
Chicago, Ill. 60637

An information clearinghouse on the Lawyer Referral Service with numerous article reprints, bulletins, and reports intended mainly for bar associations who wish to set up LRS programs.

LITERATURE: *Directory of Lawyer Referral Services;* leaflets and booklets include "Why a Lawyer Referral Service?," "Standards and Practices for Lawyer Referral Services," "Problems? You need a lawyer!," and "Ten Questions for Lawyers."

For help in consumer fraud, regardless of your ability to pay, the office of the Attorney General in your state prosecutes and defends all actions and proceedings for and against the state. A key concern is the prosecution in consumer fraud cases and most states have a separate office just for that purpose.

The following are the state offices for the attorneys general:

State Administrative Building
Montgomery, Ala. 36130

Department of Law
410 State Capital
Pouch K
Juneau, Alaska 99811

Department of Law
State Capitol
1700 West Washington Street
Phoenix, Ariz. 85007

Justice Building
Capitol Grounds
Little Rock, Ark. 72201

Department of Justice
555 Capitol Mall
Sacramento, Calif. 95814

Department of Law
1525 Sherman Street
Denver, Colo. 80203

30 Trinity Street
Hartford, Conn. 2026

Department of Justice
Wilmington Tower
1105 Market Street
Wilmington, Del. 19801

Office of the Corporation Counsel
District Building
1350 E Street, N.W., Room 329
Washington, D.C. 20004

Department of Legal Affairs
The Capitol
Tallahassee, Fla. 32304

Law Department
132 Judicial Building
40 Capitol Square, S.W.
Atlanta, Ga. 30334

State Capitol
Honolulu, Hawaii 96813

210 Statehouse
Boise, Idaho 83720

500 South Second Street
Springfield, Ill. 62701

219 State House
200 West Washington Street
Indianapolis, Ind. 46204

Capitol Building
1007 East Grand Avenue
Des Moines, Iowa 50319

State Capitol
First Floor South
Topeka, Kans. 66612

Department of Law
State Capitol
Frankfort, Ky. 40601

Department of Justice
P.O. Box 44005
Baton Rouge, La. 70804

State House
Augusta, Me. 04333

Law Department
One South Calvert Street
Baltimore, Md. 21202

1 Ashburton Place
Boston, Mass. 02108

Law Building
Lansing, Mich. 48913

102 State Capitol
Aurora Avenue and Park Street
St. Paul, Minn. 55155

Carroll Gartin Building
Jackson, Miss. 39205

Supreme Court Building
Jefferson City, Mo. 65101

Department of Justice
208 Capitol Building
Helena, Mont. 59601

Department of Justice
State Capitol
Lincoln, Neb. 68509

Central Office
Heroes Memorial Building
Carson City, Nev. 89710

208 State House Annex
Capitol Street
Concord, N.H. 03301

Department of Law and Public Safety
State House Annex, Second Floor
Trenton, N.J. 08625

Bataan Memorial Building
Santa Fe, N.M. 87501

Department of Law
State Capitol
Albany, N.Y. 12224

Department of Justice
Justice Building
P.O. Box 629
Raleigh, N.C. 27602

State Capitol
Bismarck, N.D. 58505

State Office Tower
30 East Broad Street
Columbus, Ohio 43216

112 State Capitol
Lincoln Boulevard
Oklahoma City, Okla. 73105

Department of Justice
100 State Office Building
Salem, Ore. 97310

Department of Justice
Capitol Annex, Old Museum Building
Harrisburg, Pa. 17120

Providence County Courthouse
250 Benefit Street
Providence, R.I. 02903

400 Wade Hampton Office Building
P.O. Box 11549
Columbia, S.C. 29211

Capitol Building
Pierre, S.D. 57501

Supreme Court Building
401 7th Avenue, North
Nashville, Tenn. 37219

Supreme Court Building
P.O. Box 12548, Capitol Station
Austin, Tex. 78711

State Capitol
Salt Lake City, Utah 84114

Pavilion Office Building
109 State Street
Montpelier, Vt. 05602

Department of Law
Supreme Court Building
1101 East Broad Street
Richmond, Va. 23219

Temple of Justice
Olympia, Wash. 98504

E-26 State Capitol
1800 Kanawha Boulevard, East
Charleston, W.Va. 25305

114E State Capitol
Madison, Wis. 53702

123 State Capitol
Capitol Avenue at 24th Street
Cheyenne, Wyo. 82002

Department of Justice
50 Fortaleza Street
P.O. Box 192
San Juan, P.R. 00902

Contact the following additional national legal services* for information on the educational materials and local assistance that they offer:

Center for Law and Education
6 Appian Way, Gutman Library, 3rd Floor
Cambridge, Mass. 02138

Center on Social Welfare Policy and Law
821 Fifteenth Street, N.W., Suite 638
Washington, D.C. 20005

Food Research and Action Center (FRAC)
2011 Eye Street, N.W., Suite 700
Washington, D.C. 20006

Handicapped Persons Legal Support Unit
335 Broadway, Room 803
New York, N.Y. 10013

Indian Law Backup Center
Native American Rights Funds
1506 Broadway
Boulder, Colo. 80302

Mental Disability Legal Resource Center
ABA, 1800 M Street, N.W.
Washington, D.C. 20036

Migrant Legal Action Program
806 Fifteenth Street, N.W., Suite 600
Washington, D.C. 20005

National Center for Youth Law
693 Mission Street
San Francisco, Calif. 94105

National Consumer Law Center, Inc.
11 Beacon Street
Boston, Mass. 02108

National Housing Law Project
2150 Shattuck Avenue, Suite 300
Berkeley, Calif. 94704

National Economic Development Law Project
2150 Shattuck Avenue, Suite 300
Berkeley, Calif. 94704

National Employment Law Project
475 Riverside Drive
New York, N.Y. 10027

National Health Law Program
2401 Main Street
Santa Monica, Calif. 90405

National Legal Aid and Defender Association
2100 M Street, N.W., Suite 601
Washington, D.C. 20037

National Paralegal Institute
2000 P Street, N.W., Suite 600
Washington, D.C. 20036

National Senior Citizens Law Center
1200 Fifteenth Street, N.W., Suite 500
Washington, D.C. 20005

National Social Science and Law Project
1990 M Street, N.W.
Washington, D.C. 20036

If you wish to learn about the law, contact your nearby law school to see if they offer free courses for non-lawyers, such as those courses offered by the National Street Law Institute (run by Georgetown University Law Center in Washington, D.C.). Other low-cost courses in law are offered through adult continuing education programs taught at public schools, at colleges (on a noncredit basis), or at an alternative free university.

The following free legal educational program is currently available at ten locations in three states, but more and more areas are beginning to adopt it; contact

---

* Reprinted with permission from *The Clearinghouse Review* (December 1978), National Clearinghouse for Legal Services.

488 / THE HELP BOOK

your local bar association or the Tel-Law national headquarters to find out your nearest participating telephone number:

Tel-Law
c/o Teletronix Information System
710 Brookside
Redlands, Calif. 92373

Tel-Law has about seventy five-minute tapes created for laypersons on various aspects of the law and law-related problems, such as consumer information, what to do if you are arrested, how to find a lawyer, the differences between a criminal and a civil suit, adoption procedures, senior citizen information, and so forth. In June 1977, there were ten Tel-Law systems in California, Oregon, and Arizona, usually operated through the local bar association. To use this cassette facility, all you need do is call a participating Tel-Law system and ask to hear a specific tape. Your only cost is the telephone call.

Additional sources of legal education materials are:

American Bar Association (ABA)
1155 East Sixtieth Street
Chicago, Ill. 60637

The ABA is a very active professional association sponsoring committees and publications dealing with various aspects of their profession, clients, and the system they have to work within. Some of its committees include the Consortium on Legal Services and the Public, Crime Victims, and Family Law.

LITERATURE: Various free pamphlets and booklets, write for publications list; *ABA Journal* (by subscription).

Center for Administrative Justice (CAJ)
1785 Massachusetts Avenue, N.W.
Washington, D.C. 20036

Founded in 1973, this educational organization is involved in research projects related to administrative law. It is affiliated with the American Bar Association.

Institute of Judicial Administration
1 Washington Square Village
New York, N.Y. 10012

Founded in 1952, this institute, under the sponsorship of New York University School of Law, is interested in court modernization. It also coordinates bar association and judicial council activities.

LITERATURE: Publications list upon request; annual report; *IJA Report,* quarterly newsletter.

National District Attorney's Association
211 East Chicago Avenue, Suite 1515
Chicago, Ill. 60611

Founded in 1950, NDAA's membership consists of state prosecutors and assistant district attorneys. Some of their programs include: National Center for Economic Crime Prevention; Commission on Victim-Witness Assistance; Office of National Training Coordinator. Its main educational functions are to keep prosecutors informed of developments in the criminal justice and individual civil-liberties areas.

LITERATURE: Audio cassettes on trial tactics and juvenile justice; *Prosecutor,* bimonthly journal; publications list upon request.

National Lawyers Guild
National Office
853 Broadway
New York, N.Y. 10003

A multiracial and progressive alternative to the American Bar Association, the guild publishes a labor newsletter that reports on the struggles of rank-and-file workers across the country and provides political and legal analysis of labor issues. It is also concerned with immigration, oppression of women, prisons, the American Indian's struggle, police crimes, gay rights, grand jury abuse, housing, and so on.

National Legal Data Center
100 East Thousand Oaks Boulevard, Suite 172
Thousand Oaks, Calif. 91360

The center provides technical assistance to prosecutors in the development of career criminal prosecution units and research in the social sciences, environmental protection, and other fields; it also holds conferences.

LITERATURE: *The Verdict*, newsletter; legal materials.

Women's Legal Defense Fund
1424 16th St. N. W.
Washington, D.C. 20036

The fund handles litigation of sex-discrimination cases for women and provides legal information for women; it is also an educational information clearinghouse.

If you have a complaint about legal misconduct, contact the grievance committee of your local bar association. (Most complaints are about fees or performance, which they do not handle.) Next try unofficial sources for advice. For example, contact your local citizen action group, such as PIRG (Public Interest Research Group) or consumer affairs organization to see if they will give advice or have any published material. One pertinent booklet is *How to Complain About Your Lawyer* ($.25), available from the New York Public Interest Research Group (NYPIRG), 5 Beekman Street, New York, N.Y. 10038.

ADDITIONAL LITERATURE

For a complete listing of magazines and newsletters, consult the *Index to Legal Periodicals* in your public or law school library.

American Bar Association Journal (monthly). 1155 East 60th Street, Chicago, Ill. 60637. Articles and book reviews on legal issues for lawyers, students, and interested laypersons.

Bulletin of the American Academy of Psychiatry and the Law (quarterly). Mary V. Odom, School of Law, University of Pittsburgh, Pittsburgh, Pa. 15260 ($20.00 a year). This journal examines issues in forensic psychiatry, mental health law, jurisprudence, criminology, and correctional psychiatry.

The Complete Layman's Guide to the Law by John Paul Hanna, foreword by former Justice Tom Clark (1974). Prentice-Hall, Inc., Englewood Cliffs, N.J. 07632 ($15.95).

Criminal Law for the Layman: A Guide for Citizen and Student by Fred E. Inbau and Marvin E. Aspen (1970). Chilton Book Company, Radnor, Pa. 19089 ($5.95). A clear introduction to criminal law.

Crisis at the Bar by Jethro Lieberman (1978). W. W. Norton & Company, Inc. 500 Fifth Avenue, New York, N.Y. 10036.

Directory of Legal Services Support Projects (1978). National Clearinghouse for Legal Services, 500 North Michigan Avenue, Suite 1940, Chicago, Ill. 60611. Booklet with annotated descriptions of such organizations as the National Consumer Law Center, Inc., and Center for Law and Education, Inc.; includes lists of available publications, major cases, legal activities and support services, and issue areas.

Go East, Young Man: The Autobiography of William O. Douglas, The Early Years by William O. Douglas (1975). Delta Books, Dell Publishing Company, 1 Dag Hammarskjold Plaza, New York, N.Y. 10017 ($4.25). Justice Douglas's life, from boyhood to appointment to the Supreme Court in 1939.

How to Avoid Probate! by Norman F. Dacey (1965). Crown Publishers, 1 Park Avenue, New York, N.Y. 10016 ($7.95).

How to Find the Law edited by Morris L. Cohen, 7th edition (1976). West Publishing Company, 50 West Kellogg Boulevard, P.O. Box 3526, St. Paul, Minn. 55165 ($11.95).

Juris Doctor: Magazine for the New Lawyer (eleven issues a year). MBA Communications, P.O. Box 820, Addison, Ill. 60101 (free to students, faculty, and post-1960 graduates of accredited law schools; other students, $6.00; all others, $12.00). Book excerpts, original articles and reviews on legal matters and job-related problems.

The Law for a Woman: Real Cases and What Happened by Ellen Switzer with Wendy Susco (1976). Charles Scribner's Sons, 597 Fifth Avenue, New York, N.Y. 10017 ($3.95). Covers the legal basics in education, employment, marriage, rape, divorce, and women as lawyers, women in politics, information on law schools, and reentering the job market; written in a clear style.

Law Without Lawyers by Victor Li (1977). San Francisco Book Company, 2311 Fillmore Street, San Francisco, Calif. 94116 ($8.95 hardcover; $4.95 paperback).

Legal First Aid by Henry Shain (1975). Funk & Wagnalls, 666 Fifth Avenue, New York, N.Y. 10010 ($6.95). A guide to basic law in many areas—divorce, criminal, consumer protection, accident claims—in simple language; a good home reference.

The Rights of Suspects by Oliver Rosengart with Gail Weinheimer (1974). Avon Books, 250 West 55th Street, New York, N.Y. 10019 ($1.25 plus .25 postage). In simple language, your rights when confronted by the police, when arrested, when in court, and remedies. An American Civil Liberties Union handbook.

The Story of the Law and the Men Who Made It: From the Earliest Times to the Present, revised and updated edition of *The Law*, by René A. Wormser (1962). Touchstone Books, Simon and Schuster, 1230 Avenue of the Americas, New York, N.Y. 10020 ($4.95). An entertaining and well-written survey of written law and the evolution of the modern legal system.

Super Threats: How to Sound Like a Lawyer and Get Your Rights on Your Own by John M. Striker and Andrew O. Shapiro (1977). Rawson Associates Publishers Inc., 630 Third Avenue, New York, N.Y. 10017 ($8.95).

Unequal Justice: Lawyers and Social Change in Modern America by Jerold Auerbach (1976). Oxford University Press, 200 Madison Avenue, New York, N.Y. 10016 ($3.95).

Verdicts on Lawyers, edited by Ralph Nader and Mark Green (1976). T. Y. Crowell, 10 East 53rd Street, New York, N.Y. 10022 ($10.00). A collection of articles by attorneys and journalists on various aspects of the legal profession; includes such topics as "How to Avoid Lawyers," "The Ten Worst Judges," and "The ABA as Trade Association."

What to Do Until the Lawyer Comes: An Invitation to Law by Stephan Landsman, Donald McWherter, and Alan Pfeffer (1977). Anchor Books, Anchor Press/Doubleday, Garden City, N.Y. 11530 ($2.95). A concise book providing a background to the law, covering the nature of law, lawyers, the courts, and administrative agencies, with a guide to further reading.

You and the Law, prepared by Reader's Digest Association (1976). Reader's Digest, Pleasantville, N.Y. 10570 ($12.95).

You and the Law (bimonthly). Research Institute of America, Inc., 589 Fifth Avenue, New

York, N.Y. 10017 ($36.00 a year; $3.00 a month).

West Publishing Company, 50 West Kellogg Boulevard, P.O. Box 3526, St. Paul, Minn. 55165, is one of the largest publishers of legal textbooks and annotated statutes and codes. Send for their catalog.

See also the following related chapters in *The Help Book:*

ADOPTION AND FOSTER CARE
AGING
ANIMAL RIGHTS
BATTERED ADULTS
CHILD ABUSE
CIVIL RIGHTS AND DISCRIMINATION
CONSUMER AFFAIRS
COURTS
CRIME VICTIMS AND WITNESSES
GAY LIBERATION
INFORMATION RIGHTS AND RESOURCES
JUVENILE DELINQUENCY
KIDNAPPING, MISSING PERSONS, AND RUNAWAYS
LAW ENFORCEMENT
POLITICAL ACTION

37

MEDIA AND COMMUNICATIONS

The dictionary defines *media* as simply "the plural of *medium*." But the word has the popular connotation of radio, films, television, newspapers, and magazines. Probably no other twentieth-century invention, other than mass transit, has had as great an impact on the entire world as mass media.

The first radio broadcast was heard over KDKA in Pittsburgh on November 2, 1920; by 1922, there were 500 radio stations throughout the United States. Television manufacturing began in 1939, was interrupted by World War II, and was resumed on a national basis in 1946; by 1951 limited color broadcasting had begun.

Certain types of drama, such as the soap opera, made an easy transition from the live stage to radio to television. Other formats, such as TV news reporting, have been more severely criticized because time limitations prohibit the more in-depth analysis more common in the newspaper, magazines, and even on radio.

No one yet knows if mass media is an enemy or a hero. Certainly it has been put to evil propagandist use, but it has also had positive benefits, as in the case of *Sesame Street*, a preschool educational program that has been shown to favorably influence the classroom performance of its young viewers. Nor is there conclusive evidence as to whether television violence provokes violent acts, simply mirrors those that already are prevalent in the culture, or acts as a catharsis.

But pressure from such citizen groups as the National Citizens' Committee for Broadcasting (NCCB), Action for Children's Television (ACT), and the National Parents and Teachers Association (PTA) have been effective enough to see the decrease of violence in television programming during 1977. Whether or not dramatized violence causes more actual violence will hopefully show up in future years in decreased crime statistics (although other variables may enter into that condition as well). But certainly TV and film violence is aesthetically repulsive, in addition to its unacceptability on moral grounds.

Other truisms, such as those that say television viewing deemphasizes and discourages reading, are also being debated as book and magazine sales soar. Whether the increase in reading is being carried out by a non-viewing public is unconfirmed; it still seems likely that none of the media need cancel each other out. Each one has its strengths and its limitations; unfortunately, until now, each medium and communications method has tried to compete for total number of listeners, viewers, or readers rather than trying to do its best in its special way.

Many local and national television stations compile and produce original reference booklets or community resource guides related to, or developed from, programs they have presented. For example, in 1978 NBC-TV published a booklet on working women, and additional resource one-page flyers are often mailed to viewers after consumer reports. Follow-up offers for free information are often made on the air or published in your local newspapers. If you can show a legitimate need for a transcript, you may also be able to get one following a specific broadcast. Contact your local station for specifics.

The following organizations are concerned with making the media accountable to the public:

Federal Communications Commission (FCC)
Consumer Assistance Office
Washington, D.C. 20554

An independent agency established by Congress in 1934 to regulate broadcasting radio and television stations, interstate and foreign telephone, telegraph and cable service, communications by satellite and public safety, industrial transportation, and amateur and citizen services, but not closed-circuit television operations. All stations must have their FCC application available to the public for inspection during business hours. Its Fairness Doctrine requires a controversial editorial to be "answered" by the opposing side; license renewals may be denied in which free speech has been interfered with by a production (and conversely, charges of defamation may be overturned if free speech is proven); deliberate distortion of the news requires remedial action; and the public is asked to first direct complaints to the stations.

LITERATURE: Free fact sheets; *Federal Register* reprints.

Media Access Project
1912 N Street, N.W.
Washington, D.C. 20036

A public interest law firm specializing in communications law and First Amendment issues. Work is done on behalf of local, state, and national citizen organizations desiring access to broadcast or print media for information dissemination. It also works for control of advertising campaign abuses.

Morality in the Media, Inc.
487 Park Avenue
New York, N.Y. 10022

The national headquarters for a citizens group dedicated to stopping the traffic in pornography that provides information on obscenity law enforcement.

LITERATURE: Information packet with booklets and fact sheets; newsletter ($2.50 a year).

National Advertising Review Board (NARB)
845 Third Avenue
New York, N.Y. 10022

A self-regulatory body of industry and public persons sponsored by the American Advertising Federation, the American Association of Advertising Agencies, the Association of National Advertisers, and the Council of Better Business Bureaus for the purpose of sustaining high standards of truth and accuracy in national advertising.

LITERATURE: *If You Have a Complaint About Advertising*, free booklet.

National Citizens Committee for Broadcasting (NCCB)
1028 Connecticut Avenue, N.W.
Washington, D.C. 20036

A nonprofit public interest media reform group with about 7,000 members and chaired by Nicholas Johnson, former FCC commissioner. NCCB issues violence rankings for television programs and is working to improve the quality of broadcasting. It sponsors a public affairs project and acts as an advocacy group and information clearinghouse.

LITERATURE: Free descriptive leaflets; *Media Watch*, free with $15.00 membership dues; free violence ranking brochure; *Access*, biweekly ($36.00 a year); *Citizens Media Directory* ($7.50).

National News Council
One Lincoln Plaza
New York, N.Y. 10023

Since it was founded in August 1973, the council has received more than 475 complaints, 175 of which qualified for examination. Their investigations are restricted to complaints about the accuracy and fairness of news reporting; they are also initiating studies and reports on issues involving freedom of the press. Only publicity can assure its effectiveness since it has no coercive or legal powers to enforce decisions.

LITERATURE: *In the Public Interest;* National News Council reports are published in the *Columbia Journalism Review;* fact sheet on filing complaints.

Women Against Violence in Pornography & Media (WAVPM)
2112 Channing Way
Berkeley, Calif. 94704

Founded in 1976, WAVPM has a multifaceted program to end media abuse (particularly pornography) of women. It offers a slideshow presentation and antiporn display that can be used in group situations; publishes a monthly newsletter, *Newspage*, available for $5.00 a year; and maintains extensive files on this subject that are open to all women.

LITERATURE: Information packet ($3.50).

Contact the following organizations for information on children and the media (complete descriptions are in Chapter 42, Parenting):

Action for Children's Television (ACT)
46 Austin Street
Newtonville, Mass. 02160

Committee on Children's Television (CCT)
1511 Masonic Avenue
San Francisco, Calif. 94117

National PTA TV Action Center
700 North Rush Street
Chicago, Ill. 60611

The following national organizations provide direct help for those who write and work for the media (see also Chapter 5, Arts):

MEDIA AND COMMUNICATIONS / 495

Investigative Reporters & Editors, Inc. (IRE)
220 Walter Williams Hall
University of Missouri
Columbia, Mo. 65211

A national organization of journalists (staff and freelance), educators, and others in the communications field. IRE members share problems and information through its newsletter and the annual workshop/conference that is held each year. A reference library at the University of Missouri has also been established.

(See complete listing in Chapter 5, *Arts*.)

National Academy of Television Arts and Sciences (NATAS)
National Office
291 South La Cienega Boulevard
Beverly Hills, Calif. 90211
New York Chapter
110 West 57th Street
New York, N.Y. 10019

Membership organization open to qualified producers, writers, directors, production staff, and other personnel working in television. The New York office has weekly "Drop in Lunches" with guest speakers from the media. NATAS also holds a "Drop in Dinner," special panel discussions, and "Mini-Events" in which educational, free visits to TV stations, commercial advertising agencies, and so forth are offered. Its Cinema Club has low-cost screenings, and NATAS hosts the Emmy Awards and sponsors parties, celebrity auctions, and other events. Dues are $45.00 annually.

LITERATURE: Application brochure; cover letter.

National Association of Broadcasters (NAB)
1771 N Street, N.W.
Washington, D.C. 20036

Programming and advertising codes established for the industry are available upon request; each licensee voluntarily agrees to comply.

The Newspaper Guild (TNG)
1125 Fifteenth Street, N.W.
Washington, D.C. 20005

Founded in 1933, there are eighty locals for this 33,000-member organization, which is affiliated with the AFL-CIO. The headquarters has a library with a research and information department and a section on collective bargaining and organizing.

LITERATURE: Directory, published semiannually; *Guild Reporter* Newspaper ($10.00 a year); *Thanks to the Guild* ($.15); *The Newspaperman Who Founded a Union* ($.05); *Gentlemen and Scholars of the Press* ($.10).

Women in Communications, Inc.
P.O. Box 9561
Austin, Tex. 78766

A professional organization established in 1909 for women in the communications field. Membership dues are $35.00 a year (students, $22.50). It is also a limited resource center on women's progress in communications and can recommend information sources.

LITERATURE: *Newsletter* ($6.00 a year); *Matrix*, quarterly ($6.00); free single copies of career booklets.

Writers Guild of America, East, Inc.
(Affiliated with Writers Guild of America, West, Inc.)
22 West 48th Street
New York, N.Y. 10036

A professional membership organization of writers in the fields of radio, television, motion pictures, and related areas. Initiation fee is $300.00; quarterly dues of $12.50 plus 1.5 percent of gross earnings from writing in those fields is required thereafter. It provides a credit union; group hospitalization coverage; life insurance; and business counseling on professional craft matters.

Its manuscript registration service is open to nonmembers as well as members to help establish the date of completion and the identity of unpublished literary property; work should be submitted *before showing it to a producer.* The service accepts manuscripts as well as synopses, outlines, ideas, treatments, and scenarios for registration, which is valid for ten years; send for special envelopes with specific information that must appear for registration; each registration costs $10.00 ($3.00 to members).

LITERATURE: Application; brief history of WGAE; list of agents.

Writers in the Public Interest
17 Myrtle Drive
Great Neck, N.Y. 11021

A national organization for writers and educators who are concerned about such public interest issues as poverty, civil rights, child advocacy, aging, etc. (See complete listing in Chapter 5, *Arts.*)

Contact the following organizations for television and broadcasting information:

The Advertising Council Inc.
825 Third Avenue
New York, N.Y. 10022

A nonprofit organization whose membership consists of American business, advertising, and communications industries who contribute their skills and resources in public service advertising campaigns on national problems. Very effective recent campaigns have included free advertising for booklets offered on the American economic system and exporting; others have included aging, careers, child abuse, and preventing forest fires.

LITERATURE: *Economic Communicator* (free); *Public Service Advertising Bulletin* (free).

Museum of Broadcasting
1 East 53rd Street
New York, N.Y. 10022

The first American institution dedicated to the study and preservation of the most significant programs in the fifty-year history of broadcasting. The general public, students, and scholars are invited to visit the museum during its regular hours, noon until five Tuesday through Friday; programs may be viewed on specially designed consoles equipped with color TV and radio playback equipment; groups should call ahead for reservations.

LITERATURE: Free fact sheets; membership application ($30.00 a year).

Public Broadcasting Service (PBS)
475 L'Enfant Plaza West, S.W.
Washington, D.C. 20024

A national membership organization of public television stations and distributors of public television's national programming. General information about all aspects of noncommercial broadcast media is available.

LITERATURE: Fact sheet.

Television Information Office (TIO)
745 Fifth Avenue
New York, N.Y. 10022

Established in October 1959, TIO is supported by the major networks as well as individual commercial stations and groups, educational stations, and the National Association of Broadcasters. It is an information clearinghouse for the general public and for all who work in communications and the media. An educational program includes frequent national mailings; speeches and participation in conferences; research projects, including surveys; the nation's most extensive public library and information center on social, cultural, and programming aspects of television; and *Teacher's Guide to Television*, a twice-yearly magazine.

LITERATURE: Fact sheet, publications price list; *Careers in Television* ($.20); *How Free TV Works* ($.20).

MEDIA AND COMMUNICATIONS / 497

The following is a list of just some of the companies from which you can rent or purchase films (also check your local library to see if they have a free loan program and an annotated directory):

Association Films, Inc.
866 Third Avenue
New York, N.Y. 10022

Since 1911, Association Films has been distributing free-loan sponsored films. Contact them at the above address or at other sales offices in Chicago, Ill.; Arlington, Va.; San Francisco or Sun Valley, Calif. for further information.

Green Mountain Post Films
Box 177
Montague, Mass. 01351

Film production and distribution of documentaries on political and social themes. Send for free catalog.

Learning Corporation of America (LCA)
1350 Avenue of the Americas
New York, N.Y. 10019

LCA rents and sells films for schools, colleges, and libraries. Prices range from $15.00 (rental) to $135.00 (sale) and up. Send for their extensive illustrated catalog.

Motorola Teleprograms, Inc. (MTI)
4825 North Scott Street, Suite 26
Schiller Park, Ill. 60176

MTI is a producer-distributor of more than 200 audiovisual programs, including 16mm or 3/4 videocassette motion pictures, filmstrips, and multimedia programs. Topics include executive protection and prevention and response strategies against terrorism, shoplifting, alcoholism, child abuse, women, crime prevention, and more. Films may be purchased or rented. Write for free catalog and ordering-previewing instructions.

National AudioVisual Center
National Archives and Records Service
General Services Administration
Washington, D.C. 20409

Established in 1969, the National AudioVisual Center is the central clearinghouse for all U.S. government audiovisual materials and also makes federally produced films available for use through distribution services. Sales, rental, and loan referrals are available on a variety of subjects with the center's collection concentrating in education, environmental sciences, medicine, dentistry, vocational and management training, and safety. Send for their free descriptive booklet, film rental instructions, and updated list of available films.

Time-Life Multimedia Distribution Center
100 Eisenhower Drive
Paramus, N.J. 07652

Send for their catalog of educational films available for rental or purchase covering a wide range of subjects, such as marriage, drug abuse, biography, and social studies. They are also the United States distributor for England's BBC films and programs.

ADDITIONAL LITERATURE

Backstage: TV Film and Tape Syndication Directory (updated yearly). 165 West 46th Street, New York, N.Y. 10036 ($5.00).

Broadcasting Yearbook (yearly). Broadcasting Publications, 1735 De Sales Street, N.W., Washington, D.C. 20036.

Four Arguments for the Elimination of Television by Jerry Mander (1978). William R. Morrow and Company, 105 Madison Avenue, New York, N.Y. 10016 ($11.95).

How to Appraise and Improve Your Daily Newspaper by David Bollier. Disability Rights Center, P.O. Box 19367, Washington, D.C. 20036 ($5.00 to individuals; $10.00 to institutions). Suggestions on how to make newspapers more responsive to the communities they serve.

How to Talk Back to Your Television Set by Nicholas Johnson (1970). Little, Brown & Company, 34 Beacon Street, Boston, Mass. 02106. Johnson, former FCC commissioner who became chairman of the National Committee for Citizens' Broadcasting, gives advice on how to disagree with what you see on TV.

Mediability: A Guide for Nonprofits by Len Biegel and Aileen Lubin (1975). Taft Products, Inc., 1000 Vermont Avenue, N.W., Washington, D.C. 20005. Well-written guide to how nonprofit organizations can make use of television and radio public service advertising. It explains how to produce film spots and how to use newspapers and magazines.

Media Industry Newsletter (weekly). MIN Publishing, Inc., 156 East 52nd Street, New York, N.Y. 10022 ($68.00 a year; $5.00 for single issues). Media and marketing newsletter with inside information on corporate executive changes, magazine revenues, advertising rates, and trends.

Motion Picture, TV and Theatre Directory for Services and Products (issued twice a year, fall and spring). Motion Picture Enterprises Publications, Inc., Tarrytown, N.Y. 10591 ($3.00). Names, addresses, and associations of key organizations with much advertising for products pertinent to workers in the visual field.

The New York Times Encyclopedia of Television by Les Brown (1977). Times Books, 3 Park Avenue, New York, N.Y. 10016 ($17.95). Veteran TV critic Brown describes the history of television, highlighting significant court cases and noting some of the prominent television personalities.

The Plug-In Drug by Marie Winn (1977). The Viking Press, 625 Madison Avenue, New York, N.Y. 10022 ($8.95). In this strong statement against television, Winn argues that TV threatens both the development of the child and the sanctity of the family.

Publicity: How to Get It by Richard O'Brien (1977). Harper & Row, 10 East 53rd Street, New York, N.Y. 10022 ($8.95). Practical advice from a working publicist.

Remote Control: Television and the Manipulation of American Life by Frank Mankiewicz (1977). Times Books, 3 Park Avenue, New York, N.Y. 10016 ($12.50).

Ross Reports Television (monthly). Television Index, Inc., 150 Fifth Avenue, New York, N.Y. 10011 ($15.00 a year; $1.74 each issue). For actors, writers, technicians, and other television personnel, this is an enormously valuable listing of advertising agencies, casting directors, and network studios and programs. Short write-ups include names, addresses, how to go about it, and telephone numbers; format allows this directory to keep up with the changing television world.

Television Quarterly, edited by Harriet Van Horne. The National Academy of Television Arts and Sciences, 110 West 57th Street, New York, N.Y. 10019 (free to members; others, $8.00 a year or $2.00 for single copies). Articles by television observers like Frank Mankiewicz, Eric Sevareid, and Steve Allen.

Television: The First Fifty Years by Jeff Greenfield (1977). Harry N. Abrams, Inc., 110 East 59th Street, New York, N.Y. 10022 ($35.00).

Tune In Yesterday: The Ultimate Encyclopedia of Old-Time Radio, 1925–1976 by John Dunning (1976). Prentice-Hall, Inc., Englewood Cliffs, N.J. 07632 ($17.95).

TV Guide (weekly). Radnor, Pa. 19088 ($13.56 a year; $.30 single copies). Magazine with annotated local television program listings as well as feature articles that are national in scope.

The World of Encyclopedia of Comics, edited by Maurice Horn (1977). Avon Books, 959 Eighth Avenue, New York, N.Y. 10019 ($10.00). An illustrated reference book dealing with the history of comics with biographies of comic book writers and editors (such as the late Mort Weisinger of *Superman* fame) and comic characters, such as Archie, Popeye, and Li'l Abner.

See also the following related chapters in *The Help Book*:

ARTS
CHILDREN
CITIZEN ACTION
CIVIL RIGHTS AND DISCRIMINATION
CONSUMER AFFAIRS
EDUCATION
INFORMATION RIGHTS AND RESOURCES
PARENTING
ADDITIONAL RESOURCES

38

MENTAL HEALTH

What is "normal"? Though we have concepts of what a healthy lung or healthy heart should look like, and how we could achieve physical good health, we are unable to devise or often follow a blueprint for mental health. Nevertheless there are certain general conditions that are recognized as mentally unhealthy:

- Phobias—fears so exaggerated beyond the reality of their danger that they incapacitate the sufferer. Common phobias are acrophobia (fear of heights), claustrophobia (fear of enclosed areas), and agoraphobia (fear of open spaces). Even fear of success can be a phobia if someone cannot get or keep a job because of it.
- Hypochondria—obsession with one's health to the point of imagining that one suffers from a certain illness. Excessively high medical bills without cause are often a sign of hypochondria.
- Compulsivity—addiction to a habit that overtakes one's life and health, such as alcoholism, obesity, gambling, or excessive spending.

What causes mental illness? There are many theories, ranging from chemical imbalances in the brain and the rest of the body or genes to early childhood experiences and traumatic events. But whatever the cause, the burden of regaining (or achieving) mental health is on the person afflicted. Society, through its doctors and resources, may only provide the tools. But one probable cause is extreme stress, a reaction associated with such common life experiences as death, pregnancy, marriage, divorce, and retirement. It is still uncertain exactly which life changes take their greatest toll on most people, but it is certain that numerous stress-causing events can be pinpointed. We already know that during the first year of bereavement, the death rate of widows and widowers is ten times higher than for other persons the same age; and we also know that in the year following divorce, divorced persons have an illness rate that is twelve times higher than that of married persons. So if you are going through any of the events listed below and are experiencing extreme stress, you might consider seeking help before more severe psychological or physical problems develop. Perhaps by studying how "normal" these stress-inducing events are, it will be reaffirmed that mental distress has "life" as its catalyst; but then the individual must somehow muster up his or her psychological strength, often through the assistance of a trained professional.

The scale that follows was developed from the research of Dr. Thomas H. Holmes, a psychiatrist, and his colleagues at the University of Washington School of Medicine in Seattle. Holmes evolved the scale from the rankings of hundreds of

SOCIAL READJUSTMENT RATING SCALE*

The Stress of Adjusting to Change

Events	Scale of Impact	Events	Scale of Impact
Death of spouse	100	Son or daughter leaving home	29
Divorce	73	Trouble with in-laws	29
Marital separation	65	Outstanding personal achievement	28
Jail term	63	Wife begins or stops work	26
Death of close family member	63	Begin or end school	26
Personal injury or illness	53	Change in living conditions	25
Marriage	50	Revision of personal habits	24
Fired at work	47	Trouble with boss	23
Marital reconciliation	45	Change in work hours or conditions	20
Retirement	45	Change in residence	20
Change in health of family member	44	Change in schools	20
Pregnancy	40	Change in recreation	19
Sex difficulties	39	Change in church activities	19
Gain of new family member	39	Change in social activities	18
Business readjustment	39	Mortgage or loan less than $10,000	17
Change in financial state	38	Change in sleeping habits	16
Death of close friend	37	Change in number of family get-togethers	15
Change to different line of work	36	Change in eating habits	15
Change in number of arguments with spouse	35	Vacation	13
Mortgage over $10,000	31	Christmas	12
Foreclosure of mortgage or loan	30	Minor violations of the law	11
Change in responsibilities at work	29		

Source: Dr. Thomas H. Holmes

* Reprinted with permission from "Doctors Study Treating of Ills Brought On by Stress" by Jane E. Brody in the *New York Times*, June 10, 1973, page 20, © 1973 by The New York Times Company.

persons. If 200 or more life change units occur in a single year, Holmes's studies indicate that few single individuals can withstand the consequent stress; consultation with a psychiatrist or a counselor may be advisable.

Although only a psychiatrist can diagnose mental illness, if someone demonstrates any of the following symptoms over a long period of time, psychiatric help may be necessary:*

- Lives in a separate world, refusing to face his or her problems.
- Has a delusion that people are persecuting him or her.
- Has such severe "blues" (or depression) that he or she is incapacitated.
- Suffers agonies of indecision in making up his or her mind.
- Has moods that swing from exhilaration to depression.
- Insists he or she is ill, although a thorough medical examination reveals nothing that is physically wrong.
- Needs medication to sleep.
- Excessive irritability; given to temper outbursts.
- Loses interest in his or her appearance, job, or family.
- Talks non-stop, skipping from one topic to another.
- Goes on spending sprees far beyond his or her means.
- Unfounded fears incapacitate him or her.
- Hears or sees imaginary things.

Unfortunately, the "shame" associated with mental illness has not completely vanished. Although most people openly admit it when they are having surgery for a physical problem, a much smaller number will say that they are seeing a counselor or a psychiatrist. There is still an onus of failure because someone is emotionally troubled. Although few people would contemplate operating on their own hearts, mental self-repair still seems "expected."

But what *has* changed is that the legal rights of current and former mental patients are being defined. Just within the past five years, legal cases have been won, and more are being instituted. As the public takes its time to reappraise the nature of mental illness, the courts are acting more swiftly to guarantee certain basic civil liberties of mental patients and to protect the confidentiality of medical and psychiatric records.

The following national organizations are concerned with the legal rights of mental and former mental patients:

---

*Adapted and reprinted with permission from *When Mental Illness Strikes Your Family* by Kathleen Cassidy Doyle. Copyright © 1951, 1979 by the Public Affairs Committee, Inc. (See annotated entry in Additional Literature.)

American Bar Association (ABA)
Commission on the Mentally Disabled
1800 M Street, N.W.
Washington, D.C. 20036

ABA reports on current judicial and legislative developments in the mental health case law field through its bimonthly newsletter, *Mental Disability Law Reporter*. Write for further information and/or a subscription.

Mental Health Law Project (MHLP)
1220 Nineteenth Street, N.W.
Washington, D.C. 20036

Founded in 1972, MHLP is an outgrowth of the Center for Law and Social Policy, an American Civil Liberties Union-supported organization. In addition to litigation in "right-to-treatment" and "right-to-refuse treatment" cases, MHLP is active in cases involving wages for mental patients, the right of handicapped children to attend public school, improved standards in mental hospitals, and research in the area of mental health law. An active law student internship is in operation.

LITERATURE: Newsletter.

National Commission on Confidentiality of Health Records
1211 Connecticut Avenue, N.W., Suite 504
Washington, D.C. 20036

Established in 1976 by seventeen health professional and related organizations, the protection of (and access to) records of mental health patients is one of the concerns of this national information clearinghouse. Consumer complaints are investigated; proposed legislation is analyzed. Seminars and clinics are held on specific problems; model laws and guidelines for clinics and other users of health information are prepared.

LITERATURE: *Health Records and Confidentiality: An Annotated Bibliography with Abstracts* ($4.95), see especially pages 10–15, "Confidentiality and Psychiatry"; "Your Health Records," free leaflet.

The following are a sampling of the local groups that are part of the mental patient movement; check your local directory if one is not listed for your area or contact the Network Against Psychiatric Assault (see listing that follows) for a referral:

Network Against Psychiatric Assault
558 Capp Street
San Francisco, Calif. 94110

Network Against Psychiatric Assault/Los Angeles
P.O. Box 5728
Santa Monica, Calif. 90405

Mental Health Law Project of the Legal Aid Society of Metropolitan Denver, Inc.
770 Grand, Suite 5
Denver, Colo. 80203

Mental Patients Liberation Front
P.O. Box 156
West Somerville, Mass. 02144

Mississippi Mental Health Project
P.O. Box 22571
Jackson, Miss. 39206

Mental Health Advocacy
Department of the Public Advocate/State of New Jersey
P.O. Box 141
Trenton, N.J. 08618

Mental Health Information Service
New York Civil Liberties Union (NYCLU)
27 Madison Avenue
New York, N.Y. 10010

Project Release
202 Riverside Drive
New York, N.Y. 10025

504 / THE HELP BOOK

Mental Patients Association
2146 Yew Street
Vancouver, British Columbia,
  BC V6K367 Canada

For direct help—counseling or group therapy—or referrals to treatment facilities, contact your local city or county department of mental health. Hospitals or professional mental health associations may also provide referrals. (See also the introduction to Chapter 14, *Counseling*, for suggestions on how to find a therapist.) Contact your state mental health agency for referrals to local treatment facilities and/or information.

The following are the state agencies for mental health:

Department of Mental Health
502 Washington Avenue
Montgomery, Ala. 36130

Division of Mental Health
Department of Health and Social Services
214 Alaska Office Building
350 Main Street
Pouch H-04
Juneau, Alaska 99811

Behavioral Health Services Division
Department of Health Services
Arizona State Hospital
2500 East Van Buren Street
Phoenix, Ariz. 85008

Division of Mental Health Services
Department of Social and Human
  Services
4313 West Markham Street
Little Rock, Ark. 72201

Division of Mental Health Services
Department of Institutions
4150 South Lowell Boulevard
Denver, Colo. 80236

Department of Mental Health
90 Washington Street
Hartford, Conn. 06115

Division of Mental Health
Department of Health and Social Services
Governor Bacon Health Center
Delaware City, Del. 19706

Mental Health Administration
Department of Human Resources
1875 Connecticut Avenue, N.W.
Washington, D.C. 20009

Mental Health Program Office
Department of Health and Rehabilitative
  Services
1323 Winewood Boulevard
Tallahassee, Fla. 32301

Division of Mental Health and Mental
  Retardation
Department of Human Resources
47 Trinity Avenue, S.W.
Atlanta, Ga. 30334

Mental Health Division
Department of Health
1250 Punchbowl Street
Honolulu, Hawaii 96813

Bureau of Mental Health
Division of Community Rehabilitation
Department of Health and Welfare
700 West State Street
Boise, Idaho 83720

Department of Mental Health and
  Developmental Disabilities
160 North LaSalle
Chicago, Ill. 60601

Department of Mental Health
5 Indiana Square
Indianapolis, Ind. 46204

Mental Health Services
Department of Social Services
3619½ Douglas Avenue
Des Moines, Iowa 50319

Division of Mental Health and Retardation
 Services
Department of Social and Rehabilitation
 Services
State Office Building
Topeka, Kans. 66612

Bureau for Health Services
Department for Human Resources
275 East Main Street
Frankfort, Ky. 40601

Office of Mental Health
655 North Fifth Street
Baton Rouge, La. 70802

Bureau of Mental Health
Department of Mental Health and Corrections
411 State Office Building
Augusta, Me. 04333

Department of Health and Mental Hygiene
201 West Preston Street
Baltimore, Md. 21201

Department of Mental Health
190 Portland Street
Boston, Mass. 02114

Department of Mental Health
Lewis Cass Building
Lansing, Mich. 48926

Mental Health Program Office
Bureau of Community Services
Department of Public Welfare
Centennial Office Building
658 Cedar Street
St. Paul, Minn. 55155

Department of Mental Health
607 Robert E. Lee Building
Jackson, Miss. 39201

Department of Mental Health
2002 Missouri Boulevard
P.O. Box 687
Jefferson City, Mo. 65101

Mental Health/Mental Retardation
Governor's Office
235 Capitol Building
Helena, Mont. 59601

Department of Public Institutions
P.O. Box 94728
State Capitol
Lincoln, Neb. 68509

Division of Mental Hygiene and Mental
 Retardation
Department of Human Resources
2045 California Street
Carson City, Nev. 89710

Division of Mental Health
Department of Health and Welfare
105 Pleasant Street
Concord, N.H. 03301

Division of Mental Health and Hospitals
Department of Human Services
State Office Building
135 West Hanover Street
P.O. Box 1237
Trenton, N.J. 08625

Mental Health Bureau
Health and Environment Department
Southwest Professional Plaza
Santa Fe, N.M. 87501

Department of Mental Hygiene
44 Holland Avenue
Albany, N.Y. 12229

Division of Mental Health Services
Department of Human Resources
Albemarle Building
325 North Salisbury Street
Raleigh, N.C. 27611

Mental Health and Retardation Services
Department of Health
Capitol
Bismarck, N.D. 58505

506 / THE HELP BOOK

Department of Mental Health and Mental
 Retardation
30 East Broad Street
Columbus, Ohio 43215

Department of Mental Health
408-A North Walnut Street
P.O. Box 53277
Oklahoma City, Okla. 73107

Mental Health Division
Department of Human Resources
2575 Bittern Street, N.E.
Salem, Ore. 97310

Office of Mental Health
Department of Public Welfare
P.O. Box 2675
Harrisburg, Pa. 17120

Division of Mental Health
Department of Mental Health, Retardation,
 and Hospitals
600 New London Avenue
Cranston, R.I. 02905

Department of Mental Health
2414 Bull Street
Columbia, S.C. 29202

Division of Mental Health and Mental
 Retardation
Department of Social Services
State Office Building
Illinois Avenue
Pierre, S. D. 57501

Department of Mental Health and Mental
 Retardation
501 Union Street
Nashville, Tenn. 37219

Department of Mental Health and Mental
 Retardation
P.O. Box 12668, Capitol Station
Austin, Tex. 78711

Division of Mental Health
Department of Social Services
554 South Third East Street
Salt Lake City, Utah 84111

Department of Mental Health
State Office Building
120 State Street
Montpelier, Vt. 05602

Department of Mental Health and Mental
 Retardation
P.O. Box 1797
Richmond, Va. 23214

Mental Health Division
Department of Social and Health Services
Mail Stop OB-42F
Olympia, Wash. 98504

Department of Health
Mental Health Services Section
208 State Office Building 3
1800 Washington Street, East
Charleston, W.Va. 25305

Division of Mental Hygiene
Department of Health and Social Services
534 Wilson Street State Office Building
1 West Wilson Street
Madison, Wis. 53702

Mental Health and Mental Retardation
 Services
Division of Health and Medical Services
Department of Health and Social Services
Hathaway Building
Cheyenne, Wyo. 82002

The following national organizations and federal agencies provide information on mental health issues:

Association for Rural Mental Health
University of Wisconsin—Extension
425 Lowell Hall
Madison, Wis. 53706

An information and job clearinghouse that focuses on the clinical, research, consultation, education, and administrative aspects of rural mental health. The association is developing a system by which rural mental health workers may present their needs and concerns to appropriate persons in state and federal agencies who design, implement, and fund community mental health programs.

LITERATURE: *Rural Community Mental Health* newsletter (five times a year; $10.00 by subscription or included in $10.00 membership); special bulletins of interest.

Center for Studies of Schizophrenia
National Institute of Mental Health
5600 Fishers Lane
Parklawn Building, Room 10c–26
Rockville, Md. 20857

An information clearinghouse on schizophrenia that provides research analysis and recommendations and holds conferences.

LITERATURE: Descriptive leaflet; *Treatment of Schizophrenia* and *Schizophrenia: Is There An Answer?*

Child Study Association of America
853 Broadway
New York, N.Y. 10011

Founded in 1888, this is an information clearinghouse and training center for those concerned with family mental health and education programs for underprivileged children, such as Project Head Start. It maintains a library, holds conferences and workshops for those professionals and paraprofessionals in the mental health and family life fields, and provides assistance to community groups and social service agencies.

LITERATURE: *Children's Books of the Year*, annual; numerous free pamphlets and booklets for parents and educators; *Recommended Reading about Children and Family Life*, annual.

Disaster Assistance and Emergency Mental Health Section
National Institute of Mental Health
5600 Fishers Lane
Rockville, Md. 20857

This section of the Department of Health, Education, and Welfare is aimed at helping community mental health and service organizations to respond to the mental health needs of the victims of major disasters. They also have a referrals program to counselors, physicians, lawyers, and other social services including emergency shelters; in-service training programs for hospital personnel; mental health workers, including psychiatrists.

(See Chapter 20, *Emergencies and Disasters*, for complete listing.)

The Hogg Foundation for Mental Health
The University of Texas, W. C. Hogg Building
Austin, Tex. 78712

The foundation furnishes grants to mental health projects in Texas. A free publication is sent four times a year to anyone who would like to be on their mailing list. Their library is open to the general public.

Mental Health Association
1800 North Kent Street
Arlington, Va. 22209

The association is primarily an information clearinghouse to promote citizen interest and activity on behalf of the mentally ill and for the cause of mental health.

LITERATURE: Film and publication catalog; pamphlets include *Facts About Mental Illness, What Every Child Needs, Mental Illness Can Be Prevented* and *How to Deal With Your Tensions*.

Mental Health Materials Center
419 Park Avenue South
New York, N.Y. 10016

An information resources center for mental health and family life education, a clearinghouse

National Institute of Mental Health
U.S. Department of Health, Education, and Welfare
5600 Fishers Lane
Rockville, Md. 28057

The institute acknowledges public inquiries and forwards them to the Mental Health Directory, which publishes a pamphlet listing mental health clinics throughout the United States. Sponsors the National Clearinghouse for Mental Health information.

LITERATURE: *A Consumer's Guide to Mental Health Services;* publications list.

National Self-Help Clearinghouse
c/o Graduate Center, City University of New York
33 West 42nd Street
New York, N.Y. 10036

The Clearinghouse provides an exchange of information for self-help group members, self-help practitioners, and theoreticians in the United States and abroad. The *Self Help Reporter,* a free bimonthly newsletter, is filled with valuable information on conferences, publications, and groups of interest to self-help movements and their members.

National Society for Autistic Children
1234 Massachusetts Avenue, N.W.
Washington, D.C. 20005

The Washington office is the headquarters for this national organization with local chapters throughout the United States that has meetings and conferences for parents whose children are autistic, that is, with severe communication and behavior disorders.

Network Against Psychiatric Assault
558 Capp Street
San Francisco, Calif. 94110

An antipsychiatry mental patients' rights group that publishes *Madness Network News* "All the Fits That's News to Print" (sample copy $.50 prepaid) and "Psychiatry as Social Control: An Annotated Bibliography" ($.25). An information clearinghouse on local mental patients' rights groups throughout the country.

World Federation for Mental Health (WFMH)
2075 Westbrook Crescent
University of British Columbia
Vancouver, British Columbia, Canada V6T 1W5

Founded in 1948, WFMH has 138 member organizations concerned with the promotion of mental health. Educational and scientific research are two of their goals.

LITERATURE: Quarterly newsletter ($15.00).

The following are some of the national professional associations dealing with mental health problems:

American Academy of Child Psychiatry
1424 Sixteenth Street, N.W., Suite 201A
Washington, D.C. 20036

Membership organization of child psychiatrists with thirty-six committees working on a variety of projects, such as studying the nature and problems of residential settings for disturbed children. The Academy *Journal* is published quarterly by Yale University Press.

American Mental Health Foundation, Inc.
2 East 86th Street
New York, N.Y. 10028

A nonprofit institute established in 1924 for the advancement of mental health.

American Orthopsychiatric Association, Inc.
1775 Broadway
New York, N.Y. 10019

Professional organization of those in "all of the disciplines devoted to mental health and the study of human behavior." Annual meetings. Publishes the quarterly *American Journal of Orthopsychiatry* ($20.00 a year).

American Psychiatric Association
1700 Eighteenth Street, N.W.
Washington, D.C. 20009

For complete listing see Chapter 14, *Counseling*.

American Psychological Association
1200 Seventeenth Street, N.W.
Washington, D.C. 20036

For complete listing see Chapter 14, *Counseling*.

National Association of Prevention Professionals
850 West Barry, Suite GA
Chicago, Ill. 60657

A professional association whose membership works in all phases of human services—drug and alcohol abuse, delinquency, mental health, and physical health—but only in a preventive, rather than a rehabilitative, way. It has four goals: to orchestrate prevention efforts; to educate the public about prevention; to provide training and credential granting for prevention professionals; and personal services for members.

LITERATURE: List of courses.

National Association of Community Health Centers, Inc. (NACHC)
1625 Eye Street, N.W.
Washington, D.C. 20006

This national organization (with individual and organizational membership fees from $15.00 to $500.00) is designed to promote and facilitate community health center development. A central library collection is available as well as educational and technical materials through the National Clearinghouse Program of the Community Health Institute (NCP/CHI).

LITERATURE: *Clearinghouse News;* descriptive pamphlet.

ADDITIONAL LITERATURE

Asylums: Essays on the Social Situation of Mental Patients and Other Inmates by Erving Goffman (1961). Anchor Books/Doubleday Publishing Company, Inc., Garden City, N.Y. 11550 ($2.95). Sociologist Goffman did field work in order to observe and interpret life in "total institutions."

Biographical Directory of the American Psychiatric Association, compiled and edited for the American Psychiatric Association by Jacques Cattell Press (1977). R. R. Bowker, P.O. Box 1807, Ann Arbor, Mich. 48106 ($45.00).

A Complete Guide to Therapy from Psychoanalysis to Behavior Modification by Joel Kovel, M.D. (1977). Pantheon Books, 201 East 50th Street, New York, N.Y. 10022 ($3.95).

Help: A Guide to Counseling and Therapy Without a Hassle by Jane Marks (1976). Julian Messner Division, Simon and Schuster, 1230 Avenue of the Americas, New York, N.Y. 10019 ($7.95). An exploration of the various counseling services available, this book is geared to young people (grades seven and up) and stresses the need for better coordination of all services and agencies working with youths.

I Never Promised You a Rose Garden by Hannah Green (1964). HR&W ($6.95). The poignant, wrenching, true story of one woman's fight back from mental illness. Movie edition by Joanne Greenberg (1977) New American Library ($1.75).

Man and His Symbols, edited, with an introduction by Carl G. Jung (1964). Dell Publishing

Company, Inc., 1 Dag Hammarskjold Plaza, New York, N.Y. 10017 ($1.50). This illustrated book is a collection of articles by Jung, Henderson, von Franz, Jaffe, and Jacobi that explores the unconscious, ancient myths and modern man, and symbolism in the visual arts. It is Jung's unique approach to the unconscious, dreams, the past, and the future.

The Myth of Mental Illness: Foundations of a Theory of Personal Conduct, rev. ed., by Thomas S. Szasz (1974). Harper and Row, 10 East 53rd Street, New York, N.Y. 10022 ($2.50).

Neurotic Styles by David Shapiro (1965). Harper and Row, 10 East 53rd Street, New York, N.Y. 10022 ($3.95). The impulsive, obsessive-compulsive, paranoid, and hysterical personality types are described.

One Flew Over the Cuckoo's Nest by Ken Kesey (1962, 1975) New American Library ($1.95). A novelist's penetrating look at a mental institution.

The Rights of Mental Patients by Bruce Ennis and Loren Siegel (1973). American Civil Liberties Union Handbook, Avon Books, 959 Eighth Avenue, New York, N.Y. 10019 ($1.25). A revised edition of *The Basic ACLU Guide to a Mental Patient's Rights* with basic facts about "mental illness," rights in the institution, psychoactive drugs, and the civil commitment process.

Schizophrenia Bulletin, National Institute of Mental Health (quarterly). Available from Superintendent of Documents, Government Printing Office, Washington, D.C. 20402 ($9.00 a year; $2.25 per single copy). Book reviews, reports, and articles on schizophrenia—theories and treatments.

Social Policy (September-October 1976). Special issue on self-help may be ordered for $3.00 from *Social Policy*, 33 West 42nd Street, New York, N.Y. 10036. This issue includes articles on self-help and the professional, self-help and mental health, how self-help works, and so forth.

The Strength in Us: Self-Help Groups in the Modern World by Alfred H. Katz and Eugene I. Bender (1976). New Viewpoints, c/o Franklin Watts, 730 Fifth Avenue, New York, N.Y. 10019 ($6.95). Articles on self-help with contributions by Janet Norman, Richard A. Cloward, and others.

Sybil by Flora Rheta Schreiber (1974). Warner Books ($2.25). The compelling true story of a multipersonality woman's years of struggle back to sanity.

Understanding Mental Health by the National Institute of Mental Health (1978). Consumer Information Center, Dept. 33G, Pueblo, Colo. 81009 ($.40). A booklet defining mental health and providing some of the warning signs of emotional problems that could require professional counseling or therapy.

Understanding Stress by Arthur S. Freese (1976). Public Affairs Committee, 381 Park Avenue South, New York, N.Y. 10016 (#538, $.50). Freese, a medical writer, summarizes our current information on stress, highlighting the research of Cannon, Wolff, Selye, Mason, and others. Some tips are provided in how to minimize the damage that severe stress may cause to the mind and body.

When Mental Illness Strikes Your Family by Kathleen Cassidy Doyle (1951, 1979). Public Affairs Committee, 381 Park Avenue South, New York, N.Y. 10016 (#172, $.50). A brief look at the possible causes of mental illness, some basic facts about mental health, and possible sources of private and public help.

In addition to the *Readers' Guide to Periodical Literature*, which indexes such popular psychology publications as *Psychology Today*, *Human Behavior*, and *Human Nature*, consult the *Psychiatric Abstracts* and *Psychological Abstracts*, which index and highlight articles in such professional journals as the *American Journal of Orthopsychiatry*, *American Journal of Psychoanalysis*, *Journal of Personality and Social Psychology*, *Journal of Humanistic Psychology*, *American Journal of Psychiatry*, and the *Personnel and Guidance Journal*.

See also the following related chapters in *The Help Book*:

AGING
ALCOHOLISM
BATTERED ADULTS
CHILD ABUSE
COUNSELING
COURTS
DRUGS, SMOKING, AND DRUG ABUSE
EMERGENCIES AND DISASTERS
GAMBLING
HANDICAPS
HEALTH
LEGAL SERVICES
MENTAL RETARDATION AND LEARNING DISABILITIES
MULTIPURPOSE ORGANIZATIONS
PARENTING
RAPE AND SEXUAL ASSAULT
SUICIDE PREVENTION
ADDITIONAL RESOURCES

39

MENTAL RETARDATION AND LEARNING DISABILITIES

It is estimated that about 3 percent of the population, or more than 6 million Americans, are mentally retarded. Most of those persons are "mildly" retarded; special education and treatment would enable them to fit in with the general adult population. Too often, however, because parents are ashamed or ignorant, the mentally retarded child is undiagnosed and ignored, or sent to an overcrowded institution and written off by the family.

At present about 200,000 retarded adults and children receive constant care because they cannot function without it. The quality of public services for the mentally retarded varies greatly from state to state (and within each state). Treatment for such persons must be improved, but prevention is also important. There are certain known causes of mental retardation: genetic irregularities; prenatal diseases in the mother and problems occurring during pregnancy; unusually stressful childbearing; certain childhood diseases and accidents; and other external conditions, such as lead poisoning, malnutrition, and understimulation of the brain, which leads to irreversible damage.

Learning disabilities, which are often interpreted as signs of retardation, often have no relationship to intelligence. Children with such problems often do badly in school because teachers are unable to diagnose the specific disability. Not recognizing the learning disabilities, they label the child slow or retarded. The analysis is of course self-fulfilling and eventually the child so-labeled does perform badly. Quite often tests of the child's eyesight or hearing explain the academic problems he or she may be having.

One common learning problem is dyslexia, defined as an impairment of the ability to read. Often a dyslexic child confuses the meaning of words and has difficulty with space and balance. Researchers have done studies that seem to link dyslexia to juvenile delinquency, but such conclusions should be cautiously analyzed.

Hyperactivity is another cause of learning disability. It is a biological trait and is not due to brain damage or environment. But the need for physical activity more often than other youngsters can cause a child to become an outcast. Eventually the child learns to control his or her hyperactivity—by withdrawing. The classroom may be less disrupted, but the child's behavior may develop into a severe problem for him or her.

A leaflet distributed by the Westchester, New York, Association for Children with Learning Disabilities lists some of the common symptoms that a bright child may have who is a poor learner. Exhibiting only a few of these symptoms does not necessarily mean that a child is learning disabled, but a child with many of these problems would require further examination because of a possible disability:*

hyperactive	omission of words, letters, and numbers
confusion in distinguishing between right and left	short attention span
	impulsive
poor coordination	erratic memory
easily distractible	forgetful
inability to judge space and distance	clumsy
poor reading ability	slow
sloppy writing	regularly unfinished homework
reversals of letters	unable to follow instructions
writing name backward	inability to solve simple problems
poor logic	difficulty in holding eyes on a moving object
math problems	avoids competition
poor at copying	cyclical good and bad behavior
inability to understand simple concepts	poor posture
disorganized	poor pencil position
difficulty in telling time	allergies
destructive behavior	low frustration level
poor judgment of time	constant overreaction
pronunciation problems	few or no friends
poor spelling	

Teachers and parents have to learn to understand the specifics of each condition. Then the proper help can be obtained. But no matter what the condition—inherited, biological, or environmental—love, patience, and understanding are universally needed.

Where might you go for help if you have a mentally handicapped child? Some sources are a diagnostic clinic associated with a medical center or a teaching hospital; the pediatrics department at a medical center; the school psychiatrist or

---

*Reprinted with permission from *What Is a Learning Disabled Child?*, available at cost from Westchester Association for Children with Learning Disabilities, P.O. Box 73, Mamaroneck, N.Y. 10543.

514 / THE HELP BOOK

psychologist; local mental health authorities, social welfare organizations, and medical or public library reference departments.

Another local source of direct help and information is your local or state affiliate of the following national organization:

National Association for Retarded Citizens
P.O. Box 6109
2709 Avenue E East
Arlington, Tex. 76011

The national headquarters acts as an information clearinghouse for its over 1,900 local and state units. Through the local units, direct services such as counseling, nursery schools, and recreational events are available. Each unit has its own communication tool (newspaper or newsletter), highlighting monthly meetings, events, and member news. General inquiries to the national office are answered with the booklet *Facts on Mental Retardation*. More technical and specific questions receive individual replies, wherever possible.

LITERATURE: Send $.25 and a self-addressed stamped envelope when requesting the publications price list; pamphlets include "How to Provide for Their Future," ($.50), "Take Care of Yourself" (free), and "It Can Happen to Anyone" ($.25).

For learning disabilities, contact these national organizations for information and referrals to local chapters:

Association for Children with Learning Disabilities (ACLD)
4156 Library Road
Pittsburgh, Pa. 15234

Founded in 1964, there are 48 state groups and over 700 local chapters that provide direct services and educational information on learning disabilities. The headquarters makes referrals to local chapters and also publishes a newsletter that summarizes pertinent legislative and research happenings. Write for complete publications list, but first contact your local chapter for direct help, such as schools, counseling, camps, and parent education.

LITERATURE: Descriptive brochure; publications price list.

Orton Society
8415 Bellona Lane
Towson, Md. 21204

A national organization devoted to the study and treatment of dyslexia.

The following national organizations and federal agencies also provide information on and some direct services for mentally handicapped persons:

American Association on Mental Deficiency (AAMD)
5101 Wisconsin Avenue, N.W., Suite 405
Washington, D.C. 20016

Founded in 1876, AAMD has eleven regional groups whose members include concerned citizens, physicians, administrators, social workers, students, educators, psychiatrists, and psychologists interested in the causes, prevention, and treatment of mental retardation. There are also dozens of specialized committees and an annual meeting in May.

LITERATURE: *American Journal of Mental Deficiency*, bimonthly ($40.00); *Mental Retardation*, bimonthly ($22.00).

Association for Children with Retarded Mental Development (A/CRMD)
902 Broadway
New York, N.Y. 10010

Chartered by New York State as a not-for-profit membership organization, A/CRMD has four geographical centers serving the entire spectrum of mentally retarded persons. It offers a wide range of programs, social and recreational, sheltered and vocational workshops, social rehabilitation, adult skills, and community residence. Conferences, job training and placement, and guest lecturers for schools and universities are also offered.

LITERATURE: Brochures; news reports and opinion in *On the Record* and *Children's Mandate*.

Closer Look
P.O. Box 1492
Washington, D.C. 20013

The National Information Center for the Handicapped is a project of the U.S. Department of Health, Education, and Welfare, Office of Education, Bureau of Education for the Handicapped. Closer Look provides help for parents of children with mental, emotional, and physical handicaps. Advice is provided on how to find educational programs as well as other special services and resources. Whenever possible, Closer Look provides a link with local organizations.

LITERATURE: *Common Sense from Closer Look* (free newsletter); *Practical Advice to Parents* (1974).

Division of Mental Retardation
Council for Exceptional Children
1920 Association Drive
Reston, Va., 22091

An information clearinghouse on educational programs for mentally retarded children that also supplies up-to-date roundups of available teacher training and instructional materials.

Mothers of Children with Down's Syndrome
c/o Northern Virginia Association for Retarded Citizens
105 East Annandale Road, Suite 203
Falls Church, Va., 22046

Founded in 1966, there are four state groups for mothers whose children under the age of eleven have Down's Syndrome. In addition to monthly meetings and parent-to-parent counseling, they provide information for other mothers and the general public. It holds an annual convention and raises funds for research in this area.

President's Committee on Mental Retardation
Washington, D.C. 20201

Established in May 1966 with the secretary of Health, Education, and Welfare as chairperson, the committee is a liaison between federal, public, and private activities in this area and has developed educational materials for the public to try to reduce the incidence of mental retardation. The committee reports to the president at least once annually.

Retarded Infants Services
386 Park Avenue South
New York, N.Y. 10016

Founded in 1953, this service agency is devoted to the physical well-being and development of the retarded child and the sound mental health of the parents. It helps families with retarded children with all aspects of home care, including counseling, Home Aide service, and consultation; assists in foster placement and provides ongoing case follow-up; and operates Step One Children's Center (75 Horatio Street, New York, N.Y. 10014) to prevent development of functional retardation in preschool children from disadvantaged homes. The emphasis is on working with the entire family and keeping families together where possible. It has pioneered training of nonprofessional women as Home Aides to provide supportive services in homes. The First Hope Program offers intervention for parents at the birth of a retarded child, with in-home support, guidance, and infant stimulation.

LITERATURE: RIS Newsletter, annual; brochures.

Special Olympics, Inc.
1701 K Street, N.W., Suite 203
Washington, D.C. 20006

Created and sponsored by the Joseph P. Kennedy, Jr., Foundation, Special Olympics was created in 1968 as an international program of physical fitness, sports training, and athletic competition for mentally retarded adults and children. Fourteen official sports are offered through Special Olympics; about one million mentally retarded persons now participate in them. Anyone from the age of eight up is eligible; IQ scores of the participants are usually 75 or less. Volunteers are always needed to either serve as assistant coaches at the various Special Olympics Competitions or as scorers, timers, or guides. By donating $35.00 a year, you may become a sponsor of a special athlete.

LITERATURE: Free fact sheets; publication catalog.

In addition to your city or county department of mental retardation or education, contact your state department of mental retardation for information or referrals:

Division of Mental Retardation
Department of Mental Health
502 Washington Avenue
Montgomery, Ala. 36130

Department of Health and Social Services
214 Alaska Office Building
350 Main Street
Pouch H-04B
Juneau, Alaska 99811

Bureau of Mental Retardation
Department of Economic Security
1825 East Garfield Street
P.O. Box 6760 (85005)
Phoenix, Ariz. 85006

Mental Retardation-Developmental
  Disabilities Services Division
Department of Social and Human
  Services
Waldon Building
18th and Maple Streets
North Little Rock, Ark. 72201

Division for Developmental Disabilities
Department of Institutions
4150 South Lowell Boulevard
Denver, Colo. 80236

Department of Mental Retardation
79 Elm Street
Hartford, Conn. 06115

Division of Mental Retardation
Department of Health and Social Services
Route 1
Box 1000
Georgetown, Del. 19947

Mental Health Administration
Department of Human Resources
1875 Connecticut Avenue, N.W.
Washington, D.C. 20009

Retardation Program Office
Department of Health and Rehabilitative
  Services
1311 Winewood Boulevard
Tallahassee, Fla. 32301

Division of Mental Health and Mental
  Retardation
Department of Human Resources
47 Trinity Avenue, S.W.
Atlanta, Ga. 30334

Waimano Training School and Hospital
  Division
Department of Health
Pearl City, Hawaii 96782

Developmental Disabilities Council
Division of Community Rehabilitation
Department of Health and Welfare
700 West State Street
Boise, Idaho 83720

Department of Mental Health and
  Developmental Disabilities
160 North LaSalle
Chicago, Ill. 60601

Division on Mental Retardation and Other
  Developmental Disabilities
Department of Mental Health
5 Indiana Square
Indianapolis, Ind. 46204

Bureau of Mental Retardation Services
Department of Social Services
3619½ Douglas Avenue
Des Moines, Iowa 50319

Division of Mental Health and Retardation
  Services
Department of Social and Rehabilitation
  Services
State Office Building
Topeka, Kans. 66612

Bureau for Health Services
Department for Human Resources
275 East Main Street
Frankfort, Ky. 40601

Office of Mental Retardation
P.O. Box 44215
Baton Rouge, La. 70802

Bureau of Mental Retardation
Department of Mental Health and Corrections
State House
Augusta, Me. 04333

Mental Retardation Administration
Department of Health and Mental Hygiene
201 West Preston Street
Baltimore, Md. 21201

Department of Mental Health
190 Portland Street
Boston, Mass. 02114

Department of Mental Health
Lewis Cass Building
Lansing, Mich. 48926

Mental Retardation Program Office
Bureau of Community Services
Department of Public Welfare
Centennial Office Building
658 Cedar Street
St. Paul, Minn. 55155

Division of Mental Retardation
Department of Mental Health
1404 Woolfolk State Office Building
501 North West Street
Jackson, Miss. 39201

Division of Mental Retardation and
  Developmental Disabilities
Department of Mental Health
2002 Missouri Boulevard
Jefferson City, Mo. 65101

Mental Health/Mental Retardation
Governor's Office
235 Capitol Building
Helena, Mont. 59601

Mental Retardation Office
Department of Public Institutions
State Capitol
P.O. Box 94728
Lincoln, Neb. 68509

Division of Mental Hygiene and Mental
  Retardation
Department of Human Resources
Carson City, Nev. 89710

Office of Mental Retardation
Division of Mental Health
Department of Health and Welfare
105 Pleasant Street
Concord, N.H. 03301

Division of Mental Retardation
Department of Human Services
169 West Hanover Street
P.O. Box 1237
Trenton, N.J. 08625

Mental Retardation Bureau
Health and Environment Department
Southwest Professional Plaza
Santa Fe, N.M. 87501

Division of Mental Retardation
Department of Mental Hygiene
44 Holland Avenue
Albany, N.Y. 12229

Division of Mental Health Services
Department of Human Resources
Albemarle Building
325 North Salisbury Street
Raleigh, N.C. 27611

Mental Health and Retardation Services
Department of Health
Capitol
Bismarck, N.D. 58505

Division of Mental Retardation and
  Developmental Disabilities
Department of Mental Health and Mental
  Retardation
30 East Broad Street
Columbus, Ohio 43215

Non-Hospital Medical Care and Services for
  the Mentally Retarded
Department of Institutions, Social, and
  Rehabilitative Services
Sequoyah Memorial Office Building
2400 North Lincoln Boulevard
P.O. Box 25352
Oklahoma City, Okla. 73125

Mental Health Division
Department of Human Resources
2575 Bittern Street, N.E.
Salem, Ore. 97310

Office of Mental Retardation
Department of Public Welfare
P.O. Box 2675
Harrisburg, Pa. 17120

Division of Retardation
Department of Mental Health, Retardation,
  and Hospitals
600 New London Avenue
Cranston, R.I. 02905

Department of Mental Retardation
2712 Middleburg Drive
Columbia, S.C. 29240

Developmental Disabilities Program
Division of Mental Health and Mental
  Retardation
Department of Social Services
Sirgud Anderson Building
Pierre, S.D. 57501

Department of Mental Health and Mental
  Retardation
501 Union Street
Nashville, Tenn. 37219

Department of Mental Health and Mental
  Retardation
P.O. Box 12668, Capitol Station
Austin, Tex. 78711

Utah State Training School
Department of Social Services
American Fork, Utah 84003

Department of Mental Health
State Office Building
120 State Street
Montpelier, Vt. 05602

Department of Mental Health and Mental
  Retardation
P.O. Box 1797
Richmond, Va. 23214

Division of Developmental Disabilities
Department of Social and Health Services
Mail Stop OB-42C
Olympia, Wash. 98504

Commission on Mental Retardation
309 Embleton Building
922 Quarrier Street
Charleston, W.Va. 25305

Bureau of Mental Retardation
Division of Mental Hygiene
Department of Health and Social Services
540 Wilson Street Office Building
1 West Wilson Street
Madison, Wis. 53702

Mental Health and Mental Retardation Services
Division of Health and Medical Services
Department of Health and Social Services
Hathaway Building
Cheyenne, Wyo. 82002

ADDITIONAL LITERATURE

ACLD Newsbriefs (monthly). Association for Children with Learning Disabilities, 4156 Library Road, Pittsburgh, Pa. 15234 ($3.50 a year). News, chapter highlights, legislative roundups.

Action Together/Information Exchange (newsletter, monthly). National Association for Retarded Citizens, P.O. Box 6109, Arlington, Tex. 76011 ($10.00 a year). Includes news roundups about activities of local and state ARCs.

Directory of Educational Facilities for the Learning Disabled (1978-79 edition). Academic Therapy Publications, P.O. Box 899, San Rafael, Calif. 94901 ($.35). State-by-state directory listing addresses, phone numbers, names of directors, and using letters to key in a wide spectrum of information about each facility.

Government Report (monthly). National Association for Retarded Citizens, P.O. Box 6109, Arlington, Tex. 76011 ($15.00 a year). The Governmental Affairs Office of NARC publishes this newsletter, which discusses national legislation and federal agency activities that affect the lives of the mentally retarded.

Journal of Learning Disabilities, 10 issues a year. 101 East Ontario Street, Chicago, Ill. 60611. $20.00 a year; back copies $2.00 each. A multidisciplinary journal with articles, and book reviews, on theory and practice related to learning disabilities.

The Juvenile Court Judge and Learning Disabilities by Frank N. Jacobson (1976). National Council of Juvenile Court Judges, University of Nevada, P.O. Box 8000, Reno, Nev. 89507.

Learning Disabilities: The Link to Delinquency Should Be Determined, But Schools Should Do More Now (March 4, 1977). Report to the Congress by the Comptroller General of the United States. Departments of Justice and Health, Education, and Welfare, Washington, D.C. 20548.

Learning Disability: The Unrealized Potential by Alan O. Ross (1977). McGraw-Hill Book Company, 1221 Avenue of the Americas, New York, N.Y. 10020 ($10.75).

"Learning Disabilities Checklist" (1976). The New York Institute for Child Development, Inc., 205 Lexington Avenue, New York, N.Y. 10016 ($.25). A leaflet with checklists for the preschool through high school-age child that suggests that if you answer yes to at least 10 to 20 percent of the questions, your child may have a learning disability.

Mental Retardation (bimonthly). 5101 Wisconsin Avenue, N.W. Washington, D.C. 20016 ($22.00 a year for nonmembers; $4.00 per copy). An official publication of the American Association on Mental Deficiency.

Mental Retardation News (published six times a year). National Association for Retarded Citizens, P.O. Box 6109, Arlington, Tex. 76011 ($3.50 a year).

The Mentally Retarded, 4th edition, by Thomas E. Jordan (1976). Charles E. Merrill Publishing Company, A Bell & Howell Company, Columbus, Ohio 43216. A comprehensive text on the research around mental retardation plus the dynamics of the mentally retarded—language, education, independent living, and therapeutic considerations.

New Hope for the Retarded Child by Walter Jacob (1954, 1971). Public Affairs Committee, 381 Park Avenue South, New York, N.Y. 10016 (Pamphlet No. 210A, $.50). A popular discussion of mental retardation—possible causes, diagnosing the retarded child, treatment choices, and what parents can do. A list of associations, societies, foundations, and further readings is provided.

Prevention and Treatment of Mental Retardation, edited by Irving Philips (1966). Basic Books, 10 East 53rd Street, New York, N.Y. 10022.

The Rights of Mentally Retarded Persons by Paul R. Friedman (1976). American Civil Liberties Union Handbook, Avon Books, 959 Eighth Avenue, New York, N.Y. 10019 ($1.50).

Rx for Learning Disability by Emmett C. Velten, Jr., and Carlene T. Sampson (1978). Nelson-Hall Company Book Publishers, 325 West Jackson Boulevard, Chicago, Ill. 60606 ($10.95 hardcover; $5.95 paperback). Psychologists Velten and Sampson, who have worked with learning disabled children in Tucson and Yuma, Arizona, are concerned with results, not theories. They provide clear and concise descriptions of specific learning disabilities—conceptual and perceptual deficits, visual inefficiency, hyperactivity, short attention span, and poor listening ability. They then provide specific conditions for success, reversals, and approaches to get results.

Securing the Legal Rights of Retarded Persons by Elizabeth Ogg. Public Affairs Pamphlets, 381 Park Avenue South, New York, N.Y. 10016 (Pamphlet No. 492; $.50).

See also the following related chapters in *The Help Book:*

ADOPTION AND FOSTER CARE
ALCOHOLISM
CHILDBEARING
CHILDREN
COUNSELING
COURTS
DRUGS, SMOKING, AND DRUG ABUSE
EMPLOYMENT
FAMILY PLANNING
FOOD AND NUTRITION
HANDICAPS
HEALTH
LEGAL SERVICES
MENTAL HEALTH
MULTIPURPOSE ORGANIZATIONS
PARENTING
VOLUNTEERISM

40

MULTIPURPOSE ORGANIZATIONS

The Salvation Army. The YMCA. The Girl Scouts of America. The American National Red Cross. The Boy Scouts of America. The United Nations. Familiar names. Familiar services—or are they? These successful helping agencies have become such household words that many persons today are unaware of how up-to-date and modern their programs are. In reexploring all the dynamic multipurpose organizations, formerly known as "charities," there is a lot to learn from their expertise, knowledge, and long-time experience. The Salvation Army, for example, is not just Christmas carolers ringing bells for donations. In New York alone, there are 140 Salvation Army services and centers, all of them free. There is the Outreach Program for drug addicts, staffed by five former addicts; job placement services; day care for the children of working parents; homemaker services for those unable to care for themselves; and alcoholism counseling. There are residences for senior citizens and camps for youngsters, such as Star Lake Camp in New Jersey. With the country divided into four regions and four headquarters, with the main office in New York City, the Salvation Army is accessible to all Americans with all kinds of social, psychological, physical, and emergency needs.

Multipurpose organizations, including the city and state bureau or agency for social services, are links to a wide range of problem areas, such as child abuse, alcoholism, prison reform, victim assistance, the aged, and drug addiction—hence the label "multipurpose."

For information on nonprofit multipurpose organizations, contact the following:

The National Assembly of National Voluntary Health and Social Welfare Organizations, Inc.
345 East 46th Street
New York, N.Y. 10017

The National Assembly is an association of national voluntary health and social welfare organizations that are concerned with human services. Its four goals include: promoting

522 / THE HELP BOOK

interagency collaboration; encouraging and interpreting volunteerism; exchanging information among assembly members, and increasing the effectiveness of member organizations in state and federal legislation, programs, and policies. (For a listing of member organizations, see entry in Chapter 50, *Volunteerism*.)

LITERATURE: *1978 Service Directory of National Voluntary Health and Social Welfare Organizations*, 13th edition, edited by Elma P. Cole ($5.00).

National Information Bureau, Inc. (NIB)
419 Park Avenue South
New York, N.Y. 10016

Started in 1918, NIB is a nonprofit, independent watchdog organization that reports on philanthropies, evaluating them against NIB's eight basic standards. It generally does not report on religious, fraternal, or political organizations and single or local institutions, but does report on those that regularly solicit contributions from the public. For example, of the more than 500 organizations watched, just a few that meet NIB standards for which reports are available are the Allergy Foundation of America, Asia Society, National Urban League, and Youth for Understanding. NIB will send on request up to three reports on individual agencies.

LITERATURE: *Wise Giving for Contributors* (free); *Wise Giving Guide*, monthly ($20.00 a year).

Philanthropic Advisory Service
Council of Better Business Bureaus
1150 Seventeenth Street, N.W.
Washington, D.C. 20036

The service maintains files on about 8,000 fund-raising organizations and will send up to three reports on charities, on request, free.

The following national multipurpose organizations are nonsectarian or nondenominational:

American National Red Cross
17th and D Streets, N.W.
Washington, D.C. 20006

Local chapters in nearly every community throughout the United States provide a multitude of direct and informational services, including the blood program (see listing in Chapter 30, *Health*), Disaster Relief Service (see Chapter 20, *Emergencies and Disasters*), services to the Armed Forces and Veterans, training people to care for the homebound, courses in preparation for parenthood, first aid and cardiopulmonary resuscitation, boating safety and water safety, telephone reassurance for the elderly, counseling, and emergency shelter and relief.

LITERATURE: Some free publications; *Standard First Aid and Personal Safety* ($1.95); *Advanced First Aid and Emergency Care* ($2.50).

Child Welfare League of America, Inc.
67 Irving Place
New York, N.Y. 10003

A private national organization devoted to developing standards in the areas that have been specified as child welfare services, such as adoption, foster parenting, homemaker services, juvenile delinquency, and unmarried parents. Accredited and associate member agencies around the country provide some or all of these services. A reference library is maintained at the headquarters; seminars and conferences are held throughout the year.

LITERATURE: Publications list available upon request. (See entry on page 4 for specific listings.)

Kiwanis International
Kiwanis International Building
101 East Erie Street
Chicago, Ill. 60611

Founded in 1915, Kiwanis serves communities in sixty-two nations through the committees of its more than 7,000 local clubs. These committees cover such areas as support of spiritual aims, agriculture and conservation, work with older citizens, assistance to youth, community betterment, anti-drug abuse, crime prevention, and scholarship. (For details on their crime prevention program and materials, see Chapter 16, *Crime Prevention*.)

LITERATURE: *Circle K* Magazine (free); *The Keynoter* (free); *Kiwanis Magazine* ($2.50 a year).

Family Service Association of America
44 East 23rd Street
New York, N.Y. 10010

A national organization that is a federation of about 300 local agencies offering a wide variety of direct services in the areas of family advocacy, sex therapy, marital counseling, child care, single parenting, and so forth. Consultation is provided to industry, labor unions, schools, prisons, and self-help groups; education is pursued through supervised fieldwork, institutes, workshops, and conferences.

LITERATURE: Publications list available upon request; *A Planning Handbook for Voluntary Social Welfare Agencies* ($25.00); *How to Organize a Family Service Agency* ($2.00). (See entry on page 4 for specific listings.)

National Association of Counties (NACo)
1735 New York Avenue, N.W.
Washington, D.C. 20006

A national clearinghouse for dissemination of information on county government to county, state, and federal officials, students, and other interested persons. Its committees include Aging, Rural Human Resources Program, Alcohol and Alcohol Abuse Program, Criminal Justice Program, Health Planning and Resource Development Program, Community Development Project, Higher Education Project, and Energy Project.

LITERATURE: Free fact sheets and pamphlets on NACo and various programs; publications price list; *County News*, weekly ($15.00 a year); *Welfare Reform* (free); *A Guide to Reducing Energy Use Budget Costs* (free); five reports on services to the elderly (free).

National Exchange Club
3050 Central Avenue
Toledo, Ohio 43606

Founded in 1911, the club is a national educational community service organization with more than 1,300 local chapters comprised of business and professional persons dedicated to serving fellow Americans on the local, state, and national levels. Membership is nearly 50,000. Several projects of key concern are crime prevention, Freedom Shrine, "One Nation Under God," Junior Exchange, and Youth of the Month/Year. The club has additional American citizenship programs; Project: IDEA (Drugs to Eradicate Abuse); family days; and traffic safety and fire prevention programs. See Chapter 16, *Crime Prevention*, for details on the club's program.

LITERATURE: Free descriptive booklet, *History of Exchange*; fact sheet.

Business and Professional Women's Foundation
2012 Massachusetts Avenue, N.W.
Washington, D.C. 20036

See listing in Chapter 7, *Business Information*.

United Nations Association of the U.S.A., Inc.
345 East 46th Street
New York, N.Y. 10017

An organization founded to improve public knowledge of the United Nations and those specialized agencies of the UN that have a direct effect on the lives of American citizens. Another goal is to develop ideas on how to make the UN a more effective instrument for dealing with global problems, such as housing, poverty, and hunger. It is supported entirely by membership dues ($20.00 a year) and contributions from business and labor organizations, foundations, and individuals.

LITERATURE: *The "You" in the UN* and *The World Is Our Business* (free booklets); fact sheets; UN Charter; UN Day Kit ($2.50); International Covenants on Human Rights ($.25); UN Flag Kit ($3.95); *Universal Declaration of Human Rights* ($.25); *Reference Guide to the UN System* ($2.50); *The Inter Dependent*, monthly report on world affairs issues ($5.00 a year); *The UN Everything Kit* ($3.50); *Equal Rights for Women—A Call for Action* ($.25); publications list.

United States Conference of Mayors
1620 Eye Street, N.W.
Washington, D.C. 20006

The members in this national organization are the mayors of U.S. cities. One goal is to develop better federal-city relationships. It is also an information clearinghouse for mayors and citizens. Eight standing committees are Task Force on Aging, National Community Development Association, Citizen Participation Council, Alcohol Abuse, Energy, Community Economic Development, Volunteers for Neighborhood Commercial Revitalization, and Water Quality.

LITERATURE: Descriptive brochure; publications price list; fact sheets; *The Mayor*, semimonthly newsletter ($10.00 a year); annual meeting report.

United Way of America
801 North Fairfax Street
Alexandria, Va. 22314

The United Way provides national, regional, and local program support and consultation to United Way organizations in the areas of fund raising, budgeting, allocating, planning, and communication; assists in fund raising through conduct of companywide employee campaigns and cultivation of increased corporate giving by selected companies through the National Corporate Development Program; administers staff and volunteer development training through the National Academy for Voluntarism; provides one-year internships to train new professionals well grounded in community planning, allocations, communications, and fund raising; acts as liaison between United Way organizations and governmental agencies; and provides national media support and produces campaign, promotion, and education aids for members.

Women's Information and Referral Centre
3585 St. Urbain
Montreal, Quebec, Canada

A multipurpose women's center providing peer counseling, vocational advice, public information, and referrals in a variety of areas, including self-help groups, where to sell arts and crafts, welfare, and minimum wage. The center has a speakers bureau, feminist research library, and a listing of babysitters.

LITERATURE: Brochure: newsletter ($2.00 a year).

The following are local independent or nationally affiliated religious-based multipurpose direct services, formerly known as "charities." Although the parent organization might be Catholic, Quaker, Protestant, or Jewish, generally all persons needing help are welcome. Consult your local telephone directory under the denomination or agency's name or contact these national headquarters for referrals to local branches or general information:

American Friends Service Committee (AFSC)
1501 Cherry Street
Philadelphia, Pa. 19102

Quaker faith multipurpose service organization with regional offices and branches throughout the United States that provide assistance to farm workers, criminal offenders, native Americans striving for economic survival, education, and anti-hunger programs for children. For example, a Pittsburgh affiliate operates a national clearinghouse on conflict resolution.

LITERATURE: Free pamphlets include *Toward People Power; Behind Bars;* and *The Problems of Hunger.*

Federation of Protestant Welfare Agencies
281 Park Avenue South
New York, N.Y. 10010

More than 300 member agencies: 143 provide services to children and families; 66 serve the aged; 91 help youth in neighborhood centers and settlement houses.

LITERATURE: Leaflet; annual report.

National Conference of Christians and Jews (NCCJ)
43 West 57th Street
New York, N.Y. 10019

Through its local branches, NCCJ has programs involved with youth, employment, the criminal justice system, and interreligious harmony. It holds seminars and has direct services through the initiation of programs such as crime prevention and aid to crime victims in Santa Ana, Pasadena, San Bernardino, and San Jacinto, California. NCCJ also runs the Religious News Service.

LITERATURE: *People for People,* free pamphlet; *The Employment of Persons With Arrest Records and the Ex-offender.*

National Council of Jewish Women
15 East 26th Street
New York, N.Y. 10010

Multipurpose helping organization conducting research and implementing programs in day care, justice for children, health and welfare services, including crisis centers, women's issues, and constitution rights. The council is a member organization of Women in Community Service (WICS), a volunteer program.

LITERATURE: Descriptive brochure; publications price list.

National Jewish Welfare Board (JWB)
15 East 26th Street
New York, N.Y. 10010

A federation of 370 affiliated Jewish community centers and YM-YWHAs and their branches and camps in the United States and Canada, with a combined membership of more than 800,000.

Salvation Army
National Headquarters
120 West 14th Street
New York, N.Y. 10011

Check your local directory for the nearest Salvation Army center or write to your territorial or the national headquarters for a referral. These are just some of the free programs provided: family counseling, prison counseling, disaster aid, summer camps for the elderly, information services on social security and old age assistance, settlements, day-care centers, youth clubs, employment services, residences for businesswomen, children's homes and foster care, help for unwed mothers, and a missing persons bureau.

Young Men's Christian Association (YMCA)
National Board
291 Broadway
New York, N.Y. 10007

The YMCA National Board provides program support and development, and consultative services to the local YMCA's throughout the country. Its goals include changing the conditions that foster alienation, delinquency, and crime; eliminating racism; strengthening physical and mental health; bringing together people from different countries to build an international understanding and world peace; and stimulating the development and communication of those values associated with Christian principles.

LITERATURE: *Partners in the People Business* (free).

Young Men's and Young Women's Hebrew Association (YM-YWHA)
1395 Lexington Avenue
New York, N.Y. 10028

Better known as the "92nd Street Y," this cultural center, established in 1945, has branches in New York's five boroughs. Its educational and other services include poetry readings, day camps, physical health facilities, senior citizen services, and scholarships. (Also see preceding listing for the National Jewish Welfare Board).

LITERATURE: *Bulletin,* published eighteen times a year; *Bulletin of Activities,* annual.

Young Women's Christian Association of the U.S.A. (YWCA)
National Board
600 Lexington Avenue
New York, N.Y. 10022

Contact your local YWCA to see what services are offered; workshops are offered in a variety of problem and women-related areas, including self-defense, drug addiction, and battered wives.

LITERATURE: *Interchange* newsletter.

Unlike most federal departments, such as the U.S. Department of Transportation, whose activities are confined to the transportation area, the following federal departments include subagencies or offices with a multipurpose scope. Write to the Special Assistant for Consumer Affairs for publication lists or more information.

U.S Department of Health, Education, and Welfare
330 Independence Avenue, S.W.
Washington, D.C. 20201

Office of Education
400 Maryland Avenue, S.W.
Washington, D.C. 20202

National Institute of Education
1200 Nineteenth Street, N.W.
Washington, D.C. 20208

Alcohol, Drug Abuse, and Mental Health Administration
5600 Fishers Lane
Rockville, Md. 20857

Center for Disease Control
1600 Clifton Road, N.E.
Atlanta, Ga. 30333

Food and Drug Administration
5600 Fishers Lane
Rockville, Md. 20857

Health Services Administration
5600 Fishers Lane
Rockville, Md. 20857

National Institutes of Health
9000 Rockville Pike
Bethesda, Md. 20014

Health Care Financing Administration
330 C Street, S.W.
Washington, D.C. 20201

Social Security Administration
6401 Security Boulevard
Baltimore, Md. 21235

Office of Child Support Enforcement
6401 Security Boulevard
Baltimore, Md. 21235

Office of Human Development (OHD)
330 Independence Avenue, S.W.
Washington, D.C. 20201

OHD consists of these units:
    Office for Handicapped Individuals
    President's Committee on Mental Retardation
    Office of Rural Development
    Office of Manpower
    Office of Volunteer Development
    Office of Veterans Affairs
    Federal Council on the Aging

Your state department of social services may have available a directory of services that lists the various agencies that it covers as well as free pamphlets on such federal programs as AFDC (Aid to Families With Dependent Children), Medicaid, and welfare.

The following are the state agencies for social services:

Department of Pensions and Security
Social Service Planning Unit
1 Court Square
Montgomery, Ala. 36104

Division of Social Services
Department of Health and Social Services
404 Alaska Office Building
Pouch H-05
Juneau, Alaska 99811

Social Services Bureau
Department of Economic Security
1717 West Jefferson
Phoenix, Ariz. 85007

Social Services Division
Department of Human Services
Central Office
406 National Old Line Building
Little Rock, Ark. 72201

Department of Social Services
714 P Street, MS 17–16
Sacramento, Calif. 95814

Department of Social Services
State Social Services Building
1575 Sherman Street
Denver, Colo. 80203

Department of Social Services
110 Bartholomew Avenue
Hartford, Conn. 06115

Division of Social Services
Department of Health and Social Services
P.O. Box 309
Wilmington, Del. 19899

Department of Human Resources
District Building
14th and E Streets, N.W.
Washington, D.C. 20004

Division of Social and Economic Services
Department of Health and Rehabilitative
    Services
1323 Winewood Boulevard
Tallahassee, Fla. 32301

Division of Social Services
Department of Human Resources
47 Trinity Avenue, S.W.
Atlanta, Ga. 30334

Department of Social Services and Housing
1390 Miller Street
Honolulu, Hawaii 96813

Bureau of Social Services
Division of Welfare
Department of Health and Welfare
700 West State Street
Boise, Idaho 83720

Department of Children and Family Services
160 North LaSalle
Chicago, Ill. 60601

Division of Child Welfare-Social Services
Department of Public Welfare
701 State Office Building
Indianapolis, Ind. 46204

Department of Social Services
Robert Lucas State Office Building
East 12th and Walnut Streets
Des Moines, Iowa 50319

Department of Social and Rehabilitation
    Services
State Office Building
Topeka, Kans. 66612

Bureau for Social Services
Department for Human Resources
275 East Main Street
Frankfort, Ky. 40601

Office of Family Services
P.O. Box 44065
Baton Rouge, La. 70804

Department of Human Resources
1100 North Eutaw Street
Baltimore, Md. 21201

Office of Social Services
Department of Public Welfare
600 Washington Street
Boston, Mass. 02111

Department of Social Services
300 South Capitol Avenue
Lansing, Mich. 48926

Division of Social Services
Bureau of Community Services
Department of Public Welfare
Centennial Office Building
658 Cedar Street
St. Paul, Minn. 55155

Department of Public Welfare
600 Dale Building
Jackson, Miss. 39216

Department of Social Services
Broadway State Office Building
Jefferson City, Mo. 65101

Social Services Bureau
Community Services Division
Department of Social and Rehabilitation
    Services
SRS Building 111 Sanders
Helena, Mont. 59601

Department of Public Welfare
301 Centennial Mall South
Lincoln, Neb. 68509

Department of Human Resources
251 Jeanell Drive
Capitol Complex
Carson City, Nev. 89701

Division of Welfare
Department of Health and Welfare
8 Loudon Road
Concord, N.H. 03301

Social Services Division
Human Services Department
PERA Building
Santa Fe, N.M. 87503

Department of Social Services
40 North Pearl Street
Albany, N.Y. 12243

Division of Social Services
Department of Human Resources
Albemarle Building
325 North Salisbury Street
Raleigh, N.C. 27611

Social Service Board
State Capitol
Bismarck, N.D. 58505

Division of Social Services
Department of Public Welfare
30 East Broad Street
Columbus, Ohio 43215

Department of Institutions, Social, and Rehabilitative Services
Sequoyah Memorial Office Building
2400 North Lincoln Boulevard
P.O. Box 25352
Oklahoma City, Okla. 73125

Department of Human Resources
318 Public Service Building
Salem, Ore. 97310

Office of Social Services
Department of Public Welfare
P.O. Box 2675
Harrisburg, Pa. 17120

Department of Social and Rehabilitative Services
600 New London Avenue
Cranston, R.I. 02905

Department of Social Services
North Tower Complex
1535 Confederate Avenue, Ext.
Columbia, S.C. 29202

Department of Social Services
Capitol Building
Pierre, S.D. 57501

Social Services
Department of Human Services
State Office Building
Charlotte Avenue
Nashville, Tenn. 37219

Social Services Branch
Department of Public Welfare
John H. Reagan State Office Building
Austin, Tex. 78701

Department of Social Services
10 Exchange Place
Salt Lake City, Utah 84111

Division of Social Services
Department of Social and Rehabilitation Services
Agency of Human Services
81 River Street
Montpelier, Vt. 05602

Office of Human Resources
Ninth Street Office Building, 6th Floor
9th and Grace Streets
P.O. Box 1475
Richmond, Va. 23212

Department of Social and Health Services
Office of Information and Adjustment
Mail Stop OB-44T
Olympia, Wash. 98504

Social Services
Department of Welfare
State Office Building 6
Charleston, W.Va. 25305

Department of Health and Social Services
663, 1 West Wilson Street
Madison, Wis. 53702

Department of Health and Social Services
Hathaway Building
Cheyenne, Wyo. 82002

ADDITIONAL LITERATURE

Directory of Agencies: U.S. Voluntary, International Voluntary, and Intergovernmental (1978). National Association of Social Workers, 1425 H Street, N.W., Washington, D.C. 20005. Information on the membership, purposes, and programs of more than 300 national voluntary agencies related to the profession of social work.

Directory of Jewish Federations, Funds, and Councils. Council of Jewish Federation and Welfare Funds, 315 Park Avenue South, New York, N.Y. 10010 ($3.50).

Encyclopedia of Associations edited by Mary Wilson Pair (1978). (Volume 1: *National Organizations of the United States.*) Gale Research Company, Book Tower, Detroit, Mich. 48226 ($75.00). A 1,500-page annotated directory that lists over 13,271 active organizations in seventeen subject categories including social welfare. Available at most public and college libraries. (Volume 2 rearranges this material by *Geographic and Executive Index;* Volume 3 lists *New Associations and Projects.*)

Federation of Protestant Welfare Agencies Directory: A Manual for Donors and Their Advisors, 7th edition, Ruth A. Logan, editor (1976). 281 Park Avenue South, New York, N.Y. 10010. Updated periodically since 1935, this directory contains descriptions of facilities being funded by the Federation of Protestant Welfare Agencies, such as child-care agencies and facilities for the aged.

NASW Professional Social Workers' Directory (1978 edition), Chauncey A. Alexander, executive director. 1425 H Street, N.W., Washington, D.C. 20005 ($40.00). A directory of member social workers.

National Directory of Private Social Services (updated by monthly supplements), compiled by Helga B. Croner and Kurt J. Guggenheimer. Croner Publications, Inc., 211–03 Jamaica Avenue, Queens Village, N.Y. 11428 ($18.00 a year plus $1.95 postage and handling). State-by-state brief listings; pertinent journals are highlighted.

National Trade and Professional Associations of the United States and Canada and Labor Unions: NTPA 1978, 13th edition, Craig Colgate, Jr., editor, and Patricia Broida, assistant editor (1979). Columbia Books, Inc., 734 15th Street, N.W., Washington, D.C. 20005 ($30.00). Annotated thumbnail listings and descriptions.

Public Welfare Directory, edited by Perry Frank. American Public Welfare Association, 1155 Sixteenth Street, N.W., Suite 201, Washington, D.C. 20036 ($25.00). Lists all state agencies and over 1,700 state, local, and federal agencies providing help.

Service Directory of National Voluntary Organizations (1978 edition). National Assembly of National Voluntary Health and Social Welfare Organizations, Inc., 345 East 46th Street, Room 715, New York, N.Y. 10017 ($5.00). This annotated directory describes eighty national voluntary organizations in the health and social welfare fields and tells how and where to apply for their services.

United Way of America International Directory (annual). 801 North Fairfax Street, Alexandria, Va. 22314. Listing of all local United Way social service agencies.

The Workbook, monthly. Southwest Research and Information Center, P.O. Box 4524, Albuquerque, N.M. 87106. (Subscriptions $7.00 a year to students; $10.00 to individuals; $20.00 to institutions.) Annotated descriptions of private and public local, statewide, and national organizations offering direct help and/or information in a wide range of social, consumer, and environmental problems.

Nearly every chapter in *The Help Book* lists multipurpose organizations that serve the needs discussed in that chapter, particularly under the federal and national organizations headings. Should you not find what you are looking for in *Multipurpose Organizations,* check through the other listings throughout *The Help Book.*

41

OFFENDERS AND EX-OFFENDERS

While the academics debate about whether rehabilitation "works," educational and vocational training programs are improving at many county jails and minimum- and maximum-security prisons around the country. Degree offerings in alliance with two- and four-year colleges and accelerated study toward a high school equivalency diploma are helping more inmates gain academic credentials before their release. Trained and voluntary laypersons and professionals now share their trade and general abilities in reading tutorial programs and workshops in photography, writing, and other areas. At the Suffolk County jail in Yaphank, Long Island, the farm that supplies the institution with much of its produce is not run by the inmates, as is the case at most rural institutions. Instead, outside workers are employed at $4.50 an hour so that the thirty or so prisoners may learn more relevant trades such as meat cutting and small engine and motorcycle repair mechanics, to help in post-prison job hunting.

Change comes slowly in penal institutions, but there are a few noticeable ones. Conjugal visits are permitted in only a few institutions (Mississippi State Penitentiary and the Correctional Training Facility for men in Soledad, California); but weekend furloughs for prisoners who are within a year of their release are quite common around the country. Work release is also a growing practice, facilitating the transition back into society while providing job training. Other programs, whereby the offender makes financial or service restitution to the victim of a crime, a social service agency, or the state, are gaining acceptance around the country as the economic and psychological advantages of these variations on imprisonment are being heralded.

More than ever before there is help for the ex-offender with job-related problems. Many organizations have set up cross-country networks to provide direct assistance to ex-offenders and also to break down the after-release prejudices and restrictions that can inspire further criminal activity. For example, the American

Bar Association has established the Clearinghouse on Offender Employment Restrictions of the National Offender Services Coordination Program. Its directory lists national and local organizations by state that provide ex-offender job placement services and referrals. One of the most active organizations in this area is the National Alliance of Business, whose local offices have placed thousands of job-ready ex-offenders in productive new careers. On the local level, communities are finding out that giving money to an ex-offender job placement center is far less costly than ignoring the real problems of ex-offender training and placement. One very active program is the SAFER Foundation that services the Greater Cook County area in Illinois. One of its programs is Operation DARE (Direct Action for the Rehabilitation and Employment of Ex-Offenders). In 1975, through Operation DARE, more than 1,000 ex-offenders were placed in jobs. Over a five-year period, more than 4,000 ex-offenders have been placed in jobs. More than 300 trained citizen volunteers help ex-offenders through SAFER's Challenge program.

Does rehabilitation make sense? In Illinois, it costs $14,322 to arrest, convict, and imprison an ex-offender for one year. The Safer Foundation needs only $350 to help keep each ex-offender out of prison.

You may have difficulty finding a local direct service for offenders or ex-offenders since it may not be listed in your yellow pages under the obvious heading and you need the precise name to find it in the white pages. Therefore, you may have to consult some of the directories that are listed in the Additional Literature section for a referral to a local resource. Your city or state corrections department or parole and probation agency may also make referrals to private, nonprofit helping organizations or peer counseling groups. (See listings of state agencies that follow in this chapter.)

What might you expect to find at a free offender or ex-offender association? The services offered vary widely, but here are four local groups that might provide you with some guidelines:

Delancey Street Foundation, Inc.
2563 Divisadero
San Francisco, Calif. 94115

A self-help residential program for drug addicts, alcoholics, prostitutes, and criminal offenders that is totally integrated racially, sexually, and by age. Founded in January 1971, it has helped more than 3,000 people from the jails and streets.

LITERATURE: Fact sheets.

The Fortune Society
229 Park Avenue South
New York, N.Y. 10003

Direct services of the society, such as rap sessions and ex-offender employment assistance, are local, but their information gathering and disseminating projects are national in scope. It sponsors conferences and meetings that are open to the public on various offender-related topics, such as homosexuality, prison reform, alternatives to confinement, and weekly open houses where students and concerned citizens may meet and informally talk with ex-offenders. Closed meetings are held for ex-offenders who respond to self-help peer counseling groups. Its monthly newspaper, *Fortune News,* is free to inmates; available to others for a donation ($10.00 and up). Letters and articles by inmates are frequently published. Fortune has a mail-order book service that sells the leading hardcover and paperback books in the criminal justice field, including prison memoirs, sociological studies, ex-offender projects, and psychological explorations. It also has an annual anniversary cocktail party for its members.

NAACP Project Rebound
270 West 96th Street
New York, N.Y. 10025

Started in 1971, Project Rebound provides on-the-job training with private firms for ex-offenders.

LITERATURE: Free brochure and newsletter, *Rebound.*

Self Development Group
120 Tremont Street
Boston, Mass. 02108

Founded in 1963, this is a self-help counseling group for offenders and ex-offenders that makes referrals, conducts rap sessions, and provides general information and emergency housing.

For referrals to local direct help for ex-offenders—counseling, employment, legal advice—contact the following organizations:

Clearinghouse on Offender Employment Restrictions
National Offender Services Coordination
    Program
1800 M Street, N.W.
Washington, D.C. 20036

Run by the American Bar Association, this is a research and fact-finding project that is also an information clearinghouse on ex-offender employment.

LITERATURE: Extensive publications; Directory (see Additional Literature); *Employing the Ex-Offender: Some Legal Considerations.*

National Alliance of Businessmen (NAB)
Ex-Offender Employment Program
1730 K Street, N.W.
Washington, D.C. 20006

Initiated in 1973 at the request of the White House, NAB has helped tens of thousands of ex-offenders get jobs through programs started in more than twelve states. It also sponsors conferences and publishes information.

LITERATURE: *Dictionary of Desperation* (free to bonafide employers).

National Council on Crime and Delinquency
Continental Plaza
411 Hackensack Avenue
Hackensack, N.J. 07601

Sponsors a variety of local programs to help offenders and ex-offenders and has extensive publications in this area; write for their literature price list.

National Volunteer Parole Aide Program
American Bar Association
Commission on Correctional Facilities and
    Services
1800 M Street, N.W.
Washington, D.C. 20036

Contact your state or local bar association for the nearest program that you can get involved in or that will help you.

Safer Foundation
343 South Dearborn
Chicago, Ill. 60604

Employment project for ex-offenders in Chicago and in Rock Island, Ill., area. It recruits citizen volunteers to work one-to-one with ex-offenders and has counseling and an employer and public education program.

LITERATURE: Free descriptive leaflets and brochures; *The Eddie Kendricks Story*, leaflet; *News From Safer*.

Seventh Step Foundation
P.O. Box 1261
Nashville, Tenn. 37205

Self-help and self-awareness programs for ex-offenders, parolees, and juvenile delinquents. It originated with ninety-three convicts at the Kansas State Penitentiary in 1963.

LITERATURE: *Visions of Freedom;* fact sheet.

U.S. Civil Service Commission
Bureau of Recruiting and Examining
Washington, D.C. 20415

Provides information on employment opportunities for ex-offenders with the federal government.

United States Jaycees
P.O. Box 7
Tulsa, Okla. 74102

This national organization, with over 385 chapters in correctional institutions, has a job awareness program for ex-offenders as well as potential employers. Extensive written materials are available.

LITERATURE: *Job Awareness Seminar* ($.50); *Volunteer Guide* ($.60); *Community Resource Guide* ($.50); and *Criminal Justice Print-Media Kit* ($1.00).

The following national organizations provide counseling for offenders, ex-offenders and their families:

Alston Wilkes Society
P.O. Box 363
2215 Devine Street
Columbia, S.C. 29202

More than 6,000 members belong to this national volunteer program for helping ex-offenders; it has branches in several other communities. Projects include the Prison Visitation Program, Ex-Offender Project, Juvenile Program, Family Services, Alston Wilkes Homes, and a program for providing long-term foster care for juveniles. Runaway children are a particular area of concern to this society.

LITERATURE: Free booklets on each project; annual report.

Correctional Service Federation U.S.A.
297 Park Avenue South
New York, N.Y. 10010

Affiliated with the International Prisoners Aid Association, the federation tries to coordinate services to prisoners and former inmates. It is an information clearinghouse about volunteer correctional service agencies; provides news about corrections; produces publications; and conducts research.

LITERATURE: Newsletter; *Directory of Correctional Service Agencies* (single copies free).

Prison Families Anonymous, Inc.
131 Jackson Street
Hempstead, N.Y. 11550

Self-help groups for the families of prisoners and ex-offenders in the New York and Long Island area modeled after Alcoholics Anonymous. It has a community education program, contact and outreach, referrals, and publications.

LITERATURE: Information packet including brochures, flyer, and form letter.

OFFENDERS AND EX-OFFENDERS / 535

Prison Pen Pal Program
% Lou Torok
Box 1217
Cincinnati, Ohio 45202

Lou Torok began this letter-writing program because he realized how significant just one letter from a caring outsider could mean to a convicted, imprisoned person. A list of names and biographies of men, women, and children in institutions is mailed and the correspondent makes his or her own selections. A nonprofit, all-volunteer operation, membership is $10.00 a year (including *News Bulletin*) and up.

Prisoners Union
1315 18th Street
San Francisco, Calif. 94107

A prisoner advocacy group dedicated to restoring the civil and human rights of convicts and ex-convicts with the introduction of a prevailing wage for all work done in prison and to establish uniform sentencing and abolish indeterminate sentences. It is also working to collectively bargain over inmate grievances. Branches are located in North Carolina, Minnesota, and Oklahoma.

LITERATURE: *Outlaw: The Journal of the Prisoners Union*, newspaper.

Salvation Army
National Office
120 West 14th Street
New York, N.Y. 10011

Contact your local affiliate for direct help—prisoner counseling and visitation.

Women's Prison Association and Hopper Home
110 Second Avenue
New York, N.Y. 10003

A private, nonprofit agency founded in 1884 and dedicated to providing rehabilitative services to female inmates and ex-offenders, including a no-fee halfway house facility, some financial support, intensive individual and group counseling, referrals, work placements and job development, and visits to inmates in various correctional facilities. It is also a national informational clearinghouse and educational program regarding female offenders.

The following national organizations are concerned with the rights of prisoners and with providing information and services to them while incarcerated:

American Civil Liberties Union
National Prison Project
1346 Connecticut Avenue N.W., Suite 1031
Washington, D.C. 20036

Handles class action suits involving prison conditions as well as related issues in federal and state institutions. The Project also gives advice and educational materials to others involved in prison issues.

LITERATURE: *Prisoners' Assistance Directory* ($10.00 prepaid).

American Correctional Association
4321 Hartwick Road
College Park, Md. 20740

A membership organization of correctional officials that participates nationally and internationally in correctional concerns.

LITERATURE: *American Journal of Correction* (free to members; $10.00 others); *On the Line* newsletter.

American Friends Service Committee (AFSC)
Committee on Penal Affairs
160 North 15th Street
Philadelphia, Pa. 19102

In the late 1960s, AFSC organized a national group to attack criminal justice system problems that resulted in the book *Struggle for Justice*, which suggested that offenders should organize for self-determination. AFSC is still very active in providing prisoner assistance.

American Medical Association Program to Improve Medical Care and Health Services in Jails
535 North Dearborn
Chicago, Ill. 60610

The program has extensive services and publications, including a clearinghouse of general or specific technical information and assistance. There are state and local affiliates in every community.

LITERATURE: Fact sheets; leaflets and booklets.

Howard League for Penal Reform
125 Kensington Park Road
London SE11 4JP, England

An international organization to achieve penal reforms that make the treatment of the offender fair, effective, and humane. The league has several publications and holds conferences.

LITERATURE: Descriptive leaflet; *Howard Journal* (three times a year).

National Association of Counties Research Foundation
Criminal Justice Program
1735 New York Avenue, N.W.
Washington, D.C. 20006

An information clearinghouse and research center on prisoner problems at the county level.

LITERATURE: *Programs to Re-educate, Readjust, and Restore Inmates of the County Jail; Local Alternatives to Arrest, Incarceration, and Adjudication.*

National Yokefellow Prison Ministry, Inc.
112 Old Trail North
Shamokin Dam, Pa. 17876

Founded in 1955, this national organization is funded by voluntary contributions. Trained volunteers provide in-person counseling for incarcerated men and women. Referrals to counselors, lawyers, and other social services; emergency housing; rap sessions are also provided. It helps to serve the religious needs of residents in correctional institutions and to bridge the gap between persons confined and those in the outside community. It also promotes employment aid and participates in programs to improve correctional methods.

LITERATURE: *Yoke News*, quarterly (free); *Yokefellow Manual* ($1.00); various pamphlets at nominal cost.

Offender Aid and Restoration of the United States, INC. (OAR)
414 Fourth Street, N.E.
Charlottesville, Va. 22901

A private, nonprofit organization working to help inmates by utilizing trained volunteers in a one-to-one counseling situation. OAR also has community based alternatives to imprisonment, such as work release, third-party advocacy, pretrial diversion, detoxification centers, and halfway houses. There are five state chapters and eighteen local branches.

LITERATURE: *OAR/NEWS*; OAR brochure; *OAR Volunteer's Book*.

Project ADVOCATE
American Bar Association
Section of Criminal Justice
1800 M Street, N.W.
Washington, D.C. 20036

Volunteer lawyers providing civil legal aid for offenders by working through local bars and bar associations. (ABA also sponsors the Commission on Correctional Facilities and Services, at the address above.)

LITERATURE: Fact sheets; reports.

For information on prisons and prisoners, contact the following groups:

John Howard Association
67 East Madison, Suite 1216
Chicago, Ill. 60603

A national organization founded in 1901 with local affiliates that monitor criminal justice programs and services and also support the increased use of volunteers in correctional institutions. The association also acts as information clearinghouse on prisoners and prison problems, conducts research projects, and publishes the findings.

National Moratorium on Prison Construction
324 C Street, S.E.
Washington, D.C. 20003

An information clearinghouse and research center on alternatives to prisons. Publishes *Jericho*, a free newsletter on this subject. It is a project of the Unitarian Universalist Service Committee.

The following federal agencies provide information on prisoners, prisons, and prison industries:

Bureau of Prisons
U.S. Department of Justice
320 First Avenue, N.W.
Washington, D.C.

Federal Prison Industries, Inc.
HOLC Building
101 Indiana Avenue, N.W.
Washington, D.C.

U.S. Department of Justice
Law Enforcement Assistance Administration (LEAA)
633 Indiana Avenue, N.W.
Washington, D.C. 20531

The following are the state agencies for corrections:

Board of Corrections
101 South Union Street
Montgomery, Ala. 36130

Division of Corrections
Department of Health and Social Services
129 Alaska Office Building
Pouch H-03
Juneau, Alaska 99811

Department of Corrections
Commerce Building
1601 West Jefferson Street
Phoenix, Ariz. 85007

Department of Correction
5th and State Streets
P.O. Box 8707
Pine Bluff, Ark. 71601

Department of Corrections
714 P Street
Sacramento, Calif. 95814

Department of Corrections
6385 North Academy Boulevard
Denver, Colo. 80907

Department of Correction
340 Capitol Avenue
Hartford, Conn. 06115

Department of Correction
P.O. Box 343
Smyrna, Del. 19977

Department of Corrections
614 H Street, N.W.
Washington, D.C. 20001

Department of Offender Rehabilitation
1311 Winewood Boulevard
Tallahassee, Fla. 32301

Department of Offender Rehabilitation
800 Peachtree Street, N.E.
Atlanta, Ga. 30308

Corrections Division
Department of Social Services and Housing
1390 Miller Street
Honolulu, Hawaii 96813

Department of Corrections
P.O. Box 7309
Boise, Idaho 83707

Department of Corrections
201 Armory Building
Springfield, Ill. 62706

Department of Correction
804 State Office Building
Indianapolis, Ind. 46204

Division of Correctional Institutions
Department of Social Services
Robert Lucas State Office Building
East 12th and Walnut Streets
Des Moines, Iowa 50319

Department of Corrections
535 Kansas Avenue
Topeka, Kans. 66603

Bureau of Corrections
Department of Justice
State Office Building
Frankfort, Ky. 40601

Department of Corrections
P.O. Box 44304
Baton Rouge, La. 70804

Bureau of Corrections
Department of Mental Health and Corrections
411 State Office Building
Augusta, Me. 04333

Division of Correction
Department of Public Safety and Correctional Services
One Investment Place
Baltimore, Md. 21204

Department of Correction
100 Cambridge Street
Boston, Mass. 02202

Department of Corrections
Stevens T. Mason Building
Lansing, Mich. 48913

Department of Corrections
430 Metro Square Building
7th and Robert Streets
St. Paul, Minn. 55101

Department of Corrections
723 North President Street
Jackson, Miss. 39202

Department of Social Services
Division of Corrections
911 Missouri Boulevard
Jefferson City, Mo. 65101

Department of Institutions
1539 Eleventh Avenue
Helena, Mont. 59601

Department of Correctional Services
State Capitol
P.O. Box 94661
Lincoln, Neb. 68509

Nevada State Prisons
P.O. Box 607
Carson City, Nev. 89701

New Hampshire State Prison
281 North State Street
Concord, N.H. 03301

Department of Corrections
P.O. Box 7387
Whittlesey Road
Trenton, N.J. 08625

Department of Corrections
113 Washington Avenue
Santa Fe, N.M. 87503

Department of Correctional Services
State Campus, Building 2
Albany, N.Y. 12226

Department of Correction
840 West Morgan Street
Raleigh, N.C. 27603

Director of Institutions
State Capitol
Bismarck, N.D. 58505

Department of Rehabilitation and Corrections
1050 Freeway Drive
Columbus, Ohio 43229

Department of Corrections
3400 N. Eastern Avenue
P.O. Box 1143
Oklahoma City, Okla. 73111

Corrections Division
Department of Human Resources
2575 Center Street, N.E.
Salem, Ore. 97310

Bureau of Correction
Department of Justice
P.O. Box 598
Camp Hill, Pa. 17011

Department of Corrections
250 Benefit Street
Cranston, R.I. 02903

Department of Corrections
4444 Broad River Road
Columbia, S.C. 29210

Board of Charities and Corrections
Capitol Building
Pierre, S.D. 57501

Department of Correction
First American Center, 11th Floor
326 Union Street
Nashville, Tenn. 37219

Department of Corrections
P.O. Box 99
Huntsville, Tex. 77304

Division of Corrections
Department of Social Services
2525 South Main Street
Salt Lake City, Utah 84115

Department of Corrections
79 River Street
Montpelier, Vt. 05602

Department of Corrections
22 East Cary Street
Richmond, Va. 23219

Adult Corrections Division
Department of Social and Health Services
Olympia, Wash. 98504

Department of Corrections
714 State Office Building 3
1800 Washington Street, East
Charleston, W.Va. 25305

Division of Corrections
Department of Health and Social Services
1 West Wilson Street, Room 1030
Madison, Wis. 53702

Board of Charities and Reform Staff
Hathaway Building
Cheyenne, Wyo. 82002

The following are the state agencies for probation and parole:

Probation and Parole Office
142 Washington Avenue
Montgomery, Ala. 36104

Parole Board
Department of Health and Social Services
106 Alaska Office Building
Pouch H-01E
Juneau, Alaska 99811

Board of Pardons and Paroles
1812 West Monroe Street
Phoenix, Ariz. 85007

Probation and Parole Division
Department of Correction
P.O. Box 8707
Pine Bluff, Ark. 71601

Parole and Community Services Division
Department of Corrections
714 P Street
Sacramento, Calif. 95814

Colorado Board of Parole
6385 North Academy Boulevard
Denver, Colo. 80907

Commission on Adult Probation
643 Maple Street
Hartford, Conn. 06114

Board of Parole
1228 North Scott Street
Wilmington, Del. 19806

Board of Parole
614 H Street, N.W.
Washington, D.C. 20001

Parole and Probation Commission
1117 Thomasville Road
P.O. Box 3168
Tallahassee, Fla. 32303

State Board of Pardons and Paroles
800 Peachtree Street, N.E.
Atlanta, Ga. 30308

Board of Paroles and Pardons
Department of Social Services and Housing
1390 Miller Street
Honolulu, Hawaii 96813

Commission for Pardons and Paroles
Department of Corrections
Idaho State Correctional Institution
P.O. Box 8478
Boise, Idaho 83707

Parole and Pardon Board
Department of Corrections
State Office Building
160 North LaSalle Street
Chicago, Ill. 60601

Parole Board
Department of Correction
804 State Office Building
Indianapolis, Ind. 46204

Board of Parole
Robert Lucas State Office Building
East 12th and Walnut Streets
Des Moines, Iowa 50319

Kansas Adult Authority
535 Kansas Avenue
Topeka, Kans. 66603

Division of Probation and Parole
Bureau of Corrections
Department of Justice
State Office Building
Frankfort, Ky. 40601

Division of Probation, Parole, Rehabilitation
Department of Corrections
780 North Street
Baton Rouge, La. 70802

Division of Probation and Parole
Bureau of Corrections
Department of Mental Health and Corrections
102 High Street
South Windham, Me. 04082

Division of Parole and Probation
Department of Public Safety and Correctional
  Services
One Investment Place
Hunt Valley, Md. 21204

Parole Board
Department of Correction
100 Cambridge Street
Boston, Mass. 02202

Bureau of Field Services
Department of Corrections
Stevens T. Mason Building
Lansing, Mich. 48913

Parole Board
Department of Corrections
430 Metro Square Building
Seventh and Robert Street
St. Paul, Minn. 55101

Parole Board
Department of Corrections
723 North President Street
Jackson, Miss. 39202

Board of Probation and Parole
Department of Social Services
211 Marshall Street
P.O. Box 267
Jefferson City, Mo. 65101

Probation and Parole Bureau
Corrections Division
Department of Institutions
1539 Eleventh Avenue
Helena, Mont. 59601

Parole Board
P.O. Box 94754
State Capitol
Lincoln, Neb. 68509

Department of Parole and Probation
308 North Curry
Carson City, Nev. 89701

Probation Department
11 Depot Street
Concord, N.H. 03301

Bureau of Parole
Department of Corrections
P.O. Box 7387
Whittlesey Road
Trenton, N.J. 08625

Adult Probation and Parole
Correction Division
914 Boca Street
Santa Fe, N.M. 87503

Division of Probation
Tower Building
Empire State Plaza
Albany, N.Y. 12223

Parole Commission
Department of Correction
831 West Morgan Street
Raleigh, N.C. 27603

Parole and Probation Department
P.O. Box 1497
Bismarck, N.D. 58501

Division of Parole and Community Services
Department of Rehabilitation and Corrections
1050 Freeway Drive
Columbus, Ohio 43229

Division of Parole and Community Services
Department of Corrections
3400 North Eastern Avenue
Oklahoma City, Okla. 73111

Board of Parole
2575 Center Street, N.E.
Salem, Ore. 97310

Board of Probation and Parole
3101 North Front Street
Harrisburg, Pa. 17120

Probation and Parole
Department of Corrections
250 Benefit Street
Providence, R.I. 02903

Probation, Parole, and Pardon Board
Middleburg Office Park
P.O. Box 11368
Columbia, S.C. 29211

Adult Probation and Parole
Division of Corrections
Department of Social Services
State Office Building 3
Pierre, S.D. 57501

Division of Adult Probation and Parole
Department of Correction
First American Center, 11th Floor
326 Union Street
Nashville, Tenn. 37219

Division of Juvenile Probation
Department of Correction
First American Center, 11th Floor
326 Union Street
Nashville, Tenn. 37219

Board of Pardons and Paroles
711 Stephen F. Austin State Office Building
Austin, Tex. 78701

Adult Probation and Parole
Division of Corrections
Department of Social Services
2525 South Main Street
Salt Lake City, Utah 84115

Probation and Parole
Department of Corrections
79 River Street
Montpelier, Vt. 05602

Virginia Parole Board
Willow Oaks Office Building
6767 Forest Hill Avenue
Richmond, Va. 23225

Department of Social and Health Services
Adult Corrections Division
Mail Stop FN-61
Olympia, Wash. 98504

Board of Probation and Parole
711 State Office Building 3
1800 Washington Street, E.
Charleston, W.Va. 25305

Probation and Parole
Division of Corrections
110 East Main Street
Madison, Wis. 53702

Department of Probation and Parole
2515 Capitol Avenue
Cheyenne, Wyo. 82002

ADDITIONAL LITERATURE

After Conviction: A Definitive and Compelling Study of the American Correction System by Ronald L. Goldfarb and Linda R. Singer (1973). Simon and Schuster, 1230 Avenue of the Americas, New York, N.Y. 10020 ($8.95). A comprehensive factual book on prisons.

Annual Directory of State and Federal Prisons. American Correctional Association, 4321 Hartwick Road, College Park, Md. 20740 ($11.00).

Behind Bars: Prisons in America, edited by Richard Kwartier (1977). Vintage Books, 201 East 50th Street, New York, N.Y. 10022 ($3.95).

Corrections Magazine: Covering America's Changing Prison System (monthly). Criminal Justice Publications, Inc., 801 Second Avenue, New York, N.Y. 10017 ($18.00 a year). Leading nonacademic magazine in the correctional field. It has feature articles on such topics as weekend jail plus monthly columns, book reviews, classified ads, letters, and editor's notebook, and is illustrated with photos and charts when appropriate.

The Crime of Punishment by Karl Menninger, M.D. (1969). Viking Press, Inc., 625 Madison Avenue, New York, N.Y. 10022 ($1.95). Psychiatrist Menninger's influential thesis that prisons breed more criminals, rather than rehabilitate.

Dictionary of Desperation: An Anthology of Expressions Used by Prisoners to Describe the Quality and Events of Their Daily Lives, compiled and edited by John R. Armore and Joseph D. Wolfe (1976). Communications Department, National Alliance of Businessmen, 1730 K Street, N.W., Washington, D.C. 20006 (free to employers, educations and publications interested in resolving the employment problems of ex-offenders; prepare request on company letterhead).

Directory of Criminal Justice Diversion Programs (1976). American Bar Association, 1800 M Street, N.W., Washington, D.C. 20036 (single copy free). Alphabetical state-by-state listing of diversionary programs.

Directory: Organizations Providing Job Assistance to Ex-Offenders by the American Bar Association, Clearinghouse on Offender Employment Restrictions, National Offender Services Coordination Program (1976). Order from American Bar Association, 1800 M Street, N.W., Washington, D.C. 20036 (single copy free). State-by-state and national listings.

Felony Arrests: Their Prosecution and Disposition in New York City's Courts. Vera Institute of Justice, 30 East 39th Street, New York, N.Y. 10016 ($3.50). Monograph on how felony arrests (for assault, rape, murder, robbery, burglary, grand larceny, and criminal possession of dangerous weapons) deteriorate from the arrest to the arraignment to the court disposition of the case.

Fortune News (monthly). Fortune Society, 229 Park Avenue South, New York, N.Y. 10003 (free to inmates; others, $.25 single copy, $5.00 minimum contribution for subscription, $2.00 students). Newspaper sent to inmates all over the country and interested persons and contributors. Each issue has a different theme with articles by experts, inmates, ex-offenders on the topic. It provides a mail-order service for inmates, news, letters to the editor, reports on legislation, and photos.

The Future of Imprisonment by Norval Morris (1974). University of Chicago Press, 5801 Ellis Avenue, Chicago, Ill. 60637.

Getting Busted: Personal Experiences of Arrest, Trial, and Prison, edited by Ross Firestone (1973). Pyramid Publications, Harcourt Brace Jovanovich, 757 Third Avenue, New York, N.Y. 10017 ($1.75). A collection of articles and essays about prison by such notables as Leslie A. Fiedler, Lenny Bruce, Ken Kesey, and Malcolm X.

Inside Prison U.S.A. by Tom Murton and Joe Hyams (1969, 1972). Zebra Books, Grove Press, 196 W. Houston Street, New York, N.Y. 10014 ($1.50). Murton, a penologist, took on the task of reforming the Arkansas prison system. This is a record of his efforts and insights, gleaned from his 1967–68 experience.

The Menard Time (monthly). Menard Correctional Center, Menard, Ill. 62259 ($3.00 a year). "A censored, not-for-profit penal publication . . . a project of the Menard Vocational School." This newspaper, published since 1934, contains news articles and poetry and short fiction by inmates.

The Penal Colony: Stories and Short Pieces by Franz Kafka (1948). Schocken Books, Inc., 200 Madison Avenue, New York, N.Y. 10016 ($3.95).

Prisoners' Assistance Directory (1977). National Prison Project of the American Civil Liberties Union Foundation, 1346 Connecticut Avenue, N.W., Washington, D.C. 20036 ($10.00 prepaid). National and state-by-state alphabetical listings of pertinent service organizations with brief annotations.

Prisoners' Self-Help Litigation Manual by James L. Potts, edited by Alvin J. Bronstein (1976). National Prison Project of the American Civil Liberties Union Foundation, 1346 Connecticut Avenue, N.W., Washington, D.C. 20036 ($5.00; free to prisoners). Legal self-help book for inmates that discusses parole, judicial remedies, legal research, post-conviction relief, and protecting yourself from retaliation.

Prisons: Houses of Darkness by Leonard Orland (1975). The Free Press, Macmillan Publishing Co., Inc., 866 Third Avenue, New York, N.Y. 10022 ($10.00). Professor Orland indicts the contemporary prison system, calling for a major overhaul in the post-conviction process.

Proposal for Prison Reform by Norval Morris and James Jacobs (1974). Public Affairs Pamphlets, 381 Park Avenue South, New York, N.Y. 10016 ($.50). Pamphlet no. 510.

Rehabilitation, Recidivism, and Research by Robert Martinson, Ted Palmer, and Stuart Adams (1976). National Council on Crime and Delinquency, 411 Hackensack Avenue, Hackensack, N.J. 07601. A controversial report, reprinting the article from *The Public Interest* (Spring 1974), that exploded the myth of rehabilitation in contemporary prisons.

The Rights of Prisoners by David Rudovsky, Alvin J. Bronstein, and Edward I. Koren (1973, 1977). Avon Books, 959 Eighth Avenue, New York, N.Y. 10020 ($1.50). ACLU Handbook Series.

The Right to Counsel in Criminal Cases: The Mandate of Argersinger vs. Hamlin, Executive Summary by Sheldon Krantz, Paul Froyd, Janis Hoffman, David Rossman, and Charles Smith (1976). National Institute of Law Enforcement and Criminal Justice, U.S. Department of Justice, Law Enforcement Assistance Administration, Washington, D.C. 20531.

Sane Asylum: Inside the Delancey Street Foundation by Charles Hampden-Turner (1975). San Francisco Book Company, Inc., 2311 Fillmore, San Francisco, Calif. 94115 ($10.00).

A Time to Die by Tom Wicker (1975). Quadrangle Books, 3 Park Avenue, New York, N.Y. 10016. Wicker, associate editor of the *New York Times*, was called as an "observer" mediator at the 1971 Attica riots; this is his account of what he saw and his involvement in what happened.

The Use of Volunteers in Jails (1977). American Medical Association, 535 North Dearborn, Chicago, Ill. 60610 (free). A booklet on volunteer program services in the areas of education, recreation, and exercise, chaplaincy, and counseling.

West Publishing Company, Department F., Prison Law Library Division, 170 Old Country Road, Mineola, N.Y. 11501, offers a complete selection of single volume books on a variety of pertinent topics, including penal law, family law, constitutional law, legal rights of the convicted. Write to them about lawbook needs, law library problems, or additional ordering information.

See also the following related chapters in *The Help Book:*

**CIVIL RIGHTS AND DISCRIMINATION
COUNSELING
COURTS
CRIME PREVENTION
CRIME VICTIMS AND WITNESSES
DRUGS, SMOKING, AND DRUG ABUSE
EDUCATION
EMPLOYMENT
FINANCIAL ASSISTANCE
GAMBLING
INFORMATION RIGHTS AND RESOURCES
JUVENILE DELINQUENCY
LAW ENFORCEMENT
LEGAL SERVICES
MULTIPURPOSE ORGANIZATIONS
VOLUNTEERISM**

42

PARENTING

Old and new problems confront parents today. There are many single parents—single by choice, divorce, separation, or widowhood. Adolescents, newlyweds, and couples married two or ten years all debate whether or not to have children. Other questions, such as how to raise children, have concerned parents for centuries. But added to them is a growing awareness of the influence of the media and the society on one's family and the need to control or circumvent that influence. Television, advertising, movies, comic books, pornography—all are legitimate concerns for today's parent. Education, employment, birth control, health, and mental concerns are more controversial topics than ever before. But there are some radical movements as well. Complementing the children's rights movement is the "Bill of Rights for Parents." There are even classes for those who want to learn to be a parent.

One of the more extensive studies on the American family was conducted by Yankelovich, Skelly & White, Inc. for General Mills, Inc. A sample of 2,102 persons were interviewed from 1,230 families. They included 469 children between the ages of six and twelve. Eighty-six interviews with "family experts" were also incorporated. The results about the "New Breed" and "Traditionalist" parents are summarized in the following chart and list of findings:

- Two contrasting groups of parents—the New Breed (43 percent) and the Traditionalist (57 percent)—are teaching their children the same set of traditional values.
- The New Breed parents are more self-oriented and less demanding of children than Traditionalist parents who are likely to be stricter disciplinarians.
- Nearly two out of three of all parents believe they should have lives of their own, even if it means spending less time with their children.
- Two out of three parents do not believe in staying together just for the sake of the children.

- More than one in three parents admit to uncertainty about the kind of job they are doing in raising their children.
- Mothers (70 percent) and fathers (58 percent) feel the best student should have the opportunity to go to college, regardless of sex.
- 37 percent of parents feel children today are less happy than their parents were as children.
- Children are traditional in their views—they like their mothers because they are

THE NEW BREED—43%

Not Important Values:
- Marriage as an institution
- Religion
- Saving money
- Patriotism
- Success

Characteristics and Beliefs:
- Parents are self-oriented — not ready to sacrifice for their children
- Parents don't push their children
- Parents have a laissez faire attitude — children should be free to make their own decisions
- Parents question authority
- Parents are permissive with their children
- Parents believe boys and girls should be raised alike
- Parents believe their children have no future obligation to them
- Parents see having children as an option, not a social responsibility

THE TRADITIONALISTS—57%

Very Important Values:
- Marriage as an institution
- Religion
- Saving money
- Hard work
- Financial security

Characteristics and Beliefs:
- Parents are child-oriented — ready to sacrifice for their children
- Parents want their children to be outstanding
- Parents want to be in charge — believe parents should make decisions for their children
- Parents respect authority
- Parents are not permissive with their children
- Parents believe boys and girls should be raised differently
- Parents believe old-fashioned upbringing is best
- Parents see having children as a very important value

WHAT BOTH GROUPS TEACH THEIR CHILDREN
- Duty before pleasure
- My country right or wrong
- Hard work pays off
- People in authority know best
- Sex is wrong without marriage

* Reprinted with permission from *The General Mills American Family Report, 1976–77,* "Raising Children in a Changing Society," a study conducted by Yankelovich, Skelly and White, Inc., © 1977 General Mills, Inc.

good cooks and housekeepers, and their fathers because they spend time with them and earn money.
- There is a general mood of optimism and hope among American families; 32 percent feel living standards have improved, as opposed to only 14 percent two years ago.
- 77 percent feel they can manage most money problems.
- Four out of ten parents feel they cannot rely on schools to teach children how to read and write.
- 77 percent feel women with small children should go to work *only* if money is needed.
- Three out of four parents feel children have learned good things from television—although violence on TV programs is a major concern.
- 36 percent of minority parents feel there is no reason to inoculate children against polio today since the disease has been conquered.
- Nearly half of children (44 percent) between the ages of 10 and 12 know children whose behavior has brought them into conflict with authorities.

Although the study concluded that there are two distinct types of parents, both types are teaching their children traditional values. But obviously as the society becomes more complex, and there are fewer and fewer preset "roles" to abide by, parenting becomes more and more complex and individual. Hard and fast rules of yesteryear do not seem to stand up any longer.

Direct local help and information on parenting is available from your city or county department of health, public or private school, library, hospital, media center, your pediatrician or family doctor, school counselor—or the nearest affiliate of the following national service organizations:

American Home Economics Association
2010 Massachusetts Avenue, N.W.
Washington, D.C. 20008

Founded in 1909, this national organization with over 52,000 members has fifty-two affiliates concerned with families. This is an information clearinghouse that answers inquiries on the family, forms coalitions, and maintains cooperative relationships with many organizations that share their concern with families.

LITERATURE: Write for their publications list with more than 100 titles; "A Force for Families," descriptive booklet on the organization.

Mothers-in-Law Club International, Inc.
739 Chestnut Street
Cedarhurst, N.Y. 11516

The goals of this international organization include the enrichment of family relationships and the assistance to those with depression and fears so they may get back to a normal family and community life. It is a service founded on knowledge, experience, understanding, and guidance. Inquiries receive a letter of explanation about the organization and its goals and, if someone has a problem, help is offered by mail or by phone.

National Congress of Parents and Teachers (National PTA)
700 North Rush Street
Chicago, Ill. 60611

The National PTA publishes a variety of materials dealing with education, health, and the general welfare of children; other areas of interest include reading, alcoholism, media, and careers programs.

LITERATURE: Publications price list; *How to Organize a PTA or PTSA* (free booklet); *All About National PTA Legislative Activity* ($.20); *PTA Today*, newsletter; *How to Help Your Child Select a Career* (free); *The Fine Art of Parenting* (free); *Today's Family in Focus* ($3.00).

National Council on Family Relations
1219 University Avenue, S.E.
Minneapolis, Minn. 55414

A professional organization formed in 1938 that publishes the quarterly *Journal of Marriage and the Family*, a membership directory, several books, a quarterly newsletter, a bibliography on family life, and a list of graduate programs in family studies. There are thirty-one state and twelve local groups.

National Organization of Mothers of Twins Clubs (NOMOTC)
5402 Amberwood Lane
Rockville, Md. 20853

Founded in 1960, there are 225 local groups in forty-two states. Referrals are made to local chapters, which have active direct services and newsletters. The national headquarters serves as an information clearinghouse.

LITERATURE: *MOTC's Notebook*, quarterly ($3.50); *How to Organize a Mothers of Twins Club* ($1.00); *Your Twins and You* (free brochure).

The Step Family Foundation, Inc.
333 West End Avenue
New York, N.Y. 10023

Help for the stepparent and stepchildren founded by Jeannette Lofas, who also authored *Living In Step* (McGraw-Hill Book Company, 1221 Avenue of the Americas, New York, N.Y. 10020, 1977, $3.95). Founded in December 1975, the foundation conducts workshops, lectures, training programs, and counseling for individuals and families. It serves "step" people outside of the New York City area through long distance telephone counseling and special workshops. Fees are on a sliding scale. Membership is $10.00 a year.

LITERATURE: Send a self-addressed, stamped envelope to receive a copy of the newsletter and a free descriptive brochure.

The following organizations provide help for parents of newborns (see also the listings in Chapter 10, Children, and Chapter 30, Health):

American Academy of Pediatrics
P.O. Box 1034
Evanston, Ill. 60204

Founded in 1930, there are sixty-three state groups in this national professional association of medical doctors treating diseases of children. It holds an annual convention and publishes free or low-cost booklets and leaflets on various topics in child health.

LITERATURE: Publications price list.

La Leche League International, Inc.
9616 Minneapolis Avenue
Franklin Park, Ill. 60131

A nonprofit organization dedicated to good mothering through breast feeding that provides free telephone help. In June 1977 there were 3,435 La Leche League groups in forty-two countries.

LITERATURE: Free leaflets, including "Why Breastfeed Your Baby?"; Fact folder; *La*

Leche League News, bimonthly ($2.75 a year); article reprints; publications list.

Society for the Protection of the Unborn through Nutrition (SPUN)
17 North Wabash, Suite 603
Chicago, Ill. 60602

SPUN provides professional prenatal education and counseling designed to safeguard maternal and infant health and to prevent birth abnormalities. Services include individual and group counseling, referrals, audiovisual aids, twenty-four hour telephone hotline, and answering service.

LITERATURE: Fact sheets and publications list; *The Pregnant Issue: Medicate or Educate?*, bimonthly.

For information on helping your child read, contact the following groups:

American Library Association
50 East Huron Street
Chicago, Ill. 60611

A national professional association that also publishes a wide variety of booklets, lists, and pamphlets to encourage reading.

LITERATURE: "Let's Read Together: Books for Family Enjoyment," an annotated listing for children aged two to fifteen ($2.00).

Children's Book Council
67 Irving Place
New York, N.Y. 10003

An information clearinghouse on children's literature.

LITERATURE: *Choosing a Child's Book*, four-page folder of booklets sent free with a self-addressed stamped envelope.

International Reading Association
800 Barkdale Road
P.O. Box 8139
Newark, Del. 19711

Publishes information for parents on helping children learn to read, such as "Your Home Is Your Child's First School," "You Can Encourage Your Child to Read," "Good Books Make Reading Fun For Your Child." With a self-addressed stamped envelope, single copies are free. Direct your order to the Public Information Office, Order Department.

For help or information on single parenting, contact the following groups:

Committee for Single Adoptive Parents
P.O. Box 4074
Washington, D.C. 20015

See complete listing in Chapter 1, *Adoption*.

Parents Without Partners, Inc. (PWP)
7910 Woodmont Avenue, Suite 1000
Washington, D.C. 20014

Over 900 membership chapters in all fifty states offer educational, family, and social activities. Contact your local affiliate for direct help.

LITERATURE: Free pamphlets and referrals are available; free brochures include *The Single Parent; Are You a Single Parent?; Therapy for Children and Adults; PWP and The Community; Parents Are Forever*.

Help for bereaved parents is available from the following:

The Compassionate Friends
P.O. Box 3247
Hialeah, Fla. 33013

Since 1972 this national self-help group with local chapters throughout the country has offered friendship and understanding to bereaved parents following the death of a child or children. Referrals are made to local groups.

LITERATURE: *No Death So Sad*, free folder.

National Sudden Infant Death Syndrome
310 South Michigan Avenue, Suite 1904
Chicago, Ill. 60604

A national organization that counsels and educates anyone interested in or affected by infant deaths. It also makes home visits to parents.

LITERATURE: Leaflets include "Facts About Sudden Infant Death Syndrome."

Parents who wish information on the effect of the media on their children and what they may do about it should contact the following national organizations:

Action for Children's Television (ACT)
46 Austin Street
Newtonville, Mass. 02160

A very active and influential organization started in 1968. There are now thousands of members throughout the United States who support ACT's goals—"child-oriented television without commercialism."

LITERATURE: *ACT News* (free with membership or $15.00 a year); *Nutrition Survival Kit;* article reprints, bibliography; introductory packet of ACT materials.

Committee on Children's Television (CCT)
1511 Masonic Avenue
San Francisco, Calif. 94117

A local group working with community groups that serve children of all racial and ethnic backgrounds and with television stations to try to make TV more responsive to the needs and interests of children. CCT also has extensive publications of national interest.

LITERATURE: Publications price list; descriptive brochure on CCT; *Seeking Solutions to Violence on Children's Television* ($3.50 donation); "Children and Television: A Selected Bibliography" ($1.00 donation).

Council on Children, Media, and Merchandising (CCMM)
1346 Connecticut Avenue, N.W.
Washington, D.C. 20036

Represents the consumer interests of children before Congress and federal agencies, and publishes literature on alternative ways of providing children with accurate consumer information as opposed to the ones now used by advertisers.

National PTA TV Action Center
700 North Rush Street
Chicago, Ill. 60611

An active campaign zeroing in on television violence is the result of several important resolutions concerning the influence of the media on the public that have been passed by various National PTA conventions. For further information, contact your local PTA.

LITERATURE: *The Challenge Before Us: The National PTA's Action Plan for Television* (booklet); *Mass Media and the PTA.*

For general information on parenting, contact the following national organizations:

American Institute of Family Relations
5287 Sunset Boulevard
Los Angeles, Calif. 90027

Founded in 1929, the institute has a professional staff that provides counseling for adolescents; engaged and married couples; and single, widowed, or divorced adults. Referrals are made to local counselors.

LITERATURE: Publishes 150 pamphlets on family relations—send for price list.

American Parents Committee (APC)
1346 Connecticut Avenue, N.W.
Washington, D.C. 20036

Founded in 1947, this organization is comprised of persons who are interested in federal legislation that will effect children.

LITERATURE: Annual Voting Report; Washington Report on Federal Legislation for Children; *APC Newsletter* ($10.00 a year).

Center for the Family
Home Economics Association
2010 Massachusetts Avenue, N.W.
Washington, D.C. 20036

A professional organization for those working with families that provides educational programs for counselors.

Parenting Materials Information Center
Southwest Educational Development
  Laboratory
211 East 7th Street
Austin, Tex. 78701

Gathers, analyzes, and disseminates parenting materials and information.

LITERATURE: Fact sheets; publications price list; *Parenting in 1977* ($5.00).

The following federal government departments have information available on the family:

Education for Parenthood
National Center for Child Advocacy
U.S. Department of Health, Education, and Welfare
Children's Bureau
Administration for Children, Youth and Families
P.O. Box 1182
Washington, D.C. 20013

LITERATURE: *Education for Parenthood Program, Curriculum, and Evaluation Guide*, the culmination of six years of development (1977).

National Center for Child Advocacy
Children's Bureau
Office of Child Development
U.S. Department of Health, Education, and Welfare
P.O. Box 1182
Washington, D.C. 20013

U.S. Department of Health, Education, and Welfare
Washington, D.C. 20201

U.S. Department of Labor
Women's Bureau
Washington, D.C. 20210

DAY CARE

About 50 percent of the women in America today work outside the home—some choose to, others must. Staying home to raise children is becoming a luxury; two salaries may mean the difference between barely making ends meet or those few "indulgences" such as a vacation, second car, new winter coat, or special schooling for the children. Then there are an increasing number of one-parent families—9.6 percent of all white families and 35 percent of all black families are headed by women. Single father families have also increased as men take on children in adoption or foster care or gain custody of offspring in divorce cases.

Day care—full-time private or public supervision for infants before formal education begins—has become a necessary yet controversial movement. In certain countries, such as Denmark, Sweden, and France, it is readily available; in the United States, facilities are disproportionate to current needs. There are more than 1,000 *crèches* throughout France, 80 in Paris alone. Of the 3.4 million children in France under four, 51,000 are in public crèches and another several thousand in private or religious day-care centers.

Approximately 20,000 licensed day-care centers throughout the United States currently take care of about 900,000 children, a small percentage of the number of families who need such a service. For most parents, the costs of most private day-care centers ($80–310 per month) is also prohibitive; it would mean spending most of their salaries. Sometimes babysitters, who are not licensed, will take in several infants and children, charging about $10 or $15 per child weekly. Many states have outlawed these traditional answers to the day care problem.

What are the alternatives to day care for the working parent or parents? One is the home attendant, nanny, nursemaid, or governess as the daytime or live-in assistant is called. But there are far fewer nannies than jobs—about one qualified person for each fifty requests. One reason is that new immigration laws in 1965 reduced the number of European governesses permitted to enter the country. Fewer than 10,000 trained European nannies are admitted annually to the United States, according to the U.S. Immigration Service. Even at the going salary of $150 a week those nannies are in high demand.

Another alternative is relying upon grandparents to babysit. But today's grandparent is more in touch with his or her own life and work; few are willing to be parents a second time around. Unfortunately, working women who cannot afford a nanny and do not qualify economically for day-care centers may have no other choice.

One innovation, which has had more failures than successes, are company-run day-care centers. They offer full-day facilities to working employees and others from the local community. But more close down than flourish. This is because a day care location should be, ideally, near where a woman lives, not works. An exception is the day-care center run by a shoe manufacturer. There are about forty-five children enrolled and the cost per child is about that of a year at college—$3,000 a year. For each child enrolled, employees pay 10 percent of their gross weekly salaries.

How does one go about finding a nanny or day-care center? Employment agencies are the first place to begin your search. Other suggestions include asking your cleaning lady to expand her services. A recently widowed or divorced woman in the neighborhood might also consider day care as a job alternative. You might want to organize a day-care collective—several working women join together and share the care so that each one is only responsible one day every other week. It might take a lot of organizing and planning, but there are significant benefits. You will also be able to screen who is caring for your child and have some active say in the program. Local women's groups and religious centers may provide free or low-cost space. It might be better to bring the children to the same place each time, rather than alternate mothers' homes.

Your community or city probably publishes a directory of services that are available through the local, state, and federal governments. Check out the listings under Head Start, Day Care, and Department of Social Services in your telephone book to see what is offered and what the requirements and fees are.

Some couples have found job-sharing situations so that they alternate who works and who stays at home. (See Chapter 21, *Employment*, for more information.) College students may be willing to provide child care in exchange for a salary or, as a full-time live-in sitter, with room and board.

Remember you are entrusting your most valuable treasure, so be sure to check references and facilities very, very carefully. Your child's welfare—and your peace of mind—depend on it.

For day care information, the following national organizations provide information:

Child Development Associate Consortium (CDAC)
Southern Building
805 Fifteenth Street, N.W.
Washington, D.C. 20005
Toll-free candidate hot line: 800-638-8482

Assessment system for competence of teachers working with preschool, three- to five-year-old children; qualified teachers receive Child Development Associate (CDA) status. CDAC is also an information clearinghouse on day care with publications and an annual meeting.

LITERATURE: Free pamphlets include *How to Become a Child Development Associate; The CDA Credential . . . and You; Competency Standards Report; Dateline CDAC* newspaper; *The Child Development Associate Credential and the Credential System.*

Day Care and Child Development Council of America, Inc.
1012 Fourteenth Street, N.W.
Washington, D.C. 20005

A nonprofit national organization with members all over the country that advocates legislation to improve day-care resource centers. A technical assistance staff helps establish and improve centers; field workers visit families and advise them.

LITERATURE: Publications for parents and students.

National Association for Child Development and Education
500 Twelfth Street, S.W.
Washington, D.C. 20024

The association represents day-care centers themselves; parents may contact them to complain about a member center. It also helps keep the public informed about legislative issues on day care.

National Council of Jewish Women
15 East 26th Street
New York, N.Y. 10010

The council is concerned with the need for the expansion, improvement, and coordination of quality day care service throughout the United States.

LITERATURE: *Windows on Day Care* by Mary Dublin Keyserling ($2.00).

Women's Bureau
Employment Standards Administration
U.S. Department of Labor
Washington, D.C. 20210

Day care is one of the many women-related issues that this bureau researches and reports on.

LITERATURE: *Day Care Services: Industry's Involvement* ($.25); "Day Care Facts" (1973). ($.70).

Contact the following national organization if you want information about avoiding parenting:

National Organization for Non-Parents (NON)
806 Reisterstown Road
Baltimore, Md. 21208

Founded in 1972, NON is an educational organization that seeks "to make the childfree lifestyle a realistic and socially accepted and respected option and to eliminate pronatalist social and economic discrimination."

LITERATURE: Extensive article and newspaper reprints, brochures, and pamphlets.

ADDITIONAL LITERATURE

PARENTING

Child Care Issues for Parents and Society: A Guide to Information Sources edited by Andrew Garoogian and Rhoda Garoogian (1977). Gale Research Company, Book Tower, Detroit, Mich. 48226 ($18.00). An annotated directory of organizations, publications, and audio-visual materials in a wide range of parent areas, such as exceptional children, health conditions, adoption, child abuse, general child development, sex education, and more.

The Developing Child, edited by Jerome Bruner, Michael Cole, and Barbara Lloyd (1977). Harvard University Press, 79 Garden Street, Cambridge, Mass. 02138 (4 volumes, $2.95 per volume). Experts on child behavior have assembled a body of information based on research. Volumes are: *Play* by Catherine Garvey; *Mothering* by Rudolph Schaffer; *The Psychology of Childbirth* by Aidan MacFarlane; and *Distress and Comfort* by Judy Dunn.

Families by Jane Howard (1978). Simon and Schuster, 1230 Avenue of the Americas, New York, N.Y. 10020 ($9.95). The result of two years of research, following around some 200 family units, from divorced single mothers to lesbian couples raising children.

The Family Guide to Children's Television: What to Watch, What to Miss, What to Change, and How to Do It by Evelyn Kaye (1974). Pantheon Books, 201 East 50th Street, New York, N.Y. 10022 ($2.95). How to live with television without letting it control your life and your child's mind.

The General Mills American Family Report, 1976–77: Raising Children in a Changing Society, conducted by Yankelovich, Skelly and White, Inc. (1977). General Mills, Inc., 9200 Wayzata Boulevard, Minneapolis, Minn. 55440. The Consumer Center of General Mills conducted research on the family by interviewing over 100 experts in the field and preparing a research questionnaire, which was sent to 2,102 adults and children, some of whom were in the same households. The major conclusion of the study was that "American families are divided between their belief in traditional and in new values but they are surprisingly united in their decision to pass on traditional values to their children." (See the "Today's Parents" chart at the beginning of this chapter.)

Helping Parents Help Their Children, edited by L. Eugene Arnold (1978). Brunner/Mazel, Inc., 19 Union Square West, New York, N.Y. 10003 ($17.50). Covers the gamut from abusing parents to delinquency to hyperactivity, with articles by some of the most notable researchers/writers in each field.

How to Bring Up a Child Without Spending a Fortune by Lee Edward Benning (1976). Dolphin/Doubleday, Garden City, N.Y. 11530 ($2.95). Tips on saving money on everything from baby clothes to doctor bills; also includes a resource directory.

Introducing Books to Children by Aidan Chambers (1973). The Horn Book, Park Square Building, 31 St. James Avenue, Boston, Mass. 02116 ($3.50 plus $.30 postage). A useful guide for teachers and parents to inspire the literary craving in youngsters. References and suggestions for further reading are included.

The Magic Years by Selma Fraiberg (1968). Charles Scribner's Sons, 597 Fifth Avenue, New York, N.Y. 10017 ($2.95). Best-selling popular book about early child development.

"McCall's Movie Guide for Puzzled Parents" by Lynn Minton, in *McCall's* magazine, 230 Park Avenue, New York, N.Y. 10017, or on your newsstands ($.95). The author of *Growing Into Adolescence* contributes this valuable monthly movie guide for parents. Reviews answer those questions about movies that general reviews might not bring out, such as: What values is the movie teaching? What age group would enjoy it most? How much blood and gore is there? There is also a recommended "Movie of the Month."

The Mother's Almanac by Marguerite Kelly and Elia Parsons (1975). Doubleday and Company, Garden City, N.Y. 11550 ($4.95). Popular book by two mothers covering child development, recipes, behavior, and more.

My Mother, Myself: A Daughter's Search for Identity by Nancy Friday (1977). Delacorte Press, 245 East 47th Street, New York, N.Y. 10017 ($10.00). The best selling nonfiction study of that all-important but little understood parent/child relationship.

Nobody Said It Would Be Easy: Raising Responsible Kids—and Keeping Them Out of Trouble by Dr. Dan Kiley (1978). Harper and Row, 10 East 53rd Street, New York, N.Y. 10022 ($10.00). "Protective parenting" is Kiley's suggestion for raising disciplined adults.

Ourselves and Our Children by Boston Women's Health Book Collective (1978). Random House, Inc., 201 East 50th Street, New York, N.Y. 10022 ($12.95 hardcover; $6.95 paperback). An extensive book based upon interviews with 200 male and female parents from the writers collective that created the highly successful and useful *Our Bodies, Ourselves*.

Parent Power! by John Douglas (1977). Newspaper Enterprise Association, Inc., 230 Park Avenue, New York, N.Y. 10017. How to be part of your child's learning experiences—in and out of his or her school.

A Parent's Guide to Children's Reading, 4th edition, by Nancy Larrick (1975). Bantam Books, 666 Fifth Avenue, New York, N.Y. 10019 ($1.95). The classic guidebook for parents and teachers.

Parents' Magazine (monthly). Parents' Magazine Enterprises, Inc., 52 Vanderbilt Avenue, New York, N.Y. 10017. A magazine devoted to rearing children from the crib to college. Parents' Magazine Enterprises also publishes picture books and beginning reader books through Parents' Magazine Press; produces audiovisual materials on child development, child health, and parent education through Parents' Magazine Films, Inc.; and publishes three magazines for children, *Humpty Dumpty's Magazine*, *Children's Digest*, and *Young Miss*, two specialized magazines for expectant mothers and new mothers, and *Handy Andy*, a pocket-sized do-it-yourself guide for everyone. Write for subscription prices.

Parents' Yellow Pages: A Directory by the Princeton Center for Infancy, edited by Frank Caplan (1978). Anchor Books/Doubleday, Garden City, N.Y. 11530 ($7.95 paperback). This directory of more than 500 pages is a bargain reference for any parent, with chapters on abortion, fire and fire protection, nutrition, posters for children, health problems, and more. Short articles, organizations for further information, and annotated bibliographical references accompany each section.

The Parent Test: How to Measure and Develop Your Talent for Parenthood by Ellen Peck and Dr. William Granzig (1978). G. P. Putnam's Sons, 390 Murray Hill Parkway, East Rutherford, N.J. 07073 ($9.95 plus $.75 postage and handling).

"Reading in the Home." Scholastic Magazines, 50 West 44th Street, New York, N.Y. 10036 (free). Six-page folder for parents.

Right From the Start: A Guide to Nonsexist Child Rearing by Selma Greenberg (1978). Houghton Mifflin Company, 1 Beacon Street, Boston, Mass. 02107 ($8.95). Redefining motherhood, fatherhood, parent support systems, problems with myths, what will you be when you grow up, family power plays, subliminal sex education, with source notes.

The Second Whole Kids Catalog by Peter Cardozo (1977). Bantam Books, 666 Fifth Avenue, New York, N.Y. 10019 ($7.50). An activities book geared to children from ages six to sixteen with more than 100 things to make and do and where to write for more than 100 free things.

Summerhill: A Radical Approach to Child Rearing by A. S. Neill (1977). Simon and Schuster, 1230 Avenue of the Americas, New York, N.Y. 10020 ($4.95).

Your Child From One to Six, U.S. Department of Health, Education, and Welfare (1978). Available from Consumer Information Center, Department 099F, Pueblo, Colo. 81009 ($1.75). Booklet describing the normal developmental stages that every child from one to six goes through, written from the parent's point of view and with helpful hints on coping with typical childrearing problems.

What Now? A Handbook for New Parents by Mary Lou Rozdilsky and Barbara Banet (1975). Charles Scribner's Sons, 597 Fifth Avenue, New York, N.Y. 10017 ($2.95). Advice on such situations as what to do when the baby cries, breast feeding, and reestablishing closeness as a couple.

Who Will Raise the Children? New Options for Fathers (and Mothers) by James A. Levine (1976). J. B. Lippincott Company, 521 Fifth Avenue, New York, N.Y. 10017 ($8.95). This book was begun during the author's first months of teaching preschool in California, when he was continually asked "What do you *really* do?" Levine suggests alternatives such as part-time jobs, single adoptive fathers, and househusbands.

DAY CARE

Corporation and Child Care: Profit-making Day Care, Workplace Day Care and a Look at the Alternatives by Cookie Avrin, Georgia Sassen and the Corporations and Child Care Research Project (1974). Women's Research Action Project, Box 119, Porter Square Station, Cambridge, Mass. 02140 ($2.75).

Day Care for America's Children by E. Robert LaCrosse (1971). Public Affairs Pamphlets, 381 Park Avenue South, New York, N.Y. 10016 ($.50). A booklet on the varieties of day care available, as well as some of the information parents need to make decisions about whether or not to send a child to a day-care facility.

Day Care: How to Plan, Develop, and Operate a Day Care Center by E. Belle Evans, Beth Shub, and Marlene Weinstein (1971). Beacon Press, 25 Beacon Street, Boston, Mass. 02108 ($3.95).

Family Day Care by Alice H. Collins and Eunice L. Watson (1977). Beacon Press, 25 Beacon Street, Boston, Mass. 02108 ($3.95). A step-by-step guidebook for starting and running a day-care facility.

Responsibility for Child Care: The Changing Role of Family and State in Child Development by Bernard Greenblatt (1977). Jossey-Bass, Inc., Publishers, 615 Montgomery Street, San Francisco, Calif. 94111 ($13.95).

See also the following related chapters in *The Help Book:*

**ADOPTION AND FOSTER CARE
BATTERED ADULTS
CHILD ABUSE
CHILDBEARING
CHILDREN
CONSUMER AFFAIRS
COUNSELING
DRUGS, SMOKING, AND DRUG ABUSE
EDUCATION
EMERGENCIES AND DISASTERS
FAMILY PLANNING
FOOD AND NUTRITION
HEALTH
JUVENILE DELINQUENCY
KIDNAPPING, MISSING PERSONS, AND RUNAWAYS
MENTAL HEALTH
MENTAL RETARDATION AND LEARNING DISABILITIES
MULTIPURPOSE ORGANIZATIONS
SAFETY
SEX EDUCATION AND THERAPY**

43

POLITICAL ACTION

More and more, the American people are the source of political action in this country. The two reporters on the *Washington Post* who uncovered the Watergate conspiracy are, first and foremost, private citizens employed in the private sector. The service they performed for their country should not be minimized by the fact that they were acting in the line of duty—doing their job for their newspaper.

But what options are open to the "average" person who is not a newspaper reporter or a full-time political activist? One way to express dissent is to write to government officials—from your local representatives on up to the governor of your state and even to the president. Form letters and post cards are not as effective as personal, handwritten or individually-typed, sincere expressions of concern. Another way is to write to the editor of your local newspaper or to a national newspaper. Who reads letters to the editor? *Editor & Publisher,* a trade journal for newspaper editors and writers, reported the following of 368 people interviewed by telephone: about 33 percent of newspaper readers read letters to the editor "almost always" and 12 percent read them "often." Organizations have been started from the responses generated by letters to the editor; "wrongs" have been righted by public disclosure of specific grievances.

For example, the letter reprinted below from the June 26, 1972, *New York Times* was the first published statement by this author of her concern about crime. (Six years later, that continued concern, supported by research, became the basis of *Victims* published by Charles Scribner's Sons, New York, 1978.)

Payment in Lives

To the Editor:

The cost of living in New York City is steadily rising. I am not referring to the higher prices of vegetables or fruits, but the greater payment in lives. The

Times reported on June 19 on the brutal slaying of Irma Simonton Black, chairman of publications at Bank Street College and a children's book writer, in her Greenwich Village home. I worked with Irma Black on the Bank Street Readers and knew her dedication to the education of the urban child. Her warmth and enthusiasm will be deeply missed.

Three years ago, my brother Seth, a 23-year-old freelance writer, was murdered while returning home from reviewing an Off Broadway play. What good is it to live in a city with so much exciting theater if you may never return to think about the mind-expanding experience you have just had? What persons will be listed in the obituaries in the next three years, victims of senseless acts of violence? Is there nothing that can be done by an aware, alert public to stop this growing lack of respect for life?

We could turn our backs on New York and move to a place that offers less diversity of nationalities and religions but a little more safety. That is not the solution. Somehow concerned citizens must band together to revive love and companionship in New York. Crime and brutality must become the rare exception rather than the rule.

A more radical movement afoot is the People's Lobby, a national information clearinghouse based in California, that advocates the return of direct government to the people. The passage of Proposition 13 demonstrates that the American people are demanding that government be responsible to the needs of all levels of society—the poor, the middle class, the wealthy. Bureaucratic excesses or inefficiencies will continue to be pointed out and, as one journalist suggested, there may be a time when Americans pay for only those services that they actually use.

You *can* improve small town, big city, and the federal government. Today, more than ever before, there are nonviolent and sophisticated methods open to the American people—if they will just take the initiative. Understanding just what the government of this country consists of is an important step—civic education cannot stop at the elementary school level. For information on government and politics, start at the level of government that you are specifically worried about—county, city, state, or federal. For example, the information service of your state government may have free published materials on how a bill is passed and the legislative course of a bill.

Federal Government Information Sources for the Public

To find out the status of current federal legislation, you need to know the number, author, or subject of the bill in question. A computerized system in Washington, D.C., will then provide you with information on its status. You can find out those numbers by dialing (202) 555-1212 (Washington, D.C., information) and asking for the telephone numbers of the House Bill Status Office or the Senate Bill Status Office.

THE GOVERNMENT OF THE UNITED STATES

This chart seeks to show only the more important agencies of the Government. See text for other agencies.

THE CONSTITUTION

LEGISLATIVE

THE CONGRESS

Senate   House

Architect of the Capitol
General Accounting Office
Government Printing Office
Library of Congress
United States Botanic Garden
Cost Accounting Standards Board
Office of Technology Assessment
Congressional Budget Office

EXECUTIVE

THE PRESIDENT

Executive Office of the President

White House Office
Office of Management and Budget
Council of Economic Advisers
National Security Council
Federal Property Council
Office of the Special Representative for Trade Negotiations
Council on International Economic Policy
Council on Environmental Quality
Domestic Council
Office of Telecommunications Policy
Council on Wage and Price Stability
Energy Resources Council
Office of Drug Abuse Policy
Office of Science and Technology Policy

JUDICIAL

The Supreme Court of the United States

Circuit Courts of Appeals of the United States
District Courts of the United States
United States Court of Claims
United States Court of Customs and Patent Appeals
United States Customs Court
Territorial Courts
Federal Judicial Center
Administrative Office of the United States Courts
United States Tax Court

DEPARTMENT OF STATE | DEPARTMENT OF THE TREASURY | DEPARTMENT OF DEFENSE | DEPARTMENT OF JUSTICE | DEPARTMENT OF THE INTERIOR

DEPARTMENT OF AGRICULTURE | DEPARTMENT OF COMMERCE | DEPARTMENT OF LABOR | DEPARTMENT OF HEALTH, EDUCATION, AND WELFARE | DEPARTMENT OF HOUSING AND URBAN DEVELOPMENT | DEPARTMENT OF TRANSPORTATION

INDEPENDENT OFFICES AND ESTABLISHMENTS

ACTION
Administrative Conference of the U.S.
Board for International Broadcasting
Civil Aeronautics Board
Commission on Civil Rights
Commodity Futures Trading Commission
Community Services Administration
Consumer Product Safety Commission
Energy Research and Development Administration
Environmental Protection Agency
Equal Employment Opportunity Commission
Export-Import Bank of the U.S.

Farm Credit Administration
Federal Communications Commission
Federal Deposit Insurance Corporation
Federal Election Commission
Federal Energy Administration
Federal Home Loan Bank Board
Federal Maritime Commission
Federal Mediation and Conciliation Service
Federal Power Commission
Federal Reserve System, Board of Governors of the
Federal Trade Commission

General Services Administration
Interstate Commerce Commission
National Aeronautics and Space Administration
National Foundation on the Arts and the Humanities
National Labor Relations Board
National Mediation Board
National Science Foundation
National Transportation Safety Board
Nuclear Regulatory Commission
Pennsylvania Avenue Development Corporation

Pension Benefit Guaranty Corporation
Railroad Retirement Board
Securities and Exchange Commission
Selective Service System
Small Business Administration
Tennessee Valley Authority
U.S. Information Agency
U.S. International Trade Commission
U.S. Postal Service
Veterans Administration

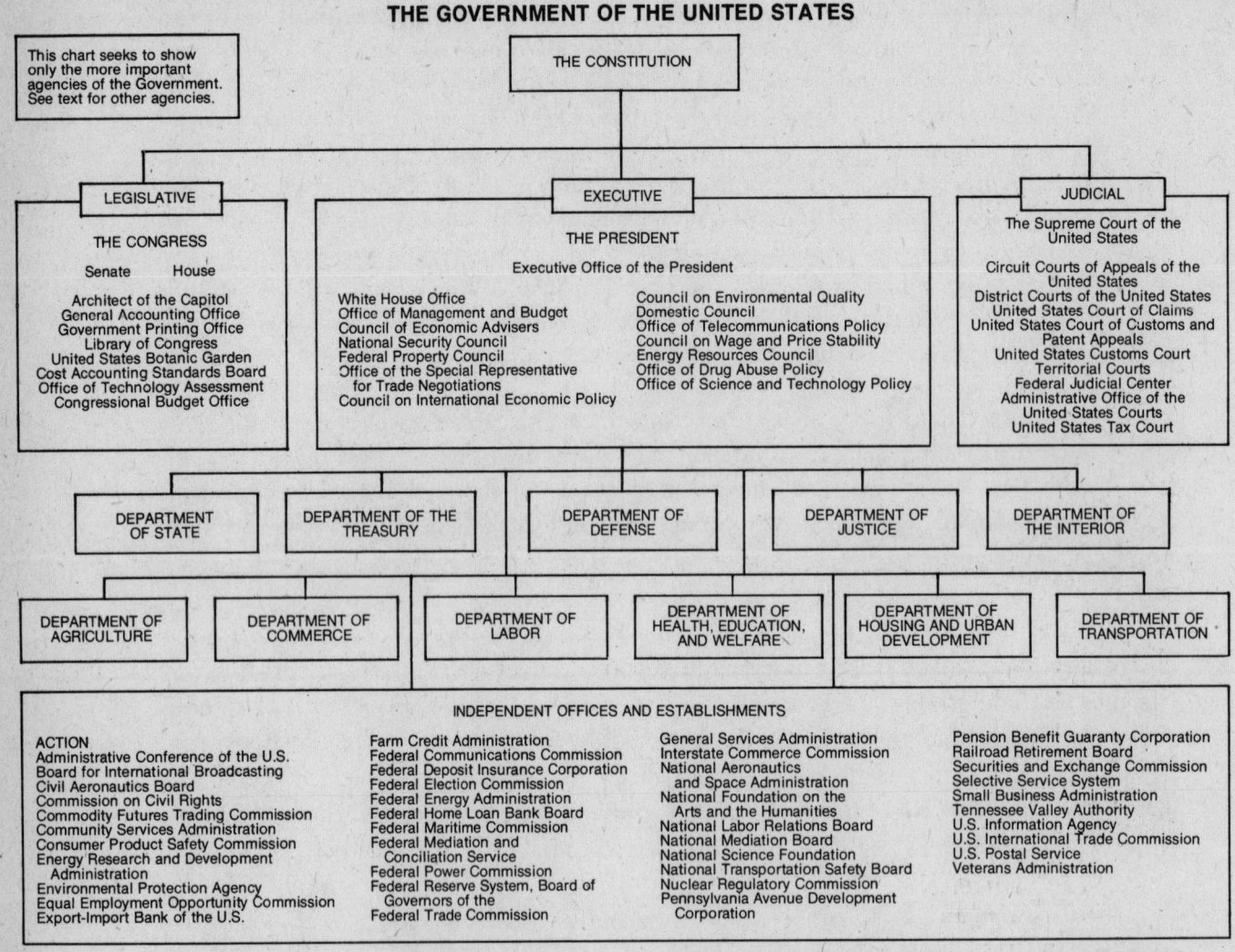

This chart and the Congress charts on page 561 are reprinted from the 1977/78 *United States Government Manual*, Office of the Federal Register, National Archives and Records Service, General Services Administration.

For general information, contact your local Federal Information Center. (See Chapter 32, *Information Rights and Resources*, for specific listings.)

The mailing addresses for Congress are:

Senator _____
Senate Office Building
Washington, D.C. 20510

Representative _____
House Office Building
Washington, D.C. 20515

Write or call the National Referral Center (Library of Congress, Washington, D.C. 20540) for their free information service on government resources.

American Statistics Index and an index to congressional information is available for a fee from: *Congressional Information Service*, 7101 Wisconsin Avenue, N.W., Washington, D.C. 20014.

UNITED STATES SENATE

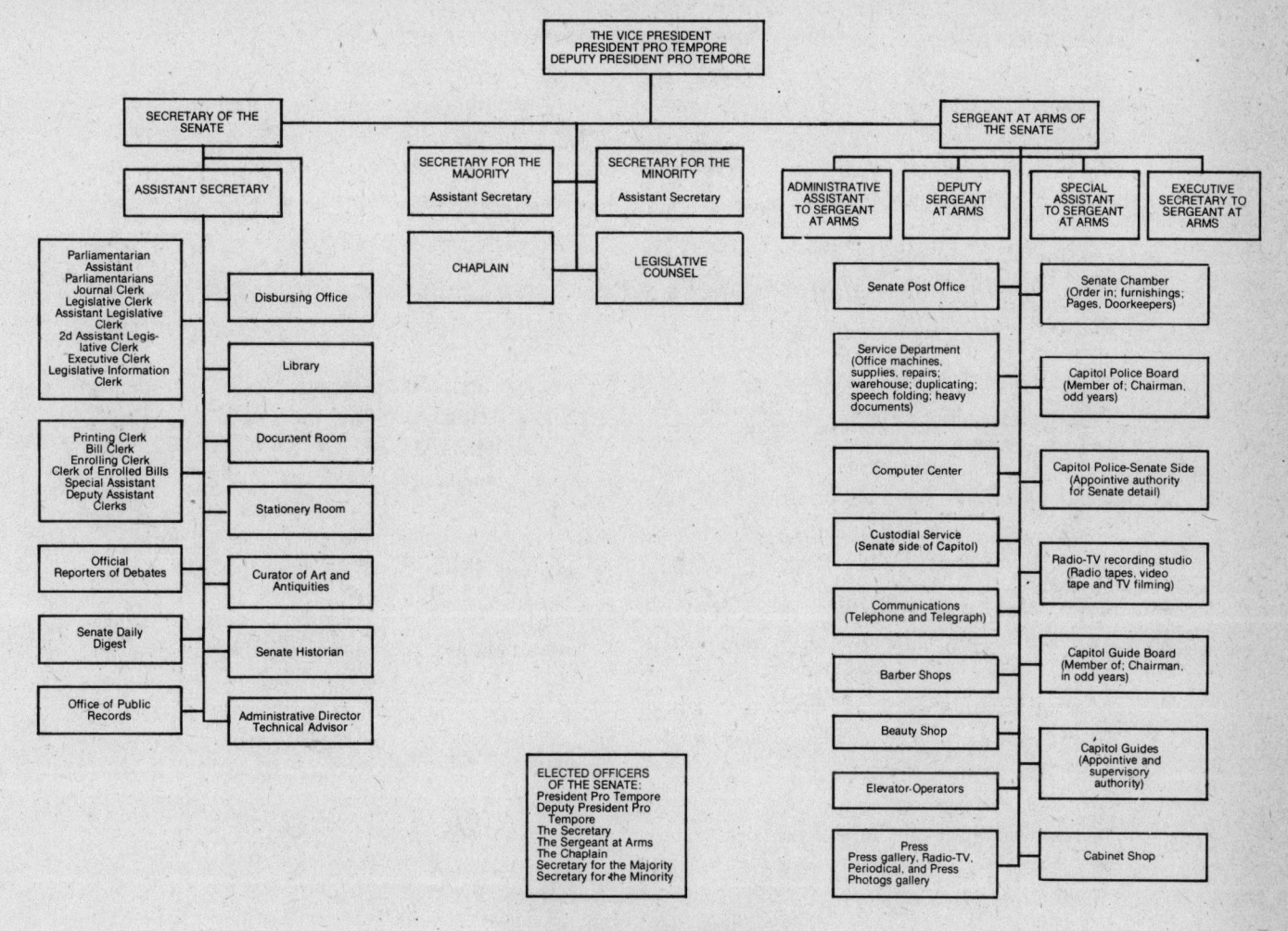

THE VICE PRESIDENT
PRESIDENT PRO TEMPORE
DEPUTY PRESIDENT PRO TEMPORE

SECRETARY OF THE SENATE

ASSISTANT SECRETARY

- Parliamentarian
  Assistant Parliamentarians
  Journal Clerk
  Legislative Clerk
  Assistant Legislative Clerk
  2d Assistant Legislative Clerk
  Executive Clerk
  Legislative Information Clerk
- Printing Clerk
  Bill Clerk
  Enrolling Clerk
  Clerk of Enrolled Bills
  Special Assistant
  Deputy Assistant Clerks
- Official Reporters of Debates
- Senate Daily Digest
- Office of Public Records

- Disbursing Office
- Library
- Document Room
- Stationery Room
- Curator of Art and Antiquities
- Senate Historian
- Administrative Director Technical Advisor

SECRETARY FOR THE MAJORITY
Assistant Secretary

- CHAPLAIN

SECRETARY FOR THE MINORITY
Assistant Secretary

- LEGISLATIVE COUNSEL

SERGEANT AT ARMS OF THE SENATE

- ADMINISTRATIVE ASSISTANT TO SERGEANT AT ARMS
- DEPUTY SERGEANT AT ARMS
- SPECIAL ASSISTANT TO SERGEANT AT ARMS
- EXECUTIVE SECRETARY TO SERGEANT AT ARMS

- Senate Post Office
- Service Department (Office machines, supplies, repairs; warehouse; duplicating; speech folding; heavy documents)
- Computer Center
- Custodial Service (Senate side of Capitol)
- Communications (Telephone and Telegraph)
- Barber Shops
- Beauty Shop
- Elevator-Operators
- Press
  Press gallery, Radio-TV, Periodical, and Press Photogs gallery

- Senate Chamber (Order in; furnishings; Pages, Doorkeepers)
- Capitol Police Board (Member of; Chairman, odd years)
- Capitol Police-Senate Side (Appointive authority for Senate detail)
- Radio-TV recording studio (Radio tapes, video tape and TV filming)
- Capitol Guide Board (Member of; Chairman, in odd years)
- Capitol Guides (Appointive and supervisory authority)
- Cabinet Shop

ELECTED OFFICERS OF THE SENATE:
President Pro Tempore
Deputy President Pro Tempore
The Secretary
The Sergeant at Arms
The Chaplain
Secretary for the Majority
Secretary for the Minority

THE U.S. CONGRESS
The Capitol
Washington, D.C. 20510

HOUSE OF REPRESENTATIVES

- MAJORITY LEADER
- HOUSE OF REPRESENTATIVES
- MINORITY LEADER
- MAJORITY WHIP
- THE SPEAKER
- MINORITY WHIP

- HOUSE OFFICE BUILDINGS COMMISSION
- COMMITTEE ON RULES
- CLERK
- PARLIAMENTARIAN
- OFFICIAL REPORTERS OF DEBATES

- LEGISLATIVE COUNSEL
- DOORKEEPER
- SERGEANT AT ARMS

- POSTMASTER
- CHAPLAIN

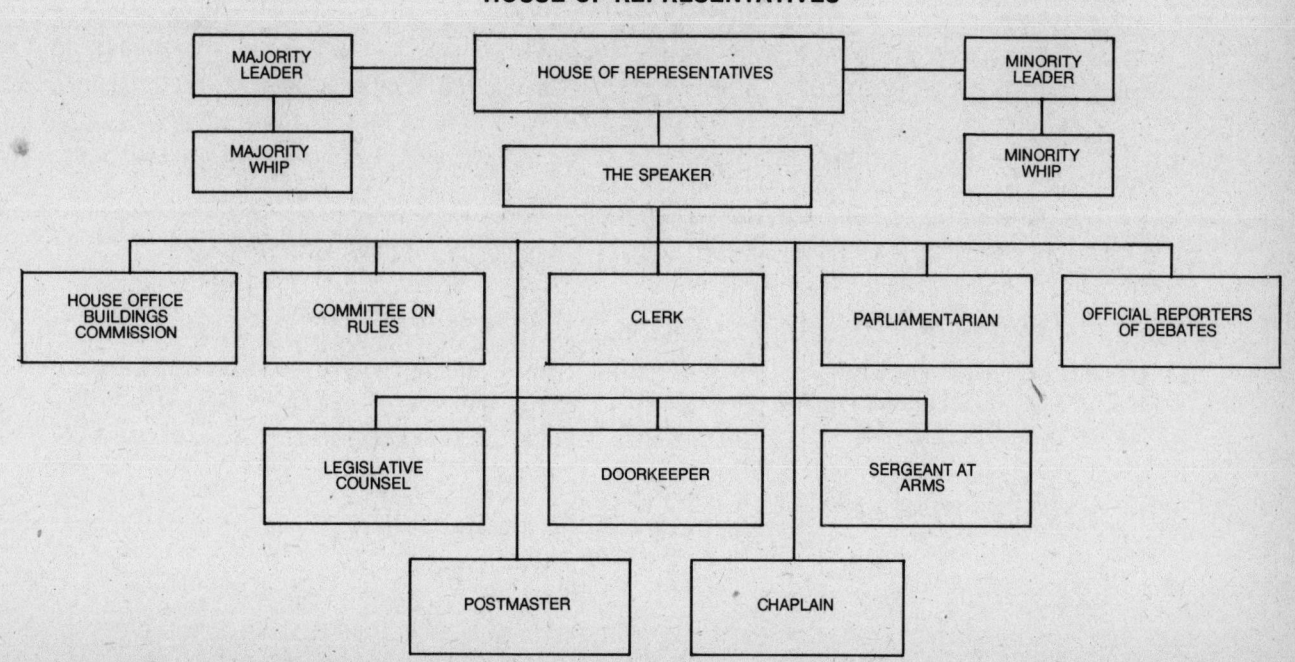

562 / THE HELP BOOK

The following publications contain government statistics:

Statistical Services of the U.S. Government ($3.40)
Statistical Reporter, monthly ($9.70 a year)
Federal Statistical Directory ($2.50)

All are for sale from the Superintendent of Documents, U.S. Government Printing Office, Washington, D.C. 20402, or your nearest government bookstore.

The following national organizations serve as information clearinghouses on government and politics:

Center for Information on America
Washington, Conn. 06793

An information clearinghouse on various topics of national or international interest, such as population, government, unemployment, black America, and the elderly.

LITERATURE: *The 95th Congress and Its Committees* ($.50); *Vital Issues*, monthly from September to June ($4.00); Grass Roots Guides for successful participation in politics published on an irregular basis ($4.50 for ten issues).

Democratic National Committee
1625 Massachusetts Avenue, N.W.
Washington, D.C. 20036

National headquarters for the Democratic Party.

Friends Committee on National Legislation (FCNL)
245 Second Street, N.E.
Washington, D.C. 20002

Started in November 1943 by a Committee of Friends (Quakers), this national information service provides monthly updates on current legislation through their monthly *Washington Newsletter* (subscriptions $10.00). They also conduct research and lobby on certain issues.

LITERATURE: Series of "how-to" pamphlets: "How to Write a Letter to the Editor"; "How to Work in Politics"; "How to Visit Your Members of Congress"; "How to Write Members of Congress and the President," and "How to Work for the Congressional Candidate of Your Choice" (first copy free, additional copies $.05 each).

League of Women Voters Education Fund
1730 M Street, N.W.
Washington, D.C. 20036

Research and information clearinghouse on national issues, such as politics, conservation, and organizing.

LITERATURE: *The Voter*, quarterly ($2.00).

National Democratic Forum
1621 Connecticut Avenue, N.W.
Washington, D.C. 20009

An independent, nonprofit educational organization based in Washington, D.C., that was founded in 1973. The forum conducts discussions, seminars, and conferences on important policy questions of national concern and publishes a magazine, *Democratic Review*. Memberships are $20.00 a year; contributions are welcomed. All forum discussions are open to the public and held at various locations around the country.

Republican National Committee
310 First Street, S.E.
Washington, D.C. 20003

The committee helps candidates with their campaigns and acts as liaison with local chapters. State party organizations deal with town and city political activities.

The following national organizations and citizens lobbies are trying to collectively influence government; contact them for general information, membership fees, and publications:

Common Cause
2030 M Street, N.W.
Washington, D.C. 20036

Started in 1970, Common Cause, a national political action citizens lobby, has more than 250,000 members and is devoted to making the processes of federal and state governments more open, responsive, and accountable to citizens. Annual membership dues are $15.00 and include subscription to *FrontLine* ($2.00 a copy to others) and *In Common*, a quarterly. Volunteers in the Washington, D.C. office perform a wide range of duties including research, writing, communication with members, and clerical activities.

LITERATURE: Write for a list of investigative studies that are available ($2.00 each).

People's Business Commission
1346 Connecticut Avenue, N.W.
Washington, D.C. 20036

Founded in 1971 as the People's Bicentennial Commission, there are six regional and sixty local groups in this research and educational organization. It is concerned with education about democratic alternatives to the American economic system. The commission has a speakers bureau, study outlines, a features service, and organizing guides.

LITERATURE: *Common Sense*, bimonthly; various brochures.

People's Lobby
3456 West Olympic Boulevard
Los Angeles, Calif. 90019

A national information clearinghouse for those asking about the initiative process—the constitutional right of people to propose laws directly to the voters by collecting signatures to put issues on the ballot; twenty-four states currently have the right of initiative. Numbers of signatures required to qualify a measure for the ballot vary from state to state, usually a percentage of those who voted for governor in the last election. People's Lobby, founded in 1968, has as its primary goal the ratification of the initiative and vote of confidence (recall) processes into the federal constitution. Local offices are located in Los Angeles and Sacramento. People's Lobby has published books and reports in this field (see Additional Literature).

LITERATURE: Position paper on initiative process and brochure (both free).

Public Citizen
P.O. Box 19404
Washington, D.C. 20036

Founded by Ralph Nader to aid citizens in informing the government of their needs and ideas, Public Citizen also includes these companion groups: Tax Reform Research Group; Litigation Group; Health Research Group; Citizen Action; Public Citizen Visitors Center; and Congress Watch. Write for publication price list.

SANE (A Citizens' Organization for a Sane World)
318 Massachusetts Avenue, N.E.
Washington, D.C. 20002

Founded in 1957, there are now about 18,000 members of SANE, whose primary goals are the reversal of the international arms race and economic conversion. Membership dues are $15.00 a year ($5.00 for senior citizens, students, GI's, and low income people). *Sane Views the World* is aired weekly over fifty radio stations; Paul Newman narrated the first SANE slide show, "Guns or Butter." It provides public education on the relationship between economics and disarmament.

564 / THE HELP BOOK

LITERATURE: Fact sheets; *The United States and Korea: Foreign Policy Choices* ($1.25); "Do You Know What Your Tax Dollar Buys?" ($.25).

The following national organizations represent the interests of neighborhoods, rural counties, or cities by coming together as unified groups and also through research, educational programs, and forums:

Council of State Governments
Iron Works Pike
Lexington, Ky. 40511

A joint agency created, supported, and directed by the states since its founding in 1933 to conduct research, publish reports, and serve as a state-federal liaison.

LITERATURE: Free descriptive brochure; send for publications price list of more than forty formal research products created annually.

National Association of Counties (NACo)
1735 New York Avenue, N.W.
Washington, D.C. 20006

A national clearinghouse for county government information in recognition of the fact that about 180 million Americans, or nine-tenths of the population, live in counties. Membership is comprised of elected and appointed officials of 1,400 U.S. counties who are encouraged to lobby and testify in Congress so that county needs are felt in the legislative process. There are thirteen steering committees: Community Development, Crime and Public Safety, Environment and Energy, Health and Education, Labor Management, Land Use, Local Determinism, Manpower, Public Lands, Regionalism, Taxation and Finance, Transportation, and Welfare and Social Services. NACo is based on the beliefs that "counties are the basic—and key—unit of state government" and that their organization "serves as the national voice of the county officials." County officials needs for technical assistance are met through conferences, data collection, individual consultations, inquiry responses, policy analysis, roundtable discussions, special briefings, and the Living Library, housing over 500 county government–related publications. Direct personal assistance by NACo staffers is available for county officials through a telephone "hotline" as well as publications keyed to the thirteen steering committee concerns and general and related topics.

LITERATURE: *County News; Outlook* supplement; *New County Times; County Manpower Report*, published six times a year; reports, including *Living Library* ($1.00); *Local Participation in Social Services; Integrated Services for Victims of Crime; County-Wide Law Enforcement; Addressing The Diverse Needs of Rural Counties: Report On The 1974–1975 Rural Human Resources Program; The NACo Book of Numbers* (free leaflet).

National Association of Neighborhoods (NAN)
1901 Q Street, N.W.
Washington, D.C. 20009

A private organization started in 1975, supported by contributions and membership fees, that is dedicated to united local neighborhood groups. It also provides legal and general information and community education.

LITERATURE: *The NAN Bulletin*.

National League of Cities (NLC)
1620 Eye Street, N.W.
Washington, D.C. 20006

NLC, an organization comprised of city officials that represent some 15,000 cities, advocates on behalf of urban interests before Congress, the White House, federal agencies, and in state capitals throughout the country. It is also an information clearinghouse providing policy analysis, federal program evaluation, and background resources on solid waste management, manpower, transportation, water quality, law enforcement,

POLITICAL ACTION / 565

and community development. There is a 30,000-volume urban affairs library shared with the U.S. Conference on Mayors. Each year there is an annual business meeting called "Congress of Cities." The Congressional-City Conference is another annual meeting. Dues range from $300 to $25,000, depending on the size of the city (from below 10,000 persons to more than 4 million). Special reports and publications are available for sale on various leadership-oriented subjects.

LITERATURE: Free pamphlet; annual "Publications & Audio Visuals" catalog; newsletters and reports (prices differ for each item and are based on whether the subscriber is a member or not).

United States Conference of Mayors
1620 Eye Street, N.W.
Washington, D.C. 20006

A national organization of city governments that provides a forum for those 750 cities with more than 30,000 population who are members or participants. The Conference concentrates on federal-city relationships. The members—by-and-large every single qualifying city—is the city's mayor. There are five standing committees—Environment, Community Development, Human Resources, Transportation, and Urban Economic Policy. Its information clearinghouse functions—for mayors and citizens alike—include the bimonthly publication *The Mayor*, special reports, Federal-City Report bulletin; send for list of extensive publications.

The state agency for state-local relations usually acts as a liaison for state-local and/or state-federal programs and affairs. It serves as an information clearinghouse on available grants, up-to-date budget information, and technical services for those towns that want to apply for grants. It will also communicate to the state what difficulties towns are having. There is usually another office for state/Washington, D.C., matters.

The following are the state agencies for state-local relations:

Division of Local Government Assistance
Department of Community and Regional
  Affairs
207 Community Building
Pouch B
Juneau, Alaska 99811

Governor's Advisory Council on
  Intergovernmental Relations
1700 West Washington
Phoenix, Ariz. 85007

Department of Local Services
900 First National Bank Building
Little Rock, Ark. 72201

Division of Local Government Fiscal Affairs
Office of the State Controller
520 Capitol Mall
Sacramento, Calif. 95814

Department of Local Affairs
Centennial Building
1313 Sherman Street
Denver, Colo. 80203

Intergovernmental Relations Division
Office of Policy and Management (OPM)
80 Washington Street
Hartford, Conn. 06115

Bureau of Local Government Assistance
Division of Technical Assistance
Department of Community Affairs
Howard Building
2571 Executive Center Circle, East
Tallahassee, Fla. 32301

Bureau of Community Affairs
Department of Community Development
7 Martin Luther King, Jr., Drive, S.W.
Atlanta, Ga. 30334

Department of Local Government Affairs
303 East Monroe Street
Springfield, Ill. 62706

Division of Municipal Affairs
Office for Planning and Programming
523 East 12th Street
Des Moines, Iowa 50319

Intergovernmental Relations and
  Administration
Department of Health and Environment
Forbes Field
Topeka, Kans. 66620

Division for Regional Affairs
Department for Local Government
909 Leawood Drive
Frankfort, Ky. 40601

Department of Urban Community Affairs
P.O. Box 44455
Baton Rouge, La. 70804

Department of Community Affairs
100 Chambers Street
Boston, Mass. 02202

Office of Local and Urban Affairs
State Planning Agency
100 Capitol Square Building
550 Cedar Street
St. Paul, Minn. 55101

Division of Community Development
Department of Consumer Affairs, Regulation,
  and Licensing
Jefferson State Office Building
P.O. Box 118
Jefferson City, Mo. 65101

Department of Community Affairs
1424 Ninth Avenue
Helena, Mont. 59601

Division of Local Government Services
Department of Community Affairs
363 West State Street
Trenton, N.J. 08625

Local Government Division
Executive Legislative Building
Santa Fe, N.M. 85703

Division of Community Affairs
162 Washington Avenue
Albany, N.Y. 12231

Division of Intergovernmental Relations
Department of Natural Resources and
  Community Development
P.O. Box 27687
Raleigh, N.C. 27611

Community Development Division
Department of Economic and Community
  Development
State Office Tower
30 East Broad Street
Columbus, Ohio 43215

Intergovernmental Relations Division
Executive Department
240 Cottage Street, S.E.
Salem, Ore. 97310

Department of Community Affairs
216 South Office Building
Harrisburg, Pa. 17120

Planning and Development Division
Department of Community Affairs
150 Washington Street
Providence, R.I. 02903

Office of Local Government
Division of Administration
State House
Columbia, S.C. 29201

Texas Advisory Commission on
  Intergovernmental Relations
Stephen F. Austin State Office Building
1700 North Congress Avenue
Austin, Tex. 78701

State Planning Coordinator
118 State Capitol
Salt Lake City, Utah 84114

Department of Community Affairs
Agency of Development and Community
  Affairs
Pavilion Office Building
109 State Street
Montpelier, Vt. 05602

Division of Local and Regional Planning
Department of Intergovernmental Affairs
Fourth Street Office Building
205 North Fourth Street
Richmond, Va. 23219

Community Planning Division
Office of Community Development
400 Capitol Center Building
410 West Fifth Street
Olympia, Wash. 98504

Department of Local Affairs and Development
Loraine Building
123 West Washington Avenue
Madison, Wis. 53702

Women who wish to get more involved in politics should contact the following groups:

Center for the American Woman and Politics
Eagleton Institute of Politics
Rutgers University
New Brunswick, N.J. 08901

An information clearinghouse concerning women in public life; library; national data bank.

LITERATURE: Fact sheets about women in politics and politics in general; descriptive literature about the center.

Democratic National Committee
Women's Division
1625 Massachusetts Avenue, N.W.
Washington, D.C. 20036

The committee emphasizes the importance of women's role in political participation.

League of Women Voters of the United States
1730 M Street, N.W.
Washington, D.C. 20036

A national organization with over 1,000 local branches committed to promoting political responsibility through active citizen participation in government. On the local level, the league is involved with law enforcement, corrections, ex-offender rehabilitation, and other programs.

LITERATURE: Catalogue of free and low-cost materials.

National Action Committee on the Status of Women
40 St. Clair Avenue East, Suite 300
Toronto, Ontario M4T 1M9, Canada

A national organization aimed at improving the status of women in Canada by maintaining a network of communication with all national women's organizations. It holds annual meetings and lobbies members of parliament for changes in legislation.

LITERATURE: *NAC Memo* (free); *Status of Women News* ($3.00 a year).

National Association of Commissions for Women
% A. Miller, National President
926 J Street, Room 1014
Sacramento, Calif. 95814

A coalition of commissions at the city, county, and state level that come together to define the goals and effective ways that commissions can operate to advance the status of women.

National Congress of Neighborhood Women
145 Skillman Avenue
Brooklyn, N.Y. 11211

A coalition of women's groups concerned with numerous problems, including battered women. It provides educational services for working class women and rap sessions and serves as an umbrella group for fifty women's services.

LITERATURE: Descriptive brochure; quarterly newspaper.

National Federation of Republican Women
310 First Street, S.E.
Washington, D.C. 20003

The federation puts people and campaigns together through its 230,000 members around the country. It has publications on every aspect of women in politics and organizations, and women as candidates.

LITERATURE: *Consider Yourself for Public Office* ($1.00).

National Organization for Women (NOW)
425 Thirteenth Street, N.W.
Washington, D.C. 20004

The national center provides organizational activities and referrals to local N.O.W. groups. It is concerned with sex discrimination, jobs, housing, rape victims, battered wives, and day care.

National Women's Education Fund (NWEF)
1532 Sixteenth Street, N.W.
Washington, D.C. 20036

The fund provides nonpartisan educational programs and materials to encourage and equip women for greater participation in the political process. NWEF conducts research, and serves as a clearinghouse on information and resources related to women in politics for the media, educational institutions, business and labor groups, membership organizations, and elected officials.

LITERATURE: *Campaign Workbook; Roster of Women State Legislators* (updated regularly).

National Women's Political Caucus (NWPC)
1411 K Street, N.W.
Washington, D.C. 20005

A national membership organization with 300 chapters in over forty states that works to increase the number of women in political office. It has grown from 271 women in 1971 to well over 35,000, and is active "talking" to legislators.

LITERATURE: Newsletter (with $15.00 dues); free descriptive brochure; *Women's Political Times*.

Women's Lobby
201 Massachusetts Avenue, N.E.
Washington, D.C. 20002

Encourages women to run for political office; lobbies on women's issues; and offers legislation updates through its newsletter, *Women's Lobby Alert* (by subscription).

ADDITIONAL LITERATURE

Directories of Government Agencies and Government Personnel

The Almanac of American Politics (issued biannually). E. P. Dutton, 2 Park Avenue, New York, N.Y. 10016 ($16.95 hardcover, $7.95 paperback). Provides information on each government representative, senator, and governor.

Congressional Directory (annual). Superintendent of Documents, U.S. Government Printing Office, Washington, D.C. 20402 ($6.50). Information on senators and representatives.

Congressional Staff Directory. Box 62, Mount Vernon, Va. 22121 ($19.50).

Congressional Yellow Book (updated quarterly). Washington Monitor, Inc., National Press Building, Washington, D.C. 20045 ($60.00 a year). Directory.

Diplomatic List. Superintendent of Documents, U.S. Government Printing Office, Washington, D.C. 20402 ($1.50). Names, titles, home addresses, and telephone numbers of members of the Washington diplomatic corps, compiled by the State Department.

Directory of Key Government Personnel (1977). Hill and Knowlton, Inc., One McPherson Square, 1425 K Street, N.W., Washington, D.C. 20005 (free booklet). A tradition that dates back to a single mimeographed sheet in 1950 listing names and numbers of the emergency agencies of the Korean War, this edition lists 1,798 persons in key government positions.

Federal Executive Telephone Directory (revised six times a year). Carroll Publishing Company, 1058 Thomas Jefferson Street, N.W., Washington, D.C. 20007 ($96.00 a year). Phone book of upper level federal employees.

The Federal Yellow Book (updated quarterly). Washington Monitor, Inc., National Press Building, Washington, D.C. 20045 ($95.00 a year). Directory.

U.S. Government Manual (updated annually). Superintendent of Documents, U.S. Government Printing Office, Washington, D.C. 20402 ($6.50). Comprehensive listing of departments and offices within the federal government; field offices are also included; services and programs are described.

Washington Information Directory. Congressional Quarterly, Inc., 1414 Twenty-second Street, N.W., Washington, D.C. 20037 ($18.00). A directory with the information arranged by subject.

Books and Booklets

The Bill of Rights: The Oliver Wendell Holmes Lectures, 1958 by Learned Hand, introduction by Charles E. Wyanski, Jr. (1958). Atheneum Publishers, 122 East 42nd Street, New York, N.Y. 10017 ($2.95). Judge Hand's explanation of the Supreme Court's relationship to the Bill of Rights.

Checking on Elected Officials by Barry Greever. The Midwest Academy, 600 West Fullerton, Chicago, Ill. 60614 ($.15). Fact sheets with questions about elected officials and where to go to get them answered.

The Community Activist's Handbook by John Huenefeld (1970). Beacon Press, 25 Beacon Street, Boston, Mass. 02108. (Currently out of print.)

The Constitution of the United States: An Introduction by Floyd G. Cullop (1969). New American Library, 1301 Avenue of the Americas, New York, N.Y. 10019 ($.75). A popular description of what the constitution guarantees.

Direct Democracy: An Historical Analysis of the Initiative, Referendum and Recall Process by Laura Tallian (1977). People's Lobby Press, 3456 West Olympic Boulevard, Los Angeles, Calif. 90019 ($7.50). Explains and uses examples of its major thesis: "We propose that the right to petition the government be made more effective," as granted in the First Amendment of the Constitution.

Have You Considered Government and Politics? Opportunities for Women are Expanding (1976). Career Options Series for Undergraduate Women, Catalyst, 14 East 60th Street, New York, N.Y. 10022 ($1.95). Booklet describing the kinds of jobs available in government, how to apply for them, educational background suggested, where to get more information, and selected publications.

It's Your Capital, Too: A Guidebook for the Congressional Witness. Hill and Knowlton, Inc., International Public Relations and Public Affairs Counsel, 150 East 42nd Street, New York, N.Y. 10017 (free leaflet).

National Initiative and Vote of Confidence (Recall): Tools for Self-Government by Alice Shader, Carol Hamcke, and Judi Phillips (1974). People's Lobby, 3456 West Olympic Boulevard, Los Angeles, Calif. 90019 ($5.00). A comprehensive book including definitions, history, and explanations of the initiative and recall processes plus a state-by-state description of what rights people have to make laws. Also includes basic background information on the People's Lobby and a bibliography.

Obedience to Authority: An Experimental View by Stanley Milgram (1975). Harper & Row Publishers, Inc., 10 East 53rd Street, New York, N.Y. 10022 ($3.45). Milgram's experiments and interpretations of why people obey authority with possible applications to politics and submission to government policies.

The Parties: Republicans and Democrats in This Century by Henry Fairlie (1978). St. Martin's Press, 175 Fifth Avenue, New York, N.Y. 10010 ($8.95).

Political Parties: A Sociological Study of the Oligarchical Tendencies of Modern Democracy by Robert Michels, translated by Eden and Cedar Paul, introduction by Seymour Martin Lipset (1962). The Free Press, Macmillan Book Company, 866 Third Avenue, New York, N.Y. 10022 ($2.45). A discussion of the inevitability of oligarchy in party life and the problems that poses for the actualization of democracy.

Political Women by Jeane J. Kirkpatrick (1974). Basic Books, 10 East 53rd Street, New York, N.Y. 10022 ($10.00).

Politics and Markets by Charles E. Lindblom (1977). Basic Books, 10 East 53rd Street, New York, N.Y. 10022 ($15.00).

Politics and Pesticides by Laura Tallian (1977). People's Lobby Press, 3456 West Olympic Boulevard, Los Angeles, Calif. 90019 ($2.50). One labor leader called this book important reading for all who are concerned about the safety of farm workers, the health of consumers, and the sanctity of the environment.

Questions and Answers About Campaign Finances. American Civil Liberties Union, 22 East 40th Street, New York, N.Y. 10016 ($.50). Pamphlet on federal laws and suggested reforms.

Successful Advocacy: A Practical Handbook. California Commission on the Status of Women, 926 J Street, Suite 10003, Sacramento, Calif. 95814 ($1.00). A concise guidebook for women who wish to become more active politically.

Understanding American Politics by R. V. Denenberg (1976). William Collins Sons and Company, Ltd., A Fontana Original, 14 St. James Place, London SW1, England ($2.95 Canada, £1.00 U.K.). An excellent, clear, and well-written guide to American politics. Denenberg makes no assumptions and spells it all out. "Democracy, political and legal equality, and individual freedom," the ideals on which America was founded, are explored through their written and systematic applications. It is especially useful for Americans who long ago studied the Constitution, Supreme Court, and the party system, or even for those who never really understood it.

Women in Politics edited by Jane Jacquette (1974). John Wiley and Sons, 605 Third Avenue, New York, N.Y. 10016 ($16.75).

Magazines and Newspapers

Dissent. 505 Fifth Avenue, New York, N.Y. 10017 ($2.50 per copy, $10.00 per subscription). "Journal devoted to radical ideas and the values of socialism and democracy."

In These Times (weekly). 1509 North Milwaukee Avenue, Chicago, Ill. 60622 ($17.50 a year). "The Independent Socialist Newspaper" with articles on nuclear waste, grassroots organizing, labor, etc.

The Nation. 333 Avenue of the Americas, New York, N.Y. 10014 ($21.00 a year). A weekly journal of political reporting with a 100-year-plus history.

Political Science Quarterly. 2852 Broadway, New York, N.Y. 10025 (subscriptions are obtained through membership in The Academy of Political Science—$16.00 a year; single copies—$4.00). "A non-partisan journal devoted to the study of contemporary and historical aspects of government, politics, and public affairs."

Seven Days (biweekly). 206 Fifth Avenue, New York, N.Y. 10010 ($15.60 a year). A political alternative news magazine. In addition to national and international news and features, there are book, television, and movie reviews. A recent issue contained articles on how the oil companies profit while we pay the bills and a two-part series on the FBI.

Society (bimonthly). Rutgers, The State University, New Brunswick, N.J. 08903 ($15.00 a year). Social science and public policy magazine for professionals, students, and laypersons.

Southern Exposure (quarterly). Box 230, Chapel Hill, N.C. 27514 ($8.00 a year, sample copy $2.50). A journal of the Institute for Southern Studies with the purpose of social change that includes stories on a variety of political and cultural topics, from labor organizing to occupational health and energy problems.

Washington Monthly. 1028 Connecticut Avenue, N.W., Washington, D.C. 20036 ($16.00 a year). In-depth articles, reviews, the "political puzzle" crossword puzzle, "memo of the month," monthly listing of new political affairs books, and, in the May 1977 edition, "Who's Who in the Carter Administration."

See also the following related chapters in *The Help Book:*

ANIMAL RIGHTS
CITIZEN ACTION
CIVIL RIGHTS AND DISCRIMINATION
CONSUMER AFFAIRS
COURTS
EDUCATION
EMPLOYMENT
ENVIRONMENT
HOUSING
INFORMATION RIGHTS AND RESOURCES
LEGAL SERVICES

44

RAPE AND SEXUAL ASSAULT

Forcible rape, as defined by the Federal Bureau of Investigation (which compiles the annual *Uniform Crime Reports* of major Index Offenses in the United States) is "the carnal knowledge of a female forcibly and against her will." Assaults or attempts to commit forcible rape by force or threat of force are also included; however statutory rape (without force), homosexual "rapes," and other sex offenses are not included in this category. It is therefore difficult to determine the numerical frequency of rape and sexual assault in this country, although it was listed officially in 1977 as 63,020, an 11.1 percent increase from the reported 56,730 offenses in the previous year.

As it is well known by now, rape and sexual assault are crimes that often go unreported by the victim. In *Against Our Will*, Susan Brownmiller argues that a figure of 255,000 rapes and attempted rapes in 1973 (when the FBI reported 51,000 cases) is an "unemotional, rock-bottom minimum." Some victims want to forget about their rape as quickly as possible; others are ashamed that they didn't fend off their attackers; and still others deny that the rape even occurred. But even if the rape is reported, the rapist is rarely convicted and imprisoned. Of the four major violent crimes—homicide, robbery, aggravated assault, and rape—only robbery, with a clearance rate of 27 percent, was lower than rape, with a clearance rate of 51 percent. (Clearance rate refers to the number of arrests made as compared to the number of complaints by victims.)

MYTHS AND FACTS ABOUT SEXUAL ASSAULT*

Myths about sexual assault prevent many victims from reporting and seeking assistance in working through the trauma of the assault. We must work to discard and dispel these myths.

---

*"Myths and Facts About Sexual Assault," "Prevention Techniques," and "What to Do if Sexually Assaulted" are reprinted with permission from *Sexual Assault: A Statewide Problem*, a booklet prepared by the Minnesota Programs for Victims of Sexual Assault (430 Metro Square Building, St. Paul., Minn. 55101), compiled and edited by Eileen Keller (1976).

Myth: Most sexual assaults are provoked by the victim.
Fact: Though provocation may consist of only "a gesture" according to the Federal Commission on Crimes of Violence, only 4 percent of reported sexual assaults involve precipitative behavior on the part of the victim.

Myth: Only women who walk alone at night are sexually assaulted.
Fact: Studies show that one-third to one-half of sexual assaults are committed in the victim's home.

Myth: Sexual assault occurs only among strangers.
Fact: In nearly 65 percent of sexual assault cases the victim and offender know each other in some way.

Myth: No person can be sexually assaulted against her will.
Fact: Studies indicate that in 75 percent of sexual assault cases the victim is faced with a weapon or threat of death or great bodily harm.

Myth: Only women are victims.
Fact: Although most victims are female, there is an increase in the number of children and men reporting. Any vulnerable man, woman, or child is a potential victim.

Myth: Sexual assault is an impulsive, uncontrollable act.
Fact: Fifty-eight percent of sexual assaults are planned in advance by the offender.

Myth: Sexual assault is primarily a sex act.
Fact: Sexual assault is primarily an act of violence. Eighty-five percent of offenders use some form of overt violence or force.

PREVENTION TECHNIQUES

No one method of prevention is completely effective in every situation. Allowing yourself to consider what you would do if attacked may be the best preparation. Consider, also, the following suggestions:
- Lock your doors and windows—car and home.
- Don't open your door to strangers; require identification of all service personnel.
- Whenever possible avoid walking alone at night.
- Don't be caught off guard—be prepared to run and scream.
- If attacked, assert yourself. Use your common sense. Do not fight against a weapon—your life is most important.
- Hitchhiking can be dangerous. If you must hitchhike try to travel in pairs and be cautious with whom you accept a ride.
- A training course in physical self-defense and assertiveness may be of help.

WHAT TO DO IF YOU HAVE BEEN SEXUALLY ASSAULTED

- REMEMBER: You are not to blame for having been sexually assaulted.
- Report the assault to the police immediately whether or not you choose to prosecute. You may save someone else from being victimized in the future.
- Do not bathe, douche, change clothes, clean up, or in any other way destroy possible evidence.
- Call a hospital or private physician to get an emergency medical exam for treatment of injuries, V.D., and pregnancy; and an evidentiary exam which is required if you decide to prosecute.
- Call a friend, family member, or a sexual assault crisis center, if available, for support.
- Write down details about the assailant and circumstances of the assault as soon as possible.

Information on rape, rape victims, and rape prevention may be available from your city or county crime prevention bureau or the state crime prevention program. State women's commissions may also have published information on rape crisis centers and rape prevention. For example, the Pennsylvania Commission for Women publishes a comprehensive booklet, *Help for the Rape Victim*, which contains a resource guide. (See additional suggestions in the introduction to "Direct Help.")

On the national level, the following organizations provide information on and for rape victims:

Center for Women Policy Studies (CWPA)
2000 P Street, N.W., Suite 508
Washington, D.C. 20036

A national information clearinghouse on rape, physically abused women, and sexually abused children. CWPA was established in 1972; the clearinghouse in 1976. It is also involved in various information-gathering projects and books.

LITERATURE: *Response* newsletter geared to the professional or worker in the fields of sensitive crimes—rape, wife abuse, sexual abuse of children (free, but subscription should be requested only if interest is that specialized).

Child Sexual Abuse Treatment Program
California Demonstration and Training Project
840 Guadalupe Parkway
San Jose, Calif. 95110

Started in 1971 by the Santa Clara County Juvenile Probation Department, this program provides direct help through individual, marriage, family, and group counseling to those involved in or affected by child sexual abuse. It provides training to other California cities and counties that wish to develop similar treatment programs. Telephone and written referrals will be made for children or adults involved in or affected by child molestation.

LITERATURE: Information packet.

Feminist Alliance Against Rape
P.O. Box 21033
Washington, D.C. 20009

An international clearinghouse on issues relating to violence against women, particularly rape and wife abuse.

LITERATURE: *Aegis* newsletter ($6.50 a year by subscription); list of publications.

National Center for the Prevention and Control of Rape
National Rape Information Clearinghouse
National Institute of Mental Health
5600 Fishers Lane, Parklawn Building
Rockville, Md. 20857

A clearinghouse of information and educational materials that deal with rape prevention and treatment. The center is studying the need for reform of state rape laws and, until a national rape victim services directory is published, the center will conduct a computer search for local groups based on telephone or written inquiries. An information packet and films on free loan are available to qualified researchers, librarians, and professionals.

LITERATURE: Send for descriptive material and information on ordering their comprehensive teaching materials.

Rape Research Group
Department of Psychology
University of Alabama
P.O. Box 2968
University, Ala. 35486

Provides "where to find it" information and is currently completing a comprehensive annotated bibliography on sexual assault that will be published by the National Center for the Prevention and Control of Rape.

LITERATURE: *Toward the Prevention of Rape*, proceedings of the January 1975 national conference on Rape: Research, Action, Prevention ($3.48 prepaid); newsletter published three times a year (free to those interested in research or action in any area of sexual assault).

DIRECT HELP

National lists of rape crisis centers are available in photocopied or published form, but since many groups relocate or start up on short notice, checking your own community services is the best way to get immediate local help. Look in your telephone directory under "rape" or ask the operator for assistance. You might also consult your local chapter of N.O.W. (National Organization for Women), Y.M.C.A. (Young Women's Christian Association), United Way, district attorney's office, police department, women's health or gynecological center, or crime victims aid center as well as women's groups for assistance.

There is a wide range of services offered by rape crisis centers, but first and foremost is counseling for victims (usually by trained volunteers) as well as an "escort" through the various after-the-rape experiences that can be especially traumatic—the hospital examination and police, pretrial, and courtroom-related interviews. Legal, general, and medical information and referrals to free or private physicians and facilities is usually also offered along with self-defense classes, rap sessions, and a speakers bureau for community education and rape prevention programs.

The following is a sampling of local rape crisis centers throughout the United States, and in Canada and England:

Anchorage Rape and Assault Center
7060 Cranberry
Anchorage, Alaska 99502

Center Against Sexual Assault (CASA)
P.O. Box 3786
Phoenix, Ariz. 85030

Tucson Women Against Rape
P.O. Box 843
Tucson, Ariz. 85702

Rape Crisis, Inc.
P.O. Box 5181
Hillcrest Station
Little Rock, Ark. 72205

Bay Area Women Against Rape
P.O. Box 240
Berkeley, Calif. 94710

Upper Solano County Rape Crisis Service
P.O. Box 368
Fairfield, Calif. 94533

Fresno County District Attorney Assault Team
1100 Van Ness
Fresno, Calif. 93721

SACWAR (Southern Alameda County Women Against Rape)
P.O. Box 662
Hayward, Calif. 94543

Marin Rape Crisis Center
P.O. Box 823
Kentfield, Calif. 94904

Women Against Sexual Abuse (WASA)
P.O. Box 8200
Long Beach, Calif. 90808

Women's Transitional Living Center, Inc.
P.O. Box 6103
Orange, Calif. 92667

Mid-Peninsula Women Against Rape
℅ YWCA
4161 Alma Street
Palo Alto, Calif. 94306

R.E.A.C.T. Hotline
78 North Marengo Avenue
Pasadena, Calif. 91101

Sacramento Rape Crisis Center Project
1230 H Street
Sacramento, Calif. 95814

San Francisco Women Against Rape
1800 Market Street, Box 139
San Francisco, Calif. 94102

Santa Barbara Rape Crisis Center
P.O. Box 458
Santa Barbara, Calif. 93102

York Street Center
Victim Support System
1632 York Street
Denver, Colo. 80207

Pueblo Rape Crisis Center, Inc.
509 Colorado Avenue, Suite G
Pueblo, Colo. 81004

Rape Crisis Service
Greater Bridgeport YWCA
1862 East Maine Street
Bridgeport, Conn. 06610

Rape Crisis Center of Wilmington
P.O. Box 1507
Wilmington, Del. 19899

Rape Information and Counseling Service
P.O. Box 13007
University Street
Gainesville, Fla. 82604

Jacksonville Rape Crisis Center
% Hubbard House
1231 Hubbard Street
Jacksonville, Fla. 32201

Metro's Rape Awareness Public Education
  Program (R.A.P.E.)
140 West Flagler Street
Miami, Fla. 33130

Tallahassee Rape Crisis Service
Florida State University
P.O. Box 6826
Tallahassee, Fla. 32313

Hillsborough County Stop Rape, Inc./Rape
  Crisis Center
1723 West Kennedy Boulevard
Tampa, Fla. 33606

Child Crisis Center
Kauikeolani Children's Hospital
226 North Khuakini Street
Honolulu, Hawaii 96817

Sex Abuse Treatment Center
Kapiolani Hospital
1319 Puahou Street
Honolulu, Hawaii 96814

Rape Crisis Alliance
720 Washington Street
Boise, Idaho 83702

Rape Crisis Center
638 Addison Avenue West
Twin Falls, Idaho 83301

Champaign County Women Against Rape,
  Inc.
112 West Hill Street
Champaign, Ill. 61820

Chicago Women Against Rape
% Loop Center YWCA
37 South Wabash Avenue
Chicago, Ill. 60603

Rape Victim Advocates
P.O. Box 11537
Chicago, Ill. 60611

DuPage Women Against Rape (DWAR)
P.O. Box 242
Clarendon Hills, Ill. 60514

Story County Sexual Assault Care Center
P.O. Box 1150
I.S.U. Station
Amers, Iowa 60010

Polk County Rape/Sexual Assault Care Center
700 East University
Des Moines, Iowa 50316

HERA (Feminist Psychotherapy Collective)
P.O. Box 28
Iowa City, Iowa 52240

Rape Victim Advocacy Program
130 North Madison Street
Iowa City, Iowa 52240

Douglas County Rape Victim Support Service
% Kansas University Information Center
105 Strong Hall
Lawrence, Kans. 66045

Northern Kentucky Rape Crisis Center
11 East 10th Street
Covington, Ky. 41011

R.A.P.E. Relief Center
604 South Third Street
Louisville, Ky. 40202

Stop Rape Crisis Center
414 Louisiana Avenue
Baton Rouge, La. 70801

YWCA Rape Crisis Service
3433 Tulane Avenue
New Orleans, La. 70119

Greater Portland Rape Crisis Center
335 Brighton Avenue
Portland, Me. 04103

Baltimore Rape Crisis Center, Inc.
128 West Franklin Street
Baltimore, Md. 21201

Rape Crisis Intervention Program
Beth Israel Hospital
330 Brookline Avenue
Boston, Mass. 02215

Boston Area Rape Crisis Center
% The Women's Center
46 Pleasant Street
Cambridge, Mass. 02139

Community Anti-Rape Effort
P.O. Box 647
Ann Arbor, Mich. 48107

Detroit Rape Crisis Line
P.O. Box 35271
Seven Oaks Station
Detroit, Mich. 48235

Rape Crisis Team
Box 6161, Station C
Grand Rapids, Mich. 49506

Women's Survival Center
171 West Pike Street
Pontiac, Mich. 48053

Saginaw County Rape Crisis Center
1765 East Genesee Avenue
Saginaw, Mich. 48601

St. Louis County Aid to Victims of Sexual
 Assault
501 Courthouse
Duluth, Minn. 55802

Rape and Sexual Assault Center
2617 Hennepin Avenue South
Minneapolis, Minn. 55408

Sexual Offense Services of Ramsey County
 (SOS)
65 East Kellogg Boulevard
St. Paul, Minn. 55101

Minnesota Program for Victims of Sexual
 Assault
430 Metro Square Building
St. Paul, Minn. 55101

Rape Crisis Center
P.O. Box 4174
Jackson, Miss. 39216

Metropolitan Organization to Counter Sexual
 Assault (MOSCA)
2 West 40th Street
Kansas City, Mo. 64111

Women's Place
1130 West Broadway
Missoula, Mont. 59801

Lincoln Coalition Against Rape
Rape Crisis Center
2545 "R" Street
Lincoln, Neb. 68503

Women Against Rape
38 South Main Street
Concord, N.H. 03301

Rape Survival Center
P.O. Box 1600
Hillside, N.J. 07205

Sex Assault Rape Analysis Unit (SARA)
20 Park Place
Newark, N.J. 07102

Albuquerque Rape Crisis Center
802 Headingly, N.W.
Albuquerque, N.M. 87107

Rape Crisis Center and Women's Center
P.O. Box 354
Binghamton, N.Y. 13902

Victims Information Bureau of Suffolk (VIBS)
501 Route 111
Hauppauge, N.Y. 11787

Eastern Women's Center
14 East 60th Street
New York, N.Y. 10022

Sex Crimes Analysis Unit
1 Police Plaza
New York, N.Y. 10038

Rape Crisis Service
24 Windsore Street
Rochester, N.Y. 14605

Rape Crisis Center of Syracuse
304 Seymour Street
Syracuse, N.Y. 13204

Bureau of Sex Crimes Analysis and
 Investigation
Westchester County Sheriffs Department
110 Grove Street
White Plains, N.Y. 10601

Emergency Room Rape Crisis Program
North Carolina Memorial Hospital
Chapel Hill, N.C. 27514

RAPE: Action, Prevention, and Education
 Center, Inc.
314 North Davie Street
Greensboro, N.C. 27401

Rape Crisis Center
1361 West Market Street
Akron, Ohio 44313

Women Helping Women/Rape Crisis Center
2699 Clifton Avenue
Cincinnati, Ohio 45220

Cleveland Rape Crisis Center
3201 Euclid Avenue
Cleveland, Ohio 44115

Project Woman
22 East Grand
Springfield, Ohio 45506

Toledo United Against Rape
P.O. Box 4372
Toledo, Ohio 43609

Oklahoma County YWCA Rape Crisis Center
YWCA Women's Resource Center
722 Northwest 30th
Oklahoma City, Okla. 73118

Women's Resource Center
908 SW Hurbert
Newport, Ore. 97365

Rape Victim Advocate Project
Multnomah County District Attorney's Office
Multnomah County Court House
Portland, Ore. 97204

Salem Women's Crisis Service
P.O. Box 851
Salem, Ore. 97308

Women Against Rape of Montgomery County
P.O. Box 182
Ambler, Pa. 19002

Harrisburg Area Rape Crisis Center
P.O. Box 38
Harrisburg, Pa. 17108

Lancaster Women's Shelter
110 North Lime Street
Lancaster, Pa. 17602

Women Organized Against Rape in Bucks
 County (W.O.A.R.)
P.O. Box 793
Langhorne, Pa. 19047

Women Against Rape of Delaware County
Box 211
Media, Pa. 19063

Women Organized Against Rape
1220 Sansom Street
Philadelphia, Pa. 19107

Pittsburgh Action Against Rape
P.O. Box 10433
Pittsburgh, Pa. 15234

People Against Rape
P.O. Box 885
Reading, Pa. 19603

Sexual Trauma and Rape Crisis Center
% Voluntary Action Center
200 Adams Avenue
Scranton, Pa. 18503

Rape Crisis Council of Chester County
Box 738
West Chester, Pa. 19380

Women Organized Against Rape of Luzerne
 County
Box 5116 (Station A)
Wilkes Barre, Pa. 18701

Rape Crisis Center of York
P.O. Box 892
York, Pa. 17405

Rhode Island Rape Crisis Center
Y.W.C.A., 324 Broad Street
Central Falls, R.I. 02863

Women's Liberation Union of Rhode Island
Committee on Criminal Sex Offenses
P.O. Box 6353
Providence, R.I. 02940

People Against Rape
109½ Church Street
Charleston, S.C. 29401

The Rape Crisis Council of Greenville, Inc.
703 East Washington Street
Greenville, S.C. 29601

Rape Crisis and Sexual Abuse Service
P.O. Box 10092
Amarillo, Tex. 79106

Austin Rape Crisis Center
600 West 28th
Austin, Tex. 78705

Rape Crisis Center of Southeast Texas
3620 Evalon Avenue
Beaumont, Tex. 77700

Rape Crisis Center
401 North Carancahua
Corpus Christi, Tex. 78401

Dallas Women Against Rape, Inc.
Box 12701
Dallas, Tex. 75225

Rape Crisis Center/Crisis Intervention
730 East Yandell
El Paso, Tex. 79902

Rape Crisis Support of Tarrant County
P.O. Box 1811
Fort Worth, Tex. 76104

Houston Rape Crisis Coalition
P.O. Box 4157
Houston, Tex. 77210

Rape Treatment, Detection, Prevention
  Program
City Health Department
1115 North MacGregor
Houston, Tex. 77030

Rape Crisis Line
c/o Crisis Center of San Antonio Area, Inc.
P.O. Box 28061
San Antonio, Tex. 78228

Salt Lake Rape Crisis Center
776 West 2nd North
Salt Lake City, Utah 84116

Roanoke Rape Crisis and Information Line
Roanoke Valley Trouble Center, Inc.
3515 Williamson Road
Roanoke, Va. 24012

Fairfax County Rape Crisis Program
7010 Calamo Street
Springfield, Va. 22150

Rape Relief
1026 North Forest
Bellingham, Wash. 98225

Thurston County Rape Relief and Reduction
220 East Union
Olympia, Wash. 98501

The Feminist Coordinating Council
5649 11th N.E.
Seattle, Wash. 98105

Rape Reduction Program
313½ First Avenue South
Seattle, Wash. 98104

Seattle Assault Center
Harborview Medical Center
325 9th Avenue
Seattle, Wash. 98104

Seattle Rape Relief
4224 University Way N.E.
Seattle, Wash. 98105

Rape Crisis Network
North 507 Howard
Spokane, Wash. 99201

Rape Information Service, Inc.
221 Willey Street
Morgantown, W.Va. 26505

Sexual Assault Center
Luther Hospital
310 Chestnut Street
Eau Claire, Wis. 54701

Green Bay Rape Crisis Center
P.O. Box 1700
744 South Webster
Green Bay, Wis. 54301

Dane County Project on Rape
120 West Mifflin Street
Madison, Wis. 53703

Rape Crisis Center
P.O. Box 1312
Madison, Wis. 53701

Sexual Treatment Center of Greater Milwaukee
2711 West Wells Street
Milwaukee, Wis. 53208

Witness Support (Anti-Rape) Unit
821 West State Street
Milwaukee, Wis. 53233

Wisconsin Task Force on Rape
P.O. Box 11408
Shorewood, Wis. 53211

CANADA

Toronto Rape Crisis Centre
P.O. Box 6597, Station A
Toronto, Ontario M5W 1X4

Rape Crisis and Information Centre
545 Broadway Avenue
Winnipeg, Manitoba R3C 0W4

ENGLAND

Rape Counselling and Research Project
P.O. Box 42
London N65 BU

ADDITIONAL LITERATURE

Against Our Will: Men, Women and Rape by Susan Brownmiller (1975). Bantam Books, 666 Fifth Avenue, New York, N.Y. 10020 ($2.75). A comprehensive book on rape and rape victims that includes the history of rape, a profile of the rapist, and how women are fighting back. Extensive footnotes and bibliography.

Aegis (six times a year). Feminist Alliance Against Rape and the National Communications Network, Box 21033, Washington, D.C. 20009 ($8.75 for individuals, $10.00 for institutions). A thorough newsletter describing legislation changes regarding rape, activities of local, national, and federal organizations and agencies. Also includes reviews of books and related media material in the area of sexual assault, battered women, and related crimes.

Fighting Back: How to Cope With the Medical, Emotional, and Legal Consequences of Rape by Janet Bode (1978). Macmillan Publishing Company, Inc., 866 Third Avenue, New York, N.Y. 10022 ($8.85). Through interviews with dozens of rape victims, the author explores how the victim and the victim's family and friends can cope with the aftermath of this crime.

Forcible Rape: Medical and Legal Information, Linda Forrest, M.A., principal author, and developed by the National Institute of Law Enforcement and Criminal Justice and the Law Enforcement Assistance Administration, U.S. Department of Justice (October 1977). Available from the Superintendent of Documents, U.S. Government Printing Office, Washington, D.C. 20402 ($1.20). This booklet, written in clear language, describes the initial police report, medical procedures, follow-up police investigation, court procedures, and victim services.

"How to Interview a Rape Victim and Survive" by Marlane Guelden, Marin Rape Crisis Center, and John Kim of Tiburon Police Department. Marin Rape Crisis Center, P.O. Box 823, Kentfield, Calif. 94909 ($.20). A well-written paper geared to police officers but also helpful to anyone counseling rape victims. This rape crisis center also sells numerous other informative materials, such as tapes of interviews with experts.

How to Say No to a Rapist and Survive by Frederic Storaska (1975). Random House, Inc., 201 East 50th Street, New York, N.Y. 10022. This book presents techniques that would-be victims can use to help them escape from a potential rapist. Based on Storaska's presentations to college audiences, some of the tactics have been the source of controversy since many women feel they would be unable to resort to such dramatic techniques, such as "pushing your thumbs into his [the rapist's] eyesockets." Contact the Learning Corporation of America, 1350 Avenue of the Americas, New York, N.Y. 10019, about the 52-minute film they rent ($250.00) or sell ($750.00) based on Storaska's methods.

How to Start a Rape Crisis Center, third edition. Rape Crisis Center, P.O. Box 21005, Washington, D.C. 20009 ($4.75). Fifty-four-page booklet with articles on fundraising, self-defense, and counseling.

Men Against Rape: What You Should Know by Carolyn K. Wickenkamp and Diane K. Rausch (1977). Direct Mail Advertising and Printing, 2461 Gardena Avenue, Long Beach, Calif. 90806 ($.50). An excellent booklet to help men understand how women feel after being raped and what a man should do if rape happens to someone he cares about. It also offers suggestions for how men can contribute to the prevention of rape by working for reform and refuting the previous "hero" myths about rapists.

The Politics of Rape: The Victim's Perspective by Diana E. H. Russell (1975). Stein and Day, Scarborough House, Briarcliff Manor, N.Y. 10510 ($3.95). Based on over eighty interviews with rape victims, sociology professor Russell explores the victim's trauma, the blaming of the victim by society, and the wide range of dynamics involved in who the rapist is ("Some Rapists Think They're Lovers" and "Some of Our Best Friends Are Rapists").

Precautions and Tactics to Avoid Rape, compiled by Muriel Solomon. Metropolitan Dade County R.A.P.E. Program, 140 West Flagler Street, Room 1503, Miami, Fla. 33130. An excellent pamphlet with common sense precautions and more specific suggestions, divided into tactics, for what to do if attacked in a populated or desolate area.

Rape: The First Sourcebook for Women by New York Radical Feminists, edited by Noreen Connell and Cassandra Wilson (1974). New American Library, Inc., 1301 Avenue of the Americas, New York, N.Y. 10019 ($3.95). Chapters on consciousness-raising on rape, legal aspects, self-defense, and sexual abuse of children.

Rape and Its Victims: A Report for Citizens, Health Facilities, and Criminal Justice Agencies. A Perspective Package by Lisa Brodyaga, Margaret Gates, Susan Singer, Marna Tucker, and Richardson White (November 1975). U.S. Department of Justice, Law Enforcement Assistance Administration, Washington, D.C. 20531 ($1.30). An extensive report on the various public and private responses to the needs of the rape victim—police programs, medical facilities, prosecutors' offices, citizen action groups—and guidelines for rendering them more responsive and helpful. Based on voluminous research, the findings in this report were submitted to recognized authorities in the field for review and comment. An annotated bibliography is also included.

The Rape Victim by Elaine Hilberman, M.D. (1976). American Psychiatric Association, 1700 Eighteenth Street, N.W., Washington, D.C. 20009 ($5.00). Hilberman, a psychiatrist who has worked extensively with rape victims, provides an excellent composite of the legal, medical, psychological, and community reactions to rape, including child rape. Also contains an excellent bibliography.

Rape: Victims of Crisis by Ann Wolbert Burgess and Lynda Lytle Holmstrom (1974). Robert J. Brady Company, Bowie, Md. ($6.95). Burgess and Holmstrom, who counsel victims at Boston City Hospital, present an excellent report on how to handle victims in the immediate crisis situation.

Self Defense and Assault Prevention for Girls and Women by Bruce Tegner and Alice McGrath (1977). Thor Publishing Company, P.O. Box 1782, Ventura, Calif. 93001 ($2.95). A complete course on basic self-defense, with an emphasis on assault prevention, written with step-by-step descriptions, enhanced by photographs.

Sexual Assault: The Target Is You!, prepared by Gary W. Flakne (1976). Available from Hennepin County Sexual Assault Services, 430 Metro Square Building, St. Paul, Minn. 55101. An excellent booklet that should serve as a model for what each state should offer. It includes a discussion of the Minnesota Criminal Sexual Conduct Law plus how to report a sexual assault and what to expect from the procedures that follow—the medical and police examinations and the prosecution. It concludes with a directory of community services, police, and helping agencies.

Victims of Violent Crimes: Sexual Assault (1977). Victims Information Bureau of Suffolk, 501 Route 111, Hauppauge, N.Y. 11787 ($.35). A pamphlet describing myths about rape, prevention tips, the rape victim's rights, what to do and where to get help if you are a victim.

Volunteer Advocate Manual. R.A.P.E. Relief Center, 604 South Third Street, Louisville, Ky. 40202. A comprehensive volunteer training manual developed by a rape crisis group. In typescript form it covers everything a crisis group needs to know about handling victims: medical information, police and court procedures, rape prevention tactics. These R.A.P.E. Relief Center forms are included: telephone log sheet, personal contact report, follow-up sheet, third-party report, court and speaker's bureau forms.

WARSTLE (monthly). Champaign County Women Against Rape, Inc. (CCWAR), 112 West Hill, Champaign, Ill. 61820 ($3.00). A good newsletter with articles, calendar of events, research reports, and other information of national concern.

FILMS

Rape: Victim or Victor, produced by the Los Angeles County Sheriff's Department and narrated by Lee Merriwether. MTI Teleprograms Inc., 4825 North Scott Street, Suite 23, Schiller Park, Ill. 60176 (one-week rental, $40.00; purchase, $275.00). This 17-minute color film on rape prevention is available in 16mm or ¾" U-matic video cassette. Through a series of vignettes, two ways of handling a threatening situation are demonstrated—how to effectively and cautiously avoid encounters and how to unwittingly make yourself vulnerable. Some of the situations include walking home alone late at night, driving alone, what to do if someone comes to the door, how to protect your home against intruders, and how to run for help. Although not all situations are as easily manipulated as the film suggests, it does show that a state of awareness about the threat of rape can often be the best defensive tactic.

"Selected Films on Rape," compiled by the Women's Crisis Center, Box 413, Ann Arbor, Mich. 48106. Write to the addresses given for rental and purchase information and more detailed descriptions for the following films:

Beware of Strangers (20 minutes). Aptos Film Production, Inc., 729 Seward, Los Angeles, Calif. 90038 (high school level).

Childhood Sexual Assault (48 minutes). Motorola Teleprograms, Inc., 4825 N. Scott Street, Schiller Park, Ill. 60176 (for counselors).

Incest: The Victim Nobody Believes (21 minutes). J. Gary Mitchell Film Company, 2000 Bridgeway, Sausalito, Calif. 94965 (high school level and up).

Meeting Strangers: Red Light, Green Light (21 minutes). BFA Educational Media, P.O. Box 1795, Santa Monica, Calif. 90406 (elementary school level).

No Tears for Rachel (27 minutes). Indiana University, Audio-Visual Center, Bloomington, Ind. 47401 (high school level and up).

Not a Pretty Picture (83 minutes). Films, Inc., 1144 Wilmette Avenue, Wilmette, Ill. 60091 (high school level and up).

Rape: A Preventive Inquiry (18 minutes). MTI Motorola Teleprograms, 4825 North Scott Street, Schiller Park, Ill. 60176 (college level and up).

Street Crime—What to Do (20 minutes). Motorola Teleprograms, 4825 North Scott Street, Schiller Park, Ill. 60176 (high school level and up).

See also the following related chapters in *The Help Book:*

- AGING
- ALCOHOLISM
- BATTERED ADULTS
- CHILD ABUSE
- COUNSELING
- COURTS
- CRIME PREVENTION
- CRIME VICTIMS AND WITNESSES
- FAMILY PLANNING
- HEALTH
- KIDNAPPING, MISSING PERSONS, AND RUNAWAYS
- LAW ENFORCEMENT
- LEGAL SERVICES
- MENTAL HEALTH

45

SAFETY

Home accidents took the lives of 24,000 Americans in 1976. Additionally, some 3,700,000 persons received crippling injuries as the result of accidents occurring in the home—a figure twice as high as that reflecting injuries on our nation's highways.

Home can be one of the most dangerous places for you and your family today unless you take the time to read and follow the simple safety hints that can make yours an accident-free home.

The National Easter Seal Society for Crippled Children and Adults, in an effort to help cut down on the number of crippling injuries occurring in home accidents, has prepared a check list (pages 586–587) to help you spot potential hazards that may exist in your home.

Educational classes on safety should be available through your local American National Red Cross, safety council, or public school. Contact the following national organizations for additional information on all safety concerns:

Industrial Safety Equipment Association (ISEA)
1901 North Moore Street
Arlington, Va. 22209

A nonprofit trade association started in 1934 whose eighty members are major manufacturers of personal protective devices. ISEA serves as an information clearinghouse on safety equipment with twelve product groups: emergency eyewash; eye and face protection; fall protection; first aid; head protection; hearing protection; machinery guards; respiratory protection; safety and health instruments; safety cans; safety wearing apparel; and warning devices.

LITERATURE: Descriptive brochure.

National Safety Council
444 North Michigan Avenue
Chicago, Ill. 60611

Founded in 1913, this private, nonprofit, nongovernmental, national organization is

Home Safety Round-Up

A Family Checklist...

Home accidents took the lives of 26,500 Americans last year. Additionally, some 4,000,000 persons received crippling injuries as the result of accidents occurring in the home — a figure twice as high as that reflecting injuries on our nation's highways.

Home can be one of the most dangerous places for you and your family today unless you take the time to read and follow the simple safety hints that can make yours an accident-free home.

The National Easter Seal Society, in an effort to help cut down on the number of crippling injuries occurring in home accidents, has prepared this check list to help you spot potential hazards that may exist in your home.

Check the following throughout your home...

yes no

1. Are electrical extension cords in good condition?
2. Are electrical extension cords kept from being stretched across heavily travelled areas of your home?
3. Are unused electrical outlets covered or locked?
4. Are electrical outlets checked regularly for overloading?
5. Do you know how to turn off gas and electricity in case of an emergency?
6. Are proper size fuses used for replacement rather than pennies or substitutes?
7. Are floor surfaces non-skid?
8. Are all floor coverings fastened down?
9. Are fireplaces screened and protected?
10. Is an approved fire extinguisher kept on each floor?
11. Are open flames such as candles kept away from walls and curtains?
12. Do you have emergency phone numbers—police, fire, doctor, utilities—handy to the phone?
13. Are frequently used items stored within safe, easy reach of adults?
14. Is a sturdy stepladder available for climbing?
15. Do interior doors such as those on closets or bathrooms have safety release locks that allow them to be opened from either side?
16. If there are small children in your home, are open windows securely screened?
17. Is lead-free paint used on all objects accessible to children?

Stairs and hallways may offer serious dangers to your family. Falls accounted for nearly half of all home injuries during the past year. Protect your family and friends by eliminating all hazards...

yes no

1. Are stairway approaches kept uncluttered and free of throw rugs?
2. Do stairways have strong bannisters or railings?
3. Are all steps in a flight the same height and width?
4. Are steps kept free of toys, tools and other objects?
5. Are stair treads or carpeting kept in good repair?
6. Is the stairway well-lighted with electrical switches located at top and bottom?
7. Are young children protected by gates placed at the top and bottom of stairways?
8. Are nightlights provided in hallways and bedroom-bathroom areas?

Keep your kitchen safe for you and your family by checking for the following...

yes no

1. Are window curtains out of the reach of the stove?
2. Are electrical appliances disconnected when not in use?
3. Is there a light over stove and sink?

---

solely dedicated to the prevention of accidents in every area from homes to farms to industries. It provides public education and has a research library, a range of membership fees starting at $15.00 a year, and the Child Safety Program. The council administered the National Disaster Survival Test that was broadcast on NBC-TV in 1977. Organizations should write for information on their letterhead.

The Youth Department sponsors various youth-oriented safety projects, such as Bicycle Safety Week, and offers this literature: *All About Bikes* packet with brochures (free); films for free loan; bicycle safety information sheet.

LITERATURE: Free publications list; descriptive brochure about the council; *National Safety News* monthly magazine ($12.00 a year); *Family Safety*, quarterly ($3.75 a year); *Traffic Safety*, monthly ($8.90 a year); newsletters;

*Home Safety Round-Up prepared by the National Easter Seal Society for Crippled Children and Adults in cooperation with the National Safety Council. Reprinted with permission.

4. Do gas appliances have flue ventilation?
5. Are freezer units and trash compactors locked to protect children?
6. Are furnaces and flues inspected regularly?
7. Are drawers and cupboards kept closed?
8. Do you keep knives in rack or compartmented tray?
9. Are pan handles pointed away from the edge of the stove and other burners?
10. Are all cleaning agents kept on shelves above children's reach?
11. Are grease, water, and other spilled liquids or foods wiped up immediately?
12. Do you have hot dish holders near stove?

The bedroom is the site of nearly 50% of all deaths due to home accidents. To keep your family safe be sure no safety hazards are allowed in your bedroom...

yes no

1. Is a light within easy reach of the bed?
2. Are room heaters turned off at bedtime?
3. Do you keep your room properly ventilated when using a room heater?
4. Is your infant's mattress firm and bed free of pillows and loose blankets?
5. Are small children's clothes checked for pins and detachable decorations which could be swallowed?

6. Are infants and toddlers' toys soft and the individual parts too large to be swallowed?
7. Are used plastic bags destroyed or kept out of children's reach?
8. Do all family members refrain from smoking in bed?

Check your bathroom to eliminate all opportunity for accidental falls, poisoning and scalding? yes no

yes no

1. Are non-skid mats used in bath tubs and shower?
2. Are all medicines kept in locked cabinets out of the reach of children?
3. Are medicines for "external use only" labeled as such and kept separate from others?
4. Do you discard prescription drugs after their use has ended?
5. Have handgrips been installed alongside the shower, tub and toilet, especially if bathroom is used by elderly or handicapped persons?
6. Are infants and toddlers watched at all times when in tub?
7. Are all electrical appliances kept away from water and unplugged after use?

To see if your yard is as safe as your home, answer the following questions...

yes no

1. Are steps and sidewalks kept free from ice, snow, toys, tools and debris?
2. Is yard free from glass, nails, yard tools and all items with jagged edges?
3. Are garden sprays non-poisonous?
4. Is play apparatus checked regularly?

5. Are clotheslines strung high enough to clear pedestrian traffic?
6. Are children kept from playing in streets and driveways?
7. Do you use charcoal lighter fluid—never gasoline—to light your outdoor grill?
8. Are children kept away from power mowers, hedge trimmers and snow blowers when such appliances are being operated?
9. Does person operating power mower wear sturdy shoes?
10. Do you limit the time you work in the hot sun?

Check your safety score...

A "yes" answer indicated a high level of safety consciousness in each question area. Each "no" answer indicated a potential hazard to your family's safety.

Create a safety climate in your home by rechecking each "no" answer and removing all hazards.

Easter Seals
SERVING THE HANDICAPPED

prepared as a public service by
THE NATIONAL EASTER SEAL SOCIETY
FOR CRIPPLED CHILDREN AND ADULTS
in cooperation with
The National Safety Council

"Where to Get Help" one-page flyer with descriptive resources and addresses.

Society for Occupational and Environmental Health
1341 G Street, N.W., Suite 308
Washington, D.C. 20005

A national membership organization of those connected with occupation and environmental health that provides a forum for discussion through conferences and workshops and publishes conference proceedings.

LITERATURE: *Women and the Workplace* ($16.00); *Dust and Disease* ($25.00).

Toy Manufacturers of America, Inc.
200 Fifth Avenue
New York, N.Y. 10010

Provides free literature on toy and game safety; prefers written requests.

LITERATURE: *The Toy Industry Fact Book* ($3.00).

Federal information sources on safety are:

Occupational Safety and Health Administration (OSHA)
U.S. Department of Labor
Washington, D.C. 20210

Established in 1971, OSHA seeks to enforce job safety and health standards for workers. There are ten regional offices throughout the country to which complaints and inquiries should be addressed. Ongoing training programs for employees and employers in correct occupational safety and health practices are available.

Occupational Safety and Health Review Commission (OSHRC)
1825 K Street, N.W.
Washington, D.C. 20006

OSHRC adjudicates cases that the Department of Labor forwards to it when there are disagreements over the results of safety and health inspections by the department in violation of the OSHA laws of 1970. OSHRC is a court, rather than an information service.

U.S. Consumer Product Safety Commission
1111 Eighteenth Street, N.W.
Washington, D.C. 20207
Toll-free hotlines.

An extensive listing of the publications and hazard-reporting procedures of the U.S. Consumer Product Safety Commission is described in Chapter 20, *Emergencies and Disasters.* In addition to hundreds of free pamphlets, fact sheets, and booklets on safety precautions and potential home and play hazards, the Consumer Product Safety Commission is the place to report complaints about unsafe products. There are field offices in thirteen cities around the country.

LITERATURE: (All free) *For Kids' Sake; Take a Close Look; Gasoline Is Made to Explode; Hazards of Flammable Liquids; Bicycling: Fun With Safety; CPSC Memo;* extensive publications list.

U.S. Food and Drug Administration (FDA)
Office of Consumer Inquiries
5600 Fishers Lane
Rockville, Md. 20857

The FDA publishes numerous pamphlets, leaflets, and memos on safety, general health, and poison prevention. See extensive listing, including how to report safety hazards and violations to the FDA, reprinted in Chapter 13, *Consumer Affairs,* and in Chapter 25, *Food and Nutrition.*

For information on health hazards of vital concern to most artists and craftspersons, contact this national organization:

Art Hazards Information Center
Center for Occupational Hazards, Inc.
5 Beekman Street
New York, N.Y. 10038

A national organization, funded by the National Endowment for the Arts and the New York State Council on the Arts, for artists, craftspeople, and hobbyists. Through the Art Hazards Newsletter ($10.00 a year) and other publications, artists are informed of potential health hazards of the materials that they are using as well as how to work with them safely. Art Hazards Information Center will answer telephone inquiries and written requests or provide speakers for lectures and workshops. Referrals will be made to occupational health physicians.

LITERATURE: Fact sheets ($.25); *Health Hazards Manual for Artists* by Michael McCann, Ph.D. ($3.50).

You may be able to get a free copy of your state Occupational Safety and Health Act from your state Department of Industrial Relations or contact the following state agencies for occupational safety and health:

Division of Safety and Inspection
Department of Industrial Relations
1816 8th Avenue, North
Birmingham, Ala. 35203

Occupational Safety and Health Division
Department of Labor
Sealaska Plaza
P.O. Box 1149
Juneau, Alaska 99811

Occupational Safety and Health
State Office Building
1624 West Adams Street
Phoenix, Ariz. 85007

OSHA Consultation Services Division
Department of Labor
Capitol Hill Building
Little Rock, Ark. 72201

Division of Industrial Safety
P.O. Box 603
Sacramento, Calif. 94101

Colorado Occupational Safety and Health (COSH)
Department of Labor and Employment
1210 Sherman Street
Denver, Colo. 80203

Division of Occupational Safety and Health
Department of Labor
200 Folly Brook Boulevard
Wethersfield, Conn. 06109

Occupational Safety and Health
Industrial Affairs Division
Department of Labor
618 North Union Street
Wilmington, Del. 19805

Industrial Safety Division
Minimum Wage and Industrial Safety Board
2900 Newton Street, N.E.
Washington, D.C. 20018

Division of Physical Health
Department of Human Resources
47 Trinity Avenue, S.W.
Atlanta, Ga. 30334

Occupational Safety and Health Division
Department of Labor and Industrial Relations
825 Milani Street
Honolulu, Hawaii 96813

Division of Industrial Hygiene and Radiological Health
Board of Health
1330 West Michigan Street
Indianapolis, Ind. 46202

Occupational Safety and Health Review Commission
Liberty Building
Des Moines, Iowa 50319

Air Quality and Occupational Health
Division of Environment
Department of Health and Environment
Forbes Field
Topeka, Kans. 66620

Occupational Safety and Health Review Commission
104 Bridge Street
Frankfort, Ky. 40601

Division of Health and Environmental Quality
P.O. Box 60630
Baton Rouge, La. 70160

Occupational Safety and Health Advisory Board
Division of Labor and Industry
Department of Licensing and Regulation
203 East Baltimore Street
Baltimore, Md. 21202

Division of Industrial Safety
Department of Labor and Industries
100 Cambridge Street
Boston, Mass. 02202

Division of Occupational Hygiene
Department of Labor and Industries
39 Boylston Street
Boston, Mass. 02116

Bureau of Environmental and Occupational
  Health
Department of Public Health
3500 North Logan Street
Lansing, Mich. 48914

Occupational Safety and Health Division
Department of Labor and Industry
Space Center Building
444 Lafayette Road
St. Paul, Minn. 55101

Occupational Safety and Health Division
Mississippi State Board of Health
2628 Southerland Street
Jackson, Miss. 39216

Bureau of Safety and Health
Division of Workers' Compensation
Department of Labor and Industry
815 Front Street
Helena, Mont. 59601

Occupational Health Bureau
Environmental Sciences Division
Department of Health and Environmental
  Sciences
224 W. F. Cogswell Building
Helena, Mont. 59601

Division of Safety
Department of Labor
550 South 16th Street
Lincoln, Neb. 68509

Occupational Health
Division of Public Health Services
Department of Health and Welfare
Hazen Drive
Concord, N.H. 03301

Occupational/Relation Protection Division
Health and Environment Department
Crown State Office Building
725 St. Michaels Drive
Santa Fe, N.M. 87503

Division of Occupational Safety and Health
Department of Labor
Building 12 State Campus
Albany, N.Y. 12240

Occupational Safety and Health Review Board
227 East Edenton Street
Raleigh, N.C. 27601

Division of Environmental Health and
  Engineering Services
Department of Health
Capitol
Bismarck, N.D. 58505

Division of Safety and Hygiene
Industrial Commission of Ohio
65 South Front Street
Columbus, Ohio 43215

Occupational and Radiological Health Service
Department of Health
N.E. 10th and Stonewall Streets
P.O. Box 53551
Oklahoma City, Okla. 73105

Occupational Health Section
Accident Prevention Division
Workmen's Compensation Board
Labor and Industries Building
Capitol Mall
Salem, Ore. 97310

Bureau of Occupational Health
Department of Environmental Resources
Fulton Building, 6th Floor
200 North 3rd Street
P.O. Box 2063
Harrisburg, Pa. 17120

Division of Occupational Safety
Department of Labor
CIC Complex
235 Promenade Street
Providence, R.I. 02908

Division of Occupational Health
Department of Health
207 State Health Department Building
75 Davis Street
Providence, R.I. 02908

[Cartoon panels:
- "KEEP DIVING PLATFORMS OUT OF CRIBS."
- "'FLYING WITH ANGEL WINGS,' ARE BABY'S THOUGHTS."
- "ALWAYS TAKE BABY OUT FIRST!"
- "NEVER, NEVER PLACE POISON IN A COMMON CONTAINER"]

Reprinted with permission from *A New Vaccine For Child Safety* by Murl Harmon, Safety Now Co., P.O. Box 567, Jenkintown, Pa. 19046.

Bureau of Occupational Health
Environmental Health and Safety
Department of Health and Environmental Control
R. J. Aycock Building
2600 Bull Street
Columbia, S.C. 29201

Division of Occupational and Radiological Health
Bureau of Environmental Health Services
Department of Public Health
C2-212 Cordell Hull Building
436 6th Avenue, North
Nashville, Tenn. 37219

Occupational Safety Division
Department of Health Resources
1100 West 49th Street
Austin, Tex. 78756

Division of Occupational Safety and Health
Industrial Commission
448 South Fourth East Street
Salt Lake City, Utah 84111

Occupational Safety Division
Department of Labor and Industry
120 State Street
Montpelier, Vt. 05602

Bureau of Industrial Hygiene
Department of Health
James Madison Building
109 Governor Street
Richmond, Va. 23219

Industrial Safety and Health Division
Department of Labor and Industries
308 East Fourth Avenue
Mail Stop 6E-11
Olympia, Wash. 98504

Industrial Hygiene Bureau
Department of Health
151 Eleventh Avenue
South Charleston, W.Va. 25303

Safety and Buildings Division
Department of Industry, Labor, and Human Relations
201 East Washington Avenue
Madison, Wis. 53702

Occupational Health and Safety Commission
200 East Eighth Avenue
Cheyenne, Wyo. 82002

The following federal agencies and national organizations are concerned with automobile and boating safety:

Action for Child Transportation Safety
400 Central Park West, #15P
New York, N.Y. 10025

Founded in 1972, there are four local chapters to this national information clearinghouse on child auto and school bus passenger safety. It also sponsors public education and citizen action and puts pressure on state and federal agencies responsible for the welfare and safety of children. It is a nonprofit organization supported by membership dues ($5.00 a year).

LITERATURE: ACTION newsletter (free to members); price list of publications; "This is the Way the Baby Rides" ($.25); "Protection for the School Bus Rider" ($.25); "Protecting Child Passengers" ($.25); free literature with a self-addressed, stamped envelope.

Center for Auto Safety
1223 Dupont Circle Building
Washington, D.C. 20036

A nonprofit public interest research organization established by Ralph Nader and Consumers Union in 1970 that became independent of its founders in 1973. It monitors extensively the U.S. Department of Transportation to ensure its adoption of strong federal safety standards for motor vehicles under the 1966 National Traffic and Motor Vehicle Safety Act.

LITERATURE: Fact sheet; *IMPACT: A Journal of Safety Litigation News; What to Do With Your Bad Car* ($2.95); price list of other publications and article reprints.

National Council on Alcoholism, Inc.
733 Third Avenue
New York, N.Y. 10017

An information clearinghouse that publishes and distributes literature on drinking and driving, including the booklets *Drinking, Drugs, and Driving*, and *Vehicle Violence: An American Tragedy*. Send for their publications price list.

National Highway Traffic Safety Administration (NHTSA)
Office of Consumer Services
U.S. Department of Transportation
400 Seventh Street, S.W.
Washington, D.C. 20590

Toll-free auto safety hotline (recording machine will take messages after business hours and callers will be contacted during the next duty day).

NHTSA's main function is to write and enforce motor vehicle safety standards and follow-up reports on vehicle defects, if sufficiently safety related to make certain manufacturers meet their responsibilities to the public. The hotline takes complaints from consumers relative to alleged safety defects in vehicles and vehicular equipment, provides information on safety-related recalls, and responds to general queries on NHTSA functions.

LITERATURE: Free descriptive leaflet on NHTSA plus a large number of free booklets and fact sheets, including "Safe Driving in Winter," "Common Sense in Buying a Safe Used Car," "How to Deal with Motor Vehicle Emergencies," "Motorcycle Safety," "What to Buy in Child Restraint Systems," "Passenger Car Brakes," "Exhaust Systems," and many others.

National Safety Council
Driver Improvement Program
425 North Michigan Avenue
Chicago, Ill. 60611

An information clearinghouse on driver safety. Contact your nearest state or local safety council (there are about 150 throughout the country that teach this course). The standardized course is taught by trained instructors. Students receive a workbook and a copy of their state rule book. The course is also used by industrial firms; federal, state, and local government agencies; and the military services.

LITERATURE: *Safe Driver* booklet; *Traffic Safety* magazine ($8.90 a year; $1.30 per single copy).

Physicians for Automotive Safety (PAS)
50 Union Avenue
Irvington, N.J. 07111

Information available upon written request on protection of children in moving vehicles, such as special child restraints and school bus safety. It was founded in 1965 to enlist the help of the medical profession in reducing highway fatalities.

LITERATURE: *Don't Risk Your Child's Life!* ($.25); brochure and fact sheet on the organization; newsletter geared to physicians ($5.00 a year).

United States Coast Guard
Office of Boating Safety
Commandant (G-B)
Washington, D.C. 20590

Inquiries answered regarding federal safety requirements, accident analyses, boat recall campaigns, and available free safe boating courses.

LITERATURE: *Free Boating Courses, Free Courtesy Examinations; Federal Requirements for Recreational Boats; (Almost) Everything You Ever Wanted to Know About Boating . . . But Were Ashamed to Ask; A Pocket Guide for Visual Distress Signals*, and many others (all free).

In 1976, there were 46,700 deaths from motor-vehicle accidents; disabling injuries numbered 1,800,000 persons. The largest concentration of victims was in the 15 to 24 age category (16,500 deaths), followed by the 25 to 44 age category (12,100 deaths.) It is estimated that motor vehicle deaths and injuries cost $24.7 billion in medical expenses, wage losses, property damage, and insurance. But what of the cost in human suffering and grief?

Nearly 1,000 children under the age of four die each year in automobile accidents that are avoidable because children are not buckled up in the car. Crash-tested car restraints can seriously reduce the number of these auto-related deaths

594 / THE HELP BOOK

and injuries. Seat belts are for grownups; infants weighing less than 40 pounds need special restraints, like the ones shown in the diagrams below.*

The following are the state agencies for highway safety:

Office of Highway and Traffic Safety
2600 East South Boulevard
Montgomery, Ala. 36116

Department of Public Safety
450 Whittier Street
Pouch N
Juneau, Alaska 99811

Office of Highway Safety
Department of Transportation
206 South Seventeenth Avenue
Phoenix, Ariz. 85007

Department of Public Safety
116 National Old Line Building
Capitol and Woodlane
Little Rock, Ark. 72201

Department of California Highway Patrol
2555 1st Avenue
Sacramento, Calif. 95818

Highway Safety Division
Department of Highways
4201 East Arkansas Avenue
Denver, Colo. 80222

Department of Transportation
24 Wolcott Hill Road
Wethersfield, Conn. 06109

Office of Highway Safety
Department of Transportation
1329 E St., N.W.
Washington, D.C. 20004

Department of Highway Safety and Motor
　Vehicles
Neil Kirkman Building
Tallahassee, Fla. 32304

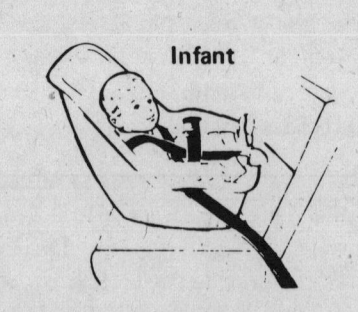

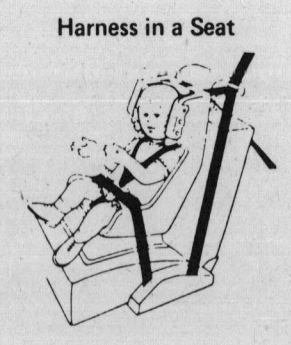

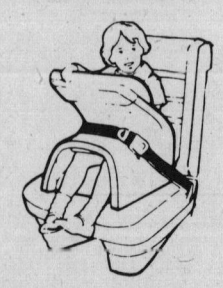

*Reprinted from *Auto Safety and Your Child*, U.S. Department of Health, Education, and Welfare, Office of Human Development Services, Administration for Children, Youth, and Families, Children's Bureau, Washington, D.C. 20201.

Office of Highway Safety
7 Martin Luther King, Jr., Dr., S.W.
Atlanta, Ga. 30334

Office of the State Highway Safety
  Coordinator
Department of Transportation
869 Punchbowl Street
Honolulu, Hawaii 96813

Traffic Safety Commission
Department of Transportation
3311 West State Street
Boise, Idaho 83707

Division of Traffic Safety
Department of Transportation
DOT Administration Building
Springfield, Ill. 62764

Department of Traffic Safety and Vehicle
  Inspection
Graphic Arts Building
215 North Senate Avenue
Indianapolis, Ind. 46202

State Patrol
Department of Public Safety
Robert Lucas State Office Building
East 12th and Walnut Streets
Des Moines, Iowa 50319

Highway Safety Coordinating Office
Department of Transportation
535 Kansas Avenue
Topeka, Kans. 66603

Department of Transportation
State Office Building
Frankfort, Ky. 40601

Highway Safety Commission
P.O. Box 44061
Baton Rouge, La. 70804

Bureau of Safety
Department of Transportation
State Office Building
Augusta, Me. 04333

Transportation Safety Division
Department of Transportation
Baltimore-Washington International Airport
P.O. Box 8755
Baltimore, Md. 21240

Governor's Highway Safety Bureau
146 Bowdoin Street
Boston, Mass. 02108

Office of Highway Safety Planning
Department of State Police
General Office Building
714 S. Harrison Road
East Lansing, Mich. 48823

Traffic Safety Section
Department of Public Safety
207 State Highway Building
St. Paul, Minn. 55155

Governor's Highway Safety Program
Watkins Building
Jackson, Miss. 39201

Division of Highway Safety
Department of Public Safety
2634 Industrial Drive
Jefferson City, Mo. 65101

Safety Unit
Department of Highways
Highway Building
6th Avenue and Roberts Street
Helena, Mont. 59601

Highway Safety Program
Department of Motor Vehicles
301 Centennial Mall South
Lincoln, Neb. 68509

Office of Traffic Safety
Department of Motor Vehicles
1923 North Carson Street, Suite 209
Capitol Complex
Carson City, Nev. 89710

Highway Safety Agency
Pine Inn Plaza, Building #2
177 Manchester Street
Concord, N.H. 03301

Office of Highway Safety
Division of Motor Vehicles
Department of Law and Public Safety
25 South Montgomery Street
Trenton, N.J. 08625

Traffic Safety Division
Department of Motor Vehicles
Manuel Lujan, Sr. Building
Santa Fe, N.M. 87503

Traffic Safety Program Coordination
Department of Motor Vehicles
Empire State Plaza
Albany, N.Y. 12228

Governor's Highway Safety Program
North Carolina Department of Transportation
P.O. Box 25201
Raleigh, N.C. 27611

Traffic Safety Programs Division
Highway Department
Highway Building
Capitol Grounds
Bismarck, N.D. 58505

Department of Highway Safety
240 Parsons Avenue
Columbus, Ohio 43215

Oklahoma Highway Safety Office
G-80 Jim Thorpe Office Building
2101 North Lincoln Boulevard
Oklahoma City, Okla. 73105

Traffic Safety Commission
895 Summer Street, N.E.
Salem, Ore. 97310

Department of Transportation
Transportation and Safety Building
Harrisburg, Pa. 17120

Council on Highway Safety
345 Harris Avenue
Providence, R.I. 02908

Highway Safety Office
P.O. Box 191
Columbia, S.C. 29201

Department of Transportation
Transportation Building
Pierre, S.D. 57501

Highway Safety Planning Division
Office of Urban and Federal Affairs
950 Capitol Hill Building
301 7th Avenue, N.
Nashville, Tenn. 37219

Office of Traffic Safety
Department of Highways and Public Transportation
804 Executive Office Building
411 West 13th Street
Austin, Tex. 78701

Highway Safety Act
Department of Public Safety
455 East 4th Street
Salt Lake City, Utah 84114

Highway Safety Program
133 State Street
Montpelier, Vt. 05602

Highway Safety Division
300 Turner Road
Richmond, Va. 23225

Traffic Safety Commission
Highways-Licenses Building
P.O. Box 1399
Olympia, Wash. 98504

Governor's Highway Safety Administration
Office of Federal-State Relations
Office of the Governor
408 Embleton Building
922 Quarrier Street
Charleston, W.Va. 25301

Division of Highway Safety Coordination
Executive Office
803 James Wilson Plaza
131 West Wilson Street
Madison, Wis. 53702

Governor's Office of Highway Safety
720 West 18th Street
Cheyenne, Wyo. 82002

ADDITIONAL LITERATURE

Auto Safety and Your Child (1978). U.S. Department of Health, Education, and Welfare, Office of Human Development Services, Administration for Children, Youth and Families, Children's Bureau, Washington, D.C. 20201 (free). This booklet first reveals the grim statistics—that "more children up to the age of four are killed each year as passengers in automobiles than any other cause of death"—and then suggests some solutions for safer driving with children. Various types of child restraints are described and illustrated. There is also a resource section.

Best's Safety Directory (updated annually). A.M. Best Company, Ambest Road, Oldwick, N.J. 08858 ($20.00). Comprehensive sourcebook of products and services that comply to OSHA regulations.

Children's Safety Lessons (1976). Kemper Insurance Companies, Long Grove, Ill. 60059 (free). Ten safety lessons in coloring book format that covers crossing the street, bicycle riding, safe places to play, flying kites, roller skating, and riding in a car.

Children's Safety Puzzles (1975). National Safety Council, 425 North Michigan Avenue, Chicago, Ill. 60611 (free). Aimed at children ages seven to ten, this is a fun way for parents to teach their children about safety. Includes twelve puzzles, one a maze entitled "Where's the Life Jacket?" with a life jacket in one corner and someone outside of a boat in the other corner.

Family Safety (quarterly). National Safety Council, 444 North Michigan Avenue, Chicago, Ill. 60611 ($3.75). This publication "for the prevention of home, traffic, and recreational accidents" is aimed at the general public. In addition to "Safety's Lighter Side" and "Letters" departments, there are articles on such topics as "Why Do Small Planes Crash?" and "Good Drivers Use Their Mirrors."

The Health of Women at Work: A Bibliography by Vilma R. Hunt (February 1977). The Program on Women, Northwestern University, 619 Emerson Street, Evanston, Ill. 60201 ($6.00). A seventeen-category bibliography with a brief introduction to each topic, such as "Accidents," "Infectious Diseases," and "Stress, Disability, Efficiency and Absenteeism."

Reprinted from "How to Take the Fun Out of Driving" by Dick Harris.

"How to Take the Fun Out of Driving." Harris and Associates, Publishing Division, 247 South 800 East Street, Logan, Utah 84321. A satirical approach to problem drivers based on six years of research—captioned cartoon vignettes are published in newspapers throughout the United States and may be ordered directly. Special rates are available for nonprofit organizations, agency newsletters, and for high school publications; write or call for samples and prices for camera-ready art.

Information Sourcebook: Occupational Safety and Health, 3rd edition (1977). Compiled and published by the Canada Safety Council, 1765 St. Laurent Boulevard, Ottawa, Canada K1G 3V4. A directory of organizations, councils, institutions, and agencies that have occupational safety and health as part or all of their function. It covers Canada, the United States, and England.

It Hurts When They Cry: Infant Safety Kit (1976). U.S. Consumer Product Safety Commission, Washington, D.C. 20207 (free). Illustrated with drawings and photographs, this very useful booklet has tear-out sheets to carry along when purchasing infant equipment and carriers to note safety features that should be present. Also includes basic facts about hazards and dangers related to such common infant-related tragedies as crib deaths.

National Safety News (monthly). National Safety Council, 444 North Michigan Avenue, Chicago, Ill. 60611. A magazine devoted to occupational safety and health with feature articles aimed at management, such as "In an Emergency—Who's in Charge?" and "Management Safety Policies." Related products in the safety field are extensively advertised (such as smoke alarms, safety shoes, step ladders, and protective glasses).

A New Vaccine for Child Safety by Murl Harmon (1976). Safety Now Co., Inc., 202 York Road, Jenkintown, Pa. 19046 ($7.50). The author, founder of Safety Now Co., offers this book as a guide to child safety. It includes state-by-state listings of poison control centers and additional sources for information. There are fourteen chapters on such subjects as safety in the first year, animals, vacationing, "Vaccinating Your Babysitter," and more.

101 Ideas That Worked (1976). National Safety Council, 444 North Michigan Avenue, Chicago, Ill. 60611 (Stock No. 192.20, $2.37). A booklet with 101 safety ideas published in previous *National Safety News* magazines.

Outdoor Safety Tips by the U.S. Department of Agriculture (July 1975). Consumer Information Center, Dept. 082F, Pueblo, Colo. 81009 ($.35). Simple tips on fire safety and what to do if you get lost in a forest, plus survival tips, first aid, and SOS signals.

Plane Safety and Survival by Eric G. Anderson, M.D. (1978). Aero Publishers, Inc., 329 West Aviation Road, Fallbrook, Calif. 92028 ($7.95). An excellent survival manual for anyone who flies, with chapters on every type of terrain and weather flying, plus particular emphasis on safety preparations for each flight. Illustrated with photos and extensive charts and drawings.

"Protecting Workers in Imminent Danger Under the Federal Job Safety and Health Law" (February 1977). U.S. Department of Labor Program Highlights, Consumer Information Leaflet No. USDL 46 (OSHA 5), Labor Department, OSHA Information Office, 200 Constitution Avenue, N.W., Washington, D.C. 20210. A two-sided flyer that describes what an imminent danger situation is, what you can do about it, and what OSHA can do. It lists your rights as an employee under the Occupational Safety and Health Act and explains why and how to file a complaint with the OSHA office.

Traffic Safety '75: A Digest of Activities of the National Highway Traffic Safety Administration (1976). U.S. Department of Transportation, NHTSA, Washington, D.C. 20590 (free). A booklet with information on traffic safety, the history of NHTSA, alcohol and driving, driver education programs, defects investigations, and research projects. Illustrated.

Unsafe at Any Speed, rev. ed., by Ralph Nader (1973). Bantam Books, Inc. 666 Fifth Avenue, New York, N.Y. 10019 ($1.95). Lawyer and consumer advocate Nader's epic work on the auto industry that prompted the adoption of the National Traffic and Motor Vehicle Safety Act of 1966. That much still has to be done is evident in Nader's introduction to this revised edition: "In the six years since the first publication of *Unsafe at Any Speed*, over three hundred and thirty thousand Americans have died on the highways and about twenty-five million more have been injured." An excellent reference for those who rightly believe auto-related deaths and injuries are preventable.

Women's Work, Women's Health: Myths and Realities by Jeanne M. Stellman (1978). Pantheon, 201 East 50th Street, New York, N.Y. 10022 ($12.95 hardcover; $3.95 paperback). Examines the misuse of restrictive policies that exclude women from certain jobs and allow men to work in unsafe environments by exploring the status of women in the job market, especially as it relates to occupational diseases and injuries.

Work Is Dangerous to Your Health: A Handbook of Health Hazards in the Workplace and What You Can Do About Them by Jeanne M. Stellman and Susan M. Daum, with a foreword by George Wald (1973). Vintage Books, 201 East 50th Street, New York, N.Y. 10022 ($1.95). An excellent book for the general public on occupational diseases, chemical hazards, controlling pollution in the workplace, and what has to be done to reduce health hazards on the job. The authors state that more than 14,000 deaths on the job are recorded and 2.2 million disabling injuries occur among the 80 million workers. Includes extensive diagrams and tables on key problems, such as back injuries and lung-related diseases. Also includes an extensive listing of health hazards by occupation and an annotated bibliography.

FILMS

Signal 30. Highway Safety Films, Inc., 890 Hollywood Lane, P.O. Box 3563, Mansfield, Ohio 44907 (puchase price $141.50). A 28-minute 16mm color/sound film showing a highway tragedy caused by misjudgment or carelessness. "It is an ugly film. It is meant to be. It is designed to drive home to those who see it that an accident is not pretty." Write for catalog of other related films, including *Mechanized Death* and *Wheels of Tragedy*.

Split Second Decision. Modern Talking Picture Service, 2323 New Hyde Park, New Hyde Park, N.Y. 11040. A 16mm color/sound film produced by 3M Company's Traffic Control Material Division. It is on one of the major causes of highway traffic fatalities—overtaking and passing other vehicles—and is available for free loan.

Trouble With the Law, edited from *Pursuit of Happiness*. Learning Corporation of America, 1350 Avenue of the Americas, New York, N.Y. 10019. A 15-minute color/sound film with E. G. Marshall, Arthur Hill, and Michael Sarrazin available for rental ($25.00) or sale ($270.00). A fictionalized account of an accidental hit-and-run, the court process, and sentencing that is a powerful statement of the dichotomy between human morality and modern laws.

See also the following related chapters in *The Help Book:*

**ALCOHOLISM
CHILDREN
CONSUMER AFFAIRS
EMERGENCIES AND DISASTERS
FOOD AND NUTRITION
GUN CONTROL
HEALTH
PARENTING
TRANSPORTATION AND TRAVEL**

46

SEX EDUCATION AND THERAPY

"Do you feel threatened by liberated women?" was the question I asked of at least fifty men of varying professions and ages. "Of course I like liberated women," they universally replied. But my questions did not stop at their obvious desire to appear with it. More intense probing revealed deep resentments of women who are more assertive than they once were.

By and large, women gave more honest reports. For example, Gail Parent, author of the best-selling novel *Sheila Levine is Dead and Living in New York*, acknowledges that there is a widespread problem; the theme of her novel is how men cope with liberated women.

"If a woman gets kicked out of bed enough times," Gail Parent says, "she'll be afraid to get in. It's enough of a problem that I thought a fictionalized account would have a wide appeal. Most women are really pseudo-liberated—they may be boss at the office, but they still sit home and wait for men to call."

Dr. Robert Chartham, a British psychologist, feels woman's liberation has a lot to do with the increasing number of male patients he sees in his London clinic—some men who are not able to ejaculate as readily as before, and others who are not able to achieve orgasm at all.

"Up to December 1971," Dr. Chartham writes, "I used to get an average of three retarded ejaculations a year. Between January 1972 and December, I had no fewer than forty-one, and the number in 1973 was even higher.

"They are all young men in their late twenties, but they all have dominant, woman's lib-type partners."

Dr. Chartham has always advocated sexual intercourse as a mutual experience. He advises partners to alternate who takes the initiative. The trouble arises when women always want to be the instigators, or the men cannot relinquish their role as aggressors.

"Men are withholding their orgasms for the same reason that women have usually withheld theirs," Dr. Chartham continues. "That is because he or she resents some aspect of the partner's sexual or other behavior."

Dr. Philip Cauthery, a British physician, feels liberated women present the greatest threat to emotionally immature men. A developed man chooses a liberated and sexually free woman. "Such a man," says Dr. Cauthery, "needs a woman who is liberated from her conventional sexual restraints, from her own sense of culturally induced inferiority, and from her own frustrations. If she isn't liberated, he will set about encouraging her to be free."

On the other hand, Dr. Cauthery thinks most men do have worries about their masculine identity, and so they "have to arrange their man-woman relationships in a way which avoids threats of domination or rejection by the woman. Liberated women pose an increased threat to such men, who have to strengthen their defenses in response."

But in summary, Dr. Cauthery puts an intriguing paradox: liberated women are more of a threat to men, but they also impose fewer tests of masculinity than the "conventional" woman.

One theory about male sexual impotence argues that some insecure men are reacting to liberated women with sexual anxiety. Though they are reluctant to admit it, many men find liberated women so threatening to their long-held dominant role that they turn off and become too inhibited to get an erection.

However, they explain it as a natural reaction to the "unfeminine" and aggressive behavior of their liberated partners, rather than their own inadequacies. In most cases, such couples simply abandon each other rather than work it out, because the anxiety and humiliation of sexual failure is intolerable.

Other men immediately become so threatened that they never even reach the sexual state. For instance, twenty-five-year-old George vacationed one August weekend on Fire Island, New York's swingers' haven.

"There were lots of nude women sunbathing," he said. "Ordinarily I would go up to an attractive woman in a bathing suit and try to start a conversation. But I felt threatened by the fact that these publicly naked women were obviously so much freer than me. I felt inadequate. I didn't know how to approach anyone."

A thirty-year-old sociology professor in Boston feels liberated women expect more sexually, and this further pressures him to perform. "Some men are even afraid to let a women get on top because it makes them feel out of control," he explained. "We're in a state of change now and liberation cannot come overnight. There'll be many battle scars before the smooth way of acting is agreed upon. It makes me feel nervous because there aren't any ground rules left."

Many men expressed hostility toward women who want it both ways. "They say they're liberated," said Andy, a twenty-nine-year-old musician. "They call me up for a date and then they still expect me to pay. That's unfair."

A young attractive female advertising copywriter explained how being liberated and straightforward can confuse a man. "I had a wonderful time with Joel on our first date," she explained. "I thought it would be pleasant to go away with him for the weekend. So I called and asked if he'd like to go with me. The only word I can use to describe his reaction is 'shocked.' Not only that, he blamed me for making him feel uncomfortable because he had to turn me down. Why didn't he tell me the truth in the first place? Probably because women always lie to him."

But for some freer women, there is less sex after liberation, though hopefully, this is only temporary. "I have fewer sexual affairs than I used to," one woman confided, "because I demand more from a man. But the sex I do have is much more fulfilling. I think I like it better this way."

In a marriage, liberation may be an extremely confusing and threatening factor. Wayne, a forty-one-year-old executive, feels it was the major reason for his divorce after eight years and two children.

"We were moving in different directions. When we got married my ex-wife wanted to have a child and teach part time. By the time we separated, she had deep resentments about doing housework and cooking. It didn't seem to be enough for her. She became hostile and felt that I had let her waste all those years. Then our sex life became masochistic. We would both abstain for a while to punish the other, and we'd follow it up with intense lovemaking and a great deal of tenderness. The warm feelings that good sex evoked would make us feel terribly guilty for punishing the other in the first place. And so the cycle went until it seemed my wife began asking herself how she could care for this beast—me. Finally, sex became perfunctory and without feeling."

Other men find that their wives become liberated only after divorce. Then these women experience problems with their new boyfriends. Carl, an editor at a publishing house, gets repeated phone calls from his ex-wife about her conflicts with men because of her newfound liberation.

"But I don't understand how she could still accept so much alimony if she's really that liberated," Carl said with bitterness.

Another man, a writer, prefers to have affairs with liberated women who assume the traditional male role of asking for sex. But at the same time he is married and says he would kill any man who covets his wife. She stays home while he goes out with "liberated" women.

Many couples are experimenting with freedom within their marriage. A thirty-year-old housewife in New Jersey told me about her compromise to liberation. "We have our separate nights out with the boys or the girls," she said as her two sons played in the yard. "We also take separate vacations. I take the kids on a trip but my husband goes off free and alone. So far I'm still content enough not to make any waves. When I do make new requests for more time alone or freedom, my husband reminds me who pays all the bills."

Perhaps one of the main sexual benefits of the women's movement is that the "slam-bam-thank-you-ma'am" type of lover is under new scrutiny. All the studies on sexuality stress foreplay and enjoyment for the woman as well as for the man. Consequently, women are demanding more from their male partners. Moreover, if the transition to a more mutually agreeable sexual relationship is arduous, one or both partners are frequently seeking professional help.

"Most men feel threatened initially by liberated women," says Dr. Edrita Fried, author of *Love and Sexuality*, who is a clinical psychologist. "But soon they see the advantages of having relationships with liberated women and they relish the change."

Dr. Fried feels the threats that liberated women pose are only temporary and that most men work them out, to find life much fuller with more independent, self-sufficient, and sexually freer women.

But there are men who cannot adjust to assertive and aggressive women; they prefer former days when men were completely in control—at least on the surface. For those men, there are still enough women around who prefer to maintain the status quo rather than take the risks of liberation.

Such men will probably never get over their threatened feelings and will continue choosing women who allow them total dominance, selfishness, and control in sexual relationships. Too frightened to risk change, growth, or experimentation, these men are "safe" as long as there are enough women who will tolerate sexual frustration and a subordinate role.

But men who are welcoming the new wave of expression from liberated women will find, though the going must be rough at first, that their partner's awakened sexuality and fulfillment is an exciting addition to their relationship, resulting in intensified experiences. And, inevitably, the outcome of these struggles to become "new" men and "new" women will be worth the effort.*

In addition to all the resources and suggestions for finding a therapist, psychiatrist, or counselor that appeared in Chapter 14, *Counseling*, or Chapter 38, *Mental Health*, you might also want to contact a sex therapist directly. Your local affiliate of Planned Parenthood of America, Inc., might make referrals. Sex education programs are also available through local public schools, women's groups, psychiatric clinics, or similar service organizations. You might also check to see if centers for sex education, like those that follow, exist in your community:

Elysium Institute
814 Robinson Road
Topanga, Calif. 92090

A human potential estate-like center with a supportive environment. Clothing is optional for singles, families, and their children. Seminars are given on various aspects of sensuality and sexuality, body self-image and acceptance of self. There are also self-help groups.

LITERATURE: *Elysium: Journal of Your Senses*, quarterly ($.30 in stamps).

---

*Adapted from "New Woman Meets Old Morality," by J. L. Barkas. © 1974 Forum International Ltd. Reprinted from *Forum: The International Journal of Human Relations*, with permission of the copyright owner.

Esalen Institute
Big Sur, Calif. 93920

The institute conducts workshops at San Francisco, Westerbeke Ranch, Yosemite, or the Sierras as well as the Big Sur headquarters. It works on developing inner consciousnesses through various programs, including Gestalt, hypnotism, yoga, meditation, massage; work-study programs; and body awareness, sensuality, and body energetics. Fees are determined on a course-by-course basis.

LITERATURE: *The Esalen Catalog* and other occasional mailings for one year ($2.00 or free to anyone attending an Esalen workshop or conference).

Human Sexuality Information and Counseling Service
Carolina Union Building, Room 256
University of North Carolina
Chapel Hill, N.C. 27514

The service provides information on sexuality; referrals to community agencies dealing with sexuality; one-to-one counseling; and a speakers bureau.

LITERATURE: Brochure. Free literature on VD and birth control.

Sexual Therapy Clinic
Lenox Hill Hospital
100 East 77th Street
New York, N.Y. 10021

Individuals and couples with sexual problems are provided with evaluation and treatment of their disorders; fees are on a sliding scale based upon ability to pay. Counseling is provided by psychiatrists and psychologists and referrals are made to physicians.

Information on sex is available through the following national organizations and institutes:

American Association of Sex Educators, Counselors, and Therapists (AASECT)
5010 Wisconsin Avenue, N.W., Suite 304
Washington, D.C. 20016

National nonprofit membership organization founded in 1967 by and for sex educators and counselors that will make referrals; it is also open to sex therapists and researchers. AASECT is also an information clearinghouse through its publications and provides training programs through American University.

LITERATURE: Free descriptive brochures; *Newsletter* to members; *Journal of Sex Education and Therapy* ($6.00 a year); *National Register of Certified Sex Educators and Certified Sex Therapists* ($3.00), updated annually; free publication list and summer institute listings.

American Personnel and Guidance Association
1607 New Hampshire Avenue, N.W.
Washington, D.C. 20009

This professional association of counselors offers publications and audio cassettes in the area of sexuality. Write for their extensive *Counseling Resources* publications catalog.

Association for Humanistic Psychology
325 Ninth Street
San Francisco, Calif. 94103

An international organization concerned with

personal growth that sponsors regional and international meetings; local groups have topical conferences concerned with sexuality and related subjects, such as women's studies, marriage, divorce, the family. Membership dues range from $35.00 (regular) to $23.00 (student) to $450 (lifetime).

LITERATURE: *Journal of Humanistic Psychology* ($10.00 a year); *Newsletter* (included in membership).

Institute for Family Research and Education (IFRE)
760 Ostrom Avenue
Syracuse, N.Y. 13210

A family and sexuality information and research center with workshops and seminars for graduate credit at Syracuse University; extensive publications; consultant services to schools, churches, clinics, agencies, and private groups and organizations; and training programs for staffs. IFRE is a program of Syracuse University's College of Human Development established in 1970. It also sponsors National Family Sex Education Week.

LITERATURE: IMPACT Newsbriefs report; free brochure; leaflets; reports; write for publications price list.

National Clearinghouse For Family Planning Information
U.S. Public Health Service
Box 2225
Rockville, Md. 20857

The clearinghouse will provide pertinent information and publications for the general public on family planning and sex education.

National Council on Family Relations
1219 University Avenue, S.E.
Minneapolis, Minn. 55414

This national professional organization of counselors working in the family field (membership dues range from $15.00 for students to $30.00 for individuals) offers the public a wide range of written and audio materials in the area of sexuality. Write for extensive publications price list.

LITERATURE: Cassette tapes—"Man and Woman as Sexual Partners" by Jay Mann, no. 28 ($7.00); "The Adult Male Sex Role and Resistance to Change" by Robert R. Bell, no. 27 ($7.00); *Journal of Marriage and the Family; The Journal of Family History; The Family Coordinator* (all by subscription).

Planned Parenthood Federation of America, Inc. (PPFA)
810 Seventh Avenue
New York, N.Y. 10019

Contact your local PPFA clinic for information, guidance, or referral to medically supervised clinics for abortion, contraception, pregnancy testing, infertility therapy, and voluntary sterilization. (See complete listing in Chapter 23, *Family Planning.*)

The Youth and Student Affairs Program provides advocacy for family planning, concentrating on the civil and medical rights of youth to sex education and information and clinical services. Technical assistance is provided to all family planning informational, educational, and clinical programs in the United States.

LITERATURE: *Getting It Together*, bimonthly newsletter ($4.00 a year); *Publications By For About Youth*, flyer; free single article reprints.

Public Affairs Committee
381 Park Avenue South
New York, N.Y. 10016

Publishes a wide range of inexpensive booklets on sex education. Write for their publications list.

LITERATURE: *Talking to Preteenagers About Sex; Sex Education: The Parent's Role; How to Tell Your Child About Sex; Sex Education for Disabled Persons;* and *Sexual Adjustment in*

Marriage (single copies of each booklet are $.50; reduced rates for bulk quantities).

Resource Center on Sex Roles in Education
1201 Sixteenth Street, N.W.
Washington, D.C. 20036

The center has projects directed toward the elimination of sex discrimination and sex bias in education, prepares and disseminates materials and information, carries out research and development projects, and provides technical assistance to groups wishing to achieve educational equity.

LITERATURE: *Research Action Notes.*

Sex Information Council of America (SICAM)
#1 Palomar Arcade
Santa Cruz, Calif. 95060

SICAM, which began in 1977, is an independent, nonsectarian, educational organization that acts as a national clearinghouse for information on sexuality and related topics. Materials are geared mainly to the general public; some are directed toward professionals in the field. SICAM is supported by contributions and the sale of materials.

LITERATURE: *Impotence: Causes and Treatment* ($.25).

Sex Information and Education Council of the United States (SIECUS)
84 Fifth Avenue
New York, N.Y. 10011

An information clearinghouse on human sexuality with sex education materials for professionals, the lay public, the aged, the handicapped, and religious workers. SIECUS reviews current books and audiovisual aids in the field. Provides leadership for better understanding of human sexuality as part of health.

LITERATURE: *SIECUS Report*, bimonthly ($9.95 for individuals, $15.00 for institutions; $7.95 introductory rate); free publications catalog from Human Sciences Press, 72 Fifth Avenue, New York, N.Y. 10011; free reprint of human sexuality bibliography for professionals.

The following organizations are concerned with providing information, referrals, and aid to prostitutes and former prostitutes:

Coyote
P.O. Box 26354
San Francisco, Calif. 94126

A national membership organization founded in 1973 whose primary goal is the decriminalization of prostitution. Other aims are to eliminate the abuses of the current situation, such as police harassment and mistreatment of prostitutes and to make the criminal justice system treat prostitutes as they do other misdemeants.

LITERATURE: *Coyote Howls* newspaper.

Scapegoat
1540 Broadway, Suite 300H
New York, N.Y. 10036

Founded in 1975 to work with all prostitutes, Scapegoat provides supportive services in New York City, including a current listing of reputable places to get legal and medical help. There are also child care drop-in services for five year olds and younger children of prostitutes. Calls and letters are handled from all over the country; the telephone service is staffed seven days a week, twenty-four hours a day.

LITERATURE: Fact sheet.

ADDITIONAL LITERATURE

The American Way of Sex by Bradley Smith (1978). Two Continents Publishing Group, Ltd., 30 E. 42nd Street, New York, N.Y. 10017 ($19.95). An illustrated survey of American sexual customs and attitudes throughout history as well as a projection for twenty-first-century behavior.

An Analysis of Human Sexual Response, edited by Ruth and Edward Brecher (1966). New American Library, 1301 Avenue of the Americas, New York, N.Y. 10019 ($.75). Sex research findings reported and described in simple, clear language. The Brecher's description of the work of Masters and Johnson is excellent and is followed by other researchers' articles, such as Isadore Rubin and William Davenport, on such topics as the Kinsey tradition, sex education, sex after forty, and teaching doctors about sex.

Community Sex Education Programs for Parents: A Training Manual for Organizers (1977). Institute for Family Research and Education, 760 Ostrom Avenue, Syracuse, N.Y. 13210 ($4.00).

The Cycles of Sex by Warren J. Gadpaille, M.D., edited by Lucy Freeman (1975). Charles Scribner's Sons, 597 Fifth Avenue, New York, N.Y. 10017 ($6.95). A discussion of psychosexual development from the womb through adolescence, parenthood, and the later years.

Getting It Together. Planned Parenthood Federation of America, Inc., Youth and Student Affairs Program, 810 Seventh Avenue, New York, N.Y. 10019 ($4.00 a year). Excellent newsletter with articles on sex education programs; book reviews; descriptions of pertinent organizations, both national and local.

A Guide to Sexuality Handbooks. Planned Parenthood Federation of America, Inc., Youth and Student Affairs Program, 810 Seventh Avenue, New York, N.Y. 10019. Concise, 15-page booklet on free and low-cost handbooks on college sexuality, non-campus booklets, "how-to" handbooks, and directories on sex education and related subjects.

The Illustrated Manual of Sex Therapy by Helen Singer Kaplan, M.D., Ph.D. (1975). Quadrangle Books, 3 Park Avenue, New York, N.Y. 10016 ($6.95). With drawings by David Passalacqua, this oversized book is a useful self-help teaching tool for those who wish to apply sexual exercises, such as "pleasuring," to try to correct sexual dysfunctions. One positive contribution of the book is that it might help the shy or fearful to seek out a sexual therapist, if there are problems that need professional help.

Journal of Sex Education and Therapy. The American Association of Sex Educators and Counselors, 5010 Wisconsin Avenue, N.W., Washington, D.C. 20016. Excellent semiannual journal with articles by professionals and reviews of pertinent books and films. One issue included the articles "The Case of the Pregnant Virgin" and "Female Sexual Dysfunction."

The Joy of Sex: A Gourmet Guide to Lovemaking, edited by Alex Comfort, Ph.D. (1972). Simon and Schuster, 1230 Avenue of the Americas, New York, N.Y. 10020 ($5.95). The first of the self-help sexual manuals that have become instant best sellers. Also, *More Joy of Sex: A Lovemaking Companion to the Joy of Sex* by Alex Comfort, Ph.D. (1974). Simon and Schuster, 1230 Avenue of the Americas, New York, N.Y. 10020 ($5.95).

The Kama Sutra of Vatsyayana, translated by Sir Richard Burton and F. F. Arbuthnot (1971). Berkeley Publishing Corporation, 200 Madison Avenue, New York, N.Y. 10016 ($.95). Based on Burton's translation that first appeared in 1883, this famous Hindu manual of the physical and emotional components of lovemaking has advice that is as sound today as when it was written sometime between the first and fourth centuries.

National Register of Certified Sex Educators and Certified Sex Therapists (updated annually). American Association of Sex Educators, Counselors, and Therapists, 5010 Wisconsin Avenue, N.W., Suite 304, Washington, D.C. 20016 ($3.00). Explains the necessary qualifications for sex educator and sex therapist certification followed by a geographic listing, state by state, of both types of professionals. Includes code abbreviations for the type of patients that they treat and in what educational site (agency, community, private practice).

Our Bodies, Ourselves, 2nd edition, by the Boston Women's Health Book Collective (1976).

Simon and Schuster, 1230 Avenue of the Americas, New York, N.Y. 10020 ($4.95). A clear and informative presentation of sexuality from a female perspective. Chapters on the anatomy and physiology of sexuality and reproduction, birth control, abortion, pregnancy, and menopause are all profusely illustrated.

The Sex Atlas: A New Illustrated Guide by Erwin J. Haeberle (1978). Seabury Press/Continuum Books, 815 Second Avenue, New York, N.Y. 10017 ($25.00). A comprehensive reference, written in plain language, on all aspects of human sexuality, with hundreds of drawings and photos.

Sex Therapy Today by Patricia and Richard Gillian (1978). Evergreen Paperbacks, Grove Press, Inc., 196 West Houston Street, New York, N.Y. 10014 ($4.95). A description of current sex therapies with later chapters discussing how to take a sexual history from a patient and ways to treat those with sexual problems.

The Sexual Self by Avodah K. Offit, M.D. (1977). J. B. Lippincott, East Washington Square, Philadelphia, Pa. 19105 ($10.00). Excellent description of normal and abnormal sexual development written in a lively but informative style.

The Student Guide to Sex on Campus by the Student Committee on Human Sexuality (1971). New American Library, 1301 Avenue of the Americas, New York, N.Y. 10019 ($1.00). A basic information source on anatomy and physiology, contraception, pregnancy, abortion, and venereal disease with sections geared specifically to the needs of students, such as deciding yes or no about sexual intercourse and student on- and off-campus services for high school and college students.

Teenage Pregnancy: Everybody's Problem by the U.S. Department of Health, Education, and Welfare (1977). Consumer Information Center, Department 087F, Pueblo, Colo. 81009 ($1.00). Statistics on the prevalence of teenage pregnancies, its consequences, how to prevent it, and what to do if contraception fails.

The Whole Sex Catalogue, edited by Bernhardt J. Hurwood (1975). Pinnacle Books, Inc., One Century Plaza, 2029 Century Park East, Los Angeles, Calif. 90067 ($6.95). A large-format paperback containing background information and illustrations about sex as well as practical listings for self-help. Sample chapters include "Sex Through the Ages," "Sex As You Like It—Heterosexual, Homosexual, Bisexual," and "Sex and Medicine."

Your Guide to Total Pleasure in Lovemaking: You Can Be Your Own Sex Therapist by Carole Altman (1976). Berkeley Publishing Corporation, 200 Madison Avenue, New York, N.Y. 10016 ($1.95). An illustrated self-help sexual manual that includes a questionnaire to help the reader understand his or her sexual preferences.

See also the following related chapters in *The Help Book:*

CHILD ABUSE
CHILDBEARING
CHILDREN
CIVIL RIGHTS AND DISCRIMINATION
COUNSELING
EDUCATION
FAMILY PLANNING
GAY LIBERATION
HEALTH
MENTAL HEALTH
MULTIPURPOSE ORGANIZATIONS
PARENTING
RAPE AND SEXUAL ASSAULT

47

SUICIDE PREVENTION

A medical receptionist in a midtown Manhattan office was typing one day when she heard a thud outside. A nurse had glanced out the window just before and seen a large form falling. They ran from the ground floor office and within minutes the nurse was feeling the pulse of the well-dressed man whose body lay on the pavement. He had jumped twenty stories.

The man had "wanted" to die. He had written a suicide note and had left his boots by the open window, perhaps to show that no one had pushed him.

The impact of suicide on society is insidious. Our attitude toward it may lead us to accept violence as a means of solving personal problems. There was a time when twice as many Americans killed themselves as killed others: about 20,000 suicides a year and 10,000 homicides. Since 1973 the figures have changed, and murder and suicide each claim over 20,000 victims yearly or 40,000 deaths a year. In England one-third of all homicides are followed by the suicide of the murderer; this phenomenon occurs less frequently in the United States. Sociologist Marvin Wolfgang reported it in 4 percent of the homicides he studied in Philadelphia in the late 1950s.

What are some of the social, legal, and cultural changes in attitudes toward suicide? Most western countries have decriminalized it. The Suicide Act in England in 1961 outlawed criminal prosecution of those who survived suicide attempts, although the aiding and abetting of a suicide attempt was punishable by up to fourteen years in prison. (The New York State Penal Code similarly defines fostering a suicide attempt as a Class E Felony, punishable by imprisonment.) As late as 1964 nine U.S. states still regarded suicide as a crime.

In the early days of Christianity suicide was sanctioned as a form of martyrdom, but St. Augustine in the *City of God* denied that self-murder was ever justified. Today, the Roman Catholic Church and some other Christian and Jewish groups still condemn suicide, but some thinkers have argued differently. David Hume's eighteenth-century essay on suicide claimed it was not sinful for a man to take his own life, and the French philosophers Montesquieu, Voltaire, and Rousseau all agreed with him. (Kant in Germany thought suicide irrational.) More recently Albert Camus in *The Rebel* (1951) noted that although murder, not suicide, seemed to be the contemporary problem, "murder and suicide are one and the same thing, and must be accepted or rejected together. . . . If the world is a matter of indifference to the man who commits suicide, it is because he has an idea of something that is not or could not be indifferent to him. . . . By the same token, if we deny that there are reasons for suicide, we cannot claim that there are grounds for murder."

The twentieth century's preoccupation with suicide is reflected in the approaches of sociologist Emile Durkheim and psychologist Sigmund Freud. Durkheim, in his most famous book *Suicide: A Study in Sociology* (1897), divided suicide into three distinct types: altruistic, egoistic, anomic. Altruistic suicide is a matter of duty, as for example the custom of suttee in India, in which a woman committed suicide following her husband's death. Egoistic suicide results from a detachment from the community; thus single people have higher suicide rates than married ones. Anomic suicides result from a drastic change in one's condition, such as sudden poverty or sudden wealth—consider the high rate during the Great Depression or the suicides of writers or artists who achieved fame overnight after long years of struggle.

Freud saw suicide as the result of an individual's mental processes rather than social conditions. In essence Freud said suicide was the acting out of an unconscious hostility toward an object of one's love—and hate. By killing oneself the victim was also killing the loved (and hated) object.

Today we have both problems—murder and suicide—in huge doses. Why does one person choose suicide and another murder? Both suicide and homicide are psychological aberrations, arising from social and mental conditions that affect each person differently. Some deal with these conditions in a socially acceptable way—through work or volunteer efforts—while others turn their rage inward or strike out against society or attack the actual object of their hate. But why?

The danger of our failure to prevent suicide is it is discouraging to think that death might become so acceptable a "solution" that the method of achieving it, whether by one's own hand or a stranger's, would be irrelevant. Of the four categories of deaths—natural, accidental, suicidal, and homicidal—only the first is beyond our control.

WARNING SIGNS OF SUICIDE*

- Suicide threats
- Statements revealing a desire to die
- Previous suicide attempts
- Sudden changes in behavior (withdrawal, apathy, moodiness)
- Depression (crying, sleeplessness, loss of appetite, hopelessness)
- Final arrangements (such as giving away personal possessions)

WHAT TO DO

- Discuss it openly and frankly
- Show interest and support
- Get professional help

Of Suicide

by John Berryman [†]

Reflexions on suicide, & on my father, possess me.
I drink too much. My wife threatens separation.
She won't 'nurse' me. She feels 'inadequate.'
We don't mix together.

It's an hour later in the East.
I could call up Mother in Washington, D.C.
But could she help me?
And all this postal adulation & reproach?

A basis rock-like of love & friendship
for all this world-wide madness seems to be needed.
Epictetus is in some ways my favourite philosopher.
Happy men have died earlier.

---

*Reprinted with permission from *Suicide in Youth and What You Can Do About It—A Guide for School Personnel*, prepared by the Suicide Prevention and Crisis Center of San Mateo County, Calif., in cooperation with the American Association of Suicidology and Merck Sharp & Dohme Health Information Services.

[†] "Of Suicide" from *Love & Fame* by John Berryman, © 1970 by John Berryman. Reprinted with the permission of Farrar, Straus & Giroux, Inc., New York. Berryman, a graduate of Columbia and Cambridge universities, was a professor of literature at the University of Minnesota at the time of his death (1972), when he himself was a suicide—he jumped off a bridge. Born in 1914, his numerous books of poetry include *Poems* (1942) and *Berryman's Sonnets* (1967).

612 / THE HELP BOOK

> I still plan to go to Mexico this summer.
> The Olmec images! Chichen Itza!
> D.H. Lawrence has a wild dream of it.
> Malcolm Lowry's book when it came out I taught to my precept at
> Princeton.
>
> I don't entirely resign. I may teach the Third Gospel
> this afternoon. I haven't made up my mind.
> It seems to me sometimes that others have easier jobs
> & do them worse.
>
> Well, we must labour & dream. Gogol was impotent,
> somebody in Pittsburgh told me.
> I said: At what age? They couldn't answer.
> That is a damned serious matter.
>
> Rembrandt was sober. There we differ. Sober.
> Terrors came on him. To us too they come.
> Of suicide I continually think.
> Apparently he didn't. I'll teach Luke.

The suicide prevention movement in the United States is mainly a community-based, grassroots, voluntary, and decentralized service with about 300 local suicide prevention or crisis counseling centers. Consult your local telephone directory—or call the operator—for the nearest twenty-four hour telephone or in-person suicide prevention free service.

For direct help, the following organizations either have local affiliates or are national in the scope of their services:

Contact Teleministries USA, Inc.
900 South Arlington Avenue
Harrisburg, Pa. 17109

Operates more than seventy-four free telephone counseling centers around the country staffed by trained volunteers. Each service is distinguished as an ecumenical Christian ministry. Telephone counseling centers have help available twenty-four hours a day, including: "Dial a Shoulder"; "Phone a Friend"; crisis intervention, suicide prevention, and information and referral. Contact Teleministries USA is a member of Life Line International, with headquarters in Toronto, Canada. Contact also has extensive publications available. (For a complete description, see Chapter 14, *Counseling*.)

The Samaritans
39, Walbrook
London EC4N 8 BP, England

355 Boylston Street
Boston, Mass. 02116

P.O. Box 386
North Falmouth, Mass. 02556

The Samaritans was started in 1953 in England, where there are now 160 branches. In the United States, there are two branches. The telephone is always answered by volunteers, although there is professional back-up by counselors and consultants. Speakers on suicide prevention are available for educational and training programs. The Samaritans also serves as a resource center for students and researchers. It is a privately funded agency depending on foundation and business grants and contributions from individuals; all donations are tax deductible.

The Boston Samaritans have telephone and walk-in befriending by trained volunteers for those who are suicidal, despairing, or lonely. They offer someone to talk to in confidence and have clients of all ages, with all kinds of problems, and at all stages of distress. In 1976, they received 45,000 calls.

LITERATURE: Free descriptive leaflet; fact sheets; annotated bibliography.

The following list is a sampling of local suicide prevention counseling services around the country:

Crisis Center of Jefferson County
3600 Eighth Avenue South
Birmingham, Ala. 35222

Suicide Prevention Crisis Center
4301 East Fifth Street
Tucson, Ariz. 85711

Suicide Prevention Center of Monterey County
P.O. Box 1304
Carmel, Calif. 93921

Suicide Prevention of Davis
618 Sunset Court
Davis, Calif. 95616

Help Line Contact Clinic
427 West Fifth Street, Suite 500
Los Angeles, Calif. 90013

Suicide Prevention Service
P.O. Box 449
Sacramento, Calif. 95802

San Francisco Suicide Prevention, Inc.
3940 Geary Boulevard
San Francisco, Calif. 94118

Suicide Prevention Center
274 West 20th Avenue
San Mateo, Calif. 94403

Pueblo Suicide Prevention Center, Inc.
212 West 12th
Pueblo, Colo. 81003

Suicide Prevention Telephone Service
1635 Central Avenue
Bridgeport, Conn. 06610

Alachua County Crisis Center
606 S.W. Third Avenue
Gainesville, Fla. 32601

Central Crisis Center
P.O. Box 6393
Jacksonville, Fla. 32205

We Care, Inc.
112 Pasadena Place
Orlando, Fla. 32804

Sarasota Guidance Clinic, Inc.
1538 State Street
Sarasota, Fla. 33577

Suicide and Crisis Center
1723 West Kennedy Boulevard #103
Tampa, Fla. 33606

Suicide and Crisis Center
% Information Referral Service
200 North Vineyard Boulevard
Room 603
Honolulu, Hawaii 96817

Call For Help—Suicide and Crisis Intervention Service, Inc.
7623 (rear) West Main Street
Belleville, Ill. 62223

Crisis Intervention and Suicide Prevention Program
4200 North Oak Park Avenue
Chicago, Ill. 60634

Suicide Prevention Center of St. Joseph County
532 South Michigan Street
South Bend, Ind. 46601

614 / THE HELP BOOK

Baton Rouge Crisis Intervention Center
Student Health Service
Louisiana State University
Baton Rouge, La. 70803

Crisis Line
1528 Jackson Avenue
New Orleans, La. 70130

Bath-Brunswick Area Rescue, Inc.
159 Maine Street
Brunswick, Me. 04011

Suicide Prevention and Drug Information Center
Detroit Psychiatric Institute
1151 Taylor Avenue
Detroit, Mich. 48202

Contact-Twin Cities
83 South 12th Street
Minneapolis, Minn. 55403

Crisis Intervention Center
Hennepin County Medical Center
Seventh and Park
Minneapolis, Minn. 55415

Life Crisis Services, Inc.
7438 Forsyth, Suite 210
St. Louis, Mo. 63105

Crisis Help and Suicide Prevention Service
508 West Main Avenue
Gastonia, N.C. 28052

Emergency Services
Central New Hampshire Community Mental Health Services, Inc.
5 Market Lane
Concord, N.H. 03301

Suicide Prevention and Crisis Center of Albuquerque, Inc.
P.O. Box 4511
Albuquerque, N.M. 87106

Suicide Prevention of Tompkins County
P.O. Box 312
Ithaca, N.Y. 14850

The National Save-A-Life League, Inc.
815 Second Avenue, Suite 409
New York, N.Y. 10017

Norman Vincent Peale Telephone Center
3 West 29th Street
New York, N.Y. 10001

Suicide and Crisis Intervention Service
P.O. Box 4068
Memphis, Tenn. 38104

Crisis Intervention Center, Inc.
2311 Ellison Place
Nashville, Tenn. 37203

Suicide Prevention Center
Luther Hospital
310 Chestnut Street
Eau Claire, Wis. 54701

The Dane County Mental Health Center
Emergency Services
31 South Henry Street
Madison, Wis. 53703

For information on suicide and suicide prevention, contact the following organizations:

American Association of Suicidology (AAS)
P.O. Box 3264
Houston, Tex. 77001

Established in 1968 following the First Annual National Conference on Suicidology, this is a multidisciplinary organization whose members consist of about 600 concerned lay people and 200 Suicide Prevention and Crisis Intervention Centers throughout the United States. Membership fees range from $20.00 for individuals to $75.00 for organizations. *Suicide*, its professional journal, is included in membership or for $7.00 for nonmembers. AAS is also an information clearinghouse that holds annual meetings; administers National Suicide Prevention Week, designated the third week of May each year; and periodically sponsors workshops and symposiums on volunteer training programs, statistical compilations pertaining to suicide prediction, and other aspects of suicidology.

LITERATURE: Free descriptive leaflet; *Before It's Too Late: What to do When Someone You Know Attempts Suicide* (see Additional Literature); *A Directory of Suicide Prevention Centers* (updated annually); *Newslink*, newsletter published three times a year on events and current organizational activities for members.

Center for Studies of Suicide Prevention
National Institute of Mental Health
Alcohol, Drug Abuse, and Mental Health Administration
Public Health Service
5600 Fishers Lane
Rockville, Md. 20857

A government-sponsored educational program in suicide prevention.

International Association for Suicide Prevention (IASP)
Central Administration Office
University of Vienna
Neuropsychiatric Clinic
Vienna, Austria

Holds a semiannual conference; has publications geared to suicide prevention workers and counselors.

ADDITIONAL LITERATURE

After Suicide by Samuel E. Wallace, M.D. (1973). John Wiley and Sons, Inc., 605 Third Avenue, New York, N.Y. 10016. Transcribed interviews with women widowed by suicide.

Before It's Too Late: What to Do When Someone You Know Attempts Suicide by Jan Fawcett, M.D., prepared by the American Association of Suicidology with MSD Health Information Services, Merck Sharp & Dohme (free in small quantities and at cost in larger quantities from American Association of Suicidology, Public Relations Office, P.O. Box 1, Gwynedd, Pa. 19436). "The shock you experience comes from the fact that this person, whom you thought you knew so well, could do such a thing," begins Fawcett's important little booklet. "Four out of five people who commit suicide have previously given clues," he also notes. There are also background facts, where to get help, and the danger signs of suicide.

Dealing With the Crisis of Suicide by Calvin J. Frederick and Louise Lague (1972). Public Affairs Pamphlets, 381 Park Avenue South, New York, N.Y. 10016 ($.50). The former chief of the Center for Studies of Suicide Prevention of the National Institute of Mental Health and a newspaper journalist have combined expertise and flowing writing to produce a compact, clear, and important roundup of the facts on suicide. Some of the topics covered are the taboo of suicide and when, how, and who can help.

The Savage God: A Study of Suicide by A. Alvarez (1971). Bantam Books, Inc., 666 Fifth Avenue, New York, N.Y. 10019 ($1.95). Alvarez, who met the poet Sylvia Plath in 1960, begins his study with an account and interpretation of Plath's suicide. He then proceeds to reveal the fallacies, theories, and feelings about suicide as well as an exhaustive study of suicide and literature. It is documented with quotations.

Separate Paths: Why People End Their Lives by Linda Pearson with Ruth Purtile (1977). Harper & Row, 10 East 53rd Street, New York, N.Y. 10022 ($7.95).

Suicide: A Study in Sociology by Emile Durkheim, translated by John A. Spaulding and George Simpson (originally published in 1897 as *Le Suicide*). The Free Press, Macmillan Publishing Company, 866 Third Avenue, New York, N.Y. 10022 ($2.95). Sociologist Durkheim's classic work on the three types of suicide dependent on the victim's relationships in the community: egoistic, anomic, and altruistic.

Suicide in Young People by Nancy H. Allen and Michael L. Peck (1976), prepared by the American Association of Suicidology and Merck Sharp & Dohme (free in small quantities; at cost in larger quantities). Write to American Association of Suicidology, Public Relations Office, P.O. Box 1, Gwynedd, Pa. 19436. A concise description of the findings of the interviews and research on youthful suicide by Peck and Litman. Some important findings are noted: 90 percent of the suicidal youths felt that their families did not understand them; nearly one-half were also involved in some form of drug or alcohol abuse shortly before their suicidal deaths.

Suicide in Youth and What You Can Do About It—A Guide for School Personnel, prepared by the Suicide Prevention and Crisis Center of San Mateo County, Calif., and Merck Sharp & Dohme (available at cost in packages of twenty-five student booklets and two teacher booklets, $4.00). Write to American Association of Suicidology, Public Relations Office, P.O. Box 1, Gwynedd, Pa. 19436. Clearly written pamphlet with statistics about the growth in student suicides, a profile of the victims, the danger signs, what to do, and how the teacher may recognize and then get help when there is a serious suicide risk.

Suicide in Youth and What You Can Do About It—A Guide for Students, prepared by the Suicide Prevention and Crisis Center of San Mateo County, Calif., and Merck Sharp & Dohme. Merck & Co., Inc., West Point, Pa. 19486 (free). Five-page well-written pamphlet summarizing what students should know about suicide.

Suicide—It Doesn't Have to Happen by Edwin S. Shneidman, Ph.D., and Philip Mandelkorn, prepared by the American Association of Suicidology with MSD Health Information Services, Merck Sharp & Dohme (free in small quantities, at cost in larger quantities from American Association of Suicidology, Public Relations Office, P.O. Box 1, Gwynedd, Pa. 19436). Informative booklet that explores answers to such questions as "why do people kill themselves," and includes discussions of prevailing attitudes, fables and facts on suicide, and clues to suicide, with a brief list of further references.

Too Young to Die: Youth and Suicide by Francine Klagsbrun (1976). Houghton Mifflin Company, 1 Beacon Street, Boston, Mass. 01207 ($6.95). As part of her research, the author tape recorded interviews with young suicide attempters to try to find out their motivations. This well-written book includes a listing of local suicide prevention centers and an annotated bibliography.

See also the following related chapters in *The Help Book*:

ALCOHOLISM
BATTERED ADULTS
COUNSELING
DRUGS, SMOKING, AND DRUG ABUSE
EMERGENCIES AND DISASTERS
GAMBLING
GUN CONTROL
KIDNAPPING, MISSING PERSONS, AND RUNAWAYS
MENTAL HEALTH
MULTIPURPOSE ORGANIZATIONS
PARENTING
VOLUNTEERISM

48

TRANSPORTATION AND TRAVEL

How America solves its transportation problems should be a key concern to private citizens, environmentalists, businesses, and government officials alike in the next decade. Many seemingly unrelated problems—such as poverty, crime, the elderly, and the handicapped—are prime considerations in transportation or travel policies. When you ponder that almost fifty thousand persons die each year as the result of motor vehicle accidents—and almost 2 million Americans receive disabling injuries—the impact of transportation even in the area of emergencies and disasters becomes apparent.

It is estimated that by 1990 there will be more than 162 million motor vehicles registered in the United States—almost a 50 percent increase from the current number. Some cities, such as Boston, are trying to increase business profits and decrease congestion and air pollution by developing downtown shopping malls that prohibit cars. Other cities, such as New York, are embroiled in controversy over proposed superhighways (Westway) running through the main downtown areas. In 1978, although bikeways had been available in New York City parks and along parkways for twenty-five years, the first Manhattan bikeways were established. One evening at rush hour, as many as 200 bikes an hour were reportedly clocked going by at 54th Street and the Avenue of the Americas. Such steps are small, but they are the beginnings of a movement that has a much longer theoretical history as it tries to reverse the one-house/two car family syndrome that characterized the post-World War II economy.

Decreasing crime is essential to increased tourism, which, in the first half of 1977, was up 7 percent over the previous year. Over eight million Canadians and other foreigners visited this country during that time; more will come as the fears of being mugged or being unfairly "ripped off" by taxi drivers and merchants are diminished. Better public transportation will definitely aid everyone, visitors and residents alike. Politicians are beginning to recognize the benefits of improved mass

A view of the Chicago Loop elevated track, looking north on Wabash Avenue from Jackson Boulevard. *Wide World Photos.*

transportation—accessible to all, including the handicapped—but it is difficult for them to obtain the necessary funds when other community concerns seem more pressing.

But transportation and travel (tourism) are statements to local residents and travelers alike as to the quality of life in a rural, suburban, or urban setting. Inefficient or unsafe vehicles unfairly jeopardize the lives of travelers and foster an unnecessary overdependence on the automobile, long a symbol of power, independence, and economic security. Mass transportation (at $.50 in Philadelphia or New York City, for example) is still one of the best bargains around. But only if it is crime-free, safe, efficient, and pleasant. Those values should be adhered to whether travel is by bicycle, foot, subway, car, rail, boat, or air. Not just conservationists and environmentalists, but all Americans have to get involved in citizen action for transportation concerns.

TRANSPORTATION

Information on local transportation regulations, as well as complaints in this area, should be directed to your county or city department of transportation. There may also be a citizen action group in your community concerned with making improvements in transportation, such as introducing bicycle lanes on roads and highways, eliminating automobile congestion, and developing more efficient buses. For example, since 1973 Transportation Alternatives, Inc., in New York City, has sponsored "bike-ins" to rally for safer cycling conditions. Look in your telephone directory, contact your government information office, or ask a larger citizen action group for referrals.

The following federal agency is concerned with all types of transportation—automobile, rail, air, and urban mass transit:

Office of Public and Consumer Affairs
U.S. Department of Transportation (DOT)
Washington, D.C. 20590

With the goal of developing and maintaining a safe, efficient, and effective national transportation system, the following operating administrations are part of an organizational grouping called DOT: U.S. Coast Guard; Federation Aviation Administration (FAA); Federal Highway Administration (FHWA); Federal Railroad Administration (FRA); National Highway Traffic Safety Administration (NHTSA); and Urban Mass Transportation Administration (UMTA). The Office of Public and Consumer Affairs provides information on all of the above and distributes free pamphlets and brochures. It also welcomes comments on consumer transportation needs for determining federal policies.

LITERATURE: *Consumer Transpotopics* newsletter (free); *Gasoline: More Miles Per Gallon* (free); press releases.

The following national organizations and federal agency provide information on auto transportation (for highway safety, see Chapter 45, Safety*):*

Automobile Association of America (AAA)
Public Information Unit
8111 Gatehouse Road
Falls Church, Va. 22042

Founded in 1902, this federation of 210 automobile clubs has nearly 20 million members with over 960 offices in the United States and Canada. They provide a touring service, emergency aid, and insurance. Auto safety programs are conducted through schools, the police, and other community groups. Extensive publications including textbooks, pamphlets, and films are available. Members and nonmembers may apply for an International Driver's Permit ($3.00) at their local AAA office.

LITERATURE: *AAA Maps and Tour Books*, updated annually (no charge to members); "Safety Belts for People Who Enjoy Living."

National Highway Traffic Safety Administration (NHTSA)
U.S. Department of Transportation
400 Seventh Street, S.W.
Washington, D.C. 20590

Enforces motor-vehicle safety standards and offers educational materials.

(See Chapter 45, *Safety*, for complete listing.)

SPEED LIMIT 55 It's a law we can live with.
U.S. Department of Transportation & The Advertising Council

A SAFE WAY TO FIND OUT HOW MUCH LIQUOR YOU CAN HOLD.

Everybody knows you shouldn't drive when you've had too much to drink. Unfortunately almost nobody knows what too much to drink is.

According to Federal standards, you're legally under the influence of alcohol when you have .10% alcohol in your bloodstream. Which means absolutely nothing to most people.

What does mean something is your weight, your physical condition, the number of drinks you've had and how long it took you to have them.

The combination of these factors can give you a more understandable way of knowing your drinking limit.

That's why we, the makers and sellers of distilled spirits, offer this chart. Use it to help find out whether you're approaching, up to, or past your limit.

It's a lot safer than finding out on the road.

For additional copies of the chart, write: Distilled Spirits Council of U.S. (DISCUS), 1300 Pennsylvania Building, Washington, D.C. 20004

KNOW YOUR LIMITS

CHART FOR RESPONSIBLE PEOPLE WHO MAY SOMETIMES DRIVE AFTER DRINKING!
APPROXIMATE BLOOD ALCOHOL PERCENTAGE

Drinks	Body Weight in Pounds								
	100	120	140	160	180	200	220	240	
1	.04	.03	.03	.02	.02	.02	.02	.02	Influenced Rarely
2	.08	.06	.05	.05	.04	.04	.03	.03	
3	.11	.09	.08	.07	.06	.06	.05	.05	
4	.15	.12	.11	.09	.08	.08	.07	.06	
5	.19	.16	.13	.12	.11	.09	.09	.08	Possibly
6	.23	.19	.16	.14	.13	.11	.10	.09	
7	.26	.22	.19	.16	.15	.13	.12	.11	
8	.30	.25	.21	.19	.17	.15	.14	.13	Definitely
9	.34	.28	.24	.21	.19	.17	.15	.14	
10	.38	.31	.27	.23	.21	.19	.17	.16	

Subtract .01% for each 40 minutes of drinking.
One Drink is 1 oz. of 100 proof liquor or 12 oz. of beer.
THIS CHART IS ONLY A GUIDE—NOT A GUARANTEE.
SUREST POLICY IS...DON'T DRIVE AFTER DRINKING!

Reprinted with permission of the Distilled Spirits Council of the United States.

National Parking Association
1101 Seventeenth Street, N.W.
Washington, D.C. 20036

Trade association representing the interests of the commercial parking industry. *Parking* magazine, *Parking World* newsletter, and NPA government reports are all available by subscription.

LITERATURE: *Better Parking for Your Town*, free pamphlet.

For information and help in aviation and air transportation, contact the following national organizations; the two federal agencies listed regulate air travel and provide information:

Aviation Consumer Action Project (ACAP)
P.O. Box 19029
Washington, D.C. 20036

ACAP is a nonprofit consumer organization advocating the interests of airline passengers before federal regulatory agencies. Consumer information leaflets are provided to airline passengers about their rights and how to register a complaint, either with the offending airline or the Civil Aeronautics Board.

LITERATURE: Free fact sheets, including "If Your Flight Is Delayed or Cancelled, Know Your Rights," "Before Checking Your Baggage—Read This," "Overbooking," and "Save Money on Air Travel—Learn About Discount Fares."

Civil Aeronautics Board
Washington, D.C. 20428

This federal regulatory agency has the following free booklets available by sending a postcard to Consumer Information Center, Pueblo, Colo. 81009: *Consumer Guide to International Air Travel; Consumers' Guide to Air Charts;* and *Air Travelers' Fly-Rights.*

Fearful Flyers
Pan American World Airways, Inc.
30 South Michigan Avenue
Chicago, Ill. 60604

Arranges seminars for a $100.00 fee for people with "fear of flying" problems.

Federal Aviation Administration (FAA)
Community and Consumer Liaison Division
800 Independence Avenue, S.W.
Washington, D.C. 20591

This federal agency is responsible for promoting and regulating aviation safety, developing and operating a national airspace system to ensure the safe and efficient use of U.S. airspace by civil and military aircraft, and protecting the environment from aircraft noise, sonic boom, and emissions. The FAA issues and enforces regulations for the certification of aircraft, air personnel, airports, and air agencies.

LITERATURE: Fact sheets; *A Flying Start; A Guide to FAA Publications* (all free).

For information about transportation by rail, contact the following:

Federal Railroad Administration (FRA)
400 Seventh Street, N.W.
Washington, D.C. 20590

The office of Public Affairs of the FRA provides information relative to program activities and railroad safety concerns. Consumer-oriented complaints are handled through the consumer affairs officer.

LITERATURE: Descriptive brochure.

National Association of Railroad Passengers (NARP)
417 New Jersey Avenue, S.E.
Washington, D.C. 20003

Founded in 1967, NARP works for the improvement and expansion of rail passenger service—long distance, corridor, and commuter.

LITERATURE: Monthly newsletter.

National Railroad Passenger Corporation (Amtrak)
400 North Capitol Street, N.W.
Washington, D.C. 20001

General information on Amtrak, which operates a nationwide system of intercity passenger trains, is available by writing to the Consumer Relations Office at the above address. Travel information (fares, schedules, package tours, group rates, etc.) may be obtained from the Amtrak Travel Center, P.O. Box 311, Addison, Ill. 60101.

The following state agencies for transportation will provide printed information and answer telephone inquiries about transportation regulations, restrictions, and problems (for the state agencies for highway safety, see Chapter 45, Safety).

Transportation Commission
Department of Commerce and Economic Development
MacKay Building
338 Denali Street
Anchorage, Alaska 99501

Department of Transportation
206 South 17th Avenue
Phoenix, Ariz. 85007

Transportation Commission
Department of Commerce
Prospect Building
1501 North University Avenue
Little Rock, Ark. 72203

Department of Transportation
Transportation Building
1120 North Street
Sacramento, Calif. 95814

Department of Transportation
24 Wolcott Hill Road
Wethersfield, Conn. 06109

Delaware Transportation Authority
Department of Transportation
Highway Administration Building
Route 113
P.O. Box 778
Dover, Del. 19901

Department of Transportation
508 Presidential Building
415 12th Street, N.W.
Washington, D.C. 20004

Department of Transportation
605 Suwannee Street
Tallahassee, Fla. 32304

Department of Transportation
2 Capitol Square
Atlanta, Ga. 30334

Department of Transportation
869 Punchbowl Street
Honolulu, Hawaii 96813

Department of Transportation
3311 West State Street
Boise, Idaho 83720

Department of Transportation
DOT Administration Building
Springfield, Ill. 62764

Department of Transportation
Capitol Building
1007 East Grand Avenue
Des Moines, Iowa 50319

Department of Transportation
State Office Building
10th and Topeka Avenue
Topeka, Kans. 66612

Department of Transportation
State Office Building
Frankfort, Ky. 40601

Department of Transportation and
Development
P.O. Box 44245
Baton Rouge, La. 70804

Department of Transportation
State House
Augusta, Me. 04333

Department of Transportation
Baltimore-Washington International Airport
P.O. Box 8755
Baltimore, Md. 21240

Executive Office of Transportation and
Construction
1 Ashburton Place
Boston, Mass. 02108

Department of State Highways and
Transportation
Highways Building
Lansing, Mich. 48909

Department of Transportation
Broadway State Office Building
High Street and Broadway
P.O. Box 1250
Jefferson City, Mo. 65101

Transportation Authority
85 Loudon Road
Concord, N.H. 03301

Department of Transportation
1035 Parkway Avenue
Trenton, N.J. 08625

Department of Motor Transportation
PERA Building
Santa Fe, N.M. 87503

Department of Transportation
State Campus
1220 Washington Avenue
Albany, N.Y. 12232

Department of Transportation
P.O. Box 25201
Raleigh, N.C. 27611

Department of Transportation
25 South Front Street
Columbus, Ohio 43215

Department of Transportation
135 Highway Building
Capitol Mall
Salem, Ore. 97310

Department of Transportation
Transportation and Safety Building
Harrisburg, Pa. 17120

Department of Transportation
State Office Building
101 Smith Street
Providence, R.I. 02903

Department of Highways and Public
Transportation
1100 Senate Street
P.O. Box 191
Columbia, S.C. 29202

Department of Transportation
Transportation Building
Pierre, S.D. 57501

Department of Transportation
Highway Building
6th and Deaderick Streets
Nashville, Tenn. 37219

Department of Highways and Public
Transportation
State Highway Building
11th and Brazos Streets
Austin, Tex. 78701

Department of Transportation
State Office Building
Salt Lake City, Utah 84114

Agency of Transportation
Administration Building
133 State Street
Montpelier, Vt. 05602

Department of Highways and Transportation
1401 East Broad Street
Richmond, Va. 23219

Transportation Division
Utilities and Transportation Commission
Highways-Licensing Building
Mail Stop PB-02
Olympia, Wash. 98504

Department of Transportation
120B, 4802 Sheboygan Avenue
Madison, Wis. 53705

TRAVEL

Your local department of tourism or city tourist office will provide useful information about places to visit, seasonal events to attend, and how to get there. To encourage more tourism—and help revitalize communities—many citizens are volunteering to participate in public relations campaigns for their areas. Contact your local citizen action group to see if such services are offered. One notable local effort is:

Public Citizens Visitors Center
1200 Fifteenth Street, N.W.
Washington, D.C. 20005

Offers personalized tours of Capitol Hill covering congressional committee hearings, the Capitol (including both the House and Senate chambers), and the Supreme Court. The purpose of these tours is to enable people to see their government at work when they come to Washington, instead of just looking at the monuments and buildings. It also acts as a consumer clearinghouse, and its staff directs complaints to the appropriate private and public agencies for help.

LITERATURE: Free leaflets; *Inside the Capitol* ($6.00 a year).

The consumer movement has affected the travel industry. More realistic travel brochures are appearing, as opposed to the previous Polyannaish full-color exaggerated claims. But you still have to carefully evaluate the free descriptive materials that are available from banks; travel agencies; county, city, or state development departments; gas stations; and tourist boards of foreign countries.

The following state agencies for tourism will also provide free brochures and leaflets about places to visit within their boundaries:

Bureau of Publicity and Information
403 State Highway Building
Montgomery, Ala. 36130

Division of Tourism
Department of Commerce and Economic
   Development
State Office Building
Pouch E
Juneau, Alaska 99811

Tourism Advisory Council
1700 West Washington Street
Phoenix, Ariz. 85007

Department of Parks and Tourism
149 State Capitol Building
Little Rock, Ark. 72201

Division of Commerce and Development
Department of Local Government
State Centennial Building
1313 Sherman Street
Denver, Colo. 80203

Tourism Division
Connecticut Department of Commerce
210 Washington Street
Hartford, Conn. 06106

Delaware State Visitors Service
Division of Economic Development
630 State College Road
Dover, Del. 19901

Washington Area Convention and Visitor's Association
1129 Twentieth Street, N.W.
Washington, D.C. 20036

Division of Tourism
Department of Commerce
505 Collins Building
Tallahassee, Fla. 32304

Tourism Division
Department of Community Development
607 Trinity-Washington Building
270 Washington Street, S.W.
P.O. Box 38097
Atlanta, Ga. 30334

Hawaii Visitor's Bureau
P.O. Box 8527
Honolulu, Hawaii 96815

Division of Tourism and Industrial Development
Office of the Governor
108 Statehouse
Boise, Idaho 83720

Division of Tourism
Department of Business and Economic Development
205 West Wacker Drive
Chicago, Ill. 60606

Division of Tourism Development
Department of Commerce
336 State House
Indianapolis, Ind. 46204

Travel Development Division
Iowa Development Commission
250 Jewett Building
914 Grand Avenue
Des Moines, Iowa 50309

Tourism Section
Development Division
Department of Economic Development
503 Kansas Avenue
Topeka, Kans. 66603

Division of Advertising and Travel Promotion
Department of Public Information
Capitol Annex
Frankfort, Ky. 40601

Office of Tourist Development
Department of Recreation and Tourism
P.O. Box 44291
Baton Rouge, La. 70804

State Development Office
State House
Augusta, Me. 04333

Division of Tourist Development
Department of Economic and Community Development
1748 Forest Drive
Annapolis, Md. 21401

Division of Tourism
Department of Commerce and Development
100 Cambridge Street
Boston, Mass. 02202

Travel Bureau
Department of Commerce
Law Building
Lansing, Mich. 48913

Tourism Division
Department of Economic Development
Hanover Building
480 Cedar Street
St. Paul, Minn. 55101

Travel and Tourism Department
Agricultural and Industrial Board
1505 Walter Sillers Building
550 High Street
Jackson, Miss. 39202

Division of Tourism
Department of Consumer Affairs, Regulation, and Licensing
308 East High Street
Jefferson City, Mo. 65101

Historical Society
Department of Education
Veterans-Pioneers Memorial Building
225 North Roberts Street
Helena, Mont. 59601

Division of Travel and Tourism
Department of Economic Development
P.O. Box 94666
Lincoln, Neb. 68509

Department of Economic Development
Capitol Complex
Carson City, Nev. 89710

Division of Economic Development
Department of Resources and Economic
  Development
State House Annex, 3rd Floor
Concord, N.H. 03301

New Jersey Office of Tourism and Promotion
P.O. Box 400
Trenton, N.J. 08625

Tourist Division
Department of Development
113 Washington Avenue
Santa Fe, N.M. 87503

Travel Development Section
Division of Economic Development
Department of Natural and Economic
  Resources
121 West Jones Street
Raleigh, N.C. 27611

Travel Division
Highway Department
Capitol Grounds
Bismarck, N.D. 58505

Office of Travel and Tourism
Economic Development Division
Department of Economic and Community
  Development
P.O. Box 1001
Columbus, Ohio 43216

Tourism Promotion Division
Tourism and Recreation Department
500 Will Rogers Memorial Office Building
Oklahoma City, Okla. 73105

Travel Information Section
101 Transportation Building
Salem, Ore. 97310

Bureau of Travel Development
Department of Commerce
431 South Office Building
Harrisburg, Pa. 17120

Tourist Promotion Division
Department of Economic Development
1 Weybosset Hill
Providence, R.I. 02903

Division of Tourism
Department of Parks, Recreation, and
  Tourism
Room 83, Box 71
Columbia, S.C. 29201

Division of Tourism
Department of Economic and Tourism
  Development
Joe Foss Building
Pierre, S.D. 57501

Tourism Development Division
Department of Economic and Community
  Development
505 Fesslers Lane
Nashville, Tenn. 37219

Tourist Development Agency
Box 12008, Capitol Station
Austin, Tex. 78711

Utah Travel Council
Council Hall, Capitol Hill
Salt Lake City, Utah 84114

Information and Travel Division
Agency of Development and Community
  Affairs
61 Elm Street
Montpelier, Vt. 05602

Virginia State Travel Service
6 North Sixth Street
Richmond, Va. 23219

Travel Development Division
Department of Commerce and Economic
  Development
General Administration Building
Olympia, Wash. 98504

Department of Commerce
1900 Washington Street, East
Charleston, W.Va. 25305

Division of Tourism
Department of Business Development
123 West Washington Avenue
Madison, Wis. 53702

Travel Commission
I-25 at Etchepare Circle
Cheyenne, Wyo. 82002

Division of Tourism
P.O. Box 1692
St. Thomas, V.I. 00801

If you are planning a trip, the following are just some of the thousands of business-run organizations that will help you with free information:

American Adventurers Association
444 N.E. Ravenna Boulevard, Suite 301
Seattle, Wash. 98115

This membership organization ($20.00 to new members; $30.00 for regular membership) includes a year's subscription to *Adventure Travel* magazine, *Adventure Travel Newsletter*, and *The 1978 International Adventure Travelguide*. Through their publications you may learn about the more than 2,000 worldwide organizations that operate more than 3,000 adventure trips each year.

LITERATURE: Send for their descriptive brochure, which lists the nonmembership subscription rates to the above publications.

American Society of Travel Agents (ASTA)
711 Fifth Avenue
New York, N.Y. 10022

Founded in 1931, there are more than 15,000 members and 25 local groups to this national association. Members have been in business at least three years and have met the ASTA's other eligibility requirements. ASTA also sponsors an annual conference.

LITERATURE: *ASTA Travel News*, monthly, membership roster, updated annually; *Astanotes*, bimonthly newsletter; pamphlets and leaflets for the general public.

American Youth Hostels, Inc. (AYH)
National Headquarters and Campus
Delaplane, Va. 22025

There are more than 4,500 low-cost hostels in the forty-nine member countries of the International Youth Hostel Federation of which AYH is a member. Two hundred hostels are in the United States. AYH arranges a variety of group trips by bicycle, land, and hiking, utilizing those hostels for overnight accomodations. Costs are $.90 to $3.50 a night, and each hostel has its own curfews and/or rules. Although few hostels are coed, there are some "family rooms." Membership dues range from junior ($5.00) to senior (over eighteen, $11) or family and life memberships. Membership includes a free listing of hostels.

LITERATURE: *Handbook* ($1.75); fact sheets; lists of trips; application for International Student Identify Card and Eurailpass.

Club Med, Inc.
40 West 57th Street
New York, N.Y. 10019

A resort chain with worldwide "vacation villages." Rates range from about $200 to $400 a week per person, double occupancy; air fares are additional. Write for free brochure.

Farm and Ranch Vacations
36 East 57th Street
New York, N.Y. 10022

Provides a comprehensive listing of vacations in this country at farms that offer a room and all meals for about $80 to $100 a week.

Holiday Exchanges
Box 878
Belen, N.M. 87002

Publishes a directory of pertinent information provided by people who want to exchange apartments or houses in a temporary arrangement. The $5.00 fee for being listed in the directory includes a copy of that issue.

LITERATURE: Descriptive brochure; *Directory* ($15.00); next twelve supplements ($15.00).

National Travel Club
Travel Building
Floral Park, N.Y. 11001

A private membership club ($10.00 a year) organized in 1906. Dues include a subscription to *Travel Holiday* magazine; travel information; a mail forwarding service; discounts on books; and a travel film library.

LITERATURE: Free descriptive brochure.

If you are planning to travel outside the United States, contact the following federal agencies:

Center for Disease Control
U.S. Department of Health, Education, and Welfare
Public Health Service
Atlanta, Ga. 30333

Provides information on necessary immunizations for foreign travel.

LITERATURE: *Health Information for International Travel* booklet, updated periodically.

Passport Office
1425 K Street, NW
Washington, D.C. 20524

Contact your regional office of this federal agency to obtain a passport. Renewals (required every five years) may be done by mail with the proper application form, usually available at the local post office. "A passport is an internationally recognized travel document attesting to the identity and nationality of the bearer and included persons. It indicates that its bearer and included persons are entitled to receive the protection and benefit of the diplomatic and consular offices of their country while abroad. In essence, it is a request on the part of the issuing government that officials of foreign governments permit the bearer and included persons to travel or sojourn in their territories and afford them all lawful aid and protection."

LITERATURE: *You and Your Passport*, booklet available from Superintendent of Documents, U.S. Government Printing Office, Washington, D.C. 20402 ($.45).

U.S. Department of Agriculture
Federal Building
Hyattsville, Md. 20782

For specific information on the entry status of certain foreign foods, plants, or animal materials, write to "Quarantines" at the above address.

The following national organizations provide medical assistance to those traveling far from home (for organizations and guidebooks especially for handicapped travelers, see Chapter 29, Handicapped*):*

Blue Cross Association
840 North Lake Shore Drive
Chicago, Ill. 60611

Publishes *A Foreign Language Guide to Health Care*, a free booklet to assist the traveler in a foreign country with common health-related phrases in German, Spanish, Italian, French, and English. (First check to see if your local Blue Cross office has copies.)

International Association for Medical Assistance to Travelers (IAMAT)
1268 St. Clair Avenue, West
Toronto, Canada M6E 1B9

Assists travelers going overseas by providing referrals to competent English-speaking physicians who charge standard fees. There is no membership fee, but IAMAT is dependent on donations ($10.00).

LITERATURE: Directory; climatic, sanitation, and risk charts for cities all over the world; immunization chart.

Intermedic
777 Third Avenue
New York, N.Y. 10017

A one-year membership ($5.00 individuals; $9.00 family) entitles you to their directory and membership card that will enable you to get medical assistance at preset low fees at any participating doctor in more than 200 foreign countries.

LITERATURE: *Directory of Participating Physicians Including Identification, Personal, Medical, Data;* leaflets.

ADDITIONAL LITERATURE

Consult your local library or bookstore for current travel guides. Some of the most popular include guides by Myra Waldo (Macmillan Publishing Company, Inc.), Fodor Guides (David McKay Publishing Company), Michelin Guides (available in the United States through French and European Publications, Inc.), and guides by Arthur S. Frommer.

Each guidebook for practically every city and country in the world provides a listing and description of places to visit, restaurants, hotels and other accommodations, travel tips, and more. Almost any traveling style—from a shoestring budget to a limitless one—will be served by any of these authors.

If you would rather write your "Having a good time, wish you were here" postcards in advance of your trip, you can buy postcards of most of the major European cities, Cairo, and Jerusalem before you leave. Write to Foreign Cards, Ltd., P.O. Box 2908, New Haven, Conn. 06515. The cost is $4.95 for twenty-five glossy cards; $9.00 for fifty; and $17.00 for one hundred.

Air Travelers' Fly-Rights, 3rd rev. ed. (February 1976). Civil Aeronautics Board, Washington, D.C. 20428 (free). Handy booklet with information on tariffs, fares, flight delays, flight cancellations, reconfirming, baggage, refunds, and charter flights.

Best $ Value Budget Motels and Hotels of America (updated annually). Budget Motels and Hotels of America, Inc., 115 East Hennepin Avenue, Minneapolis, Minn. 55414. A directory of lodging facilities that charge lower rates than other facilities in the same general area for similar accommodations. Many of the listings are part of the toll-free (800) telephone reservation plan, so that you can phone ahead for free. A written reservation form is also provided. Listings include addresses, phone numbers, descriptions of services, and rates.

The Breakdown Book. Shell Oil Company, P.O. Box 61609, Houston, Tex. 77208 (free). Available at a Participating Shell Oil dealer or from the above address. Other free titles in their series include: *The Early Warning Book; The Gasoline Mileage Book; The Car Buying and Selling Book; The 100,000 Mile Book; Rush Hour; The Driving Emergency Book; The Car Repair Shopping Book; Car Crime Prevention; The Car Fix-Up Book;* and *Foul Weather Driving.*

Budget Motels and Hotels of America (updated yearly). BMHA, Box 4203, St. Paul, Minn. 55104 ($1.00). A directory of the more than 1,300 budget motels and hotels that are members of BMHA; rooms are generally priced at $12.00 to $20.00 per night, based on double occupancy.

Common Sense in Buying a New Car, Office of Public Affairs, U.S. Department of Transportation (1978). Send a postcard to Consumer Information Center, Dept. 693F, Pueblo, Colo. 81009 (free). A booklet that points out steps to take before buying a car, such as looking up road tests in consumer or automobile enthusiast magazines.

Consumers' Guide to Air Charters, Civil Aeronautics Board (1977). Send a postcard to Consumer Information Center, Department 625F, Pueblo, Colo. 81009 (free). A booklet explaining basic information about what a charter flight is, who organizes it, and some questions for wise consumers to ask before giving their money to a charter program.

"Customs Hints—Know Before You Go." U.S. Customs Service, P.O. Box 7118, Washington, D.C. 20044 (free).

A Directory of the Leading Hotels of the World. Hotel Representative, Inc., 770 Lexington Avenue, New York, N.Y. 10021 ($1.00).

Hammond 1978 Road Atlas and Vacation Guide. Maplewood, N.J. 07040 ($1.50). In addition to maps, there are checklists for safety, what to take on your trip, preparations before leaving, and a place for emergency telephone numbers and information.

How to Buy Car Insurance (1976). Kemper Insurance Companies, Long Grove, Ill. 60049 (free). A general information booklet on why you need car insurance, what kind of protection to get, no-fault car insurance, and how the cost of insurance is determined.

"How to Fly." Air Transportation Association, 1709 New York Avenue, N.W., Washington, D.C. 20006 (free by sending a stamped, business-size envelope). A booklet geared to first-time flyers about making reservations, taking along children and pets, and other tips.

Leahy's Hotel-Motel Guide and Travel Atlas. American Hotel Registry Company, 226 West Ontario Street, Chicago, Ill. 60610 ($15.00). Lists 45,000 hotels and motels in over 8,600 cities, plus maps of each state, national parks, and more.

National Geographic Magazine, 17 and M Streets, N.W., Washington, D.C. 20036. Published by the National Geographic Society, which also produces excellent films, this magazine is still considered one of the most colorful and well-written travel-type resources in the field.

Naturalization Requirements and General Information, U.S. Department of Justice, Immigration and Naturalization Service (1978). Send a postcard to Consumer Information Center, Department 660F, Pueblo, Colo. 81009 (free). A useful booklet to have for yourself, if you are a recent immigrant, or to have on hand if any visitors are interested in the naturalization requirements.

1001 Sources for Free Travel Information by Jens Jurgen (1978). Travel Information Bureau, P.O. Box 105, Kings Park, N.Y. 11754 ($3.95). A valuable travel information guide that includes all the worldwide government tourist offices and state agencies that usually provide free maps and brochures, and hundreds of travel tips, for example, how you can use the "free stopover" to see the world at a much lower cost. Also available from the same address is Jens Jurgen's *1978 Charter Flight Directory* ($4.95).

Travel and Leisure (monthly). 1350 Avenue of the Americas, New York, N.Y. 10019 Travel magazine with regional editions as well as national articles.

The Travel Catalogue by Karen Cure (1978). Gladstone Books, Holt, Rinehart and Winston, 383 Madison Avenue, New York, N.Y. 10017 ($6.95). A good directory written in a readable style with indispensible listings of companies, published resources, and helpful advice. The author dares to give opinions, making the book even more worthwhile in a field laden with too much "all positive" industry-wide hypes.

Traveler's Guide to Luggage: How to Choose It and Use It. Luggage and Leather Goods Manufacturers of America, Inc., 220 Fifth Avenue, New York, N.Y. 10001 (free by sending a self-addressed, stamped, business-size envelope).

This booklet explains the two types of luggage—softsided and hardsided—and includes checkpoints for quality, how much luggage to take, how to clean it, and how to pack.

Traveler's Tips. U.S. Department of Agriculture, Washington, D.C. 20250 (free pamphlet).

Travel Smart. 40 Beechdale Road, Dobbs Ferry, N.Y. 10522 ($19.00 a year). A newsletter with travel tips that also publishes other travel related information and products, such as Charter Flight Directory ($3.95).

Vagabonding in America: A Guidebook About Energy by Ed Buryn and Stephanie Mines (1973). Random House, Inc., 201 East 50th Street, New York, N.Y. 10022 ($4.95). A comprehensive guide, including where to buy equipment and a bibliography, that is a celebration of life and travel. Includes essays, poetry, and photos on all types of travel within the United States from motorcycling to bicycling to hitchhiking to hiking. Also includes tips on medical matters, from rape and birth control to emergency situations.

The Whole Charter Story by TWA (1977). TWA Charters, P.O. Box 25, Grand Central Station, New York, N.Y. 10017 (free). Explains the six basic types of charters: ABC (Advance Booking Charter); OTC (One Stop Inclusive Tour Charters); ITC (Three Stop Inclusive Tour Charters); Single Entry Charters; Affinity Group Charters; and TGC (Travel Group Charters). A handy chart summarizes the key features of each charter type.

Your Vacation Checklist (1975). Kemper Insurance Companies, Long Grove, Ill. 60049 (free). Handy leaflet asking if you have checked utilities, your car, your insurance needs, and so forth before going away. Includes mileage and expense record, games for children to play, and advice on how to avoid burglaries while away.

See also the following related chapters in *The Help Book:*

AGING
ALCOHOLISM
CHILDREN
CRIME PREVENTION
EMERGENCIES AND DISASTERS
HANDICAPS
SAFETY

49

VETERANS

Five groups can find help in this section on veterans:

- The 44 of every 100 American adult males (and their dependents) who have served in the armed services and are eligible for benefits.
- Those currently enlisted in the army, air force, marines, reserves, National Guard, and navy.
- Those considering a military career.
- Friends and relatives of those still missing in action during recent wars.
- Those draft evaders not covered by President Jimmy Carter's amnesty declaration *or* veterans who wish to upgrade their discharge status.

It has been said that if the 34 million veterans who have served in the armed forces during the past thirty-five years received the benefits they are entitled to, the government would go broke. As it is, the Veterans Administration (VA) is the sixth largest federal agency, with a budget of $18.4 billion a year. The VA medical care services make up the largest health system in the country, with 171 hospitals, 217 outpatient clinics, 86 nursing homes, and 18 residences. Local offices of the VA have information booklets and applications for extensive benefits, for disability, education, health, insurance, employment and death.

The status of the enlisted person (as compared to the officer) has not advanced much, but the benefits remain excellent. Although the enlisted person's salary is not high, there is free medical, dental, and insurance coverage. After enlistment, many former military personnel go back to school or obtain jobs at a higher level than if they had stayed in the private sector.

The three college-level military academies have changed. In the class of 1981, West Point (U.S. Military Academy) has 104 women in its class of 1,961, Annapolis (U.S. Naval Academy) has 90, and the Air Force Academy 124. (The first coeducational classes were in 1976.) In September 1977, the first women to be trained as pilots were graduated from pilot school at Williams Air Force Base in Arizona, although they are not permitted to engage in combat and can only teach.

The greatest changes in the armed forces concern officers. As one captain in the Air Force notes:

> It's become a status position. All officers are required to be college graduates, and since Congress has decreased the number of officers, there's been an increase in talent and capability. Salaries are higher and you can retire after twenty years. A friend of mine who got degrees from MIT and Columbia now wishes he had joined the Armed Services. We're the same age, but he's working in a lumber yard so he can earn a position in the company. But that will take him another five or ten years. We make the same salary, but I have more benefits.

But just as his friend wished he had enlisted, some enlisted men wish they never had and want to get out of the armed services. (Desertion still happens; it is not only a phenomenon of war times.) You can learn about getting *into* the armed services at your local recruiting office, but where do you go to find out about getting out or upgrading your discharge? Various religious and nondenominational groups, such as the American Friends Service Committee and the Central Committee for Conscientious Objectors, offer free counseling and pertinent free or low-cost literature on that subject (see directory listings).

Those who wish to join the armed services should contact the nearest recruiting office of the branch of your choice, or this federal bureau for information:

Selective Service System
National Headquarters
600 E Street, N.W.
Washington, D.C. 20435

On June 30, 1973, Congressional authority for the mandatory draft terminated. This action later resulted in the closing of all local boards.

Voluntary enlistment into the armed forces is now offered, providing a wide range of jobs, salaries, and living situations. A free booklet, *Selective Service Information: Now that the Draft Has Ended* (October 1976) is available. It answers the most frequently asked questions about the Selective Service and joining the U.S. armed forces.

Contact your regional office of this federal bureau for local services; the national headquarters acts as an information clearinghouse:

Veterans Administration (VA)
Information Service
Washington, D.C. 20420

There are 96 million veterans, veteran's dependents, and survivors of deceased veterans (45 percent of the total population of the United States) who are presently or potentially eligible for VA benefits and services. The VA has 196,000 full-time employees—the second largest work force in the federal government and larger than most large corporations; there are more than 3.2 million veterans receiving disability or pension payments including 143 widows and 177 children of veterans of the Civil War. The VA has made more than

326,000 direct home loans valued in excess of $3.2 billion and also operates the largest life insurance program in the world. The National Cemetery System was transferred from the Department of the Army to the VA in September 1973.

Toll-free telephone service to the VA is available to about 90 percent of the nation's total veteran population. There is also G.I. Bill educational assistance and financial assistance to the wounded, disabled, and survivors of honorably discharged veterans.

Alcoholism and Drug Dependence Treatment Centers operate at numerous VA hospitals for free inpatient or outpatient care. Contact your local branch of the VA to find out what benefits you are eligible for and how to apply.

LITERATURE: Free fact sheets; *Federal Benefits for Veterans and Dependents* (January 1977), for sale from the U.S. Government Printing Office, Washington, D.C. 20402 ($.85).

Most cities, counties, and states have a department of veteran affairs. Consult your telephone directory or an information bureau for referrals. The following are the state agencies for veterans' affairs:

Department of Veterans Affairs
State Office Building
501 Dexter Avenue
Montgomery, Ala. 36130

Division of Veterans' Affairs
Department of Commerce and Economic Development
State Office Building
Pouch DA
Juneau, Alaska 99811

Department of Economic Security
1717 West Jefferson
Phoenix, Ariz. 85007

Division of Veterans Services
1227 O Street
Sacramento, Calif. 95814

Division of Veterans Affairs
Department of Social Services
State Social Services Building
1575 Sherman Street
Denver, Colo. 80203

Veterans' Home and Hospital Commission
287 West Street
Rocky Hill, Conn. 06067

Office of Veterans Affairs
Department of Human Resources
941 North Capitol Street, N.E.
Washington, D.C. 20421

Division of Veterans' Affairs
Department of Community Affairs
P.O. Box 1437
St. Petersburg, Fla. 33731

Department of Veterans Services
Veterans Building
Atlanta, Ga. 30334

Veterans Employment Service
P.O. Box 3680
Honolulu, Hawaii 96811

Division of Veterans Affairs
Department of Health and Welfare
320 Collins Road
Boise, Idaho 83707

Illinois Department of Veterans' Affairs
126 West Jefferson Street
Springfield, Ill. 62705

Department of Veterans' Affairs
707 State Office Building
Indianapolis, Ind. 46204

Bonus Board
Department of Public Defense
Capitol Building
1007 East Grand Avenue
Des Moines, Iowa 50319

Veterans' Commission
509 Kansas Avenue
Topeka, Kans. 66603

Kentucky Center for Veterans Affairs
Bureau of Social Services
Department of Human Resources
600 Federal Plaza
Louisville, Ky. 40202

Department of Veterans Affairs
Old State Capitol
Baton Rouge, La. 70801

Bureau of Veterans Services
Department of Defense and Veterans Services
Camp Keyes
Augusta, Me. 04333

Veterans Commission
113 Federal Office Building
31 Hopkins Plaza
Baltimore, Md. 21201

Veterans' Affairs Office
31 St. James Avenue
Boston, Mass. 02116

Veterans Trust Fund
Department of Management and Budget
300 East Michigan
Lansing, Mich. 48909

Department of Veterans Affairs
State Veterans Service Building
St. Paul, Minn. 55155

Veterans' Affairs Commission
637 North President Street
Jackson, Miss. 39201

Division of Veterans' Affairs
Department of Social Services
Broadway State Office Building
Second Floor
Jefferson City, Miss. 65101

Veterans' Affairs Division
Department of Social and Rehabilitation
  Services
SRS Building
111 Sandus
Helena, Mont. 59601

Department of Veterans' Affairs
301 Centennial Mall South
Lincoln, Neb. 68509

Office of the Commissioner of Veterans' Affairs
1201 Terminal Way
Reno, Nev. 85902

Veterans' Council
18 North Main Street
Council, N.H. 03301

Division of Veterans Programs and Special
  Services
Department of Human Services
240 West State Street
Trenton, N.J. 08625

Veterans Service Bureau
Human Services Department
440 St. Michael's Drive
Santa Fe, N.M. 87503

Division of Veterans' Affairs
Agency Building No. 2
Empire State Plaza
Albany, N.Y. 12223

Division of Veterans Affairs
Department of Military and Veterans Affairs
227 East Edenton Street
Raleigh, N.C. 27601

Department of Veterans' Affairs
1017 4th Avenue, North
Fargo, N.D. 58102

Soldiers' Claim Division
Adjutant General's Department
2825 West Granville Road
Worthington, Ohio 43085

Department of Veterans Affairs
Wiley Post Historical Building
2100 North Lincoln Boulevard
Oklahoma City, Okla. 73105

Department of Veterans' Affairs
200 General Services Building
1225 Ferry Street, S.E.
Salem, Ore. 97310

Veterans Affairs and Assistance
Department of Military Affairs
Indiantown Gap Military Reservation
Annville, Pa. 17003

Veterans' Affairs
Division of Community Services
Department of Social and Rehabilitative Services
46 Aborn Street
Providence, R.I. 02903

Department of Veterans' Affairs
227 Edgar Brown Building
1205 Pendleton Street
Columbia, S.C. 29201

Division of Veterans Affairs
Department of Military and Veterans Affairs
Capitol Building
Pierre, S.D. 57501

Department of Veterans Affairs
215 Eighth Avenue, North
Nashville, Tenn. 37203

Veterans Affairs Committee
321 Sam Houston State Office Building
201 East 14th Street
Austin, Tex. 78711

Office of Veterans Affairs
Department of Social Services
231 East 4th South Street
Salt Lake City, Utah 84111

Veterans' Administration Office
North Hartland Road
White River Junction, Vt. 05001

Division of War Veterans' Claims
Department of Law
210 Franklin Road, S.W.
Roanoke, Va. 24011

Department of Veterans Affairs
P.O. Box 9778
Olympia, Wash. 98504

Department of Veterans Affairs
612 Atlas Building
Charleston, W.Va. 25301

Department of Veteran's Affairs
77 North Dickinson
Madison, Wis. 53703

Veterans Affairs Commission
522 West Pershing Boulevard
Cheyenne, Wyo. 82001

The following national organizations provide services for veterans and their families:

Air Force Aid Society (AFAS)
National Headquarters
1117 North 19th Street, Suite 700
Arlington, Va. 22209

AFAS provides help for anyone serving active duty, or retired from active duty, in the U.S. Air Force. It also provides emergency cash funds when such situations arise, such as expenses incidental to emergency leaves, funeral costs, basic maintenance because of nonreceipt of pay, loans for travel, and life insurance payments. There is a January 31 filing deadline for education fund loans for the following fall school year, which is open to vocational training or college for dependents of air force employees. Membership and contributions are accepted.

LITERATURE: Free descriptive leaflet; *Vocational Training and College Loans*, brochure.

The American Legion
P.O. Box 1055
Indianapolis, Ind. 46206

Founded in 1919, there are more than 2.5 million members to this national veterans organization. Their efforts are community service-based with participation in children and youth programs as well as a "long opposition to communist activity." A "Jobs for Veterans" program is available to aid veterans in finding suitable employment.

LITERATURE: Fact sheet; *Need a Lift* ($.50).

Department of the Army Education Services
Army Educational Relief
HQDA (DAAG-EDD)
Washington, D.C. 20314

Provides information on available scholarship to army personnel and their dependents.

LITERATURE: Free educational scholarship pamphlet DAPAM 352-2, *Educational Scholarship Guide for Vietnam, POW/MIA Dependents;* and fact sheets.

Disabled American Veterans (DAV)
3725 Alexandria Pike
Cold Spring, Ky. 41076

(See complete listing in Chapter 29, *Handicaps.*)

Paralyzed Veterans of America (PVA)
4330 East-West Highway
Washington, D.C. 20014

(See complete listing in Chapter 29, *Handicaps.*)

Retired Officers Association
1625 Eye Street, N.W.
Washington, D.C. 20006

Founded in 1929, there are now more than 245,000 members and 300 local chapters comprised of veterans of the army, navy, air force, Marine Corps, Coast Guard, National Oceanic and Atmospheric Administration, and the Public Health Service; widows may become auxiliary members. The association lobbies on Capitol Hill for the retiree's benefits and provides the following: free employment assistance program (TOPS) to begin a second career; an information center on retiree benefits; emergency, ninety-day, interest-free loans when certain types of checks have been lost in the mail; low-cost travel programs; financial assistance for dependents under the United Student Aid Funds; biennial conventions; auto lease-purchase and automobile maintenance plan; car rental discounts; and numerous insurance plans. Membership is $10.00 a year (plus $1.00 entrance fee); auxiliary members, $4.00.

LITERATURE: Numerous free descriptive leaflets; *Our Baker's Dozen; Find Your Niche: A Practical Guide for Career Changers; Help Your Widow While She's Still Your Wife!; Roster of TROA Affiliates; The Retired Officer Magazine* (free to members, $6.00 a year to others).

Veterans Information Clearinghouse
American Association of State Colleges and Universities (AASCU)
One Dupont Circle, Suite 700
Washington, D.C. 20036

Provides information on institutions offering technical assistance to administrators and counselors trying to accommodate veteran students.

LITERATURE: *Servicemen's Opportunity College Catalog* (free).

The following national organizations are concerned with the status of conscientious objectors and/or universal amnesty:

American Friends Service Committee (AFSC)
1501 Cherry Street
Philadelphia, Pa. 19102

A national organization founded in 1917 with ten regional groups dedicated to peace education through public awareness and service projects. In some areas, there are summer volunteer programs for young people.

LITERATURE: *Quaker Service Bulletin,* three issues a year ($5.00 a year); annual reports; booklets and pamphlets.

Central Committee for Conscientious Objectors (CCCO)
National Headquarters
2016 Walnut Street
Philadelphia, Pa. 19103

Regional Offices:

CCCO Western Region
1251 Second Avenue
San Francisco, Calif. 94122

848 Peachtree Street N.E.
Atlanta, Ga. 30308

1764 Gilpin Street
Denver, Colo. 80218

Founded in 1948, this nongovernment, nonprofit organization provides information on military law, discharges, the draft and conscription, and counsels people in trouble in the military and provides factual information that is useful to counter recruitment efforts. They also train attorneys and counselors in military casework and do legal research in these areas. Extensive publications are given away or sold at cost. CCCO has a speakers bureau for public education. There are no membership dues, but contributions are welcomed.

LITERATURE: *Network News*, ten issues a year (free); *Those Who Say No: Chaplain's Guide to Conscientious Objectors* ($1.75); *Military Counselors Manual* ($10.00); *Military Counselors Directory*, 11th edition ($1.50).

Fellowship of Reconciliation (FOR)
P.O. Box 271
Nyack, N.Y. 10960

Founded in 1915, there are 200 local groups to this national educational project in nonviolence and peace. FOR maintains a 5,000-volume library on related subjects and sponsors an annual meeting.

LITERATURE: *Fellowship*, monthly; *Action* newsletter; pamphlets; booklets.

National Council for Universal Amnesty
339 Lafayette Street
New York, N.Y. 10012

The council is working for universal unconditional amnesty for all Vietnam era veterans with less-than-honorable discharges and all civilians who resisted the war (direct or indirect resistance). It is an informal network, rather than local chapters, and is funded by various religious organizations. The council also sponsors United Amnesty Action Week; reports on pertinent legislation; and has begun work in counter-recruitment, veterans issues, and GI organizing.

LITERATURE: Free descriptive leaflets; fact sheets; *Amnesty Update*, bimonthly magazine.

National Interreligious Service Board for Conscientious Objectors (NISBCO)
550 Washington Building
15th and New York Avenue, N.W.
Washington, D.C. 20005

A national organization founded in 1940 that provides professional counseling and printed literature for anyone interested in conscientious objectors—individual objectors, organizations, and churches. It has a referral service and speakers bureau and holds an annual meeting.

LITERATURE: *Words of Conscience: Religious Statements on Conscientious Objection*, 8th edition ($1.00).

War Resisters League
339 Lafayette Street
New York, N.Y. 10012

Founded in 1923, the league is an advocacy organization working toward the resolution of conflict through nonviolent means. It also has a conscientious objector counseling committee.

LITERATURE: *WIN Magazine*, weekly; *News*, bimonthly; annual desk calendar.

The following national and international organizations provide information and direct help in finding or assisting prisoners of wars:

Amnesty International USA
2112 Broadway
New York, N.Y. 10023

An organization with 50,000 supporters that has gained the release of 8,000 political prisoners around the world. It was the recipient of the Nobel Peace Prize in 1977 and is using the $145,000 prize money to help the estimated 100,000 people who are currently illegally imprisoned.

LITERATURE: Free brochures on various countries; Amnesty International Annual Report, updated yearly and available each November ($3.00).

National League of Families of American Prisoners and Missing in Southeast Asia
1608 K Street, N.W.
Washington, D.C. 20006

Organization founded by relatives of men taken prisoner and missing in Southeast Asia that is dedicated to obtaining the fullest possible accounting of prisoners of war and those missing in action from the Vietnam conflict.

The following lists of National Military Organizations, VA Recognized National Service Organizations, and Other National Service Organizations are reprinted with permission from Uniform Services Almanac (1977):

NATIONAL MILITARY ORGANIZATIONS

Association of the Army
1529 Eighteenth Street, N.W.
Washington, D.C. 20036

Air Force Association
1750 Pennsylvania Avenue, N.W.
Washington, D.C. 20006

Air Force Sergeants Association
P.O. Box 31050
Washington, D.C. 20031

Coast Guard Chief Petty Officers Association
927 South Walter Reed Drive, Suite 16
Arlington, Va. 22204

Coast Guard Enlisted Association
CG HQs
400 Seventh Street, S.W.
Washington, D.C. 20590

Fleet Reserve Association
1303 New Hampshire Avenue, N.W.
Washington, D.C. 20036

Marine Corps Association
P.O. Box 1775, MCB
Quantico, Va. 22134

Marine Corps Reserve Officers Association
888 Seventeenth Street, N.W.
Washington, D.C. 20006

National Association for Uniformed Services
956 North Monroe Street
Arlington, Va. 22201

National Guard Association of the U.S.
1 Massachusetts Avenue, N.W.
Washington, D.C. 20001

Naval Reserve Association
910 Seventeenth Street, N.W., Suite 817
Washington, D.C. 20006

Naval Enlisted Reserve Association
6703 Farragut Avenue
Falls Church, Va. 22042

Navy League of U.S.
818 Eighteenth Street, N.W.
Washington, D.C. 20006

Non-Commissioned Officers Association of USA
P.O. Box 2268
San Antonio, Tex. 78298

Reserve Officers Association
1 Constitution Avenue, N.E.
Washington, D.C. 20002

Society of the American Military Engineers
740 Fifteenth Street, N.W.
Washington, D.C. 20005

Retired Officers Association
1625 Eye Street, N.W.
Washington, D.C. 20006

U.S. Army Warrant Officers Association
P.O. Box 2040
Reston, Va. 22090

Chief Warrant Officers Association, USCG
955 L'Enfant Plaza N., S.W.
Washington, D.C. 20024

VA-RECOGNIZED NATIONAL SERVICE ORGANIZATIONS

American Legion
1608 K Street, N.W.
Washington, D.C. 20006

American Veterans (AMVETS)
1710 Rhode Island Avenue, N.W.
Washington, D.C. 20036

Catholic War Veterans of U.S.
2 Massachusetts Avenue, N.W.
Washington, D.C. 20001

Disabled American Veterans
807 Maine Street, S.W.
Washington, D.C. 20024

Disabled Officers Association
1612 K Street, N.W.
Washington, D.C. 20006

Jewish War Veterans of the United States
1712 New Hampshire Avenue
Washington, D.C.

The Marine Corps League
933 North Kenmore Street
Arlington, Va. 22201

Military Order of the World Wars
1100 Seventeenth Street, N.W.
Washington, D.C. 20036

Paralyzed Veterans of America, Inc.
7315 Wisconsin Avenue
Washington, D.C. 20014

Veterans of Foreign Wars
200 Maryland Avenue, N.E.
Washington, D.C. 20002

OTHER NATIONAL SERVICE ORGANIZATIONS

American Ex-Prisoners of War, Inc.
2620 North Dundee Street
Tampa, Fla. 33609

American Military Retirees Association, Inc.
P.O. Box 973
Saranac Lake, N.Y. 12983

Armed Forces Benefit and Aid Association
P.O. Box 2272
San Diego, Calif. 92112

Army Distaff Foundation, Inc.
6200 Oregon Avenue, N.W.
Washington, D.C. 20015

Commissioned Officers Association of the U.S.
Public Health Service
1750 Pennsylvania Avenue, N.W.
Washington, D.C. 20006

National Military Wives Association, Inc.
4405 East-West Highway, Suite 401
Washington, D.C. 20014

National Association of Concerned Veterans
1900 L Street, N.W., Suite 14
Washington, D.C. 20036

Naval Order of the U.S.
307 North Michigan Avenue, Room 2200
Chicago, Ill. 60611

Retired Armed Forces Association (RAFA)
P.O. Box 605
New London, Conn. 06320

Society of Military Widows
P.O. Box 254
Coronado, Calif. 92118

ADDITIONAL LITERATURE

Born on the Fourth of July by Ron Kovic (1977). Pocket Books, 1230 Avenue of the Americas, New York, N.Y. 10020 ($1.95). The autobiography of a man who wanted to be a war hero, like Audie Murphy in *To Hell and Back*, enlisted in the Marine Corps after high school in 1964, returned from Vietnam paralyzed for life, and became an antiwar veteran and activist.

The Causes of War by Geoffrey Blainey (1973). The Free Press, Macmillan Publishing Company, Inc., 866 Third Avenue, New York, N.Y. 10022 ($3.95). Blainey's thesis is that instead of analyzing why there have been wars, the less prevalent periods of peace should be studied.

Educational Scholarship Guide for Vietnam POW/MIA Dependents. U.S. Department of the Army, Adjutant General. For sale from the Superintendent of Documents, U.S. Government Printing Office, Washington, D.C. 20402. A booklet that describes what scholarships, grants, and other educational benefits are offered through private, state, and federal programs.

Federal Benefits for Veterans and Dependents. Consumer Information Center, Pueblo, Colo. 81009 (Item no. 844, $.85). This booklet summarizes benefits that are available for veterans and their dependents or beneficiaries. The VA regional offices are also listed.

Friendly Fire by C. D. Bryan (1977). Bantam Books, Inc., 666 Fifth Avenue, New York, N.Y. 10019 ($2.75). The best-selling nonfiction account of a journalist's search of the wartime fate of one dead GI and his family.

The Naked and the Dead by Norman Mailer (1948, 1971). New American Library, 1301 Avenue of the Americas, New York, N.Y. 10019 ($1.75).

National Guard Almanac, edited by Lt. Col. Sol Gordon and Capt. Clint Tennill, Jr. (1977). P.O. Box 76, Dept. G, Washington, D.C. 20044 ($2.90). Informational guide for members of the army and Air National Guard.

On Violence by Hannah Arendt (1970). Harcourt Brace Jovanovich, 757 Third Avenue, New York, N.Y. 10017 ($2.45). A provocative essay on the causes—and consequences—of violence.

Reserve Forces Almanac, 3rd edition, edited by Lt. Col. Sol Gordon (1977). P.O. Box 76, Dept. R, Washington, D.C. 20044 ($2.00). Prepared for members of the army, navy, air force, Marine Corps, and Coast Guard Reserves, this manual provides information on benefits, drill pay, tax highlights, and reserve components.

The Rights of Military Personnel by Robert S. Rivkin and Barton F. Stichman (1977). Avon Books, 959 Eighth Avenue, New York, N.Y. 10019 ($1.50). Useful handbook of the American Civil Liberties Union series.

Uniform Services Almanac, Inc., compiled and edited by Lee E. Sharff (updated edition available each January). P.O. Box 76, Dept. A., Washington, D.C. 20044 ($2.00). Comprehensive guide for members of the armed forces and their dependents that includes types of payments, retirement, federal income taxes, health benefits program, social security, VA benefits, reserve forces, legal holidays, and selected legislation of interest to military personnel.

Up Your Discharge: A Guide to Discharge Upgrading (October 1975). CCCO Western Region, 1251 Second Avenue, San Francisco, Calif. 94122 ($.25). Excellent booklet on preparing the DRB application and how to submit it.

See also the following related chapters in *The Help Book:*

AGING
BUSINESS INFORMATION
DRUGS, SMOKING, AND DRUG ABUSE
EDUCATION
FINANCIAL ASSISTANCE
HANDICAPS

HEALTH
HOUSING
LEGAL SERVICES
MENTAL HEALTH
MULTIPURPOSE ORGANIZATIONS

50

VOLUNTEERISM

Practically every category in this book—from adoption to veterans—has organizations with active local volunteer programs. What determines the quality of a volunteer program? First and foremost, if the organization or agency is well staffed and adequately conceived or structured, the volunteer program has something to build on. If the basic program is worth contributing to—such as the Peace Corps, the retired business person programs run by the Small Business Administration, the Association of Junior Leagues, the Salvation Army, or the American National Red Cross—volunteer efforts will be valued by the organization as well as a profitable experience for the worker.

Secondly, there must be a thorough and informative training program. This author participated in a comprehensive program run by OAR/NY (Offender-Aid-and-Restoration in New York). It included outside speakers who were experts in corrections and the criminal justice system, role playing, reading assignments, handouts of vital information, and films—in weekend fourteen-hour sessions during a one-month period. Volunteer paraprofessional counseling with juveniles awaiting trial in the city jails at Rikers Island included follow-up supervision. Many volunteers dropped out of the program even before their active counseling began because the training program was too demanding for them. Soon more volunteers became inactive because they could not make a consistent commitment to the juveniles. The volunteer "dropout" is a common problem; many volunteers forget that the first obligation must always be to the client, victim, patient, or person needing help and not to the volunteer worker's "convenience."

The third ingredient for a successful volunteer program, therefore, is continual reevaluation and retraining for the staff, both volunteer and professional. A volunteer should aim to make a contribution equal in quality to the professional's, if the program and the people it helps are to benefit.

If you want to get involved in volunteering, contact any local affiliate or separate agency of a community-based organization that delivers services in your area of interest. (Throughout *The Help Book*, thousands of such organizations are listed. Write or call the director or coordinator of volunteer services.) Or you might wish to become involved in donating your time in a county- or city-based agency, such as the executive volunteer corps. In that case, contact the volunteer office of your county or municipal government. Most states also have a Department of Volunteer Services; look in your telephone directory.

The following are some of national voluntary programs with local, direct service affiliates:

American National Red Cross
17th and D Streets, N.W.
Washington, D.C. 20006

Volunteers are used in a variety of settings, such as courts and probation programs.

(See complete listing in Chapter 40, *Multipurpose Organizations*.)

Association of Junior Leagues, Inc. (AJL)
825 Third Avenue
New York, N.Y. 10022

Area offices: 58 Sutter Street, Suite 640-650
San Francisco, Calif. 94104

1666 Connecticut Avenue, N.W.
Washington, D.C. 20009

3445 Peachtree Road, N.E., Suite 890
Atlanta, Ga. 30326

300 West Washington Street
Chicago, Ill. 60606

600 Lexington Avenue
New York, N.Y. 10022

3626 North Hall, Suite 407
Dallas, Tex. 75219

AJL is the national headquarters serving in an advisory capacity to 235 member leagues in the United States and Canada, and in Mexico City. Through the local Junior Leagues, volunteers serve in a variety of capacities—from planning, research, implementation, and direct service to evaluation—and in a wide range of areas, including health, child advocacy, and criminal justice.

LITERATURE: Free descriptive brochures on AJL and on specific association-wide programs, such as Impact, child advocacy and volunteer career development, are available from the headquarter's Information Center.

League of Women Voters of the United States
1730 M Street, N.W.
Washington, D.C. 20036

Volunteer work is available in such areas as crime prevention and environmental affairs.

(See complete listing in Chapter 43, *Political Action*.)

Literacy Volunteers of America (LVA)
700 East Water Street
Syracuse, N.Y. 13210

A nonprofit agency with twenty-nine chapters of volunteers working in thirteen states to find nonreaders and help them to read. LVA tutors go through an intensive training course. Programs are coordinated through local adult education programs, and many companies donate office space.

National Center for Voluntary Action (NCVA)
1214 Sixteenth Street, N.W.
Washington, D.C. 20036

Founded in 1970 to stimulate and strengthen voluntary action, this private, nonprofit organization provides technical assistance and training services to volunteer leaders in all areas of the voluntary sector. There are 300 local Voluntary Action Centers affiliated with NCVA which serve to expand both the quality and quantity of individual volunteer involvement in community problem-solving activities.

LITERATURE: *Voluntary Action Leadership*, quarterly ($8.00 a year); publications brochure.

National Council of Negro Women (NCNW)
1346 Connecticut Avenue, N.W.
Washington, D.C. 20036

Founded in 1935, there are more than 4 million members to this national organization with more than 167 local groups. In addition to twenty-five national organizations, interested citizens are part of its membership. NCNW acts as an information clearinghouse for and about black women and sponsors a biennial convention.

The Salvation Army
120 West 14th Street
New York, N.Y. 10011

(See complete listing in Chapter 40, *Multipurpose Organizations*.)

VIP Division
National Council on Crime and Delinquency
200 Washington Square Plaza
Royal Oak, Mich. 48067

A membership volunteer program for citizens that arranges local one-to-one direct help in crime prevention, prosecution, probation, prison, and parole. Yearly dues of $3.00 includes a subscription to the *VIP Examiner*.

Volunteers of America
National Headquarters
340 West 85th Street
New York, N.Y. 10024

Founded in 1896, there are now more than 750 local service centers in major cities throughout the United States. Volunteers help handicapped workers, homeless men, prisoners and their families, alcoholics, and the aged by assisting in telephone reassurance, school clothing programs, emergency shelters, summer camps, counseling, day care, and rehabilitation and nutrition programs.

LITERATURE: Free descriptive brochure; *The Volunteer* ($.35 a copy).

Women in Community Service (WICS)
1730 Rhode Island Avenue, N.W., Suite 400
Washington, D.C. 20036

A coalition of five organizations—Church Women United, the National Council of Catholic Women, the National Council of Jewish Women, the National Council of Negro Women, and American GI Forum Women—that screens and assists men and women aged sixteen to twenty-one who are out of school, have no job or skill, and wish to enter the National Job Corps.

LITERATURE: *American Issues Forum; This Is WICS; The WICS Friend Who Helped Job Corps Change My Life*.

(For a listing of youth-oriented volunteer-run programs, such as the Girl Scouts of America or the Big Brothers/Big Sisters International, see Chapter 10, *Children*.)

The following federal agency coordinates government programs that rely upon volunteers:

ACTION
Washington, D.C. 20525
Toll-free number

This is the U.S. government volunteer programs headquarters, with service centers in New York, Washington, Dallas, Chicago, and

San Francisco and other offices in major cities. ACTION coordinates the following federal volunteer programs.

Peace Corps: An international program that sends qualified volunteers for a two-year service period to underdeveloped countries that require technical assistance.

VISTA (Volunteers in Service to America): VISTA volunteers work to alleviate poverty in the United States. Volunteers are assigned for one- and two-year terms to assist people in need in locally sponsored projects at the request of public or private nonprofit organizations.

ACV (ACTION Cooperative Volunteers): The ACV program enables nonprofit public and private community agencies to sponsor full-time volunteers for one year; ACTION shares the cost of their services.

University Year for Action (UYA): UYA enables college students to serve off-campus for a year in low-income communities while they receive academic credit. UYA has made grants to fifty-seven colleges and universities.

Program for Local Service (PLS): PLS provides full-time volunteers the opportunity to serve within their own communities for one year, working with individual sponsors on mutually agreed-upon antipoverty projects.

RSVP (Retired Senior Volunteer Program): RSVP uses the talents of volunteers sixty years of age and over in their communities.

Foster Grandparent Program: Low-income volunteers sixty years of age and over offer friendship to children in hospitals and other institutions.

Senior Companion Program: Sixty-and-over low-income volunteers serve older persons who have special needs.

LITERATURE: Free booklet describing each program as well as the qualifications for new volunteers.

The following national organization provides information on volunteerism:

National Information Center on Volunteerism (NICOV)
P.O. Box 4179
Boulder, Colo. 80306

An independent, nonprofit organization established in 1966 to provide training, assessment, evaluation, information, and consultation to the leadership of volunteer programs in all human service areas. NICOV has extensive library and research facilities, including over 100,000 documents on volunteerism. NICOV conducts workshops and an educational program developed through a grant from the W. K. Kellogg Foundation, which by 1980 will be utilized by about 150 high schools. NICOV also offers for sale a wide range of publications written and published by a diversity of voluntary and business concerns in all fields of volunteerism, conducts literary searches, and offers Quick Reference Sheets (QRS) to answer basic questions regarding volunteer program management for beginners in the field. Service plans are available that range from $25.00 to $500.00 a year in price.

LITERATURE: Free fact sheets; *A Basic Bookshelf* (a publications catalog); information on NICOV services.

The membership of the following national organizations are mainly the volunteer agencies themselves, but concerned citizens may find their publications useful:

Alliance for Volunteerism
1214 Sixteenth Street, N.W.
Washington, D.C. 20036

Twenty-one major volunteer organizations are members of this coalition. It has these task forces: advocacy, central information service, corporate volunteerism, education and training, minority involvement, distribution center, religious involvement, research, standards, guidelines, accreditation and model development, technical assistance, and women and citizen participation. Their members, who represent over 5000 local units with ties to volunteer bureaus in about 300 American cities, included such organizations as: Association for Administration of Volunteer Services, Association of Junior Leagues, Association of Voluntary Action Scholars, Association of Volunteer Bureaus, Call For Action, Church Women United, Involvement, Inc., National Black United Fund, National Center for Voluntary Action, National Council of Negro Women, and National Information Center on Volunteerism.

LITERATURE: *The Alliance Newsletter.*

National Assembly of National Voluntary and Social Welfare Organizations, Inc.
345 East 46th Street
New York, N.Y. 10017

Founded in 1922, this is the umbrella organization for thirty-six member groups; other interested persons may join in their "colleagues" program. It sponsors a yearly meeting and publishes educational materials on volunteerism.

MEMBER AGENCIES OF THE NATIONAL ASSEMBLY

AFL-CIO, Department of Community Services
American Council for Nationalities Service
American Foundation for the Blind
American National Red Cross
Association of Junior Leagues
Boys' Clubs of America
Boy Scouts of America
Camp Fire Girls
Child Welfare League of America
Council of Jewish Federations and Welfare Funds
Family Service Association of America
Girl Scouts of the U.S.A.
Girls Clubs of America
Goodwill Industries of America
International Social Service of America
JWB (Jewish Welfare Board)
Lutheran Council in the U.S.A.
Mental Health Association
National Association for Retarded Citizens
National Conference of Catholic Charities
National Council for Homemaker-Home Health Aide Services
National Council of the Churches of Christ in the U.S.A.
National Council of Jewish Women
National Council of Negro Women
National Council on Crime and Delinquency

National Federation of Settlements and Neighborhood Centers
National Urban League
Salvation Army
Travelers Aid Association of America
United Seamen's Service
United Service Organizations
U.S. Catholic Conference
United Way of America
Volunteers of America
Y.M.C.A.'s of the U.S.A.
Y.W.C.A. of the U.S.A.

LITERATURE: Descriptive brochure with roster of member organizations; *The National Assembly News; Service Directory of National Voluntary Organizations* ($5.00; see Additional Literature).

ADDITIONAL LITERATURE

Children Are for Loving: Volunteer Involvement In the Treatment and Prevention of Child Abuse and Neglect by Isolde Chapin (1978). National Center for Voluntary Action, 1214 Sixteenth Street, N.W., Washington, D.C. 20036 ($2.95). This booklet describes programs that are available to help the abusing parent, such as SCAN, Child Protection Project, and multiple services, such as CARE, self-help groups, crisis lines, temporary homes, and therapeutic day care. Program addresses, resource groups, and additional publications are also listed for the would-be volunteer to contact.

"The Day the Volunteers Didn't," by Benjamin De Mott in *Psychology Today* (March 1978), pages 23–24, 131–132. De Mott, an English professor at Amherst College, makes a plea for the rejuvenation of American volunteerism.

Exploring Careers Through Volunteerism by Charlotte Lobb (1976). Rosen Press, 29 East 21st Street, New York, N.Y. 10010 ($4.80).

Library Journal Special Report #1: Volunteers in Library Work by Elizabeth Bole Eddison and Alice Sizer Warner (1977). R. R. Bowker Company, 1180 Avenue of the Americas, New York, N.Y. 10036 ($3.95 prepaid). Why and how to use volunteers in public school, museum, and prison libraries.

Monitoring Title IX: A Guide for the Volunteer Organization (January 1977). American Association of University Women, 2401 Virginia Avenue, N.W., Washington, D.C. 20037 ($1.50).

The New Volunteerism: A Community Connection by Barbara Feinstein and Catherine Cavanaugh (1976). Schenkman Publishing Company, Inc., 3 Mt. Auburn Place, Harvard Square, Cambridge, Mass. 02138 ($8.95). Included are chapters on paraprofessional group leaders, the new volunteerism, and a case aide handbook.

Peer Counseling Training Manual by Ned Strauss, Mimi Goldsmith, and Pat Fontaine (1976). Youth Service Board of Crittendon County, 94 Church Street, Burlington, Vt. 05401 (free with self-addressed, stamped envelope). Manual designed for twelve training sessions to help evolve in-school peer counseling by and for teenagers with an emphasis on human sexuality, career planning, and drug and alcohol concerns.

People Approach: Nine New Strategies for Citizen Volunteer Involvement by Ivan H. Scheier, Ph.D. (1977). National Information Center on Volunteerism, P.O. Box 4179, Boulder, Colo. 80306 ($5.55). This 116-page typescript spiral-bound publication describes the three years of model development at the National Information Center on Volunteerism that led to Scheier's nine-point strategy. Those strategies are: NOAH-II, MINIMAX-II, CO-MINIMAX, Self-Help and Helping (SHAH), Perceptual Recruiting, Community Linkage Process; Resources/Need; and People Approach in Volunteer Program Assessment. Two other people approach strategies that are in the process of development are also described.

The Place of Volunteerism in the Lives of Women by Arlene Kaplan Daniels. The Program on Women, Northwestern University, 619 Emerson Street, Evanston, Ill. 60201 ($2.50). An analysis of types of volunteer experiences.

"Public Affairs: The Rise and Fall of Voluntary Associations" by Amitai Etzioni in *Human Behavior* (June 1977), page 12.

Service Directory of National Voluntary Organizations (1978). The National Assembly of National Voluntary Health and Social Welfare Organizations, Inc., 345 East 46th Street, New York, N.Y. 10017 ($5.00). Annotated listings about the purpose, programs, services, and organizational structure of eighty national voluntary organizations in the health and social welfare field.

Serving Youth as Volunteers by Ivan H. Scheier, Ph.D., and Judith Lake Berry (February 1972). National Information Center on Volunteerism, Inc., P.O. Box 4179, Boulder, Colo. 80302. Excellent general volunteerism information as well as pertinent youth-oriented advice.

Voluntary Action Leadership (quarterly). National Center for Voluntary Action, 1214 16th Street, N.W., Washington, D.C. 20036 ($8.00 a year). Magazine with book reviews, a calendar of pertinent conferences, and feature articles relating to the volunteer field. "The volunteer advisor" answers typical questions. The magazine seeks to share information on how to develop volunteer programs, sharpen administration, improve fund raising and communication skills as well as updates on the latest legislative developments that affect volunteers.

Volunteerism: An Emerging Profession, edited by John Cull and Richard Hardy (1973). Charles C. Thomas, 301-27 East Lawrence Avenue, Springfield, Ill. 62717 ($9.75).

Volunteerism at the Crossroads by Gordon Manser and Rosemary Cass (1976). Family Service Association of America, 44 East 23rd Street, New York, N.Y. 10010 ($12.95).

Volunteer Programs in Prevention and Diversion by Timothy F. Fautsko and Ivan H. Scheier, Ph.D. (June 1975). National Information Center on Volunteerism, P.O. Box 4179, Boulder, Colo. 80302. A booklet describing various volunteer programs in the criminal justice field.

See also the following related chapters in *The Help Book:*

AGING
BUSINESS INFORMATION
CHILDREN
CITIZEN ACTION
COURTS
CRIME PREVENTION
CRIME VICTIMS AND WITNESSES
EDUCATION
EMERGENCIES AND DISASTERS
EMPLOYMENT
JUVENILE DELINQUENCY
MENTAL RETARDATION AND LEARNING DISABILITIES
MULTIPURPOSE ORGANIZATIONS
OFFENDERS AND EX-OFFENDERS
POLITICAL ACTION
RAPE AND SEXUAL ASSAULT
SUICIDE PREVENTION
ADDITIONAL RESOURCES

51

ADDITIONAL RESOURCES

In the four years that it has taken to develop, research, write, and recheck *The Help Book,* this author gained a great deal of specific information—about agencies, organizations, and published materials—as well as a general understanding about seeking help for oneself and for others. First and foremost is that all direct-help and information-providing organizations should be accountable to those persons whom they pledge to serve. This must be true whether in the public sector—on the local county, city, state, or federal level—or in the private one. If inefficiencies are discovered, they must be corrected. Parkinson's twenty-year-old law—that bureaucracies become less efficient as they expand—is as valid now as it has ever been. The person seeking help is therefore forced to be even more self-sufficient and imaginative in his or her approach since no "one" person may ultimately be accountable for the delays, misinformation, or poor service provided.

Second, this author learned the importance of not stopping a "call for help" because an initial written or telephone request is ignored or inappropriately answered. It might take two to ten inquiries to the same agency (but to different persons within that organization) or going to another similar helping service before success is achieved. Trying to expose the lazy or slow employee might be a bit extreme, but you should continue your pleas until you are satisfied that your questions have been answered or the services that you are entitled to have been performed. In theory, help—whether medical, educational, informational, and so forth—should be of a high quality, whether that help is provided for by publicly paid employees or privately salaried ones. In practice, that is not often the case. So if an organization is failing to help its clients, whether the funding sources are public or private, that organization should be revamped or abolished.

For example, this author sent out several hundred requests to state agencies (and administrators) around the country just to receive fifty up-to-date directories of their state agency functions (and to check missing entries). All of the following factors were widely disparate in the replies received:

- response time
- whether the answer was personalized or a form letter
- quality of the response
- quality of the state agency directory
- format, content, and production costs of the state agency directory

Some states, at the expense of their taxpayers, print and distribute elaborate, hardcover, annual directories that are illustrated with glossy photographs and contain hundreds of pages of superfluous material. In several cases, the key information that the public needs—for example, names, addresses, phone numbers, and descriptions of services provided by the state—was either missing, incomplete, inaccurate, or so badly organized that no one (probably not even the state's own governor) would find the directory of value. Other states, such as Michigan, New York, Vermont, Alaska, California, and Hawaii, provide inexpensively produced and well-done directories.

Third, the possible misappropriation of state funds in the publication of the directories of certain states is only a microcosm of what is going on around this country in both the private and public sector. Private companies spend thousands of dollars for annual reports whose flashy designs might just mean less revenues to the stockholders who are receiving those books. Private voluntary organizations often spend far too much money on fancy holiday greetings cards, personalized stationary and notepads for their employees, and unjustified business expenses when those funds should be used to provide services to their clients.

I guess what I am advocating is a return to quality rather than either excessiveness or superfluousness. That is why so many low-cost or free pamphlets and booklets are included in the Additional Literature sections throughout this book; the cost of a publication may not be related to its effectiveness. Nor does the money spent on newsletters, magazines, and publication listings improve the content of those information-giving organs if the material in it is of a poor quality.

The Help Book is just a beginning; it could never be all-inclusive or one hundred percent up-to-date. But it is a contribution to a growing movement by both consumers and administrators so that we all have more control over our lives and a better grasp of the information and resources available to us.

If you and your family are to get the help that you need and deserve, you have to know where to go for it. That means everything from the local privately run crime victim hotline to the state department of environmental concerns to the federal information and service-providing agencies. If more people were aware of what they are entitled to—and when excesses are being indulged in or functions unfulfilled—*The Help Book*'s goal will have been accomplished. This author suggests you take the time to obtain copies for your home library of local, state, regional, and federal directories ("help books"). Luckily they are either free or inexpensive and constantly updated. (If you have any doubts about where or how to obtain the local, state, regional, and federal directories that are suggested, refer back to Chapter 32, *Information Rights and Resources*.) But remember to think about directories that embrace both publicly funded government services *and* private ones. For example, if you live in Los Angeles, your at-home library might contain, in addition to your local white and yellow telephone directories, a state agency directory, such as *State of California Telephone Directory* ($3.95), *The Los Angeles People's Yellow Pages* ($2.50), the city directory for Los Angeles, and a national or regional version of the *U.S. Government Manual* ($6.00).

One way to continue the exchange of information about existing and newly formed self-help groups, as well as government and private helping agencies and organizations, is through the establishment of local self-help clearinghouses. The September/October 1978 issue of the *Self-Help Reporter*, published by the National Self-Help Clearinghouse, noted the establishment of such local self-help networks in Toronto, Canada; Huntington, West Virginia; Lincoln, Nebraska; Manhattan and Long Island, New York. If you are interested in starting such an information and referral service, or if you have established one and want to make it known, you might send an announcement to the editor of the *Self-Help Reporter* at the following address:

Self-Help Reporter
c/o National Self-Help Clearinghouse
Graduate School and University Center/CUNY
33 West 42nd Street, Room 1227
New York, N.Y. 10036

Another way to share resources and information to help others is through a "self-help fair," such as the one held in Boston in May 1978. Sponsored by the Boston University School of Social Work, twelve workshops were offered that included: "Self-Help and the Gay Community," "Alcoholism and Self-Help," "Getting Started," "Multiple Agendas of Self-Help Groups," and "Self-Help and Minorities." Similar fairs could be organized and sponsored by such public or private agencies as the mayor's office, the department of consumer or citizen affairs, a county or citywide block association, a community or four-year college or university, and so forth.

Completing this book has been personally satisfying as I realize my three hundred information-packed looseleaf notebooks, hundreds of file folders, and thousands of interviews and phone calls will be shared with others who were unable to experience firsthand the eye-opening experience of compiling this book. I have received three-page personal letters from busy administrators that provided more details and specifics than I could ever have used. I have also received briefer but still helpful replies and, of course, no replies at all. But I have gained renewed hope in the integrity of many employees and employers—both private and public—whom you will probably never read about in the financial section of your local newspaper or in national magazines. That they are performing their jobs well—and that they genuinely care about those whom they seek to help—motivates all of us to demand that high standards be maintained at a voluntary local center as well as at a county, city, state, or federally operated one.

The national organizations that follow are not easily categorized; still they seemed worthwhile enough to include in The Help Book:

Alternatives
1924 East Third Street
Bloomington, Ind. 47401

Started in 1975 because of an "outrage with the profiteering of Christmas," this group now has several refreshing projects in full swing, including the *Alternate Celebrations Catalogue* ($3.75). Alternate Celebration Resource Packets; a mail-order bookstore emphasizing voluntary simplicity; and, *Alternatives*, their alternate lifestyle quarterly newsletter ($5.00 a year). A copy of the bookstore list is mailed free.

American Mensa Limited
1701 West 3rd Street
Brooklyn, N.Y. 11223

A membership organization of 25,000 ($15.00 a year) for anyone whose standard I.Q. test score is above the 98th percentile. There are 116 local gifted children's educational chapters and facilities.

LITERATURE: *Mensa Bulletin*, published ten times a year ($5.00 to members; $10.00 to nonmembers).

Family Synergy
P.O. Box 30103
Terminal Annex
Los Angeles, Calif. 90030

A national organization founded in 1971 dedicated to the implementation of "family" groups larger than the nuclear family. Membership is $12.00 for an individual; $15.00 for a family couple. Local chapters may require additional dues. Benefits include their monthly newsletter, membership and people directories of those who want to be listed, reduced fees on Synergy events and services. Upon request, fact sheets with reading lists on communal living are available.

Good Bears of the World
P.O. Box 8236
Honolulu, Hawaii 96815

Good Bears offers love and affection to people of all walks of life by giving away teddy bears to those who are in hospitals, rest homes, and special centers. It also sponsors the Bear Poster Contest. Annual dues of $5.00 are used to purchase teddy bears and distribute the newsletter *Bear Tracks*.

LITERATURE: Fact sheets; brochure; invitation to help start a local "den" (all free).

Center for UFO Studies
Information Services
924 Chicago Avenue
Evanston, Ill. 60202

Started in 1973 as a central clearinghouse for reporting sightings of UFOs (unidentified flying objects) without "fear of ridicule or unwanted publicity." The center maintains research files about sighting reports and a computer data bank (UFOCAT).

LITERATURE: Free descriptive brochure; *International UFO Reporter*, monthly ($12.00 a year); catalog of resources ($1.00).

International Left Handers Society
Box 10198
5821 Center Street
Milwaukee, Wis. 53210

A membership organization ($10.00 a year) that includes discounts on left-hand products, a list of famous left-handers, a wall plaque, and their newsletter.

Little People of America (LPA)
National Headquarters
Box 126
Owatonna, Minn. 55060

Founded in 1968, there are twelve district chapters to this national voluntary organization providing friendship, idea exchanges, and moral support for dwarfs. Membership dues are $7.50 per person, $10.00 per family, and $5.00 per teenager or "little little."

LITERATURE: *LPA News*, published ten times a year; membership handbook.

Natural Living Switchboard Resource Center
215 North Des Plaines Street
Chicago, Ill. 60606

Started in 1974, this center is an information clearinghouse on natural living that provides referrals and telephone research. It circulates a newsletter to keep participants informed of pertinent events, such as a national nutritional food association conference or the North American Vegetarian Conference.

Procrastinators' Club of America, Inc.
Broad-Locust Building
Philadelphia, Pa. 19102

This national membership organization, with about 3,300 members in the United States and about 100 in foreign countries, was started in 1956. There are also four local subchapters in Sacramento, Calif.; Davisburg, Mich.; South Bend, Ind.; and Edwardville, Ohio. It costs $10.00 to join; annual dues are $5.00. This just-for-fun organization publishes a *Last Month's Newsletter*, which appears "late and irregularly." The goals of the group are as follows: "We promote the benefits of procrastination and we advise members how to get the most out of putting things off until later, how to relax more, how to worry less. We give awards to people, organizations, even objects (such as bridges, buildings, and railroads) who warrant such an honor for exceptional acts of procrastination." Christmas parties are held in the summertime, Halloween parties in May, and July 4th picnics in February.

LITERATURE: *Last Month's Newsletter* (with membership dues).

School of Living and Downhill Farm
P.O. Box 3233
York, Pa. 17402

Established in 1936 and incorporated in 1954, this organization sponsors week-long introductions into living in a rural community. The workshop is in the Allegheny Mountains, with music and good food. Topics include organization and legal structures, interpersonal and sexual relations, and organic gardening. There are also conferences and workshops in ecology, communal living, intimate relations, therapeutic massage, teaching your child to read, and prison reform.

LITERATURE: Descriptive leaflet; list of workshops and conferences; *Green Revolution* magazine ($8.00 a year).

Sometimes the only "help" we need is in getting out of our perennial ruts—meeting new people or trying new experiences alone, with a partner, or with our families. Here, therefore, is a totally non-therapeutic listing of some of the thousands of activities that are open to all of us. Many are available in every community or city at no cost or for very little money, or for as much as you want to spend. How many of these activities have you taken part of since you were, say, fifteen? Give yourself a new start and some self-help by trying a new sport or cultural activity this week. Or maybe two or three.

ACTIVITIES

Sports-related

Jogging
Bowling
Ice skating
Swimming
Squash
Tennis
Gymnastics
Skiing
Bicycling
Water skiing
Boating
Skateboarding
Roller skating
Horseback riding
Dancing
Pool
Shuffleboard
Basketball
Baseball
Ping Pong
Archery
Kite flying
Volleyball

Cultural

Movies
Plays
Museums
Lectures
Art galleries
Art shows
Planetarium
Dance
Non-credit classes (literature, sociology, urban affairs, cooking, arts, crafts, music)
Concerts
Poetry reading
Discussion groups
Opera
Chamber music

Social

Visiting friends
Parties (attending or giving)
Night spots
Visiting relatives
Visiting old acquaintances (elementary school teacher, college professor, your high school)
Talking

Eating places

Night Clubs
Cafes
Restaurants
Cabarets
Outdoor dining
Brunch

Miscellaneous

Reading
Acting out a play
Role playing
Word and other games (Scrabble, Bingo, cards)

Spectator sports (baseball, football, hockey, basketball)
Circus
Puppets
Psychodrama
Hiking

Window shopping
Walking
Television
Taking a short trip to somewhere you've never been

The danger in a book like this is that it will never be finished, since the absorption of each new bit of information tempted me to add even more data. But in keeping with the promise that *The Help Book* would be both compact and multiconcerned, key directories that will open up hundreds of thousands of other resources are listed in this chapter. (Those relating to only one area, such as the *National Directory of Drug Abuse Programs*, are indexed in that specific chapter, in this case, *Drugs, Smoking, and Drug Abuse*.) What follows is a list of helpful general directories, books, and multimedia materials covering a wide range of subjects. (Some of the published references in this section may have already appeared in annotated form in previous chapters. In those cases, since this section consolidates those sources that share the wide scope of *The Help Book*, only a brief bibliographic mention will be made.)

DIRECTORIES

Catalogue of Free Things, rev. ed., by Jeffrey Feinman and Mark Weiss (1976). William Morrow and Company, 105 Madison Avenue, New York, N.Y. 10016 ($6.95). Hundreds of free booklets, charts, and other items described in an entertaining style.

C/O: Journal of Alternative Human Services (quarterly). Community Congress of San Diego, 1172 Morena Boulevard, San Diego, Calif. 92110 ($8.00 a year). In addition to articles about direct services in most of the areas covered in *The Help Book*, each issue contains a valuable "Information Exchange" of current resources and organizations.

Consumer Information Catalog (quarterly). Consumer Information Center, Pueblo, Colo. 81009 (free). This booklet lists more than 200 selected free and low-cost federal consumer booklets and leaflets on such topics as energy conservation, child care, transportation, health, food, and housing. Ask to be placed on their mailing list to regularly receive the latest edition.

Consumer Sourcebook, edited by Paul Wasserman and Jean Morgan (1974). Gale Research Company, Book Tower, Detroit, Mich. 48226 ($35.00). (See complete listing in Chapter 13, *Consumer Affairs*.)

Directory of Agencies: U.S. Voluntary, International Voluntary, and Intergovernmental, rev. ed. (1975). National Association of Social Workers, 1425 H Street, N.W., Washington, D.C. 20005 ($4.00 plus $.40 postage). A comprehensive listing of agencies geared to the professional counselor or worker.

Directory of Information and Referral Services (1975). United Way of America, National Agencies Division, 801 North Fairfax Street, Alexandria, Va. 22314 (free).

ADDITIONAL RESOURCES / 657

Encyclopedia of Associations, 11th edition, edited by Margaret Fisk (1977). Gale Research Company, Book Tower, Detroit, Mich. 48226 (Volume One: *National Organizations of the United States*, $70.00; Volume Two: *Geographic and Executive Index*, $50.00; Volume Three: *New Associations and Projects*, $60.00). The third volume is the periodical supplements in looseleaf form providing information on newly formed and newly founded associations that will be included when the next edition is published. Most valuable is Volume One, which should be available at most libraries. In the 1977 edition, there are one-paragraph descriptions of nearly 14,000 organizations. Each entry provides the date the association was founded, the number of staff members, any state or local groups, a brief description of the association's goals and services, how it is supported, a list of major publications (such as magazines and newsletters), whether there is an annual meeting or convention, and the address, telephone number, and executive director or person to contact. The organizations are categorized in broad areas, such as social welfare or educational organizations, and indexed alphabetically with number keys for locating a group within this nearly 1,500-page reference book.

Encyclopedia of Ignorance, edited by Ronald Duncan and Miranda Weston-Smith (1977). Pergamon Press, Inc., Maxwell House, Fairview Park, Elmsford, N.Y. 10523 ($15.00). An anthology of writings by sixty eminent scientists on what information is still lacking in their fields.

Federal Government: A Directory of Information Resources in the United States, rev. ed., Science and Technology Division, National Referral Center (1974). Available from the Superintendent of Documents, U.S. Government Printing Office, Washington, D.C. 20402 ($4.25). Each federal agency is described with a listing of its address, areas of interest, publications, and what kind of information services it provides (such as answering inquiries or providing consultation services).

For Better, For Worse: A Feminist Handbook on Marriage and Other Options by Jennifer Baker Fleming and Carolyn Kott Washburne (1977). Charles Scribner's Sons, 597 Fifth Avenue, New York, N.Y. 10017 ($7.95). A guide for women on all aspects of marriage, including motherhood, love, money, lesbianism, spouse assault, and so forth. Casual, easy writing style and valuable annotated chapter-by-chapter resource sections in the back.

The Jewish Yellow Pages: A Directory of Goods and Services by Mae Schafter Rockland with Michael Aaron Rockland (1978). Schocken Books, 200 Madison Avenue, New York, N.Y. 10016 ($7.95). An oversized paperback with over 300 illustrations and hundreds of products and services of businesses and craftspeople throughout the United States.

Medical and Health Information Directory, edited by Anthony T. Kruzas (1977). Gale Research Company, Book Tower, Detroit, Mich. 48226 ($48.00). An exhaustive directory of organizations, associations, and health-related publications. (See complete listing in Chapter 30, *Health*.)

The National Directory of State Agencies, 1978–1979, 3rd edition, compiled by Nancy D. Wright, Jule G. McCartney, and Gene P. Allen. Information Resources Press, 2100 M Street, N.W., Washington, D.C. 20037 ($55.00 plus $2.40 for postage and handling). Listings of contact persons, addresses, and phone numbers in ninety-three functional agency categories for the fifty states, District of Columbia, and the four U.S. possessions and territories. It is divided into two parts: by state and by function.

Parents' Yellow Pages: A Directory by the Princeton Center for Infancy, general editor Frank Caplan (1978). Anchor Books, Anchor Press/Doubleday Publishing Company, Garden City, N.Y. 11530 ($7.95). Covers dozens of concerns, such as bedwetting, allergies, adoption, day care, first aid, and child abuse.

Periodicals That Progressive Scientists Should Know About. Progressive Technology, Inc.,

P.O. Box 20049, Tallahassee, Fla. 32304 (free). Science for the People (based in Boston) has a Florida group that has produced this extensive list. It covers a wide range of subjects—not just pure science—that includes the environment, citizen action, nutrition, and so forth. In addition, there are free "Reading Lists in the Making" available that focus on various scientific and related topics.

Service Directory of National Voluntary Health and Social Welfare Organizations. The National Assembly of National Voluntary Health and Social Welfare Organizations, Inc., 345 East 46th Street, New York, N.Y. 10017 ($5.00). Annotated descriptions of over eighty organizations.

Where to Get Help for Your Family by Anne M. Tansey (1977). Abbey Press, St. Meinrad, Ind. 47577 ($3.95). One hundred and fifty-seven national agencies are described (about one page per agency). Topics covered include children, the community, consumers, education, environment, the family, legal problems, medical problems, personal problems, sports, women in service, and youth.

Woman's Almanac, compiled and edited by Kathryn Paulsen and Ryan A. Kuhn (1976). J. B. Lippincott Company, 521 Fifth Avenue, New York, N.Y. 10017 ($6.95). Twelve how-to handbooks in one with excellent excerpted, reprinted material on such topics as working, education, and health.

Women in Transition: A Feminist Handbook on Separation and Divorce by Women in Transition, Inc. (1975). Charles Scribner's Sons, 597 Fifth Avenue, New York, N.Y. 10017 ($7.95). Not just for women and not just for feminists, this volume is a wealth of information, bibliographical referrals, resources, and interviews on a variety of key issues—from child abuse to divorce, from public housing to life insurance. A good reference and optimistic guide for those transitional periods that includes basic information to make sure the next step is a better one.

The Women's Yellow Pages: Original Sourcebook for Women, New England edition, edited by Carol Edry and Rosalyn Gerstein (1978). The Public Works, Inc. (formerly the Boston Women's Collective), RFD 3, Box 186, Putney, Vt. 95346 ($7.95). More than fifty articles and 3,500 directory resource listings for programs, resources, and services in a variety of areas, including employment, education, health, counseling, parenting, and consumer affairs. This is the third volume in the series; other volumes are *The New York Women's Yellow Pages* and *The West Virginia Women's Yellow Pages.*

The Workbook (monthly, except July and August). Southwest Research and Information Center, P.O. Box 4524, Albuquerque, N.M. 87106 ($1.00 single copy, $7.00 a year for students, $10.00 a year for individuals, $20.00 a year for institutions). A useful magazine for getting all kinds of help. (See annotated listing in Chapter 32, *Information Rights and Resources.*)

The World Almanac Whole Health Guide by David Hendin (1977). Plume Books, New American Library, 1301 Avenue of the Americas, New York, N.Y. 10019 ($4.95). This excellent guidebook, written by a veteran newspaper reporter, covers more than just health. There are articles on alcoholism and drug abuse, the expectant parent, the elderly, sex problems, and death. Each of the succinct sections contains follow-up information sources. The first chapter, "You and Your Doctor," explores twenty-six of the most frequently asked questions about physicians and health care.

PUBLISHERS

Ayer Press
210 West Washington Square
Philadelphia, Pa. 19106

Publishes a variety of directories and resources, such as *1978 Ayer Directory of Publications* ($56.00). Consult your library or write for their catalog.

Cassette Communications, Inc.
175 Fifth Avenue
New York, N.Y. 10010

This company produces and distributes a wide range of tapes on a variety of social-psychological topics that are narrated by experts in their fields. Sample tapes include *Fathering* by Herbert J. Freudenberger, *Children of Divorce* by Richard A. Gardner, M.D., and *Adoption: A Guide for Parents and Professionals* by Elizabeth S. Cole and Kathryn S. Donley. Each cassette is available for $9.95. Write for their catalog.

R. R. Bowker Company
1180 Avenue of the Americas
New York, N.Y. 10036

Their annotated catalog lists the hundreds of directories and reference books that they publish in such diverse fields as science, cooking, publishing, film literature, finance, research sources in military history, and so forth.

Canadian Periodical Publishers' Association
3 Church Street, Suite 407
Toronto, Ontario M5E 1M2, Canada

Publishes *Magazines*, a free booklet describing Canadian magazines of popular interest.

Feminist Book Mart
162-11 Ninth Avenue
Whitestone, N.Y. 11357

Send for their catalog, including *Girls & Boys Together, A Bibliography of Non-Sexist Children's Literature*.

The Feminist Press
Box 334
Old Westbury, N.Y. 11568

Publishes women's literature, children's books, and educational material; teaches in-service courses in nonsexist education; offers workshops, slideshows, and packets of materials for eliminating sexism within a school district; consults with school systems and libraries; and seeks to eliminate discrimination in education.

Gale Research Company
Book Tower
Detroit, Mich. 48226

Founded in 1954, this company publishes numerous directories, such as the *Encyclopedia of Associations*. A catalog is available.

Information Resources Press
2100 M Street, N.W.
Washington, D.C. 20037

Publishes numerous reference books, such as *A Guide to Sources of Educational Information* and *The National Directory of State Agencies*. Descriptive leaflets on in-print and forthcoming titles are available.

Institute for Social Research
University of Michigan
P.O. Box 1248
Ann Arbor, Mich. 48106

Established in 1946, this institute conducts research and publishes related books in areas covered by their four research centers: Survey Research Center; Research Center for Group Dynamics; Center for Research on Utilization of Scientific Knowledge; and Center for Political Studies. Write for their free annotated catalog describing books in social issues, such as juvenile courts, drugs, violence, economics, survey methodology, organizations, youth, and housing.

Involved American
P.O. Box 30169
Los Angeles, Calif. 90030

Mailing address for requesting one or more of the free booklets published by Atlantic Richfield Company's Involved American education program. The booklets include "Mandatory Retirement: A Cruel Discrimination," "American's Land: Another Depleting Resource," "Public Transportation: Getting Things Moving," "Conservation: Bridging the Energy Gap," "Offshore Drilling: What's at Stake?," "Divestiture: Non-Answer to a Real Crisis," "Our Cities: Hope for the Future," and "Guidelines to a National Energy Policy."

Know, Inc.
P.O. Box 86031
Pittsburgh, Pa. 15221

Founded in 1969 by a group of Pittsburgh NOW members, Know, Inc., publishes a feminist newsletter and information on rape, sexual abuse of children, and battered wives. Send for publications price list.

Public Affairs Committee, Inc.
381 Park Avenue South
New York, N.Y. 10016

Founded in 1935, the Public Affairs Committee is a nonprofit organization concerned with educating the American public on vital economic and social problems and issuing concise pamphlets dealing with such problems. The pamphlets (which sell for $.50 each with discounts for quantity orders) cover many topics—family relationships, child development, health and mental health, race relations, and social and economic issues. Send for their catalog.

U.S. Government Printing Office
Superintendent of Documents
Washington, D.C. 20402

All in-print government publications may be ordered from here. There is a $1.00 minimum charge for each mail order. The free monthly booklet, *Selected U.S. Government Publications*, provides comprehensive listings on new and backorder titles.

Vancouver Status of Women (VSW)
2029 West 4th Avenue
Vancouver, British Columbia, Canada

Multifaceted national organization for women with counseling, information clearinghouse, extensive publications, and referrals. *The Women's Directory*, published by VSW, is a guide to businesses owned by women and is free. They also publish *Women in British Columbia, Issues, Resources, and Services*. Write for their publications list.

Women in Distribution, Inc.
P.O. Box 8858
Washington, D.C. 20003

Distributes books and records put out by small independent presses and record companies. It has a wide range of personal, cultural, and political viewpoints of women today.

52

TELEPHONE DIRECTORY

As noted in the introduction, telephone numbers have not been included in *The Help Book* because they change so often. For local telephone numbers, check your white or yellow pages or, if necessary, call Directory Assistance.

Requests placed to out-of-state Directory Assistance bureaus are free. The accompanying national area-code map will help you to dial out-of-town information. Dial the area code for the city you are calling, plus 555-1212.

Most local telephone companies provide free published information on how to read a phone bill, how to use the telephone directory more effectively, and what to do about obscene or annoying phone calls. Contact your local business office for assistance, or to have literature mailed to you.

New telephone equipment permits the telephone company to trace phone calls that are either harassing or obscene. If you are the victim of such a call, hang up, telephone the police, and then telephone the local phone company business office. If it is after business hours, note the date and time of the call and contact the business office as soon as possible during working hours. Contact them also for written leaflets and for further information about how to handle obscene phone calls.

TOLL-FREE HOTLINES

Throughout this book, wherever appropriate and feasible, the existence of toll-free business or hotline phone numbers have been indicated. More and more, the telephone is becoming the communications tool for immediate information and help. Many private organizations, such as hotel chains and businesses, as well as service-oriented nonprofit agencies (runaway resource centers, for instance) are establishing toll-free hotlines.

662 / THE HELP BOOK

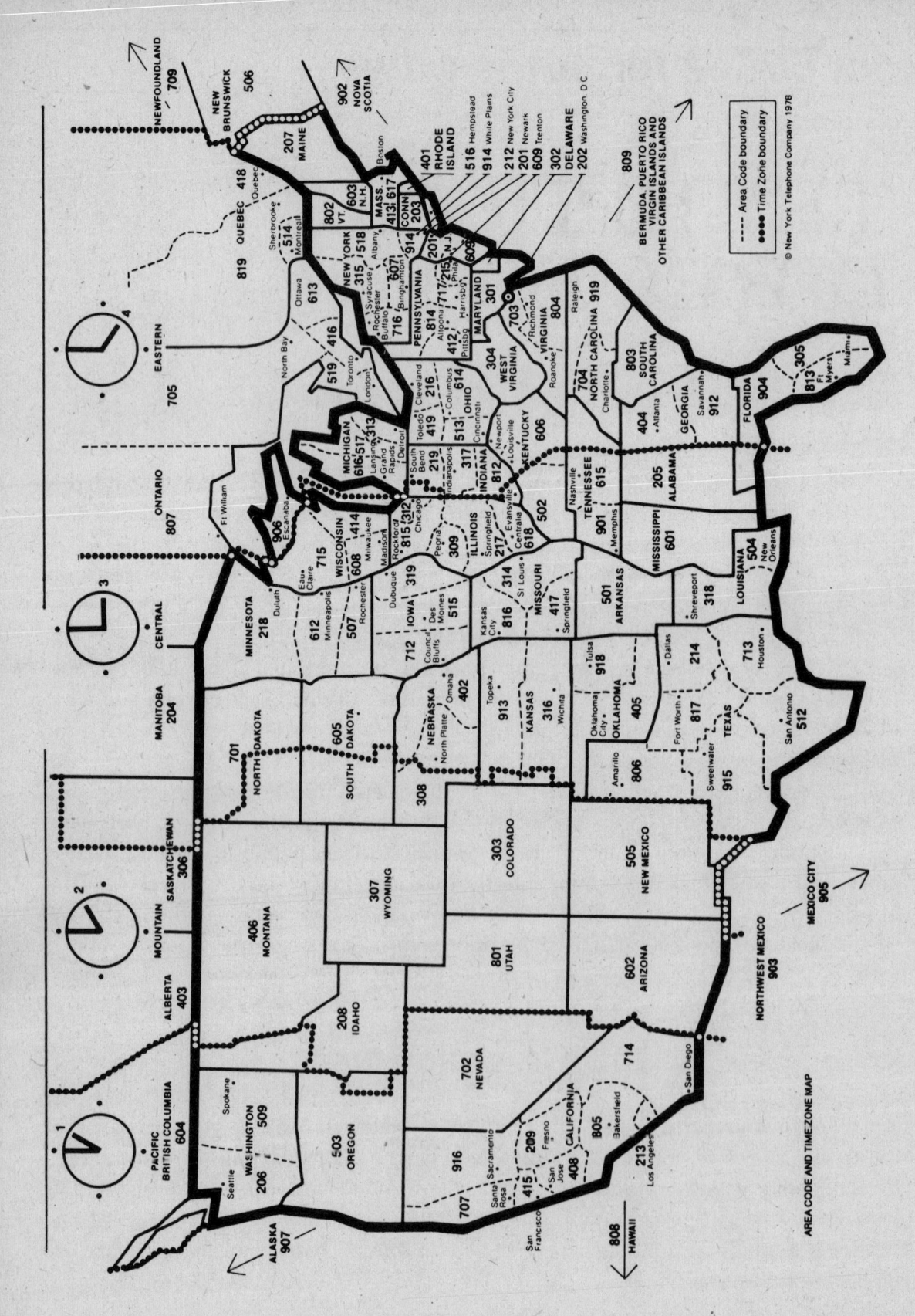

AREA CODE AND TIME ZONE MAP

Area codes for some cities

place	area code	place	area code	place	area code	place	area code	place	area code	place	area code
ALABAMA		**CALIFORNIA (Cont'd)**		**CALIFORNIA (Cont'd)**		**ILLINOIS (Cont'd)**		**INDIANA (Cont'd)**		**MASSACHUSETTS**	
All points	205	Lynwood	213	West Covina	213	Arlington Hts.	312	Indianapolis	317	Amherst	413
		Manhattan Beach	213	West Hollywood	213	Aurora	312	Kokomo	317	Andover	617
ALASKA		Menlo Park	415	Westminster	714	Belleville	618	Lafayette	317	Arlington	617
All points	907	Merced	209	Whittier	213	Berwyn	312	Marion	317	Attleboro	617
		Milpitas	408			Bloomington	309	Merrillville	219	Barnstable	617
ARIZONA		Modesto	209	**COLORADO**		Blue Island	312	Michigan City	219	Belmont	617
All points	602	Monrovia	213	All points	303	Calumet City	312	Mishawaka	219	Beverly	617
		Montclair	714			Carbondale	618	Muncie	317	Billerica	617
ARKANSAS		Montebello	213	**CONNECTICUT**		Carpentersville	312	New Albany	812	Boston	617
All points	501	Monterey	408	All points	203	Champaign-Urbana	217	Richmond	317	Braintree	617
		Monterey Park	213			Chicago	312	South Bend	219	Brockton	617
		Mountain View	415	**DELAWARE**		Chicago Hgts.	312	Terre Haute	812	Brookline	617
CALIFORNIA		Napa	707	All points	302	Cicero	312			Cambridge	617
Alameda	415	National City	714			Danville	217	**IOWA**		Chelmsford	617
Alhambra	213	Newark	415	**DIST. OF COLUMBIA**		Decatur	217	Ames	515	Chelsea	617
Altadena	213	Newport Beach	714	Washington, D.C.	202	De Kalb	815	Burlington	319	Chicopee	413
Anaheim	714	North Highlands	916			Des Plaines	312	Cedar Falls	319	Danvers	617
Arcadia	213	Norwalk	213	**FLORIDA**		Dolton	312	Cedar Rapids	319	Dedham	617
Azusa	213	Novato	415	Boca Raton	305	Downers Grove	312	Clinton	319	Everett	617
Bakersfield	805	Oakland	415	Carol City	305	East St. Louis	618	Council Bluffs	712	Fall River	617
Baldwin Park	213	Oceanside	714	Clearwater	813	Elgin	312	Davenport	319	Fitchburg	617
Bell Gardens	213	Ontario	714	Coral Gables	305	Elk Grove Village	312	Des Moines	515	Framingham	617
Bellflower	213	Orange	714	Daytona Beach	904	Elmhurst	312	Dubuque	319	Gardner	617
Belmont	415	Oxnard	805	Fort Lauderdale	305	Elmwood Park	309	Fort Dodge	515	Gloucester	617
Berkeley	415	Pacifica	415	Fort Myers	813	Evanston	312	Iowa City	319	Greenfield	413
Beverly Hills	213	Palo Alto	415	Fort Pierce	305	Evergreen Park	312	Marshalltown	515	Haverhill	617
Buena Pk.	714	Palos Verdes	213	Gainesville	904	Freeport	815	Ottumwa	515	Holyoke	413
Burbank		Paramount	213	Hallandale	305	Galesburg	309	Sioux City	712	Lawrence	617
(L.A. County)	213	Pasadena	213	Hialeah	305	Granite City	618	Waterloo	319	Leominster	617
Burlingame	415	Petaluma	707	Jacksonville	904	Harvey	312			Lexington	617
Campbell	408	Pico Rivera	213	Kendall	305	Highland Park	312	**KANSAS**		Longmeadow	413
Carmichael	916	Pleasant Hill	415	Key West	305	Hinsdale	312	Emporia	316	Lowell	617
Carson	213	Rancho Cordova	916	Lakeland	813	Hoffman Estates	312	Hutchinson	316	Lynn	617
Castro Valley	415	Redlands	714	Lake Worth	305	Joliet	815	Kansas City	913	Malden	617
Chula Vista	714	Redondo Beach	213	Melbourne	305	Kankakee	815	Lawrence	913	Marblehead	617
Claremont	714	Redwood City	415	Merritt Island	305	La Grange	312	Leavenworth	913	Marlboro	617
Compton	213	Rialto	714	Miami	305	Lansing	312	Manhattan	913	Medford	617
Concord	415	Richmond	415	Miami Beach	305	Lombard	312	Overland Park	913	Melrose	617
Corona	714	Riverside	714	Miramar	305	Maywood	312	Salina	913	Methuen	617
Costa Mesa	714	Rosemead	213	North Miami	305	Melrose Park	312	Topeka	913	Milton	617
Covina	213	Sacramento	916	North Miami Beach	305	Moline	309	Wichita	316	Natick	617
Culver City	213	Salinas	408	Ocala	904	Morton Grove	312			Needham	617
Cypress	714	San Bernadino	714	Orlando	305	Mount Prospect	312	**KENTUCKY**		New Bedford	617
Daly City	415	San Bruno	415	Panama City	904	Naperville	312	Ashland	606	Newton	617
Davis	916	San Carlos-Belmont	415	Pensacola	904	Niles	312	Bowling Green	502	North Adams	413
Downey	213	San Diego	714	Plantation	305	Normal	309	Covington	606	Northampton	413
East Los Angeles	213	San Francisco	415	Pompano Beach	305	Northbrook	312	Fort Knox	502	Norwood	617
El Cerrito	415	San Gabriel	213	St. Petersburg	813	North Chicago	312	Frankfort	502	Peabody	617
El Monte	213	San Jose	408	Sarasota	813	Oak Lawn	312	Henderson	502	Pittsfield	413
Escondido	714	San Leandro	415	Tallahassee	904	Oak Park	312	Lexington	606	Quincy	617
Eureka	707	San Lorenzo	415	Tampa	813	Palatine	312	Louisville	502	Randolph	617
Fairfield	707	San Luis Obispo	805	Titusville	305	Park Forest	312	Newport	606	Reading	617
Fountain Valley	714	San Rafael	415	West Palm Beach	305	Park Ridge	312	Owensboro	502	Revere	617
Fremont	415	Santa Ana	714			Pekin	309	Peducah	502	Roxbury	617
Fresno	209	Santa Barbara	805	**GEORGIA**		Peoria	309	Pleasure Ridge Park	502	Salem	617
Fullerton	714	Santa Clara	408	Albany	912	Rantoul	217	Valley Station	502	Saugus	617
Gardena	213	Santa Cruz	408	Athens	404	Rockford	815			Somerville	617
Garden Grove	714	Santa Maria	805	Atlanta	404	Rock Island	309	**LOUISIANA**		Springfield	413
Glendale	213	Santa Monica	213	Augusta	404	Schaumburg	312	Alexandria	318	Stoughton	617
Glendora	213	Santa Rosa	707	Columbus	404	Skokie	312	Baton Rouge	504	Taunton	617
Hacienda Heights	213	Seal Beach	213	East Point	404	South Holland	312	Bossier City	318	Tewksbury	617
Hawthorne	213	Seaside	408	Fort Benning	404	Springfield	217	Gretna	504	Wakefield	617
Hollywood	213	Simi Valley	805	Gainesville	404	Urbana	217	Houma	504	Waltham	617
Huntington Beach	714	South Gate	213	Griffin	404	Villa Park	312	Kenner	504	Watertown	617
Huntington Park	213	South Pasadena	213	La Grange	404	Waukegan	312	Lafayette	318	Wellesley	617
Inglewood	213	South		Macon	912	Wheaton	312	Lake Charles	318	Westfield	413
La Habra	213	San Francisco	415	Marietta	404	Wilmette	312	Marrero	504	West Springfield	413
Lakewood	213	South Whittier	213	Rome	404			Metairie	504	Weymouth	617
La Mesa	714	Spring Valley	714	Savannah	912			Monroe	318	Woburn	617
La Mirada	714	Stockton	209	Valdosta	912	**INDIANA**		New Iberia	318	Worcester	617
Lancaster	805	Sunnyvale	408	Warner Robins	912	Anderson	317	New Orleans	504		
La Puente	213	Temple City	213			Bloomington	812	Scotlandville	504		
Lawndale	213	Thousand Oaks	805	**HAWAII**		Columbus	812	Shreveport	318	**MICHIGAN**	
Livermore	415	Torrance	213	All points	808	East Chicago	219			Allen Park	313
Lodi	209	Upland	714			Elkhart	219	**MAINE**		Ann Arbor	313
Lompoc	805	Vallejo	707	**IDAHO**		Evansville	812	All Points	207	Battle Creek	616
Long Beach	213	Ventura	805	All points	208	Fort Wayne	219			Bay City	517
Los Altos	415	Visalia	209			Gary	219			Benton Harbor	616
Los Angeles	213	Vista	714	**ILLINOIS**		Hammond	219	**MARYLAND**		Birmingham	313
Los Gatos	408	Walnut Creek	415	Addison	312	Highland	219	All points	301	Dearborn	313
				Alton	618						

[FOR AREA CODES OF PLACES NOT LISTED, DIAL "0" (OPERATOR). THERE IS NO CHARGE FOR THE CALL.]

† © New York Telephone Company 1978

* Area code map and listings reprinted with permission of the New York Telephone Company. Neither the New York Telephone Company, the author, or the publisher assume any liability for any changes that may occur in these numbers.

Area codes for some cities (continued)

place	area code	place	area code	place	area code	place	area code	place	area code	place	area code
MICHIGAN (Cont'd)		**MISSOURI (Cont'd)**		**NEW JERSEY (Cont'd)**		**NEW YORK (Cont'd)**		**NEW YORK (Cont'd)**		**NEW YORK (Cont'd)**	
Detroit	313	Jefferson City	314	Mendham	201	Buffalo & Suburbs	716	Lindenhurst	516	Staten Island	212
East Detroit	313	Joplin	417	Metuchen	201	Callicoon	914	Livingston Manor	914	Stony Point	
East Lansing	517	Kansas City	816	Middlesex	201	Carmel	914	Lockport	716	(Rockland Co.)	914
Ferndale	313	Kirkwood	314	Millburn	201	Center Moriches	516	Long Beach	516	Suffern	914
Flint	313	Lemay	314	Millville	609	Central Islip	516	Long Island		Suffolk County	516
Garden City	313	Overland	314	Montclair	201	Chappaqua	914	(Nassau &		Syracuse &	
Grand Rapids	616	Raytown	816	Morristown	201	Cohoes	518	Suffolk Co.)	516	Suburbs	315
Hamtramck	313	Sedalia	816	Mount Holly	609	Cold Spring		Lynbrook	516	Tarrytown	914
Hazel Park	313	St. Charles	314	Newark	201	(Putnam Co.)	914	Mahopac	914	Ticonderoga	518
Highland Park	313	St. Joseph	816	Newark Int'l		Commack	516	Mamaroneck	914	Tonawanda	716
Holland	616	St. Louis	314	Airport	201	Congers	914	Manhasset	516	Troy	518
Inkster	313	Springfield	417	New Brunswick	201	Coplague	516	Manhattan	212	Tuckahoe	914
Jackson	517	University City	314	New Milford	201	Corning	607	Massapequa	516	Uniondale	516
Kalamazoo	616	Webster Groves	314	North Arlington	201	Cortland	607	Massapequa Park	516	Utica & Suburbs	315
Lansing	517			North Plainfield	201	Croton-on-Hudson	914	Massena	315	Valley Stream	516
Livonia	313	**MONTANA**		Nutley	201	Deer Park	516	Merrick	516	Wantagh	516
Madison Heights	313	All points	406	Old Bridge	201	Depew	716	Middletown	914	Watertown	315
Marquette	906			Orange	201	Dobbs Ferry	914	Mineola	516	Westbury	
Midland	517	**NEBRASKA**		Paramus	201	Dunkirk	716	Montauk Point	516	(Nassau Co.)	516
Monroe	313	Fremont	402	Passaic	201	Eastchester	914	Monticello	914	Westchester Co.	914
Muskegon	616	Grand Island	308	Paterson	201	East Hampton	516	Mount Kisco	914	Westhampton	516
Niles	616	Hastings	402	Perth Amboy	201	East Massapequa	516	Mount Vernon	914	West Hempstead	516
Oak Park	313	Lincoln	402	Phillipsburg	201	East Meadow	516	Nanuet	914	West Islip	516
Pontiac	313	North Platte	308	Plainfield	201	Eastport	516	Narrowsburg	914	Wheatley Hills	516
Portage	616	Omaha	402	Pleasantville	609	Ellenville	914	Nassau County	516	White Lake	914
Port Huron	313			Point Pleasant	201	Elmira	607	Newark	315	White Plains	914
Roseville	313	**NEVADA**		Pompton Lakes	201	Elmsford	914	Newburgh	914	Williamsville	716
Royal Oak	313	All points	702	Princeton	609	Elwood	516	New City	914	Woodbourne	914
Saginaw	517			Rahway	201	Endicott	607	New Rochelle	914	Woodmere	516
St. Clair Shores	313	**NEW HAMPSHIRE**		Red Bank	201	Endwell	607	New York City	212	Woodridge	914
St. Joseph	616	All points	603	Ridgefield	201	Fairmount	315	Niagara	716	Woodstock	914
Southfield	313			Ridgewood	201	Fallsburg	914	North Babylon	516	Wyandanch	516
Southgate	313	**NEW JERSEY**		Roselle	201	Farmingdale	516	North Bellmore	516	Yonkers	914
Sterling Heights	313	Asbury Park	201	Rutherford	201	Fire Island	516	North Massapequa	516	Yorktown Heights	914
Taylor	313	Atlantic City	609	Sayreville	201	Fishers Island	516	North Tonawanda	716		
Trenton	313	Barnegat	609	Somerville	201	Floral Park	516	Norwich	607	**NORTH CAROLINA**	
Troy	313	Bayonne	201	South Amboy	201	Franklin Square		Nyack	914	Asheville	704
Warren	313	Belleville	201	South Orange	201	(Nassau Co.)	516	Oceanside	516	Burlington	919
Westland	313	Bellmawr		South Plainfield	201	Freeport	516	Olean	716	Camp Le Jeune	919
Wyandotte	313	(Camden Co.)	609	South River	201	Fulton	315	Oneida	315	Chapel Hill	919
Wyoming	616	Bergenfield	201	Summit	201	Garden City	516	Oneonta	607	Charlotte	704
Ypsilanti	313	Bloomfield	201	Teaneck	201	Garrison	914	Ossining	914	Durham	919
		Bound Brook	201	Trenton	609	Geneva	315	Oswego	315	Fayetteville	919
		Bridgeton	609	Union City	201	Glen Cove	516	Oyster Bay	516	Fort Bragg	919
MINNESOTA		Burlington	609	Verona	201	Glens Falls	518	Patchogue	516	Gastonia	704
Austin	507	Camden	609	Vineland	609	Gloversville	518	Pearl River	914	Goldsboro	919
Bloomington	612	Carteret	201	Weehawken	201	Grahamsville	914	Peekskill	914	Greensboro	919
Brooklyn Center	612	Cliffside Park	201	Westfield	201	Great Neck	516	Pelham	914	Greenville	919
Columbia Heights	612	Clifton	201	West New York	201	Grossinger	914	Penn Station	212	High Point	919
Coon Rapids	612	Collingswood	609	West Orange	201	Hamilton	315	Piermont	914	Kannapolis	704
Crystal	612	Dover	201	Wildwood	609	Hampton Bays	516	Plainview	516	Kinston	919
Duluth	218	Dumont	201	Woodbridge	201	Harrison	914	Plattsburgh	518	Lexington	704
Edina	612	East Orange	201	Woodbury	609	Hastings-on-Hudson	914	Pleasantville	914	Raleigh	919
Fridley	612	East Paterson	201	Wyckoff	201	Haverstraw	914	Port Chester	914	Rocky Mount	919
Mankato	507	Eatontown	201			Hempstead	516	Port Jefferson	516	Salisbury	704
Minneapolis	612	Elizabeth	201	**NEW MEXICO**		Hicksville	516	Port Washington	516	Wilmington	919
Minnetonka	612	Englewood	201	All points	505	Hudson	518	Potsdam	315	Wilson	919
Moorhead	218	Ewing	609			Huntington	516	Poughkeepsie	914	Winston Salem	919
New Hope	612	Fair Lawn	201	**NEW YORK**		Huntington Sta.	516	Queens County	212		
Rochester	507	Flemington	201	Albany & Suburbs	518	Hurleyville	914	Riverhead	516	**NORTH DAKOTA**	
Roseville	612	Fort Dix	609	Amagansett	516	Irvington	914	Rochester	716	All points	701
St. Cloud	612	Fort Lee	201	Amityville	516	Islip	516	Rockville Centre	516		
St. Louis Park	612	Garfield	201	Amsterdam	518	Ithaca	607	Roosevelt	516	**OHIO**	
St. Paul	612	Glassboro	609	Armonk Village	914	Jamestown	716	Rome	315	Akron	216
White Bear Lake	612	Glen Ridge	201	Auburn	315	Jeffersonville	914	Ronkonkoma	516	Alliance	216
Winona	507	Gloucester	609	Babylon	516	Johnson City	607	Roscoe	607	Ashtabula	216
		Hackensack	201	Baldwin	516	Kenmore	716	Roslyn	516	Athens	614
		Haddonfield	609	Batavia	716	Kennedy Int'l		Rye	914	Austintown	216
MISSISSIPPI		Hasbrouck Heights	201	Bay Shore	516	Airport	212	Sag Harbor	516	Barberton	216
All points	601	Hawthorne	201	Bedford Village	914	Kerhonkson	914	Saratoga Springs	518	Boardman	216
		Hoboken	201	Bellmore	516	Kiamesha	914	Sayville	516	Brook Park	216
MISSOURI		Irvington	201	Bethpage	516	Kingston	914	Scarsdale	914	Canton	216
Affton	314	Jersey City	201	Binghamton	607	Lackawanna	716	Schenectady	518	Chillicothe	614
Cape Girardeau	314	Kearny	201	Brentwood	516	Lake Huntington	914	Seaford	516	Cincinnati	513
Columbia	314	Lakewood	201	Brewster	914	Lakeland	914	Shelter Island	516	Cleveland	216
Ferguson	314	Linden	201	Bridgehampton	516	Lake Success	516	Sloatsburg	914	Columbus	614
Florissant	314	Long Branch	201	Bronx	212	Larchmont	914	Smithtown	516	Cuyahoga Falls	216
Fort Leonard Wood	314	Madison	201	Bronxville	914	Levittown	516	Southampton	516	Dayton	513
Gladstone	816	Maplewood	201	Brooklyn	212	Liberty	914	Spring Valley	914	East Cleveland	216
Independence	816			Brookville	516						

[FOR AREA CODES OF PLACES NOT LISTED, DIAL "0" [OPERATOR]. THERE IS NO CHARGE FOR THE CALL.]

© New York Telephone Company 1978

Area codes for some cities (continued)

place	area code	place	area code	place	area code	place	area code	place	area code	place	area code
OHIO (Cont'd)		**PENNSYLVANIA**		**SOUTH DAKOTA**		**TEXAS (Cont'd)**		**WASHINGTON (Cont'd)**		**CANADA**	
East Liverpool	216	Allentown		All points	605	San Antonio	512	Seattle	206	**ALBERTA**	
Elyria	216	(Lehigh Co.)	215	**TENNESSEE**		Sherman	214	Spokane	509	All points	403
Euclid	216	Altoona	814	Chattanooga	615	Temple	817	Tacoma	206		
Fairborn	513	Beaver Falls	412	Clarksville	615	Texarkana	214	Vancouver	206	**BRITISH COLUMBIA**	
Findlay	419	Bellefonte	814	Jackson	901	Texas City—		Walla Walla	509	All points	604
Garfield Heights	216	Bethel Park	412	Johnson City	615	La Marque	713	Yakima	509		
Hamilton	513	Bethlehem	215	Kingsport	615	Tyler	214			**MANITOBA**	
Kent	216	Bloomsburg	717	Knoxville	615	Victoria	512			All points	204
Kettering	513	Bradford	814	Memphis	901	Waco	817	**WEST VIRGINIA**			
Lakewood	216	Chambersburg	717	Murfreesboro	615	Wharton	713	All points	304	**NEW BRUNSWICK**	
Lancaster	614	Chester	215	Nashville	615	Wichita Falls	817			All points	506
Lima	419	Columbia	717	Oak Ridge	615						
Lorain	216	DuBois	814			**UTAH**				**NEW FOUNDLAND**	
Mansfield	419	Easton	215	**TEXAS**		All points	801	**WISCONSIN**		All points	709
Maple Heights	216	Erie	814	Abilene	915			Appleton	414		
Marion	614	Greensburg	412	Amarillo	806	**VERMONT**		Beloit	608	**NOVA SCOTIA**	
Massillon	216	Harrisburg	717	Arlington	817	All points	802	Brookfield	414	All points	902
Mentor	216	Hazelton	717	Austin	512			Eau Claire	715		
Middletown	513	Indiana	412	Baytown	713			Fond Du Lac	414	**ONTARIO**	
Newark	614	Johnstown	814	Beaumont	713	**VIRGINIA**		Green Bay	414	Fort William	807
North Olmsted	216	Lancaster	717	Big Spring	915	Alexandria	703	Greenfield	414	London	519
Norwood	513	Lebanon	717	Brownsville	512	Annandale	703	Janesville	608	North Bay	705
Parma	216	Levittown	215	Bryan	713	Arlington	703	Kenosha	414	Ottawa	613
Parma Heights	216	Lock Haven	717	Corpus Christi	512	Charlottesville	804	La Crosse	608	Toronto	416
Portsmouth	614	McKeesport	412	Dallas	214	Chesapeake		Madison	608		
Rocky River	216	Monroeville	412	Denison	214	(Norfolk Co.)	804	Manitowoc	414	**QUEBEC**	
Sandusky	419	New Castle	412	Denton	817	Covington	703	Menomonee Falls	414	Montreal	514
Shaker Heights	216	Norristown	215	El Paso	915	Danville	804	Milwaukee	414	Quebec	418
South Euclid	216	Philadelphia	215	Farmers Branch	214	Hampton	804	Neenah	414	Sherbrooke	819
Springfield	513	Pittsburgh	412	Fort Hood	817	Hopewell	804	New Berlin	414		
Steubenville	614	Pottstown	215	Fort Worth	817	Jefferson	804	Oshkosh	414		
Toledo	419	Reading	215	Galveston	713	Lynchburg	804	Racine	414	**SASKATCHEWAN**	
Upper Arlington	614	Scranton	717	Garland	214	Newport News	804	Sheboygan	414	All points	306
Warren	216	Sharon	412	Grand Prairie	214	Norfolk	804	South Milwaukee	414		
Whitehall	614	State College	814	Harlingen	512	Petersburg	804	Stevens Point	715	**MEXICO**	
Xenia	513	Stroudsburg	717	Houston	713	Portsmouth	804	Superior	715	Las Palomas	903
Youngstown	216	Sunbury	717	Hurst	817	Richmond	804	Waukesha	414	Mexicali	903
Zanesville	614	Uniontown		Irving	214	Roanoke	703	Wausau	715	Mexico City	905
		(Indiana Co.)	814	Killeen	817	Staunton	703	Wauwatosa	414	Tijuana	903
OKLAHOMA		Warren	814	Kingsville	512	Virginia Beach	804	West Allis	414		
Altus	405	Washington	412	Laredo	512	Woodbridge	703			**BERMUDA**	
Bartlesville	918	Wayne	215	Longview	214					All points	809
Bethany	405	West Chester	215	Lubbock	806			**WYOMING**			
Dill City	405	West Mifflin	412	Lufkin	713	**WASHINGTON**		All points	307	**PUERTO RICO**	
Enid	405	Wilkes Barre	717	Marshall	214	Bellevue	206			All points	809
Lawton	405	Wilkinsburg	412	McAllen	512	Bellingham	206				
Midwest City	405	Williamsport	717	Mesquite	214	Bremerton	206	**WIDE AREA**		**VIRGIN ISLANDS**	
Muskogee	918	York	717	Midland	915	Edmonds	206	**TEL. SERV.**		All points	809
Oklahoma City	405			Nacogdoches	713	Everett	206	All locations	800		
Ponca City	405	**RHODE ISLAND**		Odessa	915	Fort Lewis	206				
Shawnee	405	All points	401	Orange	713	Longview	206				
Stillwater	405			Paris	214	Olympia	206				
Tulsa	918	**SOUTH CAROLINA**		Pasadena	713	Renton	206				
		All points	803	Port Arthur	713	Richland	509				
OREGON				Richardson	214						
All points	503			San Angelo	915						

[FOR AREA CODES OF PLACES NOT LISTED, DIAL "0" [OPERATOR]. THERE IS NO CHARGE FOR THE CALL.]

© New York Telephone Company 1978

The federal government has dozens of toll-free hotlines for requesting information, referrals, or lodging a complaint. To find out which agency you should contact, or if there is a toll-free hotline, call the Federal Information Center in your area (see listings in Chapter 32, *Information Rights and Resources*).

ADDITIONAL LITERATURE

You might want to look up articles focusing on some of the problems related to the telephone: the crank call ("The Crank-Call Caper" by Thomas Hauser, *New York*, October 3, 1977, page 92); the rise of "junk" calls—selling calls done by computer that are plaguing many Americans the way junk mail does ("Foes of 'Junk Calls' Go Into Action," *U.S. News & World Report*, March 27, 1978, page 67); the politics of the telephone ("Telephone Tyranny Puts Status on Hold" by Michael Korda, *New York Times*, July 20, 1977, pages C1, C12, or some of its related problems. ("The Long Good-bye And How to Make It Shorter" by Sally Wendkos Olds, *Family Health*, May 1978, pages 47–49.)

Crisis Intervention and Counseling by Telephone by Gene Brockopp and David Lester (1976). Charles C. Thomas, 301-27 East Lawrence Avenue, Springfield, Ill. 62717 ($11.95). A valuable anthology of articles for anyone involved in a telephone counseling service, a treatment modality whose growth is traced to the 1950s. In addition to sections on how to counsel by telephone, there is a discussion of what to do about such telephone-related situations as the obscene, nuisance, or chronic phone call.

National Directory of Addresses and Telephone Numbers by Stanley R. Greenfield (1977). Bantam Books, 666 Fifth Avenue, New York, N.Y. 10019 ($9.95). A listing of 2,785 professional and trade associations are part of the 50,000 entries in this directory that are divided into seventy-two categories. Some of the other classifications are transportation and hotels, communications and media, business services, culture and recreation, hospitals, education, foundations, religious denominations, government, politics and diplomacy, and business and finance.

Procedures Manual. Communication Help Center, Kean College of New Jersey, Union City, N.J. 07083 ($3.50). This sixty-four-page training manual is useful for Crisis Center volunteers, their agencies, and anyone else associated with a hotline.

The Pushbutton Telephone Songbook by Michael Scheff (1972). Price/Stern/Sloan Publishers, Inc., 410 North La Cienega Boulevard, Los Angeles, Calif. 90048 ($1.00). Music-making with the telephone: includes "number" and song instructions for such familiar tunes as "London Bridge" and "Strangers in the Night." Illustrated.

Self-Evaluation Handbook for Hotlines and Youth Crisis Centers by Michael Baizerman, Ph.D., James J. McDonough, Jr., Ph.D., and Mitchell Sherman, M.A. (May 1976). Center for Youth Development and Research, 48 McNeal Hall, University of Minnesota, St. Paul, Minn. 55108 ($7.00). A 500-page looseleaf binder manual designed for use by the staff at hotlines and youth crisis centers. It tries to answer such questions as: "Just what training do hotline listeners possess that qualify them to 'counsel and give advice' over the telephone?"; "How effective is a hotline?" It includes an important section on training, orienting, and evaluating the hotline volunteer and concludes with a four-part bibliography.

Toll-Free Digest (annual). Toll Free Digest Company, Inc., Box 800, Claverack, N.Y. 12513 (distributed by Warner Books, Inc., 75 Rockefeller Plaza, New York, N.Y. 10019, $1.95). A directory of more than 14,700 toll-free telephone listings.

Send any corrections, additions, comments, or suggestions for listings in future editions of *The Help Book* to the author at the address below. Please enclose a self-addressed, stamped envelope with your letter/material. Note, however, that neither a personal reply nor an actual listing is guaranteed.

J. L. Barkas
(*The Help Book*, Revised Edition)
P.O. Box 31
Cooper Station
New York, N.Y. 10003

Notes

Notes

Notes

Notes

Notes